# Creative Expression and Play in Early Childhood

## THIRD EDITION

### Joan Packer Isenberg
*George Mason University*

### Mary Renck Jalongo
*Indiana University of Pennsylvania*

DISCARD

Merrill
Prentice Hall

Upper Saddle River, New Jersey
Columbus, Ohio

 # Preface

As everyone knows, young children have active imaginations and are naturally playful. Ideally, all of the programs that are designed for young children, infancy through age eight, would capitalize on these remarkable assets of the early childhood years. The early childhood educator's knowledge of child development; repertoire of instructional strategies; and personal/professional beliefs, values, and attitudes have major ramifications for young children's creative expression and play. If adults who work with young children are too controlling, creativity is undermined and play virtually disappears from early childhood settings. If the adults are too laissez-faire, play behaviors and modes of creative expression get stalled at less mature levels. In the third edition of *Creative Expression and Play in Early Childhood*, we try to show novice and experienced early childhood teachers and caregivers the roles, responsibilities, and strategies that lead to a more child-centered, play-based curriculum—one that nurtures children's creative expression in all of its forms.

## Background

This book is an outgrowth of our combined nearly 50 years of teaching college courses on children's creativity and play to early childhood and elementary students at various stages in their careers—students seeking initial licensure or certification, whether they are enrolled in a community college, four-year teacher-preparation program, or fifth-year Professional Development School (PDS)—as well as practitioners who are seeking continuing certification or a master's degree in the field of early childhood. As is the case with many textbooks, we wrote this book because it was the one we wished we had when we first began teaching an early childhood course on children's play and creativity. We discovered that we were both searching for a text that would integrate creative expression and play into the total preschool-primary grades curriculum, a text that would treat play and creativity as fundamental to developmentally appropriate practice.

Our overarching goal in writing this book is to further the professional development of preservice and inservice teachers. We seek to prepare professionals who not only *know about* children's play and creative expression, but who also *know how* to provide these experiences and *know why* children's creative expression and play are so important. With the third edition, our goal remains the same. It has been gratifying to see the book that we conceptualized received enthusiastically by our colleagues in the early childhood profession and to see the book endure for a third rebirth. It has been a privilege as well as a labor of love to be able to revisit our work, to linger over its language, and to craft it into an even better book.

We must confess to some reluctance when our editor, Ann Davis, first suggested that it was time to begin thinking about a third edition. The first edition was published in 1993, and the ink seemed barely dry when we began discussions for the second edition in 1994. Likewise, the second edition was published in 1997, and beginning the work of revising it in 1998 seemed premature, at best. Yet, as we began to draft the revision plan, we were reminded of what a dynamic field early childhood education is. So much had happened that there really was more to say, and we felt that we could say it better and more clearly than previously. We now appreciate Ann's wisdom in nudging us into the second, and now the third, edition of *Creative Expression and Play in Early Childhood*.

## Need

We are aware that many publications exist that use the word *creative* or *play* in their titles. It distresses us that some of these "creative activities" books make minimal contributions to *teachers'* creative growth, much less *children's*. Instead, they are compilations of "cute" ideas designed to "keep little hands busy." We respect young children's ability to construct their own understandings about their world and to express their ideas in original, inventive ways. We resent the condescending message of materials that presume to give young children patterns to copy, lines to color inside, and activities that are completely initiated and directed by adults. That is why we decided to write a book that would challenge popular misconceptions about creative expression, play, and the arts in early childhood, thereby doing a better job of enabling teachers and caregivers to articulate their child-centered philosophy to families, colleagues, and administrative personnel.

## Purpose

Above all, in this third edition—as in the previous two—we want to orient both preservice and inservice teachers and caregivers to the delightful world of children's play and creativity so that they can develop a fuller understanding and richer appreciation for these traits that are so much a part of the young child's life. Glimpsing that world is the surest way that we have found to convince early childhood caregivers and teachers of play's rightful place in the curriculum and the enduring significance of creative expression. In teacher preparation, as the old proverb goes, you can give a person a fish and he will eat for a day, or teach that person to fish and he will eat for a lifetime. The first condition leads to dependence, the second to self-sufficiency. Our goal was to produce a textbook that would not stop at "giving" early childhood practitioners ideas, but rather move forward to suggest strategies and activities that would stimulate teachers' original thinking. That way, early childhood educators could learn to play with ideas and see themselves as creative individuals. Even more important, early childhood educators could model these traits for children and learn to facilitate the natural playfulness and creativity that exists in abundance among the very young. Both of us believe that it is crucial to the future of education to prepare prospective and practicing early childhood practitioners to exercise sound professional judgment based on theory, research, and exemplary practice. As a reader, you will be the judge of how close we have come to realizing these aims.

## Audience

The book is intended as a primary text for early childhood educators who are seeking teacher certification in a four-year college program or for advanced students in a two-year associate's degree program. The book is ideally suited for a course on young children's play and/or creativity. Due to the book's emphasis on the teacher as researcher, *Creative Expression and Play in Early Childhood* is equally appropriate for practicing caregivers and teachers who are enrolled in a Professional Development School, seeking professional development, participating in an inservice education program, or beginning graduate study. In our travels, we have also found that the message of *Creative Expression and Play in Early Childhood* is a universal one that communicates well to international groups of professionals who work with young children.

Instructors will find that this is an exceptionally versatile book because it includes an array of text features that can be emphasized for different audiences. Those working with more advanced students may want to stress the theoretical framework and the research articles that are part of every chapter. Those working with early childhood educators who are at the beginning of their careers may want to place greater emphasis on the case study, the interview, and the observation in each chapter in order to build students' storehouse of professional experiences. By offering instructors various features that they can use as assignments and as in-class activities, *Creative Expression and Play in Early Childhood* lends extensive support to instructors who are themselves at different levels of experience in working with early childhood practitioners.

## Description of the Book's Contents

The book begins with two chapters that form the foundation for the remaining chapters. Chapter One discusses creativity in young children: how it is defined, how it develops, and what adults can do to foster its growth. Chapter Two examines the crucial role of play in early childhood education: why it is important, how it develops, and what teachers can do to defend the child's right to play.

After establishing this base, the book covers the topics that are traditionally associated with the arts (art, music and movement, creative drama) and topics that are typically covered in a textbook on play (planning and arranging the environment, materials for creative expression and play). We also add two topics that are not typically included in books about creative expression and/or play. The first is a chapter on assessment. It is often the case that "you get what you measure" in educational settings, and early childhood is no exception. We address assessment issues directly because we know that an understanding of performance assessment is essential to the survival of play and creativity in diverse early childhood settings. The second topic that is often ignored in texts dealing with creative expression and play is guiding children's behavior. We include it because it is an understandable concern of early childhood educators at all levels, particularly novices. Chapter Ten, the final chapter, revisits the topics of the first two chapters, creativity and play, this time from the perspective of their potential for the future.

In addition, *Creative Expression and Play in Early Childhood* contains several text features emerging from our understandings about how teachers move from novice to expert practice (Jalongo & Isenberg, 1995). We begin each chapter with reflections from new and experienced teachers on the chapter content. These reflections come from journals maintained by our students in classes at George Mason University and Indiana University of Pennsylvania. Following these thoughtful remarks from our students are questions to stimulate the thinking of other students who are reading the book. The body of each chapter begins with a case study gleaned from observations in classrooms. It can serve as the basis for a class discussion. Next, there is a theoretical framework that forms the foundation for the chapter content and, new to this edition, a list of research articles on the topic as well as carefully selected websites. Each chapter also suggests ways to integrate creative, play-based activities into all subject areas; discusses inclusive and diverse early childhood settings; and concludes with a chapter summary. A set of three activities designed to expand students' understanding of the chapter content follows the body of the chapter. These activities include Discuss, a series of thought-provoking questions; Write to Learn, an issue to write about in a reflective journal; and Interview, an opportunity for students to collect firsthand information on a topic related to the chapter content. All of these materials are designed to help readers reflect upon, synthesize, apply, and solidify their knowledge.

## *New to the Third Edition*

With the third edition comes a stronger emphasis on technology, including recommended websites in the chapters as well as a website designed specifically to accompany the text (www.prenhall.com/isenberg). This website is also noted on the back cover of the text. It includes practice test questions for students in a study guide, in a self-correcting format, as well as a list of suggested outstanding children's literature to accompany the content area chapter. Another technology-based support for the instructor is access to PowerPoint transparencies that highlight key concepts from the chapters. The website contains a complete set of PowerPoint slides for each chapter. Selected PowerPoint transparencies appear in the Instructor's Manual as black-and-white handouts so that students can use them for note taking. Samples are included in the Instructor's Manual to give faculty an idea of their quality. Faculty can then go to the website and download full-color copies of the main points for each chapter, then make them into overhead transparencies or use them as a PowerPoint on-screen show using a computer and projector.

Other significant changes include greater emphasis on special needs, more thorough treatment of health and safety issues, lists of outstanding children's books to accompany the chapters, and updated information on multiple intelligences.

## Acknowledgments

We are deeply indebted to the many people who contributed to the development of this book. We wish to acknowledge the graduate and undergraduate students at George Mason University and Indiana University of Pennsylvania for their cooperation in field-testing this book and for providing us with many of the rich classroom examples that appear throughout these chapters. Natalie Conrad and Norah Hooper, our former graduate assistants, merit special recognition for their work on the Instructor's Manual that accompanies the third edition of the text. Natalie Conrad and Marjorie Stanek were responsible for compiling much of the material on the website.

We are also grateful to the many teachers, parents, and children whose photographs, art material, and stories are an integral part of this text. Thanks, too, to our many colleagues who helped us to further clarify our thinking about creative expression and play.

We want to thank our editor for this edition, Ann Davis, who urged us to consider the revision and then gave us the guidance and support to do so. We are also grateful to the rest of the staff at Merrill/Prentice Hall who made the publication of this book possible. They are a fine group of professionals and have been a pleasure to work with throughout the book's production. In addition, we appreciate the valuable input from those who reviewed the book: Pamela O. Fleege, University of South Florida; Pat Hofbauer, Northwest State Community College (Ohio); Nancy W. Wiltz, University of Maryland, College Park; and Stanley W. Wollock, William Paterson University.

Finally, we wish to acknowledge the continuous and unwavering support of our families and close friends. We are especially grateful for their encouragement, understanding, and willingness to listen through each phase of the development of the book from first to third edition.

## A Final Word

In education, there are three common misconceptions about teaching and learning—that it is all content, that it is all process, or that there is one best curriculum for all children (Eisner, 1998, 1990). Fortunately, any instructor who would choose our book for a course would also be apt to avoid these three errors. When it is approached with an open mind, the study of children's creative expression and play is a powerful reminder that coverage is not the answer, that aimlessness is not the answer, and that, clearly, there are no panaceas. Rather, the teacher must create a classroom learning community that emphasizes quality over quantity of materials, that balances freedom with control, and that respects children as individuals while socializing them into an increasingly diverse society and global village. By bring-ing these perspectives to teaching, early childhood faculty and their students not only avoid the pervasive pitfalls of which Eisner speaks, but also become more ef-fective, reflective, and child-centered practitioners.

*Joan Packer Isenberg*
Fairfax, Virginia

*Mary Renck Jalongo*
Indiana, Pennsylvania

### References

Eisner, E. (1988). The ecology of school improvement. *Educational Leadership, 45,* 24–29.

Eisner, E. (1990). Who decides what schools teach? *Phi Delta Kappan,* 71, 523–525.

Jalongo, M. R., & Isenberg, J. P. (1995). *Teachers' stories: From personal narrative to professional insight.* San Francisco: Jossey-Bass.

# Discover the Companion Website Accompanying This Book

## The Prentice Hall Companion Website: A Virtual Learning Environment

Technology is a constantly growing and changing aspect of our field that is creating a need for content and resources. To address this emerging need, we have developed an online learning environment for students and professors alike—Companion Websites—to support our textbooks.

In creating a Companion Website, our goal is to build on and enhance what the textbook already offers. For this reason, the content for each user-friendly website is organized by chapter and provides the professor and student with a variety of meaningful resources. Common features of a Companion Website include:

## For the Professor—

Every Companion Website integrates **Syllabus Manager**™, an online syllabus creation and management utility.

- **Syllabus Manager**™ provides you, the instructor, with an easy, step-by-step process to create and revise syllabi, with direct links into Companion Website and other online content without having to learn HTML.
- Students may logon to your syllabus during any study session. All they need to know is the web address for the Companion Website, and the password you've assigned to your syllabus.
- After you have created a syllabus using **Syllabus Manager**™, students may enter the syllabus for their course section from any point in the Companion Website.
- Clicking on a date, the student is shown the list of activities for the assignment. The activities for each assignment are linked directly to actual content, saving time for students.
- Adding assignments consists of clicking on the desired due date, then filling in the details of the assignment—name of the assignment, instructions, and whether or not it is a one-time or repeating assignment.
- In addition, links to other activities can be created easily. If the activity is online, a URL can be entered in the space provided, and it will be linked automatically in the final syllabus.

- Your completed syllabus is hosted on our servers, allowing convenient updates from any computer on the Internet. Changes you make to your syllabus are immediately available to your students at their next login.

## *For the Student—*

- **Chapter Objectives**—outline key concepts from the text
- **Interactive Self-Quizzes**—complete with hints and automatic grading that provide immediate feedback for students

  After students submit their answers for the interactive self-quizzes, the Companion Website **Results Reporter** computes a percentage grade, provides a graphic representation of how many questions were answered correctly and incorrectly, and gives a question by question analysis of the quiz. Students are given the option to send their quiz to up to four e-mail addresses (professor, teaching assistant, study partner, etc.).

- **Message Board**—serves as a virtual bulletin board to post—or respond to—questions or comments to a national audience
- **Chat**—real-time chat with anyone who is using the text anywhere in the country—ideal for discussion and study groups, class projects, etc.
- **Web Destinations**—links to www sites that relate to chapter content
- **Additional Resources**—access to chapter-specific or general content that enhances material found in the text.

To take advantage of these resources, please visit the *Creative Expression and Play in Early Childhood,* Third Edition, Companion Website at

**www.prenhall.com/isenberg**

# Contents

## Part 3     Contexts for Creative Expression and Play     247

NOTE: Every effort has been made to provide accurate and current Internet information in this book. However, the Internet and information posted on it are constantly changing, so it is inevitable that some of the Internet addresses in this textbook will change.

# PART 1
# THE YOUNG CHILD:
# DEVELOPING FLEXIBLE
# AND DIVERGENT THINKING

# Chapter 1

## Creativity and the Young Child

*"The common language of creativity transcends race, country, culture, and economic level."*

Karen Meador, 1999, p. 324

*"Students have experiences that are similar in complexity, challenge, and creativity to those of creative experts."*

Renata Caine and Geoffrey Caine, 1996, p. 117

# TEACHERS' REFLECTIONS ON CREATIVITY

Before beginning to read the chapter on creativity, consider these preservice and inservice teachers' reflections as they completed a course on creativity:

### Preservice Teachers

"My knowledge of creativity was really limited. I knew that it was beneficial, but I didn't really have any facts to back it up—just a vague feeling that it's basically good. Now I have reasons why creativity benefits the whole child in all areas of development."

"I have learned that creative expression in young children should be taken seriously; that it is important to provide a stimulating environment and materials that motivate young children to explore, discover, and feel supported in meeting new challenges. This enables children to express themselves freely and interact cooperatively with others. I have also learned that it is important for teachers to focus on the process in young children's work rather than exclusively on the product. The teacher's role is to bring out children's creativity, not to 'show off' her or his own."

### Inservice Teachers

"I have always believed that creative expression was important to young children and their development, but I think I only considered the content—art, music, dance, etc. I think I viewed these subjects as something to be appreciated rather than in terms of what they could provide for children."

"I guess I never realized how important creative expression is. Studying this topic has changed my thinking permanently. Now I can't plan anything or respond to a lesson/activity planned by others without thinking, 'Does this allow for creative expression?' I never realized how easily creativity can be hindered by outside influences!"

## Your Reflections

- How do these teachers think about creativity?

- What are your assumptions and understandings about creativity?

- What role might creativity play in teaching and learning?

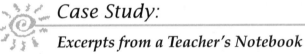

## Case Study:

### Excerpts from a Teacher's Notebook

As part of her study of children's creative expression and play, Fran observes young children in three different settings: a suburban nursery school, a rural church-affiliated preschool, and an urban public school kindergarten. Some of her observations include the following.

Two 5-year-old boys put empty margarine tub dishes on their heads and moved around the table where children were playing with puzzles. As they balanced the tubs on their heads, they pretended to be band members who lifted their knees up high and marched while playing imaginary instruments and humming. The teacher told them that the plastic tubs were for holding puzzle pieces and directed them to put everything away. They did. I think the boys showed creativity and a fine sense of motor control. Their teacher seemed annoyed.

Several preschoolers, ages 4 to 5, were looking out the window and saw several pigeons walking outside. A girl yelled for the other children to come and watch. Soon, all 12 children began imitating the birds' walk and flapping their arms around like a flock of pigeons. One young boy yelled out, "Uh-oh! A pigeon pooped on me!" The children all laughed and screamed, pretending to wipe themselves off. The teacher told the children to settle down and pulled the boy aside to talk to him about his behavior.

I recorded this dialogue among a group of kindergartners as they played house in their kindergarten classroom. I was surprised by some of the themes in their play—the absent father, going to jail, the homemaker mother, and the child who insisted on being the baby. These themes are very different from what I recall as a young child. Where do children's ideas for play come from, I wonder?

**Girl 1:** (Speaking to a boy while running a toy sweeper) "Get out, you're making a mess!"

**Boy:** "I didn't do anything wrong. I'm playing by myself."

**Girl 2:** "Don't, honey. I already swept the floor, now I'll have to do it again." (Sweeps the floor, picks up a doll and speaks to the boy.) "You're her daddy. Our little girl needs to see you. You're her daddy."

**Boy:** "No, I'm not. I have ten brothers and we are going to see a movie that's rated PG.

**Girl 1:** "Daddy, Dad come here."

**Boy:** "This is stupid. I didn't do anything bad. Let's play." (Moves a wooden ramp across the entrance to the housekeeping area.) "Honey, pretend this is a jail and I can't get out. See, I got on handcuffs." (Puts wrists together.)

**Girl 1:** "I can get you out. See, I just did."

**Girl 2:** "Daddy, Daddy. I want to be baby."

**Girl 1:** "No, you will not be the baby."

**Girl 2:** "I am the baby—goo, goo, ga, ga." (Grabs baby bottle and crawls on the floor with it in her mouth.)

**Girl 1:** "Then who's going to be the father?"

**Boy:** "Not me, I'm going to work."

These observations raise many questions about creativity, including what creativity is, how children's creativity might differ from adults', and what adults do to help or hinder children's creative growth. In this chapter, we explore the role of creativity in young children's lives and its rightful place in the early childhood curriculum.

## THEORETICAL AND RESEARCH BASE: DEFINING CREATIVITY

The word *create* comes from the Latin word *creare,* which means "to make a thing which has not been made before; to bring into being" (Barnhart & Barnhart, 1983). Based on these origins, the word *creative* is used in contemporary society to refer to having the power to create, invent, or produce; approaching the realm of art (imaginative, artistic, literary); and involving something useful or worthwhile (constructive, purposeful). **Creativity** is a thinking and responding process that involves connecting with our previous experience, responding to stimuli (objects, symbols, ideas, people, situations), and generating at least one unique combination (Parnes, 1963). E. Paul Torrance, one of the leading researchers in the field of creativity, defined creativity as "the process of sensing problems, forming ideas, and deriving unprecedented solutions of unique problems with elaboration and embellishment" (cited in Tennent & Berthelsen, 1997, p. 91).

The children who were described in the teacher's notebook, for instance, connected with their previous experiences (e.g., an absent father), responded to objects (e.g., making margarine tubs into band hats), used symbols (e.g., hands joined to represent handcuffs), used ideas (e.g., a PG-rated movie), collaborated with other people (e.g., the flock of pigeons), and responded to situations (e.g., playing house in the housekeeping area). As we look at children's play, it is also apparent that creativity is both a cognitive (thinking) process and an affective (feeling) process (Feldhusen, 1995) that is dependent upon a complex interplay of biological, psychological, and social factors (Craft, 1999; Dacey & Lennon, 1998). Figure 1.1 summarizes the cognitive and affective dimensions of creativity.

From a psychologist's point of view, creativity is the ability to make something new out of available and stored information. With young children, that "something new" may be something that is old and familiar to adults, but more than a copy to the child. When 3-year-old Ruiz paints a "mandala" (a circle shape with sunlike rays emanating from it), it is new to him even though adults have seen it many times in other young children's drawings. When children create, they draw upon their previous experiences, respond to internal and external stimuli, and express themselves in inventive, symbolic ways. Consider, for example, the spontaneous play of two preschoolers. Arwen, a 5-year-old, is pretending to be invisible, and Jessica, a 30-month-old, has wrapped a block in a blanket that she now refers to as "baby." Because they are using experience and stimuli for self-expression, we would say that they are thinking creatively.

Yet, as the comments depicted in Figure 1.2 illustrate, the word *creativity* is interpreted many different ways. Everyday understandings of the term can also be full of contradictions. People may:

- Say that creativity is an asset, but have difficulty explaining it.
- See it as an everyday thing, but limit it to the arts.
- Suppose that it is irrational, yet treat it as if it were "super-rational" or inspired.
- Believe it is impractical, yet credit it with great solutions to life's most perplexing problems (Harrison, 1984).

The next section examines children's creative behavior in greater detail.

## *Criteria for Creativity*

In order for a behavior to be creative, it must meet four basic criteria (Guilford, 1984; Jackson & Messick, 1965). These criteria are described below using examples of young children's behavior.

### *Criterion 1: Creative behavior is original; it has a low probability of occurrence.*

Two-year-old Adam attended a college hockey game with his father, and the toddler now wants to be a hockey player. When Adam asked for hockey equipment, his parents told him he was too little and that it was too expensive, so Adam in-

**Figure 1.1**
Dimensions of
Creativity

**Four Cognitive Dimensions**
*Creativity as a Thinking Process*
**1. Fluency**
   - Generating a large quantity of relevant responses
   - Following a train of thought
   - Building up collections of related ideas
**2. Flexibility**
   - Approaching things in alternative ways
   - Changing categories as appropriate
   - Viewing the problem from a different perspective
**3. Originality**
   - Producing unusual, novel, unique, or clever ideas
   - Combining known ideas into some new form and connecting the seemingly unconnected
**4. Elaboration**
   - Filling out ideas and adding interesting details
   - Stretching or expanding on an idea

**Four Affective Dimensions**
*Creativity as a Feeling Process*
**1. Curiosity**
   - Wondering, puzzling about something
   - Playing with ideas
   - Following intuition to see what happens
**2. Complexity**
   - Feeling challenged to do things in detailed ways
   - Seeking many different alternatives
   - Bringing order out of chaos
   - Seeing missing parts between what is and what could be
**3. Risk-Taking**
   - A willingness to express ideas to others
   - The courage to expose self to criticism or failure
   - The confidence to follow a hunch and "invest" in a humble idea
**4. Imagination and Fantasy**
   - The ability to form rich and varied mental images ("what if"/"as if")
   - The ability to put one's self in another place, time, or person's shoes
   - An intuitive sense of what might be or what something might become

*Source:* Adapted from Guilford (1984) and Sternberg (1997).

**Figure 1.2**
Views of Creativity

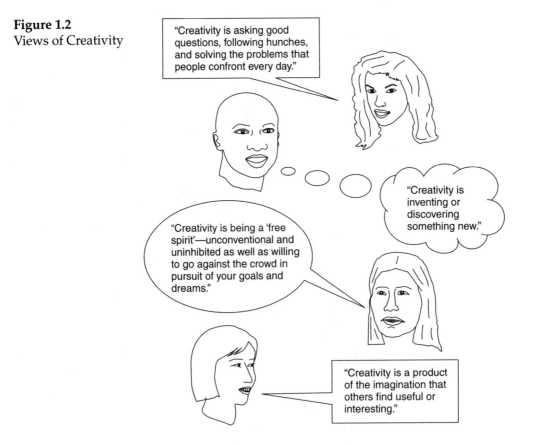

vented his own. He used a wooden spoon for a hockey stick, his sister's empty lip gloss container for a puck, socks for hockey gloves, and the open door to a closet as the goal mouth. Now, "playing goalie" while his dad or older brother does the sports commentary is Adam's favorite game. Adam's behavior is unusual and surprising rather than typical and predictable. Thus it has a low probability of occurrence, and it is original.

*Criterion 2: Creative behavior is appropriate and relevant.*
Six-year-old twins Becky and Belinda both love Hans Christian Andersen's "The Little Mermaid." They want to look like mermaids and need to create long, flowing hair, so Becky suggests using scarves attached with bobby pins. Their mother is delighted by their inventiveness and happily supplies these materials. To create a tail, Belinda has the idea of using a sock. Once again, their mother helps out and gives them an old pair of socks to use. Belinda cuts off the foot portion and stretches the ankle part over both of her ankles, turning her feet outward to represent "fins." The twins' behavior is a good illustration of appropriateness. In order for behavior to be creative, it needs to be relevant to the goals of the person who produced it.

*Criterion 3: Creative behavior is fluent; it results in many new, meaningful forms.*

Four-year-old Louie likes to invent things and does so frequently. One day he was fixing his own cereal at the breakfast table while his mother chatted on the telephone in the next room. He held up a sealed plastic sandwich bag filled with milk and cereal for his mother to see. "Look," Louie announced, "I just invented portable cereal. Now I can eat breakfast without missing cartoons!" Instead of scolding Louie, his mother described his behavior to her friend over the telephone, then added proudly, "He's my little inventor." By combining several apparently unrelated elements—two foods, television viewing, convenience, and a plastic bag—Louie has created a new, meaningful form. Fluency in creativity is comparable to fluency with language; it means that the child can generate one idea after another with apparent ease.

*Criterion 4: Creative behavior is flexible; it explores and uses nontraditional approaches to problem solving.*

Lucia is seated next to Tomas, a fellow kindergartner who is disassembling a grease pencil. He pulls the string and unwraps the paper coiled around the lead. Lucia watches as Tomas throws the curls of paper in the trash can, then she retrieves them. She cuts two pieces of curled paper, glues them on her drawing, and attaches a piece of string to each one. "There," she says aloud. "The windows of my house have shades just like this." Lucia's teacher comments on Lucia's picture, saying, "And the shades on the windows you drew really roll up and down, too! This looks like a very special picture—will you choose it for your portfolio?" Lucia's behavior is a good example of flexibility. She wanted to make her drawing three-dimensional and saw possibilities in material that others considered useless. She also used a nontraditional method when she rummaged through the trash can in order to achieve her goal.

As the behaviors of these young children suggest, behavior is creative when it is original, appropriate, fluent, and flexible.

## Creativity During Early Childhood

Creative behavior in adults or older children and creative behavior in young children are somewhat different. When we talk about more mature people's creativity, we usually emphasize things such as expertise, which involves the technical skill, artistic ability, talent, or knowledge of useful information that they bring to whatever they produce; and work habits, which include work style, concentration and persistence, the ability to generate new possibilities, and openness to new ideas (Amabile, 1983; Kohn, 1987). Children, on the other hand, obviously have less experience than adults and therefore less expertise, and their work styles are less well developed. But whatever young children may lack in terms of expertise or style, they more than compensate for in their unique ways of thinking and approaching a task. Here is what Caitlin, a 3 1/2-year-old, says out loud as she draws a picture. Notice Caitlin's vivid imagination as she describes the many different pictures she draws as well as her lack of inhibition about revealing her inner thoughts:

*I'm makin' a butterfly. This is grass, this green stuff is grass. I'm making a bridge this time. The butterfly's gonna go over the bridge—under the bridge, I mean. . . . Now I'll make myself. I need some pink. Hmm, no pink. [she chooses a red crayon.] I'll just have to color light if I want to make some pink. There, that's my honker [nose]. This is my hair. I'm going to make some hair. There I am! [She smiles.] I want black. Purple will do. I have some blush on—there! Ha-ha! I'll have to make a sidewalk here. Those are drainers [drains], like little logs. [In a sing-song voice] I need a blue log log, blue log, blue log log. Can you make a flower, Samantha? Blue will do it! Blue water. See, this is a log. I forgot to make the sunshine. I'll pretend this is Rudolph [the Red-Nosed Reindeer]. Sunshine. There! Now I'm going to make an elephant. . . ."*

### Unique Features of Children's Thought.
As the preceding glimpse of Caitlin's thinking suggests, children excel at three characteristics thought to be related to creative genius: (1) sensitivity to internal and external stimuli, (2) lack of inhibition, and (3) the ability to become completely absorbed in an activity (Holden, 1987).

Marina, a 3-year-old, is a good example of a child with sensitivity to stimuli. She was at a very important gathering where the bishop of her Greek Orthodox church was visiting the congregation. All of the adults were a bit intimidated and felt awkward; Marina "broke the ice" by walking up to the bishop and asking, "Do you know how to color? Would you like to draw pictures with me?" Marina seemed to sense that welcoming the bishop was important; she used her knowledge of "how to make friends" in a way that the entire congregation still remembers fondly. Marina's response illustrates the sensitivity to stimuli that is a characteristic of the very young.

Keiko, a 4-year-old, reveals his spontaneity and lack of inhibition during a testing situation. When the examiner asks him if he is "very happy, happy, not very happy, a little sad, or very sad," Keiko says, "Happy!", whirls around, takes the pen from the examiner, and circles the "smiley" face on the test form himself. Like Keiko, most young children are less self-conscious and freer in their responses than adults would be in a similar situation.

Lauren exemplifies the young child's complete absorption in an activity. She has created an imaginary friend named "Mousie," and before her family travels anywhere, she lifts the gas tank door and puts her hand, palm up, next to the opening so that Mousie can crawl inside. Lauren talks aloud to her imaginary pet and gives him instructions on how to behave, completely unconcerned that anyone might overhear her. She is fully absorbed in her play and, unlike most adults, she reveals her imaginative thinking to others rather than attempting to conceal it.

As the behavior of Lauren, Keiko, and Marina illustrates, young children can become totally absorbed in pretending. They surprise us by their thinking, spontaneity, and playfulness. Because they are newer to the world, their sensory impressions are particularly keen. When you think about it, these are some of the characteristics that lead us to seek careers working with young children, traits that endear the very young to us as adults. Of all the characteristics that young children manifest through behavior, perhaps none is more charming than their world of make-believe, the world of imagination and fantasy that we will explore next.

*Imagination and Fantasy.*
In the estimation of both experts and laypersons, imagination and fantasy are the great creative assets of early childhood. These assets differ from those generally attributed to adults—literal, factual thinking. Because literal thought is the preferred mode of adults, adults sometimes push children into literal thought rather than respecting and appreciating young children's propensity for imagination and fantasy. Contrasting the behaviors of two teachers is a good way to show how teachers can do a better job of capitalizing upon the young child's active imagination. One kindergarten teacher is reminding the children that they must be quiet while walking down the school hallway to lunch because they might disturb students in other classes. The other kindergarten teacher reminds her group of students about the fall leaves they saw drifting down when they were outside on the playground together. She tells them that they are going to "float down the hallway as slowly and quietly as the leaves." As you might guess, the second teacher, the one who tapped into the children's imagination, is more successful in obtaining the desired result. Because her students are concentrating on expressing the gentle motion of the leaves through their bodies, they remain relatively quiet. The children in the other class must be reminded several times to stay quiet and to walk instead of running. This example also helps to illustrate why it is common to say that young children have "active imaginations"—the boundaries between reality and fantasy are not as clearly demarcated for children as they are for adults, and imaginative thought comes as readily to the young child as literal thought comes to the adult. In fact, it has long been the opinion of experts on creativity that, for most human beings, imagination peaks during early childhood.

What, exactly, is imagination and why might it be more active early in life? **Imagination** is defined as the ability to form rich and varied mental images or concepts of people, places, things, and situations that are not present. Kindergartner Mallory's drawings in Figure 1.3 offer a good example of the imagination at work. She has become intrigued by flowers—not just ordinary flowers, but flowers that exist only in her imagination. As she imagines what she calls "an acrobatic flower" and "a flower with pineapple teeth," Mallory uses both objective thought (what she knows) and intuitive thought (what she feels). In addition, Mallory must think about how to communicate that knowledge, those feelings, and those possibilities to others. For this reason, "imagination is to the young child what problem solving is to the adult"; it is an "as if" situation (Weininger, 1988, p. 142). Mallory has seen pineapple chunks before; now she draws "as if" they were in the flower's mouth as teeth. She has seen acrobats on television; now she draws her flower "as if" it too had the physical skills of an acrobat. By examining how Mallory has combined apparently unrelated elements in her drawings to produce surprising new forms, we can glimpse Mallory's imagination at work.

**Figure 1.3**   Mallory's Flowers

Fantasy is a subset of imagination. Fantasy occurs when a person uses the imagination to create particularly vivid mental images or concepts that have little similarity to the real world. Fantasy explores the realm of make-believe, of the impossible—or at least the not yet possible. Fantasy is a "what if" situation (Weininger, 1988, p. 144). Here is how one mother described her son's use of fantasy as he created a pretend companion:

> My son, who just turned four, became fascinated by deer. This happened, I
> think, because while we were visiting friends out in the country, a doe and her
> fawn came into the yard. Now Scott has created a pretend friend named

*Imagination and fantasy are the great creative assets of early childhood.*

"Fawnbelly." His bedroom window faces the front porch, and that, according to my son, is where she sleeps. He feeds her by putting a plastic apple on the windowsill, and in return, she protects him at night. When he talks about Fawnbelly, I can picture this gentle, expectant doe with huge brown eyes keeping watch over our house.

This mother obviously values the vivid imagination and rich fantasy life of her child, and rightly so. Harvard psychologist Howard Gardner (1993) has described how young children are freer in their thinking, moving easily between and among the various modes of thought: "The young child is not bothered by inconsistencies, departures from convention, nonliteralness . . . which often results in unusual and appealing juxtapositions and associations" (p. 228). In fact, many adult artists report that they must struggle to get back in touch with those feelings and attitudes of early childhood in order to realize their creative potential. It is this nonliteral mode of thinking, so prevalent during early childhood, that balances and complements literal thinking. As the next section will describe, it is the skillful combination of the two that is necessary to produce great ideas.

## Modes of Thinking

The process of examining our own thinking—when we "think about thinking"—is referred to as metacognition. One way of thinking about thinking that is especially useful in a discussion of creativity is to compare/contrast different types of thought and their relationships to the creative process. Types of thinking may be broadly categorized as convergent or divergent. The creative process relies upon them both.

### Convergent Thinking

Just as the word *converge* implies, convergent thinking leads to one, and only one, acceptable answer. Convergent thinking can be conceptualized as "vertical" because it involves moving back and forth between higher and lower levels of thought. Basically, convergent thinking "digs the same hole deeper" (De Bono, 1971, p. 5). A good example of a convergent problem-solving task is a group of primary grade children using a simple scale to weigh various objects and arrange them from lightest to heaviest.

### Divergent Thinking

Divergent thinking has a different focus from convergent thinking. Just as the word *diverge* implies, divergent thinking searches for many different ways of defining or interpreting a problem. Divergent thinking can be conceptualized as "lateral" thinking; it "is concerned with digging the hole in another place" (De Bono, 1971, p. 5). A good example of divergent thinking is the teacher who encourages children to write and illustrate their own books. The teacher expects a wide variety of responses and anticipates that no two student-created books will be exactly alike. Table 1.1 is a summary of the distinctions between convergent and divergent thinking.

### TABLE 1.1   Modes of Thinking

| Convergent | Divergent |
|---|---|
| Analytical—correctness is valued | Generative—information is valued for its ability to stimulate ideas |
| Selective—one correct path; rejects the irrelevant | Explorative—many possible paths, irrelevancies are seen as potential sources of inspiration |
| Predictable—follows a logical sequence | Unpredictable—relies on intuition as much as logic; makes psychic leaps |
| Leads to good answers | Is necessary for great answers |

*Source:* Adapted from Dacey (1989).

When children create, they use both types of thinking and learn to switch from one mode to another at appropriate times in the creative process. They need appropriate experiences that allow both types of thinking to develop and flourish. In other words, imagination and fantasy are just as useful and valuable in everyday life as literal thinking. The same brain that calculates a math problem can listen to the story "The Three Billy Goats Gruff" and visualize the troll crouching underneath the bridge; the same brain that processes print in order to read can imagine what will happen if the lids are left off the paste jars without actually allowing the paste to dry out. It is the blending of literal and imaginative thought that is necessary for problem solving (De Bono, 1992). Young children also need teachers who understand that creativity is a skillful blend of divergent and convergent modes of thought.

## The Theory of Multiple Intelligences

Over the past decade, our view of human intelligence has expanded and enlarged. In the past, there was a tendency to think of intelligence as a singular trait—the general capacity of the human being for storing, retrieving, and processing information. Howard Gardner (1993) defines intelligence as "the ability to solve problems, or to fashion products that are of consequence in a particular cultural setting or community" (p. 15), and he has proposed that there are at least eight types of intelligence. He argues that each of those ways of thinking is sufficiently distinctive to warrant a special category. Those eight types of intelligence are:

1. *Verbal/linguistic*—intelligence with words and language, such as the skill possessed by a writer or a person who can speak several languages fluently.
2. *Logical/mathematical*—intelligence with sequential thinking and numerical reasoning ability, such as the abilities possessed by a mathematician or scientist.
3. *Bodily/kinesthetic*—wisdom about one's own body and its movements, such as the intelligence possessed by a figure skater or a wide receiver in football.
4. *Visual/spatial*—intelligence in using "the mind's eye" to work with images and see their interrelationships, such as the intelligence needed by an architect.
5. *Musical/rhythmic*—intelligence having to do with sound patterns, mastery of musical notation, and musical talent, such as the skills of a composer/performer.
6. *Interpersonal*—intelligence in dealing with human interaction and perceptivity about how to resolve social problems, such as the abilities of a skilled counselor or therapist.
7. *Intrapersonal*—wisdom about the self that leads to self-knowledge and personal growth, such as the intelligence of a person who fully understands how he or she learns.
8. *Environmental/naturalist*—intelligence having to do with adapting to and learning about the physical environment, both natural and man-made (Checkley, 1997). This type of intelligence is needed by a marine biologist, a city planner, or a forest ranger.

Furthermore, Gardner argued that only the first two forms of intelligence—verbal/linguistic and logical/mathematical—were routinely emphasized in American schools and that, as a result, much human potential was being wasted. Many other educators and researchers have concluded that other forms of intelligence have been undervalued in our society and that we need to plan programs that respect these different ways of knowing (Hatch, 1997; Reiff, 1997). To get an idea of what an early childhood theme that provides for all eight types of intelligence might look like, see the MI theme on pets in Table 1.2.

Gardner urges educators who seek to apply his theory to use their creative thinking processes and aim for three important goals: (1) to cultivate skills that are valued in community and society, (2) to approach new concepts and subjects in a variety of ways, and (3) to personalize instruction as much as possible (Latham, 1997).

**TABLE 1.2   Teaching Themes Based on Multiple Intelligences**

| The Eight Intelligences | Preschool MI Theme on Colors | First-Grade MI Theme on Patterns | Third-Grade MI Theme on Pets |
|---|---|---|---|
| **Verbal/ Linguistic** | Read concept books about colors (e.g., *Who Said Red?* [Serfozo, 1992]), produce class books about various colors (e.g., What Is Green? Our Favorite Colors), learn to recognize the names of the primary colors, conduct a simple survey to discover favorite colors of classmates and family members, invent a class version of a book that features colors, such as *Brown Bear, Brown Bear, What Do You See?* (Martin, 1995), learn color names in a different language, read *Naming Colors* (Dewey, 1995), learn the chant *My Crayons Talk* (Hubbard, 1996). | Define the concept of patterns by finding examples of patterns in the classroom, explore word patterns (e.g., chants, rhymes, and raps), write couplets, listen for patterns in story language (e.g., "but it was too small," "but it was too large," "and it was just right"), recite a poem with a refrain in unison, search for patterns in groups of words that rhyme (e.g., mall, hall, fall, wall), read and perform a story in rhyme such as *Chicka Chicka Boom Boom* (Martin & Archambault, 1989) | Identify animal sounds, discuss chapter books about pets, maintain a detailed observational log about a classroom pet, create group booklets with practical information about the care and feeding of pets, tape-record reports about a particular type of pet, read the classified section of the newspaper to see what pets are for sale, visit pet rescue Web sites to see what pets are available (e.g., mustangs, greyhounds), make a vocabulary book of words for groups of animals (e.g., flock, herd). |

TABLE 1.2 *(continued)*

| The Eight Intelligences | Preschool MI Theme on Colors | First-Grade MI Theme on Patterns | Third-Grade MI Theme on Pets |
|---|---|---|---|
| **Logical/ Mathematical** | Use paint samples to arrange hues from light to dark and produce color "families," develop a color chart after experimenting with food coloring (e.g., blue and red make _____), play sorting games with attribute blocks—flat, plastic blocks in 3 colors (red, yellow, and blue), 3 shapes (circle, triangle, square), and 3 sizes (small, medium, large), play a matching game with the color word on one side of a puzzle piece and a picture of a crayon that color on the matching piece. | Examine patterns in mathematical equations (e.g., adding 1 to a number), recognize the fact that subtraction problems can be checked by adding the two bottom numbers, produce pictorial patterns on the computer using various types of software, use a number line on the floor to count by ones, twos, and so forth, watch the video *How the Leopard Got Its Spots* and note the patterns in animals' fur (e.g., zebra stripes, giraffe spots), as well as the patterns in the African choir's music. | Count the number of pets owned by everyone in the class, create a simple bar graph of the favorite pets owned by the class, list the common features of domesticated animals, rank-order pets from most to least popular, identify the most unusual pet owned by anyone in the group, match various pets to their preferred food choices, analyze the consequences of neglecting pets' care, figure out how much it would cost to raise a cat or dog for a year, make lists of pet-care tips after consulting reference materials. |
| **Bodily/ Kinesthetic** | Make finger and hand prints of different colors, use a simplified computer keyboard with keys in different colors, play a simple teacher-made color game on a plastic shower curtain or tablecloth on the floor, group children according to the color of their clothing for an activity, decorate plain cloth dolls for each child so that the doll's features can be made to match the child's hair color, eye color, etc., use hard candy to match colors to flavors (e.g., red for cherry, yellow for lemon), take a color walk after reading *Colors Everywhere* (Hoban, 1997). | Invent patterns of sound (e.g., clapping, tapping feet), create a product using a pattern (e.g., in and out for weaving), make pattern cards for others to follow using large wooden beads and string, give children a chance to arrange their bodies into letter patterns (e.g., a task card that asks 3 children to make their bodies into a capital letter A), make patterns using an ink pad and stamps constructed from styrofoam, use wallpaper book samples to search for repeated patterns and sort them into groups on the floor, make rubbings of patterns (e.g., bottom of shoe). | Compare the relative sizes of pets to one another and one's self, invent a dance that characterizes a particular animal's style of moving, give a demonstration of how to groom a pet (e.g., a 4-H student showing how to care for a cow's feet), research and analyze how pets move (e.g., how a horse runs, a snake slithers). |

*(continued)*

TABLE 1.2 *(continued)*

| The Eight Intelligences | Preschool MI Theme on Colors | First-Grade MI Theme on Patterns | Third-Grade MI Theme on Pets |
|---|---|---|---|
| **Visual/ Spatial** | Use word configuration (the outline or shape of the word) to match color words to the correct shape; use swatches of fabric to match colors, sort individual boxes of crayons into plastic containers of all the same color of crayon, identify the colors that typically go with various foods (e.g., apples as yellow, red, green or combinations of these), sort plastic fruits and vegetables by colors, discover the magic of mixing colors in *White Rabbit's Color Book* (Baker, 1995). | Create designs using parquetry blocks, design patterned borders for original picture books, make and follow cue cards to show the gestures that accompany an action song (e.g., "Little Cabin in the Woods"), print out common signs in various colors from the computer and make into a color-sorting game, look at a piece of landscaping software to see how patterns are used, take a virtual field trip to a museum to look for patterns in art, use architectural blocks to build a structure and make a diagram of the structure. | Make sculptures of various pets, examine a pet closely and create life-size silhouettes, identify animal tracks and match them to the animals that made them, design a poster to encourage responsible pet ownership, create diagrams of pets labeled with the proper terminology (e.g., mane, withers, and fetlock for a horse), take a video visit to a veterinarian's office, go on a virtual field trip to a pet supplies store online. |
| **Musical/ Rhythmic Interpersonal** | Sing color songs (e.g., "Jenny Jenkins" or "Mary Wore Her Red Dress"), learn a color song in another language (e.g., "De Colores"), use a toy xylophone with colored keys and a color-coded piece of music for a simple nursery tune and learn to play a song. | Participate in simple dances and musical games (e.g., square dance steps), move "in time" with music (e.g., swaying), lead a rhythm band, watch a musical video with a bouncing ball that shows the pattern for singing; recite a cumulative rhyme (e.g., The House That Jack Built), sing a song with a chorus or a refrain. | Find or invent an instrumental selection that captures the feelings associated with various pets, sing songs about animals, choose a rhythm that matches the characteristic movement of a pet, compose a song about a pet using music software. |

**TABLE 1.2** *(continued)*

| The Eight Intelligences | Preschool MI Theme on Colors | First-Grade MI Theme on Patterns | Third-Grade MI Theme on Pets |
|---|---|---|---|
| **Interpersonal** | Work with a partner or a small group to develop a poster collage of colors, read a story about different skin tones, make a big poster-sized book on colors and share it with another class, use color paddles (wooden frames with tinted plastic inside) to look at things with a partner and discuss how a change in color changes the object. | Infer the steps in a process by observing others (e.g., how to operate a videotape, learn a jump rope game, play hopscotch), work with a partner to learn a rhyme with a clapping pattern ("Miss Lucy"), use coffee can drums to follow a tapping pattern, solve a simple secret code, such as numbering the letters of the alphabet, learn about patterns and fabrics of different cultures in *Kente Colors* (Chocolate, 1996). | Participate in a class project designed to safeguard the welfare of pets in the community, interview a pet shop owner, arrange a classroom visit with an expert on animal care, correspond over e-mail with volunteers at the local animal shelter, put on a pet show with a wide variety of forms of recognition for pets (e.g., furriest, friendliest, etc.). |
| **Intrapersonal** | Think about the feelings associated with various colors (e.g., red as fiery, yellow as sunshine), choose dress-up clothes based on favorite colors, use the paint feature of a piece of art software to try out several colors for an object or a picture before deciding which one to save or print out. | Look for daily routines that are patterns of behavior (e.g., getting ready for school), identify patterns of sound that are pleasant (e.g., ticking of a clock), experiment with a piece of software to make patterns until a satisfying combination is produced. | Maintain a journal of activities enjoyed with a pet, describe reasons for choosing a particular pet as a favorite, prepare a statement of beliefs about animal rights, write a persuasive argument for choosing a mature animal rather than a baby animal or an animal without a home rather than a pedigree. |
| **Naturalist/ Environmental** | Take a color walk, sort fallen leaves by color, search for animals who are hidden by their protective coloration in pictures, look at how different book illustrators use color and compare/contrast (e.g., Tomie de Paola and Ed Young), document how colors in nature change (e.g., watching an amaryllis bulb grow). | Look for repeated patterns in the environment (e.g., sunrise/sunset, a picket fence), listen for patterns of sound in nature (e.g., ocean waves) and patterns of sound from objects invented by people (e.g., train), make a collection of logos and look for patterns. | Research appropriate habitats for different kinds of pets, compare and contrast pet habitats with those of wild animals, investigate the illegal sale of exotic or endangered species pets, learn more about animals whose habitats are threatened by humans, investigate the Web site of the Humane Society. |

*Source:* Based on Gardner (1993) and Armstrong (1987).

## Stages in the Creative Process

According to the classic theory of creativity, the creative process consists of four stages (Wallas, 1926). The stages are recursive, meaning that a person may move back and forth between and among them, rather than following them in an invariant sequence from first to last. As we look at each stage, we will follow the behavior of a classroom woodworking project.

   **1.** *Preparation or brainstorming.* During this stage, the person applies knowledge, skill, and understanding to materials, objects, problems, or combinations of these things. Creative individuals "engage" with the materials, objects, or problems with a playful or experimental attitude. Engagement with the ideas may be deliberate or accidental.

   Ms. Levenstein is planning to set up a woodworking area in her classroom for the first time. She begins by consulting the professional literature about how to go about developing such a center (Skeen, Garner, & Cartwright, 1992). The center now includes a workbench, white glue, a set of simple tools, wood scraps of various sizes and shapes, crosscut sections of tree trunks, and milled wooden wheels. She introduces the center by explaining its purpose—to create things out of wood. She emphasizes that the saw blade is very sharp and the need to be careful when driving nails with the hammer. As she explains the appropriate use of the tools, she asks children to come forward and demonstrate each tool's use. When she is finished with the demonstration, she lets the children know that they may work at the bench no more than two at a time and reminds them that the classroom aide will be there to help. At first, children are just interested in examining the tools more closely, holding the pieces of wood in their hands, and pounding a few practice nails into a section of a log with the aide's help. The children are in the stage of preparation.

   **2.** *Incubation.* During this stage, the mind begins to formulate and work on a problem, often through images and associations. Tyrell has been playing with a wheeled vehicle and is now trying to figure out how to make a car using scraps of wood and the wooden wheels with predrilled holes. He tries gluing together four scraps of wood into a boxlike shape for the car. Now the challenge is to figure out how to get the wheels on at the right level so that the car will actually move. He can visualize in his mind's eye what he wants to accomplish; the challenge is to figure out how to engineer the car so that it will roll.

   **3.** *Illumination.* This is an evaluative phase where the person selects some ideas and rejects others. In planning his car, for example, Tyrell thought about something that he had seen his father do many times around the house—use a pencil to mark the place where he wanted to put a nail hole. Using a pencil, Tyrell marks all four places on the wood where the wheels will need to go. One of the classroom aides has brought in a cordless electric drill and is showing the children how to use it. With careful supervision, Tyrell drills four holes on the sides of his car, then hammers the nail through the predrilled hole in the wheel and into the pilot holes he made with the drill. As Tyrell's experience with the illu-

**Figure 1.4**
Stages in the
Creative Process

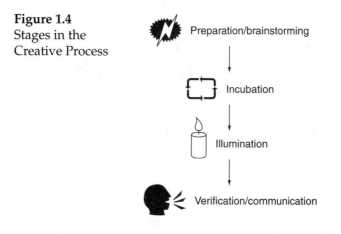

Preparation/brainstorming

Incubation

Illumination

Verification/communication

mination stage of creativity illustrates, it is a time in the process when the ideas that are chosen are rearranged into a satisfying form. Sometimes, illumination is experienced as a flash of insight (aha!), which is instantly recognized as a harmonious and complete way of approaching the task. The Japanese call this moment of enlightenment that comes after long periods of preparation, training, and practice *satori* (Torrance, 1979). That moment of discovery, that "aha!" experience, happens for Tyrell when he begins to think about the finishing touches for his car. He decides to paint the wheels black and the body red, just like his family's car. He also draws on the headlights and taillights with a pencil, then paints them, too. From his facial expression, it is clear that Tyrell is satisfied with the results of his efforts.

    **4.** *Verification/communication.* Now the person tests the product of creative thought in terms of usefulness, completeness, and correctness—in Tyrell's case, he takes his new vehicle "out for a run." He tries it on the floor, then on a ramp, and outside on the playground. One of the wheels seems to be on too tight. It isn't rolling as freely as the others and, as a result, the car is moving rather slowly. Tyrell takes the car back to the woodworking area, explains the situation, and asks for advice. Actually, Tyrell is going through an important, final stage in creativity, one in which the critical, judgmental side of convergent thought goes into action and the idea is fine-tuned, often through feedback from others. This is the stage when the outcome of the creative process "goes public" and is shared with others. By consulting with a more experienced woodworker, Tyrell makes a slight adjustment by loosening the nail on the slow wheel. With encouragement from adults, access to interesting materials, and the time to explore alternatives, Tyrell has moved through all four of the classic stages in the creative process to produce a homemade wooden car that is a source of pride and accomplishment. These stages in the creative process are summarized in Figure 1.4.

## Research on Creativity

Campbell, B. (1997). Variations on a theme: How teachers interpret MI Theory. *Educational Leadership, 55*(1), 14–19.

Cramond, B., & Uusikyla, K. (1994). Are expressions of creativity culturally dependent? *Gifted and Talented International, 9*(1), 8–10.

Dinca, M. (1999). Creative children in Romanian society. *Childhood Education, 75*(6), 355–358.

Ebbeck, M. (1996). Children constructing their own knowledge. *International Journal of Early Years Education, 4*(2), 5–27.

Hearne, D., & Stone, S. (1995). Multiple intelligences and underachievement: Lessons from individuals with learning disabilities. *Journal of Learning Disabilities, 28*(7), 439–448.

Newberger, J. (1997). New brain development research: A wonderful window of opportunity to build public support for early childhood education! *Young Children, 52*(4), 4–9.

Policastro, E. (1995). Creative intuition: An integrative review. *Creativity Research Journal, 8*(2), 99–113.

Poole, C. R. (1997). Maximizing learning: A conversation with Renate Nummela Caine. *Educational Leadership, 54*(6), 11–15.

Rodd, J. (1999). Encouraging young children's critical and creative thinking skills: One approach in an English elementary school. *Childhood Education, 75*(6), 350–354.

Runco, M. A., & Pritzker, S. (1999). *Encyclopedia of creativity.* San Diego, CA: Academic Press.

### Web Sites

National Association for Gifted Children

*http://www.mplc.co.uk/orgs/index1.html*

National Art Education Association

*http://www.naea-reston.org*

Inclusion Web Site

*http://www.uni.edu/coe/inclusion*

Quotations Related to Creativity

*http://www.ozemail.com.au/~caveman/Creative/Resources/crquote.htm*

Resources for Gifted Education

*http://www.ced.sped.org/fact/gt-asso.htm*

## ❀ IDENTIFYING CREATIVITY

The creative process has been studied in various ways. Isaksen (1992) refers to these approaches as "the four Ps of creativity":

- Study of the *people* involved, including their traits, characteristics, or attributes (Sheldon, 1995).
- Study of the creative *process,* including how a task is approached and performed (Runco, 1994).
- Study of creative *products,* including the quality and usefulness of the final outcome (Simonton, 1996).
- Study of the *press*—all the external, context-specific variables that exert an influence on people engaged in creative processes (Sternberg, 1997).

But whether we study creative contexts, products, processes, or people, the basic question is: Why? Why do people create? Many experts have attempted to explain what urges people to be creative (Simonton, 1996; Torrance, 1995). Theoretically speaking, explanations for why people create can be conceptualized as humanistic, psychoanalytic, or constructivist. From a humanistic perspective, people create because creativity is a feature of human thought that differentiates us from other forms of life; creative behavior makes us "more fully human." From a psychoanalytic perspective, people create out of a need to satisfy inner emotional drives. From a constructivist point of view, creativity is a concept-building and problem-solving strategy that depends on the child's level of intellectual functioning. Figure 1.5 is an overview of these three theoretical orientations and the theorists most closely associated with each.

## *Children's Creative Abilities*

All children have creative potential. In programs where teachers and parents believe this, children's creativity flourishes (Duffy, 1998). Based on a review of the research, when children are using their creative abilities, they typically are:

*Playful, Persistent, and Intrinsically Motivated*

- Become intensely absorbed in activities, persist at work or play, and concentrate on a single task for a relatively long period of time.
- Explore, experiment, manipulate, play, ask questions, make guesses, and discuss findings.
- Use imaginative role-playing, language play, storytelling, and artwork to solve problems and make sense out of their world.

*Curious, Intuitive, and Resourceful*

- Ask many questions.
- Are capable of tolerating ambiguity as they explore alternatives.

**Figure 1.5**
Theories of
Creativity

---

### Classical Theories

**Theory: Humanistic**
- **Carl Rogers: The creative person is fully functioning.**

**Implications for Early Childhood:** If the young child's natural curiosity, passion for learning, and active imagination are deadened by adults who insist on quiet, calm, and facts, then an avenue for self-expression is closed off and the child becomes less rather than more capable from a creative standpoint over time.

- **Abraham Maslow: The creative person is self-actualized.**

**Implications for Early Childhood:** In order to be creative, a person needs some measure of self-direction. When schedules are rigid and tasks are predetermined, children do not have an opportunity to make choices or solve interesting problems. Over time, they learn to depend on others for ideas rather than trusting their own ideas.

- **Rollo May: Being creative is courageous.**

**Implications for Early Childhood:** Young children's ideas often seem outrageous or silly to adults who seek large amounts of predictability and control. Yet children need permission to pursue their unorthodox ideas so that they can "dare to be different" throughout life.

**Theory: Psychoanalytic**
- **Alfred Adler: Creativity is a way of compensating for perceived physical or psychological inferiority.**

**Implications for Early Childhood:** Rather than having a "talent scout" mentality, in which only those children with potential to become great artists or inventors are afforded opportunities for creative expression, teachers need to cultivate the creativity in all children.

- **Carl Jung: Creative ideas emanate from a deeper source, from the "collective unconscious."**

**Implications for Early Childhood:** Each child has a propensity to connect with human history and traditions, such as an interest in stories. Therefore, it is essential that children become familiar with the creative processes and products of other times, cultures, ethnic groups, and races so that they can begin to perceive their personal connections with the sum of human creativity.

- **Otto Rank: The development of creativity requires supportive significant others during the first 5 years of life.**

**Implications for Early Childhood:** The early years generally are regarded as the imaginative peak of life and a time when naïve responses to works of art are honest and spontaneous. When adults fail to capitalize on these rich resources and cultivate the child's sense of wonder, only the strongest-willed child can sustain his or her own creativity in the absence of support.

**Figure 1.5**
*(Continued)*

---

**Theory: Constructivist**
- **Jean Piaget: Creativity is type of problem solving that is dependent upon the child's thinking processes.**

**Implications for Early Childhood:** Developing the young child's problem-solving processes gives children the time and opportunity to explore materials and use hands-on approaches in pursuing solutions to interesting challenges.

**Contemporary Theories**

---

**Multiple Intelligences Theory**
- **Howard Gardner: Creativity consists of a constellation of 8 different intelligences.**

**Implications for Early Childhood:** Every young child possesses at least 8 distinctive ways of knowing that must be considered and valued when planning any curriculum that claims to meet individual needs.

**Triarchic Theory of Creativity**
- **Robert J. Sternberg: Creativity is a cluster of 3 types of abilities; synthesizing (seeing connections others miss, producing novel ideas), analyzing (recognizing which ideas are good ones), and practicing (translating ideas into practical accomplishments).**

**Implications for Early Childhood:** Young children need to have role models of creativity, raise questions, have time to use trial-and-error, take sensible risks, define and pursue their own problems, puzzle over ideas, overcome obstacles, earn support for their ideas, and be evaluated in ways that respect creativity.

**Optimal Experience or "Flow" Theory**
- **Mihalyi Csikzentmihalyi: Creative individuals are people who acquire competence in a domain of interest and pursue that interest with passion and enjoyment in a frame of mind where they are completely absorbed, lose track of time, and engage in a task for its own sake ("flow").**

**Implications for Early Childhood:** Throughout the world, young children will play spontaneously and persist at their play even though no one is directing it or reinforcing them. In studies of eminently creative adults, one consistent finding is that the lines between play and work are blurred and they tend to approach their work playfully.

---

- Are strongly intuitive and perceptive.
- Enjoy thinking and working independently.

*Resourceful, Nonconforming, and Adventuresome*

- Tend to challenge assumptions or authorities based on well-reasoned differences of opinion.
- Formulate hypotheses and conduct trials to test their ideas.

- Try to bring order out of chaos by organizing their environment.
- Do something new with the old and familiar and display interest in new ideas.
- Use repetition as an opportunity to learn more from an experience rather than becoming bored with it (Davis & Rimm, 1994; McAlpine, 1996; Healy, 1996; Maxim, 1989).

Note that each of these clusters of behavior might also be interpreted in a negative way by uninformed or insensitive adults. The child who is playful, energetic, and intrinsically motivated could be labeled as "hyperactive," the child who is independent, perceptive, and confident as a "smart aleck," and the child who is original, nonconforming, and adventuresome as "strange" or "stubborn." Similarly, adults may prefer children who are subdued, compliant, quiet, neat, polite, and who fit in easily with peers.

This is one reason why it is so important for teachers to be well informed about young children's creativity. You cannot afford to make such an error in judgment because it will damage the child's self-esteem and thwart creative growth.

Notice that these behaviors are generally (1) active rather than passive, (2) child-initiated rather than adult-initiated, and (3) displayed by all children at various times or in particular situations. Does this mean that everyone is creative to some extent? Yes. While there are different dimensions and levels of creativity, everyone is creative if given the chance to be. One early childhood program that gives children this opportunity can be found in a section of Italy called Reggio Emilia.

## *Reggio Emilia: Nurturing Creativity*

Of all the early childhood programs in the world today, those in a municipality of Italy called Reggio Emilia are recognized as some of the very finest (Edwards, Gandini, & Forman, 1993; 1998; Edwards & Springate, 1995). Providing opportunities for children's creative expression is a cornerstone of the early childhood programs in Reggio Emilia, and educators from around the globe travel there to marvel at the creative genius of children that is expressed through their work (Caldwell, 1997). The first question that this raises is: Why? What occurs in these programs that supports children's creative expression? Surely no one would argue that Italian children are innately more creative than other children! So what is the teaching philosophy, what is the curriculum, and what are the conditions that lead to such impressive work from young children? As you read this description of the schools written by Frankie DeGeorge (personal communication, January 30, 1996), think about all of the ways that the schools of Reggio Emilia support creative expression and play.

> The Reggio Emilia approach to early childhood involves a system of interrelationships among children, parents, teachers, and the environment. Central to the approach is the view of the child as an active seeker and builder of knowledge (Edwards, 1993).
>
> Children's interests determine what will be investigated, experienced, and interpreted. This display of interest can be initiated in various ways: by a book, a local happening, or a problem that presents itself within the group. Children's

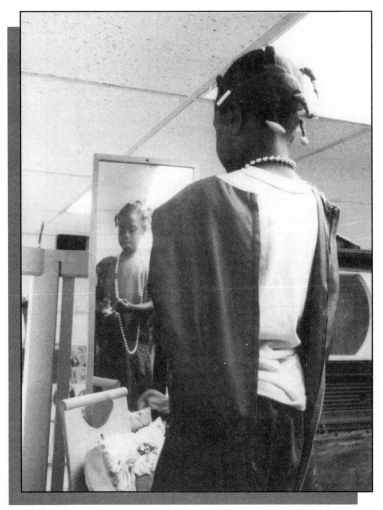

*All children display creative behaviors at various times or in particular situations.*

interest in these projects may last only a few days, be sustained over several weeks, or appear intermittently over a number of months.

The teachers play an important role in these projects—as inquirers to encourage thinking, as co-learners who construct knowledge along with the children, as projectors of the possible directions of a project and as resources for equipment or experiences to support the children's initiatives. It is important to mention here the role of the *atelierista,* or arts educator, who assists the children and the teachers in providing the appropriate art medium for the children's use in expressing and creating, thereby documenting their own work as the project unfolds.

This idea of documentation is another essential element in the Reggio Emilia approach. It begins in the *asili nido* (infant center) for children approximately one to three years of age. Each child has an album filled with photographs, teacher descriptions of events, developmental milestones, and children's scribbles. Seeing these albums gives visitors, and surely parents, an overwhelming sense of the respect and value that teachers have for children. Quotations from parents were seen over each crib in one center. They had been gathered from interviews and conversations with parents. These words, held to be so special by the teachers, conveyed this same feeling for the parents.

Documentation for ages three to five involves the display of children's artwork, which remains at school. It is comprised of photographs, questions and comments of the children as they investigate, experience, and create, all beautifully displayed on classroom walls.

Seeing this documentation contributes to the children's understanding that their words and work are valued by the adults around them. This knowledge engenders a continued interest in creating and participating by the children.

Indeed, this documentation has a positive effect on parents, who can see the whole scope of a project and their child's development through it. This knowledge fuels interest in their child's work and furthers parental participation in the school.

Displays of children's artwork and photograph panels also play an important part in the interior decor of Reggio Emilia schools. The children's artwork is displayed with all the attention and care given to the work of professional artists. Mobiles hang from the ceiling, translucent works were attached to glass, some works were framed on a wall-mounted light box, and many sculptures were neatly arranged on shelves. The effect is delightful.

*A bear with his eyes closed, by a 4-year-old boy.*

The environments draw the children, as well as the adults, into a world of light, reflection, and involvement. Mirrors are seen everywhere—at entrances, along stairwells, under blocks, and, particularly, in the totally mirrored, small triangular houses where a child can see multiple reflections. All the schools visited included a large, tiled, central square or *piazza,* where gatherings take place and special play centers are available. These areas were lovely, with plants, artifacts, and equipment neatly and artistically arranged.

Each of the schools also provided a puppet stage frequently used by the municipal puppeteer, who entertains and intrigues the young children with issues of reality versus fantasy, "It is and it isn't." This recurring theme is also played out in the dress-up centers where, to quote a teacher, "A child goes in one person and comes out another." A large shadow screen where children can create settings and dramatize is also provided.

Other materials found in the schools include blocks with many props, table games, comfortable book corners, housekeeping areas, water-play activities, music rooms for listening and creating, and inside climbing equipment.

The dining rooms were especially inviting with decorative items that added a homelike touch. Small tables were covered with cloths. Each table was graced with a centerpiece; at one school, it was an African violet, at others, children's creations.

In the art rooms, varieties of paper, art supplies, and various materials were neatly stored on open shelves for everyone's use. The tops of the storage units held divided trays of bits and pieces, beads, seeds, buttons, sequins, and marvelous collections of items to be used creatively. Wire and other metal fencing materials were available for shaping and weaving. Also in supply were translucent papers for painting and transparent material for encasing three-dimensional works of art. One display of clay sculptures created by children showed adults, each holding a child in a different way. One adult held a child's hand, one carried a child on his back, one held a child in her arms, and one bounced a child on his extended leg. The pieces were individually designed, detailed, well-proportioned, and expressed sensitivity to feelings.

The *atelierista* (art teacher) explained that the children are encouraged to be attentive to the details of the object they are representing. The teachers may point out the shape or curve or other specifics to the children. In addition, the children are given the opportunity to "revisit" their previous works in the same area and improve upon them, since the work remains at school. This practice allows children to see mistakes or missed details as their knowledge of the subject matter improves and their project continues. Learning and creativity are purposely intertwined in the program.

As this description suggests, creative expression and play are at the heart of practice in the exemplary schools of Reggio Emilia.

Every person needs the opportunity to be creative. This does not mean that everyone will invent something, perform on stage, or see his or her art displayed in a gallery. A teacher who invents a new activity is being creative. A mother who provides nutritious, tasty meals on a very limited food budget is being creative. A child who fashions an imaginary dinosaur out of clay is being creative. When we meet life's challenges and resolve problems, we are being creative (Ripple, 1989; Runco, 1996). In the next section, we will look at the conditions that enable creativity to flourish.

*Every child needs the opportunity to be creative.*

## ✿ UNLOCKING CREATIVE POTENTIAL

There is a story told about a visiting efficiency expert who reported that one of the Ford Motor Company's well-paid employees sat with his feet propped up on the desk and appeared to be daydreaming most of the time. Henry Ford reputedly replied that that was exactly how the employee looked when he had an idea that saved the company more than enough money to cover his salary in the years to come.

Valuing creativity as Ford apparently did is a prerequisite to understanding it. Warnock (1977) says that being more creative is analogous to being more healthy. We do not ask, "Why become more healthy?" because being healthy is simply good. The same holds true for creativity, for once we understand it, we know that being creative is an end in itself, just like being healthy.

Unlocking creative potential is largely dependent upon two sets of internal psychological conditions: (1) psychological safety and (2) psychological freedom (Rogers, 1991).

### *Psychological Safety*

Psychological safety is external; it is dependent upon a low-risk environment. Children feel psychologically safe when significant others accept the child as having unconditional worth, avoid external evaluation, and identify and empathize with the child. Consider how this mother provides psychological safety for her preschool son Lance's behavior:

> Lance [age 5] loves farming and he inherited a lot of toy farm equipment that used to belong to his dad and big brothers. One day he was playing farmer and took his toy manure spreader into the kitchen, filled it up with coffee grounds, and began spreading "manure" on his land, which just happens to be the kitchen floor!

Lance's mother knew that he was completely wrapped up in his farm fantasy and that his intentions were good, even if the outcomes were bad from an adult perspective. She did insist that Lance help her clean up the coffee grounds, yet she did not punish him or make him feel ashamed of his desire to really "test out" his farm equipment. When adults respond sensitively to children's behavior, they contribute to the child's feelings of psychological safety.

## Psychological Freedom

Psychological freedom is internal. It emanates from within the child. When children feel free to play with symbols and to use these symbols for self-expression, they have developed an inner state of psychological freedom. According to Rogerian theory, one person becomes more creative than the next because he or she has learned to play with ideas, to toy with elements and concepts, to be open to experience and receptive to ideas, and to rely more on self-evaluation than the evaluations of others.

## Social Support

Lev Vygotsky (1933), a Russian theorist, has argued that learning is fundamentally a social activity: that children learn and grow with and from "the company they keep" (Smith, 1992). One of the basic precepts of Vygotsky's theory is the "zone of proximal development," the level at which the child feels reasonably confident in pursuing an activity, yet not bored by it; the level at which the child feels challenged intellectually, yet not frustrated. Vygotsky argued that real learning takes place when the child is functioning at this level. Children need to pursue activities that urge them to move to higher levels of functioning. This is one reason why giving children preprinted pictures to color and/or cut out while sitting quietly at their seats—a very common activity in American schools—is not recommended. True, this activity keeps children occupied, but it does nothing to challenge children intellectually, it undermines creativity, and it offers no social support. Such an activity creates no feeling of functioning in a community of learners; it is simply busywork that is frequently performed in quiet isolation as the teacher insists on children "doing their own work" with "no talking."

Vygotsky further argued that learning is fundamentally social and interactive in nature. Through social interaction, children internalize the cultural tools that the world of others presents to them (Davis & Gardner, 1992). For example, if we examine the drawings by a Japanese child or a Navajo child, we will see that their early representational drawings resemble the art from the culture they know; their style has been influenced by the art that they have experienced in their societies. Remember Mallory's fanciful flowers? They illustrate another way in which creativity, imagination, and fantasy are social—children give their mental representations a public form that can be communicated to others (Davis & Gardner, 1992). As we have seen, psychological safety, psychological freedom, and social support are essential to promote optimal creative growth in children. How well are the schools meeting these requirements?

## CREATIVITY AND EDUCATION

Society in general and schools in particular have been criticized for failing to provide the environmental conditions for psychological safety and helping children to acquire a sense of psychological freedom (Egan & Nadaner, 1988; Westby & Dawson, 1995). Although it is sad to think that education would be responsible in any way for thwarting the child's creative potential, there is considerable support for this point of view:

> Schools suppress creativity. How can this be stated so categorically? The reasoning goes as follows: most young children are naturally curious and highly imaginative. Then, after they have attended school for a while, something happens. They become more cautious and less innovative. Worst of all, they tend to change from being participators to being spectators. Unfortunately, it is necessary to conclude from the investigations of many researchers (most of whom have been professional educators) that our schools are the major culprit. (Dacey, 1989, p. 200)

Are school personnel deliberately suppressing children's creativity? Actually, it is more often the case that adults have misconceptions about creativity and act upon those erroneous beliefs (Williams, Brigockas, & Sternberg, 1997). For example, in a study that compared the results of a thorough assessment of preschoolers' creativity with their teachers' ratings of the children's creativity, Nicholson and Moran (1986) concluded that teachers are not very good judges of creativity. The three mistakes most commonly made by teachers of young children are:

**1.** *Confusing measures of intelligence with measures of creativity.* Intelligence as measured by tests and grades is very different from creativity. Tests and grades focus on convergent thought (right answers), while tests of creativity focus on divergent thought (many possible answers). So, the child with a record of high academic achievement and high intelligence test scores is not necessarily the same child who does exceptionally well on tests of creativity. In the real world, apart from testing, creativity and intelligence apparently interact rather than function as separate entities (Runco, 1986). Creativity is a form of intelligence, but it is not the form usually assessed by tests and grades. Yet teachers sometimes incorrectly infer that students who receive the highest grades are automatically the most creative students in their classes.

**2.** *Being overly influenced by socially desirable behavior.* Academic environments are not always accepting of children who "dare to be different." History is full of examples of people who were called "daydreamers," "underachievers," or "troublemakers" during childhood only to become highly creative or even creative geniuses in later life, such as the politician Winston Churchill, the actress Sara Bernhardt, the scientist Albert Einstein, the inventor Alexander Graham Bell, and the dancer Isadora Duncan. When convergent thinking dominates the schools, divergent thinking can be undervalued and teachers can become intolerant of children who do not "go along with the program" (Sternberg & Lubart, 1995; Sternberg, 1997).

**3.** *Being overly influenced by the child's rate of development.* Adults react more readily and more favorably to children's uncommon (advanced) behavior than to children's unconventional (creative) behavior (Nicholson & Moran, 1986). Compare the behavior of Aaron and Matt, both preschoolers. At age 3, Aaron can identify several words printed on flashcards. His parents think that he is exceptionally creative. But even though Aaron has been pushed into recognizing a few written symbols before his peers (advanced for his age), this is not an indicator of extraordinary creativity. Contrast this with the experiences of Matt, another 3-year-old. His parents try to encourage independence and creative problem solving. In fact, one of Matt's favorite expressions is "I have an idea. We could . . . " Of the two children, Matt is getting more support in developing creativity. Aaron, on the other hand, is being conditioned to imitate adult behavior as rapidly as possible. He may be precocious, but his creativity is being compromised in the process.

How does acting upon these common misconceptions about creativity influence teachers' behavior? Suppose that a teacher is presenting a unit on basic shapes—circles, triangles, squares, and rectangles. When introducing a review lesson, she asks children to suggest the names of shapes that they know. Robert suggests, "There's an egg shape, only it's called an ellipse." How would you as a teacher handle this response? A teacher who is overly concerned about confusing the other children might say, "Robert, that isn't one of the shapes we learned." If you do, what will happen to Robert? He will feel rejected. Over time, Robert will probably begin to "play the game" and tell teachers what they want to hear. He may even quit contributing in class. Situations such as these, repeated day after day, not only undermine children's creativity but also distort teachers' perspectives on what constitutes creative behavior.

The goal of studying children's creativity and play is to change teachers' perspectives—to prepare a new generation of teachers who will do a better job of meeting children on their own terms rather than trying to mold them prematurely into performing adult behaviors. Figure 1.6 compares/contrasts educational environments that deter or support creativity (Burton, 1989).

**Figure 1.6**
Negative and Positive
Environments for
Creativity

**Environments That Thwart Creativity**
- Push children to think literally rather than working to children's imaginative strengths
- Overvalue conformity and follow established traditions
- Reward children only when they follow directions, discourage them from taking risks, or make them feel ashamed of mistakes
- Control time strictly by following inflexible schedules and setting time limits on every task
- Avoid children's questions and discourage exploration of ideas
- Overemphasize memorization, imitation, and rigidly planned tasks

**Environments That Support Creativity**
- Promote equity and reciprocal respect
- Welcome the contribution of original ideas
- Regard differing points of view as a resource for learning rather than as a waste of time or a threat
- Seek new approaches to problems
- Encourage fantasy and imagination
- Develop research and inquiry skills
- Create learning communities that build feelings of trust and minimize risks

*Source:* Adapted from Burton (1989).

## *Schools That Nurture Creativity*

When schools do respect and develop creativity in children, theory and research have shown that several conditions exist.

**1.** *School personnel strive to reduce stress and anxiety in children and in themselves.* Adults recognize the importance of positive affect—feeling good about being in school, treating one another with respect, and building self-esteem among children and colleagues (Isen, Daubman, & Nowicki, 1987).

**2.** *Process is valued over product.* This means that children are encouraged to play with ideas and explore solutions rather than being pushed into premature conclusions. Creativity and productivity may actually be inversely related. When children are pressured to dash something off to meet someone else's schedule, they are not afforded the "luxury" of seeking many alternatives and refining the most promising ones. Rather, they are taught to value the quantity of work produced over the quality of the finished product (Amabile, 1989).

**3.** *Time limits are removed from activities in which children are deeply involved.* Children are free to become absorbed in what they are doing. In a school committed to creative expression, children follow their interests and enjoy what they are doing along with their peers, teachers, and other school personnel. This condition of being able to pursue an idea is the "labor of love" aspect of creative processes (Amabile, 1986).

**4.** *A free, open atmosphere is established where self-expression is encouraged and valued.* Creativity is fostered when teachers enjoy experiences along with children rather than singling out particular products for praise or rewards. Teachers support children's creativity by providing a wide variety of interesting materials and keeping activities open-ended; they give help when needed, but they do not interfere with children's creative processes.

**5.** *The children are encouraged to share ideas, not only with the teacher but also with one another.* "Creative individuals see themselves as being creative" (Katz, 1987). One of the ways that children begin to regard themselves as creative is in their reflected selves—in the responses that others have to them and their ideas. This is one reason why it is important for children to give and receive supportive feedback, not only from adults but also from peers. Children need to experience the verification/communication stage of the creative process as well as preparation, incubation, and illumination.

**6.** *Competition and external rewards are minimized.* When children are informed that there will be a contest, that some will win a tangible reward and others will lose, three things happen. First, they become more cautious and tend to "play it safe"; second, they feel pressured to please someone else and lose their intrinsic motivation; and third, they tend to rush to get the reward. All of these things result in less spontaneous, less complex, and less varied products; in other words, less creative responses.

**7.** *Children's creativity, imagination, and fantasy are valued.* Remember the student teacher's journal entries that introduced this chapter? She found that teachers often disapproved of children's departure from routines and literal thinking. Young children's creative expression is supported in programs where teachers are inclined to notice and accept evidence of young children's active imaginations at work. Table 1.3 provides examples for children of different ages.

Two first-grade teachers who are making puppets with their students help to illustrate how these seven features of schools that nurture creativity are put into practice. Ms. Poole shows children a paper bag puppet that she has made and demonstrates how it was assembled. She then distributes copies of a pattern that she found in a book to the children and instructs them to work quietly, color neatly, cut out on the lines, and paste in the designated areas. Ms. Poole reminds the children that she has just one pattern for each child, and that anyone who does not follow directions will not get another copy. When the puppets are completed, the children print their names on them and they are posted on the bulletin board. If colleagues stop by, the teacher points out the "good" ones and ignores the "bad" ones.

In another first-grade classroom, children are getting ready to invent their own puppets. Ms. Kastenbaum, their teacher, uses a four-phase strategy that begins with awareness, then moves to exploration, next to inquiry, and finally to utilization

**TABLE 1.3   Evidence of Children's Imagination**

**Typical Behavior**

**Toddlers**
- Replays familiar behaviors, such as pretending to go to sleep by briefly lying down and shutting eyes
- Mimics the behaviors of adults through play, such as pretending to sing a lullaby to a baby doll by rocking the baby and babbling
- Easily frightened by nightmares and may experience night terrors caused by particularly vivid dreams

**Ages Three and Four**
- Replays sequences of behavior that have been observed frequently, such as feeding a baby
- May ritualistically repeat routines, such as insisting on putting on the plastic firefighter's hat every morning
- Plays with words and makes up silly songs, such as a song about spaghetti
- Tends to respond imaginatively to what is experienced, such as crawling around and wanting to eat from a bowl on the floor like the family pet
- Treats toys as if they were alive, such as pretending to teach a group of stuffed toys
- May invent a pretend friend or imaginary companion that is treated as if it were alive. These invisible companions are often either naughty or very powerful
- Begins to take on roles and assign roles to others in order to play, as when playing house
- Invents stories and dialogue while playing with miniature toys, such as a toy farm
- Often uses objects in surprising ways as props, such as using the bathroom rug to represent a frog's pond
- Tends to be fascinated by games of chase and rescue, such as a group of children who played jaguars by chasing others
- Intrigued by good/bad behavior, such as playing the role of wrestlers who have a reputation for being evil or good
- Tends to view gender roles inflexibly and be intolerant of others who do not play, such as girls who chase boys away from the housekeeping area
- Often uses self-guiding speech (expressing thoughts out loud while performing a task) such as talking aloud while drawing a picture
- Often uses artwork as a prop for talking about an experience or to make up a story
- Frequently afraid of monsters or other powerful, imaginary creatures, such as believing there is a witch under the bed at night

**TABLE 1.3**   *(Continued)*

**Ages Five and Six**

- Becomes more adept at assuming the characteristics of a role and remaining in role while playing out a theme, and play is more likely to involve extensive interaction with other children, such as using old jewelry to create a jewelry store equipped with various props
- Often carries over play themes from one day to the next, such as hospital play
- Uses imagination to invent new worlds represented as pictures, stories, plays, puppets, and so forth, such as putting on a puppet play
- Constructs more elaborate and detailed projects, such as attempting to make a stuffed toy
- May use music and movement to invent own performances, such as pretending to be a ballerina
- Greatly influenced by adult and peer models of creative problem solving, such as striving to solve a puzzle after watching others try it
- Easily frightened by imaginary things that are brought to life through the media, such as advertisements for horror movies
- Capable of monologues based on opportunities to observe something, such as pretending to be a sports announcer doing the play-by-play
- Intrigued by jokes and riddles and people's responses to them, such as knock-knock jokes, and tries to make jokes
- May try to invent things from available materials, such as using a tree, a length of rope, and a pillow to make a swing
- May develop puzzles for others to solve, such as making a birthday card for a family member that is cut into puzzle pieces
- Uses expanding vocabulary to make intentionally humorous comments, such as the child who saw fuzz on her mother's sweater and said, "Mommy, you're molting."
- Often pursues construction with materials, such as making a doll house out of cardboard
- With opportunity, may begin training in an area of the arts, such as playing a musical instrument or woodworking
- With encouragement, may offer creative solutions to problems, such as helping the teacher organize the room

(Bredekamp & Rosegrant, 1992). She builds the children's awareness by asking, "What is a robot? How are robots made? What is special about robots? What robots have you seen?" Krish says that robots are "sort of like people, only they're machines." Taro mentions R2D2 from *Star Wars,* and Joelle expresses a wish for a toy robot. Exploration begins as the children share and discuss a collection of robot pictures, and the teacher summarizes by asking, "What have you learned about robots? What questions do you still have about robots?" Now Ms. Kastenbaum moves the group into inquiry as she invites them to examine a wide array of recycled materials and invent a robot puppet. One child begins with an old sock, another with a cardboard box; one child uses styrofoam egg carton cups for "buggy eyes," another chooses aluminum foil and cardboard tubes for arms. All of the children experiment with different fixatives such as glue, staples, tape, and sewing. The activity turns to utilization after the robots are completed, and the children are invited to make their puppets move to electronic music.

As you have surely surmised, the second classroom supports creativity while the first classroom does not. As teachers, we may know this intuitively, but it is also important to understand the underlying reasons why this occurs, something that will be explored further in the sections that follow.

## TEACHERS' ROLES AND RESPONSIBILITIES IN PROMOTING CREATIVE EXPRESSION

In order to foster creative processes, teachers need to provide a low-risk environment, one that meets the conditions of psychological freedom, psychological safety, and social support. Research suggests that either too much or too little structure can interfere with the development of creative expression (McLeod, 1997). If a classroom is regimented, there is too much structure. On the other hand, if a classroom is "anything goes," there is too little structure to provide proper guidance. How do teachers find the right mixtures and balances?

First of all, teachers need to *share power,* to function as facilitators who allow children to help plan (Jones, 1986). When every outcome is predetermined, as with Ms. Poole's puppet pattern, the underlying goal is to control children, to avoid any surprises, to monitor busywork. To get a sense of what this power-sharing notion is all about, think about how teachers respond to the initial writing attempts of young children. Children have the least autonomy when they are required to trace on a piece of paper or copy from the chalkboard. They have somewhat more autonomy when they dictate a story to an adult. They have the highest level of autonomy when they are actively applying whatever they know about writing at the time. At this highest level of power-sharing with teachers, children in the same kindergarten class may make scribbles or squiggles, some may invent letterlike forms (mock letters), some may write combinations of actual and mock letters, and still others may write in more conventional ways. By supporting the children in their writing instead of dictating their every move, the teacher is sharing power and authority.

In the creative classroom, teachers *encourage risk-taking* because they know that authentic learning results in a change in behavior (Chenfeld, 1995). Making those changes involves risks. Children need to exert control over their own processes and have the freedom to take the necessary risks. Too many teachers subscribe to what Paulo Freire (1973) calls the "banking model" of education, the view that it is our job to make regular deposits of information into the student's brain and that the accumulation of that information will result in an educated person. But we know that children cannot simply absorb someone else's ready-made answers; children must build their own understandings about the world, and that path to understanding is littered with "errors." If we make learners self-conscious about mistakes, their progress will be slowed or even halted. Nothing of value can be learned in an environment where everything that the children do is predictable and plodding.

A third key responsibility for teachers is to fully *understand creative activities*. Too many teachers assume that "creative activities" are all focused on the teacher when, in reality, the value of creative activities is determined by the quality of the children's responses. Creative activities are not something that teachers do for children, such as designing "cute" games for them to play. There is nothing wrong with a teacher creating a beautiful visual aid to use during a lesson, but whose creativity was being developed, the teacher's or the children's? Although it is important for teachers to unlock their own creative potential, they should not do so exclusively in the name of "creative teaching," nor should they do so at the expense of the children. Unless children are responding in their own unique ways, unless each child's response is an original (rather than a copy), "creative teaching" is not occurring in any sense of those words. This should be good news for teachers who worry about their singing voices, their inability to draw, their clumsiness at dance, their inexperience with drama, or the fact that they never learned to play a musical instrument. Your goal in creative teaching is to set children's creativity free, to create the conditions for them to create, not to put on a polished performance for them.

Another important role for teachers of young children is to *use praise judiciously and defer judgment* (Klein, 1984). Effusive praise can actually suppress children's creativity. Suppose that a child paints an orange pumpkin with black triangle eyes and nose and a toothy grin. If adults shower the child with praise, saying, "Oh, that's so wonderful! It's just the cutest little pumpkin!" the child may get "stalled" at this stage because he or she is trying to please the adult. It is better to show genuine, personalized interest than to overdo it with generalized praise. You can show interest in children's work by commenting specifically on the child's work ("Carla, that pumpkin looks really happy") or by asking questions about it ("How did you make the stem?"). Figure 1.7 suggests appropriate comments about children's creative work. As you use these comments and add to the list, remember to leave much of the evaluative function to the child so that he or she can learn the skills of self-evaluation.

Every child needs opportunities to express his or her creativity in many different contexts. If teachers limit their assessment of children's potential to academic subjects and formal learning situations, they will have little idea of how creative the students in their classes can truly be.

**Figure 1.7**
Responses to
Children's Work

How did you get the idea for this work?

This makes me feel . . .

I like the way you used _____ because . . .

This reminds me of . . .

What were you trying to do?

Maybe you could combine . . .

This interests me because . . .

How does this work compare with other work you have created?

I wonder what would happen if . . .

I like the part where . . .

I'd like to know more about . . .

You used some powerful ideas such as . . .

The part where you explained . . .

This is like your . . .

You are really good at . . .

*Source:* Adapted from Cecil & Lauritzen (1994).

## PRACTICAL APPLICATIONS FOR YOUR CLASSROOM

What kinds of activities offer a genuine creative problem-solving challenge for children? Activities stimulate creative thinking when they:

- Are relevant to the learner, meaning that they are developmentally appropriate, understandable to the learner, and have "real world" applications
- Meet the needs of children at different levels of development because the challenges have multiple answers (rather than one right answer)
- Enable students to engage in long-term, open-ended projects and pursue a narrower range of ideas and materials in greater depth
- Capitalize on children's interests, curiosities, and passions and allow the child to set the pace and take the lead
- Support children as they use the processes of exploring, selecting, combining, and refining a form
- Are framed by teachers and students, with teachers structuring or limiting as necessary
- Give the students something practical and worthwhile to do that engages thoughts and feelings, mind and body
- Encourage children to look for models and make connections, emphasizing the influence and the works of others

*Teachers encourage learners to value diversity by providing opportunities for activities that are reflective of different cultural and ethnic backgrounds.*

- Make use of a variety of perspectives (e.g., the critic, the philosopher, the inventor)
- Help students to develop a set of standards for evaluating their performance and peers' performance that goes beyond "good" or "bad" and carefully analyzes the dimensions of a work
- Expand opportunities for learning and lead to new, interesting challenges (Jalongo & Stamp, 1997; Lindstrom, 1997).

## *Experiences to Support Cultural and Ethnic Diversity*

The essence of meeting children's needs is being alert to opportunities for them to excel. Ms. Reagon's observations of her second graders on the playground offer another opportunity for a teacher to see her students in a different context. She notices that, as a group, the students from low-income homes are much more adept at inventing games and playing cooperatively than the children who come from economically advantaged homes. Rather than allowing this important strength to go unnoticed, Ms. Reagon asks the children to show the class some of their games, which involve syncopated hand clapping and original jump rope chants. When the other children try to participate in the games these students have created, they gain a new appreciation for their classmates' skills. Ms. Reagon further supports and extends the children's activity by sharing several books of jump rope jingles, by inviting each child to discuss favorite childhood games with various family members, by giving children the opportunity to share what they learned from their interviews, by inviting parents to come in to demonstrate favorite childhood games, and by teaching the children new games from other eras and lands. As a result of Ms. Reagon's interest and encouragement, all of her students' outdoor play has become richer, more cooperative, and more reflective of different ethnic and cultural backgrounds.

## Experiences to Support Inclusion

The key to unlocking the creative potential in children with disabling conditions is, once again, the search for opportunities for every child to experience success. This typically involves focusing on children's strengths and adapting the environment to enable them to express those abilities. For example, the visually impaired child may not be able to use crayons to produce a drawing that is pleasing to the eye, but the child can use fabrics to create a fabric collage that is pleasing to the touch. Likewise, the child whose physical condition prohibits the requisite fine motor skills for sculpting or painting at an easel may be able to mold large objects with clay or use hand and arm movements to fingerpaint. Mr. Robinson is a first-grade teacher who believes that his role is "to give every child a chance to shine." Rex, a child in his inclusive classroom, has been a deaf mute since birth and sometimes gets frustrated when the other children do not understand him, but he excels as a communicator through his art and through dramatization. Throughout the year, Mr. Robinson has been doing pantomime and playing charades related to the themes the class is studying. Often, Rex is the one who brings a particularly challenging idea to the class. Through creative dramatics, Mr. Robinson has afforded Rex the opportunity for creative expression, and Rex has acquired a leadership role among his peers.

## Adaptations for Individual Learners

What about gifted and talented children? As we have seen, academic achievement and creativity are not the same thing. In fact, the child who has the highest scores in reading or mathematics has often learned to succeed on multiple-choice item tests by relying almost exclusively on convergent thinking. Even enrollment in special programs for the gifted and talented does not guarantee that the conditions of psychological freedom and psychological safety are being met. One parent described an incident involving her daughter that helps to illustrate this point:

> When Marjorie was a first grader in the gifted and talented program, her teacher gave them the assignment of keeping a journal. Marjorie's idea was to write George Washington's diary by looking up things in books in the library and "imagining the rest," but the teacher insisted that if the journal could not be historically accurate in every detail, it would be better to select a different topic. Marjorie's older sister, wise in the ways of school, advised her to "make the teacher happy so you get a good grade," but Marjorie was determined to pursue

*Teachers build understanding and acceptance when they focus on each child's abilities and emphasize cooperation.*

her original idea. She was only 6 years old, and she had such integrity! As it turned out, Marjorie proved herself right and *she* taught the *teacher* something about respecting children's creativity.

This mother defended her daughter's right to creative expression rather than focusing exclusively on her child's mastery of "facts." As Marjorie's experience illustrates, sometimes creativity is seen as a "given" in children who are gifted and talented and adults assume that it requires no further development. Clearly, this is not the case.

Whenever a child does not perform as well as peers on academic tasks, adults sometimes lower their expectations for the child's performance in all areas and the child's creativity remains unrecognized. Second grader Evelyn is a good example. She was retained in both kindergarten and first grade and has been diagnosed as developmentally delayed. Yet if we observed her and her classmates fashioning things from clay, we would be impressed by Evelyn's originality. While most of the other students are making coils or baskets, Evelyn creates a mother bird and a nest filled with a combination of eggs and hatching chicks. If the teacher had limited Evelyn's play with clay to art class, she might never have glimpsed just how imaginative this child is.

As teachers work in inclusive and multicultural settings, it is essential that they provide opportunities for every child to experience success. By focusing on each child's abilities and emphasizing cooperation, teachers build understanding and acceptance among all of the children in the class.

As you consider young children's creativity, keep in mind that "young children live ferociously. Their senses—taste, touch, vision, hearing, smell—are turbocharged, in overdrive at all times except during sleep. . . .They sing, paint, play with imaginary friends, animate inanimate objects and tell richly woven, epic-length falsehoods. They fulminate with creative intensity" (Barasch, 1997, p. 54).

## CHAPTER SUMMARY

1. Creativity is a behavior characterized by originality, relevance, fluency, and flexibility.
2. Young children's thinking is different from adults' thinking because, generally speaking, children are highly sensitive to stimuli, are more uninhibited, and can become completely absorbed in imagination ("as if") and pretend ("what if").
3. If teachers regard the dimensions of children's creative behavior—originality, appropriateness, relevance, fluency, and flexibility—they can further develop children's creative potential.
4. Metacognitive theories suggest that creative thinking processes can be conceptualized as convergent or divergent. Creativity, imagination, and fantasy are all interrelated types of thinking that are largely dependent upon the ability to use symbols in inventive ways. Literal thought and imaginative thought are distinctive, yet complementary.
5. Theories that attempt to explain the desire to create may be categorized as humanistic, psychoanalytic, and constructivist.
6. The creative process can be described in four stages: preparation, incubation, illumination, and verification/communication.
7. Some ways that classroom environments support creativity include providing psychological safety by reducing stress and anxiety, valuing process over product, removing time limits, valuing self-expression, encouraging peer interaction, and minimizing competition and external rewards.
8. Active, child-initiated experiences give the child authentic opportunities for creative expression and, in so doing, build the child's inner sense of psychological freedom. When teachers provide a classroom environment in which children feel safe to experiment, to take the risks associated with learning something new, and to learn from their mistakes as an accepted part of the learning process, the condition of psychological safety has been met.
9. Teachers and parents play a crucial role in fostering the creative process in children. One recommended teaching strategy is to begin by building children's awareness, then move next to exploration, then to inquiry, and finally to utilization.

10. All children are creative. If all children are to develop their creative potential to the fullest extent, every classroom must provide a wide range of opportunities for creative expression. This means that teachers will need to respect children's ethnic and cultural diversity, acknowledge the role of multiple intelligences, adapt materials to each child's needs, and encourage authentic self-expression.

## EXPANDING YOUR THINKING ABOUT CREATIVE EXPRESSION AND PLAY

 *Discuss: Perspectives on Creative Expression*

1. Teachers are often advised to "work to children's strengths." How does an understanding of children's creativity enable you to do this more effectively?

2. How do the schools in Reggio Emilia differ from the American classrooms with which you are familiar? Do you agree that schools in the United States sometimes actively discourage creativity? Why or why not? What lessons can we learn from the exemplary programs in Italy?

3. Sometimes children's creativity is mistaken for misbehavior. Did you ever experience this yourself as a child? Did it ever happen to a child you know? How do you plan to avoid this when you are teaching?

4. Cite several current examples of imagination and creativity at work in various fields (e.g., medical research, business, new inventions, film, music). What role did divergent thinking apparently play? What role did convergent thinking play? How would an education that fosters creativity prepare children for the workplace of the future?

5. Experts in the field of early childhood education are generally advocates of play in the curriculum. How would play meet the criteria for creativity and the conditions for nurturing creativity discussed in this chapter?

## *Interview: The Creative Family*

Arrange to interview parents about their young child's creativity. First, make it clear to the parent that you are seeking examples of behaviors that are original, imaginative, and creative rather than examples of their child's academic achievement on tests or grades in school subjects. Then ask the following questions and transcribe the answers:

1. Please describe some specific examples when your child's behavior was particularly imaginative, original, or inventive.

2. Why do you think this particular behavior illustrates creativity?

3. What do you do to encourage problem solving, independent thinking, and originality in your child?

4. Do you consider yourself (or any other members of your family) to be creative in any way? If yes, how? If no, why not?

5. Do you feel that your child is being taught creatively? Why or why not?

6. Do you think that creativity is important in everyday life? Why or why not?

## Write to Learn: A Classroom for Creativity

Using the section in this chapter on classroom conditions and teachers' roles in nurturing creativity, imagine an ideal "classroom for creativity." Make sure that your scenario incorporates all of the characteristics of teachers and environments that foster creativity (see Figure 1.6). Imagine such things as the physical arrangement of the room, some sample activities that you might observe, examples of the teachers' comments and questions, and so forth. Share your description with the group. Imagine that you are the teacher in this classroom and someone is challenging your curriculum, saying that it is not sufficiently "academic." Formulate a philosophy statement that you could use to respond to this criticism.

## REFERENCES

Amabile, T. M. (1983). *The social psychology of creativity.* New York: Springer-Verlag.

Amabile, T. M. (1986). The personality of creativity. *Creative Living, 15*(3), 12–16.

Amabile, T. M. (1989). *Growing up creative.* New York: Crown.

Armstrong, T. (1987). *In their own way.* New York: St. Martin's Press.

Barasch, D. S. (1997, November). Creativity. *Family Life,* 54–59.

Barnhart, C. L., & Barnhart, R. K. (1983). *The world book dictionary.* Chicago: Thorndike-Barnhart.

Bredekamp, S., & Rosegrant, T. (1992). *Reaching potentials: Appropriate curriculum and assessment for young children, Volume 1.* Washington, DC: National Association for the Education of Young Children.

Burton, L. (1989). Musical understanding through creative movement. In B. Andress (Ed.), *Promising practices: Pre-kindergarten music education* (pp. 97–104). Reston, VA: Music Educators National Conference.

Caine, R. N., & Caine, G. (1996). *Education on the edge of possibility.* Alexandria, VA: Association for Supervision and Curriculum Development.

Caldwell, L. B. (1997). *Bringing Reggio Emilia home: An innovative approach to early childhood education.* New York: Teachers College Press.

Cecil, N. L., & Lauritzen, P. (1994). *Literacy and the arts for the integrated classroom: Alternative ways of knowing.* New York: Longman.

Checkley, K. (1997). The first seven . . . and the eighth. *Educational Leadership, 55*(1), 8–15.

Chenfeld, M. B. (1995). *Creative experiences for young children* (2nd ed.). Fort Worth, TX: Harcourt Brace Jovanovich.

Craft, A. (1999). *Teaching creativity: Philosophy and practice.* New York: Routledge.

Csikszentmihalyi, M. (1996). *Creativity: Flow and the psychology of discovery and invention.* New York: HarperCollins.

Dacey, J. S. (1989). *Fundamentals of creative thinking.* Lexington, MA: D. C. Heath.

Dacey, J. S., & Lennon, K. H. (1998). *Understanding creativity: The interplay of biological, psychological, and social factors.* San Francisco, CA: Jossey-Bass.

Davis, J., & Gardner, H. (1992). The cognitive revolution: Consequences for the understanding and education of the child as artist. In B. Reimer & R. A. Smith (Eds.), *The arts, education, and aesthetic knowing* (pp. 92–123). Chicago: University of Chicago Press.

Davis, G., & Rimm, S. (1994). *Education of the gifted and talented* (3rd ed.). Needham Heights, MA: Allyn & Bacon.

De Bono, E. (1971). *New think.* New York: Avon.

De Bono, E. (1992). *Teach your child how to think.* New York: Viking.

Duffy, B. (1998). *Supporting creativity and imagination in the early years.* Buckingham, UK: Open University Press.

Edwards, C. (Ed.). (1993). *The hundred languages of children: The Reggio Emilia approach to early childhood education.* Norwood, NJ: Ablex.

Edwards, C., Gandini, L., & Forman, G. (Eds.). (1993). *The hundred languages of children: The Reggio Emilia approach to early childhood education.* Norwood, NJ: Ablex. (ERIC Document Reproduction Service No. ED 355 034)

Edwards, C., Gandini, L., & Forman, G. (Eds.). (1998). *The hundred languages of children: The Reggio Emilia approach—Advanced reflections.* Greenwich, CT: Ablex.

Edwards, C. P., & Springate, K. W. (1995). The lion comes out of the stone: Helping young children achieve their creative potential. *Dimensions of Early Childhood, 23*(4), 24–29.

Egan, K., & Nadaner, D. (Eds.). (1988). *Imagination and education.* New York: Teachers College Press.

Feldhusen, J. F. (1995). Creativity: Knowledge base, metacognitive skills, and personality factors. *Journal of Creative Behavior, 29*(4), 255–268.

Freire, P. (1973). *Pedagogy of the oppressed.* New York: Seabury.

Gardner, H. (1993). *Frames of mind: The theory of multiple intelligences* (10th anniversary ed.). New York: Basic Books.

Gardner, H. (1995). Reflections on multiple intelligences: Myths and messages. *Phi Delta Kappan, 77*(3), 200–209.

Guilford, J. P. (1984). Varieties of divergent production. *Journal of Creative Behavior, 18*, 1–10.

Harrison, A. (1984). Creativity, class and boredom: Cognitive models for intelligent activities. *Journal of Education, 166*(2), 150–169.

Hatch, T. (1997). Getting specific about multiple intelligences. *Educational Leadership, 54*(6), 26–29.

Healy, J. (1996). How to uncover the natural creative abilities in your child. *Brown University Child and Adolescent Behavior Letter, 12*(4), 5–6.

Holden, C. (1987, April). Creativity and the troubled mind. *Psychology Today, 21*(4), 9–10.

Isaksen, S. G. (1992). *Nurturing creative talents: Lessons from industry about needed work-life skills.* Buffalo, NY: The Creative Solving Group.

Isen, A. M., Daubman, K. A., & Nowicki, G. P. (1987). Positive affect facilitates problem solving. *Journal of Personality and Social Psychology, 52,* 1121–1131.

Jackson, P. W., & Messick, S. (1965). The person, the product, and the response: Conceptual problems in the assessment of creativity. *Journal of Personality, 33,* 309–329.

Jalongo, M. R., & Stamp, L. N. (1997). *The arts in children's lives: Aesthetic experiences in early childhood.* Boston: Allyn & Bacon.

Jones, E. (1986). Teaching adults. Washington, DC: National Association for the Education of Young Children.

Katz, A. (1987). Self-reference in the encoding of creative-relevant traits. *Journal of Personality, 55*(1), 98–120.

Klein, B. (1984). Power and control of praise and deferred judgment. *Journal of Creative Behavior, 17,* 9–17.

Kohn, A. (1987, September). Art for art's sake. *Psychology Today, 21*(9), 52–57.

Latham, A. S. (1997). Research link: Quantifying MI's gains. *Educational Leadership, 55*(1), 84–85.

Lindstrom, L. (1997). Integration, creativity, or communication? Paradigm shifts and continuity in Swedish art education. *Arts Education Policy Review, 99*(1), 17–25.

Maxim, G. (1989). *The very young: Guiding children from infancy through the early years* (3rd ed.). Upper Saddle River, NJ: Merrill/Prentice Hall.

McAlpine, D. (1996). Characteristics of gifted children. In D. McAlpine & R. Moltzen (Eds.), *Gifted and talented: New Zealand perspectives* (pp. 43–62). Palmerston North, NZ: Massey University ERDC Press.

McLeod, L. (1997). Young children's metacognition: Do we know what they know? And if so, what do we do about it? *Australian Journal of Early Childhood, 22*(2), 6–11.

Meador, K. (1999). Creativity around the globe. *Childhood Education, 75,* 324–325.

Nicholson, M. W., & Moran, J. D. (1986). Teachers' judgments of preschoolers' creativity. *Perceptual and Motor Skills, 63,* 1211–1216.

Parnes, S. (1963). Creativity. In C. W. Taylor & T. Barron (Eds.), *The identification of creativity and scientific talent* (pp. 225–255). New York: John Wiley.

Reiff, J. C. (1997). Multiple intelligences, culture, and equitable learning. *Childhood Education, 73*(5), 301–304.

Ripple, R. E. (1989). Ordinary creativity. *Contemporary Educational Psychology, 14,* 189–202.

Rogers, C. (1991). Toward a theory of creativity. In A. Rothenberg & C. Hausman (Eds.), *The creativity question* (pp. 296–305). Durham, NC: Duke University Press. (Original work published 1954.)

Runco, M. A. (1986). Predicting children's creative performance. *Psychological Reports, 59,* 1247–1252.

Runco, M. A. (1996). *Eminent creativity: Everyday creativity and health.* Norwood, NJ: Ablex.

Runco, M. A. (Ed.). (1994). *Problem finding, problem solving, and creativity.* Norwood, NJ: Ablex.

Sheldon, K. M. (1995). Creativity and self-determination in personality. *Creativity Research Journal, 8*(1), 25–36.

Simonton, D. K. (1996). *Selected papers in genius and creativity.* Norwood, NJ: Ablex.

Skeen, P., Garner, A. P., & Cartwright, S. (1993). *Woodworking for young children.* Washington, DC: National Association for the Education of Young Children.

Smith, F. (1992). Learning to read: The great debate. *Phi Delta Kappan, 73*(6), 432–435, 438–441.

Sternberg, R. J. (1997). *How to develop student creativity.* Alexandria, VA: Association for Supervision and Curriculum Development.

Sternberg, R. J., & Lubart, T. I. (1995). *Defying the crowd: Cultivating creativity in a culture of conformity.* New York: Free Press.

Tennent, L., & Berthelsen, D. (1997). Creativity: What does it mean in the family context? *Journal of Australian Research in Early Childhood Education, 1,* 91–103.

Torrance, E. P. (1979). *The search for Satori and creativity.* Buffalo, NY: The Creative Education Foundation.

Torrance, E. P. (1995). *Why fly? A philosophy of creativity.* Norwood, NJ: Ablex.

Vygotsky, L. S. (1933). The role of play in development. In M. Cole, V. John-Steiner, S. Scribner, & E. Souberman (Eds.), *Mind in society* (pp. 92–104). Cambridge, MA: Harvard University Press.

Wallas, G. (1926). *The art of thought.* New York: Harcourt Brace.

Warnock, M. (1977). *Schools of thought.* London: Faber & Faber.

Weininger, O. (1988). "What if" and "as if" imagination and pretend play in early childhood. In K. Egan & D. Nadaner (Eds.), *Imagination and education* (pp. 141–149). New York: Teachers College Press.

Westby, E., & Dawson, V. (1995). Creativity: Asset or burden in the classroom? *Creativity Research Journal, 8*(1), 1–10.

Williams, W. M., Brigockas, M. G., & Sternberg, R. J. (1997). *Creative intelligence for school.* New York: HarperCollins.

## Children's Books

Baker, A. (1995). *White rabbit's color book.* Phoenix, AZ: Kingfisher.

Chocolate, D. (1996). *Kente colors.* New York: Walker.

Dewey, A. (1995). *Naming colors.* New York: HarperCollins.

Hoban, T. (1997). *Colors everywhere.* New York: Greenwillow.

Hubbard, P. (1996). *My crayons talk.* New York: Scholastic.

Martin, B., & Archambault, J. (1989). *Chicka chicka boom boom.* New York: Simon & Schuster.

Martin, B. (1995). *Brown bear, brown bear what do you see?* New York: Holt.

Serfozo. (1992). *Who said red?* New York: Simon & Schuster.

Zion, G. (1956). *Harry the dirty dog.* New York: Harper.

# Chapter 2

# Play and
# the Young Child

*"All theorists recognize that pretense permits children to become familiar with social role possibilities in their culture, providing important insights into the link between self and wider society."*

Laura E. Berk, 1994, p. 30

*"Everything a child is, does, and becomes may at one time or another be demonstrated through play."*

Garry Landreth and Linda Homeyer, 1998, p. 193

 # TEACHERS' REFLECTIONS ON PLAY

## Preservice Teachers

"I never before realized that there were so many aspects of play. I was surprised that a whole course could be designed around play. I've also learned some of the reasons why so many people do not believe that play is important."

"I always felt that play provided enjoyment and emotional release for children, but now I realize that play can also help children's intellectual and social development."

"I never really thought of play as a learning tool. Rather, I thought of it as just something to take up time with the children. Now I realize that play benefits children in many ways. It is an excellent tool for learning, not just something they do with no real consequences."

## Inservice Teachers

"I realized I needed play in my classroom when the children began complaining of headaches and I was having no fun. I haven't changed any of my curriculum objectives; I've just looked for better ways to teach the children and for better ways for them to be learners.

"The importance of children's self-expression through play is something I've thought a lot about this year as I continue to learn how best to teach children in first grade. I am struggling with my own philosophy of teaching that keeps swinging back and forth between play-centered environments and teacher-directed ones."

## Your Reflections

- What role do you think play has in the early childhood curriculum?

- Can you envision different types, functions, and purposes of play in an early childhood curriculum?

- How might your beliefs about play enhance or inhibit children's growth and development?

## Case Study:

### Restaurant Play

Jonah, Dylan, and Sarena are three kindergartners who are playing in the dramatic play center. Their teacher, Ms. George, recently read the book *Days of the Week* by Eric Carle, and the children are re-creating their own version of it. During their play, the children pretend to be different workers in a restaurant and talk extensively about their roles. As you read the following excerpts from this play episode, think about the following questions:

- Who assumed leadership roles?
- How does the play relate to these children's past experience?
- What opportunities for physical, social, emotional, language, or cognitive growth are evident?

**Jonah:**   I think we should make this a restaurant. This is our food (points to the play food that's in the basket), and over there is where you pay.

**Dylan:**   We're going to need some money.

**Sarena:**   Yeah, and someone has to cook all the food.

**Dylan:**   I think we should make a menu.

**Jonah:**   Today is Thursday so that means we should make roast beef (referring to the Eric Carle book the children have recently heard).

**Dylan:**   (Stirring the pot on the stove) Here is your alphabet soup. I added some more alphabets to it!

The children continue pretending to cook, serve food, and collect money from the patrons.

**Sarena:**   Don't you think we should lock up the store since we don't have anything to eat except onions?

**Jonah:**   Yes, it's closing time. Pull in the menu so we can close up the restaurant.

**Dylan:**   But wait, we didn't get to collect all the credit cards.

**Sarena:**   Look, we got all these credit cards (pointing to all the playing cards from the card drawer).

**Jonah:**   OK. Everyone out! I've got to lock up.

**Dylan:**   Wait a minute, that man didn't pay.

**Sarena:**   Oh, we have to clean up the kitchen and wash all the pots and pans and put the dishes away.

**Jonah:**   Let's pretend all of that is already done. Like, we already put everything in the dishwasher and now it's time to lock up.

**Dylan:**   OK. Restaurant's closed. Go home.

Throughout this play sequence, the children spontaneously developed and role-played a familiar restaurant theme. When Jonah announced, "I think we should make this a restaurant," he initiated the restaurant play sequence. Sarena and Dylan immediately joined the play. The children also made connections to the Eric Carle book they had recently heard. They checked their own imaginative play against the reality of restaurants when they talked about needing to "lock up the store . . . clean up the kitchen . . . and put the dishes away." Their words, actions, and gestures reflected their understandings of the elements needed for a restaurant based on their actual experiences, the media, and the content in which the play occurs. Beyond having fun and playing out a restaurant theme, Jonah demonstrated what he knew about restaurants and practiced that role by announcing what the food was going to be and identifying a place to pay. Dylan demonstrated his knowledge by stating they needed money, and Sarena showed her knowledge by noting that they needed someone to cook the food. This chapter explores the role of play as an important childhood activity that helps all children master their developmental needs.

## ✤ THEORETICAL AND RESEARCH BASE: WHAT IS PLAY?

Over the years, theorists, researchers, and educators across different disciplines and perspectives have documented that play is the optimal vehicle for learning and development in the early childhood years. They also suggest that the *absence of play* is often an obstacle to the development of happy, healthy, and creative individuals. Although those who study play have proposed a variety of definitions and functions of play, experts disagree on some aspects. Despite these differences, there is genuine agreement on some of the characteristics that distinguish play from other types of human behavior (Bretherton, 1984; Fromberg, 1992, 1990).

### *Characteristics of Play*

There are at least five essential elements that characterize play. Each one of these components was illustrated in the opening case study with Jonah, Dylan, and Sarena.

**1.** *Play is voluntary and intrinsically motivated.* In play, children are free to choose the content and direction of their activity. The play is self-satisfying because it does not respond to external demands or expectations. In their self-chosen roles as cook and restaurant workers, Jonah, Dylan, and Sarena controlled how to play them out.

**2.** *Play is symbolic, meaningful, and transformational.* Play enables children to connect their past experiences to their current world. It empowers them to transform themselves into others' roles as they switch back and forth and in and out of different situations. By pretending to be others, they assume a "what if" or "as if" attitude. When Dylan imagined himself as a cook making alphabet soup, he assumed a "what if" attitude by imagining what a cook might say or do. When he pretended to be a cook, he transformed himself into a cook by imagining cooking, stirring, and serving soup as a cook would do. This "as if" attitude (the play) is the behavior that facilitates the further generation of ideas.

**3.** *Play actively involves the players.* In play, children explore, experiment, investigate, and inquire with people, objects, or events. Notice how Jonah decided on the restaurant theme, Dylan added the need for money and a menu, and Sarena noted the need for a cook. Together, these children actively collaborated to enact their version of a restaurant.

**4.** *Play is rule-bound.* Children are governed by either explicit or implicit rules during play. Younger children create and change rules in play that apply to appropriate role behavior and object use. Older children accept predetermined rules that guide the play. In this play scenario, the kindergartners created their own rules about paying, cooking, and cleaning up.

**5.** *Play is pleasurable.* When children play, they pursue an activity for the intrinsic pleasure it brings—not for an extrinsic reward. That is, these children were playing because they chose to, how they wanted to, and with total concentration on what they were doing (Fromberg & Bergen, 1998; Johnson, Christie, & Yawkey, 1999). Clearly, these children were pursuing their play because it was meaningful and made sense to them.

Play enables children to construct understandings of their world from their own experiences and strongly influences all aspects of their growth and development. Children become empowered in play to do things for themselves, to feel in control, to test out and practice their skills, and to affirm confidence in themselves. The play context is an important one for children's developing sense of competence (Wassermann, 1990).

These five characteristics of play explain what play is. Remember, the more choice children have in being in control of their play, the more opportunity they have to engage in or withdraw from activity, and the more possibilities children have in safely bending reality to fit their needs, the closer the behavior is to a pure play activity. While it is important to understand what play is, it is equally important to consider what play is not. Table 2.1 lists a continuum of behavior from play to work that will help you differentiate between play and nonplay behaviors.

**TABLE 2.1  Continuum of Behavior from Play to Nonplay**

| | Child-Initiated Play, Freely Chosen | Facilitative Play | Directed Play | Work Disguised as Play | Work (Nonplay) |
|---|---|---|---|---|---|
| **Focus of Play** | Child has greatest degree of control over situation, event, or other players. Can freely interact. | Child plays within a flexible environment of social rules, requiring players to attend to externally imposed control. Adults monitor play more closely than free play and often redirect, challenge, and add materials. | Adults impose play elements and often lead the play. Players do not usually choose whether to play, what to play, how to play, or when to play. | Task-oriented activities that are not inherently playful but that can be transformed into directed or guided play activities if the potential for internal control, motivation, and reality can be tapped. | An activity designed to reach an externally defined goal and for which motivation is external. No opportunity to bend the reality. Adult's expectations are central and often evaluated. |
| **Example** | Child freely chooses when to play, how to play, what to play, and with whom to play. High levels of social and pretend play occur during free play. For example, child can be a baby in the family living area. | Players may have limited number of choices or be expected to engage in a specified number of play activities within a particular time period. | Group games, fingerplays, directed story reenactment. | Rote memory activities such as singing ABC songs, spelling games, addition facts races. | Adults decide when to work, how to work, where to work, or what to work at. Goal-oriented tasks, such as worksheets. |

*Source:* Adapted from Bergen (1987) and Wing (1995).

## Controversies Surrounding Play

With agreed-upon characteristics of play, why would there be any controversy about its definition and purposes? First, theorists and researchers have differed in their assumptions about play and its primary purpose, yet all have attested to its significance in children's physical, social/emotional, language, and intellectual growth and development. Freud (1958) and Erikson (1963) emphasized the *emotional* significance of play, the way children use play to express and release powerful emotions; Piaget (1962), on the other hand, emphasized play's *cognitive* significance, the way *individual children* use play to practice known information and construct understanding. Vygotsky (1967; 1978) emphasized the way children use play as a vehicle for *social and cultural learning* and the development of the social tool called language.

Second, our own culture makes a clear distinction between play and work (Johnson, Christie, & Yawkey, 1999; Fromberg, 1998, 1990). Today's children are pressured more and more to participate in teacher-directed, structured, formal lessons leaving little, if any, time to learn through play. Many early childhood teachers believe that play activities should be the centerpiece of their curricula. Yet they feel pressured to justify the use of play with the phrase "Play is children's work." While this statement equates play with work, it also implies that work is serious and play

*Play with objects empowers children to do things for themselves, to feel in control, to test and practice skills, and to develop a sense of competence.*

is trivial. This misconception equates "real" school with paper-and-pencil activities. Yet, if we look at the best practices in each area of the curriculum, such as hands-on science, math manipulatives, music laboratories, or writers' workshops, it is easy to see that all of these approaches are play-based.

An illustration of how teachers' orientations to play affect the early childhood classroom comes from the following two very different first-grade classrooms. In Ms. McGill's room, children plan their daily schedules with their teacher during their morning meeting. Then, during a 90-minute uninterrupted block of learning experiences, the first graders complete some teacher-selected stations and then choose freely among a wide variety of accessible and well-organized materials. Some build with blocks, paint at easels, play in the family-living corner, construct with manipulatives, write in their math or writing journals, or investigate science ideas. There is a quiet buzz from the children's interactions with these diverse activities. They also have daily opportunities for outdoor play.

Mr. Sampson's first graders, on the other hand, sit in desks in neat rows. He directs his 6-year-olds to work in whole-group experiences to complete teacher-prepared activities, such as coloring in worksheets, tracing letters, and making an art project by copying the sample Mr. Sampson made. His first graders are reminded to do their own work, and there is little time to talk with one another about what they are doing, thinking, or making. Outdoors, children play organized ball games or practice motor skills on the climbing equipment. How do these classrooms reflect each teacher's assumptions about play?

In a classroom like Mr. Sampson's, little attention is given to the powerful relationship of play to learning and development. His classroom experiences deny children the opportunity to work on challenging tasks in a playful context. Historically, early childhood educators have valued the centrality of play and supported children's natural play activities in the early childhood classroom (Johnson et al., 1999; Isenberg & Quisenberry, 1988). However, recent societal and educational developments have emphasized a more academic, structured orientation and have undermined the role of play in the curriculum. Classroom practices such as the use of stations, centers, or cooperative problem-solving activities in today's curriculum offer one way of including play-based experiences in the curriculum.

## *The Educational Role of Play*

If we could travel back in time and interview three leaders in early childhood education about the value of play, what would they say? John Dewey, Patty Smith Hill, and Susan Isaacs were all strong advocates of play in the early childhood classroom. Dewey (1916, 1938) believed that children learn about themselves and their world through play. While children build on what they know in their play, their play is continually changed by their ongoing experiences. For Dewey, play becomes a recurring cycle of learning that is essential to what children know and can do. Through meaningful, firsthand experiences with concrete materials coupled with opportunities to think and talk about these experiences, children build new understandings. Through peer interaction and the negotiations that inevitably occur during play, they enhance

*(a) John Dewey believed that children learn about themselves and their world through their play. (b) Patty Smith Hill invented the large hollow blocks that are an integral part of today's early childhood settings.*

their social growth. Dewey's ideas about **active learning** continue to permeate to-day's early childhood curriculum.

Patty Smith Hill (1923), strongly influenced by Dewey's ideas, recognized the importance of play for children's learning. She invented the large hollow blocks that are still an integral part of most early childhood classrooms and believed that large classroom spaces enhance children's learning through play. In her work-play period, her kindergarten children freely explored the objects and materials in their environment, initiated and carried out their own ideas, and engaged in cooperative learning groups with their peers.

Susan Isaacs (1933) is another historical figure who believed that play contributes to all aspects of children's growth and development. Her work was especially helpful to teachers as they observed children's developing mastery of their emotions. Isaacs ardently defended children's right to play and challenged parents to support play, which she regarded as children's natural resource for learning.

Prior to the large-scale societal and educational reforms beginning in the 1960s, most early childhood practitioners recognized the importance of play. They believed that play reflects children's experiences, is meaningful and relevant, and is thus a rich resource for learning. The translation of Piaget's (1962) work in the 1960s began to find support for the idea that children are active learners.

At the same time, other researchers documented the importance of the early years for influencing intellectual development (Bloom, 1964; Bruner, 1966; Hunt, 1961). Educators soon began putting these research ideas into practice with the growing numbers of disadvantaged children but did so in inappropriate ways. Early childhood classrooms at all levels became more academic and rigorous. As curriculum designers became driven by the belief that earlier is better, academic skills replaced play as central to the curriculum, to the grave concern of many early childhood educators.

But the educational climate is once again changing. As educational leaders look to the skills and abilities workers will need in the new millennium, they are raising questions about rote learning. Schools and curricula at all levels are being refashioned with learning outcomes for children in mind. They invite children's initiative and planning and focus on developing their problem-solving ability, divergent thinking, and social skills. Play provides the vehicle for young children to develop such competencies. Teachers who care for and educate young children must be conversant about the crucial role of play in the lives of all children. As teachers, we must advocate strongly the restoration of play to the early childhood curriculum by exploding the myth that play is frivolous and trivial. As the next section details, play is what childhood is all about.

## ✿ WHY IS PLAY IMPORTANT?

Guidelines from the Association for Childhood Education International and the National Association for the Education of Young Children, two respected professional associations, affirm that play is essential for all children's healthy growth and development. Play:

- Enables children to make sense of their world.
- Develops social and cultural understandings.
- Allows children to express their thoughts and feelings.
- Fosters flexible and divergent thinking.
- Provides opportunities to meet and solve real problems.
- Develops language and literacy skills and concepts (Bredekamp & Copple, 1997; Bredekamp & Rosegrant, 1992; Isenberg & Quisenberry, 1988).

In the following play vignettes, consider how play contributes to children's cognitive, language, literacy, social/emotional, and creative development.

## *Cognitive Development*

Ellen, Taralyn, and Jasmine are first graders. On this day early in the school year, they come into their classroom, hang up their backpacks, and then choose to play school at the chalkboard. Ellen decides that Jasmine and Taralyn should get a chair and bring it up to the board. They each also find a yardstick.

*Ellen:*   *We better have two chairs.*
*Taralyn:*   *(Writing on the chalkboard) Today is . . .*
*Jasmine:*   *I need to check the size. (Using the yardstick, she begins to measure herself while sitting down.) I am the big teacher. My size is up to here (pointing to where she measured herself).*

*Ellen gets up from the chair, ready to be the teacher.*

*Ellen:*   *I will write it. You sit down.*
*Jasmine:*   *Today is what? (Gets up.) I want to be the teacher. First you sit down. Sit down.*
*Ellen:*   *It's my turn first. You can be the teacher next. (Begins to write where Taralyn had started.) Today is Thursday, October 1999.*

*As Ellen looks at the calendar to find the words she wants to use, Taralyn measures herself with the yardstick.*

*Taralyn:*   *Today is October 7, 1999.*
*Jasmine:*   *Ellen, can I write, too?*
*Ellen:*   *After I am finished. (Taralyn and Jasmine begin giving Ellen weather words to write.)*
*Taralyn:*   *Read the calendar sentence. Hey, you forgot the 7.*
*Ellen:*   *Yeah. (She goes back and inserts the number 7. Then she writes* Tody *and* wet.)
*Jasmine:*   *It's my turn to be the teacher. I am a children. (Gets up, erases the board and writes* ROL EOYF ONM. *She looks at what she wrote and says, "Today." Ellen sits down where Jasmine was sitting. Jasmine looks at what she has written and says, "Today.")*
*Taralyn:*   *What is the weather? It's my turn.*
*Ellen:*   *Raise your hand for the weather.*
*Taralyn:*   *Today the weather is sunny.*
*Ellen:*   *(Writing on the board, she asks Taralyn for help.) What comes after s-u-n?*
*Taralyn:*   *N-n-y.*

The first graders in this scenario are using play as a tool for cognitive development. When we talk about cognitive development, we refer to how children make sense of their world. They do this by building upon what they already know to interpret new experiences. In their play, Ellen, Taralyn, and Jasmine demonstrate the following four essential elements of cognitive development (Perkins, 1984):

1. *Problem-solving.* Using the yardstick to measure herself sitting down and standing up, Jasmine figures out the concept of size.
2. *Mental planning.* When Ellen comes to the chalkboard area, tells Taralyn and Jasmine to get two chairs, sits down in front and stands at the chalkboard to

write, she clearly plans to play school. Mental planning also occurs when Ellen states she will be the teacher first.

3. *Self-monitoring.* We see Ellen checking her own spelling skills when she asks Taralyn for help spelling the rest of the word *sunny.*

4. *Evaluation.* When Taralyn is reading the calendar sentence and notices that Ellen forgot the 7, she demonstrates her understanding of writing the date.

Much of the research on play shows its relationship to the development of children's thinking and more sophisticated classification skills (Johnson, Ershler, & Lawton, 1982; Perkins, 1984; Resnick, 1987) and the ability to use what they already know to construct new knowledge. In this case, these first graders are building on what they already know (e.g., the routines of school, specific teacher behaviors, and basic literacy concepts and skills) and extending it through playful interactions. They play with words and letters as they test out the spelling of weather words and the way to record the day and date.

The cognitive skills children use in pretend play are essential for their success in school (Smilansky, 1968; Smilansky & Shefatya, 1990). All subjects and problems include cognitive skills children use to pretend, yet many subjects (e.g., social studies) are those with which children have limited experience. To illustrate, after a teacher shares books about the Chinese New Year such as *Lion Dancer* (Walters & Slovenz-Low, 1990) or *China's Bravest Girl* (Chin, 1997), children's imaginations are stimulated. During play we might observe that the children are able to *imagine* a Chinese New Year celebration with its special dances to ward off evil spirits, colorful dragons and decorations, and special Chinese festival foods, because they are using their *make-believe ability* to play. In this way, real and pretend become complementary as children use make-believe to enhance their cognitive understanding (Berk, 1994; Johnson et al., 1999; Smilansky & Shefatya, 1990).

## Language Development

Evan and Anna are preparing a birthday celebration for their mother in the housekeeping area of their Head Start classroom. When they realize they need a present, Anna says, "Let's ask Mr. Bear." This is a reference to the book *Ask Mr. Bear* by Marjorie Flack (1932), in which Danny tries to find the perfect birthday present for his mother by asking several different animals for suggestions. After locating the book in the library corner, Evan and Anna become the goose, the goat, the cow, the hen, and the bear as they search for the perfect present. The book becomes the content for their play as they assume the roles of the animals, experiment with the intonations and inflections of the different animals, and use language to guide their own behavior and direct the behavior of others. Evan and Anna's play is contributing to their language growth and vice versa.

Proficiency in oral language is essential for all children's success in school. Studies of how children learn both their first and second language describe language *use* as a major influence on language *development* (Gibbons, 1993). In the previous scenario, we see at least four ways in which Anna and Evan's play of a birthday celebration enables them to practice important language skills:

1. *Communication.* In pretend play, children use role-appropriate statements and metacommunication, language used to maintain the play episode, plan a story line, and assign roles. Pretending to be someone else enables children to use voice inflections and language in situations they may or may not have ever encountered. Play helps children to internalize the many rule systems associated with the language they are speaking. It also helps them generate multiple ways of expressing their thinking (Santrock, 2000).

2. *Forms and functions.* During play, children learn to use language for different purposes in a variety of settings and with different people. Michael Halliday (1975) calls this process "learning how to mean," as children discover that what they say translates to what can be done. Talking in play settings allows children to practice the necessary forms and functions of language (Halliday, 1975) and helps them think about ways to communicate (Garvey, 1977). Moreover, for children whose native language is not English, play offers children opportunities to build upon and practice fluency in their home language in safe and informal settings (Owocki, 1999). Table 2.2 describes these functions, provides a language example, and identifies play contexts that support these language forms and functions.

3. *Purposeful verbal interaction.* In play with others, children often use language to ask for materials, ask a question, express ideas, explore language, or establish and maintain the play. For younger children, verbal give-and-take during sociodramatic play needs to be highly developed because children plan, manage, problem-solve, and maintain the play by verbal explanations, discussions, or commands (Smilansky & Shefatya, 1990).

4. *Play with language.* Both younger and older children enjoy playing with language because, in doing so, they feel in control of it. Play is their arena for experimenting with and coming to understand words, syllables, sounds, and grammatical structure (Cazden, 1976). Language play for school-aged children manifests itself in the jokes, riddles, jump rope rhymes, and games of elementary age children (Athey, 1984). Elementary school children are intrigued by the sound and meaning ambiguity of "knock-knock" jokes as well as by the humor of enacting scripts that include dialogue involving multiple meanings and rhymes (Isenberg, 1995; Owocki, 1999). These forms of language play require the transformational ability to explore the phonological, syntactic, and semantic rules of language.

## Literacy Development

There is a growing body of evidence to show how children's play contributes explicitly to their literacy development (Christie, 1998). We know that children's literacy development—their reading and writing abilities—occurs from infancy along with their oral language development. By the time they come to school, they already possess a well-developed spoken language in their native tongue as well as a wealth of understanding and knowledge about print (Owocki, 1999; Stone & Christie, 1996). We also know that children learn to read and write in "meaningful, functional social settings" (Morrow, 1993, p. 110) that involve both social and cognitive abilities (Owocki, 1999).

**TABLE 2.2  Halliday's Functions of Language with Language Samples from Three Kindergarten Girls Building with Blocks**

| Function | Language Usage and Sample | Play Experiences |
|---|---|---|
| Instrumental (Get things done) | "I want . . ." "Let me have all the orange ones for turrets." | Choosing materials; entering a play situation |
| Regulatory (Control others' behavior) | "Do this . . ." "Only 3 people can play here; don't knock that over." | Dramatic play; games; story retellings |
| Personal (Tell about self) | "I like this . . ." "Oh no, this is hard to build. I really like castles." | Role playing; choosing roles |
| Interactional (Maintain relationships with others) | "Let's do this . . ." "Let's build a moat around the castle and a bridge to go across it." | Play with language; puppetry; cooperative play; sociodramatic play |
| Heuristic (Find out information) | "How come this is. . . ?" "How come this castle doesn't have a moat?" | Questioning games; investigations; TV shows |
| Imaginative (Use pretend language) | "Pretend we are . . ." "Let's pretend there are snakes in the moat and we need to escape." | Role-play; dramatic play; constructive play |
| Informative (Provide information to others) | "This is how I made . . ." "You have to have one turret for each part on the wall. There are lots of castles in fairy tales." | Projects; investigations |

*Source:* Adapted from Halliday (1975, pp. 19–21). Language samples courtesy of Kim Rose.

Children's first attempts at reading and writing often occur during dramatic play as they read environmental print, make shopping lists, or play school. Their play can reveal the following literacy understandings:

**1.** *Interest in stories, knowledge of story structure, and story comprehension.* Evan and Anna demonstrated an interest in stories (e.g., choosing to retell *Ask Mr. Bear*), displayed a knowledge of story structure (e.g., character, plot, setting, goal, and conflict), and exhibited story comprehension in their pretend dramatization of preparing for a birthday. Most beginning readers rely on their oral language to gain meaning from books as they internalize the structure and meaning of language. Dramatic play develops improved story comprehension (Pellegrini & Galda, 1982; Stone & Christie, 1996; Williamson & Silvern, 1984) and an increased understanding of story structure (Pellegrini, 1980; Roskos, 1988).

**2.** *Understanding fantasy in books.* In dramatic play, children enter the play world "as if" they were another character or thing. The ability to transform oneself in play enables children to enter the world often created in books featuring talking animals (e.g., *Ask Mr. Bear* or *Charlotte's Web*) or to write stories in which they create hypothetical characters (Berk, 1994; Monighan-Nourot & Van Hoorn, 1991; Stone & Christie, 1996).

**3.** *Use of symbols to represent their world.* As children reinvent or construct their own versions of stories, they naturally come to understand their world and make it their own. Through play, children represent their understandings of the world symbolically. Children's language, role enactment, or use of props provides evidence of children's representational competence or ways to represent their knowledge (Berk, 1994; Johnson et al., 1999).

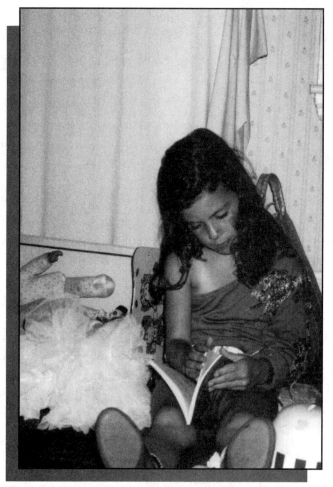

*Children's first attempts at reading and writing often occur during dramatic play.*

Although play is often viewed as an activity for very young children, older children also require opportunities for "collaborative, social, and interactive learning" (Morrow, 1993, p. 112) through playful story retellings, writing, word play, and conversations. Early childhood teachers have an important role in helping parents understand the many ways children's play contributes to their language and literacy development. Figure 2.1 is a checklist for documenting children's literacy development through play.

## Social and Emotional Development

During play, children also increase their social competence and emotional maturity. Smilansky and Shefatya (1990) contend that school success largely depends on children's ability to interact positively with their peers and adults. Play is vital to children's social development. It enables children to:

**Figure 2.1**
Documenting Children's Literacy Learning Through Play

---

Child's Name: _____

*Demonstrates "reading-like," literate behaviors*
- ✓ Looks at books and other print materials
- ✓ Does pretend writing
- ✓ Shares reading/writing ideas with friends
- ✓ Uses sound spelling to write notes
- ✓ Practices reading familiar stories
- ✓ Chooses books and magazines that reflect their interests
- ✓ Other

*Shows understanding of stories and narrative language*
- ✓ Acts out pretend stories
- ✓ Tells a story through drawing or other media
- ✓ Uses puppets to retell a story dramatically
- ✓ Engages in dramatic retellings that include _____ characters, _____ setting, _____ conflict, _____ plot, and _____ solution
- ✓ Dramatic retellings use story structure (e.g., beginning, middle, and end)
- ✓ Other

*Explores conventions of print*
- ✓ Writes messages in dramatic play center
- ✓ Copies letters and words from other print materials
- ✓ Reads messages to others during dramatic play or story retellings
- ✓ Other

*(continued)*

**Figure 2.1**
*(Continued)*

---

*Investigates book knowledge and the language of books*

  ✓  Holds book right side up

  ✓  Turns pages left to right

  ✓  Pretends to read while turning pages

  ✓  Distinguishes between pictures and print

  ✓  Makes up words and stories to match pictures

  ✓  Reads books with familiar patterns or repetitive language

  ✓  Names some print while reading

  ✓  Other

*Experiments with a variety of forms of written language*

  ✓  Announcements

  ✓  Calendars

  ✓  Money/cash registers

  ✓  Coupons

  ✓  Labels

  ✓  Invitations

  ✓  Library cards

  ✓  Notes/Recipes

  ✓  Signs

  ✓  Tickets

  ✓  Other

*Statement of literacy behaviors demonstrated.*

*Ideas for furthering literacy development.*

*Suggestions for parents.*

---

*Source:* Adapted from Owocki (1999).

- Practice both verbal and nonverbal communication skills by negotiating roles, trying to gain access to ongoing play, or appreciating the feelings of others (Spodek & Saracho, 1998).
- Respond to their peers' feelings while waiting for their turn and sharing materials and experiences (Sapon-Shevin, et al., 1998).
- Experiment with roles of the people in their home, school, and community by coming into contact with the needs and wishes of others (Creasey, Jarvis, & Berk, 1998; Garvey, 1977; Spodek & Saracho, 1998).
- Experience others' points of view by working through conflicts about space, materials or rules positively (Smilansky & Shefatya, 1990).

*We went bowling, by a*
*4-year-old girl.*

Play supports emotional development by providing a way to *express* feelings and a context to *cope* with them. Pretend play helps children to express feelings in the following four ways (Piaget, 1962):

1.  *Simplifying events* by creating an imaginary character, plot, or setting to match their emotional state. A child afraid of the dark, for example, might eliminate darkness or night from the play episode.
2.  *Compensating for situations* by adding forbidden acts to pretend play. A child may, for example, eat cookies and ice cream for breakfast in play, whereas in reality, this would not be permitted.
3.  *Controlling emotional expression* by repeatedly reenacting unpleasant or frightening experiences. For example, a child might pretend to have an accident after seeing a real traffic accident on the highway.
4.  *Avoiding adverse consequences* by pretending another character, real or imaginary, commits inappropriate acts and suffers the consequences. Children whose television viewing is monitored at home, for instance, can pretend to allow the doll to watch indiscriminately and then reprimand the "bad child" for unacceptable TV viewing habits.

In addition to expressing feelings, children also learn to *cope* with their feelings as they act out being angry, sad, or worried in a situation they control (Erikson, 1963). Pretend play allows them to think out loud about experiences charged with both pleasant and unpleasant feelings (Fein, 1985). A good example is Alexander, a 4-year-old whose dog was recently hit by a car. In his dramatic play in the pet hospital, his teacher heard him say to another child, "I'm sad because the car hurt my dog." Here he was trying to cope with unpleasant feelings from a frightening situation. Play enabled Alexander to *express* his feelings so that he could *cope* with his worry about his dog (Landreth & Homeyer, 1998).

## *Physical Development*

Play contributes to children's fine and gross motor development and body aware-ness as they actively use their bodies. Learning to use a writing tool, such as a marker, is an example of fine motor development through play. The natural pro-gression in small motor development is from scribbles to shapes and forms to rep-resentational pictures. Playing with writing tools helps children refine their fine motor skills. Gross motor development, such as hopping and skipping, develops in a similar fashion. When children first learn to hop, they practice hopping on dif-ferent feet or just for the pure joy of hopping. As school-aged children, their hop-ping skill is integrated into many games. Using their bodies during play also en-ables them "to feel physically confident, secure and self-assured" (Isenberg & Quisenberry, 1988, p. 139).

While all children need active play for healthy physical development, the physical benefits are particularly valuable for children with joint or muscular ill-nesses such as juvenile rheumatoid arthritis or multiple sclerosis. These children cannot engage in repeated strenuous exercise; they can, however, engage in active play. Active play helps them build or maintain energy, joint flexibility, and mus-cular strength (Majure, 1995). Side benefits of active play for these children in-clude the development of social skills and an increasing ability to endure stress-ful situations.

## *Creative Development*

In Chapter One we talked about the important role of creativity and divergent thinking in children's development. The play context is ideal for supporting children's creative and imaginative growth because it offers a risk-free envi-ronment. Research supports the notion that play and creativity are related because they both rely upon children's ability to use symbols (Johnson et al., 1999; Singer & Singer, 1998; Spodek & Saracho, 1998). In research conducted by Jerome and Dorothy Singer (1985, 1998), they describe the ability to engage in make-believe as essential to children's developing ability for internal imagery, stimulating curiosity, and experimenting with alternative responses to different situations (Monighan-Nourot & Van Hoorn, 1991). This capacity, practiced in play settings, enhances children's ability to engage successfully in new situations.

Creativity can be viewed as an aspect of problem solving, which has its roots in play. When young children use their imaginations in play, they are more cre-ative, perform better at school tasks, and develop a problem-solving approach to learning (Dansky, 1980; Dansky & Silverman, 1973; Pepler & Ross, 1981; Singer, 1973; Sutton-Smith, 1986).

The importance of play in children's lives is well documented. As young children grow and change, play develops with them according to a developmen-tal sequence.

## Research Studies about Play

Bagley, D. M., & Kass, P. H. (1997). Comparison of preschoolers' play in housekeeping and thematic sociodramatic play centers. *Journal of Research in Childhood Education, 12*(1), 71–77.

Kontos, S. (1999). Preschool teachers' talk, roles, and activity settings during free play. *Early Childhood Research Quarterly, 14*(3), 363–382.

Stone, S. J., & Christie, J. F. (1996). Collaborative literacy learning during sociodramatic play in a multiage (K–2) primary classroom. *Journal of Research in Childhood Education, 10*(2), 123–133.

Trawick-Smith, J. (1998). Why play training works: An integrated model for play intervention. *Journal of Research in Childhood Education, 12*(2), 117–129.

Wing, L. A. (1995). Play is not the work of the child. *Early Childhood Research Quarterly, 10*(2), 223–247.

### Web Sites

Early Years Are Learning Years (Block Play: Building a Child's Mind, 1977).

*www.naeyc.org/naeyc*

Early Years Are Learning Years (Toys: Tools for Learning, 1996).

*www.cyfc.umn.edu/Children/naeyc2.html*

Catalogue of toys for children with disabilities.

*www.dftoys.com*

## HOW DOES PLAY DEVELOP?

Meet Jessie, a child who is starting third grade in the fall. If you could go back through her play life and catch glimpses of her behavior, this is what you would see:

*As a 10-month-old, Jessie plays pat-a-cake with Grandma Marji. At age 2, Jessie pours sand back and forth into different-sized plastic containers. When Jessie is 4, she pretends to make pizzas and take delivery orders over the telephone with her friends, Lara and Michelle. At age 6, Jessie and two friends pretend to eat space food in a spaceship they have constructed. And now, at age 8, Jessie plays a card game, "I Doubt It," and is becoming quite adept at Rummy.*

As Jessie's experiences illustrate, play occurs in a sequence. The development of play at all ages has been studied from two major perspectives, cognitive and social. Both parallel and strengthen children's overall development. Think about the following questions as you read the next section: What types of play do children demonstrate at different ages? Do these types of play reappear at later ages? How does play reflect and promote children's cognitive and social development?

## Developmental Stages of Cognitive Play

Cognitive play reflects children's age, conceptual understandings, and experiential background. The ideas of Piaget (1962), Smilansky (1968) and Smilansky & Shefatya (1990) describe the following cognitive stages of play: functional play, symbolic play, constructive play, and games with rules. Although each of these types of play peaks at a particular age, it continues in some form throughout life, has unique characteristics, and contributes to children's growing understanding of themselves, others, and their world. Table 2.3 provides an overview of the four categories of cognitive play, their typical behaviors, and an age-appropriate example.

### Functional Play

**Functional play** (birth to age two) is characterized by simple, pleasurable, repeated movements with objects, people, and language to learn new skills or to gain mastery of a physical or mental skill. It is also referred to as sensorimotor, practice, or exercise play (Piaget, 1962; Smilansky & Shefatya, 1990). Functional play dominates the first two years of development, about one-third of the play of preschoolers, less than one-sixth of the play of elementary school children (Rubin, Fein, & Vandenberg, 1983), and continues in some form through adulthood.

Through functional or practice play, children develop coordinated motor skills and begin to feel confident and competent with their bodies, like the:

One-year-old who stacks and unstacks rings on a pole.

Four-year-old who incessantly repeats "I'm the king of the castle."

Five-year-old who deliberately places pegs in a pattern on a pegboard.

Seven-year-old who practices bicycling skills on a two-wheeler at every available minute.

### Symbolic Play

**Symbolic play** (2 to 7 years), also called pretend, dramatic or sociodramatic, fantasy, or make-believe play, emerges during the second year and continues in different forms throughout adulthood. It arises when children are able to transform their world into symbols and usually contains three elements: props, plot, and roles (Garvey, 1977). Symbolic play reflects children's growing mental ability to make objects, actions, gestures, or words stand for something or someone else (Monighan-Nourot & Van Hoorn, 1991; Piaget, 1962). Play at this stage is called "symbolic" because it focuses on social roles and interactions (Smilansky &

| TABLE 2.3 | Types, Characteristics, and Examples of Cognitive Play | |
|---|---|---|
| **Type** | **Characteristics** | **Example** |
| Functional Play | Repetition of movements when new skills are being learned, with or without objects. | *Infants and toddlers:* grasping and pulling a mobile |
| | | *Preschoolers and kindergartners:* repeating a pattern on a pegboard |
| | | *School-aged children:* practicing throwing, catching, or doing acrobatics |
| Symbolic Play | Use of imagination and role play to transform the self and objects and to satisfy needs. | *Infants and toddlers:* pretending to drink from a baby bottle |
| | Early symbolic play: mental representation that transforms one object for another. | *Preschoolers and kindergartners:* pretending a block is a broken car and pretending to fix it |
| | Later symbolic play: mental representation that transforms self and objects. | *School-aged children:* using secret codes or made-up languages to communicate |
| Constructive Play | Manipulation of objects or materials to make something. Combines functional play repetitive activity with symbolic representation of ideas. Occurs when children regulate their own creations or constructions. | *Preschoolers and kindergartners:* constructing a hospital room for a sick animal<br>*School-aged children:* creating an exhibit of a project just studied or designing virtual games and figures with electronic icons |
| Games with Rules | Activities with predetermined rules that are goal-oriented and often competitive with one or more individual. | *Infants and toddlers:* playing pat-a-cake with an adult<br>*Preschoolers and kindergartners:* playing simple singing and circle games<br>*School-aged children:* tag, marbles, hopscotch, or contests such as relay races |

*Sources:* Adapted from Piaget (1962) and Smilansky & Shefatya (1990).

Shefatya, l990) and reveals children's ability to play with ideas or symbols. In symbolic play, children make mental and verbal plans of action, assume roles, and transform objects or actions to express their feelings and ideas (Monighan-Nourot & Van Hoorn, 1991).

Infants and toddlers imitate actions associated with a particular prop in symbolic play, learn to substitute one thing for another, and act as if they were someone else who is familiar to them. For example, as a young toddler, Naomi picks up her toy cup and pretends to drink from it. As an older toddler, she may offer her

*Using their bodies during play enables children to feel competent and confident.*

doll a drink from the cup. Her symbolic play shifts from pretense about herself to pretense about others.

Preschool and kindergarten children's symbolic play is more complex. They pretend alone or with others, use nonrealistic objects, assume roles, and use objects as symbols in addition to what they stand for (Bergen, 1988). Three-year-old Miriam uses her hand as a pretend hairbrush for the baby's hair. Five-year-olds Jimbo and Celeste become firefighters as they collaborate to rescue people from a burning building. These transformations are essential for symbolic play to occur (Weininger, 1988). Symbolic play peaks during the preschool years, the golden age of make-believe.

Elementary school children's symbolic play is different from the play of children at other ages because now their thinking is less public. They can integrate their symbols into age-appropriate, socially acceptable mental games and language play. Riddles, number games, secret codes, and daydreaming form the structure of symbolic play for elementary school children (Berk, 1994; Johnson et al., 1999). It is not uncommon to find 7-year-olds delighting in the use of secret code, a form of symbolic and language play.

Research shows that symbolic play increases children's memory (Newman, 1990), enriches language and expands vocabulary (Fromberg, 1992), enhances children's ability to reason with contradictory facts (Fromberg & Bergen, 1998), and fosters flexible and inventive thinking (Pepler & Ross, 1981).

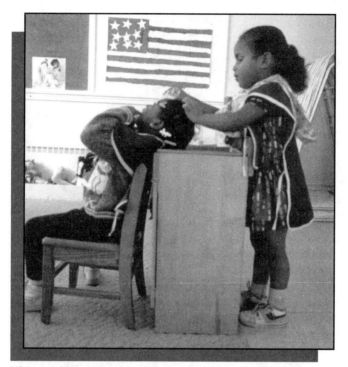

*These girls are transforming their world into symbols by using props, creating a story, and assuming new roles as they re-enact a "beauty shop."*

### Sociodramatic Play

When symbolic play involves two or more children who communicate verbally about the play episode, it is called **sociodramatic play.** Because it is person-oriented rather than object-oriented, sociodramatic play is considered a higher level of symbolic play behavior. Here children exchange information and ideas during a jointly elaborated play sequence or theme; they can also simultaneously be actors, interactors, and observers (Smilansky & Shefatya, 1990). Repeated opportunities to engage in this type of play offer children a rich arena for developing and refining concepts, solving problems, feeling in control by making things happen, and enhancing peer relationships. Sociodramatic play correlates highly with children's intellectual and social abilities (Smilansky & Shefatya, 1990). Table 2.4 describes Smilansky's six criteria for determining dramatic and sociodramatic play.

It is the last two characteristics (interaction and verbal communication) that define symbolic play as sociodramatic. A discussion of the Smilansky scale for evaluating sociodramatic play elements can be found in Chapter Nine.

*In sociodramatic play, children imitate familiar roles and develop social skills.*

### Constructive Play

In **constructive play,** children create something or engage in problem-solving behavior according to a preconceived plan. Constructive play often combines functional and symbolic play and predominates during the preschool years (Forman, 1998; Rubin, Fein, & Vandenberg, 1983). The following example occurred during center time in Ms. Mitsoff's multi-age kindergarten and first-grade classroom.

Emily, Porsche, and Elizabeth chose to play in the block center. They had just visited the Washington, D.C., memorials and decided to build the Jefferson Memorial. To do this, they negotiated and discussed which blocks would be appropriate for the entrances, where to place them, how to make the river, and who would be

**TABLE 2.4    Smilansky's Characteristics of Dramatic and Sociodramatic Play**

| Play Behavior | Characteristics | Examples | Levels |
|---|---|---|---|
| Imitative Role Play | Child assumes a make-believe role of a person or object and expresses it in imitation and/or verbalization | "Let's pretend that I am the baby." | Beginning: Role relates to the familiar world (e.g., mommy, daddy, baby) |
| | | | Advanced: Role relates to world outside the family (e.g., doctor, teacher, police) |
| Make-believe with regard to objects | Child substitutes movements, verbal declarations, and/or materials or toys that are not replicas of the object itself or real objects | Uses Lincoln Logs to make a house for the baby and uses chimneys from Lincoln Logs to make beds for the dogs. | Beginning: Real objects or replicas used (e.g., real toy car) |
| | | | Advanced: Uses prop as part of play scenario (e.g., stirs soup with a block) |
| Verbal make-believe with regard to actions and situations | Child substitutes verbal descriptions or declarations for actions and situations | Uses Lincoln Logs to outline a square for the house and says "This is a house for the baby." | Beginning: Imitates simple actions of adult (e.g., holds vacuum and moves back and forth) |
| | | | Advanced: Child's actions are integral to the play episode (e.g., "I'm vacuuming this floor so the baby can crawl around and not hurt herself.") |
| Persistence in role play | Child stays within a role or play theme for at least 10 minutes | Plays role of baby, mother, and daughter within a family play theme for 10 minutes. | Beginning: Short, sporadic involvement (e.g., child enters area, picks up the baby and leaves) |
| | | | Advanced: Child stays involved in area and the theme for more than 10 minutes |
| Interaction | At least two players interact within the context of a play episode | | Beginning: Plays alone with no obvious awareness of others nearby |
| | | | Advanced: Cooperative effort to work together around a common theme |
| Verbal communication | There is some verbal interaction related to the play episode | | Beginning: Simple dialogue around the use of toys (e.g., "Give me the bottle.") |
| | | | Advanced: Dialogue about the roles, props, plot of the play scenario |

*Sources:* Adapted from Smilansky (1968) and Dodge & Colker (1992).

*In constructive play, the child becomes absorbed
in the process of creating a lasting end product.*

the statue. After they built their structure, which resembled the "real" Jefferson
Memorial, they engaged in symbolic play. In this play episode, the girls combined
constructive play (building a memorial) with symbolic play (visiting the memorial)
by representing their ideas with the materials (blocks) and elaborating on them in
symbolic play (playing house inside the memorial). In constructive play, the child
focuses on a lasting end product (Forman, 1998; Smilansky & Shefatya, 1990).

Elementary school children engage in some constructive play in the school
setting because it is easily accommodated in work-oriented settings (Forman, 1998;
Bergen, 1988). Typical constructive activities might include creating a play around
a social studies topic (e.g., occupations), writing a story, creating an interactive exhibit, using invented spelling, building virtual systems on a computer screen, or
making a mobile out of recycled materials. In order for the play to qualify as constructive, however, children must maintain a playful attitude (for instance, keeping the focus on "What if I do this?" rather than "Why won't it do that?"), must become absorbed in the process, and must find it pleasurable. In that way, the child
keeps the goal in mind, but it does not dominate the play.

### Games with Rules
**Games with rules** rely upon prearranged rules that guide acceptable play behav-
ior of reciprocity and turn taking. Games with rules such as board games (e.g.,
Clue), card games (e.g., Rummy), or outdoor games (e.g., kickball) are the most

prominent form of play among school-aged children. School-aged children's more logical ways of thinking and advanced social skills make it possible for them to follow a set of rules and negotiate with peers. Games with rules (see Chapter Seven for detailed discussion) enhance children's physical coordination, refine their social and language skills, build conceptual understandings, and increase children's understanding of cooperation and competition (DeVries, 1998).

In the following example of the card game Addition War, think about the rules Tom and Chang use and how they reason their way through problems. The boys are sitting side-by-side so they can see each other's addition facts and lay their cards down like a vertical math problem.

> **Tom:**   *I have 18. How many do you have?*
> **Chang:**   *I have 17.*
>
> *Tom picks up all four cards and places them at the bottom of his stack, face down. They each put down two more cards and Tom says, "I win."*
>
> **Chang:**   *I have 9 and 8. You know what that is? That equals 17 so I win this time.*
> **Tom:**   *We haven't had a war yet.*
> **Chang:**   *I have 18; what do you have?*
> **Tom:**   *I have 11 and 8.*
> **Chang:**   *11 and 8 is 19.*
> **Tom:**   *How much is an ace worth?*
> **Chang:**   *11. Oooh, you win! (They lay down more cards.) A jack and king equal 20. I have 20. I have 20. I have 20. Let me see. You have 16 and I have 20. I win. (When the game ends, the boys count their cards to see who has the most. Chang quickly counts his and says, "I have 39 and that means I win because it's more than half the deck.")*

In this card game, Tom and Chang use their knowledge of addition facts to engage in a rule-based game with each other. They demonstrate understanding of prearranged rules (acknowledging the winner of each round and assigning a numerical value to the ace), conceptual understanding (that the winner holding 39 cards has more than half the deck), and turn taking (knowing who goes next after each pair is placed on the table).

In sum, children use all types of cognitive play at different ages and for a variety of purposes. The unique nature of each type of cognitive play reflects what children know and are able to do. Because much of children's play occurs with or around others, the next section describes how play contributes to children's social competence.

## *Developmental Stages of Social Play*

Social play, the ability of children to interact with their peers, also develops in age-related stages. This kind of play often develops rapidly during the preschool years.

The now classic ideas of Mildred Parten (1932) have focused attention on the social aspects of play during early childhood. Parten identified six types of play, beginning with the least socially mature (solitary play) and moving toward the most socially mature (cooperative play). Today, most researchers consider Parten's "levels" as descriptive of *styles* of play rather than social maturity because as children grow older, they cycle back and forth between the types of social play (Monighan-Nourot, Scales, Van Hoorn, & Almy, 1987). Table 2.5 describes the characteristics of Parten's six levels of social play.

Knowledge of the stages of play helps teachers and caregivers provide appropriate environments that support children's development. It also enables them to enjoy, encourage, and appreciate age-appropriate play behavior. Play is children's natural resource for developing social and cognitive skills that affect their present and future interactions. To appreciate the essential role of play in children's lives, it is important to understand the different theories of why children play and how these theories influence teachers' views of play.

**TABLE 2.5   Levels of Social Play**

| Type of Play | Characteristics of the Child |
| --- | --- |
| Unoccupied behavior | Is not engaged in play and does not seem to have a goal. Plays with body, gets on and off chairs, walks about aimlessly. |
| Onlooker behavior | Observes, ask questions, and talks to other children but does not enter play itself. Stands within speaking distance to see and hear. May use onlooker behavior to decide when to enter an ongoing play group or to choose an activity. More active interest and involvement than unoccupied behavior. |
| Solitary play | Plays independently and is not involved with other children. Playing with own toys is the primary goal. Most typical of 2- and 3-year-old children. Older children use solitary play for needed privacy and for elaborate individual dramatic play. |
| Parallel play | Plays alongside or nearby, but not with, others. Uses shared toys but plays independently. Does not share toys. Typical of young preschool children. Often considered the beginnings of group play. |
| Associative play | Plays with others in a similar, loosely organized activity. Conversation involves asking questions, using one another's toys. Some attempts made to control who may join the group. Is often the transition from parallel to cooperative play. |
| Cooperative play | Involves complex social organization with shared common goals. Uses negotiation, division of labor, differential role taking, and organization of play themes. Reciprocal role taking (e.g., turn-taking) and a strong sense of belonging to the group. Organizes group for the purpose of making a product, dramatizing a situation, or playing a formal game. |

*Source:* Adapted from Parten (1932).

# WHY DO CHILDREN PLAY?

For over 150 years, theories of play have been proposed, yet none adequately explains why children play. Some suggest that children play because they feel physically safe in the play setting (e.g., the house is not really burning so they can escape); others suggest that children play because they feel safe emotionally (e.g., playing out events in a war-torn country provides a way for children to confront the realities of their environment). Still others suggest that play enables children to assimilate new information and make it their own, such as using invented spelling to write a message. Collectively, however, these theories represent a vision for the powerful role of play in children's development, which has greatly influenced teachers' thinking about its importance. These theories can be categorized as **classical** (e.g., those theories that were prominent in the nineteenth century through World War I) and **modern** (those that were prominent after World War I) (Johnson et al., 1999).

## *Classical Theories*

Classical theorists sought to explain the causes and purposes of play through surplus energy, recreation/relaxation, practice, and recapitulation (Ellis, 1973). We can see evidence of these theories in the way teachers currently view children's behaviors.

**Surplus-energy theory** suggests that human beings have a certain amount of energy to be used for survival. Energy not used for survival is spent on play and becomes surplus energy. When children have limited opportunities to move around, they seem to have bursts of energy that relieve stress and tension so they can settle down again. Teachers' views about "getting rid of excess energy on the playground" support this theoretical perspective.

**Recreation/relaxation theory,** in contrast to surplus-energy theory, suggests that play *replenishes* energy used in work. The influence of this theory is evident in early childhood classrooms where children alternate between quiet and active activities.

**Practice theory,** also known as instinct theory, proposes that play prepares children for the *future* roles and responsibilities needed to survive in their culture. When young children pretend to be a mother, father, or teacher and invent ways to use materials to represent adult tools, they are practicing the behaviors and characteristics of significant adults in their lives. Even when no play materials are available, children will use available objects to create play episodes.

**Recapitulation theory** also focuses on innate instincts. In contrast to practice theory, it posits that play enables children to *revisit* developmental stages observed in their ancestors and shed any negative behaviors. Play is seen as a way of preparing children for living in today's world. Popular games of chase and pursuit can be categorized within recapitulation theory.

## Modern Theories

The major difference between classical and modern theories of play is that modern theories emphasize the consequences of play *for the child* rather than focusing on the consequences *for the culture at large.* These three major theoretical orientations are psychoanalytic, supporting emotional development; cognitive-developmental, supporting cognitive development; and sociocultural, focusing on social development.

**Psychoanalytic theory** views play as an important vehicle for emotional release (Freud, 1958) and for developing self-esteem as children gain mastery of their thoughts, bodies, objects, and social behaviors (Erikson, 1963). Play enables children to enact feelings, without pressure, by actively reliving experiences and mastering them in reality. Moreover, it provides the teacher or caregiver with clues to children's individual needs (Weber, 1984). After the birth of a new baby, it is not uncommon to hear a preschool brother or sister at play saying to a doll, "I'm taking you back to the hospital." Expressing resentment through play enables children to gain control of it in real situations.

**Cognitive theory** examines play as a mirror of children's emerging mental abilities (Bruner, 1966; Piaget, 1962; Sutton-Smith, 1986). Piaget proposes that children *individually* create their own knowledge about the world through their interactions with people and materials. They practice using known information while consolidating new information and skills, test new ideas against their experiences, and construct new knowledge about people, objects, and situations.

Bruner (1966) and Sutton-Smith (1986) interpret play as flexible thinking and creative problem solving in action. Because children focus on the *process* of play, they engage in multiple combinations of ideas and solutions that they use to solve relevant life problems.

**Sociocultural theory** (Vygotsky, 1967, 1978) emphasizes the centrality of the *social and cultural contexts* in development. Vygotsky (1978) believes that pretend play is a "leading factor in development" (p. 101) and observes that "in play a child behaves beyond his average, above his daily behavior; in play it is as though he were a head taller than himself" (p. 102). Because children first encounter knowledge in their social world that *later* shapes their conceptual understandings, play acts as a mental support that enables children to think through and solve problems in new ways. This *"zone of proximal development"* (Vygotsky, 1978) provides children with the freedom to negotiate reality and do things in play that they are often unable to do on their own outside the play setting. When 4-year-olds David and Molly use paper, tape, markers, and stickers to make dwarf hats for their game of Snow White and the Seven Dwarfs, they do not need to create real fabric hats in order to act "as if" they were really the dwarfs.

Each of these theorists supports the essential role of play in children's developing abilities. Angelo, a 4-year-old who is playing with the figures from the manger scene beneath the Christmas tree, illustrates each of these theories in his play. He picks up one, inspects it closely, then says, "Here's Baby Jesus in his car seat." Angelo has looked at the mounds of hay surrounding the infant and related them to the cushion that protects and surrounds his baby sister while she rides in the family car. Clearly, he is *constructing knowledge* (Piaget, 1962), affected and sup-

**TABLE 2.6   Theoretical Perspectives of Children's Play**

| Theories | Theorists | Purpose of Play |
|---|---|---|
| Classical | | |
|   Surplus-energy | Schiller and Spencer | Expend excess energy to survive |
|   Recreation/relaxation | Lazarus | Restore energy used in work |
|   Practice/instinct | Groos | Practice future survival skills |
|   Recapitulation | Hall | Reenact ancient activities |
| Modern | | |
|   Psychoanalytic | Freud | Master unpleasant experiences |
| | Erikson | Master physical and social skills to build self-esteem; express wishes and needs |
|     Cognitive | Piaget | Practice and consolidate known information and skills through different types of play<br>Functional play (repeated motions)<br>Symbolic play (make-believe)<br>Games with rules (predetermined rules) |
| | Bruner and Sutton-Smith | Promote flexibility and creative problem-solving through symbolic transformations |
|   Sociocultural | Vygotsky | Foster abstract thinking and self-regulation through symbolic play. Contribute to potential development (performance with a more capable peer or an adult or the zone of proximal development). Enable child to grapple with unrealizable desires. |
|   Other | Bateson | Operate on two levels at the same time. On one level, children are engrossed in pretending; on another level, they are aware of their true identities |

ported by his *social context* (Vygotsky, 1967) and using his *creative problem-solving* skills (Bruner, 1996; Sutton-Smith, 1986).

Table 2.6, Theoretical Perspectives of Children's Play, lists the major theories, theorists, and purposes of play. Collectively, these theories provide teachers with a research base that guides the specific roles they assume in promoting the development of children's play and play skills in the classroom.

# TEACHERS' ROLES AND RESPONSIBILITIES

One question that teachers of young children often ask is, "Should I intervene in children's play?" When adults support children's play, everything they do can be considered a kind of intervention. Whether, how, and when teachers intervene determines if play is enriched or disrupted.

Research tells us that children's play becomes more elaborate, richer, and complex when adults support children in their play (Smilansky & Shefatya, 1990; Trawick-Smith, 1998; Vygotsky, 1978). A good blend of intervention strategies means that teachers are neither too directive nor too unaware about their role in children's play. When teachers are too controlling, children lose the opportunity to self-regulate their behavior. On the other hand, when teachers intervene in situations where children can already perform a task, they discourage children's self-regulatory behavior by fostering dependence on adults.

## Why Should Teachers Intervene in Children's Play?

Guidance in answering this question comes naturally from the theories of Lev Vygotsky (1978), who suggested that play is a critical scaffold that enables children to advance to higher ability levels in all developing areas. Scaffolding is particularly important as we examine the range of teachers' roles in play settings. Often there are tasks that a child cannot accomplish independently but can accomplish with the assistance of an adult or a more capable peer. This "zone of proximal development" is the optimum time for teachers to assist children in their learning.

## When Should Teachers Intervene in Children's Play?

Although there are times when teachers are most likely to want to intervene explicitly in children's play, under no conditions should teachers assume a role that dominates the direction of children's play, nor should teachers participate in play when children clearly do not want them there. Usually, teachers intervene when:

1. Play is absent from children's behavior (e.g., aimless wandering and inability to engage with another child or material).
2. A child finds a task far too difficult (e.g., being unable to make a bridge out of blocks).
3. A child needs assistance to get something done (e.g., playing a board game).
4. A child has limited knowledge of the role, object, or situation (e.g., reenacting a scene from a literature selection).
5. Children ask them to participate (e.g., teachers may assume the role of ticket taker at an imaginary airport) (Trawick-Smith, 1994, 1998).

As you read each of the different roles teachers assume, think about *when* and *how* to use each role as an intervention.

## What Are Teachers' Roles in Children's Play?

The following seven roles describe the various kinds of interventions teachers can use.

### Teachers as Observers

Teachers must be good observers of children's play so that they can determine whether or not children need help with a problem; if toys or materials are adequately stimulating; and how play situations are contributing to children's developing social, motor, and cognitive skills. Skilled observers note which child plays what role, which child chooses particular themes, how children enter and exit a play setting, which children seem to "get stuck" in a play theme and can't move forward with it, who needs one-to-one interaction, and which children are developing the ability to participate in group activity. Skilled observers also note when *not* to intervene, such as when children are already engaging in cooperative play or when they do not seem interested in adult participation. Careful observation and interpretation are the bedrock of all the other roles teachers assume in facilitating the play process (Trawick-Smith, 1994, 1998). For an extended discussion of informal observation measures to study play, see Chapter Nine.

### Teachers as Collaborators

Sometimes children continuously repeat actions and cannot move forward with a role, theme or idea. Teachers can extend their play by adding a new toy, prop, or by asking a question that elaborates on but does not change the theme. One kindergarten teacher had a fast-food restaurant in her theme corner. After a week of play, she added a "Drive Thru" sign and a cardboard window that the children used to add a new dimension to their play. She also suggested adding the role of "cashier." In doing so, she extended children's thought processes and imagination without undermining the children's original intentions (Fromberg & Bergen, 1998; Stooke, 1998).

### Teachers as Planners

Teachers must also plan for children's play. An environment conducive to play provides enough *time* to develop and carry out a play theme; enough *space* for children to enact a theme or to construct something; a variety of *materials* that encourage all forms of play; *common and familiar experience* so that children can enact roles they understand; and an *appropriate ratio of adults to children* who respond sensitively and knowledgeably to children's needs (Johnson et. al, 1999).

Selma Wassermann (1990) describes a K–2 multi-age classroom that shows the teacher's careful attention to planning for play. She writes about "breathing out," the first 45 minutes of the day when children make an easy transition from home to a school environment that absorbs their interest and prepares them for a day of learning. This environment includes plenty of space for learning stations including blocks, construction materials, dramatic play, and art; investigative play centers that operate later in the day where children explore explicit content; and a choosing board where children select how they will spend their time at centers. As children become absorbed in their play activities, teachers work individually with children on particular skills. Orchestrating this kind of play activity requires considerable skill.

### Teachers as Responders

When teachers verbally describe children's actions and words or ask questions about the role or theme, they provide feedback on what the children are doing and saying. Making statements such as, "I see you have bought a large bag of groceries" or "I noticed the tower is as tall as you are" gives children an opportunity to elaborate on that behavior if they choose. Asking questions, making suggestions, and helping children make contact with others are all ways in which teachers can respond to children's play (Trawick-Smith, 1998; Smilansky & Shefatya, 1990). These interventions, however, must address the *role* of the child and not the *child*. In this way, the intervention maintains a child's dramatic or sociodramatic play and validates that playing is a valued activity.

### Teachers as Models

Sometimes it is appropriate for teachers to actively join the play and model a particular behavior or role relevant to the ongoing play theme. In this way, teachers can teach individuals or groups of children a needed play skill or behavior. Consider the following example. In Ms. Blum's preschool special needs class, two 4-year-old girls are playing house in the housekeeping area. Ms. Blum notices that one child rocks with a doll while the other repeatedly opens and closes the oven door. She enters the play, sits at the table and announces: "It is time for lunch." She asks, "What smells so good in the oven?" and later asks, "Could I help set the table?" Ms. Blum's modeling of family roles and behaviors encourages children to practice some of those skills, which children will then be able to transfer to other settings on their own.

### Teachers as Mediators

Teachers of young children frequently encounter children's conflicts and disputes in play situations. Very young children often have disputes about toys or space for play, while older preschool children may have disputes about role play or rules. School-aged children often argue over rules of the game, participation, and friends. Most teachers feel the need to either prevent such conflicts or intervene immediately. Teachers who mediate children's disputes use strategies that help children develop peaceful resolutions. These can include being aware of children's intentions; helping children use their words to express their needs and feelings; making play spaces accessible and providing enough materials to share; and giving children enough time to negotiate their own solutions to the problems (Wheeler, 1994).

### Teachers as Monitors of Children's Safety

Teachers have an ongoing responsibility to create and maintain safe environments for children both inside and outside the classroom. The following safety checklist will help you analyze the environment for safety:

1.  Check the environment for such hazards as exposed outlets and cords, dangerous plants, and non-childproof gates.
2.  Make sure the equipment and materials are in good repair and free of sharp edges, protrusions, or broken parts that toddlers could swallow or put in their ears or noses. Discard any materials that are worn out or damaged.
3.  Store toys and materials on shelves that children can easily reach. If you have materials that you do not wish children to use, store them in locked cabinets or on high shelves that are not accessible.

4.  Periodically disinfect materials and equipment to keep things sanitary. Use warm, soapy water followed by a disinfectant solution of 2 tablespoons chlorine bleach to one gallon of water. (Be certain to store the bleach in a locked cupboard where children cannot reach it.)
5.  Supervise all children's play to ensure that materials are being used as expected and that the materials hold their interest and are appropriate to their needs.
6.  Practice emergency procedures and encourage children to enact them or talk about them in "what if" situations in their play.

When teachers attend to their roles as monitors of children's safety, they exert a positive influence on early childhood curriculum and wean themselves away from a skills-based curriculum. As so aptly stated by Fromberg (1990), "The teacher's most useful direct intervention is maintaining a playful attitude and accepting and encouraging children's independent problem-solving and connection-making" (p. 238).

## PRACTICAL APPLICATIONS FOR YOUR CLASSROOM

With greater frequency, today's early childhood settings includes children whose native language is not English, children who come from other cultures, children who have identified disabilities, children who are extraordinarily needy, and children who may be extremely gifted or talented. Play can help all children cope more easily with their uniqueness, identify their strengths, and develop an awareness of the needs of others. Play connects children and ideas that help them come to understand and deal with differences—a valuable life skill. Hence, play for all children is necessary and integral to the early childhood curriculum.

### Experiences to Support Cultural and Ethnic Diversity

Young children's play provides information about who they are and enables them to better understand others. Jalongo (1991) offers the following suggestions to help teachers realize play's potential for children from different cultures, races, and ethnic backgrounds.

**1.**  *Accept children's cultural differences.* Teachers and caregivers need to ask themselves some difficult questions to discover their basic attitude toward others. Questions that help reveal those attitudes may include the following: Am I aware of my own biases toward different populations? For example, do I know that each subgroup of Asian-Americans is unique or do I make the mistake of believing there is an "Oriental" culture? Do I recognize that different child-rearing practices affect a child's play? How can I show respect to families with different configurations or from different economic levels?

**2.** *Help children explore their cultural backgrounds through appropriate play centers and materials.* As a teacher of young children, you need to have enough knowledge about children to make informed curriculum decisions. Learning the background and culture of the children helps bridge the gap between school and home. Teachers and caregivers have a responsibility to find out the following: For how long have families been in this country? What toys do children use at home? What experiences have children had outside the home (e.g., eating in a certain kind of restaurant or observing cars being repaired at a gas station)? And how do the parents feel about play? Inviting children and their families to supply cultural materials for thematic centers is one way of helping children explore different cultural backgrounds. This information is critical to providing relevant and familiar play experiences.

**3.** *Be particularly sensitive to gender and racial issues as children enact familiar roles.* Play is a powerful vehicle for understanding gender and racial issues. How you as teachers and caregivers communicate messages about what girls, boys, and people of color can do affects how children view themselves and their competencies. In preparing children for today's and tomorrow's world, be sure to use culturally diverse materials such as puppets, dolls, puzzles, music, art, and books in the room; that they provide enough novelty and challenge for all; and that children are free to enact different roles.

## Experiences to Support Inclusion

As early childhood classrooms become more inclusive, early childhood teachers are wondering how they can adapt their curriculum to include all children in meaningful play experiences. The following suggestions show how play supports the developmental needs of children with language, motor, cognitive, or social disabilities (Deiner, 1993; Dolinar, Boser, & Holm, 1994; Mindes, 1998; Rappaport & Schultz, 1998).

**1.** *Provide opportunities for children to practice specific skills.* Aaron, a first-grade child with spina bifida, was thrilled by the discovery that he could use his walker and participate as a goalie in the class game of kickball. As a kindergartner, Aaron was equally excited when his teacher rearranged the housekeeping area with a wide entry so he could gain access to the dramatic play area in his wheelchair.

**2.** *Assist children with language development.* Often, children with hearing impairments are reluctant to use language in large group settings. In pretend play settings, however, a child with a hearing impairment has the opportunity to use language during interactions with both peers and adults. Kendra, a 5-year-old child in an after-school-care program, was particularly intrigued by puppetry because she could use the puppet as her alter ego and communicate more comfortably with her friends.

**3.** *Reduce the effects of stress in children's lives.* After a repeated hospitalization or a family disruption, play provides a powerful vehicle for helping children to regain a sense of control over their lives. After Bernice was diagnosed as having diabetes, she became fascinated by the plastic syringe in the doctor's kit and wanted to administer shots to everyone else. She also made special food in the housekeeping area and fed her dolls on a regular schedule. In this way, she used play to help her cope with her need for daily shots and dietary restrictions.

## *Adaptations for Individual Learners*

Gifted learners often are the most difficult children for teachers to work with. Many gifted children often exhibit creative, divergent thinking that clearly needs to be challenged and enriched. Equally important is their need to feel part of the group, to experience a range of feelings, and to become comfortable with their bodies (Deiner, 1993). We suggest the following guidelines that capitalize on gifted learners' need for inquiry, decision making, and socialization.

**1.** *Provide for peer interaction.* All children need opportunities to develop social competence through peer interaction. Teachers and caregivers need to encourage children's active involvement in dramatic play (e.g., a fast-food theme corner); constructive play (e.g., building roads for a city); and games with rules (e.g., card games like Go Fish) that provide opportunities to develop and practice social skills. In these play contexts, all children can and do play together. There is no place or need for ability grouping.

**2.** *Adjust to the children's ability levels.* Suppose that a class is creating a Big Book in small groups. Gifted learners may invent new uses for the materials, such as creating a lift-the-flap book or smaller books for other children in the class to share. Because they need autonomy, they may also be expected to make their own decisions in investigative and inquiry-oriented play experiences in science, mathematics, and social studies. They may write, illustrate, and enact poems about different job functions in a social studies unit or invent new ways to measure distances and amounts in mathematics.

Although we have suggested experiences for specific populations of children, the teaching/learning ideas for play apply to all children. All children need to feel good about themselves, to feel physically and psychologically safe in their environments in order to take risks, and to feel a sense of mastery over their increasingly complex world. Play is the major way children grow and learn.

## CHAPTER SUMMARY

1. Play has been studied from different perspectives, yet experts have not arrived at consensus about its definition or primary purpose. There are, however, accepted identifiable characteristics.
2. Both classical and modern theories have influenced how play is viewed in the early childhood curriculum. These theories are essential to understanding why children play and must be used as a basis of curriculum planning.

3.  Play contributes to all areas of children's development. It is the primary vehicle through which their cognitive, language, literacy, social/emotional, and creative development occurs. Play has been studied primarily as an aspect of social and cognitive development.

4.  Teachers and caregivers have at least seven clear roles and responsibilities in children's play—observer, collaborator, planner, responder, role model, mediator, and monitor of children's safety. Each of these roles and responsibilities must be fulfilled in order to support children's learning and development through play.

5.  Teachers and caregivers must adapt their curriculum so that all children can benefit from the power of play. Play can be utilized to enhance the cultural and ethnic aspects of their classrooms; to challenge the imagination of gifted learners; and to integrate children with disabilities into the mainstream.

# EXPANDING YOUR THINKING ABOUT PLAY

## Discuss: Perspectives on Play

1.  This chapter has described the difficulty surrounding the study of play. Explain to your colleagues how the assumptions about play and the play/work distinction have contributed to this confusion. Describe how you used to think about play before reading this chapter and the questions you now have after reading this chapter. How can you begin to find answers to these questions?

2.  Your role as an early childhood teacher is crucial in supporting play. Review the seven roles of the teacher discussed in this chapter. Of what significance is it to assume these different roles? Cite some examples from your own experience or from your field experience that illustrate these roles. Were these the most useful roles to assume? Why or why not?

3.  Reread the teachers' reflections on play at the beginning of this chapter. In what ways are these teachers' reflections similar in their thinking about play? What differences did you notice? Talk about which of these teachers' reflections made an impression on how you think about play after reading this chapter. Of what importance are teacher reflections?

4.  An appropriate play environment is essential for children to grow. What principles and practices would you adopt to assure children's healthy development?

5.  In the new millennium, many educators believe that the play context will be considered as fundamental to learning as basic skills are today. How do you think the play context can help children develop the necessary knowledge and skills they need to be successful in school and in the workplace of the future? What do you believe about the importance of play? Why do you believe so?

## Interview: An Early Childhood Teacher's Commitment to Play

Early childhood educators expect play to be an integral part of the curriculum. This demands a teacher's commitment for its appropriate implementation, because "teachers must take the lead in articulating the need for play in children's lives, including the curriculum" (Isenberg & Quisenberry, 1988, p. 139).

To determine teachers' level of commitment to play in the curriculum, interview an early childhood teacher and record her or his responses to each of the following questions. Ask any additional questions that emerge from your interview. As a class activity, compare your responses with those of your classmates and identify the common elements.

1.  How would you define and describe children's play?
2.  What kinds of practices do you believe enrich or disrupt children's ability to play?
3.  How do you relate play to developmentally appropriate practice?
4.  On a scale ranging from "Extremely Important" to "Unimportant," how would you rate play for children's overall development? Describe how you structure your day for children's learning. How do you think play relates to learning?
5.  How do you inform parents about the role of play in your classroom?

## Write to Learn: The Teacher's Role in Play

An essential aspect of your professional responsibility in support of play is to assume different teacher roles. Select three of the seven teacher roles described in this chapter and write about your feelings and experiences with them. Think about where you experienced/observed these roles, under what conditions, how you (the teacher) assumed the roles, and why they were helpful or disruptive to the children's play. Share your writing with the group. Which roles seem to occur most often? Least often? In what form of play? Summarize this information in a chart. Have you identified other roles that recur and that were not mentioned in the chapter? If so, describe them.

## REFERENCES

Athey, I. (1984). Contributions of play to development. In T. D. Yawkey & A. D. Pellegrini (Eds.), *Child's play: Developmental and applied* (pp. 9–29). Hillsdale, NJ: Lawrence Erlbaum.

Bergen, D. (1988). Using a schema for play and learning. In D. Bergen (Ed.), *Play as a medium for learning and development: A handbook of theory and practice* (pp. 169–180). Portsmouth, NH: Heinemann.

Bergen, D. (Ed.). (1987). *Play as a medium for learning and development: A handbook of theory and practice.* Portsmouth, NH: Heinemann.

Berk, L. E. (1994). Vygotsky's theory: The importance of make-believe play. *Young Children, 50*(1), 30–39.

Bloom, B. (1964). *Stability and change in human characteristics.* New York: Wiley.

Bredekamp, S. & Copple, C. (Eds.). (1997). *Developmentally appropriate practice in early childhood programs* (Rev. ed.). Washington, DC: National Association for the Education of Young Children.

Bredekamp, S. & Rosegrant, T. (Eds.). (1992). *Reaching potentials: Appropriate curriculum and assessment for young children.* (Vol. 1). Washington, DC: National Association for the Education of Young Children.

Bretherton, I. (Ed.). (1984). *Symbolic play: The development of social understanding.* New York: Academic Press.

Bruner, J. S. (1966). What we have learned about early learning. *European Early Education Research Journal, 4*(1), 5–16.

Cazden, C. (1976). Play with language and metalinguistic awareness: One dimension of language experience. In J. S. Bruner, A. Jolly, & K. Sylva (Eds.), *Play—its role in development and evolution* (pp. 603–608). New York: Basic Books, 1976.

Christie, J. F. (1998). Play as a medium for literacy development. In D. P. Fromberg & D. M. Bergen (Eds.), *Play from birth to twelve and beyond: Contexts, perspectives, and meanings* (pp. 50–55). New York: Garland.

Creasey, G., Jarvis, P., & Berk, L. (1998). Play and social competence. In O. Saracho and B. Spodek (Eds.), *Multiple perspectives on play in early childhood education* (pp. 116–143). Albany: State University of New York Press.

Dansky, J. L. (1980). Make-believe: A mediator of the relationship between play and associative fluency. *Child Development, 51*, 576–579.

Dansky, J. L., & Silverman, I. W. (1973). Effects of play on associative fluency in preschool children. *Developmental Psychology, 9*, 38–43.

Deiner, P. L. (1993). *Resources for teaching young children with diverse abilities* (2nd ed.). New York: Harcourt Brace College Publishers.

DeVries, R. (1998). Games with rules. In D. P. Fromberg & D. M. Bergen (Eds.), *Play from birth to twelve and beyond: Contexts, perspectives, and meanings* (pp. 409–415). New York: Garland.

Dewey, J. (1916). *Democracy and education.* New York: Macmillan.

Dewey, J. (1938). *Experience and education.* New York: Macmillan.

Dolinar, K., Boser, C., & Holm, E. (1994). *Learning through play: Curriculum and activities for the inclusive classroom.* Albany, NY: Delmar.

Ellis, M. J. (1973). *Why people play.* Englewood Cliffs, NJ: Prentice Hall.

Erikson, E. H. (1963). *Childhood and society.* New York: Norton.

Fein, G. G. (1985). Learning in play: Surfaces of thinking and feeling. In J. L. Frost & S. Sunderlin (Eds.), *When children play* (pp. 19–28). Wheaton, MD: Association for Childhood Education International.

Forman, G. (1998). Constructive Play. In D. P. Fromberg & D. M. Bergen (Eds.), *Play from birth to twelve and beyond: Contexts, perspectives, and meanings* (pp. 392–400). New York: Garland.

Freud, S. (1958). *On creativity and the unconscious.* (I. F. Grant Doff, trans.). New York: Harper & Row. (Original work published in 1928.)

Fromberg, D. P. (1990). Play issues in early childhood education. In C. Seefeldt (Ed.), *Continuing issues in early childhood education* (pp. 223–243). Upper Saddle River, NJ: Merrill/Prentice Hall.

Fromberg, D. P. (1992). A review of research on play. In C. Seefeldt (Ed.), *The early childhood curriculum: A review of current research* (2nd ed.) (pp. 35–74). New York: Teachers College Press.

Fromberg, D. P., & Bergen, D. M. (Eds.). (1998). *Play from birth to twelve: Contexts, perspectives, and meanings.* New York: Garland.

Garvey, C. (1977). *Play.* Cambridge, MA: Harvard University Press.

Gibbons, P. (1993). *Learning to learn in a second language.* Portsmouth, NH: Heinemann.

Halliday, M. A. K. (1975). *Explorations in the function of language.* London: Edward Arnold.

Hill, P. S. (1923). *A conduct curriculum for the kindergarten and first grade.* New York: Scribners.

Hunt, J. M. (1961). *Intelligence and experience.* New York: Ronald Press.

Isaacs, S. (1933). *Social development in young children.* London: Routledge & Kegan Paul.

Isenberg, J. P. (1995). Whole language in play and the expressive arts. In S. Raines (Ed.), *Whole language across the curriculum: Grades 1, 2, 3* (pp. 114–136). New York: Teachers College Press.

Isenberg, J., & Quisenberry, N. (1988). Play: A necessity for all children. *Childhood Education, 64*(3), 138–145.

Jalongo, M. R. (1991). Children's play: A resource for multicultural education. In E. B. Vold (Ed.), *Multicultural education in the early childhood classroom* (pp. 55–63). Washington, DC: National Education Association.

Johnson, J. E., Christie, J. F., & Yawkey, T. D. (1999). *Play and early childhood development* (2nd ed.). Glenview, IL: Scott, Foresman.

Johnson, J. E., Ershler, J., & Lawton, J. (1982). Intellectual correlates of preschoolers' spontaneous play. *Journal of Genetic Psychology, 106,* 115–122.

Landreth, G., & Homeyer, L. (1998). Play as the language of children's feelings. In D. P. Fromberg & D. M. Bergen (Eds.), *Play from birth to twelve and beyond: Contexts, perspectives, and meanings* (pp. 193–198). New York: Garland.

Majure, J. (1995). It's playtime. *Arthritis Today, 9*(1), 46–51.

Mindes, G. (1998). Can I play too? Reflections on the issues for children with disabilities. In D. P. Fromberg & D. M. Bergen (Eds.), *Play from birth to twelve and beyond: Contexts, perspectives, and meanings* (pp. 208–214). New York: Garland.

Monighan-Nourot, P., Scales, B., & Van Hoorn, J., with Almy, M. (1987). *Looking at children's play: A bridge between theory and practice.* New York: Teachers College Press.

Monighan-Nourot, P., & Van Hoorn, J. L. (1991). Symbolic play in preschool and primary settings. *Young Children,* September 1991, 40–50.

Morrow, L. M. (1993). *Literacy development in the early years* (2nd ed.). Boston: Allyn & Bacon.

Newman, J. (Ed.). (1990). *Finding our own way.* Portsmouth, NH: Heinemann.

Owocki, G. (1999). *Literacy through play.* Portsmouth, NH: Heinemann.

Parten, M. (1932). Social participation among preschool children. *Journal of Abnormal and Social Psychology, 27*(2), 243–269.

Pellegrini, A. (1980). The relationship between kindergartners' play and achievement in pre-reading, language, and writing. *Psychology in the schools, 17*(4), 530–535.

Pellegrini, A. D., & Galda, L. (1982). Playing about a story: Its impact on comprehension. *The Reading Teacher, 36*(1), 52–55.

Pepler, D., & Ross, H. S. (1981). The effects of play on convergent and divergent problem-solving. *Child Development, 52,* 1202–1210.

Perkins, D. (1984). Creativity by design. *Educational Leadership, 42,* 18–25.

Piaget, J. (1962). *Play, dreams and imitation in childhood.* New York: Norton.

Rappaport, L., & Schulz, L. (1998). *Creative play activities for children with disabilities: A resource book for teachers and parents.* Champagne, IL: Human Kinetics.

Resnick, L. B. (1987). *Education and learning to think.* Washington, DC: National Academy Press.

Roskos, K. (1988). Literacy at work in play. *The Reading Teacher, 41,* 562–566.

Rubin, K. H., Fein, G. S., & Vandenberg, B. (1983). Play. In E. M. Hetherington (Ed.) and P. H. Mussen (Series Ed.), *Handbook of child psychology: Vol. 4. Socialization, personality and development* (pp. 698–774). New York: Wiley.

Santrock, J. W. (2000). *Children* (6th ed.). New York: W. C. Brown.

Sapon-Shevin, M., Dobbelgere, A., Carrigan, C., Goodman, K., & Mastin, M. (1998). Everyone here can play. *Educational Leadership, 56*(1), 42–45.

Singer, D. G., & Singer, J. L. (1998). Fantasy and Imagination. In D. P. Fromberg & D. M. Bergen (Eds.), *Play from birth to twelve and beyond: Contexts, perspectives, and meanings* (pp. 313–318). New York: Garland.

Singer, J. L. (1973). *The child's world of make-believe.* New York: Wiley.

Singer, J. L. & Singer, D. C. (1985). *Makebelieve: Games and activities to foster imaginative play in young children.* Glenview, IL: Scott Foresman.

Smilansky, S. (1968). *The effects of socio-dramatic play on disadvantaged preschool children.* New York: Wiley.

Smilansky, S., & Shefatya, L. (1990). *Facilitating play: A medium for promoting cognitive, socio-emotional and academic development in young children.* Gaithersburg, MD: Psychosocial and Educational Publications.

Spodek, B., & Saracho, O. N. (Eds.). (1998). *Multiple perspectives on play in early childhood education.* Albany: State University of New York Press.

Stone, S. J., & Christie, J. F. (1996). Collaborative literacy learning during sociodramatic play in a multiage classroom. *Journal of Research in Childhood Education, 10*(2), 123–133.

Stooke, R. (1998). Teaching through play. *Research in Drama Education, 3*(2), 272–277.

Sutton-Smith, B. (1986). The spirit of play. In G. Fein & M. Rivkin (Eds.), *The young child at play: Reviews of research* (Vol. 4, pp. 3–16). Washington, DC: National Association for the Education of Young Children.

Trawick-Smith, J. (1994). *Interactions in the classroom: Facilitating play in the early years.* New York: Macmillan.

Trawick-Smith, J. (1998). Why Play Training Works: An Integrated Model for Play Intervention. *Journal of Research in Childhood Education,*12(2), 117–129.

Vygotsky, L. S. (1967). Play and its role in the mental development of the child. *Soviet Psychology, 12,* 62–76.

Vygotsky. L. S. (1978). Mind in society. The development of higher psychological processes. Boston: Harvard University Press.

Wassermann, S. (1990). *Serious players in the primary classroom.* New York: Teachers College Press.

Weber, E. (1984). *Ideas influencing early childhood education: A theoretical analysis.* New York: Teachers College Press.

Weininger, O. (1988). "What if" and "As if": Imagination and pretend play in early childhood. In K. Egan & D. Nadaner (Eds.), *Imagination and education* (pp. 141–149). New York: Teachers College Press.

Wheeler, E. J. (1994). Peer conflicts in the classroom: Drawing implications from research. *Childhood Education, 70*(5), 296–299.

Williamson, P. & Silvern, S. (1984). Creative dramatic play and language comprehension. In T. D. Yawkey & A. D. Pellegrini (Eds.), *Child's play: Developmental and applied* (pp. 347–358). Hillsdale, NJ: Erlbaum.

Wing, L. (1995). Play is not the work of the child: Young children's perceptions of work and play. *Early Childhood Research Quarterly 10*(2), 223–247.

## *Children's Literature Cited*

Chin, C. (1997). *China's bravest girl.* Emeryville, CA: Children's Book Press.

Flack, M. (1932). *Ask Mr. Bear.* New York: Macmillan.

Walters, K., & Slovenz-Low, M. (1990). *Lion Dancer: Ernie Wan's Chinese New Year.* New York: Scholastic.

White, E. B. (1952). *Charlotte's Web.* New York: Harper & Row.

# PART 2
## THE CREATIVE ARTS CURRICULUM

# Chapter 3

# Art in the Early Childhood Curriculum

*"Once I drew like Raphael, but it has taken me a whole lifetime to learn to draw like children."*

Pablo Picasso

*"Educators have always recognized that the arts provide children with cultural advantages that contribute to their creativity. Now it is clear that they contribute to children's overall development as well. . . . [The arts] provide children with many opportunities to succeed, thereby helping them to develop positive attitudes toward themselves and learning. Through interactive experiences with the arts, children engage in the learning processes of exploring ideas, creating meaning, constructing knowledge, and communicating concepts, thoughts, and feelings."*

Dolores Varnon, 1997, p. 325

# TEACHERS' REFLECTIONS ON ART

## Preservice Teachers

"After we talked about children's art in class, I decided to use what I am learning to plan the activities for my volunteer work at the Community Center program. It was a theme that I had used with success before, during my first prestudent teaching experience. In it, I recited a poem about the gingerbread man prior to making gingerbread cookies. That part still seemed good, so I kept it. But the art activity I had chosen to do while we were waiting for the gingerbread to bake seemed inappropriate after taking this class. Originally, I had planned to make copies of a gingerbread person that I found in a book. It had decorations to cut out and paste on the pattern. Instead of doing this, I decided to let the children create their own drawings and decorations. I was so impressed by what they produced on their own!"

"I knew that art was appropriate for children before, but now I know why because I understand how it affects children and enhances their overall development. I also have many ideas about how to use art in my classroom."

### Inservice Teachers

"I never really knew how important art activities are for young children. Until now, I thought they were just enjoyable things for children to do. Now I realize that the things I thought were art—like the teacher making models for children to copy or duplicating pictures to color—really are not art in any sense of the word. They are just exercises in following directions and are really the opposite of art."

"Because I graduated in elementary education two years ago and have been substitute teaching while I work on a second certification in early childhood, I have done many of the things that were criticized in this chapter. Usually, I have to follow plans left by the teacher, and most things are 'product art' that results in exactly the same thing from each student—a cut-and-paste Christmas stocking, an Easter egg picture to color, a Valentine's Day heart to trace. But, to be honest, even if I didn't have the plans, I probably would have done 'art' activities like those anyway because they are so common and accepted. Now I feel encouraged to break away from teacher-dominated approaches and really support children's creative expression."

## Your Reflections

- What is a creative art activity in early childhood? What criteria can be used to differentiate between art activities and other types of classroom activities?

- What contributions does art make to every child's overall development?

- What concerns do you have about making art an integral part of your curriculum?

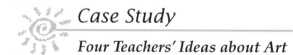 ## Case Study

### Four Teachers' Ideas about Art

In a large metropolitan area, four teachers are engaged in doing what each of them defines as art.

Mr. Evanko has been teaching a lesson on safety in his public school kindergarten. Each child will make a "traffic signal" from a rectangle of black construction paper and red, yellow, and green paper circles. When the activity is completed, each child's traffic signal looks nearly identical to the ones cut and pasted by the other children. Is this art?

In Ms. Carr's private nursery school, children can choose painting, clay, drawing with crayons, or construction paper and glue every day. She describes her philosophy as creative because she gives the children no guidance in the use and care of materials, nor does she discuss their work. Is this art?

In Ms. Lenninger's parochial school second-grade classroom, children are busily preparing for spring parent-teacher conferences. Ms. Lenninger has the idea of placing large tree branches into a flowerpot filled with plaster of Paris and involving her students in making paper dogwood flowers. She directs the children to trace carefully around the patterns she has provided, and even with 20 students, it takes quite some time before the branches are covered with paper blossoms. Is this art?

Mr. Ortiz's first graders have been collecting what he calls "beautiful junk" for several weeks. Included in these materials are items such as bits of fabric, yarn, buttons, lace, felt, boxes, and plastic bottles of various sizes and shapes. The children have been listening to stories about amiable monsters, including *Where the Wild Things Are* (Sendak, 1963); *The Very Worst Monster* (Hutchins, 1985); *There's a Nightmare in My Closet* (Mayer, 1968); and *Harry and the Terrible Whatzit* (Gackenbach, 1977). Mr. Ortiz's challenge to his students is simply this: "Using any of the materials we have collected here or others you may have at home, create your own monster. Think about questions like these: What is a monster? What is special about your monster? What does it eat? Are people afraid of it? Why? Where does it live now? What makes it happy? What makes it sad? What does it like to do? After you have created your monster, you will tell the class all about it. Then you will make up a story about your monster." Is this art?

Each of these teachers is operating on a set of assumptions about art. The first three teachers (the one who was making paper traffic signals, the one who believed in complete nonintervention, and the one who was making "dogwood trees") have committed the three most common errors in teaching art: (1) advocating formulas and requiring conformity in copying, (2) mistaking lack of guidance for freedom, and (3) unduly emphasizing copying and neatness (Gaitskell, Hurwitz, & Day, 1982). Of the four examples given, only the last, Mr. Ortiz's "monster-inventing activity," could be categorized as art, because it is the only activity that enables the children to respond in an individual and creative way using art materials. In fact many, if not most, of the "art" activities that adults do with young children are not art (Szyba, 1999).

## THEORETICAL AND RESEARCH BASE: WHAT IS ART AND AESTHETIC EXPERIENCE?

Actually, it is easy to avoid some of the worst activities masquerading as art by asking four simple questions (Jalongo & Stamp, 1997).

**1.** *Are the children's responses predetermined?* If so, it is not art. A teacher who distributes patterns to color, trace, copy, or cut out in some designated way is not providing an art activity, no matter how clever it might be. It is an exercise in following directions, not an aesthetic experience.

**2.** *Will one child's work look nearly identical to another's?* If so, it is not art. When you can scan a display of children's work and see nothing original or surprising, it is not really children's work. Young children are naturally imaginative and creative. If their efforts do not reflect this quality, then the activity was not an aesthetic experience.

**3.** *Who is the activity for?* If it is simply to convince parents that their child is keeping busy at school or to fool parents into believing that their child is doing something precocious, it is not art. For example, the teacher who "fixes" children's cut-and-paste pictures by rearranging them to look more presentable for display has not only selected an inappropriate activity but also is undermining children's confidence in their ability to be makers of art.

**4.** *Will the child's efforts lead to the creation of a new form that is satisfying to the child at his or her level of development?* If a child is being pushed, it is not art. An adult who grasps a three- or four-year-old's hand and forces the child to produce a stick figure is *not* "teaching" the child to draw! Most young children will strongly resist such impositions, and understandably so. When a child is at the scribbling stage, scribbles are satisfying because they are something new and interesting. When adults have to do an activity for the child, it is not suited to the child's developmental level, and it is definitely not art. Table 3.1 describes in greater detail what does and does not qualify as an art activity.

In order to understand the visual arts in early childhood more fully, you must first understand the underlying philosophy of art, called aesthetics. Aesthetics is a branch of philosophy that deals with the fundamental questions "What is beauty? What is worthy of the label 'art'?" "What works of art merit being displayed in the museums of our culture?" and, with regard to young children, "How do we help children to understand and appreciate beauty and works of art?" Figure 3.1 provides some highlights of aesthetic theory and its implications for curriculum.

As a test of your assumptions about children's art and aesthetic experiences, indicate whether you think each statement below is true or false.

*True or False?*

1. Artistic ability unfolds naturally and children are best left to follow their own inclinations.
2. Producing art is an emotional process rather than a cognitive one.
3. Art is valued primarily because it allows children to "act out" their feelings.
4. Any sensory experience is an art experience.
5. Artworks need to be produced in a solitary fashion, otherwise children will "copy" the work of their peers.
6. The primary purpose of art projects in school is and should be to make gifts or holiday ornaments.

**TABLE 3.1    Is It Art? How to Decide**

| | |
|---|---|
| **Not Art** | |

| Category | Examples |
|---|---|
| **Assembly tasks** | gluing a magnet on a clothespin, collections of craft store items that are assembled at school, making houses out of Popsicle sticks |

*Why isn't this art?* There is no creativity involved. Each child's work will appear very similar. The emphasis is on following directions.

| | |
|---|---|
| **Using Food as Art** | macaroni necklaces, "painting" with pudding, making a "house" out of graham crackers and icing, "painting" on bread with food coloring, gluing beans, rice, and other food items onto paper |

*Why isn't this art?* Real artists do not use these materials. These projects waste good food and may be perplexing or offensive, particularly to people from communities where food is in short supply.

| | |
|---|---|
| **Copy Work** | coloring pictures from coloring books, follow-the-dots drawing, using clip art, tracing patterns or using templates, painting by the numbers |

*Why isn't this art?* These activities emphasize conformity and fine motor control rather than resourcefulness and originality

| | |
|---|---|
| **Art** | |

| Category | Examples |
|---|---|
| **Creative Problem Solving** | designing an original picture book, meeting the challenge of sculpting a dinosaur from clay, constructing a well-balanced mobile |

*Why is this art?* Each child's work will be a one-of-a-kind original. Children are choosing their own artistic challenges, making decisions about the medium, and determining ways to share and display their work.

| | |
|---|---|
| **Aesthetic Responses** | pairs of children examining art postcards and notecards and discussing them; describing/comparing/contrasting the artistic style of picture books, responding to beauty outdoors or in nature photographs |

*Why is this art?* Children are developing emergent skills in art criticism and insights about style.

You may be surprised to learn that all six of these statements are false. Here is why: Children need to learn techniques, such as preschoolers learning how to use just a bit of white glue so that wooden items will hold together and dry quickly or third graders learning how to sketch or build a scale model of a display of their work before actually constructing the display.

Art is every bit as much a cognitive (thinking) process as it is an affective (emotional) one. When a group of children plans a display of their work, they are engaging in problem solving (Where will we place our display? How will we organize it?) as well as responding to affective responses (How does this look?).

Although art can be an outlet, it can also be a source of frustration, such as when a weaving unravels or a clay sculpture breaks after it is fired in a kiln. So even

**Theoretical Perspective:** Emphasis on aesthetic objects and their makers. Aesthetic experiences are fundamentally gratifying because they are experienced as whole, complete, and satisfying. The artistic goodness of a work exists in its capacity to evoke pleasure, enjoyment, and powerful responses.

**Theorist:** Monroe C. Beardsley

**Curricular Connection:** Teach children to observe closely and consider what makes an object beautiful and worthy of appreciation (Smith and the Drawing Study Group, 1999). Surround children with the work of mature artists, particularly those that parallel the efforts of child artists. Engage them in provocative dialogues about works of art that begin with scrutiny and description of the visible qualities. Introduce these ideas very concretely and dramatically at first (e.g., showing an illustration with many fine lines versus one with bold, dramatic lines, showing types of lines—straight, curved, zigzag, spiral, etc.). Next, encourage children to analyze relationships among the qualities (e.g., repetition, rhythm, variation, balance, contrast, dominance/emphasis, unity). Next, focus on interpretation—the ideas, feelings, and moods of the work. Finally, arrive at a conclusion or judgment of the work (Cole & Schaefer, 1990).

**Theoretical Perspective:** Emphasis on the way that aesthetic objects affect the audience. Knowing art results in an integrative vision. Repeated aesthetic experiences result in percipience, a highly developed form of appreciation and aesthetic judgment.

**Theorist:** Harold Osborne

**Curricular Connections:** Begin by understanding some basic findings on children's responses to art. We know that young children (1) respond to the sensory qualities of art work (e.g., responding to bright, intense colors), (2) relate the subject matter in art reproductions to their experiences, (3) invent stories about the shapes, colors, and images found in works of art, (4) respond more to what is pictured (subject or theme) than to the artist's style (Kerlavage, 1995). Design activities that build upon these assets of early childhood and that give the child opportunities to verbalize the reasons for their preferences and to grow more capable of responding to complex works, more sensitive to style, and more perceptive about works of art. Guide children in discovering themes in works of visual art (e.g., fantasy, realism, multiculturalism, portraits, caricatures, land/city/seascapes, still life).

**Theoretical Perspective:** Emphasis on the attenders' interpretations of aesthetic objects. Aesthetic experiences are a way of understanding. Things of beauty are symbols that need to be interpreted. Through the interpretation of aesthetic objects, enlightenment is achieved.

**Theorist:** Nelson Goodman

**Curricular Connections:** Help children develop the symbolic tools of literacy in the visual arts and learn to "read" the aesthetic symbols of their culture. Emphasize thinking about art (e.g., compare, recall, analyze, visualize, summarize, predict, infer, evaluate, interpret, synthesize) as children study art. Investigate the strategies that are used in the schools of Reggio Emilia to see how children are taught to interpret and produce aesthetic objects.

**Theoretical Perspective:** Emphasis on the cultural context in which works of art are produced. Art cannot exist independent of culture and values. Art is part of a rational and moral life. Art is defined by the culture and determined by community values.

**Theorist :** Marcia Eaton

**Curricular Connections:** Engage children in closely examining different categories of works of visual art (e.g., photographs, sculpture, textile art, architecture) as well as styles and periods of art (e.g., commercial art, modern art, folk art), and concepts of art (craftspersonship, art & technology, decoration, art & nature). Give children multicultural experiences with art history and art criticism. Introduce them to artists and works of art from different cultural, ethnic, religious, and social class backgrounds. Show respect for works of art by avoiding disparaging terminology such as "primitive" in reference to tribal cultures' art.

**Figure 3.1**  Theories of Aesthetic Experience: Curricular Connections
*Sources:* Adapted from discussion in Smith (1995), Cole and Schaefer (1990), Dunn (1995), London (1994), and Spodek (1993).

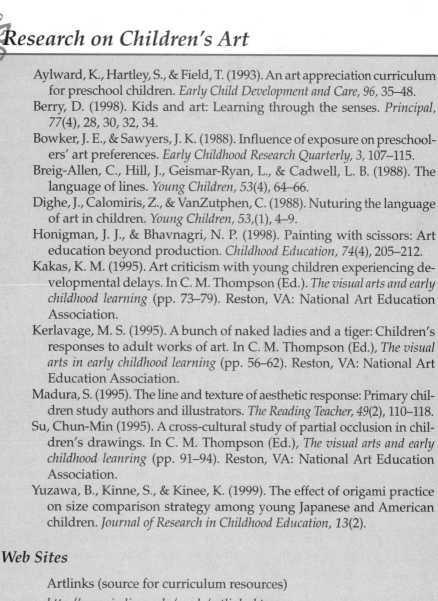

## Research on Children's Art

Aylward, K., Hartley, S., & Field, T. (1993). An art appreciation curriculum for preschool children. *Early Child Development and Care, 96,* 35–48.

Berry, D. (1998). Kids and art: Learning through the senses. *Principal, 77*(4), 28, 30, 32, 34.

Bowker, J. E., & Sawyers, J. K. (1988). Influence of exposure on preschoolers' art preferences. *Early Childhood Research Quarterly, 3,* 107–115.

Breig-Allen, C., Hill, J., Geismar-Ryan, L., & Cadwell, L. B. (1988). The language of lines. *Young Children, 53*(4), 64–66.

Dighe, J., Calomiris, Z., & VanZutphen, C. (1988). Nuturing the language of art in children. *Young Children, 53,*(1), 4–9.

Honigman, J. J., & Bhavnagri, N. P. (1998). Painting with scissors: Art education beyond production. *Childhood Education, 74*(4), 205–212.

Kakas, K. M. (1995). Art criticism with young children experiencing developmental delays. In C. M. Thompson (Ed.). *The visual arts and early childhood learning* (pp. 73–79). Reston, VA: National Art Education Association.

Kerlavage, M. S. (1995). A bunch of naked ladies and a tiger: Children's responses to adult works of art. In C. M. Thompson (Ed.), *The visual arts in early childhood learning* (pp. 56–62). Reston, VA: National Art Education Association.

Madura, S. (1995). The line and texture of aesthetic response: Primary children study authors and illustrators. *The Reading Teacher, 49*(2), 110–118.

Su, Chun-Min (1995). A cross-cultural study of partial occlusion in children's drawings. In C. M. Thompson (Ed.), *The visual arts and early childhood leanring* (pp. 91–94). Reston, VA: National Art Education Association.

Yuzawa, B., Kinne, S., & Kinee, K. (1999). The effect of origami practice on size comparison strategy among young Japanese and American children. *Journal of Research in Childhood Education, 13*(2).

### Web Sites

Artlinks (source for curriculum resources)
*http://www.indiana.edu/~ssdc/artlinks.htm*

Americans for the Arts
*http://www.artsusa.org/education/artslnk73.htm*

National Art Education Association
*www.naea.org*

though there are emotional outlets associated with the arts, there are also emotional stresses when the work is not going well. There is a problem-solving dimension to the arts that teaches children how to respond to complex challenges with tenacity and grace.

There is a useful distinction between "messing about" with materials and art experiences. A baby who plays with his food is not having an art experience, because the behavior serves no purpose related to the arts. Likewise, a preschooler who plays with soap bubbles in a dishpan is not having "an aesthetic experience," because the activity is not elevated above the ordinary by being linked with creative expression. Children are often inspired by their peers to try new things in art, just as real artists are influenced by the works of artists they admire. Art is a social activity, not merely a means of talent testing or promoting individual accomplishment.

Art is not a commodity. If children paste cotton ball beards on a preprinted copy of a Santa face, it is not art, it is an assembly task. Likewise, children who color predrawn pictures are not producing art any more than an adult whitewashing a fence is producing art. In all cases, it is simply a task to be dashed off to schedule and there is little opportunity for creative expression or problem solving (adapted from Kindler, 1996).

## HOW CHILDREN LEARN THROUGH ART

Like language, art is a symbol system that can be used to generate meaning and as a tool for learning. Art activities "provide a means of expression for children, a vehicle for creative development, a way of symbolizing and communicating knowledge gained in other activities, a vehicle for teaching and learning about aesthetics, and a way to help children access academic knowledge" (Spodek, 1993, p. 12). When we speak about art, we are talking about something that is perceptual, cognitive, developmental, graphic, and affected by the context and culture. Consider Figure 3.2, an original picture book by Vickie, a first grader, whose mother is expecting a baby. Vickie's original picture book reveals her understandings and feelings about this important event.

Artistic responses are *perceptual* because artists of any age must be keenly aware of sensory input. It is clear from Vickie's story that she is aware of the changes in her mother's body. This leads to the second characteristic of art, its *cognitive* or intellectual aspect. When Vickie forms symbols, she must know the material (in this case, the media of paper and crayons), know the referent (in this case, the mother and baby), and use that material/medium to express something about that referent (in this case, original drawing and writing) (Smith, 1982).

Vickie's art is *developmental*, meaning that as she matures and gains experience, her art changes along with her. Drawings created by 6-year-olds are distinctly different from the scribbles produced by toddlers, for example. A drawing by a primary grade child typically resembles what it represents and includes many details—a reflection of an emerging sense of realism. This is not to say that a drawing is inherently "better" than a scribble, only that drawings are more characteristic of older children.

**Figure 3.2**
Vicki's Book

My mom is fat because
She's haveing a Baby

by vickie RYan

a.

She's geting fat

She's not fat yet

b.

I Love my mom

c.

d.

now it's        ready
to be born

We went to the
hospital to wate for it to
be born

e.

f.

and it was born

it was so tiny

g.

h.

Vickie's art is also *graphic,* meaning that it is a representation and an interpretation of her reality. Her depiction of the hospital, her pregnant mother, and the new baby show that she is learning the art techniques necessary to give form to her feelings, ideas, and experiences. These techniques include color, line, arrangement, proportion, and placement.

Finally, Vickie's art is affected by culture and the context. Because the birth of a new child is celebrated as an important life event in her family, she has chosen it as a worthy subject for her art.

To summarize, children learn the following things through the arts:

- To observe carefully and record their observations
- To organize ideas and express their feelings
- To work with purpose and maintain a focus
- To solve unstructured problems through trial and error
- To respect themselves and their achievements
- To communicate feelings and ideas with others
- To discover their own points of view while appreciating different points of view
- To appreciate the contributions of different cultural groups
- To create change in their environment using a wide range of media
- To make aesthetic discoveries and render evaluative judgments (Cohen & Gainer, 1995; Jalongo & Stamp, 1997).

As you work to support children's growth in art, keep in mind four important themes: (1) emphasizing the process as well as the product, (2) valuing originality, (3) allowing children to retain ownership of their artwork, and (4) striving for an appreciation of mixtures and balances.

## Process As Well As Product

The Greek philosopher Aristotle once said that "the aim of art is to represent not the outward appearance of things, but their inward significance; for this . . . is true reality." When children are pushed to make their work represent the superficial aspects of an object or experience, product is being emphasized. The most common type of product requires children to color pictures neatly in designated areas, cut out predetermined shapes on the lines, paste them onto paper in some preordained way, and take the result home to decorate a refrigerator door. Activities such as these communicate the message that children's original artwork is not valued and that their art processes are inferior to adults'.

## Originality Rather Than Conformity

Stan overheard his second-grade teacher saying that she wanted to do an art activity in February. Stan thought about President's Day, Flag Day, and Valentine's Day and invented a new kind of flag. Instead of using stars to represent the states, Stan used red hearts on a white background. For this 8-year-old, creating the flag was an original activity. But if the teacher requires every child in the class to copy Stan's idea, she is demanding conformity rather than encouraging originality. As stated so clearly by Alfred North Whitehead (1967): "Art flourishes where there is a sense of adventure, a sense of nothing having been done before, of complete freedom to experiment; but when caution comes in you get repetition, and repetition is the death of art" (p. 55).

Real art activities encourage different responses from each child; they celebrate uniqueness. The goal of art is to break stereotypes rather than to perpetuate them. Art is not coloring pages and following the dots; art is not a hand-traced turkey for Thanksgiving, a tree that looks like a lollipop, or a square-plus-triangle house. If it isn't original, it isn't art.

## Children Retain Ownership

Children retain ownership of their artwork when they (1) choose their own ideas or subject matter, (2) have the freedom to express their ideas in their own way, and (3) have the right to organize their art in their own way (Jefferson, 1963). Children need the latitude to use many different art media. The goal is not to compete and make comparisons between and among children by singling out one child's work (or the teacher's model) as the standard for all to follow.

*Authentic art experiences emphasize the process, value originality, and allow children to retain ownership of their artwork.*

## An Appreciation for Mixtures and Balances

Suppose that you wanted to watch a movie, but moviemaking hadn't been invented yet. Think about how different your life would be without the visual art of film. So much would be missed. Now think about a film that you have watched many times. What was it about the style of the film that captured your imagination? Are there other films by this same director that you also like? Answers to questions such as these illustrate the importance of a concept in aesthetics called mixtures and balances. Clearly, many films can be made, but it is the particular combination of ingredients and the interplay of those elements that creates a satisfying whole. Skillful mixtures and balances transform the ordinary into the extraordinary, the mundane into a work of art. That is something that children first need to experience for themselves in order to recognize and appreciate it in others. The art experiences that you provide for young children should develop this understanding. Asking children questions such as "Why did you choose this painting for your portfolio?" or "How is the mural going?" helps children to reflect on mixtures and balances, a fundamental concept in the arts.

Generally speaking, there are four types of learning promoted through the arts. Figure 3.3 provides an overview of the four major types of learning promoted through the arts.

## CRITICAL ISSUES IN TEACHING ART

Phyllis is a 5-year-old who has just started kindergarten. One day the preschooler comes home from school looking distraught. She bursts into tears, reaches in her pocket, and takes out a tissue with a broken crayon wrapped inside. It seems that the teacher had been especially harsh in cautioning children about taking care of school supplies and not breaking the crayons. Phyllis knew she had committed the unpardonable sin—"pressing too hard." To avoid punishment, she had resorted to concealing her "crime." Phyllis's experience illustrates how important it is for an art program to (1) respect and encourage children's efforts, (2) give children time to explore and to develop control and sensitivity to materials, and (3) give children independent access to materials (Clemens, 1991).

## Providing a Safe and Healthy Art Environment

Teachers are often unaware of the potential hazards of art materials and activities. Figure 3.4 provides a checklist that you can use to assess your knowledge about safety issues in working with art materials.

## Selecting and Presenting Materials and Experiences

Although the ownership of art should rest with the child, teachers do have a responsibility to demonstrate the appropriate use of materials. Take, for example, painting at the easel. When children first begin using paints, a teacher might present

1. **Knowledge about the arts** *is developed by:*

sensory experiences and the exploration of materials.

meeting real, live artists and watching them at work.

thoughtful examination and discussion of works of art.

**What Practitioners Can Do:**

Select high-quality art materials that children will want to return to again and again.

Teach children to respect and care for art materials (e.g., cleaning up, proper storage).

Use community resources to provide role models of craftspersonship.

Use the library, media center, Internet, and museum-quality reprints and reproductions to stimulate children's thinking about art.

Extend children's vocabulary by using descriptive words when talking about art.

2. **Skills in the arts** *are developed by:*

experimenting with arts materials, tools, and processes in a low-risk environment.

gentle guidance from others who have already acquired the skills.

a certain amount of trial and error; making mistakes and learning from them.

**What Practitioners Can Do:**

Provide a wide variety of high-quality art materials.

Make time for art experiences every day.

Experiment yourself with the materials that you provide for children.

Emphasize the process that children use to create art products.

3. **Dispositions toward the arts** *are developed by:*

interaction with role models—more competent peers, teachers, and professional artists.

experiencing the arts alongside enthusiastic arts advocates.

participating successfully in the arts.

**What Practitioners Can Do:**

Encourage children to use their own imaginations and ideas in their work and to find their own ways of responding to lesson objectives.

Teach children to be observant and aware of the visual arts in their surroundings.

Invite children to select their best work and display artwork created by every child.

4. **Feelings about the arts** *are developed by:*

a sense of belonging to a community and feeling support from the group.

opportunities to respond to works of art created by others.

the sense of efficacy that results when a child's artistic efforts evoke a positive response from others.

**What Practitioners Can Do:**

Teach children to respect the work created by peers.

Model for children ways to respond thoughtfully to the works of professional artists.

Invite children to consider why their work evoked particular responses from others.

**Figure 3.3** Four Types of Learning Promoted Through the Arts
*Sources:* Cohen & Gainer (1995), Jalongo & Stamp (1997), and State of Florida Department of State (1990).

| | Yes | No |
|---|:---:|:---:|
| **The Environment** | | |
| Is the area free of dirt, debris, and dust? | ☐ | ☐ |
| Is the floor clean and dry to avoid slipping and falling? | ☐ | ☐ |
| Is equipment arranged to avoid tripping, falling, and pulling items down (e.g., electrical cord taped to baseboard)? | ☐ | ☐ |
| Is ventilation (e.g., fresh air, open window, fan) adequate? | ☐ | ☐ |
| Is the lighting adequate? | ☐ | ☐ |
| Is protective gear (e.g., dust masks, plastic gloves, eye protection) in use? | ☐ | ☐ |
| Are safety rules posted (e.g., no running, no using art tools as weapons)? | ☐ | ☐ |
| Are emergency procedures posted and is the Poison Control Center number displayed? | ☐ | ☐ |
| **Supplies and Storage** | | |
| Are the items to which children need independent access stored so that children can obtain them readily? | ☐ | ☐ |
| Are materials that require teacher supervision stored in a locked cabinet? | ☐ | ☐ |
| **Health and Safety Practices** | | |
| Are health and safety considerations part of the planning of activities? | ☐ | ☐ |
| Are health and safety issues part of the explanation of activities to children? | ☐ | ☐ |
| Is there evidence that children have been taught safe and healthy practices (e.g., pictorial warning signs, a poster about washing hands)? | ☐ | ☐ |
| Are the art materials and equipment that children use maintained and inspected regularly? | ☐ | ☐ |
| **Instructional Practices** | | |
| Does the teacher use good sense in selecting activities that are both age appropriate and individually appropriate (e.g., "painting" with shaving cream is *not* appropriate for toddlers, who may attempt to taste it or accidentally rub their eyes)? | ☐ | ☐ |
| Are children taught the way to use tools properly? | ☐ | ☐ |
| Is the teacher aware of environmental toxins and their effects? | ☐ | ☐ |
| Does the teacher know about the ratings of art supplies (e.g., nontoxic, AP/Approved Product or CP/Certified Product of the Art and Craft Materials Institute) and avoid using inexpensive imported products that may be hazardous? | ☐ | ☐ |
| Are policies and procedures clear (e.g., handling scissors, distributing or collecting tools, no horseplay with art materials)? | ☐ | ☐ |
| Is the teacher aware of potential hazards due to ingestion, inhalation, or absorption through the skin? | ☐ | ☐ |

**Figure 3.4**   Health and Safety Issues in Art: A Checklist
*Sources:* Qualley (1986) and Center for Safety in the Arts, http://artswire.org: 70/1/csa; National Safety Council, www.nsc.org/ehc/airqual.htm.

| **Special Needs** | **Yes** | **No** |
|---|---|---|
| Does the teacher have detailed information about which children have allergies, chemical sensitivities, respiratory problems, fine or large motor impairments, etc.? | ☐ | ☐ |
| Has the teacher carefully considered the characteristics of students, such as their manual dexterity or familiarity with the tools, when planning art activities? | ☐ | ☐ |
| Is there evidence of low-tech and high-tech adaptations that will enable young children with special needs to participate in art activities? | ☐ | ☐ |

**Teacher Knowledge**
Did you know that . . .

| | **Yes** | **No** |
|---|---|---|
| Clay is 60% silica, and if clay dust becomes airborne, it can aggravate respiratory problems or even cause lung disease with prolonged exposure? | ☐ | ☐ |
| Powders and mixtures that are often used to make art materials (e.g., flour, cornstarch, plaster of paris) can be inhaled and precipitate an asthma attack in children with this disease? | ☐ | ☐ |
| Even if children do not deliberately eat art supplies, they can accidentally ingest them by touching their mouths, biting their fingernails, or putting an art tool in their mouths? | ☐ | ☐ |
| Food dyes, once believed to be completely harmless, are now considered carcinogenic (cancer-causing)? | ☐ | ☐ |
| Real clay, dug from the earth, can contain molds and bacteria that may trigger allergies or cause infections? | ☐ | ☐ |
| Children may rub their eyes and accidentally get dyes, paints, ink from markers, and other substances in their eyes, causing swelling and irritation? | ☐ | ☐ |
| The main ingredient in play dough and paste is wheat flour, and the main ingredient in white glue is milk. Therefore, if children with an allergy to wheat (celiac condition) or milk products (lactose intolerance) ingest these substances, they can become very ill? | ☐ | ☐ |

**Figure 3.4**   *(Continued)*

the basic concepts of using protective clothing, putting the brush back in the same color, and cleaning up after painting. As they gain some experience, the teacher could present the strategy of wiping each side of the brush on the rim of the paint container to avoid drips and grasping the brush with the fingers (rather than the fist) above the metal rim, which increases the child's control over the brush. Next, the teacher could show children how to avoid smearing by letting one color dry before putting wet paint over or very close to it, how to use different-sized brushes for different purposes (narrow/pointed for details, wide/flat for large areas), and how to rinse brushes in cool water and store them with bristles up. As children gain experience with paints in the primary grades, they can be taught different brush strokes or how to sketch before painting.

## Evaluating Materials and Experiences

Walk down the hall of an elementary school, look at children's artwork, and you will notice a definite trend. In kindergarten and first grade, there is a freshness and spontaneity to children's work. Most kindergartners and first graders will tackle nearly any illustration challenge—a suspension bridge, a giraffe, or a trailer court. By second or third grade, however, many children have begun to trace and copy rather than create their own drawings. One student teacher even reported that a girl in her class began to cry when a classmate wouldn't share a picture book so that she could trace it too. This is what happens when adults push children in art by comparing, correcting, and making excessive value judgments. Children take the safe route of making their picture look like someone else's rather than creating a new form.

It is particularly important, then, to avoid singling out art that looks like something and identifying it as the only good artwork. When adults do this, children lose confidence in themselves and resort to stereotypes, such as drawing stick figures. A much better strategy is simply to say to the child, "Tell me about your painting." If a 4-year-old says, "I painted it at the easel and the paint ran down the page. Red is my favorite color," then the teacher can reply, "Yes, I see the way you used red. Let's hang it up to dry so that you can take it home."

In many ways, the process of supporting children's art is similar to supporting their efforts in writing (Rowe, 1987). Just as teachers maintain a portfolio of children's writing efforts, they should keep a folder of children's artistic efforts. One-dimensional art can be filed or copied for inclusion in the folder, while three-dimensional art such as sculpture or puppets can be photographed.

As teachers, we know we are providing quality art materials and experiences when:

- Children use art materials and request specific materials.
- Children confidently accept new challenges in art.
- Children pursue art activities during free time at home and at school.
- Children express positive attitudes toward art and artistic abilities during class discussions.

## TEACHERS' ROLES AND RESPONSIBILITIES

Teachers must do more than go through the motions of offering art; they must fully appreciate its value. One classroom teacher expressed it this way:

> I offer children artwork as a preventive measure, a benign alternative to letting them express themselves in destructive ways. I offer them art because they love it. I offer them art because it makes my survival in the classroom more likely. What we hear from the worst people in our field is that you have to control children, you have to make them behave. The best people will tell you that if you give children interesting choices, your class, home or life will run more smoothly. For all these reasons, art takes a prominent place in my daily class. (Clemens, 1991, p. 4)

Sadly, some teachers miss out on the rich contributions of art to the curriculum. They may rely entirely on work disguised as art or, if they teach in an elementary school, they may delegate all of the responsibility for teaching art to the art teacher. The outcome of both behaviors is that art is further segregated from the child's total life experience. Treating art as a second-class subject is a contradiction of what we know about the holistic learning processes of young children.

The National Art Education Association (1999) has identified nine key opportunities that teachers should provide to students of art.

**1.** *Examining extensively both natural and human-made objects from many sources.* Mrs. Petit, a kindergarten teacher, has a collection of ceramic, wood, metal, plastic, and fabric elephants. When she brought the collection to school, the children had an opportunity to see a carved wooden elephant from India, a stuffed toy of the storybook character Babar, and a ceramic elephant bank, to name a few. In this way, children were able to examine these objects closely and to compare/contrast the various depictions of elephants with photographs of the actual animals.

**2.** *Expressing individual perceptions, ideas, and feelings through a variety of art media suited to the manipulative abilities and expressive needs of the student.* When a teacher provides large sheets of moistened paper and fingerpaints for young children, that teacher is providing materials that are well suited to the developmental levels of the students. Most young preschoolers create **nonrepresentational art,** meaning that the art does not look like the item being represented. They are more interested in the feel of the materials (e.g., swirling the paint with a brush), in expressing their emotions (e.g., pounding clay when they are angry), and in expressing real and imaginary images (i.e., using dramatic colors and lines to depict a thunderstorm). If the teacher in-

*Sensory experiences are the foundation for later artistic understanding and appreciation.*

vites children to try some different hand movements (i.e., palms, fingertips, fists, and forearms), the children have many opportunities to express themselves through an artistic medium. Older children may plan a design and become very deliberate and controlled in their use of color, form, and line to develop a particular composition.

**3.** *Experimenting with art materials and processes to understand their potentials for personal expression.* When a second-grade teacher invites his students to make a gift collage, it results in extensive experimentation with materials. Cellina makes a collage that characterizes her mother's personality. The second grader begins with a scrap of "country colors" fabric over a piece of cardboard, then adds lace, dried flowers, an old snapshot, and ribbon. As Cellina searches for other materials, she is experimenting with art media; as she figures out the most satisfying way to arrange and fasten them, she is determining her effectiveness; and when she is finished, she has succeeded in creating a new form.

**4.** *Working with tools appropriate to the students' abilities to develop manipulative skills needed for satisfying aesthetic expression.* Beginning teachers are sometimes surprised to encounter preschoolers who do not know how to cut with scissors. Rather than insisting that all children begin using scissors immediately, skilled teachers give children options such as tearing paper, cutting pieces of modeling dough rolled thin, tearing at the paper with scissors, resting the scissors on the desk while cutting, and making simple cuts (e.g., paper fringe) (Schirrmacher, 1988). A skilled teacher also knows that it is too difficult for young children to cut out small interior spaces (such as the eye holes for a mask), partly because they lack the fine motor control needed for such a task, and partly because they need sharp, pointed scissors to do the job, which can result in injury. Teachers also wait until children have gained experience with scissors before expecting them to cut on lines or to use special equipment such as pinking shears, which must be kept at a right angle to the fabric in order to function properly. Figure 3.5 supplies an overview of the developmental sequence in making art for young children.

---

**Art-Making Activities**

Art-making activities in the visual arts typically include such things as:

Painting, drawing, printmaking, collage

Sculpture, including mobiles, assemblages, and light

Photography, films, television, theater design, videography, and digital imagery

Crafts—ceramics, fiber arts, jewelry, metalwork, enameling, works in wood, paper, plastic, and other materials

Environmental arts—architecture, urban design, landscaping, interior design, product design, clothing design, and graphic communication in both personal and public environments

Technology—computer-generated graphics, multimedia design, and the use of the Internet as a resource (National Art Education Association, 1999)

---

**Figure 3.5**   Developmental Sequence for the Making of Art

**NONREPRESENTATIONAL/SCRIBBLING STAGE**

**Approximate Age:**  2 years
**Art Skills:**  Explores media through all the senses
Makes random marks on paper
Begins scribbling

**Figure 3.5**   *(Continued)*

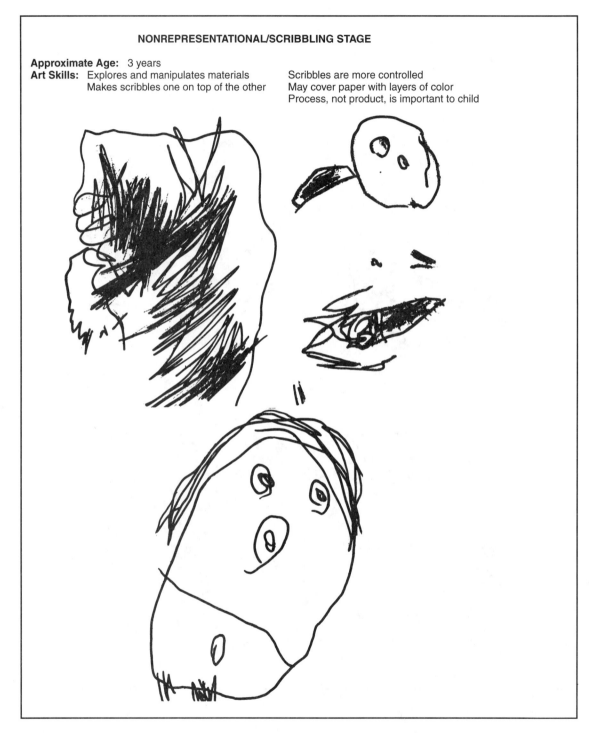

**NONREPRESENTATIONAL/SCRIBBLING STAGE**

**Approximate Age:** 3 years

**Art Skills:**   Explores and manipulates materials     Scribbles are more controlled

Makes scribbles one on top of the other     May cover paper with layers of color

Process, not product, is important to child

**Figure 3.5**   *(Continued)*

---

### Infants and Toddlers

**Developmental Profile:** The child communicates directly through body movements, such as enjoying the medium of fingerpaint and observing the effects of different hand movements on the patterns on the paper. For the very young, visual artworks are more of a happening, more of an experience and an event than a means of communicating with others. An infant's attempt at drawing tends to be random. If the drawing implement makes contact with the paper, that is what is produced.

**Typical Art Activities:** Infants tend to engage in sensory experiences—touching, tasting, smelling, and mouthing objects. During early infancy, they begin to focus their gaze and then track objects with their eyes. Young infants have a definite preference for high-contrast pictures (e.g., black and white patterns) and the human face. During later infancy, they study objects intently and manipulate toys and objects that interest them. They frequently are fascinated by variation in what they see (e.g., a mobile over the crib, a blinking light). Toddlers begin to explore simple art materials in ways that do not demand high levels of manual dexterity, such as fingerpaints, play dough, scribbling with a fat crayon on paper, and so forth.

### Preschool and Kindergarten

**Developmental Profile:** The child begins to learn how to communicate through symbols and to use one thing to represent another. The drawings typically produced by 3-year-olds are **controlled scribbles,** because the child is better able to deliberately make marks on paper. Although a young preschooler's scribble in response to a cat may not look anything like a cat, that scribble might represent all of the child's sensory impressions of an experience with a cat—sandpapery tongue, beautiful fur, the sound of its purr, and its playfulness. The child may announce, "That's kitty," hence this stage is referred to as naming of scribbles. As control of drawing increases, typically developing threes and fours often begin to produce repeated small shapes, almost like geometric designs. By the time that most children are in kindergarten, they recognize that art has the power to communicate. They often use artwork as a "narrative prop"—as a way of telling a story. Their drawings and play-dough creations begin to resemble the objects that they have in mind. This is referred to as **representational art.**

**Typical Art Activities:** Basic art materials such as crayons and paper; fingerpaints and wet paper; large paintbrushes, tempera paints and easels; modeling dough or clay; white glue and wood; torn paper constructions; simple collages; crayon rubbings of objects (e.g., leaves, shoe sole); painting with objects (e.g., marbles dipped in paint and rolled around in a box on paper); learning to use scissors; simple printmaking with Styrofoam shapes dipped in paint. Learning to use crayons, scissors, paste, and paint to design, cut, arrange, and paste various items, such as child-made books, murals, simple masks, replicas of objects (e.g., a large cardboard box transformed into a house), considering ways of displaying art.

**Figure 3.5**   *(Continued)*

**Figure 3.5**   *(Continued)*

**EMERGING REPRESENTATIONAL**

**Approximate Age:**  4–5 years
**Art Skills:**  Combines two shapes, often a circle and a cross, to make "mandalas"
Draws "suns"
Represents humans as a circle with arms and legs, a "tadpole" person
Figures appear to float on the page
Art is used to represent feelings and ideas
Represents what has made an impression, rather than everything that is
seen or known

**Figure 3.5**   *(Continued)*

**REPRESENTATIONAL**

**Approximate Age:** 6–8 years
**Art Skills:** Child's art clearly resembles whatever it represents
Baseline begins to appear in drawings
More preplanning and inclusion of details
Child strives to master various art skills and begins to evaluate own work
Work tends to be more realistic in terms of proportion and arrangement

**Figure 3.5** *(Continued)*

| **First Grade** |
| --- |
| **Developmental Profile:** The child becomes more confident as a symbol maker. With greater mastery of language, the child frequently chooses to weave symbols together (e.g., making a picture book). <br> **Typical Art Activities:** New and more involved techniques such as papier-mâché, paper weaving, and collage construction are introduced. Materials and techniques involving yarns, fabrics, and stencils are experienced. More sophisticated clay construction techniques (e.g., using coils of clay to construct items, planning constructions that will stand and stay together). Simple stitchery (e.g., yarn and plastic needle on burlap), puppets (e.g., rod and sock puppets). |
| **Second and Third Grade** |
| This stage corresponds to the industry-versus-inferiority stage of Erikson's psychosocial theory. The child seeks to build competence by undertaking a wide variety of art activities. Crafts such as toymaking, painting with acrylics, fashioning items from fabric, and making ceramic items or holiday decorative items are all common during this stage that Davis and Gardner (1992) refer to as "youth as craftsperson." <br> **Typical Art Activities:** Students learn more complex uses of art tools (e.g., the clay sculpting tools used by artists). More manual control and ability (e.g., exploring watercolors and fine brushes). Children begin to explore stitchery (e.g., making a class quilt or a simple stuffed toy), create more elaborate props (e.g., paint on fabric to create a scenery backdrop), investigate design problems (e.g., creating posters for an event), explore multistep group projects that are fashioned to scale (e.g., using chicken wire and papier-mâché to construct a dinosaur). |

**Figure 3.5**   *(Continued)*
*Source:* Adapted from Feeney, Christensen, & Moravcik (1991).

   **5.**   *Organizing, evaluating, and reorganizing works-in-process to gain an understanding of the formal structuring and expressive potential of line, form, color, and texture in space.* One way of glimpsing young children's thinking about art is to encourage them to talk as they work with materials and listen to what they have to say. Lynn, a 4-year-old, is drawing a picture for her sister. She explains her selection of materials as follows: "Crayons make fat lines I do not want; colored pencils are 'thins' that make pretty pictures." By listening to Lynn, we can better understand how she is thinking about her work-in-process and how she will go about selecting art materials and art elements that will best enable her to express her ideas.

   **6.** and **7.**   *Reading about, looking at, and discussing works of art and design from contemporary and past cultures using a variety of educational media and community resources; Seeing artists and designers at work in their studios and in the classroom through the use of technology.* Every community offers examples of sculpture, constructions, architecture, industrial, and handcrafted products. Four residents of the senior center (which meets in the same building as the county-supported after-school-care program) are making a quilt for the church bazaar. When Mr. Donlevy learns of this, he invites the women to talk with the children. On the first visit, the ladies develop the concept that a quilt can tell a story. They show the children several actual quilts as well as examples in quilt pattern books. Next, the ladies share their plans and pattern for the quilt and give each child a small scrap of fabric to keep.

Mr. Donlevy uses educational media to extend and enrich the project, including several picture books about quilts—*The Quilt* (Jonas, 1989), *Quilt Story* (Johnston, 1984), and *The Patchwork Quilt* (Flournoy, 1985)—and excerpts from a movie about quilting borrowed from the library. On the second visit, the ladies demonstrate how a quilt is put together. The children learn about stitching, appliqués, polyester fiberfill, and a quilting frame. On the third visit, a portion of the quilt is finished and a piece is added while the children observe closely. On the fourth and final visit, the ladies show the children the completed quilt and donate a tiny quilt for the baby's crib in the housekeeping corner. Through this simple project, children have looked at, discussed, and directly experienced folk art using educational media and community resources.

**8.** *Evaluating art of both students and mature artists, industrial products, and home and community design.* As part of a unit on consumer education, a group of third graders decides to compare/contrast the features of three pieces of educational print-shop software. The students establish a rating sheet for the product, which includes such things as the quality and variety of pictures available and the number of different tasks possible (i.e., banner, invitation, greeting card, or letterhead). They compile their data and then, using published software reviews as a guide, write a critique for each. In this way, children have gained firsthand experience in the evaluation of industrial/technical products.

**9.** *Engaging in activities that provide opportunities to apply art knowledge and aesthetic judgment to personal life, home, and workplace.* Ms. Sandstrom has decided that her second-grade classroom needs to be rearranged to accommodate and display some of their new projects. One of those projects is a scale model of their main street, because they have been studying simple maps. Rather than reorganizing the room herself after school, she uses this as an opportunity to build the children's aesthetic judgment. She makes a scale model of the classroom on separate pieces of colored overhead transparencies. The children experiment with many different room arrangements by shifting the items around on the overhead projector until they decide on the best classroom layout.

## Establishing Rules and Limits

As explained in the introduction to this chapter, teachers sometimes go to one extreme or the other with art, either being excessively controlling or completely laissez-faire. Ideally, teachers should establish rules and limits that enable children to get the most from their art experiences. Figure 3.6 is a suggested list of classroom management considerations in art (Schirrmacher, 1988).

## Talking with Children about Their Art

As we have seen, children's drawings may be broadly categorized as nonrepresentational or representational (Kellogg, 1979). Both types of art are authentic means of self-expression. Consider, for example, 2-year-old Katie's drawing of Kirstie, a border collie. Katie likes to curl up with the dog while she is looking at

**Figure 3.6**
Establishing Rules
and Limits in Early
Childhood Art
Programs

1. Decide upon a few important general rules rather than many insignificant specific rules.

2. Limit the number of children at a center at any one time. This avoids disputes over materials and accidental damage to a child's work caused by overcrowding.

3. Impress upon children the need to wear protective clothing. Provide smock, aprons, or simply a man's old shirt worn backwards with sleeves rolled up.

4. Teach children how to use and care for art tools, such as rinsing paintbrushes, putting the lid on paste, and returning materials to their original location when finished.

5. Model for children the importance of conserving materials and using only what is needed. You could give them a dab of white glue on an old margarine tub lid, for example, rather than the whole bottle.

6. Teach children to share supplies and respect others. Model for children, asking rather than grabbing ("May I use the stapler next?" "Are you finished with the pink Play-doh?"). Discuss with children the importance of accepting the art activities of other children.

7. Rather than simply announcing "time to clean up," demonstrate how children are supposed to clean up after each art activity.

*Source:* Adapted from Schirrmacher (1988).

books. Maybe Katie's scribble goes beyond the visual image that she has of the dog and represents the softness of the animal's fur or the pleasurable feeling of being surrounded by warmth and closeness. The adult who remarks "Very good, but what happened to the dog's tail?" or demands "What is it?" fails to appreciate young children's early forms of artistic expression. The answer, of course, is that it isn't supposed to be anything! Sometimes, children are simply exploring an artistic medium—for example, the sensory pleasure of squishing clay into different shapes or gliding a crayon across the page. Children do not separate their sensory impressions from one another, nor do they dichotomize feelings and ideas as adults are prone to do. In fact, Davis and Gardner (1992) reported that when they asked a young preschooler to draw "a scary house," the child obliged by drawing a regular-looking house, but growled all the while he drew it!

As you respond to children's artwork, keep the following guiding principles in mind:

**1.** *Present several alternatives.* Rather than turning art into an "assignment," provide children with choices, not only of how the finished product will look, but also of the process they will use to get there.

**2.** *Treat child artists and their work with respect.* Let children know that their work is valued by displaying it proudly, helping them to transport it home safely, and finding something positive to say about their work (Rankin, 1995).

**3.** *Emphasize feelings and responses.* Rather than treating art as an assembly task or an exercise in following directions, encourage children to explore emotions via the arts.

**4.** *Intervene when children seem stalled or frustrated.* Ask questions that will help children to take a different approach or perspective rather than falling into a rut or quitting in frustration. Encourage children to persist when tasks are challenging rather than becoming discouraged if the way to proceed is not clear or obvious.

**5.** *Help children to sort out what is essential from what is unnecessary.* Teach them the skills of emphasizing what is most important in their creative products and help them to understand that many times "less is more" and aesthetic experiences are improved by the elimination of extraneous details.

**6.** *Recognize children's efforts, but do not accept slapdash work.* Guide children in doing their best and give recognition to their achievements, not as a highly competitive contest, but as a "bonus" after the work is produced. When it is clear that children did not make a real effort to explore the materials or produce their best work, try to find out why and give them another chance to excel (adapted from Cohen & Gainer, 1995).

Generally speaking, it is best to rely on artistic elements when discussing art with very young children. You could comment on color ("Look at all that yellow, Ishaka!"), on arrangement ("Lester, you covered the whole page with paint"), texture ("This clay feels smooth now that you rolled it out"), line ("I see the interesting patterns you made with the toothpick and paint on your paper, Claudia"), or shape ("Stevie and Alexei made lots of small round bubbles. Kerri and Man-Li made one big long bubble"). For older children who are creating representational art, it is best to follow the children's lead. You might begin by saying, "Tell me about your picture," and then relate subsequent comments to whatever the child says.

Six-year-old Twila understands how the artwork of others invites us to think and to respond in individual ways. When the teacher asks the children what Vincent van Gogh might be trying to tell us in his painting *Sunflowers*, Twila remarks, "It depends on when you see the picture; one picture can mean different things." Henrik, a 5-year-old, has figured out what painters do: "First they see their think, then they paint it." Both of these children are developing their vocabularies of art and learning how to discuss art.

*Making windsocks by a 4-year-old girl.*

## Developing Concepts and a Vocabulary of Art

Developing a child's vocabulary of art involves three things:

1. *Encouraging children to discuss the artwork first in ordinary language.* If children discuss art in their own words first, it permits an equal sharing of adult and child perceptions. Five-year-old children who examined a large, colorful book of American artist Mary Cassatt's paintings made interesting observations such as "She must like little kids" and "The pictures look soft." By allowing children to make these observations first, the teacher can follow their lead, explaining briefly about the artist's life ("Deidra was right, Mary Cassatt did love little children. Sometimes she used her own family as models for her paintings"). Teachers might pose interesting challenges such as "What could an artist do to lines to make the picture 'look soft,' like Harrold said? Let's try to make some pictures that way, pictures without dark lines, pictures that look softer."

2. *Introducing the vocabulary in context.* If children use new words in conjunction with direct experience, they are more likely to make the words part of their active vocabularies. When Jenny's mother demonstrated her cake-decorating talents to second graders, they used the words **thick, thin, food coloring, pastry bag,** and all of the names for the different metal tips used. The children examined a real rose, talked about its parts (petals, leaves), then watched Jenny's mother create icing roses on the cake. Finally, each child had an opportunity to decorate a cupcake using the pastry tips, techniques, and colors of their choice.

3. *Using accurate, appropriate vocabulary.* Teachers need to provide new vocabulary words quickly and unobtrusively so that they underscore the child's experience rather than impose the teacher's opinions (Dixon & Chalmers, 1990). This might explain why young children tend to prefer abstract works of art over realistic ones—abstract works of art allow children to suggest a wider range of interpretations for the same work (Bowker & Sawyers, 1988). A simple material such as cornstarch and water can build the art vocabulary of preschoolers. The recipe for cornstarch and water is simple:

*Cornstarch and Water*

2 cups of warm water
3 cups of cornstarch
Mix the ingredients with hands
(Clemens, 1991)

What makes the material interesting is that it is solid when it is left standing, but turns to liquid when handled. Rather than simply mixing the material and making it available, teachers can turn the experience into an art vocabulary lesson. First, let the children handle the dry cornstarch and have them describe it. Words such as *powder, smooth,* and *silky* may be introduced here. Then add a little of the warm water and ask the children for descriptors. Words such as *lumpy* and *thick* may be introduced here. Next, invite the children to hold a chunk of the material as they watch it transform from solid to liquid. Add the rest of the water and make statements such as "Let your fingers drift down. Try to punch your way down. How do your hands feel now?" Let the mixture stand overnight, then add water

again to watch the material change from liquid to solid and to practice the new vocabulary in context again.

Building a vocabulary of art is important because "we sometimes take it for
granted that children who do not respond verbally are incapable of appreciation or
criticism, when in fact they may not have the appropriate words to discuss their
own work and involvement or the work of others. Without being able to draw easily on a descriptive vocabulary, children are frequently unwilling to enter into a
discussion" (Dixon & Chalmers, 1990, p. 16).

## *Ways of Discussing Art*

In early childhood programs that support children's development in art, young
children not only create original art, they respond to the art of others. Figure 3.7 is
an overview of discussion strategies to be used in discussing works of art and art
reproductions.

---

**Types of Questions**

Questions on aesthetics—Look at the lines on your paper. On the ceiling. Can you find other lines?
Thin lines? Thick lines?

Questions on art criticism—Here are pictures of some famous buildings in the world. If you could
choose one to be built in our town, which one would it be? Why?

Questions about art history—Which of these sculptures was made a long time ago? Why do you think so?

Questions on art production—What are some ways artists can make their pictures look smooth? Rough?

1. *Who made it?*

*Situation:* looking at a UNICEF calendar of children's art work.

*Question:* "Do you think these drawings were made by adults or children? What are you seeing right
now that can give you a clue?"

2. *How was it made?*

*Situation:* looking at a large metal sculpture

*Question:* "Does anyone know how pieces of metal are joined together?"

3. *When was it made?*

*Situation:* looking at an ancient piece of sculpture

*Question:* "If you look at this carefully, you will notice that some of the pieces are broken off. Do you
think this sculpture is new or old? Why?"

4. *For whom was it made?*

*Situation:* looking at a wooden toy

*Question:* "One of my neighbors makes toys out of wood like the ones I brought today for you to play
with. Who do you think he makes the toys for?"

---

**Figure 3.7**   Questions About a Work of Art
*Sources:* Adapted from Amann (1993), Heberholz (1974), Jalongo & Stamp (1997), and Rowe (1987).

5. *What is the message or meaning, if any?*

*Situation:* looking at a heritage quilt

*Question:* "Do you know anyone who makes their clothes by sewing them instead of buying them already made at the store? The owner of this quilt said that her great-grandmother made it from scraps of fabric that were left over from the sewing she did for her family. Why would their grandmother do all of this work to make a quilt?"

6. *What is its style?*

*Situation:* looking at the art in picture book illustrations

*Question:* "On this table, we have several books written and illustrated by the same person. These three are by Rosemary Wells, these by Keith Baker, these by Jerry Pinkney, and these by Diane Goode. What can you say that explains what each artist's work is like? How are these drawings by Rosemary Wells alike? How are they different from all the others?"

7. *What is the quality of experience it affords?*

*Situation:* after viewing a film

*Question:* "You all know the book *Frog Goes to Dinner* by Mercer Mayer (1975). Which did you like better, the movie or the book?"

8. *What was its place in the culture in which it was made?*

*Situation:* watching a Navajo sand painter at work from the video on sight by Diane Ackerman from the PBS series *Mystery of the Senses*

*Question:* "Were you surprised to see that someone could paint with sand? Why are these sand paintings made?"

9. *What is its place in the culture or society of today?*

*Situation:* visit to an art museum

*Question:* "How do you decide which of your art projects or paintings to keep and which ones to throw away? One of the people we will be meeting has a special job in taking care of these paintings. The paintings need to be cleaned, and sometimes they need to be fixed. Can you think of some reasons why people think these paintings are important enough to keep?"

10. *What peculiar problems does it present to understanding and appreciation?*

*Situation:* looking at an art print that uses pointilism

*Question:* "Some of you were wondering why this picture looks so different close up than it does from a distance. If you look very closely, you will see that the picture is made up of hundreds of dots. Did any of you ever experiment with dots as a way to make pictures? When you work at the computer to make a picture, the computer actually makes the dots for you. Use this magnifying glass to look at one of the pictures you made last week. Now look at this piece of a newspaper. You can see that the print is made of dots too."

**Additional Questions about a Work of Art**

What is this work of art?

What is it made from?

What is the most interesting thing about this work of art?

What is the artist trying to tell us?

*(continued)*

**Figure 3.7**   *(Continued)*

Is there a story here? What is it?

Does the artist suggest new ways of seeing things?

How does the work make you feel? Why?

What does it make you think of?

What did the artist use (medium, techniques, tools, ways of organization, effects, composition)?

How is this the same (or different) from other pieces you have seen by this artist? By other artists?

What makes a work of art great?

What makes an artist great?

Do you like this work of art? Why or why not?

**Sources for Art and Art Reproductions**

Children's picture books, prints of famous works of art borrowed from the library, picture postcards of art, walls of a local gallery, an artist's studio, a display of children's work at a public building, a museum exhibit, a university, slides, art history books, encyclopedias, film. Specific sources include:

*Full-size* (approximately 22″ × 28″)
Metropolitan Museum of Art
New York, NY 10028

Modern Learning Press
P.O. Box 167
Rosemont, NJ
(800) 627-5867

*Miniature* (such as postcard size)

| Art Visuals | Parent Child Press | University Prints |
|---|---|---|
| P.O. Box 925 | P.O. Box 675 | 21 East Street |
| Orem, UT 84059 | Hollidaysburg, PA 16648 | Winchester, MA 02138 |

**Figure 3.7** *(Continued)*

Understanding children's artistic development, the role of art in promoting meaningful self-expression, and the basic principles of a high-quality art education is essential to a well-balanced early childhood curriculum (Wright, 1997). Skillful teachers have learned to use the arts, not as an afterthought or add-on, but as a basic foundation of the developmentally appropriate early childhood curriculum (Rasmussen, 1998).

## Locating Resources and Storing Materials

Few teachers have the luxury of purchasing whatever art materials they please. More often, it is a matter of making choices among many possible alternatives. Materials such as paints, paper, crayons, clay, and wood are usually referred to as consumable because they need to be replenished constantly. When budgets are tight, the focus is often on nonconsumables, materials that need replacement less often. Many times, adults are not particularly unhappy to see these messy materials go. But these art materials are a basic means of self-expression and something that children should have access to every day. Rather than eliminating them altogether, teachers need to be creative problem solvers and seek out art materials wherever they can find them. An added bonus to this approach is that it teaches children the value of responsible recycling.

Art materials should:

1. *Extend children's experience.* In order to foster creative expression, children need to learn the same elements and principles of design understood by artists. Naturally, it is important that design elements and principles be presented in developmentally appropriate ways. Figure 3.8 highlights ways that children's picture books can be used to teach elements and principles of design.

2. *Be plentiful.* To acquire an ample supply of free paper, all you need to do is find an office and recycle. Newspaper printers will sometimes give away the ends of paper rolls, and wrapping paper from gifts can be saved by everyone in the class. For special papers, make contact with a printer who prints stationery and invitations or get in touch with a frame shop. Another way to achieve greater variety in classroom resources is to send home a list at the beginning of the year asking for such things as sewing and craft materials (buttons, trim, pieces of fabric, yarn, and ribbon) and throwaway materials that can be put to another use (plastic bottle caps, detergent bottles, food containers, six-pack holder rings, and foil canisters of various sizes).

3. *Be accessible.* It is important for children to use materials when they wish, rather than being completely dependent upon adults for access to materials. Be alert to inexpensive or throwaway materials that can be put to another use. An old microwave cart, divided trays, or a lazy susan can all help provide children access to many different materials, keep the materials organized, and make the collection mobile. One teacher went to a hospital sale and purchased several metal wheeled carts with low, wide shelves, which she used to store her art materials; another scavenged a discontinued display rack from a drugstore, which enabled her to hang up children's paintings on hooks. The goal of using such materials is to allow children to become more independent by making materials more accessible to them.

4. *Be age-appropriate.* When a mother volunteered to work in her son Jaime's Head Start classroom, both she and the teacher were surprised to observe the boy take the paper off the easel and put it on newspaper on the floor to paint. Apparently, Jaime's only experience with painting was on a horizontal rather than a vertical surface. Jaime's behavior illustrates why it is so important to accept children's efforts rather than impose an adult perspective on them. If Jaime's mother had appeared embarrassed or the teacher had reprimanded Jaime, he may have avoided using the materials. But because they both watched and listened, they were able to gradually extend Jaime's experience to painting at an easel.

A story guide is a set of activities designed to accompany and extend a particular children's book. A good story guide integrates content areas and invites children to respond to the book in meaningful ways (McClure & Kristo, 1994). Below are two story guides that emphasize the arts, play, creativity, and imagination.

### Story Guide for *Tar Beach*

**Book** *Tar Beach,* by Faith Ringgold.

**Summary** City apartment dwellers pretend that their apartment building roof is a beautiful beach. On their "tar beach," they have a picnic and enjoy one another's company. Then the narrator, a young African American girl, and her younger brother go on a flight of fancy through the neighborhood before returning safely home. Illustrations for the book come from a quilt created by the author.

**Introduction** Today we are going to hear a story about pretending. What are some make-believe games that you play? Look at the cover of this book by Faith Ringgold. It is about a girl and her brother who like to pretend. The pictures in this book are very special. Instead of drawing the pictures, Faith Ringgold sewed them. Then she put them all together into a quilt.

**Questions**

1. What are some things that you like to pretend?
2. Why did the people in the story pretend to have a beach?
3. If you could fly, what would you choose to fly over? Why?
4. Who would you choose to go with you?

**Props** A real quilt or a book of quilts with picture patterns.

**Follow-up**

- Look at other books with unusual illustrations—the plasticine illustrations in *Have You Seen Birds?* by Joanne Oppenheim and Barbara Reid; the collage in *The Snowy Day,* by Ezra Jack Keats; or the moving parts in *The Wheels on the Bus,* by Paul O. Zelinsky.
- Try sewing some pictures of your own with burlap, large plastic needles, and yarn.
- Look at a book or calendar or magazine pictures of prize-winning quilts. Take a survey on which quilt each member of the class likes best and why.
- Ask someone who makes quilts to visit the class and bring several quilts in different stages of completion.
- Read some other books about quilts that tell a story, such as Patricia Polacco's *The Keeping Quilt,* Tony Johnston's *Quilt Story,* and Lauren Mills's *The Rag Coat.*
- Read another book about another flight of fancy, such as *Abuela,* by Arthur Dorros, or watch a video of Raymond Briggs's *The Snowman.*
- Watch the movie *Peter Pan.* Then read *Amazing Grace,* a story by Mary Hoffman about an African American girl who wants to play Peter Pan in the school play.

### Story Guide for *Seven Blind Mice*

**Book** *Seven Blind Mice,* by Ed Young.

**Summary** In this variant of the Indian tale "The Blind Men and the Elephant," each mouse examines one small portion of the elephant's anatomy (ear, tusk, tail, etc.) and draws an incorrect conclusion about the total object. It is only after the seventh mouse examines the entire elephant and puts all of their observations together that they realize what the object really is!

**Figure 3.8** Using Children's Picture Books to Develop Arts Awareness

**Introduction**  Make a pair of old sunglasses into a blindfold by gluing black paper over the lenses. Let children wear the "blindfold" while attempting to guess what various objects are by touch alone.

**Questions**

1. Why were six of the mice wrong in their guesses about what the object was?

2. What did the last mouse do that was different from the other six mice? How did that help him to make a good guess?

3. Did your eyes ever play a trick on you? Did you ever see one thing and think it was something else?

**Props**  Create a large silhouette of an elephant and seven felt finger puppets or paper stick puppets of mice.

**Follow-up**  After you read the story, have children retell the story using the elephant silhouette and mice puppets they have created.

- Create a "guess what" class book using children's drawings or photographs cut out from magazines. Cover each picture with a piece of card stock and create small, numbered flaps to lift. Children should try to guess what is pictured by seeing only a small portion of the total picture. After guessing what the picture is, they can lift the entire sheet to see the total picture. Bind each child's page into a large class book.

- Try using bright acrylic paints on a black background to create some of the same effects that the artist used in the book.

- Read other stories with surprises, including *Boo! Who?* by Colin and Jacqui Hawkins (1984) or the *I Spy* picture riddle books series by Jean Marzollo.

- Look at several optical illusions. (Psychology books or reference books about vision are good sources.) Also look at some books that show how animals hide using various types of camouflage.

**Exploring Art Media through Picture Books**

(Amann, 1993; Kiefer, 1995)

**Watercolor**  Transparent paint mixed with water. It is usually painted on a white background, giving it a luminous quality.

***Examples of watercolor illustrations from children's books***

Julie Vivas (*I Went Walking*)

Uri Shulevitz (*Dawn*)

Allen Say (*Grandfather's Journey*)

***Experiencing watercolor with children***  Teach children how to control the color intensity by the amount of water that they use to mix with the paints; teach them to rinse the brush out thoroughly when switching from one color to another.

**Pastel chalk**  A stick of color made from powdered pigment in soft hues.

***Examples of pastel chalk illustrations from picture books***

Judith Hendershot/Thomas Allen (*In Coal Country*)

***Experiencing chalk with children***  Use sidewalk chalk to create a life-size board game, to draw a hopscotch board, to advertise an upcoming event in the classroom, to guide a walk around the playground, to draw oversized pictures, or to make giant scribbles.

**Pen and ink**  Pigment (usually black) applied with a pen to paper (usually white).

*(continued)*

**Figure 3.8**  *(Continued)*

*Examples of pen and ink illustrations from picture books*

Chris Van Allsburg (*Two Bad Ants*)

Mercer Mayer (*Frog Goes to Dinner*)

*Experiencing pen and ink with children*   Give children white shelf paper or shirt or hosiery cardboard and an assortment of black ballpoint pens and black felt-tip pens so that they can create pictures in black and white; look at sketches done by artists in black and white.

**Acrylic paints**   Pigments bound with vinyl that resemble oil paint but are faster drying.

*Examples of acrylic from picture books*

Donald Hall & Barbara Cooney (*Ox Cart Man*)

*Experiencing acrylics with children*   Visit an artist's studio or a display of art at a local bank, museum, or university. If you have access to some acrylics, allow the children to experiment with them on a small scale (these paints are rather expensive), but be sure to protect the children's clothing (these paints will not wash out).

**Airbrush**   A mechanical tool used by commercial artists that looks like a pen. An airbrush takes a small amount of paint and sprays it very evenly on a surface using a small compressor.

*Examples of airbrush techniques from picture books*

Donald Crews (*Freight Train*)

Leo and Diane Dillon (*Why Mosquitoes Buzz in People's Ears*)

*Experiencing an airbrush with children*   To see an airbrush in use, watch *A Video Visit with Donald Crews,* published by Trumpet Book Club. Invite a commercial artist to demonstrate the use of the airbrush and let children use it. Try mixing thin tempera and using a pump spray (like the ones used for hairspray) to create outlines of shapes created by the children.

**Collage**   The use of an assemblage or collection of materials and textures to create a picture.

*Examples of collage illustrations from picture books*

Eric Carle (*The Very Hungry Caterpillar*)

Ezra Jack Keats (*The Snowy Day*)

*Experiencing collage with children*   Invite children to create books using collage illustrations; to create a collage that represents a feeling or characterizes a person; or to make a nature collage of leaves, seed pods, branches, dried flowers, etc.

**Resist**   The technique of masking a surface so that it repels paint, dye, or ink. Batik uses this process with fabric.

*Examples of batik illustrations from picture books*

Roni Scholter & Marcia Sewall (*Captain Snap and the Children of Vinegar Lane*)

Margaret Mahy & Patricia MacCarthy (*17 Kings and 43 Elephants*)

*Experiencing resist with children*   Use crayon resist and paste batik.

**Linoleum or block prints**   A pattern or picture is cut into metal, wood, or linoleum so that raised lines and shapes are created. Then paint or ink is applied to the surface of the block and the pattern is printed on paper.

**Figure 3.8**   *(Continued)*

*Examples of prints from picture books*

Gail Haley (*A Story, A Story*)

Ashley Wolff (*A Year of Birds*)

*Experiencing prints with children*   Use a cut-out piece of Styrofoam glued onto a block of Styrofoam to create a stamp, use a small screwdriver to create a shape on the Styrofoam, and make a print.

**Photography**   The technique of using film to record a picture of something.

*Examples of photography in picture books*

Tana Hoban (*A Children's Zoo*)

Dav Pilkey (*Dogzilla*)

*Experiencing photography with children*   Get children involved in using inexpensive, durable cameras to take pictures during a special event; ask children to bring in family snapshots.

**Oil paint**   Paint that uses oil as a base for the pigment.

*Examples of oil paintings in picture books*

Hans Christian Andersen & Thomas Locker's (*The Ugly Duckling*)

Jacob W. Grim & Paul O. Zelinsky's (*Rumplestiltskin*)

*Experiencing oil paints with children*   Collect scraps of canvas board so that children can paint on the same surface that real artists use. Use a plastic lid from a small jar as a palette and place a small daub of various colored oil paints inside. Invite children to comment on the texture and rich colors oil paints produce.

**Plasticine**   A modeling material similar to clay that does not harden when exposed to air.

*Examples of plasticine in picture books*

Joanne Oppenheim and Barbara Reid (*Have You Seen Birds?*)

Barbara Reid (*Two by Two*)

*Experiencing plasticine with children*   Use various types of modeling material, including plastic clay. Invite children to study the illustrations and invent some pictures with bits of brightly colored clay.

**Children's picture books about art experiences**

Carle, E. (1992). *Draw me a star.* New York: Philomel.

Cohen, M. (1980). *No good in art.* New York: Greenwillow.

de Paola, T. (1988). *The art lesson.* New York: Putnam.

Lionni, L. (1991). *Matthew's dream.* New York: Knopf.

Rylant, C. (1988). *All I see.* New York: Orchard.

Velthuijs, M. (1992). *Crocodile's masterpiece.* New York: Farrar, Straus & Giroux.

Wolkstein, D. (1992). *Little mouse's painting.* New York: Morrow.

**Figure 3.8**   *(Continued)*

The thing to remember in providing age-appropriate experiences is to consider whether the child can complete the artwork without excessive adult interference. If the teacher must draw, cut out, or assemble things for the child, then the activity is not age-appropriate.

**5.** *Be of high quality.* As the poet Walter de la Mare once observed, only the rarest and best kind of anything is good enough for the very young. Sometimes tempera paint is thinned to save money, but it becomes so runny that children have difficulty controlling it. It is better to use a paint extender/thickener, such as this recipe:

*Powdered Paint Extender*

1 cup Bentonite
1/2 cup Ivory Snow (flakes)
2 quarts warm water

Mix the ingredients well and let them stand in a large jar for about three days. Stir the mixture each day. The mixture is jelly-like and can be thinned to the desired consistency. Mix it with water and add powdered paint when you are ready to use it (Clemens, 1991).

Adults sometimes insist that children use crayons rather than markers, but young children often prefer the bright color and control of a water-based marker. True, markers are expensive and can easily be ruined by leaving the caps off or pressing too firmly. But rather than ruling them out, teachers need to demonstrate how to use and care for them. One way to help children with the task of putting on the caps is to make a marker stand by sinking the caps into a lump of wet plaster of paris or clay so that children can replace the markers with one movement (Clemens, 1991).

As you organize art materials in your classroom, differentiate among those that are used daily, occasionally, and infrequently. Store materials for daily use, such as crayons, scissors, or paper, on low, open shelves where children can see and reach them. You will also want to consider storing materials that are new and not supposed to be opened yet in an area less accessible to children, such as in a cabinet on a high shelf.

## Displaying Children's Art

Some general guidelines for displaying children's art include placing the work at children's eye level where they can enjoy it, rotating art regularly, and utilizing a variety of spaces—not just walls or bulletin boards, but also cardboard box panels, doors, windows, shelves, and display cases. Consider also how you will deal with works-in-progress as opposed to finished projects. Usually, the works-in-progress need to be out on a low table so that children can return to them again easily, while the finished projects can be placed in a slightly less accessible area, such as on the windowsills. A part of displaying children's art that is often neglected is the finishing touch, such as a frame for a picture. Frames for children's

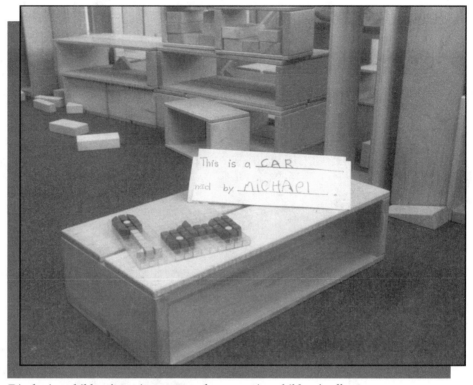

*Displaying children's art is one way of encouraging children's efforts.*

art can be colored paper, Styrofoam meat trays, plastic microwave food trays, plastic coffee can lids, or boxes and lids of every description. Figure 3.9 contains two pieces of framed art: a picture of three imaginary characters by Sharyl Lynn (age 6) and a picture of Robin Hood and his horse created by Justin (age 5). With older children, you may want to develop an art gallery of their framed art, tape-record children's descriptions of their art, or even make a walking-tour tape similar to that used in a museum.

Remember, displaying art is for everybody, not just the small percentage of children who might become professional artists someday. Rather than functioning as a talent scout who singles out only a few children's work to be displayed, teachers should recognize every child's efforts at self-expression. It is important to respect the children's wishes to take their work home and display it there too. Children should be permitted to take their work home immediately or at least within a reasonable period of time. Teachers who care about children's art make sure that the paint is dry before rolling up the picture or, if the art is three-dimensional, plan a way for the child to transport the item home safely. Clean, recycled milk cartons with the lids cut off are good carriers for clay creations, for example.

*Three imaginary characters by Sharyl Lynn, age 6*

*Robin Hood and his horse by Justin, age 5*

**Figure 3.9**
Examples of Framed Art

## LEARNER-CENTERED ART EXPERIENCES

When children are engaged in creating works of visual art, they rely primarily upon their visual/spatial intelligence (Gardner, 1993). The outcomes of developing visual/spatial intelligence include such things as sensitivity to visual stimuli and facility in seeing, manipulating, and producing images in the mind's eye. The three major considerations in selecting **learner-centered art** experiences are (1) letting children direct their own work, (2) valuing the process more than the product, and (3) encouraging originality rather than conformity. The next section offers several examples of learner-centered activities in art.

## *Paper*

Some art activities with paper include:

**1.** *Picture Making.* Young children can create pictures with crayons, paints, markers, torn paper of various colors, and colored pencils on large pieces of paper. Primary grade children can use materials that are more difficult to control, such as watercolors and nonwashable colors such as oil pastel crayons, oil paint, or ink. As children gain greater control over their drawing, they can experiment with drawing on different types of paper, such as a mural taped to the wall, tiny cartoon-style pictures on strips of adding-machine tape, or pictures drawn on paper plates. You may want to try a "pass it on" picture, in which each child draws something, then turns it over to another child, and so forth, until the picture is complete. Arranging bits of paper into a unified design offers children another opportunity to explore with paper. Generally speaking, preschoolers will tend to use larger pieces of paper, while primary grade children will have developed the skill and patience to work with smaller, mosaic-like pieces.

**2.** *Printmaking.* Preschool children can make simple prints by dipping objects (a bolt, the heel from an old shoe, a plastic cap, Styrofoam shapes) into thin tempera paint and stamping them onto paper. Primary grade children can create stamps or gift wrap or monograms by cutting and gluing pieces of Styrofoam or rubber into interesting shapes and using a stamp pad or sponge moistened with tempera. Even very young children can create "marble track pictures." Get an empty box and put one sheet of construction paper in the bottom. The child drops a marble dunked in tempera paint inside the box and gently rolls it around until the pattern looks pleasing. Children can do crayon rubbing prints by placing a leaf under a sheet of paper and rubbing it with a crayon. Kindergarten or primary grade children can create splatter prints by taping an item to a sheet of paper and dragging a toothbrush dipped in paint over a piece of screen in front of it to create an outline.

**3.** *Local Art.* Use your community resources to give children experiences with art exhibits. In addition to art museums, art exhibits can be seen at shopping malls, colleges, banks and brokerage houses, and many other public buildings. One local chamber of commerce used elementary school children's winter scenes to enhance their holiday luncheon. The framed pieces were then transferred to a nearby mall where everyone in the community could appreciate the children's winter art for the entire month.

**4.** *Paper Sculpture.* In three-dimensional art with paper, children can experiment with glue and paper and learn simple paper folding (origami). Young children might create hats out of paper. Older children can learn some basic paper sculpture techniques, browse through books that illustrate paper sculpture, and watch a person who knows origami demonstrate these skills.

## Sculpture and Pottery

Modeling materials such as clay or play dough are standard items in schools because they introduce children to the basics of sculpting and pottery design. Because these materials are flexible, pliable, and open-ended, they also enable children to "start again" as they create and recreate using the same material.

**1.** *Clay.* If possible, give children the experience of using commercially marketed clay, seeing a pottery wheel in use, or seeing how clay items are fired in a kiln. Often these experiences can be arranged in a high school or college art department or at a commercial crafts store. For more suggestions on using clay, see Koster (1999).

**2.** *Wood Sculptures.* Children can use scraps of wood, white glue, and a hammer and nails to create three-dimensional wood sculptures. These unified, balanced designs can be fixed (stabiles) or movable (mobiles). Encourage children's inventiveness by adding other materials such as tongue depressors, cotton swabs, toothpicks, popsicle sticks, or milled wooden wheels that can be affixed with one nail and are available from early childhood art supply companies.

## Fabric

Textiles include such things as sewing, dyeing fabrics, and weaving.

**1.** *Sewing.* Even very young preschoolers can begin sewing with plastic needles threaded with yarn if the material being stitched is easy to work with. Squares of burlap or felt with holes punched in it are good materials for early experiences with sewing. Most first graders can stitch various designs on heavy cloth with yarn and work together to create a wall hanging or individually to create a bookmark. With adult supervision, second and third graders can design simple stuffed toy pillows, first on paper, then on fabric. After an adult volunteer stitches the outline on a sewing machine, the children can stuff the toy and stitch the opening closed.

**2.** *Dyeing.* To give children experiences in dyeing fabric through the ancient art of color resist, follow this procedure:

*Paste Batik*

Mix in a blender:
1/2 cup flour
1/2 cup water
2 teaspoons alum

Pour the mixture into squeeze bottles (discarded plastic shampoo or squeeze mustard bottles work well). Tape pieces (8″ × 10″) of an old white sheet to corrugated cardboard and let children "draw" pictures using the squeeze bottles. Paint the fabric with food dye or watercolors and let it dry. Remove the paste mixture by rubbing. All areas covered by the paste remain white.

**3.** *Weaving.* After children have mastered the under-over aspect of weaving with strips of paper, they can begin weaving with cloth or yarn. Pieces of heavy yarn or string tied to a frame of popsicle sticks can serve as the loom. Plastic rings from a six-pack of soft drink cans can be joined together with yarn, twist ties, or pieces of pipe cleaners. When connected together in this way and used by the class as the frame for weaving strips of cloth, these recycled materials become a wall hanging.

## INTEGRATING ART INTO THE SUBJECT AREAS

### Media and Technology

When children draw on blank slides and then show them on the projector, put on a light show, create puppets and a stage to perform a play, use film, or create imaginative pictures at the computer, they are exploring the media/technology aspect of art.

Miss Karen's class of 5-year-olds created peep-face boards for their improvised versions of favorite folktales. The teacher used heavy corrugated cardboard cut large enough to cover the children. She measured and cut out circular holes for the children to put their faces and hands through. The children painted the boards to represent the characters and used them to enact "Little Red Riding Hood," "The Three Bears," and "The Three Little Pigs."

Hutinger (1997) describes a project that enabled children with severe and multiple disabilities to create pictures on the computer and print a hard copy of their drawings using a color printer. Software such as *Kid Pix, HyperStudio,* and *EA\* Kids Art* Center was augmented with special switches and keyboards to make these programs accessible to children with special needs.

### Mathematics and Science

Mr. Kasatonov's third grade participated in their home state's "Adopt a Highway" program. The goal of the project was for groups of children to assume responsibility for keeping a small portion of the median strip on a highway beautiful

*Integrating art experiences into the subject areas enhances learning of both.*

by planting flowers and keeping it clean. Before the children decided how to fulfill this responsibility, Mr. Kasatonov took the class on a field trip where they picked wild-flowers and used materials from the Agricultural Extension office to label, classify, and learn about them. In art class, the children created vases to display the flowers. Afterward, they used reference materials to find out which of the flowers were the most colorful, long blooming, disease resistant, and heat tolerant and then tabulated their findings on a chart. The students searched for the best hybrid in seed catalogs, then did some test plantings of seeds from different companies in a flower bed in front of the school and graphed the results. Children also used art to create cross-sections of plants, labeled diagrams, and a web of their entire project that was posted in the hallway. For more on the links between visual imagery, mathematics, science, and critical thinking skills, see Stix (1995) and McCoubrey (1994).

As a culmination to their study and classification of rocks, Ms. Lovell invited a man who makes jewelry out of semiprecious stones to bring his rock-polishing equipment to her kindergarten class. The children had been taught how to find small stones with quartz in them, which they could put into the polishing drum. In this way, the children had an opportunity to appreciate natural beauty. Similarly, the teacher who shares picture books about colors, such as *Mouse Paint* (Walsh, 1989), *Colors and Things* (Hoban, 1989), or *Color Zoo* (Ehlert, 1989), and then invites children to go in search of these colors in nature on a "color walk" is linking art with science. Other activities to teach elements and principles of design include those listed in Figure 3.10.

| | **Elements of Design** |
|---|---|
| **Line** | *Preschool*—Use an overhead projector to illustrate basic types of lines: fat/thin, straight/curvy, zigzag, wavy. Let children experiment with paintbrushes of various widths and markers with different point styles (e.g., chisel point, fine point) to create different lines. |
| | *Primary*—Use calligraphy markers with special tips (e.g., double, triple, thick, and thin) to identify different types of lines; invite children to use the markers to create signs, cards, and bulletin boards. Use cartoon characters to illustrate how a few lines (e.g., mouth, eyebrows) can change facial expression. |
| **Color** | *Preschool*—Use Easter egg dye or food coloring to identify and match primary colors. |
| | *Primary*—Mix white tempera paint with colors to form pastels; mix black with colors to darken them. Create a secondary colors wheel through experimentation with color mixing. Use paint samples to arrange primary and secondary colors by hues. |
| **Shape** | *Preschool*—Identify basic shapes (circle, square, rectangle, triangle, diamond), read several picture books about shapes (e.g., *Color Farm* [Ehlert, 1990]), and search for examples of those shapes in the environment (e.g., the top of a drum is a circle, a box is a square or rectangle, a sandwich turned sideways and cut diagonally is a diamond and two triangles). |
| | *Primary*—Help children to discover the properties of less-familiar shapes (e.g., using lengths of yarn to create polygons or blocks to create trapezoids). Differentiate between one-dimensional and three-dimensional shapes (e.g., cylinders, pyramids). |
| **Space** | *Preschool*—Provide flexible materials, such as collage, and encourage children to experiment before deciding upon a use of space. Give children real experiences in organizing space, such as planning a new arrangement of the housekeeping area on the chalkboard, then rearranging the furniture. |
| | *Primary*—Invite children to analyze the works of their favorite picture book illustrators in terms of the use of space. Have children categorize the techniques (e.g., words and illustrations on facing pages; illustrations at the top, words at the bottom; words and illustrations interspersed all over the page). |
| **Texture** | *Preschool*—Use real objects, such as the vegetables to be used in cooking or material scraps from an upholsterer, and invite children to describe the textures of each. Experiment with ways of altering the texture of art materials (e.g., adding sawdust to clay, daubing paint on instead of spreading it on). |
| | *Primary*—Examine the texture of artwork at a museum, in a gallery, or in a schoolwide display of student artwork. Invite children to create a work of art with textural interest. |

*(continued)*

**Figure 3.10**  Activities to Extend Children's Experiences with Design

*Source:* Based upon the Department of Defense Dependents Schools (DODDS) Visual Arts Program Guidelines, Scope and Sequence for Kindergarten—2nd grade (ERIC Document Reproduction Service No. ED 291 641).

| **Principles of Design** | |
|---|---|
| **Emphasis** | *Preschool*—Use several works of art with a clear focal point and ask children, "Where does your eye go first?" |
| | *Primary*—Ask children to analyze the use of the two-page spread in picture books. How is it used to emphasize something important to the story? Invite children to create original picture books that have a clear emphasis. |
| **Rhythm** | *Preschool*—Use unit blocks or plastic beads to develop the concept of a repeated design. |
| | *Primary*—Using a microcomputer, invite each child to create a repeated design; children can use their vocabularies of art to describe each one. Using a wallpaper catalog and/or samples, evaluate the rhythm of the designs and compare how often the patterns are repeated. |
| **Balance** | *Preschool*—Use felt shapes on the flannel board to illustrate dramatically the concept of balance in design. Begin with all of the figures piled up at one end, then invite children to come up and create more visually appealing arrangements. |
| | *Primary*—Develop the concept of symmetry through the use of paper shapes with identical sides cut from folded paper. Use catalogs and magazines to locate fashions and home-decorating ideas that illustrate symmetrical and asymmetrical arrangements. Invite children to find examples of balanced designs at home, in books, in storefront displays, and in architecture. |
| **Contrast** | *Preschool*—Use photo negatives and the contrast button on the black and white setting of a television set or computer monitor to illustrate the concept of contrast. Make high-contrast pictures using black, white, and gray. |
| | *Primary*—Present children with several art prints and ask them to categorize them into one of five high-contrast groups: works that use light and dark dramatically, works that use contrasting sizes, works that use contrasting shapes, works that contrast textures, and works that contrast colors. Challenge children to create a high-contrast picture, sculpture, pottery, or fabric. |
| **Proportion** | *Preschool*—Use the familiar folktales "The Three Bears" and "The Three Billy Goats Gruff" to develop the concept of relative sizes. |
| | *Primary*—Create illustrated books of comparisons (e.g., big, bigger, biggest); look at grocery store products, such as eggs or laundry detergents, for words to describe sizes. |

**Figure 3.10**   *(Continued)*

## Language, Literacy, and Art

When children ages 5 to 9 were interviewed about the connection between their drawing and writing, their responses fell into four basic categories. The children used drawings (1) as objects to label, (2) as catalysts for generating ideas, (3) as ways of making the abstract concrete, and (4) as aids to their thinking (DuCharme, 1991). Many young children who are drawing representationally use narrative art, pictures that tell a story. Sometimes their storytelling depends entirely on the pictures; sometimes the pictures are combined with captions or complete written stories. Five-year-old Isabell explained the advantage of drawing over writing this way: "I'll draw you what I would write, but drawing is funner." Even before children are writing alphabetically, teachers can develop the concept of pictures accompanied by print—squiggles, letterlike forms, or letters and numbers that the child happens to know. An activity that is very appropriate for linking art with literacy is creating a web for a work of art. At the center of the web might be a print or photograph of the work. Radiating out from the center might be categories such as works of similar type (e.g., other sculptures), works with a similar subject or theme (e.g., animals), works by the same artist (e.g., Van Gogh), works of similar style (e.g., picture books that use collage), and so forth. In this way, children are using both the skills of literacy with print and their visual literacy skills.

## Social Studies, Health, and Nutrition

In Mrs. Browne's community, a young woman teaches classes on making stained glass. Mrs. Browne prepared the children for her visit by going on a "stained glass tour" through an area of town with several churches and old homes. They also looked at some smaller examples of stained glass supplied by the craftsperson, including suncatchers, trinket boxes, and picture frames. When the craftsperson visited the class, she brought a small window she was repairing for a local homeowner, demonstrated the process of putting together the pieces of glass, and talked about the safety measures necessary when working with the material. Other opportunities to see art being produced in the community might include a visit to a potter's studio to see what pottery looks like at various stages in its production, watching a Native American crafting jewelry, observing a weaver spinning yarn into cloth, and interviewing a craftsperson who makes musical instruments.

Mrs. Bleakney's first-grade children were studying Native Americans. After she shared several books about totem poles, the children became fascinated by the concept of a totem pole telling a story. They asked the local ice cream store to save large cardboard containers and used them as the base for their totem pole. The children studied a collection of pictures about totem poles provided by the librarian and then used paper, cardboard, paint, and fabric scraps to produce a simulated totem pole.

## PRACTICAL APPLICATIONS FOR YOUR CLASSROOM

There are several important variables that affect children's artistic expression, including (Henkes, 1989):

- Prior experience with art materials. Do children have access to materials and art tools? Is the range, supply, or quality of materials limited?
- Cultural opportunities. Do children have the opportunity to see various types of art in their environment? For instance, do they visit studios or museums, examine different types of architecture, or appreciate the folk art traditions of their culture and other cultures?
- Family discipline. How do parents react to the child's artistic efforts? Is a child severely punished for drawing on the wall, for instance? Are boys actively discouraged from artistic pursuits?
- Visual skills, mental capacity, and motor coordination. What strengths and abilities does the child bring to the art activity? Can the activity be adapted to challenges or the special strengths of the child?

### *Experiences to Support Cultural and Ethnic Diversity*

The visual arts support multicultural education by helping children understand (1) the relevance and significance of art in human experience, (2) the perspectives posed by people of various backgrounds, (3) the commonality and diversity of humankind, and (4) the child's personal power as a creator of and responder to art, as well as the responsibilities that come with that power (Delacruz, 1995).

As the preceding points illustrate, communication and acceptance are linked to the child's creative expression (Henkes, 1989). In order for all children to flourish as artists themselves, they must communicate about a wide range of artistic styles and forms, see those styles and forms accepted by others, freely experiment with art media, and learn to accept one another's art. Art offers a way of communicating and accepting other cultures. Mexican piñatas, African masks, or Ukrainian decorated eggs—each of these artifacts gives children insight into the history, values, and aesthetic sensibilities of others.

It has been rightly said that the language of art is universal. Art gives children an authentic, satisfying form of self-expression. The newly immigrated child with limited English proficiency can express ideas, thoughts, and feelings nonverbally through paper, sculpture, pottery, and fabric. One way to support art activities at home is through the use of an ARTtache as described by Hutinger (1997). These were take-home bags of expressive art materials accompanied by notes inviting families to work with their children on projects at home that could then be brought to school and shared. Also included in the ARTtache kits were a comment page for children to draw or write about what they liked best and a family questionnaire to evaluate the kits.

## *Experiences to Support Inclusion*

Creative teachers adapt art activities to accommodate children with physical disabilities. It might mean a "low-tech" solution, such as putting clay on a wheelchair tray rather than at the table, or giving a child larger or longer paintbrush handles or crayons that can be held in the palm of the hand. It could also mean a high-tech solution such as equipping a computer software program with a TouchWindow, a Big Red switch, or kidDraw so that children with physical limitations can operate the program. In every case, the key is sensitivity to the child, knowledge about the child's abilities, and creative problem-solving techniques. Art experiences should help all children to see that everyone is differently abled. The visually impaired child, for example, may be even more adept than peers at discerning different textures through touch alone.

All children need the challenge and excitement of working with new art media. It is thrilling to draw with brand-new, sharply pointed, soft-leaded colored pencils or to draw and color a picture with watercolor markers that include unusual colors such as silver or gold. Unusual papers are appealing too. Paper that is heavy, embossed, glossy, or foil, such as that used in greeting cards and wrapping paper, can often be recycled for a lasting supply of high-quality material. Many children do not have access to art materials (other than crayons and paper) at home. Materials such as oil pastels, colored chalk, washable acrylic paints, and clay are generally unavailable because parents cannot afford them, do not recognize their value, or are

*Skillful teachers adapt art activities to children's developmental levels. These children with Down syndrome are preparing crafts for a parade.*

concerned about the mess. Even fewer children have access at home to artist's tools such as an easel, woodworking tools, or crafts materials. Real sculptors, for example, do not usually rely exclusively on their hands for making clay sculptures. Consider supplying some of the real tools used by artists, demonstrate how they are used with clay, and make them available to children. Figure 3.11 lists some of the adaptations that need to be made in order for young children with special needs to participate more fully in the arts.

## Adaptations for Individual Learners

Research on young gifted children suggests that they may (1) strive for realistic portrayals, many details, and complete accuracy in what they represent, (2) become intensely interested in particular topics not routinely of interest to peers (e.g., meteors, sea creatures), (3) go beyond what is immediately observable and explore the subject in greater depth (e.g., making a cross-section drawing of the *Titanic*), (4) display exceptional sensitivity to emotion and ways of expressing it (e.g., choose to explore the subtleties and complexities of humor), or (5) produce works of visual art that display types of perception not commonly found in young children's work (e.g., light and shade, near/far perspective) and that require advanced development in the physical domain (Harrison, 1999). A challenging activity for primary grade children is using art as a basis for practicing their emerging research skills. A child with an interest in wood carving could, for instance, study different types of wood carvings: those from various regions of the United States, those from different types of wood (e.g., ebony, teak, mahogany), and those from different historical periods.

For children who are struggling with academic subjects, art can become a refuge where competition is minimized and self-esteem is built. Year after year, the majority of children report that art is one of their favorite subjects in school. It is not difficult to understand why when we consider how ways of teaching art in elementary school differ from traditional ways of teaching subjects geared to children's verbal and mathematical intelligences. In art, children have a greater opportunity to make meaningful choices, to work at their own pace, to spontaneously seek new challenges. There is no right or wrong answer, but there is satisfaction in work well done and the chance to develop skill in self-evaluation. Through art, children learn that pride in craft is essential, that details are important (Eisner, 1992).

Every child, at one time or another, must deal with angry feelings. Through art, that child can hammer at the woodworking bench or pound clay into a satisfying shape and turn that energy to creative rather than destructive ends. In this way, art offers a medium for expressing powerful emotions and coping with a sometimes confusing or hostile environment. That outlet is particularly important for children with special needs.

Eisner (1976) has defined the personal inclinations for the arts as those abilities that enable us to "play with images, ideas and feelings, to be able to recognize and construct the multiple meanings of events, to perceive and conceive of things from various perspectives, to be able to be a clown, a dreamer, a taker of risks" (p. vii). As early childhood educators, we need to build these attributes in ourselves, in our colleagues, and, most importantly, in our students.

**Figure 3.11**
Making Art Activities
Accessible to Young
Children with Special
Needs

**Children with Learning Disabilities or Attentional Difficulties**
Provide encouragement.

Establish and maintain routines.

Give directions one step at a time.

Provide quiet areas for children who are easily distracted.

Offer a choice of media for exploring techniques or skills.

Help the child deal with frustration productively.

Let the child work with a partner but do not let the partner do the work for the child.

**Children with Orthopedic (Physical) Impairments**
Make materials easily accessible.

Use low-tech adaptive devices to increase independence (e.g., rubber grip for paintbrush).

Use high-tech adaptive devices as available and appropriate (e.g., special foot switch for a computer).

Ask if the child needs help before giving it.

Ensure that facilities do not pose obstacles to wheelchairs, crutches, or other equipment.

Allow more time for movement.

**Children with Emotional Disabilities**
Provide lessons that are structured yet flexible.

Plan activities that enable the child to capitalize on positive energy.

Promote confidence by building on small successes.

Keep only those supplies that are necessary within reach.

Encourage the child to express emotions in socially appropriate ways.

Defend each child's right to personal space where the student feels safe and protected.

Establish a few simple rules and expectations and follow them consistently.

**Children with Visual Impairments**
Help children to achieve greater mobility by standing next to and a little ahead of the child. Bend your arm at the elbow and ask the child to place his or her hand on your forearm. Walk slowly, giving verbal cues and advance warnings about any obstacles.

Teach aides and peers the procedure above.

Get in the habit of identifying yourself and letting the child know you are talking to him or her.

Announce that you are leaving before you walk away.

*(continued)*

*Source:* Adapted from: Pappalardo, R. G. (1990).

**Figure 3.11**
*(Continued)*

**Children with Visual Impairments, *(continued)***

Speak in a normal tone of voice.

Invite children to touch objects as well as to listen to very detailed, concrete description.

When describing sizes, relate it to something with which the child is very familiar (e.g., "It's about as tall as your chair").

**Children with Hearing Impairments**

Avoid changing your message suddenly.

If the child reads lips, make sure he or she can see and avoid turning away or covering your mouth.

Use simple, basic language, speaking clearly and at an even pace.

Emphasize nonverbal communication, such as facial expressions and gestures, to communicate your thoughts.

Keep paper and pencil handy to quickly sketch a picture or write a word that might help the child to understand.

If the child speaks, listen carefully and strive to get the gist of the message. If you cannot understand the child, ask him or her to repeat it slowly. If there is a chance that the group may not understand, repeat what the child said.

Try to avoid coming up suddenly or making quick movements. You may startle the child or make him or her dizzy.

Give the child ample opportunity to view and handle objects before explaining. Remember that many children with hearing impairments cannot listen and look at the object at the same time because they need to watch a person talking.

**Children with Mental Retardation**

Keep directions simple, break the task into sequential steps, demonstrate each task.

Offer frequent praise and encouragement.

Be patient and allow the child extra time to observe and think.

Repeat directions and identify all materials verbally.

Deal in concrete ideas and familiar terminology.

Use multisensory approaches.

Use the child's ability range as a guide in planning lessons rather than basing them on chronological age.

When giving verbal instructions, establish eye contact first.

Guide a child through the motions of the task.

Encourage cooperation among students.

## CHAPTER SUMMARY

1. In order for a classroom activity to qualify as art, it must value process over product, emphasize originality rather than conformity, allow children to retain ownership of their work, and develop an appreciation of mixtures and balances.

2. Understanding children's art depends upon an appreciation of the child as artist, a knowledge of the developmental sequence in children's art, an understanding of the principles of art education, and a recognition of the many contributions art makes to children's overall development.

3. In a quality art program, children not only learn to become artists but also learn to appreciate the artwork of others.

4. To support the goals of art education, teachers should locate quality art and art reproductions from many sources and discuss these works skillfully with children. Critical issues in art programs for young children include health and safety considerations as well as the selection, presentation, evaluation, storage, and display of art and art materials.

5. Teachers in child-centered classrooms believe that quality art experiences with a variety of materials build every child's artistic sensibilities and skills.

6. Art is a true curricular basic, a way of knowing that is just as valuable in the real world as other types of know-how.

7. Art must be integrated into different subject areas so that it receives the attention that it merits.

## *EXPANDING YOUR THINKING ABOUT ART*

### *Discuss: Supporting Children's Art*

1. A friend or relative asks you how to tell if his or her child is artistic. How would you respond, based upon what you have read in this chapter?

2. Reread the quotations that introduced this chapter. How has your understanding of them been enriched?

3. Suppose that a parent volunteers to work in your classroom and you observe the parent with his or her hand on top of a child's hand and paintbrush, forcibly showing the child how to paint a flower. After the children leave, the parent tells you that the child was rude and unappreciative. How would you respond?

4. A colleague criticizes you for letting your primary grade children make things out of clay, saying, "I leave that sort of thing to the art teacher." How would you articulate your position on this issue?

## Interview: Teachers' Beliefs About Child-Initiated Art Activities

Arrange to interview a teacher of young children about the art experiences he or she provides for children. Write down the teacher's response to each of the following questions:

1. Do you see yourself as being responsible for children's growth in art? Why or why not?

2. How did your teacher education program prepare you for teaching art? How have you extended your learning about art?

3. What kinds of art experiences do you provide for children? Could you describe an activity that was particularly successful?

4. How do you feel about your own artistic ability? How have these beliefs about yourself influenced your ideas about children's art?

5. Was there ever a child in your class who you considered to be especially artistic? Why did this child impress you with his or her artistic ability?

## Write to Learn: Building Your Arts Background

If a classmate mentions that her friend is an art major, does your mind immediately jump to a stereotype? Far too often, we forget that "the artist, no less than the scientist, is the observer/thinker/believer" (Engel, 1983, p. 8). Write in response to one or more of the following questions:

1. What biases do I have about art and artists?

2. How do I respond to the art I see in my campus or community environment, for instance?

3. How would I describe my background in art?

4. Have I taken a course in art appreciation? Read about famous artists and their works? Visited museums, craft shows, galleries, or other types of art exhibits? What can I do to increase my knowledge of art and use my knowledge to teach more effectively?

## REFERENCES

Amann, J. (1993). *Theme teaching with great visual resources: How to involve and educate students using large, high-quality, low-cost art reproductions.* Rosemont, NJ: Modern Learning Press.

Booth, E. (1998). *The everyday work of art: How artistic experience can transform your life.* Naperville, IL: Source Books.

Bowker, J. E., & Sawyers, J. K. (1988). Influence of exposure on preschoolers' art preferences. *Early Childhood Research Quarterly, 3,* 107–115.

Clemens, S. G. (1991). Art in the classroom: Making every day special. *Young Children, 46*(2), 4–11.

Cohen, E. P., & Gainer, R. S. (1995). *Art: Another language for learning* (3rd ed.). Portsmouth, NH: Heinemann.

Cole, E., & Schaefer, C. (1990). Can young children be art critics? *Young Children, 45*(2), 33–38.

Davis, J., & Gardner, H. (1992). The cognitive revolution: Consequences for the understanding and education of the child as artist. In B. Reimer & R. A. Smith (Eds.), *The arts, education, and aesthetic knowing* (pp. 92–123). Chicago: University of Chicago Press.

Delacruz, E. M. (1995). Multiculturalism and the tender years: Big and little questions. In C. M. Thompson (Ed.). *The visual arts and early childhood learning* (pp. 101–106). Reston, VA: National Art Education Association.

Dixon, G., & Chalmers, F. G. (1990). The expressive arts in education. *Childhood Education, 67*(1), 12–17.

DuCharme, C. C. (1991, April). *The role of drawing in the writing processes of primary grade children.* Paper presented at the Association for Childhood Education International Study Conference, San Diego, CA.

Dunn, P. (1995). *Creating curriculum in art.* Reston, VA: National Art Education Association.

Eisner, E. (1976). *The arts, human development and education.* Berkeley, CA: McCuthen.

Eisner, E. (1992). The misunderstood role of the arts in human development. *Phi Delta Kappan, 73*(8), 591–595.

Engel, M. (1983). Art and the mind. *Art Education, 36*(2), 6–8.

Feeney, S., Christensen, D., & Moravcik, E. (Eds.). (1991). *Who am I in the lives of children?* Upper Saddle River, NJ: Merrill-Prentice Hall.

Gaitskell, C. D., Hurwitz, A., & Day, M. (1982). *Children and their art: Methods for the elementary school* (4th ed.). Dubuque, IA: Brown.

Gardner, H. (1993). *Frames of mind: The theory of multiple intelligences* (10th anniversary edition). New York: Basic Books.

Harrison, C. (1999). Visual representation of the young gifted child. *Roeper Review, 21*(3), 189–195.

Heberholz, B. (1974). *Early childhood art.* Dubuque, IA: Brown.

Henkes, R. (1989). The child's artistic expression. *Early Child Development and Care, 47,* 165–176.

Hutinger, P. L. (1997). *The Expressive Arts Project: A final report.* Macomb, IL. (ERIC Document Reproduction Service No. ED 415 646)

Jalongo, M. R., & Stamp, L. N. (1997). *The arts in children's lives: Aesthetic experiences in early childhood education.* Boston: Allyn & Bacon.

Jefferson, B. (1963). *Teaching art to children: The values of creative expression.* Boston: Allyn & Bacon.

Kellogg, R. (1979). *Children's drawings/children's minds.* New York: Avon.

Kiefer, B. (1994). *The potential of picturebooks: From visual literacy to aesthetic understanding.* Englewood Cliffs, NJ: Prentice Hall.

Kindler, A. M. (Ed.). (1997). *Child development in art.* Reston, VA: National Art Education Association.

Koster, J. B. (1999). Clay for little fingers. *Young Children, 52*(5), 18–22.

London, P. (Ed.). (1994). *Exemplary art education curricula: A guide to guides.* Reston, VA: National Art Education Association.

McCoubrey, S. (1994). *Art and thinking skills.* Vancouver, British Columbia. (ERIC Document Reproduction Service Number ED 404 221)

Miller, E. (1994). Letting talent flow: How schools can promote learning for the sheer love of it. *The Harvard Education Letter, 10*(2), 1–3, 8.

National Art Education Association. (1999). *Purposes, principles, and standards for school art programs.* Reston, VA: Author.

Nyman, A. L., & Jenkins, A. M. (Eds.). (1999). *Issues and approaches to art for students with special needs.* Reston, VA: National Art Education Association.

Pappalardo, R. G. (1990). Curricular issues: The visual arts and students with disabilities. In A. L. Nyman & A. J. Jenkins (Eds.), *Issues and approaches for art students with special needs* (pp. 42–54) Reston, VA: National Art Education Association.

President's Committee on the Arts and the Humanities (1996). *Eloquent evidence: Arts at the core of learning.* Washington, DC: National Endowment for the Arts.

Qualley, C. (1986). *Safety in the art room.* Worcester, MA: Davis Publications.

Rankin, B. (1995, February). Displaying children's work. *Scholastic Early Childhood Today,* 34–35.

Rasmussen, K. (1998). Arts education: A cornerstone of basic education. *ASCD Curriculum Update,* Spring, 1–3, 6–7.

Rollins, J. (Committee Chair). (1994). *The national visual arts standards.* Reston, VA: National Art Education Association.

Rowe, G. (1987). *Guiding young artists: Curriculum ideas for teachers.* Portsmouth, NH: Heinemann.

Schirrmacher, R. (1988). *Art and creative development for young children.* Albany, NY: Delmar.

Seefeldt, C. (1995). Art—Serious work. *Young Children, 50*(3), 39–45.

Smith, N. R. (1982). The visual arts in early childhood education: Development and the creation of meaning. In B. Spodek (Ed.), *Handbook of research in early childhood education* (pp. 87–106). New York: Free Press.

Smith, N. & The Drawing Study Group (1997). *Observation drawing with children.* New York: Teachers College Press.

Smith, R. A. (1995). *Excellence II: The continuing quest in art education.* Reston, VA: National Art Education Association.

Spodek, B. (1993). Selecting activities in the arts for early childhood education. *Arts Education Policy Review, 94*(6), 11–18.

State of Florida Department of State. (1990). *Children and the arts: A sourcebook of experiences for Florida's pre-kindergarten early intervention program.* Gainesville, FL: Author. (ERIC Document Reproduction Service No. ED 330 454)

Stephens, D. (1994). Learning what art means. *Language Arts, 71,* 35–37.

Stix, A. (1995). *The link between art and mathematics.* (ERIC Document Reproduction Service No. ED 398 170)

Szyba, C. M. (1999). Why do some teachers resist offering appropriate, open-ended art activities for young children? *Young Children, 54*(1), 14–20.

Thompson, C. (Ed.). (1995). *The visual arts and early childhood learning.* Reston, VA: National Art Education Association.

Varnon, D. (1997). Enriching remedial programs with the arts. *Reading and Writing Quarterly, 13*(4), 325–332.

Whitehead, A. N. (1967). In G. Selden (compiler), *The Great Quotations.* New York: Pocket Books.

Wright, S. (1997). Learning how to learn: The arts as core in an emergent curriculum. *Childhood Education, 73*(6), 361–365.

## *Children's Books*

Briggs, R. (1978). *The snowman.* New York: Random House.

Carle, E. (1969). *The very hungry caterpillar.* New York: Harper Collins/World.

Crews, D. (1978). *Freight train.* New York: Greenwillow.

Dillon, L., & Dillon, D. (1983). *Why mosquitoes buzz in people's ears: A West African tale.* New York: Puffin.

Dorros, A. (1995). *Abuela.* New York: Dutton.

Ehlert, L. (1989). *Color zoo.* New York: Harper/Lippincott.

Flournoy, V. (1985). *The patchwork quilt.* New York: Dial.

Gackenbach, D. (1977). *Harry and the terrible whatzit.* New York: Seabury.

Haley, G. E. (1988). *A story, a story.* New York: Simon & Schuster.

Hall, D., & Cooney, B. (1984). *Ox-cart man.* New York: Live Oak Media.

Hawkins, C., & Hawkins, J. (1984). *Boo! Who?* New York: Holt.

Hendershot, J. (1987). *In coal country.* New York: Knopf.

Hoban, T. (1989). *Colors and things.* New York: Greenwillow.

Hoffman, M. (1991). *Amazing Grace.* New York: Dial.

Hutchins, P. (1985). *The very worst monster.* New York: Greenwillow.

Johnston, T. (1984). *The quilt story.* New York: Putnam.

Jonas, A. (1989). *The quilt.* New York: Greenwillow.

Keats, E. J. (1962). *The snowy day.* New York: Viking.

Mahy, M., & McCarthy, P. (1993). *Seventeen kings and forty-two elephants.* New York: Dutton.

Marzollo, J. (1994). *I spy: A book of picture riddles.* New York: Scholastic.

Mayer, M. (1968). *There's a nightmare in my closet.* New York: Dial.

Mayer, M. (1977). *Frog goes to dinner.* New York: Dial.

Mills, L. (1991). *The rag coat.* Boston: Little, Brown.

Oppenheim, J., & Reid, B. (1988). *Have you seen birds?* New York: Scholastic.

Pilkey, D. (1993). *Dogzilla.* San Diego: Harcourt Brace.

Polacco, P. (1988). *The keeping quilt.* New York: Simon & Schuster.

Ringgold, F. (1991). *Tar beach.* New York: Scholastic.

Say, A. (1993). *Grandfather's journey.* Boston: Houghton Mifflin.

Schotter, R., & Sewall, M. (1988). *Captain Snap and the children of Vinegar Lane.* New York: Orchard.

Sendak, M. (1963). *Where the wild things are.* New York: Harper.

Shulevitz, U. (1988). *Dawn.* New York: Farrar, Straus & Giroux.

Van Allsburg, C. (1988). *Two bad ants.* Boston: Houghton Mifflin.

Walsh, E. S. (1989). *Mouse paint.* San Diego, CA: Harcourt Brace Jovanovich.

Williams, S. (1992). *I went walking.* San Diego, CA: Harcourt Brace.

Wolff, A. (1984). *A year of birds.* New York: Dodd.

Young, E. (1992). *Seven blind mice.* New York: Putnam.

Zelinksy, P. O. (1986). *Rumplestiltskin.*

# Chapter 4

## Music and Movement in the Early Childhood Curriculum

*"We now have sufficient research yielding a new view of music in the schools. At the most basic level, music has deep biological roots. Thus, infants have great competency in the perceptual and cognitive processing of fundamental components of music. Parents and caregivers instinctively communicate with infants in a musical fashion because, although infants don't understand words, melodic stimulation always gets their attention. Young children clearly enjoy music, engaging in musical behavior spontaneously. In addition, the human brain contains identifiable musical building blocks. "*

Norman M. Weinberger, 1998, p. 3

*"Dance in early childhood provides concrete experiences in which children become more aware of the movement they see in their world, try it on for themselves, and notice how it feels."*

Susan W. Stinson, 1990, p. 35

# TEACHERS' REFLECTIONS ON MUSIC AND MOVEMENT

### Preservice Teachers

"I realize now that music is an important factor in a child's life. Music can provide an emotional release. Children learn so much through music! It opens their imaginations and creativity. As a result, music allows children to express themselves in their own ways."

"To be honest, when I first scheduled this class I wasn't really sure that it would be beneficial. Now I think it was very beneficial. It's not that my ideas have changed that much, but now I feel that I have a basis for what I believe and I will feel more secure in explaining to parents and administrators why I provide music and movement activities."

### Inservice Teachers

"Until I learned more about music for young children, I relied almost exclusively on a few well-known (and well-worn) records. In comparison to the recordings recommended in this chapter, the music I had been using sounded dull and ordinary. I had no idea that there was so much variety in music. You haven't really enjoyed 'The Hokey Pokey' until you've heard Sharon, Lois, and Bram's rock version and compared it to Michael Doucet's zydeco version! And you have forgotten how 'Skip to My Lou' is supposed to be sung until you've listened to John McCutcheon's lively version!"

"After reading this chapter and contrasting it with what happened in the name of music at the day-care center where I worked last summer, I can see that we were really missing the whole point. We basically used music as a 'cheap filler' or tried to drill children on some skill through music, like 'The Alphabet Song.' Now I see how much more we could have been doing in terms of selecting, presenting, and simply enjoying music together."

## Your Reflections

- How would you characterize your current thoughts about how music and movement activities contribute to children's lives and their overall development?

- What types of musical experiences, artists, and resource materials, both traditional and contemporary, would you choose for young children? Why?

- What concerns do you have about your own abilities to foster young children's creative expression through music and movement?

## Case Study:

### Raphael

When Raphael was a newborn, he could be comforted by nestling against his mother's chest and listening to the sounds of her heartbeat, something that was familiar to him even before birth. By 3 months, he had a favorite song, "Arorro Mi Niño." When his mother sang it, he listened intently. Often, the song helped him settle down to sleep. At 18 months, Raphael bounced delightedly on his father's knee to the rhythms of marching bands during the "Battle of the Bands," a competition among the area high schools. At age 3, he attended nursery school where he could be observed rocking in the wooden boat with friends, inventing nonsense chants, and giggling. Aunt Otilla brought Raphael a set of brightly painted maracas direct from Mexico when he was 4. When Grandma Diaz babysat, they would listen to her folk music records while Raphael sang, danced, and played his maracas. At age 5, Raphael took the maracas to "show and tell," and the teacher invited him to use them while the class sang. Later, Raphael taught the class a song in Spanish, "De Colores." By the time that Raphael was in first grade, he had learned to sing melodiously and enjoyed singing in church. Uncle Jorge invited 7-year-old Raphael to come up on stage and sing along with the band at their cousin's wedding. As a reward for having done so well in second grade, Raphael's father surprised him with a guitar—the one that Uncle Jorge had used as a boy when he first learned how to play.

For Raphael, music is more than listening to prerecorded selections and more than making music—it is a social event: "Musical ability is developed in a relationship, in a succession of relationships—musical self in relation to musical selves" (Bernstein, 1990, p. 401).

## MUSIC, MOVEMENT, AND THE YOUNG CHILD

For centuries, people have used lullabies and a rocking motion to calm a fussy infant or action songs and gentle bouncing to entertain a toddler or preschooler. They operated on the assumption that these activities were good for children based on children's responses—the baby being lulled to sleep, the toddler or preschooler laughing delightedly and asking for more. But contemporary research goes beyond an "art for art's sake" approach, providing extensive study of the many ways that the connections between the cells of the brain, called synapses, are strengthened through use. Evidently, enjoying and participating in music and dance appear to be particularly stimulating to the brain (Gromko & Poorman, 1998).

Look in on any high-quality program from toddler through the primary grades and you will see children chanting, singing, clapping, swinging, tapping, marching, skipping, doing simple dances—all kinds of music and movement activities.

## THEORETICAL AND RESEARCH BASE: WHAT IS MUSIC AND MOVEMENT?

Music has a long history in early childhood education. In 1883, Jean-Jacques Rousseau invented an "everychild" named Emile. When Rousseau wrote about Emile's music education, he recommended that the mother sing simple, interesting, developmentally appropriate songs to make the child's voice accurate, uniform, flexible, and sonorous; to make the child's ear sensitive to meter and harmony. Near the turn of the century, Maria Montessori applied her concept of the prepared environment to the child's music education. She advocated sound exploration activities for children and invented a set of mushroom-shaped bells that helped children to discover musical concepts.

Later in the twentieth century, several music experts designed music programs specifically for young children. Carl Orff, a German music educator, developed creative musicianship by engaging children in spontaneously producing and creating their own music, rhythmic responses, and imaginative actions. Zoltan Kodaly, a Hungarian music educator, promoted musical literacy through a carefully sequenced program of folk music that began with 3-year-olds. Shinichi Suzuki, a Japanese educator, originated a talent education program that taught very young children to play the violin or cello and required extensive parental involvement.

Today's early childhood educator typically takes an eclectic approach to music that draws upon the best features of each tradition. We recognize the importance of early experience as Rousseau did, we prepare a musical environment as Montessori did, we emphasize spontaneity and originality as Orff did, we attend to the developmental levels of children as Kodaly did, and we appreciate the importance of parental involvement as Suzuki did. Even though there are many published music curriculum guides (Andress, 1998; Snyder, 1995), skilled early childhood educators use music throughout the day and incorporate a wide variety of musical experiences, rather than slavishly following a particular program.

In recent years there has been a greater emphasis on music and movement for young children. In large part, this is due to the influence of research on the human brain from the fields of neuroscience and cognitive science. With advanced technology, it is actually possible to determine which areas of the human brain are activated by certain activities. Perhaps you have heard that activity in the right hemisphere of the brain dominates when performing logical, sequential tasks such as mathematics and that the activity in the left hemisphere of the brain tends to dominate when processing language. Thanks to PET (positron emission tomography), we now know that when children are participating in music, scans of the brain's functioning "light up like a Christmas tree" (Parr, Radford, & Snyder, 1998) because many different areas of the brain are activated (Nash, 1997).

You may not have conceived of it this way previously, but music and dance are important ways for children to demonstrate their intelligence. Musical/rhythmic intelligence refers to sensitivity to sounds and patterns of sound that results in the ability to appreciate, participate in, and perform music. Perhaps you have heard about the "Mozart Effect," the contention that playing classical music for babies can increase the brain's capacity by strengthening the connections among neurons. Although more research would be needed to make any such claims, there is evidence to support that musical experiences provide a unique form of cognitive stimulation in the early years (Caulfield, 1999).

Dance is linked with kinesthetic or bodily intelligence. Kinesthetic intelligence refers to the ability to coordinate the body and orchestrate one's physical movements in space and time; it is a physical/spatial/temporal intelligence possessed to a high degree by dancers and athletes. Where young children are concerned, dance is often referred to as creative movement to differentiate it from formal lessons and on-stage performances. To illustrate, consider this observation of Teresa:

*For young children, the connection between movement and understanding is very strong.*

The scene is a spring elementary school concert and Teresa, a 24-month-old, is in the audience. The family members and teachers look on with pride as the children play songs on their instruments. Some adults are snapping pictures or running videotape equipment. Teresa has a very different response. The toddler is standing on a chair so that she can see, and as soon as her brother participates in playing a lively song, she kicks the sandals off her chubby feet and begins to dance. Her body and sundress skirt sway in response to the music. The final song is about a bird, and Teresa moves her arms and hands expressively, like a bird gliding through the air. She is completely unselfconscious in her response even though many adults in the audience are pointing her out and smiling at her reaction to the tunes she has heard her brother practice at home so often. Teresa has not been taught to dance, she simply allows her feelings to be her guide. (Jalongo & Stamp, 1997, pp. 30–31)

For the very young, dance "begins with an awareness of the movement of the body and its creative potential. At this level, students become engaged in body awareness and movement exploration that promote a recognition and appreciation of self and others" (Consortium of National Arts Education Associations, 1994, p. 23). The connection between movement and understanding is so strong that when children are asked to physically rotate their bodies, they are then able to understand the mental concept of rotation (Wohlschlaeger & Wohlschlaeger, 1998).

## Research on Music and Movement

Achilles, E. (1999). Creating music environments in early childhood programs. *Young Children, 54*(1), 21–26.

Caulfield, R. (1999). Mozart effect: Sound beginnings? *Early Childhood Education Journal, 27*(2), 119–122.

Feierabend, J. M., Saunders, T. C., Holahan, J. M., & Getnick, P. E. (1998). Song recognition among preschool-age children: An investigation of words and music. *Journal of Research in Music Education, 46*(3), 351–359.

Gharavi, G. J. (1993). Music skills for preschool teachers: Needs and solutions. *Arts Education Policy Review, 94*(3), 27–30.

Klinger, R., Campbell, P. S., & Goolsby, T. (1998). Approaches to children's song acquisition: Immersion or phrase-by-phrase? *Journal of Research in Music Education, 46*(1), 24–34.

LaFuente, M. J., Grifol, R., Segarra, J., Soriano, J., Gorba, M. A., & Montesinos, A. (1997). Effects of the Firstart method of prenatal stimulation on psychomotor development: The first six months. *Pre- and Peri-Natal Psychology Journal, 11,* 151–162.

Lamb, S. J., & Gregory, A. H. (1993). The relationship between music and reading in beginning readers. *Educational Psychology, 13,* 19–26.

Raushcer, F. H., Shaw, G. L., Levine, L. J., Wright, E. L., Dennis, W. R., & Newcomb, R. L. (1997). Music training causes long-term enhancement of children's spatial-temporal reasoning. *Neurological Research, 19,* 2–8.

### Web Sites

American Music Conference. Music and Early Childhood Development/Research

*http://www.amc-music.com/maecrf.htm*

Azar, B. (1996). Musical studies provide clues to brain functions. *APA Monitor* [on-line]

*http://www.apa.org/monitor/apr96/neural.html* [1996, April]

## THE EDUCATIONAL ROLE OF MUSIC AND MOVEMENT

A child's early experiences with music and movement shape later knowledge, skills, attitudes, and values. We know that music and movement education for young children is most effective when it respects the learning characteristics of young children and has enjoyment as its foundation (see Figure 4.1).

**Figure 4.1**
A Framework of
Beliefs about Young
Children, Music, and
Movement

- All children have potential in music and movement.
- All children bring their own unique interests and abilities to the music and movement learning environment.
- Very young children are capable of developing critical thinking skills through musical ideas and movement activities.
- Children come to early childhood music and movement experiences with diverse backgrounds.
- Children should experience exemplary musical sounds, activities, and materials.
- Young children should not be pressured to perform on stage with an audience.
- Children's music and movement activities should be enjoyable and inaugurate a lifelong appreciation for music and movement.
- Children learn best in safe, pleasant physical and social environments.
- Diverse learning environments and varied opportunities are essential in order to serve the developmental needs of many children.
- Children need effective, enthusiastic adult models.

*Source:* Adapted from Palmer & Sims (1993).

Affirming the value of music in children's lives is important, but it is not enough. Educators also need to understand the basic philosophy of music education. In a democratic society, the goal of teaching music is not to single out those who are gifted in music. Rather, the goal is to maximize the musical abilities of every child. Achieving this purpose involves an understanding of (1) the child musician and the musical experience, (2) musical development theory, and (3) the connection between music and movement.

Do we value children's music only for its imitation of adult musical behaviors, or do we appreciate it in its own right? Identifying young children as musicians should not be based on the expectation that they will demonstrate precocious musical behavior (Fox, 1991) or on the hope that they will become concert pianists, successful rock singers, or ballet prima donnas someday. Rather, the focus should be on music for today and every day, music for everyone.

Too many children's so-called musical experiences are thinly disguised schoolwork. There is drill disguised as music, such as math facts set to music to make practice more palatable. There are ditties that are heavy-handed lessons, such as songs about safety rules. At the other extreme, there are the adult purists who contend that classical/symphonic music is the only music of any value and who try to restrict children's musical experiences to that category alone. Some adults neglect their responsibility for seeking quality children's recordings and simply use whatever is readily available or heavily advertised. All of these approaches are ill conceived and inadvisable. Figure 4.2 highlights the ways that teachers use music effectively. Likewise, when early childhood practitioners think

**Figure 4.2**
How Early
Childhood Teachers
Use Music and
Movement

- To begin the day and greet one another
- To create a warm, positive atmosphere
- To establish a particular mood
- To ease transitions from one activity to another
- To link the arts with other subject areas
- To focus children's attention
- To make special events even more special
- To celebrate diversity
- To establish social solidarity
- To refresh and relax
- To sharpen thinking skills
- To promote creative expression
- To bring the day or an event to a satisfying conclusion

*Source:* Adapted from Hildebrandt (1992).

about children's physical movement, they often take the approach of letting children race around aimlessly to expend surplus energy or, at the other extreme, urge children to perform acrobatic stunts. Figure 4.3 provides recommendations for age-appropriate dance.

## THE EDUCATIONAL VALUE OF MUSIC AND MOVEMENT

Music contributes to the child's total development: psychomotor, perceptual, affective, cognitive, social, cultural, and aesthetic. Specific contributions of music and movement experiences to these areas of development are described below.

**1.** *Psychomotor skills*—Children are using the small muscles of their hands and arms, or fine motor skills, when they strike the keys on a toy xylophone or tap lightly on a tambourine. They are using the large muscles of their bodies when they invent actions to go along with a song or interpret the mood of a musical selection through creative dance. Activities such as these build kinesthetic/bodily intelligence.

**2.** *Perceptual skills*—A baby who recognizes her mother's voice or a 3-year-old who requests a favorite folk song are demonstrating their abilities to perceive music. For the very young child, sensory perceptions of music may be so striking that they do not expect them to be perceived by hearing alone. Rather, the child expects all senses to be involved, so that a teacher might play a note on the piano and realize that a toddler is searching for that note, expecting to see and touch as well as hear it.

---

### Infants

**Music**

Sensitive to *dynamics,* the loudness or softness of a sound; startle at loud sounds and are comforted by soft, rhythmic, melodious sounds (e.g., musical toys, lullabies). Respond to the human voice, especially the primary caregiver's voice; respond in more lively ways to action songs and more subdued ways to lullabies.

**Movement**

Tend to respond to music with the entire body. "Lap babies" will bounce to lively music; babies who are standing may rock side-to-side, sway back and forth, or bounce up and down by flexing their knees.

### Toddlers

**Music**

Discriminate among sounds and may attempt to imitate sound or to approximate pitches; listen to music and respond more enthusiastically to certain songs. Explore sound making with household objects (e.g., hitting a pan with a wooden spoon), musical toys, (e.g., a toy xylophone), or musical instruments; express greater interest in recordings. Can demonstrate knowledge of sounds and music by identifying familiar sounds or instruments played on a tape or outside their view. Experiment with songs and voice and gain some control of the singing voice; occasionally match melody and may join in on certain phrases of familiar songs; sing or hum improvisationally during play.

**Movement**

Use primarily arms and legs and can move in response to the tempo (fast/slow) of a rhythm instrument (e.g., run, walk, "freeze"). Will often "dance" on request while music is playing and show more control over physical responses. Respond well to large and small motor musical activities that emphasize repetition and rhyme—simple fingerplays and action songs.

### Three-Year-Olds

**Music**

Have better voice control, rhythmic responses, and mastery of song; most have names for their favorite tunes, can recognize familiar tunes, and can sing portions of them with a fair degree of accuracy (Day, 1988). With experience, most can play a simple rhythm instrument in ways that reveal an emerging awareness of beat, tempo, and pitch in response to songs with simple, definite rhythm patterns.

**Movement**

Move in a more coordinated way to music (usually running) and may experiment with different types of body movements, such as walking on tiptoe; movements tend to be more graceful than previously. Usually try to participate in action songs and fingerplays by performing the gestures; often combine creative drama with song.

---

**Figure 4.3**
Developmental Sequence for Music and Movement

---

**Four-Year-Olds**

---

**Music**

Capable of learning some basic musical concepts such as pitch (high/low), duration (long/short), tempo (fast/slow), and loudness (soft/loud) and can use language to express these ideas; can classify musical instruments by sound, shape, size, pitch, and quality. Sing complete songs from memory with greater pitch control and rhythmic accuracy; sing both original songs and structured songs spontaneously. Vocal range, rhythmic ability, and vocabulary expand rapidly; can sing an average of five notes. Usually enjoy group singing games and more complex songs. Longer attention span in guided listening to records.

**Movement**

Movements suggesting rhythm (e.g., swinging on a swing) are likely to be accompanied by spontaneous song. Master new movements and can switch rapidly from one type of movement to another when the word is substituted (e.g., "Hop, hop, hop to my Lou").

**Five-Year-Olds**

---

**Music**

Sense of pitch, rhythm, and melody emerge; usually understand some melodic contours and intervals (skips and steps in a melody); can demonstrate some musical concepts (e.g., fast/slow, high/low, short/long duration) on a small keyboard. Enjoy longer songs with predictable structures (e.g., colors, numbers, repetition, rhyme). Can reproduce the melody in an echo song and have a vocal range of five to six notes.

**Movement**

Movements have a more rhythmic quality than previously. Fives can march around in a circle while playing in a rhythm band and participate in a variety of group singing games with simple dance movements to songs such as "Looby Lou."

**Six-, Seven-, and Eight-Year-Olds**

---

**Music**

Singing voice is at nearly mature level (Davidson, 1985). Sing "in tune," with a vocal range of approximately eight to ten notes; are aware of a song being pitched at a comfortable singing level. Sense of harmony is emerging. By second or third grade, can sing a round and may master a simple two-part harmony if given adult direction. Enjoy silliness and begin to understand word play in song lyrics; learn to read song lyrics; able to master songs that place greater demands on memory and sequencing skills. Greater awareness of printed music and its relationship to the way that music is sung or played; usually able to conceptualize musical notes as "stairsteps." Musical preferences are fairly well established; may express an interest in learning to play a musical instrument.

**Movement**

Able to improvise movements and match movements to the beat of the music (i.e., clapping "in time," playing a rhythm instrument "to the beat"). Capable of following more complex instructions and can learn simple folk dances with adult direction.

**Figure 4.3**   *(Continued)*

3. *Affective skills*—Music evokes emotional responses. A toddler who delights at hearing her name inserted into a song sung at day care is showing how music affects her. A kindergartner who remarks that "The Flight of the Bumblebee" sounds "buzzy" is showing how the music affects him. As children gain experience with music and language, they can better articulate their emotional responses to music. A group of primary grade children heard the mournful tune "Ashokan Farewell," the theme song for the Ken Burns's *The Civil War* series on PBS. When the teacher introduced the selection, she asked the children to listen carefully and explain why it was used as a goodbye song. The children were quiet, then responded with statements such as: "It's kind of slow and sad" and "It makes you feel the way you feel if your friend moves away."

4. *Cognitive skills*—As mentioned earlier, musical intelligence involves children's ability to process mentally the tonal aspects of rhythm and melody. The child who learns to sing "This Old Man," for instance, has learned to focus on a task, sequence material, and link words with actions. Musical experiences, such as creating a tune at a keyboard, can develop all the higher-level thinking skills of application, analysis, synthesis, and evaluation. There are cognitive connections between learning music and learning to do mathematics or learning to read, since all of these tasks depend on learning to interpret symbols.

5. *Social skills*—Music and movement activities encourage participation, sharing, and cooperation; it is part of the early bonding process in cultures around the globe and a memorable part of most peoples' childhoods. Through a simple musical activity such as the group singing game "London Bridge," children learn to subordinate their individual wishes to the goals of the group—the essence of cooperation.

6. *Cultural skills*—Music familiarizes children with the musical heritage of various geographic regions, cultures, and ethnic groups. A group of second graders who heard the Grammy-award-winning African music group Ladysmith Black Mambazo were captivated by their majestic Zulu harmonies. Those children with African roots felt renewed pride in their ethnic heritage, while those children with a different cultural heritage felt admiration for the music of a culture different from their own. Likewise, when a Lakota Sioux group performed their breathtaking ceremonial dances at a university and a beautifully synchronized troupe of Irish step dancers demonstrated the power of their art at an ethnic festival, their audiences were not only enthralled, but filled with admiration.

7. *Aesthetic skills*—When music and movement contribute to children's aesthetic sensibilities, it leads children to consider questions such as the following:

What do we hear in the music and notice in the dance?

Why do we respond the way that we do to what we hear and see?

What is beautiful in music and dance?

How might we appreciate and participate in music and dance?

There are three compelling reasons for teaching music. First, music education is vital to the individual development of children; second, musical experience is a particular type of knowledge and form of intelligence; and third, the richness of musical experiences justifies itself (Koopman, 1996).

## HOW DO MUSIC AND MOVEMENT DEVELOP?

Jerome Bruner (1968) hypothesized that children proceed through three cognitive stages: (1) enactive, (2) iconic, and (3) symbolic. Each of these stages suggests developmentally appropriate music experiences for children.

At the **enactive stage,** physical activity and music are intertwined. Consider all of the rhythmic games that adults play with infants and toddlers, and how they combine physical activity with music. We rock babies to sleep with a lullaby such as "Rock-a-bye Baby," tickle a child's toes to the chant of "This Little Piggy," or begin sharing simple action songs such as "Eency Weency Spider" with toddlers. Bruner's enactive stage relates to Piaget's (1952) sensorimotor stage and Erikson's (1950) trust-building stage. When we think about the enactive music stage of babies and toddlers, it is clear that the activities adults select not only stimulate the child's senses and foster cognitive development, but also build social relationships by communicating warmth and acceptance.

At the **iconic stage,** children begin to use objects and pictures to represent ideas (Bruner, 1968). During preschool, children are highly imaginative (Piaget, 1962) and are asserting their autonomy, yet want to be accepted by the group (Erikson, 1950). Musical experiences that are appropriate for this stage recognize all of these characteristics of preschoolers. Consider, for example, a teacher who extends the musical game "The Farmer in the Dell" by providing toys to represent each character in the game. The children use these toys to symbolize or represent their experience of directly participating.

At the **symbolic stage,** children begin to use abstract symbols, primarily language, to represent ideas. School-age children think more logically and realistically (Piaget, 1952). They also have a sense of industry, which is manifested in their drive to master many different skills (Erikson, 1950). Returning to the "Farmer in the Dell" example, school-age children might interpret the song's familiar words on a song chart or in a book. As children enter the symbolic stage, they rely less on icons (pictures) and learn to use the systems of symbols such as the printed word or musical notation. Illustrated song charts, song collections, and song picture books (illustrated versions of song lyrics) are particularly useful because they link the symbolic stage with the previous iconic stage (Jalongo & Ribblett, 1997).

Intellectual development from birth through the school years runs the course of the enactive, iconic, and symbolic systems "until the human being is able to command all three" (Bruner, 1968, p. 12). As children mature, they attain many milestones in music and movement. Figure 4.3 presents an overview of musical development and suitable music and movement activities for each age/stage.

As a result of developmentally appropriate music and movement activities throughout the early childhood years, children should acquire the following attitudes (adapted from Hall, 1989):

- *I can listen to music and watch dance*—recognizing different ways of using their senses to hear and differentiate among various types of music, such as identifying the music made by different instruments or voices.
- *I can join in music and movement*—knowing that they can use movement as a form of nonverbal communication, like 9-month-old Burkely, who moved animatedly in her car seat and made cooing sounds whenever her favorite Christmas carol, "The Holly and the Ivy," was played on a cassette tape.
- *I can create music and movement*—feeling free to explore sounds and confident about their musical intelligence, such as playing with a toy xylophone.
- *I can understand the language of music and dance*—using a vocabulary of music to describe experiences with tone, timbre, rhythm, and harmony, such as identifying loudness/softness or differentiating between a slow and fast beat.
- *I can compose music and choreograph movements*—knowing that music is a form of creative expression and doing such things as spontaneously creating and singing original songs, inventing dances to accompany musical selections, and creating rhythm band compositions.
- *I can perform music and dance*—believing that they are capable of producing pleasing sounds and music on homemade or real instruments, such as using "sleigh bells" to accompany a Christmas song or playing a tom-tom to accompany a song.

Children grow musically when adults provide (1) a supportive physical and emotional environment, (2) opportunities for social interaction, and (3) role models to emulate. A supportive physical and emotional environment is in evidence when children feel free to take risks and do not feel pressured to perform. "Musical activities should give pleasure to all who are participating, and if they don't, they are probably worse than useless" (Boyd, 1989, p. 8). It is not enough to simply "bathe" children in music, because, to the young child, music is both active (something that you do) and interactive (something that you share with others).

Early childhood musical experiences maximize social interaction when they are adjusted to the particular child's level of development and behavioral responses. Think about the traditional singing game "Ring Around the Rosy." As a toddler, Regina's version of the song was simply "rindaround . . . pocketful . . . boom," and she participated with her mother by moving in a circle and dropping to the floor at the song's end. As a 3-year-old in nursery school, she mastered all of the words (substituting "Ashes, ashes, we all fall down" for "boom") and learned how to move together with the other children around the circle.

Role models are equally important in the child's overall musical development. Many studies, both of exceptionally talented musicians and adults in general, suggest that early experiences that were relaxed, informal, and enjoyed in the company of supportive adults contributed to the child's early attachment to music (Wilson & Roehmann, 1990). A team of researchers who studied infant musical development concluded that the parents' own singing might be the single most important influence on an infant's musical activity (Kelley & Sutton-Smith, 1987).

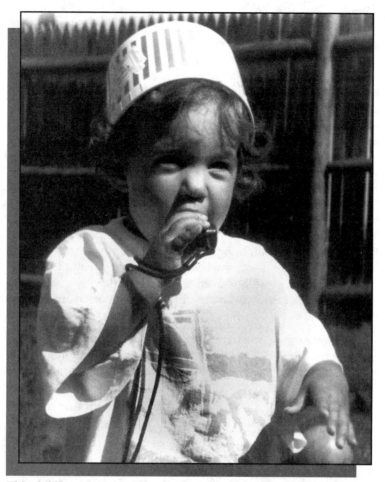

*This child's exploration of musical sounds illustrates her emerging understandings about music.*

In contrast, when significant others express disdain for certain musical activities, it tends to narrow children's range of interests. Consider the parent who is proud of an inability to carry a tune or a parent who ridicules males who are interested in dance or music. The child who naturally admires the parent soon devalues these activities too. Clearly, the models we provide at home and at school exert an influence on the child's attitudes about music and dance. A high school stage band, an elementary school ballet class, a choral group from the senior center, or an organist from the music store at the mall are all potential music and dance role models whom children can listen to and admire, enjoy, and emulate.

## *The Music-Movement Connection*

Children naturally connect music with body movement. The direction and flow of music invite children to respond to music with their bodies and express their feelings and thoughts in ways that words cannot express. When children move their bodies in response to music through creative dance, they use and integrate their bodies, minds, emotions, and spirits (Ririe, 1980). Even a baby who has not learned to crawl will usually raise his arms and legs up off the floor and make rapid swimming motions in response to lively music.

It is not necessary for teachers to be dancers themselves in order to lead children in movement activities. It is important, however, to include some type of movement activity in every musical experience for young children (Turner, 1999). One of the best ways to encourage creative movement is by making comments and asking good questions at the right time. Try beginning with a word, such as *happy.* Say to children, "Show me how your face looks when you open a present and it's just what you've been hoping for. Now add your arms. Next, show your whole body being happy. Show me how happy moves around the room. Now choose a prop that makes your look even happier, joyful."

A teacher could stimulate different types of creative movement with questions such as these:

Can you show me with your body that the music is getting louder? softer? higher? lower? Can you show me with just your hands? Can you show me with your whole body that it is getting faster? with just your head? with just your feet?

Can you show me giant steps as you move around the circle? baby steps? How would an elephant dance to this music? a mouse?

Show me how a snowflake moves with your whole body. Can you show me with a paper streamer? with just your arms?

The use of simple props is another way to combine music and movement. Toddlers can rock a teddy bear to a lullaby, preschoolers can make "dancing dolls" (empty detergent bottles and fabric skirts) and swirl them about in response to a Strauss waltz, and primary grade children can lope along to a cowboy song as they hold the reins of their horse (a length of ribbon or yarn encircling the waist of a partner). Naturally, the selection of both music and movement activities depends upon the developmental levels of the children.

## CRITICAL ISSUES IN TEACHING MUSIC AND MOVEMENT

Chances are, you will discover that there is limited support for music and movement activities in the early childhood settings in which you teach. At one time, teachers were required to complete as many as 15 credits in the arts prior to teaching. Now it is commonplace for teachers to have just one or two classes and hope that a music and art specialist will be available. Yet even when these services are available, they are typically scheduled for just 20–30 minutes per week. Therefore, no matter what your training or setting, you will have responsibility for providing quality music and movement experiences for young children. The information in Figure 4.4, How to Create a Music and Movement Program in Your Classroom or Center, should help you to get started.

## Identifying Appropriate Content

Before beginning to incorporate music into your program, you will first need to make some important decisions about what is appropriate and understand the basic musical concepts and content that young children are expected to acquire. Figure 4.5 summarizes the musical elements—dynamics (soft/loud), tempo (fast/slow), pitch (high/low), rhythm (the patterns of sounds), and harmony (the blending of complementary sounds) and some strategies for helping children to acquire these important understandings.

---

**General Principles**

- Base the program on four elements: listening (e.g., playing the music of different cultures in the background), moving (e.g., inviting children to experiment with dance steps that accompany musical selections with distinctive beats), playing (e.g., teaching children a story song and inviting them to dramatize it), singing (e.g., encouraging joyful, spontaneous singing in response to activities such as swinging on a swing).

- Provide a balance of large group, small group, partner, and individual music and movement activities. Adapt the environment and materials to give children with special needs opportunities to participate. Also provide a balance of teacher-facilitated and child-initiated activities.

- Expect children's responses to vary and invite children to respond in their own ways to music and dance rather than requiring everyone to do the same thing. For instance, balance the use of songs that have the motions predetermined (like "Eency Weency Spider") with opportunities for children to invent their own actions to accompany songs.

- Build the children's self-confidence as people who can enjoy, participate in, and respond to music and dance. Invite children to share their ideas, but do not force them to perform or ask the group to critique their performance.

- Avoid generic praise ("That's great, everyone!") and use personalized encouragement instead ("I notice that you are using your whole body, Jason, and I see that Chelsea decided to use mostly her arms.").

*(continued)*

---

**Figure 4.4**   How to Create a Music and Movement Program in Your Classroom or Center
*Sources:* Bennett, Wood, & Rogers (1997), Gold & Cuming (1999), Greenberg (1979), Persellin (1998), and Turner (1999).

**General Principles,** *continued*

- Actively seek to build the children's vocabularies related to music and movement. While toddlers may focus on simpler concepts (e.g., fast/slow, turning around), older children can learn the terminology used by artists (e.g., dynamics, pirouette).

- Encourage and support the child's spontaneous songs and dances by observing and documenting what they have created on audio or videotape. Invite the child to teach her or his song or dance to you.

- Join in as appropriate, by offering to sing with a child or accompany the child's song or dance on whatever instrument you can play (e.g., a drum, a kazoo, a guitar, a keyboard).

- For children who seem reluctant to express themselves through music and movement, model joyful responses and invite the child to sing or move with you in response to music.

- Avoid a talent-scout mentality, in which you focus on a few children who appear to be precocious in music or dance. Give all children opportunities to engage in music and movement to the best of their abilities.

**Preparation**

- For safety's sake, when children are engaged in movement activities, make sure that they are wearing shoes with nonslip soles. Make certain also that children are not being asked to sing during snack or meal times as food may get caught in their throats and cause them to choke.

- Select a space that will accommodate the activity. During creative movement activities, use a large, open, uncluttered area and tell children to behave like peanut butter and s-p-r-e-a-d out! Even if space is more limited, ask each child to extend arms and turn slowly about to be sure that they will not bump into anyone else. You will need a large group area for playing circle games (e.g., "Ring Around the Rosy"), and a listening center equipped with high-quality sound equipment and musical selections from throughout the world. Remember to include outdoor musical experiences, such as galloping to music with stick horses.

- When you set up learning centers, make certain that you provide music and movement opportunities every day (e.g., a listening center, a music center) as well as centers that change periodically (e.g., a musical prop-making center, materials for making sandpaper blocks at the woodworking center). Be certain to have a center that includes scarves, ropes, balls, streamers, and other materials that encourage movement and dance. Consider a special dramatic play area for conducting music that includes a music stand, baton, and podium. Plan a music laboratory where children can invent their own music, equipping it with a set of bells, a keyboard, xylophone, drums, and rhythm band set. Add music to the home-life center by including a cassette or CD player, musical stuffed toys, a music box, or some musical instruments.

- At various times, combine music and movement with all other subject areas and centers in the classroom (e.g, a work song playing in the woodworking area for preschoolers, or a group of second graders who invent a song parody about energy in science, or a third grade class that composes and performs a musical puppet play on sets and subsets for first grade).

**Figure 4.4**   *(Continued)*

**Materials and Resources**

- Don't choose a book, recording, or piece of software simply because it is "popular"—much of the "children's music" in wide use is of inferior quality and simply well marketed. Strive to provide the very best. Choose high-quality materials and sound equipment. You might be able to use the CD player on a computer to provide better sound quality than that provided by old records or cassette tapes, for example.

- Song lyrics should be matched to the interests and developmental levels of *children* (e.g., romantic songs are not appropriate). Songs need to be pitched at the child's singing range.

- When young children sing or move to music, they should be responding sincerely and genuinely rather than mimicking adults. Strive for a neat, clean appearance and avoid makeup, suggestive song lyrics or risqué costumes.

- Teach children to respect and care for props, instruments, equipment, and software. Organize your classroom so that it is easy for children to see where things belong and how they are to be put away.

- Give children independent access to musical experiences by providing a listening center, a place to record music, a center or cart with homemade and real musical instruments, and computer software about music and dance. Teach children how to operate the equipment and provide posters with illustrated instructions.

- Expand children's appreciation for different types and styles of music and dance by introducing the music and dance of many eras, ethnic groups, and cultures throughout the entire year.

- Use community resources to provide a wide array of recorded and live performances in music and dance. Collaborate with families, colleagues, and professionals in other fields. Send out a request to those who have skill in music, asking them to share their talent and level of accomplishment with children.

- Begin a file of on-line and print resources for parents/families about young children's music and dance. When parents turn to you for advice about lessons in music or dance, have authoritative answers ready.

**Presentation**

- Don't reserve music and movement activities for one specific time block. Rather, use music and creative movement throughout the day, particularly during transition times such as arrival/departure at the school or center; as children move in and out of free play; before, during or after a story session; or as children move inside and outside for outdoor play.

- Remember that young children enjoy repeating familiar songs and dance movements. Feel free to revisit the familiar as well as introduce something that is new.

- When young children are moving to music, the emphasis should be on developing techniques rather than on displays of athleticism or stunts. Incorrect technique can cause physical damage to the young child's body.

- Pay attention to variety and pacing. Even a brief music or creative dance time period will require several different activities. Stop an activity before the children grow tired of it and save some of that enthusiasm for next time.

*(continued)*

**Figure 4.4**   *(Continued)*

---

**Evaluation**

- Quality music and movement programs help all children develop positive attitudes and emotional responses. Early musical experiences should inaugurate a lifelong love of music and dance.

- Closely observe how children respond to particular music and movement activities. Make some brief notes about what was particularly well received and what was not.

- Realize that a lukewarm response to a song or a movement experience may mean that it was not developmentally suited to the children at that time. Perhaps if it is introduced later on, children will respond more favorably.

- Don't allow yourself to get caught up in high-pressure, on-stage performances for large audiences. Even people who have extensive musical training may not understand the needs of young children very well and you will need to advocate for the children's needs. Remember, you aren't selling tickets, you are teaching children.

- Exercise good judgment about how formal a music or dance experience should be for children. Help parents and community members to understand that when children are acting tense and anxious, rather than enjoying the activity, it is time to reconsider.

- Remain current with the recommendations of leading organizations in music and movement, such as Music Educators National Conference, and use their guidelines as a basis for ongoing self-evaluation.

- You will know your music and movement program is achieving its goals when children learn to listen and observe appreciatively, sing tunefully, move expressively and rhythmically, play classroom instruments, develop age-appropriate musical concepts, create self-satisfying responses, and value music and dance as part of everyday life.

---

**Figure 4.4**   *(Continued)*

## *Providing Musical Materials and Experiences*

As teachers, we have a responsibility to extend children's musical experiences and preferences. This long-term interest in music can be achieved by creating a classroom music laboratory, by offering a balanced selection of high-quality materials, and by providing a variety of musical experiences.

The modern-day version of Montessori's "prepared environment" is the music laboratory. A music laboratory functions much like a scientist's laboratory—it provides children the equipment, time, and opportunity to investigate music. Recent research with toddlers, preschoolers, and school-aged children (Fox, 1989; Upitis, 1990) suggests that one of the best ways of leading children to music is to provide an environment where they have the materials, time, and opportunity to discover and build their own knowledge about music.

A music laboratory emphasizes active involvement. Children explore and experiment with sounds and classroom musical instruments in an environment that supports their play; they use a variety of resources to invent simple musical instruments, such as making sandpaper blocks, using different types of containers to

---

### Musical Element: Dynamics (Soft/Loud)

---

**Reception**

Even before birth, during the last months of pregnancy, infants have a hearing ability comparable to that of an adult, although the sounds they can hear while immersed in amniotic fluid are muffled. They startle to loud, sudden noises and are comforted by soft sounds, such as quiet music or a lullaby. Newborns and young infants benefit from listening to music of different types, including classical music, traditional lullabies, and music of many different types and cultures.

**Imitation**

Toddlers and young preschoolers can be helped to understand the distinction between loud and soft if these concepts are made sufficiently concrete. Allow children to directly experience what happens when the volume is turned down low and then turned up high on a piece of listening equipment. Try tapping a drum very softly, then loudly. Invite them to slap their thighs very softly, then louder, or tap their feet softly, then stomp their feet loudly. Get them to use the words *loud* and *soft* to refer to their experiences (e.g., the thunderstorm was loud, the sound of rain falling was soft).

**Production**

Most preschoolers are capable of demonstrating their understandings of dynamics by producing sounds. You might construct a large, cardboard dial that the children can see and ask them to begin singing, then allow a child to operate the dial and "turn up" or "turn down" their voices.

### Musical Element: Tempo (Fast/Slow)

---

**Reception**

While still in the hospital nursery, infants respond differentially to slow music, such as lullabies, and lively music, such as action songs. Babies become more active when lively music is played. (Wilcox, 1994).

**Imitation**

Make the fast/slow aspect concrete by looking at things in nature. Look at animals that move quickly, others that move slowly. Ask children to show how they move slowly and quickly by walking/running or by making the wheels of their wheelchair move faster. Get children moving around the circle and ask them to change how they move in response to the music. Then play slow songs followed by fast songs.

**Production**

Invite children to work at the music center to create fast and slow songs using the props provided there. Children may, for example, create a lively chant or cheer to go along with pom-poms and create a slow song to accompany scarves or paper fans.

*(continued)*

**Figure 4.5**   Strategies for Building Understanding in Music and Movement

---

**Musical Element: Pitch (High/Low)**

---

### Reception

Even young infants are apparently able to distinguish between high and low pitches. If the same pitch is played repeatedly, the infant grows accustomed to it. But when a new pitch is introduced, babies will often begin to suck on a pacifier vigorously, indicating that they detect the difference and are interested again.

### Imitation

Differences in pitch are often introduced to preschoolers as stair steps because this gives them a concrete way of relating to high and low pitches. Try using a wooden rocking boat set upside down and a set of tonal bells or a toy xylophone as a prop. Begin with very dramatic differences between pitches. After several demonstrations of moving up on top of the boat when the music goes higher, give children a chance to play this high/low game. The game can be made more challenging by choosing notes on the scale that are closer in pitch or by adding steps.

### Production

Using a pitch pipe, keyboard, bells, or xylophone, play each note on the scale and ask children to "match" it with their voices. Teach children the song "Do Re Mi."

**Musical Element: Rhythm (The Patterns of Sounds)**

---

### Reception

Even before birth, infants grow accustomed to rhythmic sounds of the mother's heartbeat and respiration. Hospital nurseries sometimes have toys or sound equipment that plays similar sounds to comfort newborns. Babies frequently relax and drift off to sleep from the rhythmic motion of a caregiver's gentle rocking, a car, a stroller, or a swing.

### Imitation

Rocking and gently bouncing babies and toddlers as a part of playful games and nursery tunes teaches them the rudiments of rhythm. A child who learns to play "Pat a Cake" is imitating the rhythm.

### Production

Even preschoolers can begin to move their bodies "in time" to the rhythm of the music if it is modeled for them. A good rhythm song for kindergarten and primary is "Horsey, Horsey" by Sharon, Lois, and Bram. The entire song follows the clip-clop of the horse's hooves, which can be produced by using rhythm sticks or tapping together the shells of an empty coconut.

**Figure 4.5**   *(Continued)*

---

**Musical Element: Harmony (The Blending of Complementary Sounds)**

**Reception**

From the earliest days of life, children are immersed in the harmonies of their cultures. There is ample evidence to suggest that an understanding of harmony is accelerated by early exposure and atrophies with disuse.

**Imitation**

An understanding of harmony is generally considered the last to develop. Make the complementarity of sounds concrete by playing two musical notes together on a keyboard. Ask children whether the notes sound better together or not. Consider watching a video of an African choir or inviting musicians whose work relies on close harmony, such as a barbershop quartet or folksingers, to perform for the class.

**Production**

It is not until elementary school that most children are taught to sing a song in two or three parts and harmonize their voices. A good recording is the Chenille Sisters.

---

**Figure 4.5**   *(Continued)*

create drums, or making shakers out of containers with rice, beans, sand, etc., inside. The music laboratory is supported by adults who function in the role of teacher/facilitator, adults who observe, model, support, and make comments or ask questions about the child's activities. Additionally, the music laboratory contributes to a more balanced program by equalizing unstructured music play and teacher-facilitated music and movement activities; individual activity (e.g., experimenting with bells) is moderated by group music making (e.g., playing in a rhythm band). Naturally, the type of music laboratory provided in the classroom must take into consideration the developmental levels of the children. Music and movement activities are adjusted to the child's developmental level (e.g., moving from primarily enactment to iconic representations and finally to symbols). When using the music laboratory, teachers should allow children to explore sounds, experiment with instruments, and orchestrate sounds, such as leading a homemade rhythm band.

As the research from the music laboratory suggests, even high-quality background music is not enough. Young children need opportunities to create, produce, and respond to music at an early age. Classroom teachers who bring relevant broad and varied musical elements into the curriculum will affect children's musical behaviors throughout their lives.

The general categories of materials that should be a part of every early childhood classroom include music-playing equipment such as CDs and a CD player or

*In high-quality early childhood settings, the emphasis is on children's musical activity. These primary grade children are playing simple instruments and singing with a partner.*

tapes and a tape recorder; rhythm band materials; visual aids to accompany songs such as song charts, puppets, flannel board figures, and rebus song sheets; and simple musical instruments such as bells, xylophones, a recorder, and an autoharp. Figure 4.6 provides a more detailed description.

A well-balanced program contains many different types of music. Research suggests that children generally prefer music and songs that have dominant

*Circle time by a 4-year-old girl.*

**Figure 4.6**

Types of Classroom
Instruments

*Sources* for classroom
instruments: Suzuki,
Rhythm Band, Inc., and
Music for Little People.

**RHYTHM**

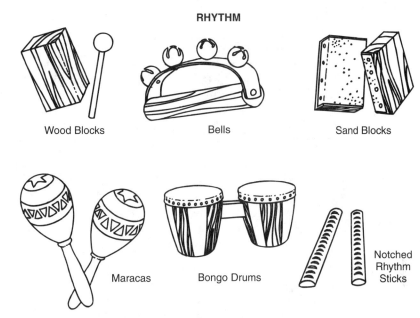

Wood Blocks      Bells      Sand Blocks

Maracas      Bongo Drums      Notched Rhythm Sticks

Clicking (tone blocks, wood blocks, coconut shells)
Ringing (bells, gong, jingle taps, wrist bells)
Rattling or swishing (sand blocks, rattles, gourds, maracas, cabasa)
Booming or thudding (drums—tom-tom, bongos, African drums)
Scratching or scraping (notched rhythm sticks, gourd rasp, washboard)

**MELODY**

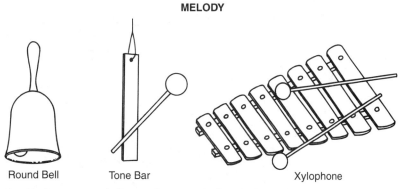

Round Bell      Tone Bar      Xylophone

Hand bells, resonator bells, tone bars, step bells, xylophone

**HARMONY**

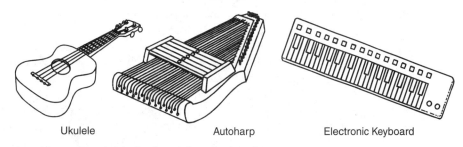

Ukulele      Autoharp      Electronic Keyboard

Accordion, guitar, ukulele, banjo, autoharp, keyboards

rhythm patterns, repetition, and nonsense syllables; evoke a mood (e.g., calm, lively); emphasize enjoyment; suggest enactment and movement; and tell a story (Bayless & Ramsey, 1990). Figure 4.7 is an overview of the types of music that ought to be included and examples of each.

## Selecting Teaching Strategies

Teachers often operate under the mistaken impression that they must be able to sing beautifully and accompany themselves on an instrument in order to share music with young children. Actually, very few adults possess such performance skills. It is important to remember that the major focus is on the children's musical activity rather than on your talents in music. Some ways of compensating for a lack of musical background include the following:

   **1.** *Use your voice.* Judge your voice by the ability to sing children's songs, not adults' songs. The great majority of songs for preschoolers have a range of about five notes. An ordinary singing voice coupled with extraordinary enthusiasm is perfectly adequate to sing most songs for young children. You probably know many of the songs already or can quickly learn them by singing along with a tape or record.

   **2.** *Use recorded music.* There are many excellent CDs, tapes, and children's concert videotapes that teachers can obtain through their public library. To avoid fumbling around to find a particular selection on a tape or CD, make copies on tape with just the songs you will be using that day or use the counter on the videotape machine and write down the exact location of each song. This will enable you to move smoothly from one selection to another.

   What if you find the sheet music to a song in a book but cannot find a recorded version? Find a person who plays an instrument well to make a tape for you. You might ask the person to sing the song the first time so that you can learn it, then play just the background music the second time. Videotapes of skilled children's musicians in action are not only for children's viewing, but are also useful self-teaching tools for early childhood educators. Tapes such as *A Young Children's Concert with Raffi* model the enthusiasm and ways of presenting material that achieve maximum audience participation.

   **3.** *Use simple instruments.* Teachers quickly recognize that any instrument they find difficult to play only diverts their attention from the children and interferes with the musical experience. Perhaps you are familiar with the chorded zither called an autoharp. Instead of having to learn the chords by positioning the fingers (as with a guitar), teachers can simply press a button corresponding to that chord. Place the autoharp on a table or hold it upright against you, then strum down with your thumb and up with your finger in time to the music. The major drawback to the autoharp is that it must be tuned. The best way for nonmusicians to tune it is to ask a musician to do it for you or, better yet, learn to do it for yourself by matching each string's sound to those on a CD or tape (Peterson, 1979). Another alternative is the Omnichord, an electronic

**Lullabies—Traditional and Original, American and Multicultural**

Examples: *Baby's Morning Time* (July Collins), *Lullaby Berceuse* (Connie Kaldor & Carmen Campagne), *Star Dreamer* (Priscilla Herdman), *Earthmother Lullabies I* and *Earthmother Lullabies II* (Pamala Ballingham), *Lullabies for Little Dreamers* (Kevin Roth), *Nitey-Night* (Patti Ballas & Laura Baron), *Nightsongs and Lullabies* (Jim Chappell)

**American Folk Songs—Children's Chants, Play Songs, and Singing Games**

Examples: *Let's Sing Fingerplays* and *Activity and Game Songs* (Tom Glazer), *Circle Time* (Lisa Monet), *Family Tree* (Tom Chapin), *Doc Watson Sings Songs for Little Pickers* (Doc Watson), *Stories and Songs for Little Children* and *American Folk Songs for Children* (Pete Seeger), *The Best of Burl's for Boys and Girls* (Burl Ives), *Come on In* and *Fiddle Up a Tune* (Eric Nagler), *This a way, That a way* (Ella Jenkins), *Stay Tuned* (Sharon, Lois, & Bram), *American Children* (various artists), *Peter, Paul, & Mommy* (Peter, Paul, & Mary)

**Nursery Tunes and Songs for the Very Young**

Examples: *Mainly Mother Goose* (Sharon, Lois, & Bram), *Singable Songs for the Very Young* and *More Singable Songs for the Very Young* (Raffi), *Baby Songs* and *More Baby Songs* (Hap Palmer), *The Baby Record* (Bob McGrath & Katherine Smithrim), *Lullabies and Laughter* (Pat Carfra), *Shake It to the One You Love the Best: Play Songs and Lullabies from Black Musical Traditions* (Cheryl Warren Mattox)

**Multicultural Music From Around the World and Music of the Child's Ethnic Heritage**

Examples: *Children's Songs of Latin America* and *Cloud Journey* (Marcia Berman), *All for Freedom* (African-American) (Sweet Honey in the Rock), *Family Folk Festival: A Multicultural Sing-Along* (various artists), *Mi Casa es Su Casa* (Michele Valeri), *Beyond Boundaries: The Earthbeat! Sampler* (various artists), *Miss Luba and Kenyan Folk Melodies* (Muungano National Choir of Kenya), *Shake Shugaree* (various cultures) (Taj Mahal), *Le Hoogie Boogie: Louisiana French Music for Children* (Michael Doucet)

**Holiday, Religious, and Seasonal Music**

Examples: *Leprechauns and Unicorns* and *Oscar Brand and His Singing Friends Celebrate Holidays* (Oscar Brand), *Holiday Songs and Rhythms* (Hap Palmer), *Songs for the Holiday Season* (Nancy Rover), *Just in Time for Chanukah* (Rosenthal & Safyan), Mormon Tabernacle Choir, Vienna Boys Choir, Gregorian Chant (Benedictine Monks), Reverend James Cleveland, Mighty Clouds of Joy

**Contemporary Children's Music**

Examples: *Evergreen, Everblue* (Raffi), *Rosenshontz* (Gary Rosen & Bill Shontz), *Sillytime Magic* (Joanie Bartels), *All of Us Will Shine, Hug the Earth,* and *Circle Around* (Tickle Tune Typhoon), *1-2-3 for Kids* (The Chenille Sisters), *Little Friends for Little Folks* (Janice Buckner), *Singin' and Swingin'* (Sharon, Lois, & Bram), *Collections* (Fred Penner), *Take Me with You* (Peter Alsop)

**Popular Music—Rock, Jazz, New Age, Pop, Electronic, Movie Music, Show Music**

Examples: *Sebastian the Crab* (from *The Little Mermaid*) (various artists), *Peter and the Wolf Play Jazz* (Dave Van Ronk), *Star Wars Trilogy Soundtrack* (London Philharmonic), *Electronic Music II* (Jacob Druckman), *Really Rosie* (children's musical) (Carole King/Maurice Sendak), *Baby Road* (Floyd Domino), *Fresh Aire I* and *Fresh Aire II* (Manheim Steamroller), *The Lion King* (Elton John)

*(continued)*

**Figure 4.7**   Types of Music

**Chants, Rhymes, and Rap**
Examples: "The Little Shekere" from *All for Freedom* (Sweet Honey in the Rock), "Fiesta Musical" from *Music for Little People Sampler* (Maria Medina Serafin), various playground chants and African chants from *Where I Come From!* (Cockburn & Steinbergh)

**Classical Music**
Examples: *Peter and the Wolf* (Sergio Prokofiev), *Sorcerer's Apprentice* (Dukas), *Carnival of the Animals* (Camille Saint-Saens), *Sleeping Beauty* (Peter Ilyich Tchaikovsky), *The Firebird* (Igor Stravinsky), *Fiedler's Favorites for Children* and *More Fiedler Favorites* (Arthur Fiedler and the Boston Pops Orchestra), *G'morning, Johann: Classical Piano Solos* (Ric Louchard), *Nutcracker Suite* (Peter Ilyich Tchaikovsky), *Symponie Fantastique* (Hector Berlioz), *La Mer* (Claude Debussy), *Mr. Bach Comes to Call* (Toronto Boys Choir and Studio Arts Orchestra)

**Music for Dancing, Patriotic Songs, and Marching Songs**
Examples: *Play Your Instruments* (Ella Jenkins), Sousa marches, Strauss waltzes, *Swan Lake* (Peter Ilyich Tchaikovsky)

**Music from Various Historical Periods**
Examples: *Dance of the Renaissance* (Richard Searles & Gilbert Yslas), *Shake It to the One You Love the Best: Play Songs and Lullabies from Black Musical Traditions* (various artists), *Harpsichord Music* (Jean-Philippe Rameau)

**Music by Contemporary Artists**
Examples: *Who's Afraid of Opera* video (Joan Sutherland), Beverly Sills, Stevie Wonder, Luciano Pavarotti, *Songbird* (Kenny G)

**Story Songs for Quiet Listening**
Examples: "The Ugly Duckling" from *A Child's Celebration of Song* (Danny Kaye), "Puff the Magic Dragon" from *Peter, Paul, & Mommy* (Peter, Paul, & Mary), "My Grandfather's Clock" from *Family Folk Festival: A Multicultural Sing-Along* (Doc Watson), "Mail Myself to You" from *Special Delivery* (John McCutcheon), "The Circus Song" from *Family Folk Festival: A Multicultural Sing-Along* (Maria Muldaur)

**Sources for Children's Recordings**

Children's Circle
Weston, CT 06883
(800) KIDS-VID

Educational Record Center
Building 400, Suite 400
1575 Northside Drive
Atlanta, GA 30318-4298
(800) 438-1637

Music for Little People
Post Office Box 1460
1144 Redway Drive
Redway, CA 95560
(800) 346-4445

Redleaf Press
450 North Syndicate Suite 5
St. Paul, MN 55104-4125
(800) 423-8309

**Figure 4.7**   *(Continued)*

version of the autoharp that requires no tuning—you need only to push a button and stroke a pressure-sensitive keyboard. There are many different models of the Omnichord, and the smaller ones are reasonably priced.

**4.** *Match musical experiences to teaching goals.* As early childhood music expert Sharron Lucky has concluded, "It's important for non-musicians to remember that we are not expected to teach music, but we need to learn better ways to teach with music" (Lucky, 1990, p. 4). When you make choices about musical activities, try to focus on your purpose. Is your goal to emphasize rhythm? If so, you could use a simple chant such as the Big Book version of *Peanut Butter and Jelly* (Wescott, 1987) to emphasize the rhythmic patterns of language. To pose a rhythmic challenge to third graders, you could select a complicated rap such as "The Little Shekere" on Sweet Honey in the Rock's *All for Freedom* album (1989). If your goal is to improve children's memory, you might select a song with several verses, such as Peter Spier's *The Fox Went Out on a Chilly Night* (1961) for first or second graders, or something simpler such as "If You're Happy and You Know It" for preschoolers. Suppose that you want to create a mood through music. Once again, you can make choices that match your goals—an Irish jig to evoke a lively response, a Polish march (polonaise) to inspire hearty marching, a blues guitar to slow down the pace, or New Age music to relax. Music is also ideal for fostering multicultural appreciation as children listen to a collection of songs, chants, and poems from a wide array of ethnic and cultural groups through a musical collection such as *Where I Come From! Poems and Songs from Many Cultures* (Cockburn & Steinbergh, 1991).

**5.** *Talk with children about their music.* Leading children to an understanding of musical concepts requires you to identify with the child. Students might be led to understand rests in music by asking them to "freeze" their bodies for a moment when the music pauses. A group of children might understand the concept of rhythm better if it is related to a concrete experience many of them already have, such as the ticking of a clock. A teacher might pass around a clock, tell children to listen, and then ask, "How can we make our rhythm sticks sound like a clock?" Alternatively, the children might listen to the song "My Grandfather's Clock" or the music of the "Syncopated Clock" and move their heads, hands, or feet to the sounds of the clock. If a group of school-age children want to present a story such as "Coppelia" by Leo Delibes (1986) with musical sound effects, the teacher can relate it to their picture-symbol knowledge with questions such as "How could you help the players remember when to play?" Children may decide to provide the director with pictorial cue cards of each instrument, to make a large story chart coded with the symbols, or to provide each player with the text of the story coded with the instrument symbols.

## *Evaluating Musical Materials and Experiences*

Children are accustomed to hearing music—at shopping malls, in radio jingles, on computer web sites, or from wind-up musical toys—but these experiences do not really teach children to listen to music. In fact, these experiences may be doing just the opposite: teaching children to disregard music by bombarding them with poor quality. Browsing through the display booths at any large professional conference will quickly point out how difficult the job of evaluating musical materials can become, particularly for the nonmusician teacher. Hundreds of records, tapes, and other musical materials have been created for children, and the choices can sometimes be overwhelming. Fortunately, there are many sources of support for teachers.

With recorded music, look for award-winning materials. Two of the major awards in children's recordings are the Parent's Choice Award and the American Library Association's Notable Recording; look, too, for favorable reviews from newspapers and endorsements from various professional organizations. Where musical instruments or sound exploration equipment is concerned, deal with reputable manufacturers and school supply companies. Fisher-Price, for example, has an all-in-one rhythm band that is reasonably priced, durable, and versatile. Use the library to locate professional journal and magazine articles about music, curriculum guides for early childhood music, song books, music methods textbooks, and children's picture books that include songs. Finally, talk with teachers, both music specialists and regular classroom teachers, about those early childhood musical materials that they have found particularly useful.

## ✎ TEACHERS' ROLES AND RESPONSIBILITIES

The teacher's role is more complex than merely playing a CD at various times of the day. Teachers fulfill their musical roles and responsibilities when they function as motivators, planners, co-participants, and observers.

### *Motivator*

Too often, teachers assume that they have done their part when they set up a music center with some rhythm instruments and a listening station. But children need to be introduced to musical experiences in an engaging way, just as with a story or lesson. The motivation for a music activity should include a concrete object, thought-provoking questions, and active participation. Mrs. O'Malley introduced a new song to her kindergarten class by placing a four-sided wooden object with one pointed end and a stem in the center of the circle. The children were not really sure what it was or why it had unusual markings on it. When she gave the object a twirl and it began to spin around, they called out delightedly "a top!" Mrs. O'Malley then explained that it was a very special type of top, a dreidel, that it was a traditional toy of Jewish children, and that the markings on the top were Hebrew letters. Then the children learned to sing "My Dreidel" while each child took a turn spinning the top. Additional motivational ideas include introducing "The Teddybears' Picnic" with a picnic basket, arranging chairs in bus seat formation to introduce "The Wheels on the Bus" (Zelinsky, 1990) or singing "I'm Being Swallowed by a Boa Constrictor" with a snake sock puppet.

Providing simple rhythm band instruments for children to play is naturally motivating. Even if resources are limited, rhythm sticks can be made from dowel rods, sandpaper blocks from scraps of wood and sandpaper, and drums from pieces of inner tube stretched over coffee cans. For many ideas on making simple instruments, see *Listen!* (Wilt & Watson, 1977).

## *Planner*

Planning a musical experience involves preparation, pacing, and variety. Preparation includes identifying your purpose, deciding what to include, and assembling all of your materials. If you are using recording equipment, make certain that it is in working order. Careful preparation will enable you to keep your attention on the children rather than on the book, musical instrument, or recording equipment. Another aspect of preparation is getting the children assembled and ready. The children should be seated comfortably where they all can see. A circle is usually the best arrangement. Teach the children a signal that it is music time, such as a clang of the finger cymbals or an introductory song. Strive to reduce background noise and other distractions before beginning.

Pacing is important too. Do not drag out an activity or race through it. It is generally best to alternate "mostly listening" activities with "mostly movement," to limit the amount of unfamiliar material at any one session, and to conclude with a quiet song or a song that leads into the next activity planned. If children ask to sing a song again, honor their request but stop before interest wanes.

Variety is another consideration. Give children a variety of opportunities to participate by listening, singing, using creative movement, and playing rhythm instruments. Remember that the goal is to extend and balance children's musical experiences, so include many different types of musical selections (see Figure 4.7), not only during music time, but also throughout the day.

It is also important to develop a variety of strategies for achieving learning goals. If you want to teach children a new song, for example, you could:

- Play the song in the background for several days so children will be familiar with it when it is introduced.
- Teach children the chorus while you sing the verses (at first).
- Sing along with a recording and tell children to join in singing with whatever portions of the song they feel comfortable with.
- Use lined poster paper to create a song chart that older students can read.
- Create a rebus (words and pictures) song sheet for children to use so that picture cues remind them of the content of each verse.
- Teach children the song one phrase or sentence at a time, then combine the phrases.
- Teach children the actions to an action song first, then teach them to sing the words (or vice versa).

Variety, both in your music/movement teaching strategies and in the materials you select, will help to maintain children's interest and encourage participation.

*Participating in a rhythm band teaches both musical skills and cooperation.*

## Co-Participant

The best early childhood teachers of music recognize that they are co-participants. These teachers share and enjoy music with children rather than perform for them. "Teachers who enjoy music and sing with enthusiasm, regardless of ability or training, are the ones who receive the greatest response and involvement from children" (Eliason & Jenkins, 1977, p. 245).

## Observer

When sharing music with young children, watch for these behaviors (Jalongo & Collins, 1985):

**1.** *What parts of the activity generate the most response?* Without prompting, children may clap, sway side to side, bounce up and down, or associate specific words with actions. When singing, children do not usually sing every word. They may join in by singing just one word, a phrase, the first word of a verse, or the chorus.

**2.** *When do children follow along best?* Experiment with different methods of presenting concepts to children and note which are most effective. Try to relate explanations to something that the children have all experienced, asking, for example: "Can you make your coconut shells sound like the clip-clop of a horse's feet?"

3. *How do children use music spontaneously?* Note when and where children burst into song, dance around, or use musical instruments. If talk with a parent reveals that a child who never sings at circle time is singing away as she rides home in the car, an audiotape of the class singing might be sent home to build the child's confidence. If children seldom engage in song outdoors, teachers might plan an outdoor music activity, such as singing "The Bear Went over the Mountain" while climbing an obstacle course. If children seek a quiet corner in the classroom to play their instruments, a new music center and better room arrangement might be the answer. By keeping in mind that the purpose is to support children's growth, teachers can provide the best possible experiences for their students.

## Resource Manager

The local record store or bookstore probably will not carry the high-quality music resources that teachers need for their classrooms. Usually, the best ways of locating these high-quality productions include the following:

1. *Use the library.* Many of the most popular children's musicians, such as Ella Jenkins; Hap Palmer; Wee Sing; Tickle Tune Typhoon; Sharon, Lois, and Bram; and Raffi, have concert tapes that you can borrow from the public library. Weston Woods has several song picture books on tape, including Pete Seeger's *The Foolish Frog,* Aliki's *Hush Little Baby,* and Maurice Sendak's *Really Rosie,* and some commercial videotapes, such as Walt Disney's *Fantasia,* are of good quality. With videotapes becoming more affordable, your school may want to invest in some of these materials.

Another source is to tape quality children's television programs. *Reading Rainbow* often includes songs, and there are musical programs for children, such as *The Elephant Show.* Occasionally there are children's concerts or seasonal music specials for children.

2. *Attend professional conferences.* At conferences, you can often attend music workshops by children's musicians. Usually, there are display booths where you can listen to a CD or tape, assess the quality of rhythm instruments, or look over song picture books or song collections before investing in them.

3. *Contact children's music distributors.* One important resource for quality children's recordings and musical instruments is the catalog. Usually, the catalogs will indicate which recordings have earned awards. These catalogs often include authentic music from other lands and simple instruments from around the world that children can play. (See Figures 4.6 and 4.7 for sources).

4. *Read the professional literature.* Publications such as *Booklist,* published by the American Library Association, regularly review picture books, videotapes, and CDs and tapes for children. Each year, *Booklist* publishes a "Nonprint Editor's Choice," as well as periodically featuring special listings such as "Best in Kidvid." After teachers have located high-quality materials, the next step is to infuse music and movement activities throughout the curriculum.

## ✵ INTEGRATING MUSIC AND MOVEMENT INTO THE SUBJECT AREAS

As long as music is kept separate from "academic" subjects, it will be considered a "frill" and will remain neglected. By integrating music into all subject areas, teachers provide richer musical and movement experiences for young children.

In general, appropriate music activities include singing songs together, playing and listening to records and tapes, learning the names and uses of musical instruments, discovering ways of making sounds, experiencing the different ways that music makes us feel, learning to participate with music through physical action and song, discovering rhythms in everyday life, observing different instruments being played, and playing simple musical instruments (Taylor, 1991). This chapter contains a sample thematic unit on the topic of African Rhythms and Harmonies suitable for second- or third-grade children (see pages 191–192). As you look over the activities, you will see how all of the musical experiences recommended in this chapter are included and integrated with all other areas of the curriculum. Activities that integrate music, movement, and all other areas of the curriculum are suggested below.

## *Mathematics, Science, and Technology*

There are many ways of integrating mathematics, science, and technology into music activities.

### *Musical Sets*

In mathematics, children could seriate instruments from large to small; they could also classify instruments into sets and subsets (e.g., woods, metals, drums, sticks). The teacher could provide experience with one-to-one correspondence by asking a child to distribute one rhythm band instrument to each classmate or could create a momentary rhythm instrument shortage to get across the idea of unequal sets.

### *Sounds of Nature*

In science, children could listen to nature's music: bird songs, the rhythms of the ocean, or the sounds created by whales and dolphins. A good follow-up to identifying the song of a real mockingbird on tape is learning a song such as "Mockingbird Hill" (Muldaur, 1990).

### *Sound Shake Match*

Use empty potato chip or 35mm film canisters and make two cans that contain distinctive-sounding materials such as popcorn, rice, beans, and sand. The children could listen to the sounds and try to find the matching pairs.

### Sound Quality

Children could conduct simple sound vibration experiments: listening to and observing the vibrations of rubber bands stretched across cardboard, experimenting with tuning forks, or trying different ways of beating a drum (with fingertips, with the palm, with a stick). In technology, children might compare/contrast symphonic and synthesizer versions of the same selections, produce different types of sounds on a computer or electronic keyboard, or compare the sound of the same recording played on a record player or cassette player and a portable compact disc player.

## Language, Literature, and Literacy

The child's growth in music and the language arts of listening, speaking, reading, and writing are connected in that both are symbolic systems. Some child-centered experiences that connect these systems include the following:

### Musical Storytelling

Storytelling often lends itself to musical accompaniment. We can read "Jack and the Beanstalk" and use a slide whistle to represent characters' ascent and descent on the stalk, use drums of different sizes to represent Jack's and the giant's footsteps, or set "Fee Fi Fo Fum . . ." to music. Most high-quality recordings for young children contain at least one story with sound effects and music, such as "Bear Hunt" (Bayes, 1983).

### Song Picture Books

One category of picture book for young children is the song picture book, an illustrated version of a song (Jalongo & Ribblett, 1997). Often these books contain the music for the song, such as *On Top of Spaghetti* (Glazer, 1982); sometimes they are accompanied by a record, such as *Over in the Meadow* (Keats, 1965); and sometimes they tell the history of the song, such as *Follow the Drinking Gourd* (Winter, 1988). Of course, teachers and/or children can also design original illustrations to accompany song charts or books.

### Creative Movement and Literature

A teacher might connect music with stories or picture books by asking:

> Can you show me how Baby Bear might go for his walk as you move around the circle? Now let's see Papa Bear's walk. Now Mama Bear's.

> Which rhythm instrument will you choose for each billy goat? Who can show me how the little billy goat would cross our balance beam bridge to this music?

> In the book *Color Dance* (Jonas, 1989), the dancers made colors with their scarves. Can you mix the colors while you dance, too?

### Song Parodies

A teacher might invite children to invent new verses for a song, beginning with simple substitutions such as "If you're happy and you know it, ____," then listening to a parody of "She'll Be Comin' Round the Mountain," "All for Freedom" (Sweet Honey in the Rock, 1989). Teachers in the primary grades might ask children to create an entirely new version, as Raffi did for "Old MacDonald Had a Band" or "Baa Baa Black Sheep," in which he sings, "One for your sweater, one for your rug. One for your blanket to keep you warm and snug." In order for children to accomplish this task, they must synthesize and evaluate what they know about lyrics, melody, rhythm, and rhyme. Writing a song parody is a complex, intellectually demanding activity (D'Angelo & Jalongo, 1984).

### Vocabulary Enactment

The language of creative dance includes words that describe the body, space, time, energy, and relationships (Stinson, 1990). Combining concrete, physical movements with abstract, verbal symbols helps to build children's active vocabularies. It is one thing to use descriptors such as *flexible, energetic, agile, graceful,* or *powerful* and quite another to see these attributes in action. By looking at several different types of movement on tape, such as a gymnast, a tap dancer, a modern dance troupe, or a scene from a ballet, children can incorporate these words into their vocabularies and then respond to them through dance.

## Social Studies, Health, and Nutrition

The music of a culture communicates information about that culture, because every social group uses music to celebrate, to worship, and as a vehicle for creative expression. Warner (1999) notes that many areas of the United States are famous for their unique brand of music, whether it is jazz, blues, tejano, or bluegrass. She suggests inviting children to construct a chart of where they hear music as a way to make children aware of how music is infused throughout their lives.

### Restaurant Play

A teacher who transforms her housekeeping area into a Mexican restaurant with authentic music, a menu, and equipment is extending children's understandings about other cultures and building the self-esteem of those children who are already familiar with the materials and theme.

### Visiting Musician

Teachers should use community resources to extend children's concepts about music. One Head Start teacher, for example, invited an African college student to her class. He arrived in traditional costume, taught the children a simple game from Nigeria, played the mbira (a thumb piano made of graduated metal strips over a wooden sound board), and taught them to sing a Nigerian children's song.

*Health and Nutrition Songs*
Practically every activity has a musical component if you only look for it. As part of a dental health unit, teachers might use a chant such as Raffi's "Brush Your Teeth." One teacher used the song "Today is Monday" as a culmination to her unit on the four food groups. Each child created a version of the song by drawing pictures using different healthful foods for each day of the week.

## PRACTICAL APPLICATIONS FOR YOUR CLASSROOM

When sharing music with special populations of young children, it is imperative that teachers first understand each child's strengths and limitations (McDonald & Simons, 1989).

## *Experiences to Support Cultural and Ethnic Diversity*

Oscar Wilde once said, "Art says nothing, art expresses everything." Throughout history and in every culture, music and movement have been regarded as an art form, a part of religious rituals, a type of recreation, and a form of therapy (Schwartz, 1989). As a result, music and movement provide a common vehicle for children to know about, understand, appreciate, and preserve cultural traditions. Children can respond to dances from other cultures through recordings. Simple dances from the Far East, India, Africa, the Americas, and continental Europe can be taught using the Nonesuch Explorer series (Numbers 7–11) as a guide. Songs such as "Tortillitas Para Mama" (Griego, 1980), a Spanish work song, or "Moonsong Lullaby" (Highwater, 1981), a Native American lullaby, expose children to the language and music of other cultures. Here is a sample teaching theme on African music.

## *Sample Teaching Theme on African Rhythms and Harmonies*

### *What Is a Teaching Theme?*
A teaching theme begins with the concepts that children are expected to acquire as a result of the theme. Using those concepts as a foundation, the teacher identifies a variety of activities that will further develop those concepts. Other concepts suggested by the experiences can also be identified and elaborated upon as they emerge from the experiences and the children's interests.

### *Concepts to Be Developed*

*Concept #1: Rhythm is the pattern that we hear in music; rhythm is what some people call the beat.*

Introduction to Concept #1: Use a drum to demonstrate a clear, steady rhythm and a random bunch of sounds. Then play a song with a strong, steady beat that children can easily pick out and replicate on their drums. Ask children to invent rhythms on coffee can or oatmeal box drums.

*Concept #2: Harmony is what makes music blend together well; harmony makes music pleasing to the ear.*

Introduction to Concept #2: Use a simple musical instrument, such as a toy xylophone, to illustrate two notes played simultaneously. After each combination of notes, ask children whether the two sounded good together or not so good. Explain that when the notes complement one another and sound good together, it is called harmony.

### Activities

**Pulling Together**   Tie a rope around a relatively heavy object, such as a small desk, and ask several of the children to pull it across the floor. Listen to "Harambe," an African chant that means "Let's all pull together," from the album *Evolution of Gospel,* by The Sounds of Blackness. Point out to the children that this is a work song, one that will enable them to work more effectively because they can tug in rhythm to the song. Play the song again and tap the rhythm on a drum or sticks. Tell the children to coordinate their pulling and to tug only when they hear the beat. Compare the progress that they made in moving the object in an uncoordinated way with the progress they made when they synchronized their pulling and worked together. Measure the distance that the object moved each time and contrast the two.

**Talking Drums**   Tell the children that you are going to answer their questions yes or no by playing a drum. Invite them to guess whether your answer is yes or no by listening alone. Demonstrate with a simple question (e.g., Can a dog fly?). Hit the drum sharply once for *no.* Then demonstrate with another question (e.g., Can a cow moo?) and play a light roll of the drum with your fingertips to mimic the sound of the word *yes.* Use the *All for Freedom* recording by Sweet Honey in the Rock (1989) to explain why drums are so important to the African culture. For older children, invite them to generate a list of other nonverbal methods of communication (e.g., smoke signals, the flash of a mirror, a telegraph, or signal flags). Then ask them to make a list of devices we use to amplify, transmit, and enhance verbal communication (e.g., a cellular phone, microphones, walkie-talkies, letters, or a paper cup and string telephone). Look at a chart of the universal symbol codes for school crossing, danger, stop, etc. and/or look at books that combine pictures with words to communicate, such as Marc Brown's *Hand Rhymes* (Brown, 1985), *If You're Happy and You Know It* (Weiss, 1987), or *"I Can't," said the Ant* (Cameron, 1961). Ask children if they are aware of any other cultures that used pictures to communicate (e.g., Egyptian hieroglyphics, Native Americans).

**Sets and Subsets**   Make a list of activities and ask the children to classify them into two groups: things they can do all by themselves (e.g., roller skating, riding a bike, reading a book, or putting together a puzzle) and things that they cannot do without others (e.g., playing a lotto game, playing in a rhythm band, or using a see-saw). For older children, introduce the concept of the intersection of sets using hula hoops or circles of yarns as Venn diagrams. Include a list of things that lend themselves to individual and group participation, such as jumping rope.

**Chants and Rap**   Listen to a recorded chant on an album by the Grammy-award-winning Zulu a capella choral group Ladysmith Black Mambazo, or watch their performance on Paul Simon's *Graceland* video. Then teach the children to sing the African nonsense chant "Che Che Koolay" and compare/contrast it with American children's playground chants on the album *Where I Come From! Poems and Songs from Many Cultures* (Cockburn & Steinbergh, 1991). Use the work chant/song "There Come Our Mothers" by Ladysmith Black Mambazo and a children's chorus (1994) to sing a song in two languages. Use "Fiesta Musical" (Serafin, 1994), a Latino rap song, as an introduction to rap.

**Life in Africa**   Develop children's understanding of African culture by reading books such as *A is for Africa* by Ifeoma Oneyefulu, *A Country Far Away* by Nigel Gray, *Darkness and the Butterfly* and *The Village of Round and Square Houses* by Ann Grifalconi, *When Africa Was Home* and *Galimoto*, both by Karen Williams.

## Experiences to Support Inclusion

Children with special needs can enjoy and participate in music if teachers are sensitive to ways of adapting musical experiences that emphasize children's abilities. Even teachers who are relatively untrained in music and movement—even those who feel they have very little ability in music or dance—can, with the right attitude and resources, provide a high-quality musical program for young children with special needs. Take, for example, a child with a physical challenge such as cystic fibrosis, which can cause a deterioration in breath control and affect singing. You may find that a child with physical limitations can participate in singing if given an opportunity to rest for a moment, or you might invite the child to sing just one part of the song. A child's cognitive limitations can make it difficult for him or her to recall words and melodies, focus on the music activity, or follow directions to an action song (Darrow, 1985). You could help such a child by using visual, verbal, and physical cues; providing more repetition; reducing distractions and background noise; breaking tasks into smaller segments; and ritualizing procedures (Darrow, 1985). Cerebral palsy affects a child's motor skills and may prevent participation in certain movement activities. Yet teachers who are alert to each child's capabilities might discover that the child with cerebral palsy sometimes has more motor control on one side of the body than on the other and can therefore participate to some extent in motor activities. That child might enjoy clapping along with the music by using one hand to tap on the table or slap her or his knee, for example. Often, children with special needs are so motivated to participate in music that they function at the highest possible level.

*Music often motivates the child with a physical disability to function at the highest possible level.*

Hearing impairments of various types obviously affect listening capacities and pose another challenge to the child (Darrow & Loomis, 1999). But you may find, for instance, that the hearing-impaired child has enough residual hearing to perceive a song played on earphones or that the child has low-frequency acuity and can hear low-pitched sounds, such as a bass drum. Even a child who is deaf can feel the rhythm of the vibrations by gently touching the speakers of the record player. For the child with attention disorders, creative dance is a highly motivating way to concentrate because "dancing involves making movement significant in and of itself. The first step in making movement dance is to pay attention to it" (Stinson, 1990, p. 35). Although we can make these general statements about limitations, each child is an individual. Teachers should check with specialists to determine each child's particular capabilities.

## Adaptations for Individual Learners

Because musical intelligence and bodily/kinesthetic intelligence are two distinctive "kinds of smart," children who perform well in academic subjects may or may not be gifted musically or kinesthetically. In a special project involving elementary school students that was designed to identify talent in the performing arts, 62 percent to 82 percent of those identified as gifted in dance had reading levels in the bottom half of the class, and 34 percent were below grade level in mathematics (Kay & Subotnik, 1994). This finding illustrates, once again, that schools are failing to recognize all eight kinds of know-how in the curriculum. Furthermore, children who are gifted musically may or may not have exceptional bodily/kinesthetic abilities. It is important for music and creative dance to be available to all children, not only to the privileged child whose parents can afford private lessons or to the child who is gifted in music and movement. Still, teachers need to be alert to opportunities for children to pursue new challenges in music and movement. Some students may be ready for more formal musical experiences such as leading a group of classmates as they play pitched bells or composing original songs at an electronic keyboard. If children are at least given the opportunity to try various kinds of music and movement activities, they can begin to appreciate more fully the rich diversity among their classmates and to recognize the fact that each person has unique strengths and talents.

We also know that some children whose academic achievement falls below their peers' in certain areas can recall and retain information better when they use more than one modality (e.g., visual, auditory, tactile). Music and movement offer multimodal approaches to learning, enabling children to practice and solidify information and concepts.

Sometimes the learning problems of children are more social and emotional than cognitive. Socio-emotional difficulties can be addressed through music as well. Psychologists have found that music is especially useful for children who have difficulty gaining social acceptance from peers, such as children who are aggressive and uncontrolled and those who are timid and withdrawn (Hughes, 1999). Creative dance in response to music builds self-esteem because a young child who moves in response to music does not move the wrong way or take the wrong step (Stinson, 1990).

## Conclusion

There are some music and movement activities suitable for every child, regardless of age, talent, or physical limitations. Leading children to music and movement is also for all early childhood educators, regardless of their performance skills in music or dance. Early childhood music specialist Marvin Greenberg (1976) contends that preschool teachers who have limited musical backgrounds and apparently low effectiveness can do as well in sharing music and movement activities with young children as teachers with extensive musical backgrounds, but only if the nonmusician teachers are conscientious and enthusiastic about following a daily musical curriculum. When teachers make music and movement an integral part of the school day, children's development in all areas—emotional, social, physical, and cognitive—is supported and enriched.

## CHAPTER SUMMARY

1. Children develop their music and movement abilities through interaction with significant others and enjoyment of a wide variety of music and movement activities.
2. The goal of early childhood music and movement activities is to support every child's growth in music and movement from the earliest days of life. Music and movement experiences should be both developmentally appropriate and individually appropriate for young children.
3. Children proceed through the enactive, iconic, and symbolic modes in their understandings about music.
4. Music and movement activities have a long tradition in early childhood education and contemporary programs tend to be eclectic.
5. Factors that contribute to the child's growth in musicality are a supportive physical and emotional environment, opportunities for social interaction, and adult role models.
6. Teachers fulfill their roles and responsibilities in music education when they select, present, and evaluate musical experiences effectively; when they function as motivators, planners, co-participants, and observers; and when they integrate music throughout the school day and across various subject areas.

## EXPANDING YOUR THINKING ABOUT MUSIC AND MOVEMENT

### Discuss: *Your Ideas About Music*

1. Compare/contrast the beliefs, values, and attitudes that underlie a program to maximize every child's musical talent versus those that seek to identify precocity in music. Use your readings to support the philosophy of building every child's abilities.
2. A parent tells you, "I don't sing to my child because I never learned to play an instrument, but I play his song tape for him at night." How would you respond? Why?
3. An administrator observes the children briefly during your lesson, then asks, "Why are they having music during social studies?" How would you support your decision without becoming defensive?
4. If money were available through the budget, a donation, or a small grant, what music materials would you purchase first for each age group—infants, toddlers, preschoolers, and primary grade children? Why?

## Interview: Children's Favorite Songs

The purpose of this assignment is to study young children's musical preferences. Arrange to interview the parents of a young child (5 to 8 years old) and the child individually. Try to interview a child who knows you well and who will not be too shy to sing on tape. Ask the parent about the child's favorite lullaby, nursery rhyme, children's song, or popular song at various times during the child's development. Then interview the child and invite him or her to name, describe, and/or sing some of the songs he or she prefers today. (If the child is uncomfortable doing this, you might ask the parent to do it.) Tape-record the child's responses. Ask the child to tell you what he or she likes about each song.

In class, make a list of the songs selected by children. What categories of music are generally preferred? What features do they tend to have in common? Are there any surprising choices? Which songs are mentioned most frequently as favorites?

## Write to Learn: Integrating Music and Movement Across the Curriculum

Imagine that you are responsible for planning a thematic mini-unit for a group of children. The unit must include all of the traditional academic subjects (language arts, mathematics, science, social studies, health/nutrition) as well as sociodramatic play, art, and music. Begin with the music and movement characteristics of a particular age group of children (refer to Figure 4.3). Sketch out a plan for your theme and unit.

## REFERENCES

Andress, B. (1998). *Music for young children.* Philadelphia: Harcourt Brace.

Bennett, N., Wood, L., & Rogers, S. (1997). *Teaching through play: Teachers' thinking and classroom practice.* Buckingham, England: Open University Press.

Bernstein, P. (1990). On breaking 100 in music. In F. Wilson & F. Roehmann (Eds.), *Music and child development: Proceedings of the 1987 Denver Conference* (pp. 400–419). St. Louis, MO: Mosby.

Bayless, K. M., & Ramsey, M. E. (1990). *Music: A way of life for the young child.* Upper Saddle River, NJ: Merrill-Prentice Hall..

Boyd, A. E. (1989, July–August). *Music in early childhood.* Paper presented at the 21st International Conference on Early Education and Development. Hong Kong. (ERIC Document Reproduction Service No. ED 310 863)

Bruner, J. (1968). *Toward a theory of instruction.* New York: Norton.

Caulfield, R. (1999). Mozart effect: Sound beginnings? *Early Childhood Education Journal, 27*(2), 119–122.

Consortium of National Arts Education Associations. (1994). *National standards for arts education: Dance, music, theater, and visual arts: What every young American should know and be able to do in the arts.* Reston, VA: Music Educators National Conference.

D'Angelo, K., & Jalongo, M. R. (1984). Song picture books and the language disabled child. *Teaching Exceptional Children, 16,* 114–120.

Darrow, A. A. (1985). Music for the deaf. *Music Educators Journal, 71*(6), 33–35.

Darrow, A., & Loomis, D. M. (1999). Music and deaf culture: Images from the media and their interpretation by deaf and hearing students. *Journal of Music Therapy, 26*(2), 88–107.

Eliason, C., & Jenkins, L. (1977). *A practical guide to early childhood curriculum.* St. Louis, MO: Mosby.

Erikson, E. (1950). *Childhood and society.* New York: Norton.

Fox, D. B. (1989). Music TIME and music times two: The Eastman infant-toddler music program. In B. Andress (Ed.), *Promising practices in prekindergarten music* (pp. 13–24). Reston, VA: Music Educators National Conference.

Fox, D. B. (1991). Music, development, and the young child. *Music Educators Journal, 77*(5), 42–46.

Gold, R., & Cuming, G. J. (1999). Age-appropriate dance. *Dance* Magazine, 78.

Greenberg, M. (1976). Research in music in early childhood education: A survey with recommendations. *Bulletin of the Council for Research in Music Education, 45* 1–20.

Greenberg, M. (1979). *Your children need music.* Englewood Cliffs, NJ: Prentice Hall.

Gromko, J. E., & Poorman, A. S. (1998). The effect of music training on preschoolers' spatial-temporal task performance. *Journal of Research in Music Education, 46*(2), 173–181.

Hall, M. A. (1989). Music for children. In B. Andress (Ed.), *Promising practices in prekindergarten music* (pp. 47–57). Reston, VA: Music Educators National Conference.

Hildebrandt, C. (1992). Creativity in music and early childhood. *Young Children, 53*(6), 68–74.

Hughes, F. (1999). *Children, play and development* (3rd ed.). Boston: Allyn & Bacon.

Jalongo, M. R., & Collins, M. (1985). Singing with young children! Folk music for nonmusicians. *Young Children, 40,* 17–22.

Jalongo, M. R. (1996). Teaching young children to become better listeners. *Young Children, 51*(2), 21–26.

Jalongo, M. R. (1996). Using recorded music with young children: A guide for nonmusicians. *Young Children, 51*(5), 6–14.

Jalongo, M. R., & Ribblett, D. (1997). Using song picture books to support emergent literacy. *Childhood Education, 74*(1), 15–22.

Kay, S. I., & Subotnik, R. F. (1994). Talent beyond words: Unveiling spatial, expressive, kinesthetic and musical talent in young children. *Gifted Child Quarterly, 38*(2), 70–74.

Kelley, L., & Sutton-Smith, B. (1987). A study of infant musical productivity. In J. C. Peery, I. W. Peery, & T. Draper (Eds.), *Music and child development* (pp. 35–53). New York: Springer-Verlag.

Koopman, C. (1996). Why teach music at school? *Oxford Review of Education,* 22(4), 483–494.

Lucky, S. (1990). *Music-movement-make-believe: The link between creativity and thinking skills.* Paper presented at the 41st annual conference of the Southern Association for Children Under Six, Dallas, TX.

McDonald, D. T., & Simons, G. M. (1989). *Musical growth and development: Birth through six.* New York: Schirmer/Macmillan.

Nash, J. M. (1997, February). Fertile minds. *Time, 149,* 48–56.

Palmer, M. & Sims, W. L. (Eds.). (1993). *Music in prekindergarten: Planning and teaching.* Reston, VA: Music Educators National Conference.

Parr, N. C., Radford, J., & Snyder, S. (1998). Kaleidoscope: Building an arts-infused elementary curriculum. *Early Childhood Education Journal, 25*(3), 181–188.

Persellin, D. (1998). Quoted in M. P. Pautz, Teaching prekindergarten music. *Teaching Music, 5*(5), 40–43.

Peterson, M. (1979). *Stay in tune* (record/cassette). Summit, NJ: Meg Peterson Enterprises.

Piaget, J. (1952). *The origins of intellect.* New York: International University Press.

Piaget, J. (1962). *Play, dreams and imitation in childhood.* C. Gategno & F. M. Hodgson (Trans.). New York: Norton.

Ririe, S. R. (1980). Individual arts: Dance. In J. J. Hausman (Ed.), *Arts and the schools* (pp. 270–279). New York: McGraw-Hill.

Rousseau, J. J. (1883). *Emile, or treatise on education.* W. H. Payne (Trans.). New York: Appleton.

Schwartz, V. (1989). Dance dynamics—A dance for all people. *Journal of Physical Education, Recreation, and Dance, 60*(9), 49–64.

Snyder, S. (1995). *Share the music, K–6.* New York: Macmillan/McGraw-Hill.

Stinson, S. W. (1990). Dance for education in early childhood. *Design for Arts in Education, 91,* 34–41.

Taylor, B. (1999). *A child goes forth: A curriculum guide for preschool children.* Upper Saddle River, NJ: Merrill/Prentice Hall.

Turner, M. E. (1999). Child-centered learning and music programs. *Music Educators Journal, 86*(1), 30–35.

Warner, L. (1999). Self-esteem: A byproduct of quality classroom music. *Childhood Education, 76*(1), 19–23.

Weinberger, N. M. (1998). The music in our minds. *Educational Leadership, 56*(3), 36–40.

Wilcox, E. (1994). Unlock the joy of music. *Teaching Music, 2,* 34–35, 46.

Wilson, F., & Roehmann, F. (Eds.). (1990). *Music and child development: Proceedings of the 1987 Denver Conference.* St Louis, MO: MMB Music.

Wilt, J., & Watson, T. (1977). *Listen!* Waco, TX: Creative Resources.

Wohlschlaeger, A., & Wohlschlaeger, A. (1998). Mental and manual rotation. *Journal of Experimental Psychology: Human Perception and Performance, 24*(2), 387–412.

Wolf, J. (1994). Singing with young children is a cinch. *Young Children, 46*(2), 20–25, 36–41.

Zdzinski, S. F. (1999). Sound Advice: Involving parents in music. *Our Children, 25*(3), 12–13.

## Children's Books and Records

Aliki. (1968). *Hush little baby.* Englewood Cliffs, NJ: Prentice Hall.

Bayes, L. (1983) "Bear Hunt," on *Circle around.* Seattle, WA: Tickle Tune Typhoon.

Brett, J. (1986). *The twelve days of Christmas.* New York: Trumpet Club.

Brown, M. (1985). *Hand rhymes.* New York: Dutton.

Cameron, P. (1961). *"I can't," said the ant.* New York: Coward.

Cockburn, V., & Steinbergh, J. (1991). *Where I come from! Poems and songs from many cultures.* Chestnut Hill, MA: Talking Stone Press.

Collins, M. (1982). *Sounds like fun.* Rochester, NY: Sampler Records.

Delibes, L. (1986). Coppelia. In M. Greaves, *Petrushka (A little box of ballet stories).* New York: Dial.

Glazer, T. (1982). *On top of spaghetti.* New York: Doubleday.

Greigo, M. (1980). *Tortillitas para mama.* New York: Holt, Rinehart & Winston.

Highwater, J. (1981). *Moonsong lullaby.* New York: Lothrop, Lee & Shephard.

Jonas, A. (1989). *Color dance.* New York: Greenwillow.

Keats, E. J. (1965). *Over in the meadow.* New York: Scholastic.

Kennedy, J. (1983). *Teddy bear's picnic.* La Jolla, CA: Green Tiger Press.

Muldaur, M. (1990). *On the sunny side.* Redway, CA: Music for Little People.

Raffi (1987). *Down by the bay.* New York: Crown.

Seeger, P. (1973). *The foolish frog.* New York: Macmillan. (Also on Weston Woods video.)

Sendak, M. (1975). *Carole King's Really Rosie.* Hollywood, CA: A&M.

Sounds of Blackness (1991). *The evolution of gospel.* New York: Polygram Records.

Spier, P. (1961). *The fox went out on a chilly night.* New York: Doubleday.

Sweet Honey in the Rock (1989). *All for freedom.* Redmond, CA: Music for Little People.

Wescott, N. B. (1980). *I know an old lady who swallowed a fly.* Boston: Atlantic/Little.

Winter, J. (1988). *Follow the drinking gourd.* New York: Knopf.

Zelinsky, P. (1990). *The wheels on the bus.* New York: Dutton.

## Big Books

Weiss, N. (1987). *If you're happy and you know it.* New York: Greenwillow.

Wescott, N. B. (1987). *Peanut butter and jelly.* New York: Dutton.

## Videotapes

Raffi. (1984). *A young children's concert with Raffi.* Hollywood, CA: Shoreline/Troubadour.

# Chapter 5

## Creative Drama
## in the Early Childhood Curriculum

*"Of all of the arts, drama involves the participant most fully: intellectually, emotionally, physically, verbally, and socially. As players, children assume the roles of others, where they learn and become sensitive to the problems and values of persons different from themselves. At the same time, they are learning to work cooperatively in groups, for drama is a communal art, each person necessary to the whole. As spectators, children become involved vicariously in the adventures of the characters on stage."*

Nellie McCaslin, 2000, p. 4

*"If I could no longer use drama, I would become an impoverished teacher. Drama releases imagination and creates opportunities for learning unlike any other medium."*

Brian Edmiston, 1998, p.xxii

# TEACHERS' REFLECTIONS ON DRAMA

## Preservice Teachers

"I now know there is an important role for an audience when using some forms of creative drama in the classroom. The children will always have some special involvement."

"I wish that all teachers valued creative drama in the classroom. I wonder how I would explain dramatic play to a parent who believes in an academic program."

"I learned how drama helps make language arts more concrete because the child can actually interpret the character."

## Inservice Teachers

"I tried using story drama in my first-grade class for the first time this year. I found that the children are empowered by either retelling or re-creating versions of their own. I also noticed that they had a much clearer understanding of sequential story events, and their retellings grew increasingly more accurate."

"I learned that I need to address the *role* of the child rather than the *child* when intervening in dramatic play. For instance, if John is playing the role of the wolf, I say, "Wolf, what are you going to do now that . . .""

"I now understand why I felt so uncomfortable having my kindergartners participate in our annual, elaborate kindergarten play for the parents. It just was not appropriate for this age child, caused too much stress for the children and the teachers, and was not meaningful to many of the children."

## Your Reflections

- What role do you think drama has in the early childhood curriculum?

- How would you go about integrating different creative drama activities and experiences in the early childhood curriculum?

- How might your knowledge and beliefs about drama enhance or inhibit children's self-expression?

 ## Case Study:

### Reenacting a Story

It is February in Ms. Clark's urban first-grade classroom, and five children have asked to enact "The Little Red Hen." Florence, a nonreader, has volunteered to be the narrator. Jesse, a shy, obese African-American boy, has asked to play the role of the hen. When Ms. Clark comes by, she helps the children to plan by asking good questions:

> **Ms. Clark:**   Let's do some brainstorming about what we might need for costumes and I'll write it down.
> **Jesse:**   I need some feathers.
> **Ms. Clark:**   How do you want to use the feathers? How would you put them on?
> **Tory:**   (Holding up a fringed, red scarf) We can use this for the head part.
> **Ms. Clark:**   (Writes down what each child chooses to wear, how each will invent a simple costume and props, and then announces) I need to know what you're going to work on tomorrow so I can have my supplies ready.

This group of students is ethnically diverse and lives in a low-income area of the city. Why would Ms. Clark devote time to drama? Wouldn't her time be better spent on teaching phonics and addition skills?

Ms. Clark knows how important child-initiated activity is for young children. Her first graders thought of dramatizing a favorite, familiar story. They also selected and negotiated roles, jointly planned costumes, and chose their audience. Rather than giving her students seatwork to complete after reading the story (such as cutting and pasting pictures in correct sequence), Ms. Clark capitalized on their interests, involved them in purposeful and meaningful activities, and supported their learning through dramatization. A simple enactment activity, such as dramatizing "The Little Red Hen," enables children to learn about themselves and others, to develop a sense of belonging in a community of learners, to gain self-confidence, and to master skills and concepts in meaningful situations. Analyzing the children's behavior reveals how important these goals are in every classroom.

Remember Jesse? He usually speaks softly and does not enunciate clearly, but because he wanted to be the Little Red Hen, he practiced and refined his speaking skills. Florence is not yet reading, but her role as narrator has prompted her to listen to a tape recording over and over again until she can rely upon familiarity with the story to read the book aloud.

## THEORETICAL AND RESEARCH BASE: WHAT IS CREATIVE DRAMA?

When most adults think about drama, they think about formal productions: a small group of performers who memorize lines and use props and costumes while entertaining an audience. Formal drama often causes both teachers and students to feel anxious, self-conscious, and constrained by the script. Consequently, many teachers are reluctant to use formal drama in their classrooms (Fox, 1987).

Creative drama, often called enactment, on the other hand, differs significantly from formal drama. It emerges from the spontaneous play of young children and uses the art of theater to enhance the participants' awareness of self, others, and the world in which they live (Pinciotti, 1993). In creative drama, children act "as if" their imagined world were an actual world and represent familiar feelings, thoughts, and actions for themselves rather than memorizing a script for an audience (McCaslin, 2000; Wilhelm & Edmiston, 1998). Creative drama not only provides children with a meaningful form of communication and an opportunity to imagine possibilities, but also becomes a useful learning resource for higher-order thinking, problem solving, feelings, and reflection as children show what they know through oral communication. Many teachers believe that creative drama provides an excellent foundation for literacy development, because it supports all four of the language arts—listening, speaking, reading, and writing (Cecil & Lauritzen, 1994; Heller, 1996; McMaster, 1998; Wilhelm & Edmiston, 1998).

Drama experiences tap into three kinds of intelligences that capitalize on children's learning potential: (1) bodily/kinesthetic, (2) interpersonal, and (3) intrapersonal intelligence (Gardner, 1993a, 1993b). Gardner's work suggests that people develop and learn in many ways and that neither children nor adults possess intelligence that is "fixed" in one area. Children, like adults, depend upon different areas of their brain in different situations, at different times, and for different reasons. As children act out stories, situations, and ideas, they use their *bodily/kinesthetic intelligence* to express themselves through gesture, voice, or movement. They also use their *interpersonal intelligence* to work cooperatively to determine how to dramatize a favorite story or interact with an audience, and they use their *intrapersonal intelligence* to access their own feelings through different forms of role play and pantomime. These ways of expression are also better checks on comprehension than most other classroom activities. Table 5.1 lists and defines these three types of intelligences, relates them to enactment, and supplies some enactment examples.

### TABLE 5.1   Multiple Intelligences Most Related to Enactment

| Type | Definition | Relation to Enactment | Enactment Examples |
|---|---|---|---|
| Bodily-Kinesthetic | The ability to use body to express feelings and thoughts and solve problems; to use hands to handle objects skillfully. | Offers children a concrete, specific, and personal way for developing abstract thought and to represent their understanding of concepts and ideas through "hands-on" experiences. | ° Role play<br>° Story re-enactments<br>° Pantomime<br>° Dramatic play<br>° Dance and movement |
| Interpersonal | The ability to distinguish among the intentions, moods, and feelings of others by being sensitive to voice, gesture, and facial expressions, and to respond sensitively to others' feelings and moods. | Enables children to explore feelings, moods, and points of view of others and to respond sensitively to them. | ° Improvisation<br>° Pantomime<br>° Role play<br>° Pretend<br>° Puppets |
| Intrapersonal | The ability to detect one's own moods, needs, desires, and to look both inward and outward. | Enables children to reflect on and explore their own feelings and moods in socially acceptable ways and to test out their own feelings and emotions as well as their responses to others. | ° Dramatic play<br>° Pantomime<br>° Improvisation<br>° Readers theater<br>° Puppets |

Experiences with enactment help all children to succeed in school by uncovering their hidden strengths or by challenging undeveloped areas of learning. Consequently, opportunities for drama belong everywhere in the early childhood curriculum (Fox, 1987; Heller, 1996; Bromley, 1998).

## The Meaning of Enactment

Five-year-old Haley has heard and was captivated by the story of *Perfect the Pig* (Jeschke, 1985). In this story, a homeless, flying piglet is found, loved, and cared for by a young woman who decides to name the pig Perfect. Perfect is stolen and abused by a man who operates a carnival sideshow, then is happily reunited with the woman when a judge awards her custody. After hearing this dramatic story, Haley pretends to be Perfect, experiencing the feelings and thoughts of the pig during the story. She also decides which props ("I'll need wings") and behaviors ("This is how he oinks when he needs help") she needs to enact that role.

**Enactment** occurs when children adopt the actions, feelings, thoughts, and behaviors of people in particular situations. This ability emerges at about age 3 and signals the child's developing imagination. Enactment is potentially the most powerful kind of learning because children can:

*   Assume roles, create dialogue, feel emotions, use their bodies, and make decisions.
*   Use their past and present experiences to talk about and solve problems.
*   Develop knowledge of appropriate roles, actions, and behaviors.
*   See others' points of view.
*   Try out new and emerging skills.
*   Explore the forms and functions of language (Shaftel & Shaftel, 1983; Wilhelm & Edmiston, 1998).

Children learn about their physical and social worlds not only from their interactions with these worlds, but also from the way these worlds interact with them. These concrete, personal experiences provide the basis for their developing abstract, interpersonal knowledge, which comprises much of the learning that goes on in schools today (Gardner, 1993a). Because drama is always concrete, specific, and personal, it helps children more easily understand how their physical and social worlds work and interact (Johnson, 1998; Dillon, 1988). In other words, the dramatic mode is a powerful way of knowing about the world.

Very young children (e.g., toddlers) enact events that they have directly experienced, such as diapering and feeding; preschool and kindergarten children add to these incidents with more imaginative and make-believe situations, such as preparing meals for a family or taking care of a baby. Primary grade children most often imagine themselves in real-life, problem-solving situations, such as controlling a space shuttle in outer space. Through enactment, all children stretch their imaginations, share experiences that help them understand their world in a low-risk setting, and explore feelings, emotions, and ideas in socially acceptable ways (Heinig, 1993; Heller, 1996).

*Enactment is a powerful kind of learning.*

## Forms of Enactment

Enactment occurs in three forms in the early childhood years: (1) informal drama, (2) story or interpretive drama, and (3) formal or scripted drama. These drama forms can be differentiated according to their degree of spontaneity versus formality (Tompkins, 1998). Following are the characteristics and an example of each form.

    **1.   Informal drama** is the earliest and most spontaneous type of enactment. It includes dramatic and sociodramatic play as well as pantomime and some movement activities. In informal drama, young children spontaneously take on a role or behavior of someone else (such as pretending to direct traffic as a police officer), use an object to stand for something else (such as sitting on a block and driving an "imaginary tractor" around fields), and use make-believe to act out familiar events (such as enacting a trip to a fast-food restaurant). There is no audience and the teacher serves as an observer or facilitator. Older children who enact their own scripts base them on familiar life situations (such as family celebrations of holidays), literature (such as a play based on the dramatic story of a little fruit bat, *Stellaluna* (Cannon, 1993), or media experiences (such as the film *Jumanji*).

2. **Story or interpretive drama** involves interpreting someone else's ideas and words rather than creating new ideas and words. Children in the primary grades often enact favorite stories they have heard and read or they create original stories. Take, for example, the picture book *Amazing Grace* (Hoffman, 1991). Grace is an African-American child with a flair for drama. She pretends to be a nurse whose patients' lives are in her hands, imagines that she is the African trickster, Anansi the Spider; and pretends to be a peg-legged pirate. When the class decides to enact Peter Pan, her peers tell Grace that she cannot play the lead role because she is a female and black. With her mother's and grandmother's support, Grace does pursue her dream. This story really lends itself to interpretation because Grace is practicing some form of enactment on every page. Story drama is particularly valuable in stimulating children's oral language and literacy learning.

3. **Formal or scripted drama** is the most structured form of drama. It involves a polished production of a prepared script before an audience (McCaslin, 2000). In scripted drama, the children memorize lines and the teacher directs. Because scripted drama is product-oriented, it focuses more on technique rather than spontaneous self-expression (Bolton, 1985). Current thinking in the field of early childhood education is against the use of formal or scripted drama for young children through the primary grades unless, of course, children choose to create and produce their own plays. Otherwise, formal, scripted plays are not considered to be the most developmentally appropriate form of drama for young children (Tompkins, 1998). Table 5.2 arranges these types of enactment from least to most formal, compares the preparation time needed for each form, contrasts the role of the players and audience, analyzes materials needed, and examines implications for teachers.

Informal drama and story dramas are the only forms of creative drama that belong in the early childhood curriculum. They offer purposeful ways to develop children's oral language, literacy understandings, imagination and thinking, nonverbal communication, and self-confidence. In the next section we will see how drama supports children's learning.

## THE IMPORTANCE OF CREATIVE DRAMA IN THE CURRICULUM

For all children, creative drama is a powerful vehicle for understanding difficult concepts through playing with ideas that are enacted in drama, engaging in genuine dialogue that is based upon shared meaning, and thinking and feeling about oneself and others (Fennessey, 1995; Furman, 2000; Verriour, 1994; Wilhelm

**TABLE 5.2   Three Types of Drama Activities**

| Informal Drama/Dramatic Play | Story or Interpretive Drama | Formal/Scripted Drama |
|---|---|---|
| Least Formal ◄──────────────────────────────────────────► Most Formal | | |
| **Characteristics** | | |
| Unrehearsed, spontaneous, invented enactment of roles and behaviors of familiar people or characters; includes verbal and nonverbal activities (facial expressions, gestures, body movements, and vocal changes) to enact feelings and ideas; important first step in uses of enactment; most characteristic of 3-8 year-olds. | Invented, improvised interpretation of ideas and stories using voices, gestures, and facial expressions.<br><br>Involves some rehearsal and is more formal. | Memorizing a written script; performing polished plays before an audience. |
| **Preparation Time** | | |
| Minimal: children initiate roles and behaviors; and invent actions, dialogue, and movements based on knowledge of the world and/or a familiar story. | Moderate: children rehearse reading, interpret story, and enact roles | Extensive: children memorize parts, dialogue, and gestures. |
| **Roles of Players and Audience** | | |
| Active: children move freely from role of audience to that of player; not designed for an audience. | Active: children read parts individually or as members of a group. | Passive: roles must be rehearsed to play; audience watches. |
| **Materials** | | |
| Simple, familiar props; some realistic. | Simple props. | Elaborate costumes, prop, scenery. |
| **Implications for the Classroom** | | |
| Exerts powerful influence on children's social and cognitive understandings; can be used with children's favorite or original stories; children practice both verbal and nonverbal communication and begin to see others' points of view. | Increases children's confidence in using scripted drama; allows for cooperative work with peers. | Should be used only at the children's suggestion and be child-directed. |

& Edmiston, 1998). This is a particularly important strategy for second-language learners. Creative drama develops understanding in four main ways.

**1.** *Creative drama values and respects children's individuality and creative expressiveness.* Drama builds positive self-concepts in children as they participate in experiences that have no right or wrong answers (McCaslin, 2000). Each child's interpretation of a role is unique. One child might play the role of the wolf in "Little Red Riding Hood" as sly, another as mean, and still another as foolish. These possibilities enable each child to feel good about involvement in a group experience. Children's languages and cultures gain respect as children participate in drama activities both in their native language and in the majority language of the culture.

**2.** *Creative drama offers a means for cooperative learning and teamwork through shared experiences* (Heller, 1996). Two third-graders wanted to use a secret code to "put on a show" for their friends. During recess, they decided on the theme of eating and sleeping in space and then figured out a code based on colors. After collecting props such as sleeping bags, self-sealing plastic bags, and a pillow, they invited some of their peers to watch their skit and try to figure out their code.

**3.** *Creative drama enables children to make abstract situations meaningful and personalize real-life situations* (Verriour, 1994). After 4-year-old Mary's puppy died, she initiated an animal rescue theme play. In her dramas, unlike the real-life situation, Mary was always able to save the animal's life, enabling her to understand loss and cope with grief.

**4.** *Creative drama provides opportunities to be spectators and actors.* Whether children are enacting or watching others enact, they are simultaneously imagining the situations and problems of others (Furman, 2000; Heller, 1996). After hearing a story about a Kwanzaa celebration, a small group of kindergartners shared dances, poetry, songs, and food to celebrate the bounty of the earth. As a result, the children functioned as actors for their peers during some parts of the events and as spectators of their peers during others.

In addition to supporting children's overall learning, creative drama explicitly contributes to all other academic areas and enhances children's ability to learn in school settings. In the following enactment of a restaurant theme, Kellie and Tammie, 4-year-old twins, and Brenda, a college student, are co-playing. Consider how this dramatic play episode contributes to the twins' developing imaginative thinking, problem-solving ability, language and listening skills, perspective-taking ability, and appreciation of drama as an art form.

**Kellie:**   Oh, here's your table. (She gestures toward the table.)

**Brenda:**   Well, what should we eat, Tammie? What do you have here, Kellie?

**Kellie:**   Well, we have pork chops, lima beans, and fish sticks.

**Tammie:**   That sounds good. We'll take it. (Kellie exits and returns with a "tray"—two parts of a plastic sweater-drying rack.)

The girls continue their play, name their restaurant "King's," order drinks, and then ask for a check.

**Tammie:**   I want my check to be five dollars.

**Kellie:**   Five dollars . . . and eighty-six cents.

**Tammie:**   Okay.

**Brenda:**   Do you have any money?

**Tammie:**   Oh, yeah. I have a lot of money. Oh. I forgot. I don't have a lot of money. (Starts rummaging through her purse and begins to giggle.)

First, think about how creative drama develops children's *imaginative thinking.* In this restaurant scene, Kellie and Tammie both had a strong mental image of a restaurant, which enabled them to create and enact the roles of customer and server as well as to embellish and ad lib the scenario they created. When Kellie needed a tray to serve the food in the restaurant, she was problem-solving as she used two parts of a plastic sweater drying rack for this prop. Through drama, children relive their experiences by creating their own worlds and experiment with solutions to real-life problems (Heller, 1996; McCaslin, 2000).

Drama also provides meaningful opportunities for children to practice *literacy skills.* It elicits more verbal play and richer language than in any other setting (Christie & Johnson, 1983; McMaster, 1998), develops narrative competence when

*Some creative drama experiences provide opportunities for children to be both actors and spectators.*

*We played Humpty*
*Dumpty sat on a wall,*
*by a 4-year-old boy.*

children invent stories that contain essential story elements, displays children's knowledge of the functions of reading and writing (McMaster, 1998; Wiltz & Fein, 1996), and increases both children's confidence in their abilities to speak language and the value they place on communicating precisely (McMaster, 1998). When Kellie and Tammie communicate about what to order and how to pay, they use both verbal and nonverbal communication. Play episodes such as this one give children opportunities to use all of the various forms and functions of language (Halliday, 1975).

Role enactment also develops children's perspective-taking ability. When children actually become someone else, they not only learn the behaviors and feelings of that character or role but also study how people affect others. Even very young children may glimpse insights that help in understanding people and, therefore, in living (McCaslin, 2000). In the restaurant episode, Kellie and Tammie practiced appropriate behaviors for eating in a restaurant. They also watched Brenda, the college student, model the customer role by asking, "Well, what should we eat, Tammie? What do you have here, Kellie?"

Through early drama experiences, children learn to appreciate drama as an art form. According to drama expert Nellie McCaslin (2000), drama activities "offer children their first taste of the magic and make-believe of the theater" (p. 16). Today's children are tomorrow's audiences and players. School provides an important context for them to gain an understanding of what drama is and how it comes into being.

Drama, in its many forms, is an important stimulus for children's healthy growth and development. It enables them to express their thoughts, feelings, and ideas in both verbal and nonverbal ways. As so poignantly stated by Gavin Bolton (1985), a recognized expert in drama education: "Drama allows children to experience the complexities of today's world and to be prepared to live in the twenty-first century" (p. 156). Therefore, creative drama is not a "frill"—it is a curricular basic.

## Research Studies on Creative Drama

Carlson-Sabelli, L. (1998). Children's therapeutic puppet theatre—Action, interaction, and cocreation. *International Journal of Action Methods, 51*(3), 91–112.

Galda, L. (1982). Playing about a story: Its impact on comprehension. *The Reading Teacher, 55*(1), 52–55.

Howe, N., Moller, L., Chambers, B., & Petrakos, H. (1993). The ecology of dramatic play centers and children's social and cognitive play. *Early Childhood Research Quarterly, 8*(2), 235–252.

Krafft, K. C., & Berk, L. E. (1998). Private speech in two preschools: Significance of open-ended activities and make-believe play for verbal self-regulation. *Early Childhood Research Quarterly, 13*(4), 637–658.

Moore, B., & Caldwell, H. (1993). Drama and drawing for narrative writing in primary grades. *Journal of Educational Research, 8*(2), 100–110.

Stone, S., & Christie, J. (1996). Collaborative literacy learning during sociodramatic play in a multiage (K–2) primary classroom. *Journal of Research in Childhood Education, 10*(2), 123–133.

Williamson, P. A., & Silvern, S. B. (1992). "You can't be grandma; you're a boy": Events within the thematic fantasy play context that contribute to story comprehension. *Early Childhood Research Quarterly, 7*, 75–94.

## CRITERIA FOR INTEGRATING DRAMA INTO THE CURRICULUM

Teachers exert a powerful influence over children's dramatic expression. When teachers are open to children's creative efforts and work to establish a safe, supportive, child-centered environment, they have a powerful, positive influence on creative drama and the total curriculum (Edwards, 1997). An early childhood curriculum must contain a variety of opportunities for children to dramatize familiar experiences and to share enactments with both peers and adults.

### Selecting and Presenting Experiences and Materials

Some considerations that enhance creative drama and capitalize on children's multiple intelligences include space, materials, and an enthusiastic teacher (McCaslin, 2000). Here are six brief examples of how to release children's creative potential through drama. See if you can provide others.

1. *Large, pleasant spaces.* How space is arranged sends strong messages about how to use that space for drama. Providing specific space for dramatic activity (such as a puppet stage), as well as clear pathways to enter and exit those spaces, is important.

2. *A large assortment of hands-on materials.* Materials influence the content of children's enactments and support their ability to initiate and sustain informal and story drama activities. A group of first graders was playing out a rescue operation in a medevac helicopter they had constructed with blocks. Using the accessible props of buttons, plastic cups, and a steering wheel, they took their helicopter into the air and onto the hospital landing platform while using their control panel to communicate with the hospital emergency room.

3. *Accessible and easily stored materials.* Three first-grade children were role-playing in their classroom grocery store and decided to make signs for the "weekly specials." Their teacher provided folders and table easels to save or reuse their work. Prop boxes, discussed in the section on dramatic play in this chapter, offer another type of accessible storage. Accessible and easily stored material gives children autonomy in pursuing dramatic interests.

4. *Adequate time.* Children need ample time to plan, carry out, and sustain their dramatic activity. Drama requires recruiting players, locating materials and props, negotiating roles and plots, and carrying out agreed-upon ideas. To enable this, we, as teachers, need to schedule ample blocks of time for creative drama (Johnson, Christie, & Yawkey, 1999).

5. *Opportunity for cooperative group learning.* When children engage in dramatic activities, they tap into their "interpersonal intelligence" (Gardner, 1993b). In a thematic unit on the Brazilian rainforest, for example, second graders shared key ideas and information about plant life and ecology as a basis for determining how to dramatize their final project. Such opportunities, whether with peers or in small groups, enable children to work together as a unit—an important life skill for functioning in social settings.

6. *Personal involvement.* Students' levels of personal engagement in drama are important (Morgan & Saxton, 1987). For drama to be an effective learning medium, children must be interested, engaged, and committed to the enactment.

Let's look at Mr. Sanchez's first grade, which is enacting a camping theme. Think about the six considerations for selecting and presenting drama experiences—space, "hands-on" materials, storage, time, cooperative learning, and personal involvement. As you read about the camping theme in Mr. Sanchez's classroom, consider how these variables affect the children's enactments.

Because camping is a relatively inexpensive family vacation, many children have had some direct experience with this activity. Mr. Sanchez began by reading several camping stories, including *Bailey Goes Camping* (Henkes, 1985), *Three Days on a River in a Red Canoe* (Williams, 1981), and *Stringbean's Trip to the Shining Sea* (Williams, 1988), to help them elaborate their dramatic play. Next, the children brainstormed a list of ideas about camping and grouped their list into a concept map on poster board. They came up with categories of *where you go* (backyard, state park, campground, lake), *how you get there* (walk, car, trailer, truck with camper, motor home), *where you sleep* (in a camper, in tents, in sleeping bags), *what you eat* (trail mix, food from cans, fish you catch, hot dogs, marshmallows), and *things to do* (swim, sing songs, bike, hike, explore, tell stories). In planning a camping theme, Mr. Sanchez cleared a corner of the classroom so that it could be left in place for as long as the children's interest allowed. Next, with Mr. Sanchez's support, the children used, made, or brought in various props to represent a campground with tents, a campfire, trees, a lake, trails, and a stuffed wildlife toy. Following a few days of play, Mr. Sanchez observed the children repeatedly reenacting the same sequence of putting up and taking down their tents. After talking with them about other camping activities, such as how they were preparing their meals, he decided to add some cooking equipment and empty boxes of real food products for a camp store. Clearly, this episode illustrates the teacher's key role in creative drama in the classroom.

## *Teachers' Roles and Responsibilities*

Teachers often wonder how much, if at all, they should intervene in children's enactments. As facilitators who enhance and encourage drama and dramatic play, teachers assume an important role in the preparation and follow-up to children's dramatizations (Wilhelm & Edmiston, 1998). One common error is for teachers to become too intrusive, to act as "directors" who disrupt the children's spontaneity. A second common error is the reverse—to completely ignore the children's drama and work on other routine tasks such as putting out the paints or arranging a bulletin board display.

The following strategies will help you avoid both of these extremes and will allow you to extend drama throughout your classroom. As you explore these strategies, remember that your role as a teacher strongly influences how children use drama.

**1.** *Ask thoughtful questions that provoke creative thinking.* Before any drama activity, find out what children know or want to know about the content and roles. During the activity, be curious and be a good listener. When Mr. Sanchez's first graders were planning their camping theme corner, he asked them to talk about what they knew about camping. He also asked them questions such as "Where will you all sleep?" "How will you prepare your food?" and "What will you do for fun on your trip?" By understanding the experiences of the children in his class, Mr. Sanchez challenged their thinking, which helped them enact more complex camping themes.

**2.** *Reflect with children.* Talking about specific roles and situations during and after the drama helps children clarify their thoughts and feelings. Ms. Wengel's second graders had created a shoe store as part of their unit on clothing. The shoe store contained a variety of styles of real shoes, such as slippers, boots, running shoes, and ballet shoes. It also contained shoe catalogs and photos of old-fashioned shoes and boots that the children used to sort, classify, measure, and make purchases. Ms. Wengel helped the children reflect on their play by asking them to think about how the old-fashioned shoes differed from today's styles and to imagine how shoes might change in the future when they become adults. In their reflections, the children thought about shoes of the future, such as "jet shoes" that could help you take off and fly. They also listened to others' ideas and responses, which they then incorporated into future dramatizations in the shoe store.

**3.** *Model a behavior or attribute.* One of the most effective strategies for empowering children through drama is to model certain behaviors for them. Watch, however, for the appropriate moment to do this. In creative drama, teachers should not impose their ideas on children. Rather, they should encourage children to develop their own ideas, value their responses, support their improvisations, and encourage them to believe in themselves and their abilities (Heller, 1996; Wilhelm & Edmiston, 1998). When Mr. Martinez's first graders wanted to enact a firefighting scene, they needed a prop to use as a firehose. He invited them to problem-solve, asking, "What should the object do?" Children suggested that it should be long, rounded, skinny, and sort of stretchy. They decided to use a plastic Slinky.

Talking with children about their drama, assuming different roles, and providing time, space, and resources are the building blocks of the early childhood drama program. This foundation provides children with the needed opportunities to explore appropriate drama activities.

## APPROPRIATE CREATIVE DRAMA ACTIVITIES AND EXPERIENCES

As discussed earlier, informal, unrehearsed, process-oriented drama activities are the most appropriate for the early childhood years (Bromley, 1998; Tompkins, 1998). Some of these activities include dramatic and sociodramatic play, story play, pantomime, puppets, story drama, and readers theater. These drama activities help children to:

1.  Develop improved skills in reading, listening, speaking, and writing.
2.  Develop skill in thinking analytically, in acting decisively and responsibly.
3.  Increase and sustain the ability to concentrate and follow directions.
4.  Strengthen self-concept by cooperative interaction with others.
5.  Increase motivation to learn.
6.  Develop individual and group creativity (Joint Committee on the Role of Informal Drama in the Classroom, 1983, pp. 370–371).

### Dramatic and Sociodramatic Play

Three-year-old Michelle dons a surgeon's cap, hangs a stethoscope around her neck, and examines "Spotty," a large teddy bear. She uses a spoon to give her patient a shot, scribbles a prescription on a scrap of paper located in the play area, and hands it to her playmate, David.

A group of kindergartners are being air traffic controllers and helping planes land during a blizzard. Their conversation includes negotiations and decisions about how many controllers can fit into the control tower and which planes belong to which controller. These children are engaged in *dramatic and sociodramatic play.*

### Why Use Dramatic and Sociodramatic Play?

In dramatic and sociodramatic play, children can be both actors and directors. As actors, children actually experience the feelings, thoughts, and behaviors of the roles they are playing. As directors, they imagine the thoughts, feelings, and behaviors associated with a role and coach the actors. Playing both roles in dramatic and sociodramatic play helps children:

- Construct their own understandings of how the world works by stepping into the shoes of another person (Jalongo & Isenberg, 2000; Corbey-Scullen & Howell, 1997).
- Act out social situations requiring negotiation with players with different needs and views (Furman, 2000).
- Express their inner feelings (Mayesky, 1998).
- Communicate in meaningful ways and develop social skills by negotiating roles, locating props, and agreeing on a common theme (Furman, 2000).
- Develop the confidence to explore freely and imaginatively the more structured forms of drama (McCaslin, 2000; Shaftel & Shaftel, 1983).

### Suggestions for the Classroom

Ms. Senack has set up a beach theme center that includes assorted, related materials such as a large ocean poster, a child-sized beach chair, a small umbrella, a collection of shells, water toys, and cassette tapes for her 4-year-old class. Ari spreads his towel along the sand, then checks his bag for sunglasses and sand toys. Shayna locates her portable radio and skips over stations until she finds the appropriate music. "Hey, Ari!" Shayna asks, "do you like this song? Let's pretend we are teenagers!" Eventually, they use towels to bury themselves and call themselves "Dancing Sand People." At the sand table, they engage in the following dialogue:

> **Ari:**  Put all the shells you want in your pile. Don't get them mixed up. These are mine! (Gets a magnifying glass from the science table.) Look, this one is really dirty!

> **Shayna:**  Let me see! (Ari hands her the magnifying glass, and Shayna examines the shell.) That's not dirt! That's the way the shell is. It comes like that! You just don't know 'cause only if you have a 'fying glass can you see what it looks like underneath.

> **Ari:**  My mom sometimes uses shells for plates. She has really big shells and puts all our food on it.

> **Shayna:**  Here's some macaroni and cheese! (Hands Ari a shell with some sand on it.)

*In dramatic play, children experience the actual feelings, thoughts, and behaviors of the roles they enact.*

This beach theme play illustrates the use of two strategies for enhancing role play—*prop boxes*, or dramatic play kits, and *theme corners*, or play centers.

**Prop Boxes and Dramatic Play Kits.**   **Prop boxes,** or dramatic play kits, contain a collection of real items that are related in some way, such as a picnic basket, plastic food, a tablecloth, and plastic ants. Using real items can stimulate children's imaginative play with particular concepts, situations, and roles. Prop boxes:

- Promote experiences with real materials and tools related to a theme (e.g., a toolbox).

- Extend interest so that children can sustain their theme play (e.g., books, posters, records, and tapes related to the theme).
- Increase opportunities for families to be involved in story drama through contributing materials and using literature-based prop boxes from school in the home setting (Stone, 1995).
- Provide opportunities to enact familiar roles (e.g., deposit slips and checks for a banker or boots, a net, and a fishing pole for a fisherman).
- Develop career awareness (e.g., a medical kit or a briefcase) (Myhre, 1993).

Well-planned prop boxes enhance dramatic and sociodramatic play opportunities. Younger children need adequate props, space, and time to pursue dramatic play even though their roles and themes shift frequently. Older children, who are more sophisticated in their play, can plan their theme and often negotiate roles and responsibilities. At all ages, children use the props in many different ways. Be certain, however, that all of the items are safe to use and free of dangerous or loose parts.

The following guidelines will help you create and use prop boxes and dramatic play kits to extend units of study and to support children's enactments.

1. *Brainstorm themes that interest the children.* Choose some themes that are very familiar, (e.g., a grocery store or a farm), others that are somewhat familiar, (e.g., a gas station or a TV studio), and still others that are even less familiar to children (e.g., a travel agency or a construction project). Be certain to provide adequate background experiences that will support children's play in theme centers.

2. *Collect storage containers.* Strong boxes with lids (such as those that contain photocopy paper) or clean, dry five-gallon ice cream tubs work well for this purpose. Label the outside of the container with the theme (e.g., "The Three Bears" or "Chinese New Year") and draw a picture or paste on a photo that will help children identify each container's contents. You might also invite the children to paint and decorate these boxes.

3. *Generate with your children a list of possible items to include in the prop box.* Ask children, parents, colleagues, and local businesses to contribute items. Clothing, especially old uniforms and costumes, and recycled materials such as old toys and household articles are generally useful. Invite families to provide materials such as clothing, accessories, or props for a particular piece of literature to be studied in the classroom. Stories such as *The City Mouse and the Country Mouse* (Stevens, 1987), *Sylvester and the Magic Pebble* (Steig, 1969), and *Stone Soup* (Brown, 1975) are some of children's favorites that lend themselves to family involvement (Stone, 1995).

4. *Think about your goals for the theme or unit.* What vocabulary could children use in their drama? How will you introduce the theme and related activities so that they capitalize on what children know? You may want to include some books that correspond to the theme or an audiotape of appropriate background music or sounds. Record these ideas and tape them inside the cover of the prop box to serve as a guide for parents, substitute or student teachers, or administrators. These ideas will help keep the dramatic play well connected to the goals of the unit. Figure 5.1 shows a properly labeled prop box containing an assortment of related

**Figure 5.1**
Properly Labeled
Prop Box

| Information to be taped inside the lid or cover of the prop box | Theme: _____ <br> Goals for Center: _____ <br> Vocabulary:_____ <br> Introduction Procedure: _____ <br> Field Trips and Resource People: _____ |
| --- | --- |
| Information on the outside of the prop box | Theme: _____ <br> Props (costumes, <br> real things, objects): _____ <br> Materials in Box:_____ <br> Suggested Supplements: _____ <br> Child-Made Materials: _____ |
| Suggestions for Adults | Observer: Watch play. <br> Collaborator: Add a new toy, prop, or ask a question, if needed. Help children gain entry to play without intruding on the ongoing play of the others. <br> Model: If invited, join the play and model a role or action and then leave. <br> Mediator: Help children develop peaceful solutions to conflicts. <br> Safety Monitor: Check for hazards, worn or damaged materials, clutter. |

items. Figure 5.2 gives examples of what to include in a Puppet and a Medical Prop Box. Appendix A shows how to use a dance prop box and contains ideas for additional prop boxes.

**Theme Corners or Play Centers.**   Theme corners or play centers contain materials focused on a topic familiar and interesting to a particular group of children. They encourage children's spontaneous interactions with a variety of roles (Howe, Moller, Chambers, & Petrakos, 1993; Woodward, 1985). Theme corners make a subject of study, such as nutrition or careers, more real to children, and build interest in the topic.

Use the following five guidelines to encourage children's dramatizations. Teachers who create theme corners or play centers need to:

**Figure 5.2**
Materials for Puppet
and Medical Prop
Boxes

**Puppet Prop Box:**
Paper plates, paper bags, craft sticks, tongue depressors, buttons, sequin pieces, wallpaper pieces, cotton balls, construction paper, pipe cleaners, yarn, glue, scissors, markers, tape, books about puppetry and puppet making.

**Medical Prop Box:**
Dolls, stuffed animals, doll-sized furniture, doctor kit, stethoscope, plastic digital thermometer, plastic syringes, bandages, eye chart, white shirts for uniforms, pad, pencil, telephone, appointment book, shower cap, empty pill containers, scale, patient folders, coupons for medical supplies and products, magazines, books about doctors and nurses, posters of doctors and nurses.

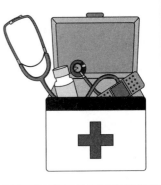

1.   *Provide a variety of background experiences.* Use pictures, stories, and discussion centered on the theme to build background knowledge. Children need to be familiar with roles in order to enact them.

2.   *Create an attractive physical setting.* Posters, books, and materials can transform an area of the classroom. The physical setting can invite children to enter the area and can stimulate their imaginations.

3.   *Provide safe, simple, and durable props.* Select props and materials that are well suited to children's ages, interests, and abilities. You will want to check periodically that your props are in good repair and are being used properly. Simple props such as a cape or a magic mirror inspire children to enact roles and behaviors.

4.   *Intervene only when necessary.* When introducing a new theme corner, jointly establish limits such as the number of children who can be there at any one time.

5.   *Involve children in planning.* Encourage children to suggest ideas for themes and to develop new theme corners periodically. Children can make and collect the necessary props. (Adapted from Woodward, 1985, pp. 291–295.)

Figure 5.3 shows a theme corner for a fast-food restaurant that incorporates goals, materials, and related activities. Figure 5.4 lists other ideas for theme corners and shows a doctor's office, bakery, and fix-it shop.

| Goal | Vocabulary | Teacher-Provided Props |
|---|---|---|
| To increase children's ability to choose and enact roles | Restaurant<br>Drive-through<br>Cashier<br>Cook<br>Menu<br>Food<br>Hamburger<br>Customer<br>Trash Can<br>Cash register<br>Tables and chairs | Uniforms<br>Play money<br>Trash can, dishcloth, mop<br>Stove<br>Cups, straws, trays<br>Assorted containers<br>Cooking utensils<br>Pencils<br>Cards for taking orders<br>Wall posters of food & prices |
| **Child-Provided Props** | **Introducing the Theme Corner** | **Related Activities** |
| Hats<br>Aprons<br>Menus<br>Signs<br>Decorated car made from box<br>Price list<br>Styrofoam containers | 1. Discuss experiences of eating in a fast-food restaurant.<br>2. Discuss roles of workers and customers.<br>3. Discuss appropriate behavior in restaurant. Introduce imprinted items from different restaurants and have children sort and classify them. | 1. Take a field trip and eat in a fast-food restaurant.<br>2. Invite employees to talk with the children about their work.<br>3. Collect cups, napkins, hats, and other objects.<br>4. Cook and taste different kinds of potatoes. |

**Figure 5.3**    Theme Corner for a Fast-Food Restaurant
*Source:* Adapted from Isbell (1995).

## Story Play

**Story play,** also called *story dictation,* is a form of guided drama that uses children's own stories as the content for enactment (Paley, 1981). In this kind of drama, children can be both writers and actors by dictating stories to an adult or by writing their own stories that later become plays to dramatize. As the authors, children choose which of their friends might play certain roles as the teacher reads the original stories. Story play in the preschool and kindergarten years is a natural transition to the journal writing and shared reading and writing typically encountered in the primary grades.

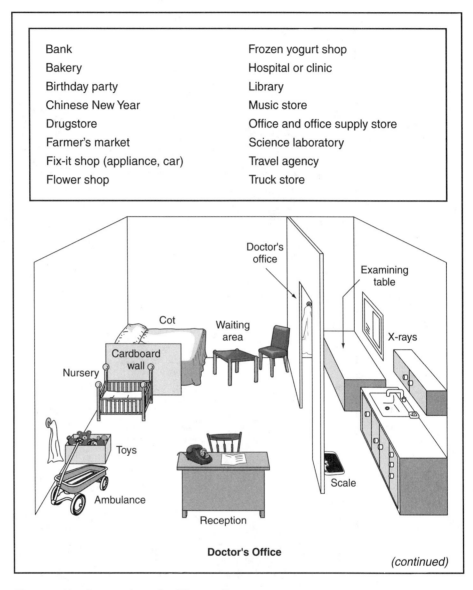

| | |
|---|---|
| Bank | Frozen yogurt shop |
| Bakery | Hospital or clinic |
| Birthday party | Library |
| Chinese New Year | Music store |
| Drugstore | Office and office supply store |
| Farmer's market | Science laboratory |
| Fix-it shop (appliance, car) | Travel agency |
| Flower shop | Truck store |

**Doctor's Office**

*(continued)*

**Figure 5.4**  Suggestions for Theme Corners

*Why Use Story Play?*

Vivian Paley (1981) reports that children who see their own stories enacted are motivated to write other stories for dramatization so that they can become story players. Many teachers use children's own stories to dramatize in order to support children's language and literacy development and to build a strong sense of community in the classroom. In this way, enactment provides all children an opportunity to be "story tellers," to engage in both verbal and nonverbal expression

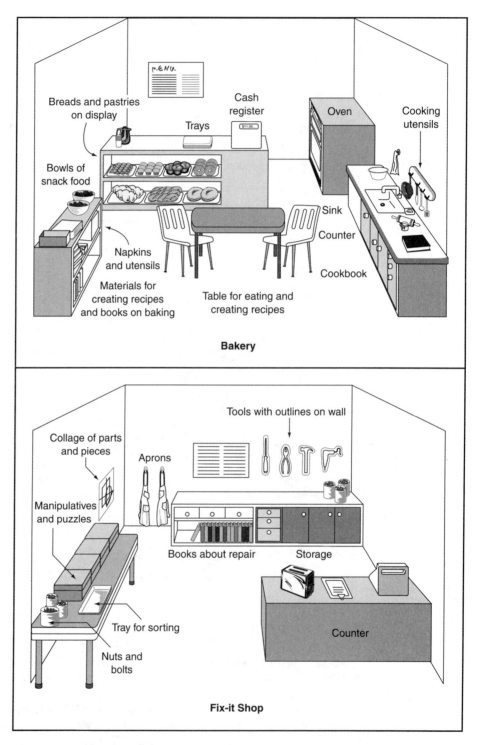

**Figure 5.4** *(Continued)*

of ideas, to increase their communicative competence, and to participate in a simple yet powerful dramatic experience (Wiltz & Fein, 1996). Story play is predicated on the idea that children can learn to read and write more easily if they are using their own words because they have more meaning for them. Story play is one way to include shy children, second-language learners, and children with special needs into classroom drama.

### Suggestions for the Classroom

Story play begins by encouraging children to write their own stories or to dictate stories to an adult who writes them down. Older children can use their invented spelling to write their own stories for later enactment to a small group or to the whole class. Children are then invited to share their original stories with the rest of the class. One by one, each child author chooses a role to play from his or her story and selects classmates to play different roles. The child author may also serve as the director as the teacher reads the child's story aloud. Periodically, select an original story to keep in each child's portfolio so that you can see his or her storytelling abilities progress over time.

The story play procedure validates children's attempts at writing and telling stories. The more opportunities children have to elaborate their own ideas, the more complex their stories will become and the better insight they will have about the structure of narrative.

## Pantomime

Pantomime, a type of informal drama, is a good starting point for creative drama. In pantomime, children use gestures and movement to communicate ideas, feelings, and actions—all without words. As part of their unit on the circus, a group of second graders were pantomiming eating cotton candy. Some children held their hands in front of their faces and bit off chunks of the cotton candy; others pulled some candy off of the cones with their hands and ate it; still others just licked their hands and fingers. The teacher encouraged responses from the onlookers by asking, "How did you know it was cotton candy?" or "What else might the mimers have done to show you it was cotton candy and not an ice cream cone?" In this way, the second graders and their teacher used pantomime to give form to their ideas.

### Why Use Pantomime?

Pantomime helps children feel comfortable with their bodies while interpreting ideas, feelings, and actions. Because it begins with physical experience, it makes concepts more concrete. More specifically, it helps children:

1. Develop the confidence needed for later story dramatization.
2. Become aware of the importance of nonverbal communication.
3. Convey their actions, thoughts, and feelings through gesture and movement.

4.  Develop skills in listening, language, remembering, acting, and audience awareness (Hennings, 2000; McCaslin, 2000).

Because mime uses no words or dialogue, it is particularly valuable for children who are nonnative English speakers, who have speech or hearing problems, or who are very shy. It helps them develop confidence in their abilities to express themselves through body language. In pantomime, all children can be successful because they do not have to be concerned about verbal communication. "Learning that takes place in words alone, without the foundation of understanding derived from experience, is in fact too rote and superficial to be called 'learning' " (San Jose, 1989, p. 33).

### Suggestions for the Classroom

It is a good idea to first introduce pantomime as a whole group activity. Once children feel comfortable in using their bodies to act out situations, small groups of children can begin to explore simple characterizations and role-play common experiences. Children express themselves more freely when many children and the adults participate. Younger children need help getting started with pantomime. The less experienced children are, the more background and modeling they need to stimulate their imaginations before they can create their own interpretations. Children respond positively to teachers' suggestions such as "Show me with your body that it is cold outside" or "Let's pretend you are a helicopter in the sky, or a stick floating down a quiet stream." Young children also like to interpret their actions and gestures to music or pantomime characters from a favorite story, such as "The Three Billy Goats Gruff."

Older children enjoy making up original and humorous skits for group pantomime. They also can be encouraged to pantomime individuals currently in the news, such as politicians or sports figures. In this way, they explore sophisticated variations of actions or feelings and respond favorably to teachers acting as choreographers in changing their actions (Hennings, 2000). The more children are able to observe nonverbal behaviors, the more able they are to add body language and gestures to their own nonverbal repertoire. One third-grade class, for example, was pantomiming ways of walking in response to these teacher's calls: "You are walking on slippery ice . . . through the muddy jungle . . . in the very hot desert . . . and in a very dark alley." As the context changed, the children interpreted and invented the appropriate movements, such as tiptoeing, sliding, staggering, or walking rapidly.

Here is an example of a beach activity that all ages like to pantomime.

#### THE BEACH

Let's pretend we're at the beach at lunchtime. It's hot! The sun is right overhead. Put on some sunburn lotion. Don't lose the top of it in the sand. Put the top on and rub in the lotion. What about some for your nose? Pick up the tube and squeeze out some lotion. Smear it over your nose and under your eyes. Super!

It's too hot for me! We don't want to get burned, so let's put up an umbrella— a striped beach umbrella. Ooh, it's heavy and it's difficult to put up. There! I've done it. Mine is red and orange. What color is yours? And yours? And yours?

(Ask some of the children to tell you the colors of their umbrellas.)

Look at the shadow that the umbrella's made. Let's all lie down in it. Aah, that's better.

Come and sit by me. Wasn't it great at the beach? (Fox, 1987, pp. 64–65).

Because all children like to make and do things, miming actions interests them. Children will be most able to mime those actions they have experienced and that they can easily imagine. Some appropriate mime activities for young children are:

1. Acting out familiar nursery rhymes such as "Jack and Jill" or "One, Two, Buckle My Shoe."
2. Showing what it is like to do your favorite after-school activity, such as riding a bike or working in the family garden.
3. Being a character or an animal in favorite songs. Short songs, such as "I'm a Little Teapot," are good introductions to mime and song.
4. Modeling familiar actions such as brushing teeth, washing hands, riding on a crowded bus, or eating in the school cafeteria. Have the children try to model the action after they guess it. Children also like to mime throwing balls of different sizes, eating a dripping ice cream cone, or washing dishes.
5. Imagining they are other creatures, such as a tiger stalking through the jungle looking for food, a kitten lapping some milk, or a wriggling worm.

Older children who have little experience with mime also need practice and modeling before they feel free enough to mime. Group experiences of the same action convey the message of multiple interpretations with no right or wrong response.

## Puppets

Puppets make powerful teaching tools. Even though the word *puppet* comes from the Latin word for doll, puppets are more than dolls. They invite children to explore their imaginations and share their imaginings with others. Puppets are the perfect props for all forms of creative drama!

### Why Use Puppets?

Puppets add life to the classroom and are a natural vehicle for creativity, imagination, and self-expression. In today's product-oriented world, they help children convey feelings, emotions, values, and ideas. They are particularly motivating for the listener because they carry a bit of mystery with them.

For children, the process of creating and using puppets makes the learning valuable rather than focusing on the puppet as a finished product. Teachers can also use puppets to enhance their own creativity, view children in different roles, and nurture affective development (Hunt & Renfro, 1982).

A puppet can become a nonthreatening vehicle for:

- Self-expression, storytelling, improvisation, and enactment (Mayesky, 1998, Hunt & Renfro, 1982).
- Risk taking and building confidence in speaking abilities (Hennings, 2000).

*Puppets are the perfect props for all forms of creative drama.*

- Social negotiation (McCaslin, 2000).
- Releasing emotions, distinguishing between reality and fantasy, and practicing life experiences (Hunt & Renfro, 1982).

Many puppets are simple, safe, and easy for children to create and use. A wooden spoon easily becomes a person when given a face; a mitten can be transformed into an animal by adding eyes and a nose. If puppets are to become real tools for unlocking children's creative potential, they must be easily accessible. Consequently, storing puppets is an important consideration. Figure 5.5 lists ideas for making and storing puppets.

### Suggestions for the Classroom
Here are some suggestions for classwork with puppets.

**1.** Provide many opportunities for children to experiment with different puppets before they create their own. Have them hold the puppets in front of them or over their heads. Introduce a mirror so that they can explore the puppet's movements, voice, and gestures. Young children find it easiest to manipulate puppets with moving mouths so that they can use dialogue if they choose (Hunt & Renfro, 1982).

### Finger, Glove, and Mitten Puppets

Draw characters on fingers with washable markers.

Cut fingers from old work gloves or rubber gloves.

Cut a hole in old ping-pong balls and draw a face.

Bottle lids that are large and deep may be painted or decorated.

Use commercial finger puppets.

Decorate cardboard tubes (e.g., old bandage tube).

### Box Puppets

Assorted small boxes (e.g., small candy carton, pudding, or cereal boxes for hand and finger puppet)

Assorted large boxes (e.g., cereal) for larger puppets

Assorted envelopes of all colors and sizes

### Paper Bag Puppets

Assorted brown and white bags to be decorated with materials for face puppets

Assorted brown and white bags to be decorated for the body and use the fingers through the flattened bottom as the face.

Grocery bags become body puppets (called humanettes: half people, half bag)

### Stick Puppets

Draw faces on assorted sticks (e.g., tongue depressors, popsicle sticks).

Draw faces on wooden clothespins to make storytelling puppets.

Draw faces on lightweight cardboard.

Use a tongue depressor attached to a paper plate for a paper plate puppet.

Make pipe cleaner and wooden spoon puppets.

### Ball Puppets

Use styrofoam ball for the head.

Decorate old tennis balls.

(continued)

**Figure 5.5**  Ideas for Making Puppets

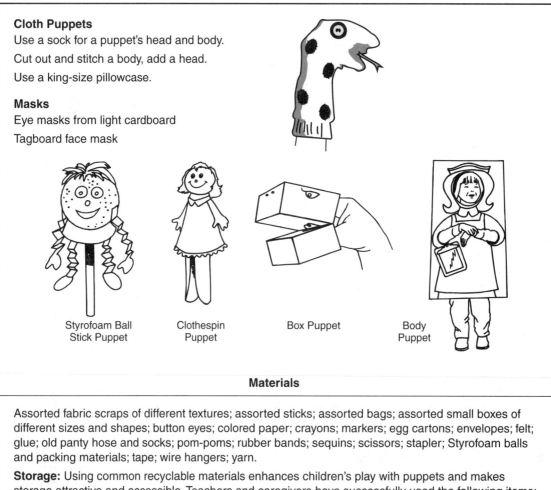

**Cloth Puppets**

Use a sock for a puppet's head and body.

Cut out and stitch a body, add a head.

Use a king-size pillowcase.

**Masks**

Eye masks from light cardboard

Tagboard face mask

Styrofoam Ball
Stick Puppet

Clothespin
Puppet

Box Puppet

Body
Puppet

**Materials**

Assorted fabric scraps of different textures; assorted sticks; assorted bags; assorted small boxes of different sizes and shapes; button eyes; colored paper; crayons; markers; egg cartons; envelopes; felt; glue; old panty hose and socks; pom-poms; rubber bands; sequins; scissors; stapler; Styrofoam balls and packing materials; tape; wire hangers; yarn.

**Storage:** Using common recyclable materials enhances children's play with puppets and makes storage attractive and accessible. Teachers and caregivers have successfully used the following items: aprons with pockets; cardboard six packs; egg cartons; expanding hanging baskets; hat or wine rack; photocopy paper boxes; multiple skirt hangers; plastic gallon containers or 2 liter plastic bottles; shoe box, bag, or rack.

**Figure 5.5**   *(Continued)*

2.   Create a puppet center with a box of puppet-making materials such as scraps of fabric, paper tubing and plates, recycled buttons, yarn, and popsicle sticks. Locate the center away from the normal traffic pattern so those children can gather and use their puppets in informal enactments (Bromley, 1998). Preschoolers enjoy using paper plates or other recycled materials to invent new types of puppets. First-grade children often use the puppet center to create silhouette stick puppets of favorite book characters to share informally with one another. Notice

the confidence in first grader Brittany's comments while working with a friend in the puppet center.

> **Brittany:**   Oh, I love puppets. They are so cute. Hmmm . . . what can I make? I think I'll make a girl. Can I make two? Okay, then I'll make a girl and a boy. We can do a little play then. I'll be the girl and you can be the boy.

**3.**   Use puppets to help children express feelings with their voices. Children can be encouraged to use high- or low-pitched voices, or animal sounds such as squeaking, growling, or chirping (Bromley, 1998; Hunt & Renfro, 1982). For example, a kindergarten teacher uses paper plate puppets with happy, sad, surprised, and frightened faces on them. She tells a short story, stops, and asks a child to respond using one of the puppets and an appropriate voice.

**4.**   Suggest that children audiotape a story if they are going to do a puppet show. Primary grade children often have difficulty manipulating puppets and saying the words at the same time. Making a recording in advance gives them the chance to focus on the puppet's actions.

**5.**   Provide guidelines for safety and management. To maximize the value of puppets in the classroom, be sure to involve children in establishing limits and responsibilities in using puppets. For example, puppets can be used for talking with one another, creating a puppet show, or retelling a story. Teachers and caregivers should not allow puppets to be used as action figures in "hand-to-hand" combat.

## Story Drama

**Story drama,** a type of interpretive drama, is based upon the reenactment of familiar stories, poems, fables, or original stories. Sometimes referred to as story retelling, story drama often consists of a teacher-led group experience with children creating scenes from familiar literature that use both dialogue and movement (Morado, Koenig, & Wilson, 1999). Younger children enjoy dramatizing cumulative tales such as *Henny Penny* (Galdone, 1968) or *Over in the Meadow* (Keats, 1971). Older children enjoy dramatizing scenes from longer stories such as *Ramona the Brave* (Cleary, 1975), *Dr. De Soto* (Steig, 1982), or *Knots on a Counting Rope* (Martin & Archambault, 1987).

### Why Use Story Drama?

Story drama supports children's understanding of story structure and helps them see how language affects others. For the teacher, it offers a natural and authentic form of literacy understandings. Research shows that enacting stories (1) improves reading comprehension by enabling readers to clarify concepts and gain a deeper understanding of the literature (Bromley, 1998; Jalongo, 2000); (2) promotes speaking, listening, critical, and creative reading skills by interpreting familiar material (Hennings, 2000); (3) heightens students' interest in reading (Diamond & Moore, 1995); and (4) enables children to experience the feelings and behaviors of others (McCaslin, 2000). Story drama meets the needs of children at all developmental levels because the children control the length and interpretation of the particular retelling.

*Suggestions for the Classroom*

When choosing and adapting stories to dramatize, think about the following characteristics.

**1.** Choose stories with *immediate action, a simple plot, few characters, and appealing dialogue* that children can easily put into their own words. Students must be familiar with the story and characters if they are to re-create the plot and the conversation. Folk tales such as *How Many Spots Does a Leopard Have?* (Lester, 1990) or *Fables* (Lobel, 1980) fit this criterion.

**2.** *Involve children* actively in the selection of the story. Allowing them to choose stories to enact will build interest in dramatization. Stories suitable for dramatization, such as *The Mixed-up Chameleon* (Carle, 1984) or *One Fine Day* (Hogrogrian, 1971), interest many children and should be readily available in the classroom library.

**3.** *Adapt familiar stories* and enthusiastically support children's spontaneous interpretations. Young children will have simple and often loose interpretations; older children will have more sophisticated understandings and a more coherent plot that follows the original story more closely. One effective technique is to use "yarn-tug stories," where children hold on to knotted pieces of yarn and sit in a semicircle around a child who starts the story. That child then tugs at the knot of another child, who continues the retelling. The process continues until all children have participated in the retelling and the story is complete.

**4.** *Be a facilitator.* Prepare questions in advance to help children focus on story elements and to gain distance from the story. For example, in reenacting the story of "The Three Bears," you might ask, "I wonder how Goldilocks got into the bears' house? How do you suppose the bears felt when they came home and saw their porridge, chairs, and Goldilocks sleeping in their bed? If you were Goldilocks, what would you have done? Why?"

**5.** *Provide ample time and space for children to plan the dramatization, decide which parts to read or enact, and explore the dimensions of their characters.* Each child must determine how a character feels and thinks before trying to act like that character. In one first-grade reenactment of *Caps for Sale* (Slobodkina, 1947) children asked one another these questions to help them better understand the character of the peddler: Where do you live? Where did you get your caps? How will you shake your fingers, shake both hands, stamp your feet, and throw your caps on the ground? How will you act like a monkey in the trees?

**6.** *Evaluate the reenactment.* By second grade, children can evaluate their story dramatizations. Always begin with the strengths of the drama. What did you see that you liked? Then ask questions that will help children reexamine the drama elements of voice, action, diction, and movement of the characters.

## Readers Theater

**Readers theater,** another form of interpretive drama, is a presentation of a story or script by a group of readers. In selecting literature for readers theater, choose stories with a simple plot; a clear ending; interesting characters; and clear, simple dialogue. Readers then assume a role, read aloud, and interpret the parts of the script that relate to their particular role. Props are not necessary. This form of drama enables children to use facial and vocal expressions, gestures, and their imaginations to interpret a play or story in a nonstaged performance to communicate shades of meaning. Sometimes a narrator sets the tone, but this is not necessary. Because readers theater incorporates practice before presentation, less-proficient readers can often be successful in oral reading and interpretation (Forsythe, 1995; Hennings, 2000). Although readers theater was designed for older children, it is easily adaptable to primary grade children and nonreaders using a memorized big book on an easel (Jalongo & Stamp, 1997).

### Why Use Readers Theater?

In readers theater, children focus only on the oral interpretation of the material, facial expressions, and simple gestures. Unlike formal, scripted drama, they are not pressured to memorize lines or use elaborate props. During readers theater, the audience receives information and responds to the participants. Readers theater is a particularly useful form of drama for:

1.  *Incorporating multicultural stories,* such as *Abiyoyo* (Seeger, 1986) or *Listen Children: An Anthology of Black Literature* (Strickland, 1982).

2.  *Developing language proficiency.* Readers theater reinforces word meanings, helps children understand the relationship between sounds and symbols, and extends children's comprehension of plot and character interpretation. Using books such as *Chicka Chicka Boom Boom* (Martin & Archambault, 1989), first-grade children like to find and enact words that begin with certain sounds, such as the *b* in button. They suggest "Beat . . . I'll beat you to the top of the coconut tree" or ". . . Chicka chicka boom boom" (Diamond & Moore, 1995).

3.  *Practicing reading in a supportive environment.* Readers theater allows less-able readers to experience fluency and comprehension in a low-anxiety setting, and fosters language acquisition for second-language learners (Dixon, 1996).

### Suggestions for the Classroom

Early childhood teachers typically use the following procedure for readers theater:

1.  Have readers sit on the floor or stand, with their books in front of them, while they read and follow along with the material.

2.  Make sure that children can read the material without help (Bromley, 1998). Many of the predictable books children use as big books or language experience stories from their reading program are a rich source for readers theater because children have memorized the stories from repeated readings.

3.  Select material that is action based, exciting, and capable of interpretation in a dramatic fashion (Bromley, 1998). Folktales such as "Chicken Little" and "The Magic Fish" and stories in verse such as *The Cat in the Hat* (Seuss, 1957) and *The Adventures of Taxi Dog* (Barracca & Barracca, 1990) are appealing and meet the criteria for readers theater. For a more complete list of appropriate materials to use in readers theater, see Busching (1981). In addition, the Readers

Theater Script Service provides scripts for readers theater at the elementary level, such as *The Tale of Peter Rabbit* (Potter, 1986) and *The Emperor's New Clothes* (Andersen, 1982).

Creative drama experiences during early childhood develop children's understanding of the forms and functions of language, nonverbal communication, possibilities in dealing with life, while simultaneously building self-esteem, and self-confidence. These activities can be used across the curriculum to enhance and reinforce learning in all subject areas. For further information about readers theater, contact:

Readers Theater Script Service
P.O. Box 178333
San Diego, CA 92117
(619) 276-1948

# INTEGRATING CREATIVE DRAMA INTO THE SUBJECT AREAS

Drama experts recommend that drama activities be infused into the subject areas (Bolton, 1985; McCaslin, 2000; Wilhelm & Edmiston, 1998). In this way, children come to understand abstract ideas by enacting them concretely. The activities that follow are grouped by subject area and may be adapted across ages and subject areas.

## *Mathematics, Science, and Technology*

Children enjoy creative drama activities that focus on mathematics and science. Examples of these activities follow:

### *Bodyplays and Fingerplays*

Young children are particularly fond of these activities. While studying animals, they enjoy inventing their own gestures and acting out rhymes, such as this one about an elephant:

> His name is Elmer elephant, (Point to self as elephant)
> His lip and trunk are one. (Put two fists in front of mouth)
> And when I went to pick him up, (Bend way down)
> I knew he weighed a ton! (Lift up arms enclosed in a semicircle and make
> facial gestures)

They also enjoy changing their bodies into all kinds of shapes—shapes for objects (e.g., a bridge or a ball), shapes that change (e.g., an egg to a chicken), or shapes that move (e.g., a top) (Chenfeld, 1995).

### Pantomime

Young children enjoy pantomiming seasonal changes with their bodies. They can show Spring by miming planting seeds in a garden, Summer by making sand castles, Fall by falling leaves blowing in the wind, and Winter by pretending to be an ice skater, skier, or an ice hockey player. As part of their study of life cycles, primary grade children can cooperatively plan a pantomime of the life cycles, for example, of the caterpillar and the frog. Their classmates may provide feedback.

### Theme Corners

As part of a grocery store theme corner, children's dramatic play can include counting items on the shelves, sorting and classifying empty boxes and containers of different foods, counting money and making change, or designing a recycling bin for clean, used grocery bags. Environmental awareness can be introduced through questions such as "Do you want plastic or paper bags?"

### Readers Theater

In a unit on time, one third-grade class invented their own story of the future and presented it as readers theater. They created third-grade characters in a school setting in the year 2000 along with dialogue that might be used in the next century and compared their story to what life was like for them today.

### Movement

One primary grade teacher had her children develop rhythmic patterns to different number bases in mathematics. Divided into different bases, the group rhythmically grouped and regrouped themselves according to their base. They enjoyed working with the concept on paper after they had interpreted it physically.

Ms. Green used body movements to teach the concept of shadows to her first graders. The children used their bodies to do "shadow dancing" and to "show shadows at different times of the day."

## Language, Literature, and Literacy

Try the following common drama activities to enrich your language, literature, and literacy curriculum.

### Pantomime

Ms. Poretz's 2-year-olds like to act out action words. They choose an action picture from her shoebox collection and then do what they see in the picture. Some popular pictures include a child jumping, an airplane flying, a kitten lapping up milk, a horse galloping, and a mother cuddling a baby.

Primary grade children respond positively to pantomiming action words that relate to favorite books or book characters, feelings, and skill lessons in which they are engaged. They like unusual words such as *glide, hammer, inside out, jiggle, knead,*

*These children enjoy enacting their original stories as part of their study of animals.*

*limp, meander, nod* and *quake*. Older children can do more complicated charades based on poetry, folktales, and fairytales such as "Hey Diddle Diddle," "Jack and the Beanstalk," or "The Princess and the Pea."

### Role Play and Dramatic Play
Young children can role-play an event, such as a trip to the farm, through drama that begins by sharing personal knowledge of what a farm is like, followed by enactment of roles, such as a farmer, farm animals, and visitors. Teachers then discuss the enactment and may also read a book on the topic. Many teachers place real telephones in the theme or housekeeping area for children to converse freely with an imaginary person.

Encourage children to create situations where they have to relay messages, such as taking a sick child to the doctor, asking for information about a movie, or making a reservation at a restaurant. These role-plays in the early years successfully build children's prior knowledge, so critical to literacy development.

### Bodyplays

Vocabulary enacted through drama provides children with a strong mental image of the word that has been experienced visually, aurally, and kinesthetically. Older children enjoy enacting parts of speech, such as antonyms, synonyms, or homonyms, and having someone else guess the opposite or provide a matching word. They also enjoy enacting the same words but with different characteristics. For example, several groups of primary children formed the word *DOG*. There were *FAT* dogs, *SKINNY* dogs, *SCARY* dogs, *SHORT* dogs, *SAD* dogs, and *LITTLE* dogs.

### Storytelling

Second and third graders enjoy inventing beanbag stories. With children sitting in a circle, a child begins to tell a story. After a few sentences, the storyteller stops and throws a beanbag to another child, who continues the story. When no more ideas can be generated, another person starts a different story.

### Characterization

With their favorite story in hand, third-grade children like to create a "Literature Talk Show" and become the talk show host. Other children call in and ask questions about the characters in the book, the characters' feelings and actions, or the resolution of the story.

Other children make book characters come to life with sock puppets as they portray Frog and Toad, for example, from a favorite book, *Frog and Toad Are Friends* (Lobel, 1970).

## Social Studies, Health, and Nutrition

Creative drama helps to solidify important social studies, health, and nutrition concepts, such as the four food groups, community workers, valuing different cultures, geography, and maps.

### Role Playing

Using gestures, facial expressions, intonation, and movement, young children can communicate social studies concepts (e.g., enacting parenting behaviors), health and safety concepts (e.g., dramatizing safe and unsafe ways to cross the street), and nutrition concepts (e.g., preparing a puppet play about balanced meals and the four food groups). Mr. Arakaki's first graders were comparing similarities and differences between Japanese and American families. After extensive background experiences, including reading *The Boy of the Three Year Nap* (Snyder, 1988), Mr. Arakaki observed the children dramatizing scenes from each culture's home life and enacting different ways of sleeping, eating, and greeting people.

*Props and other materials make it easy to integrate drama across the curriculum, adapting oral language experiences to the skills, abilities, and interests of all children.*

As their final project for a unit on explorers, one third-grade class chose to role-play preparing for an expedition to an unknown location. They negotiated and discussed how to dramatize each crew member's role and responsibility, what supplies they needed, how to call for help in an emergency, how to maintain records, and the strategies to use for communicating with their families.

### Fingerplays

Young children enjoy songs, fingerplays, and poems related to nutrition. Try having children enact "I'm a Little Teapot," "Little Jack Horner," "The Muffin Man," or "To Market, to Market."

### Identifying and Expressing Feelings

During a unit on families, preschool and kindergarten children enjoy enacting how family members feel when they are hungry, hurt, afraid, lonely, or tired. Children of all ages can relate to the different emotions exhibited by the Seven Dwarfs—Bashful, Grumpy, Sneezy, Sleepy, Dopey, Doc, and Happy. Using a mood cube made from a box like the one in the following illustration also encourages the expression of feelings. Children roll the cube and enact a situation that elicits the emotion depicted on the cube.

### Prop Boxes

As part of her unit on the post office, Ms. Packer and her kindergarten children prepared a prop box. They located scales, stamps and stamp pads, mailers, wooden mail boxes, a mail carrier's bag, and a cap. The children enacted the roles of the postal worker, mail carrier, and customer and wrote letters and cards to mail at the post office.

### Body Movement and Nonverbal Communication

While studying maps, second and third graders can use body movements to demonstrate map symbols and directions. One child becomes the hands of the compass pointing north; another lays down and faces east. They can also use their bodies to show such map symbols as mountains, roads, and railroads.

### Puppetry

Following a unit on careers and vocations, primary grade children can use puppets to interview one another about their careers. Using simple hand, finger, and face puppets, create a set of interview questions such as, Why did you choose this career? What do you do in your job? How long does it take you to get to work? What do you like about your work? Is your boss nice? What is the hardest part of your work?

Without this vital understanding of how drama can be integrated across the curriculum, it is easy to see how many teachers overlook its possibilities. Certainly all children benefit from relevant, meaningful learning activities that focus on intensive oral language experience and use imagination to deal with abstract ideas. Drama, in particular, is easily adapted for the skills, abilities, and interests of all children.

## 🦋 PRACTICAL APPLICATIONS FOR YOUR CLASSROOM

Creative drama is a powerful teaching and learning strategy that enables all children to participate, portray, and react spontaneously to an idea. It has been used positively with children with learning disabilities (Snyder, 1977); second-language students (Diamond & Moore, 1995); and timid, fearful, and aggressive children (Hennings, 2000). Since the goal of drama is to release children's creative potential, children choose how they will participate.

## *Experiences to Support Cultural and Ethnic Diversity*

Drama enables all children to work together in groups or teams to create, direct, and interpret meaningful situations. Its social nature provides opportunities for children with limited proficiency in English to initiate and engage in conversation with fluent English speakers, to improve their oral language skills, and to develop positive attitudes toward each other. According to McCaslin (2000), "The most common error in dealing with [limited English-speaking] children is underestimating their ability and overestimating their verbal skill" (p. 339).

The following suggestions use drama as a foundation for developing children's oral language ability while simultaneously improving their self-image.

**1.** *Use body movement, choral speaking, and pantomime to develop vocabulary.* These activities utilize children's concentration without the pressure of verbalization. Movement activities, such as people sculptures, require a physical response to oral language; pantomime connects actions to words when the spectator guesses what the person is doing; and choral speaking provides practice in oral interpretation and pronunciation without identifying a less-capable speaker (Diamond & Moore, 1995; McCaslin, 2000).

**2.** *Use children's literature to enhance oral language development.* It is well known that reading aloud to children is a powerful way to expand their language. With children from all cultural groups, extend read-aloud sessions with creative drama activities such as puppetry, story drama, and dramatic play. The younger the children, the more quickly they acquire and expand their language. Cumulative folktales and fables such as *Millions of Cats* (Gag, 1956) or *The Very Hungry Caterpillar* (Carle, 1969) are good books for younger children to enact because they are repetitive and predictable. Older children can dramatize scenes from *Mrs. Frisby and the Rats of NIHM* (O'Brien, 1971) or important events from famous people's lives with *Columbus* (d'Aulaire & d'Aulaire, 1955).

**3.** *Immerse children in oral language.* Drama is one of the most natural means of bathing young children in oral language. In dramatic play, children have the richest opportunity to use language. Provide daily experiences where children can create and interpret familiar situations, character roles, and events.

## Experiences to Support Inclusion

Alicia, a third grader with a hearing impairment, used sign language to communicate outside of school. Mr. Ubek, her teacher, invited Alicia to share her knowledge of sign language using pantomime. Her hearing peers acted as spectators as they interpreted the signs that Alicia shared. For the child with a hearing impairment, pantomime and movement are the easiest mediums for success (McCaslin, 2000).

Children with other physical disabilities can still participate in drama activities. Often, these children take the role of the narrator in a retelling, the puppeteer in a dramatization, or a group member in choral speaking.

All children with disabilities can participate in and feel successful in drama activities. They, too, must experience the rewards from creative drama.

## Adaptations for Individual Learners

Gifted learners comprehend quickly and easily and often see many possibilities in their activities. They need an environment that encourages risk taking, occasions to be producers rather than consumers of information, and varied formats for project work (Cohen, 1987). The following example of third graders illustrates how drama, with its many possibilities, challenges gifted learners' thinking skills while meeting these basic needs.

A group of third graders had been learning about the basic concepts of economics—the study of choices and decision making in their own daily lives. For their project, they brainstormed, created, and enacted two different skits about decision making in their classroom using small puppets. One play told the story of planning an entire school day with playing games, watching movies, listening to music, and eating snacks as children's only choices; the other skit described a school day with more variety in activities. The children incorporated sign language, jokes, and vocal changes as they applied creative problem-solving processes to their decision making. The skits ended with the puppets discussing the impact of three major economic concepts on their lives: how choices affect the quality of life; the impact of limited resources on our choices; and the recognition that choosing one thing requires giving up something else.

## CHAPTER SUMMARY

1. Creative drama contributes to every child's learning and is an essential part of a child-centered, early childhood curriculum. Enactment enhances the development of children's imaginative thinking, problem solving, communication, and perspective-taking abilities, as well as their appreciation of drama as an art form.
2. Creative drama focuses on children's natural expression of thoughts, feelings, and ideas rather than on a polished, theatrical performance.

3. Drama activities can be characterized on a continuum from least to most formal. Informal drama uses children's natural, pretend behavior to enact roles, behaviors, and actions. It relies upon participants' inventions or creations in such activities as role play or pantomime. Story or interpretive drama involves some rehearsal, and participants use voice, gestures, and facial features to interpret someone else's ideas and words. Scripted or formal drama uses a memorized script performed for an audience.

4. Teachers possess the most powerful influence over children's dramatic expression. How teachers select and present drama activities and experiences significantly influences how children will develop their creative potential.

5. Appropriate creative drama experiences and activities for children include sociodramatic and dramatic play, story dictation, pantomime, puppets, story drama, and readers theater. All of these drama forms can be integrated with every subject area.

# EXPANDING YOUR THINKING ABOUT CREATIVE DRAMA

### Discuss: Perspectives on Creative Drama

1. Many educators and parents believe that the answer to our educational problems is a "back to basics" philosophy. What arguments would you put forth to convince other educators that drama is basic to an early childhood curriculum?

2. The teacher and caregiver have an important role in developing and sustaining creative drama as an integral part of the curriculum. What teaching behaviors would you expect to see from a teacher who supported children's growth through drama?

3. Review the opening case study of first-grade children preparing to enact the story "The Little Red Hen." Why do you think Ms. Clark devoted one week to this activity? If a colleague of Ms. Clark's criticized her for "wasting time," how might Ms. Clark respond without being overly defensive?

4. Have you ever performed a scripted drama on stage in front of an audience? Describe your feelings. How do you think children feel when engaged in this kind of activity?

5. As a beginning teacher, how much experience with drama do you need to have? What are the minimum skills and values you will need to incorporate drama successfully into your curriculum?

6. Research describes the positive effects of dramatization on children's reading comprehension. Name some stories or picture books that you would use to encourage children at different age levels to reenact. Why did you select these particular stories? How can teachers encourage story drama in their classrooms?

## Interview: Teachers' Beliefs about Drama

Experts in creative drama agree that classroom teachers must value creative drama for it to be integrated into the curriculum (Wilhelm & Edmiston, 1998). In light of this conclusion, arrange to interview an early childhood teacher about his or her beliefs concerning forms of drama in the classroom. Ask the following questions and record the teacher's responses. You may want to tape-record your interview and transcribe the responses after the interview.

1. Do you use drama and puppetry in your classroom? If so, could you provide an example of a drama activity your children enjoy? If not, why?

2. How did your teacher education program prepare you to teach drama in the classroom?

3. In an ideal curriculum, how much importance would you attach to drama in the curriculum?

4. What factors discourage teachers from using more drama in the classroom?

## Write to Learn: Sharing Drama Ideas with Colleagues

As a second-grade teacher who integrates drama in all subject areas, you have been asked by your building principal to share your ideas and beliefs about drama in the curriculum with your grade-level colleagues. Do some free writing in which you explore how you will share these ideas, what your main points will be, and how you will function as a resource person for your peers. Then share your reading with a partner and plan to share your main points with the rest of the class.

## REFERENCES

Bolton, G. (1985). Changes in thinking about drama in the classroom. *Theory into Practice, 24*(3), 151–157.

Bromley, K. D. (1998). *Language arts: Exploring connections* (3rd ed.). Boston: Allyn & Bacon.

Busching, B. A. (1981). Readers theater: An education for language and life. *Language Arts, 58*(3), 337.

Cecil, N. L., & Lauritzen, P. (1994*). Literacy and the arts for the integrated classroom: Alternative ways of knowing.* New York: Longman.

Chenfeld, M. (1995). *Creative experiences for young children* (2nd ed.). New York: Harcourt Brace.

Christie, J. F., & Johnson, E. P. (1983). The role of play in social-intellectual development. *Review of Educational Research, 53*(1), 93–115.

Cohen, L. M. (1987). Thirteen tips for teaching gifted students. *Teaching Exceptional Children, 20,* 34–38.

Corbey-Scullen, L., & Howell, J. (1997). Out of the housekeeping corner and onto the stage: Extending dramatic play. *Young Children, 52*(6), 82–88.

Diamond, B. J., & Moore, M. A. (1995). *Multicultural literacy: Mirroring the reality of the classroom.* White Plains, NY: Longman.

Dillon, D. (1988). Dear readers. *Language Arts, 65*(1), 7–9.

Dixon, N. (1996). Learning with readers theater: Building connections. (ERIC Document Reproduction Service No. ED 396 341)

Edwards, L. C. (1997). *The creative arts: A process approach for teachers and children* (2nd ed.). Upper Saddle River, NJ: Merrill/Prentice Hall.

Fennessey, S. (1995). Living history through drama and literature. *The Reading Teacher, 49*(3), 16–19.

Forsythe, S. J. (1995). It worked! Readers theater in second grade. *The Reading Teacher, 49*(3), 264–265.

Fox, M. (1987). *Teaching drama to young children.* Portsmouth, NH: Heinemann.

Furman, L. (in press). In support of drama in early childhood education, again. *Early Childhood Education Journal.*

Gardner, H. (1993a). *Frames of mind: The theory of multiple intelligences* (10th anniversary ed.). New York: Basic Books.

Gardner, H. (1993b). *Multiple intelligences: The theory in practice.* New York: Basic Books.

Halliday, M. A. K. (1975). *Explorations in the functions of language.* London: Edward Arnold.

Heinig, R. B. (1993). *Creative drama for the classroom teacher* (4th ed.). Upper Saddle River, NJ: Prentice Hall.

Heller, P. G. (1996). Many ways of knowing: Using drama, oral interaction, and the visual arts to enhance reading comprehension. *The Reading Teacher, 45*(8), 580–584.

Hennings, D. G. (2000). *Communication in action: Teaching the language arts* (7th ed.). Boston: Houghton Mifflin.

Howe, N., Moller, L., Chambers, B., & Petrakos, H. (1993). The ecology of dramatic play centers and children's social and cognitive play. *Early Childhood Research Quarterly, 8*(2), 235–252.

Hunt, T., & Renfro, N. (1982). *Puppetry in early childhood education.* Austin, TX: Nancy Renfro Studios.

Isbell, R. (1995). *The complete learning center book.* Beltsville, MD: Gryphon House.

Jalongo, M. R. (2000). *Early childhood language arts* (2nd ed.). Boston: Allyn & Bacon.

Jalongo, M. R., & Stamp, L. N. (1997). *The arts in children's lives: Aesthetic experience in early childhood.* Boston: Allyn & Bacon.

Jalongo, M. R., & Isenberg, J. P. (2000). *Exploring your role: A practitioner's introduction to early childhood education.* Upper Saddle River, NJ: Merrill/Prentice Hall.

Johnson, A. (1998). How to use creative dramatics in the classroom. *Childhood Education, 75*(1), 2.

Johnson, J. E., Christie, J. F., & Yawkey, T. D. (1999). *Play and early childhood development* (2nd ed.). Glenview, IL: Scott, Foresman.

Joint Committee on the Role of Informal Drama in the Classroom of the National Council of Teachers of English and the Children's Theater Association. (1983). Forum: Informal classroom drama. *Language Arts, 60,* 370–371.

Mayesky, M. (1998). *Creative activities for young children* (6th ed.). Albany, NY: Delmar.

McCaslin, N. (2000). *Creative drama in the classroom* (7th ed.). New York: Longman.

McMaster, J. C. (1998). "Doing" literature: Using drama to build literacy. *The Reading Teacher, 51*(7), 574–675.

Morado, C., Koenig, R., & Wilson, A. (1999). Miniperformances, many stars! Playing with stories. *The Reading Teacher, 53*(2), 116–123.

Morgan, J., & Saxton, J. (1987). *Teaching drama: A mind of many wonders.* Portsmouth, NH: Heinemann.

Myhre, S. M. (1993). Enhancing your dramatic play area through the use of prop boxes. *Young Children, 48*(5), 6–11.

Paley, V. (1981). *Wally's stories.* Cambridge, MA: Harvard University Press.

Pinciotti, P. (1993). Creative drama and young children: The dramatic learning connection. *Arts Education Policy Review, 94*(6), 24–29.

San Jose, C. (1989). Classroom drama: Learning from the inside out. In S. Hoffman & L. Lamme (Eds.), *Learning from the inside out* (pp. 69–76). Wheaton, MD: Association for Childhood Education International.

Shaftel, F. R., & Shaftel, G. (1983). *Role playing in the curriculum* (2nd ed.). Englewood Cliffs, NJ: Prentice Hall.

Snyder, A. B. (1977). Let's do drama. *The Pointer, 21*(3), 36–40.

Stone, S. J. (1995). Wanted: Advocates for play in the primary grades. *Young Children, 50*(6), 45–54.

Tompkins, G. E. (1998). *Language arts: Content and teaching strategies* (4th ed.). Upper Saddle River, NJ: Merrill/Prentice Hall.

Verriour, P. (1994). *In role: Teaching and learning dramatically.* Markham, Ontario: Pippin.

Wilhelm, J. D., & Edmiston, B. (Eds.). (1998). *Imagining to learn: Inquiry, ethics, and integration through drama.* Portsmouth, NH: Heinemann.

Wiltz, N. W. & Fein, G. (1996). Evolution of a narrative curriculum: The contributions of Vivan Gussey Paley. *Young Children, 51*(3), 61–68.

Woodward, C. (1985). Guidelines for facilitating sociodramatic play. In J. Frost & S. Sunderlin (Eds.), *When children play* (pp. 291–295). Wheaton, MD: Association for Childhood Education International.

## Children's Literature Cited

Andersen, H. C. (1982). *The emperor's new clothes.* New York: Crowell.

Barracca, D., & Barracca, S. (1990). *The adventures of Taxi Dog.* New York: Trumpet.

Brown, M. (1975). *Stone soup.* New York: Scribners.

Cannon, J. (1993). *Stellaluna.* San Diego, CA: Harcourt Brace Jovanovich.

Carle, E. (1969). *The very hungry caterpillar.* Cleveland, OH: Collins-World.

Carle, E. (1984). *The mixed-up chameleon.* New York: Harper Collins.

Cleary, B. (1975). *Ramona the brave.* New York: Morrow.

d'Aulairé, I., & d'Aulairé, E. P. (1995). *Columbus.* New York: Doubleday.

Gag, W. (1956). *Millions of cats.* New York: Coward McCann (Putnam Publishing Group).

Galdone, P. (1968). *Henny Penny.* New York: Seaburg.

Henkes, K. (1985). *Bailey goes camping.* New York: Greenwillow.

Hoffman, M. (1991). *Amazing Grace.* New York: Dial.

Hogrogrian, N. (1971). *One fine day.* New York: Macmillan.

Jeschke, S. (1985). *Perfect the pig.* New York: Holt.

Keats, E. J. (1971). *Over in the meadow.* New York: Four Winds Press.

Lester, J. (reteller). (1990). *How many spots does a leopard have?* New York: Scholastic.

Lobel, A. (1970). *Frog and Toad are friends.* New York: Harper & Row.

Lobel, A. (1980). *Fables.* New York: Harper & Row.

Martin, B., & Archambault, J. (1987). *Knots on a counting rope.* New York: Holt.

Martin, B., & Archambault, J. (1989). *Chicka chicka boom boom.* New York: Simon & Schuster.

O'Brien, R. (1971). *Mrs. Frisby and the rats of NIMH.* New York: Atheneum.

Potter, B. (1986). *The tale of Peter Rabbit.* New York: Viking.

Seeger, P. (1986). *Abiyoyo.* New York: Macmillan.

Seuss, Dr. (1957). *The cat in the hat.* New York: Random House.

Slobodkina, E. (1947). *Caps for sale.* New York: Scott.

Snyder, S. (1988). *The boy of the three year nap.* New York: Scholastic.

Steig, W. (1969). *Sylvester and the magic pebble.* New York: Prentice Hall.

Steig, W. (1982). *Dr. DeSoto.* New York: Farrar, Straus & Giroux.

Stevens, J. (1987). *The city mouse and the country mouse.* New York: Holiday House.

Strickland, D. (Ed.). (1982). *Listen children: An anthology of black literature.* New York: Bantam.

Williams, V. B. (1981). *Three days on a river in a red canoe.* New York: Greenwillow.

Williams, V. B. (1988). *Stringbean's trip to the shining sea.* New York: Greenwillow.

# PART 3
## CONTEXTS
## FOR CREATIVE
## EXPRESSION AND PLAY

# Chapter 6

# Planning and Managing the Creative Learning Environment

*"Children's self-esteem, sense of belonging, and ambivalent needs both for control over their world and for boundaries to guide that control can be shaped through the thoughtful design of the school and classroom environments."*

Elizabeth Hebert, 1998, p. 70

*"Today's children do need planned playgrounds to compensate for crowded conditions in urban areas, to provide reasonable safe play areas, and to help ensure that children play."*

Joe Frost, 2000, p. 177

# TEACHERS' REFLECTIONS ON CREATIVE ENVIRONMENTS

### Preservice Teachers

"I have seen a diverse set of classrooms this semester. I was able to work with my cooperating teacher to make some classroom adjustments that were aesthetically pleasing and functional. One was a messy coat closet that was in full view. Since these elements were movable, we rearranged them so that the back of the closet provided an area to set up the new 'artist center.' "

"I used to think that how a teacher decided to use climate, space, and time in the classroom would not really affect children's learning, but now I know that this is quite false. As a result of my internship and reading, I now think about these elements as I view how to create centers in the elementary classroom. I noticed that because of the short blocks of time my cooperating teacher allotted for center activity, the children often had to start cleaning up almost as soon as they initiated an activity. I know that this seriously affected the learning and creative potential. During my student teaching, I was able to extend the time blocks and can see the benefits of this on children's learning and creative expression."

"Before reading this book, I thought that schools and classrooms should be serious, no-nonsense environments. I now believe that warm, homey climates are more beneficial to fostering creative expression because they help children feel comfortable in the classroom. I have seen the benefits of this firsthand this semester, and I plan to implement similar practices in the future."

### Inservice Teachers

A preschool teacher says: "I used to think of the classroom environment largely in terms of space—the aesthetic value and room arrangement that made the best use of that space and invited independence. Since studying about creative environments, my thinking has also been focused on the features of *climate* and *time*. I believe that my own attitudes about the value of play, authentic interactions with children, and respect for their thinking has laid the groundwork for a supportive climate in my preschool classroom."

A kindergarten teacher reveals: "I had not really thought about the idea of the environment as the 'third teacher.' Being exposed to this idea has prompted joyful wanderings in my own head of the possibilities associated with this notion. How to make this happen is daunting to me now, but I am convinced of the need for it and am pursuing it."

A school board member and former preschool teacher reflects: "I was asked to examine the playground space at one of our elementary schools and hesitated at first. Playground space just didn't shout out 'creative thinking' or 'priority' to me. Now, as I finished my study, I realized that too many practitioners feel the way I did. I have seen how the playground can hold the key to hands-on extensions and expand children's view of their life, the world, and the future."

## Your Reflections

- What do you think are the effects of the physical environment on children's and teachers' behavior?

- How might your knowledge and beliefs about a creative learning environment influence children's self-expression and learning?

- How would you go about planning and arranging your own creative early childhood learning environment?

## Case Study:

### The Creative Classroom

When Ms. Ring had surgery, she missed two weeks of school and a substitute taught her kindergarten class. On the day Ms. Ring returns to her classroom, she is shocked by what she sees. There may be a place for everything, but nothing is in its place. Puzzle pieces are in the toy box, on the floor, and buried in the sand table. Dolls and stuffed toys are sticky with glue, raisins are squashed into the carpet, and crayons are mixed in with the woodworking tools. The substitute had brought in sieves, sifters, and soil so that the children could categorize and label the soil as rocks, gravel, or sand. Now those materials are everywhere. Before Ms. Ring took sick leave, she conferred with the substitute and felt confident that she was a creative teacher. Now Ms. Ring has doubts. Her classroom is no longer a context for creative expression and play. It is, in her words, a "disaster area"—unsupervised, unstructured, and unplanned.

This scenario dramatically highlights how a classroom can become a poor context for learning. Teachers who design creative environments do more than supply a setting for learning. They view the environment holistically, as "a planned arrangement of ideas, people, time, space, and resources" (McLean, 1995, p. 7) that is essential to the teaching and learning process. The creative classroom is carefully planned and supervised; it encourages children's self-expression, builds upon children's natural curiosity and joy of learning, and allows personal initiative to flourish, yet develops respect for others.

The choices teachers make in planning, arranging, and managing the environment strongly affect how children interact with one another, with adults, with materials, and with the learning experiences. If we compare Ms. Ring's concept of a creative environment with that of the substitute, it is easy to see how contexts for creative expression and play reveal our own beliefs, values, and attitudes about creativity. Planning, arranging, and managing the classroom is as important as planning for instruction. Each must harmonize with the goals of the program.

# THEORETICAL AND RESEARCH BASE: FEATURES OF CREATIVE ENVIRONMENTS

There are three basic elements of creative learning environments: *climate, space,* and *time* (Caples, 1996; Frost, Shinn, & Jacobs, 1998; Garreau & Kennedy, 1991; Johnson, Christie, & Yawkey, 1999; Jones, 1977). These features have a considerable influence on children's play behavior. They should be considered in creating a supportive, respectful place for learning that has high appeal to children.

## *Climate*

**Climate** refers to the feeling one gets from the environment and dictates to what extent children can be productive, engaged learners. In many ways, the child's environment can be compared to the adult's work environment (Frost et al., 1998; Jones, 1977). Young children respond best to classrooms that have:

- *Design features* that evoke a warm, homelike quality, such as carpeted surfaces, soft, light colors, and comfortable furniture.
- *Materials* that capture and sustain children's interest and imagination and that are stored attractively on shelves.
- *Teachers* who show genuine interest in children's activities and support children's efforts.
- *Children* who are absorbed in learning, have choices, and make decisions about work to be done.

On the other hand, classrooms that hinder children's creative expression are product-oriented and have:

- *Design features* that evoke an institutional feeling, such as neutral colors, unmovable furniture, or an abundance of uncoordinated patterns.
- *Materials* that elicit one correct answer, suggest a "hands-off" approach to learning, and are stored on crowded shelves.
- *Teachers* who have little physical contact with children and strive for complete control through numerous verbal commands.
- *Children* who are passive learners, have few choices, and rarely make their own decisions.

Consider these characteristics as you think about the feeling emanating from two second-grade classrooms. In Mr. Kaminsky's class, desks are aligned in neat rows; children are quiet and work individually on the same tasks while the teacher reads with a reading group in the back of the room. Teacher-made bulletin boards, cartoon figures, and posters of classroom rules dominate the room. Mr. Kaminsky divides his daily schedule into five subject-area time blocks. When he rings the bell, the children move quietly to the next activity.

In the class across the hall, Ms. Reiks arranges her classroom into learning and interest centers, each identified by inviting and colorful hanging signs. When the children arrive each morning, they talk with one another and plan their instructional day with selections on a planning board. They move easily and freely around the room, independently accessing materials and placing completed assignments in designated, labeled boxes. Active and quiet activities occur simultaneously. Some children are reading to one another in the library corner; others are constructing scenery for a play they have created; still others are working with Ms. Reiks on a three-dimensional community map. Displays of children's original work, mounted attractively and placed at the children's eye level, fill the room. At planned times during the day, they gather together for group experiences and sharing.

Clearly, Ms. Reiks's classroom has a climate that is more conducive to creative expression. The context she has created is more **child-centered**—more responsive

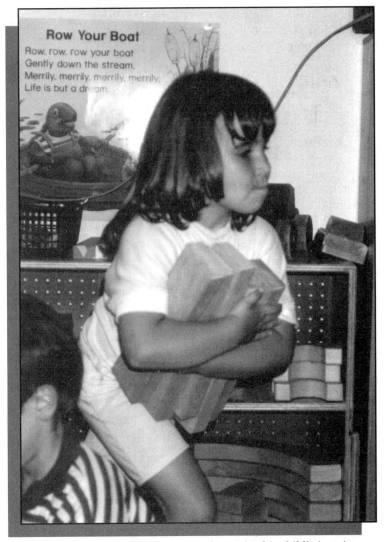

*Notice how these materials capture and sustain this child's imagination and interest.*

to children's needs and interests and more respectful of children's ability to participate in making decisions.

Classroom climate is also greatly influenced by an environment's aesthetic appeal (Edwards, Gandini, & Forman, 1993; Gestwicki, 1999; Sanoff, 1995). Classrooms for young children should be beautiful places to learn. The schools in the Reggio Emilia section of Italy have learning environments that are explicitly created to appeal to children's aesthetic senses. A visitor to such a school might see environments full of light, color, plants, and mirrors selected for their aesthetic characteristics. Great care is taken to create a beautiful environment—detail is given even to such seemingly inconsequential considerations as how the bathroom is decorated, how materials are stored, and how lunches and snacks are presented. The environment in Reggio Emilia schools is one of warmth and beauty, and it is taken as seriously as planning instruction (Edwards et al., 1993).

There are published rating scales and guidelines that support teachers' design of appropriate environments for children of all ages. Using one or more of these scales will provide the salient criteria needed to arrange and assess children's creative environments. Appendix B lists and describes several such scales.

The process of planning, arranging, and managing the creative learning environment is not completed by the previous teacher or finished before school begins. Rather, it is a continuous process based on the children's and teacher's changing needs, interests, and abilities. Environments that are responsive to children can and should be modified periodically.

## *Space*

**Space** includes the degree to which the physical environment is arranged and organized to develop active, creative thinkers and has a strong influence on how children function and learn. To play productively and to minimize disputes, children need at least 25–30 feet (Rettig, 1998; Smith & Connolly, 1980). Children feel more connected to those settings that have adequate space, anticipate their needs, and respect them as individuals.

In good early childhood settings, teachers use easels, movable cabinets, storage shelves, and tables to define areas so that children can work individually, in small groups, or in a large group at circle time. The more flexible the materials and furnishings are within a space, the more possible it is to maximize the potential of any room regardless of its size or shape. If, for example, children are in a school building that is undergoing renovations and want to reconstruct what they are seeing with blocks or other large materials, flexible furnishings allow for spaces to be increased and decreased in response to the children's current project needs.

Well-balanced classroom space separates quiet and boisterous activity and creates safe traffic patterns. It also provides small spaces necessary for children to create imaginative playworlds in which they can engage for long periods of time. These arrangements give both children and teachers more control and choice over their play (Johnson et al., 1999; Kritchevsky, Prescott, & Walling, 1977; Wellhousen, 1999) and maximize the use of time available for play (Tegano, Moran, DeLong, Brickey, & Ramassini, 1996). Many teachers and caregivers are quite inventive in using classroom space in creative and appropriate ways (Wellhousen, 1999). Figure 6.1 lists ways of creating small spaces in your setting to increase the quality and length of children's play and creative expression.

Teachers and caregivers sometimes underestimate the young child's need for private space. Some children need a periodic rest from the action and interaction of the classroom in a place to restore energy or to think quietly before resuming classroom activity. Certain activities, such as listening to a story tape, are enjoyed more fully in a secluded place. If classrooms lack such places, children often

**Figure 6.1**
Suggestions for
Creating Small Play
Spaces

- **Lofts,** which use both upper and lower spaces at the same time.
- **Alcoves,** which often occur between shelves.
- **Closet,** with the door removed, which can become a learning center.
- **Screens** that create a cozy space and enable teachers to monitor children.
- **Appliance boxes,** which become another center or an imaginary place.

*Source:* Adapted from Wellhousen (1999).

create their own. One first-grade teacher who seldom used her desk put it in the corner and found that the space underneath it was a favorite place to read. When teachers insist upon private behavior in a nonprivate space, such as demanding absolute quiet at worktables, it is often stressful for young children (Jones, 1977; Readdick, 1993).

How children use materials within arranged spaces can also enhance or inhibit original thinking. One preschool teacher modeled different uses of materials by moving her easel outdoors in good weather and moving the tricycles indoors when the weather was inclement. A kindergarten teacher placed the workbench near the art center, encouraging the children to build, glue, and paint their constructions. Children could then see materials being used in a variety of settings and in a variety of ways rather than being limited to a single setting or use. Even though room size and shape are important, how space is arranged is even more important.

## Time

**Time** conveys a clear message about the importance of an activity or experience and affects teachers' short-term and long-term planning. When children have long blocks of time, their play is more constructive, cooperative, and expressive than with short, interrupted time periods. In a full-day preschool or kindergarten, 30 minutes per day of play is a minimum (Christie & Wardle, 1992). Teachers who are sensitive to time factors must be able to decide when to extend or stop an activity or when to capitalize on a "teachable moment." Time exerts an important influence on three dimensions of creative behavior—self-expression and self-directedness, attention span, and more complex play.

- *Time influences children's self-expression and self-direction.* Mr. Moore, a teacher of 4-year-olds, planned his schedule to meet his goal of developing children's imagination. He provided a long block of time each day during which children were free to select dramatic play activities, among others. Knowing that there would be time each day to act out familiar roles and events such as playing house, doctor, or restaurant without interruption contributed to children's creative and playful expression. When children are continuously interrupted by many teacher-directed activities in short time blocks, they lose valuable time waiting and are disengaged in learning (Johnson et al., 1999). In contrast, when children have enough time during the school day to choose some learning activities, they become more self-directed learners. Effective early childhood teachers plan creative environments that have a comfortable climate, flexible space, and ample time to foster children's imaginative spirit.

- *Time affects children's attention span.* Early childhood teachers often refer to children's short attention spans when describing children who are not interested in or motivated to complete a project. Many teachers erroneously believe that because children have short attention spans, activities must be changed constantly. When young children are engaged in meaningful activities, however, they are capable of concentrating for long periods of time. In the schools of Reggio Emilia, for example, children remain with a topic for as long as they show an interest in it. Often these topics last for several months (Edwards et al., 1993).

- *Time affects the complexity of children's play.* Higher levels of play, such as sociodramatic and constructive play, require considerable amounts of time to plan and carry out an activity that is particularly engaging and meaningful to the child (Edwards et al., 1993; Garreau & Kennedy, 1991; Tegano et al., 1996). Long blocks of time increase children's ability to move from exploration to more complex forms of play with materials, people, and events. A good example is Robin, a 4-year-old Sioux girl. Her favorite game is "Pow," short for "powwow," and she has participated in a number of these Native American gatherings. Powwows usually last for a few days and include such experiences as dancing, storytelling, selling wares, and judging costumes. In her lengthy play scenarios, Robin takes her daughter (a Native American doll) to see the "powwow" events and invites her friends to play the roles of dancer and storyteller (Jalongo, 1992). Because Robin's teacher provides large blocks of time for Robin to pursue her activities in a meaningful and responsible fashion, she is motivated, interested, and has a longer attention span.

Planning for the physical environment, which includes the element of time, is just as important as planning the instructional program, and it cannot be overlooked. When the physical environment allows time for children to explore, inquire, and utilize its contents, it supports children's creative expression. Without this time, the richest environment has little benefit for children's learning and development (McLean, 1995).

Elizabeth Jones (1977) and Elizabeth Prescott (1984) describe key dimensions of the physical environment that affect children's creative expression and play. These key features are described in Figure 6.2.

1. **Softness**                                        **Hardness**

This dimension describes the feeling of the environment.

Carpeted areas                                          Hard surfaces (wood or linoleum)
Soft, comfortable, and mobile furniture                 Immobile furniture
Animals to hold                                         Drab colors
Messy materials (water, sand)
Laps for sitting
Warm, soft vocal tones

2. **Open**                                            **Closed**

This dimension describes how materials, storage patterns, and program structure enhance or restrict children's creative interactions with materials and with each other. The more ways materials can be used and the more choices children have in the play, the more open the environment becomes.

Open materials offer unlimited possibilities            Limited alternatives (e.g., puzzles and
  for use (e.g., collage and water)                       matching games)
Relatively open materials offer a number of             No visible or reachable storage
  possibilities (e.g., construction materials)          Materials to be used in one way
Visible and accessible storage

3. **Simple**                                          **Complex**

This dimension describes the extent to which materials and equipment sustain children's interests. Simple environments encourage children to focus on task completion and do not hold children's attention very long; complex environments contribute to children's imagination.

Single use not fostering manipulation                   Combine two different materials (e.g., art,
  (e.g., slides, puzzles, swings)                          dramatic play); supercomplex materials:
                                                          combine three or more materials (e.g., sand,
                                                          tools, and water)

4. **High Mobility**                                   **Low Mobility**

This dimension concerns the degree of children's physical activity.

Gross motor, active physical activities                 Small motor, sedentary activities (e.g., drawing,
  (e.g., climbing, jumping)                                writing)

5. **Intrusion**                                       **Seclusion**

This dimension concerns boundaries and opportunities for privacy.

Adds new people and materials to the                    Defined private sectors
  environment; children free to move about;
  cross-age grouping and teachable moments

6. **Risk**                                            **Safety**

This dimension concerns opportunities for risk taking and environmental safety.

Opportunities to experiment with new materials,         Protects children from hazards
  ideas, and ways of playing in careful ways

7. **Large Group**                                     **Individual**

This dimension addresses the balance between large and small group learning opportunities throughout the day.

Story-time, musical experiences, Group                  Lap reading, one-to-one reading, Individual
  games, morning meeting                                  activities

**Figure 6.2**   Key Features of Creative Learning Environments
*Sources:* Adapted from Jones (1977) and Prescott (1984).

# Research Studies on Planning and Managing the Creative Environment

Bagley, D. M., & Kass, P. H. (1997). Comparison of preschoolers' play in housekeeping and thematic sociodramatic play centers. *Journal of Research in Childhood Education, 12*(1), 71–77.

Barbour, A. C. (1999). The impact of playground design on the play behaviors of children with differing levels of physical competence. *Early Childhood Research Quarterly, 14*(1), 75–98.

Hartle, L. (1996). Effects of additional materials on preschool children's outdoor play behaviors. *Journal of Research in Childhood Education, 11*(1), 68–81.

Petrakos, H., & Howe, N. (1996). The influence of the physical design of the dramatic play center on children's play. *Early Childhood Research Quarterly, 11*(1), 63–67.

Rettig, M. (1998). Environmental influences on the play of young children with disabilities. *Education and Training in Mental Retardation and Developmental Disabilities, 33*(2), 189–194.

Tegano, D. W., Lookabaugh, S., May, G., & Burdette, M. P. (1991). Constructive play and problem solving: The role of structure and time in the classroom. *Early Childhood Development and Care, 68*(1), 27–35.

## Web Sites

Handbook for Public Playground Safety

*www.cpsc.gov*

SAFE brochures and other materials

*www.uni.edu/playground*

Early Years Are Learning Years (Block Play: Building a Child's Mind, 1997)

*www.naeyc.org/naeyc*

Early Years Are Learning Years (Playgrounds: Keeping Outdoor Learning Safe, 1996)

*www.cyfcc.umn.edu/Children/naeyc5.html*

Encouraging Creativity in Early Childhood Classrooms

*www.ericece.org/reggio/edward95.html*

## PLANNING AND MANAGING THE INDOOR ENVIRONMENT

In creative environments, children engage in a balance of self-selected, self-directed, and teacher-selected activities. Picture these two kindergarten environments in which the daily schedule is posted. In Mr. Lee's room, the day begins with centers containing thematic activities and projects selected by the children. After cleanup, the children gather together as a group. Mr. Lee places traditional, interesting whole-group activities (e.g., story, calendar, sharing) after cleanup to reserve the morning for creative expression and play activities and to capitalize on children's high interest in starting to learn early in the day. Across the hall in Ms. Gorman's room, the children spend the first hour and a half of each day in circle activities. They are required to remain seated on a piece of masking tape that marks their place on the rug. Each day begins with a good-morning song, attendance, the calendar, and the weather. This is followed by a lesson and a lengthy period of teacher's questions to individual children about the lesson. Children are constantly reminded to pay attention and several are isolated from the group by being sent to the "thinking chair" as punishment for becoming distracted.

Notice how the room arrangement in Mr. Lee's room is flexible, interest centers are provided, transitions are managed well, and routines are established to meet children's needs. In Ms. Gorman's room, on the other hand, the room arrangement is invariant, there are no interest centers, one activity blurs into another, and routines are established for teacher convenience. In this case, Ms. Gorman's teacher-directed environment does not provide opportunities for children to assume responsibility for their own learning, while Mr. Lee's arrangement encourages and supports child-initiated learning.

### Room Arrangement

Room arrangement refers to the way space is organized for children's learning and movement. It can be planned, such as the art center and the area around it, or unplanned, such as a cubbyhole between two shelving units that attracts children. Space also affects both children's and teachers' behaviors and attitudes (McLean, 1995; Prescott, 1984).

When children use space in ways that do not occur to us as teachers, it is time to reexamine room arrangement. One kindergarten teacher who observed her kindergartners using the coatroom for a play space realized this. She responded to their discovery by converting empty space, first dividing the space with a screen and then adding dramatic play materials (Loughlin & Suina, 1982). Now, when the children entered the coatroom, their activity was primarily guided by the materials available in that area.

When arranging or rearranging the environment, keep in mind the following principles:

**1.** *Consider how the environment communicates messages about appropriate behavior.* If you are invited to dinner, you would behave differently at a cookout with paper plates and plastic utensils than at a formal dinner party with china, silver, and crystal. Space works in the same way with children. It dictates how they may interact and use materials and affects their work pace (Jalongo & Isenberg, 2000; Johnson et al., 1999). Well-organized space facilitates freedom of movement, creative expression, and learning. In contrast, poorly organized space invites ongoing interruptions, decreases children's attention spans, increases the likelihood of conflicts, and demands more teacher direction about rules and regulations (Prescott, 1984).

**2.** *Space must be easy to supervise* (Bredekamp & Copple, 1997; Kritchevsky et al., 1977). When children are involved in a variety of activities simultaneously, teachers must be able to scan the room from all vantagepoints. Carefully arranged space enables teachers to observe and monitor children's behavior. In this way, teachers can facilitate those behaviors that support program goals and redirect those behaviors that do not.

**3.** *Materials must be accessible and easy to use* (Crosser, 1992). Ms. Reich arranged the manipulative toys in her class of 2-year-olds—such as large Tinkertoys, puzzles, shape sorters, rings, and links—along low, open shelves that faced a carpeted area away from traffic flow. In this class, the 2-year-olds' typical behavior dictated the room arrangement. Because toddlers usually dump manipulatives on the floor to play with them, Ms. Reich provided the space for them to do so. From a developmental perspective, it is unrealistic to expect every 2-year-old to carry materials to a table, so this teacher made her toys easy to use. When materials are accessible to children, they enhance children's sense of ownership of the classroom, encourage creative problem solving, and foster exchanges of materials from one part of the classroom to another.

**4.** *Be alert to behaviors that conflict with your goals.* Sometimes children's behaviors do not match teachers' intentions. When that happens, think about whether the problem lies with the children or with the room arrangement (McLean, 1995). For example, when Fernando, a kindergartner, repeatedly ran through the dramatic play center to feed the guinea pig, he disrupted the ongoing play. Upon observation and questioning, his teacher discovered that the easiest and fastest route to the guinea pig cage went directly through the dramatic play area. Together, they figured out a different location for the guinea pig, and the problem of using the dramatic play area as a thoroughfare was solved.

**5.** *Distinguish between the child's and the adult's environment.* Teachers and children view their surroundings from different perspectives. Both usually attend to what is at their eye level. Obviously, that space is different for adults and children due to differences in their height, experience, and movement patterns. The best way to understand the child's environment is to kneel down and view the space from the child's perspective (Loughlin & Martin, 1987; Loughlin & Suina,

1982). Adopting a child's-eye view can enable you to plan a more child-centered room arrangement.

**6.** *Be alert to traffic patterns.* Well-arranged rooms provide clear pathways for a smooth and easy flow of traffic throughout the room. A path is visible, empty floor space through which people move from place to place. When activity centers are too close to one another and children cannot freely move among them, children interfere with each other. This usually causes conflict. To maintain freedom of movement that enables children to focus on their play, paths should not be used for any other purpose. Unclear paths often distract children on their way to a space or disrupt activities by leading children to intrude in others' ongoing play or to accidentally knock over materials.

Room arrangement is a powerful tool in the creative environment. It requires knowledge of how space affects behavior and how space must be designed for special purposes and interests. Figure 6.3 shows room arrangements for toddlers, preschoolers and kindergartners, and primary grade children.

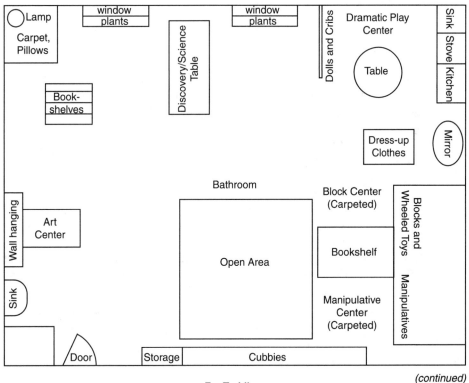

**For Toddlers**

*(continued)*

**Figure 6.3**   Room Arrangements

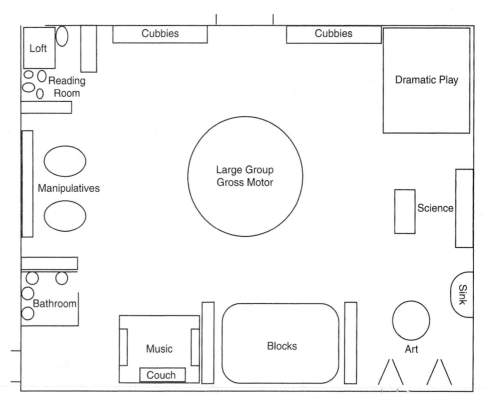

**For Preschoolers/Kindergartners**

**Figure 6.3**   *(Continued)*

## *Centers*

Most creative environments for children organize space into well-defined, thematic interest areas or centers. Centers are a valuable educational tool, enabling teachers to integrate the curriculum, overlap subject areas, develop multicultural awareness, teach to all of children's intelligences, and nurture children's spontaneity and originality (Isbell, 1995; Sloane, 1998). Carefully designed centers contain a variety of books and real and manipulative materials that:

- Promote active learning, planning, decision making, problem solving, originality, and interaction throughout the subject areas (Casey & Lippman, 1991; Isbell, 1995).
- Increase social and verbal interaction and various forms of play among peers (Bredekamp & Copple, 1997; Isbell, 1995).
- Require children to make choices of how to spend and manage their time and decide when to move to another activity (Johnson et al., 1999).
- Reflect children's interests and cultural backgrounds.

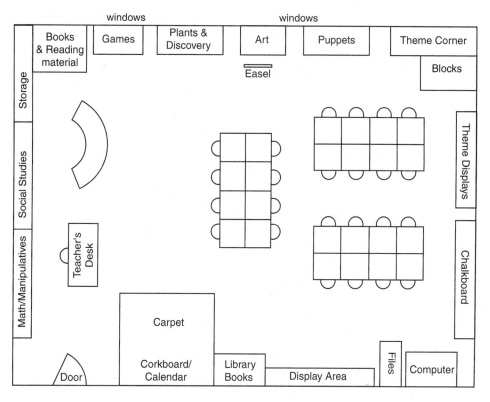

**For Primary Grade Children**

**Figure 6.3**  *(Continued)*

## Planning Centers for Different Age Levels

Planning and arranging centers focuses on the question, "What will children do and learn?" A center arrangement is appropriate for all children. Centers not only integrate learning but also provide an organized system for teaching to children's multiple ways of learning. Some adaptations, however, must be made to meet the needs, abilities, and interests of children at different ages.

*Toddlers* need centers that contain a variety of play materials with different levels of complexity, as well as time for exploration (Bredekamp & Copple, 1997; Buffin, 1998; Rettig, 1998). They must:

*   Have low, open shelves to display and help the children find materials.
*   Have materials that reflect familiar people and places matched to the children's developmental level to encourage and extend play.
*   Encourage exploration and large motor development with climbing, push-pull, and ride-on toys.
*   Provide a private space to watch others play or to rest with a soft toy.

- Offer sensory and creative experiences with music, science, dramatic play, construction, manipulatives, and sand and water to encourage different types of play. Chapter Seven details the variety of developmentally appropriate materials toddlers can use in these areas.

*Preschool children and kindergartners* need centers that meet all of the requirements for toddlers and contain a variety of interesting materials and supplies that can be used to role-play pretend games (e.g., hats, shoes) and to construct (e.g., wood and glue, wooden blocks). The materials must reflect the expanding world of their community, their culture, and their increasing interest in all subject areas (Bredekamp & Copple, 1997; Gestwicki, 1999).

*School-age* children need centers that support their need to develop logical thinking skills, create an orderly environment, belong to a peer group, and demonstrate competence in a particular area. They need learning experiences that capitalize on their need to be active learners and that enable them to feel competent and successful. School-age children like resources that include literacy materials, challenge cards, and additional space for ongoing projects (Sloane, 1998).

In planning and arranging centers, teachers and caregivers need to consider three essential elements: space, special requirements, and supervision. *Spatial aspects* include planning to ensure visible, defined areas; clear pathways created by using the backs of large pieces of furniture or movable screens; private space by providing a cozy area; and centers arranged by type of activity (e.g., large or small group, active or quiet interaction). *Special requirements* might include water, electricity, large floor space, or privacy. *Supervision* entails organizing materials close to their appropriate centers and maintaining a proper vantage point for observation (Isbell, 1995; Petrakos & Howe, 1996; Sloane, 1998). The following section provides suggestions for managing learning centers in your creative learning environment.

### Managing a Center-Based Classroom

Incorporating centers into the creative learning environment requires planning in order to capitalize on children's natural need for self-directed behavior. The following six techniques are necessary to organize and manage a center-based environment (Crosser, 1992; Rybcynski & Troy, 1995; Sloane, 1998). These are:

**1.** *Select centers that are appropriate for a particular group of children.* Knowing the needs, interests, and background of your students is important for establishing a center that invites children's participation. You might ask, "What is appropriate for individual children to learn while using this center?" "How will the children who use this center be able to express what they know?" Planning a center involves assessment of what students know and where a child is in the learning process. It is important to solicit children's ideas about a theme before items are collected. Getting the children involved in the planning builds excitement and influences procedures for its use.

**2.** *Introduce the center with guidelines for its use.* Some teachers provide mini "field trips" before using the centers. These excursions help children understand the boundaries of the center, highlight the materials and equipment available for use, and give children a sense of how much time they have for sustained play and exploration. They also help individual children know what learning goals are expected.

3.   *Use a planning or choice board.* Planning or choice boards encourage children to recognize the beginning and end of an activity, develop planning and organizational skills related to their own activities, manage their time, work independently and with others, assume responsibility for their own activities, and reflect on their decisions (Casey & Lippman, 1991; Gestwicki, 1999; Sloane, 1998). They also help teachers limit the number of children in a center or activity at any one time, evaluate and change centers as needed, and observe children's choices. Planning or choice boards provide teachers with a great deal of flexibility.

A planning board can be easily constructed from pegboard or any freestanding object (such as a bulletin board), pictures or labels for centers, and name tags. Some teachers use a magnetic board with small magnets or magnetic tape strips on the board and paper clips glued on the back of cards. For preschool and kindergarten children who are not yet readers, children's names and the names of the centers can be illustrated pictorially. Figure 6.4 illustrates a planning board used with preschoolers; Figures 6.5 and 6.6 illustrate planning sheets used with kindergartners and first graders.

4.   *Assume specific teacher roles to facilitate learning through centers.* The teacher's roles are critical to an appropriate use of learning centers. Teachers and caregivers can use centers to observe children for social or skill use and document their progress. They should also meet with individual children to guide their center choices that are related to specific learning goals. Moreover, teachers and caregivers can use center time to model behavior for children who are reluctant to participate in the center project, support children's ideas and projects through listening or participating as a co-player where needed, or pose questions that will keep children engaged in their experiences.

5.   *Document children's progress.* Documentation helps teachers identify what children are learning through center activity. Because children are engaged in a variety of learning experiences at the same time, it is important to have a system in place to show what children can do. Refer back to Figure 2.1 in Chapter Two for a checklist for documenting children's literacy learning through play.

6.   *Evaluate how the center is being used.* In center-based classrooms, teachers continually need to ask themselves whether or not children are engaged in meaningful activity and whether there are ongoing opportunities and challenges for them in the centers. Moreover, a key part of the evaluation is to watch for children's waning interest. It may be that they need additional props or materials or need to start brainstorming ideas for a new theme.

### A Center-Based Classroom

Consider how Mr. Kennedy uses centers in his first-grade classroom. There are two large, child-created displays relating to their unit on insects. One display contains a variety of three-dimensional, imaginative insects created by the children at the art center. Another presents children's illustrated stories about their creations. Mr. Kennedy's centers contain interesting and accessible materials

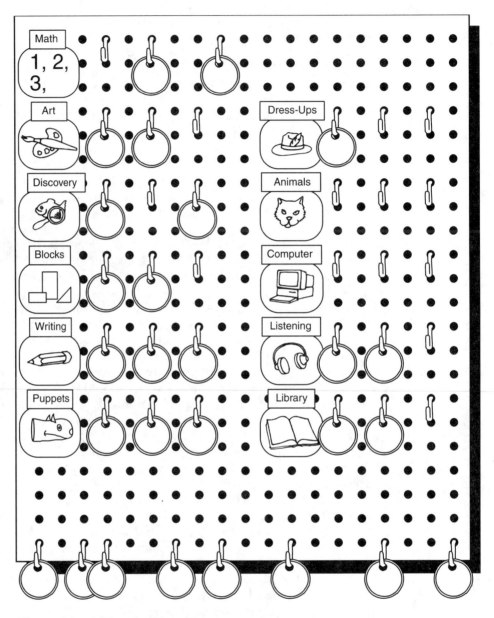

**Figure 6.4**    A Planning Board

that invite children's participation. They are attractively stored in color-coded plastic baskets and tubs and have pictures to assist children in keeping them properly organized.

Mr. Kennedy has placed centers for dramatic play, blocks, and the work-bench near each other because children's play here is often noisy; he has grouped

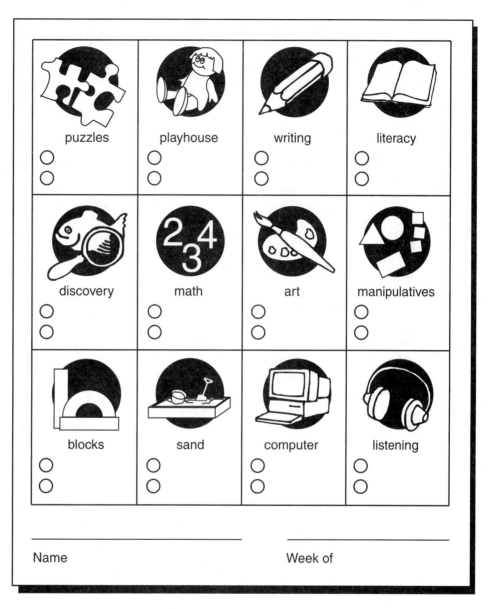

**Figure 6.5**   Planning Sheet for Preschoolers/Kindergartners

the discovery and art centers next to the sink because they need water; and he has clustered the literacy, writing, and listening areas together because they demand a quieter environment. He has even arranged a small, cozy corner with a beanbag chair and colored pillows for those times when children seek solitude. Because of these groupings, children commonly use materials from one center as they work

Name _____    Week of _____

| Art | | Math | |
|---|---|---|---|
| _____ ○ | | _____ ○ | |
| _____ ○ | | _____ ○ | |

| Writing | | Science | |
|---|---|---|---|
| _____ ○ | | _____ ○ | |
| _____ ○ | | _____ ○ | |

Skill Group

| Lunch | Story | Recess | |
|---|---|---|---|
| Blocks | ○ ○ | Literacy | ○ ○ |
| Manipulatives | ○ ○ | Sand | ○ ○ |
| Listening | ○ ○ | Puzzles | ○ ○ |
| Projects | ○ ○ | Computer | ○ ○ |

**Figure 6.6**   Planning Sheet for Primary Grade Children

in another (e.g., using pots and pans from the dramatic play center in the "trailer" they constructed from blocks in the block center).

Mr. Kennedy organizes his materials in cabinets close to where they are going to be used. This enables him to add new materials quickly and efficiently when children show special interest. It also enables him to rotate materials regularly to keep children engaged and involved in their center experiences. Rotating materi-

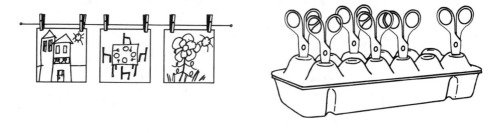

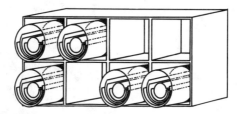

als provides opportunities for children to practice known skills and also to develop new ones.

In addition to organizing materials, Mr. Kennedy also organizes children's work. He uses individual mailboxes made from recycled two-liter or gallon jugs with the tops cut off, uses an egg carton as a scissors holder, and uses a clothesline to display children's art. Organizing children's work provides children with a sense of order that fosters their ability to gain a sense of control over their environment.

Mr. Kennedy's environment has been prepared to foster children's learning through play and creative expression. Through active, concrete experiences and numerous opportunities for peer and adult interactions, these first graders can express themselves in developmentally appropriate ways.

### Types and Uses of Centers

Indoor centers include some of the following commonly found centers and materials to support children's self-expression. The best centers include a rich variety of materials that invite exploration and experimentation.

**Art Center.**   The art center enables children to investigate and create using a wide variety of materials. Some teachers even display works from famous artists in or near the center to enhance aesthetic appreciation. The art center should be located near a water source. If not, use plastic sheeting to cover carpeted areas or tables when children are using messy materials.

Most art materials should be organized and accessible on low, open shelves. This arrangement enables children to use them in other centers as needed. For example, in one first-grade classroom, two children were designing a menu and a cover for their Mexican restaurant theme center. They used the menu to elaborate on their play. In a third-grade class, Horace used the art center to create a glove

*A workbench and tools are an important part of a center-based classroom.*

finger puppet as a prop for his story on dragons. In these rooms, the centers provided a vehicle for integrating the curriculum while supporting children's creative expression. Chapter Three contains a detailed list of appropriate uses of art materials.

**Block Center.**   Blocks help children develop essential classification and seriation skills and concepts, as well as increase their social and problem-solving skills. The block center should be located away from busy traffic areas and in an area where there is ample space for construction. It should contain a wide assortment of blocks and accessories (such as human figures, road signs, and small-wheeled vehicles). Literacy materials and tools are another important addition. Children may want to sketch their "blueprints" on paper, label a building they've created, or write a story about their experience. Blocks should be accessible on open shelves marked with paper silhouettes of each block size and shape. Placing the center adjacent to the dramatic play center increases the interchange among centers (Hirsch, 1996; Kinsman & Berk, 1979). Chapter Seven contains more detailed information on blocks.

*Cleaning up blocks, by
a 4-year-old boy.*

**Discovery and Science Center.**   In this center, children actively explore materials that help develop scientific and conceptual understandings, such as shape, size, number, and volume. Children gain firsthand experiences with, for example, animals, vegetation, minerals, and the equipment used to study them such as scales, magnets, and simple measurement tools. Materials for experiments include boxes of collected items (such as shells or rocks) for sorting, classifying, comparing, and contrasting. Literacy materials and tools also support reading and writing across the subject areas. Often children use these materials for ongoing projects in other centers. To illustrate, one kindergartner took the magnifying glasses from the discovery center to examine sick animals she was tending in the dramatic play area. A second grader added information about his plant's growth to the classroom graph.

The discovery and science center also includes experiences with sand, rice, and water. Appropriate tables or plastic tubs with plastic containers and tubing of all shapes and sizes provide opportunities for scientific exploration with such concepts as volume, buoyancy, and displacement.

**Dramatic Play Center.**   The dramatic play center offers a rich setting for extending children's exploration and expansion of roles, behaviors, social skills, and language. It also promotes career and cultural awareness as children explore various occupations and cultures. Dramatic play centers are often transformed into thematic units of study such as a bakery during a unit on economics, a shoe store during a unit on measurement, and a photographer's studio during a unit on color and

*Children can develop scientific understandings through exploration with a variety of plastic containers and tubing and a large water table.*

shapes. Regardless of the theme, dramatic play centers provide rich opportunities for building literacy skills and concepts. When pencils, pads, telephone books, literature books, and other print materials are added to this center, children's voluntary use of literacy is encouraged (Ferguson, 1999). Prop boxes, described in Chapter Five, are appropriate in this center and enhance children's play.

**Library and Literacy Center.**   This center invites children to read a variety of print materials in a relaxing way and should be located in a quiet area of the classroom. It should be a soft, cozy place. Some teachers have used a rocking chair, a seat removed from a car, or an old bathtub filled with pillows in their literacy centers. A variety of familiar and interesting books should be displayed on bookshelves. There should also be books in different formats such as story and information books, wordless and predictable books, riddles, rhymes, and child-made books. The center should also contain printed signs and questions that invite children to explore the book selections. Some teachers include the Sunday comics, old catalogues, puppets and prop boxes for retelling stories, recycled copies of children's magazines, and mobiles of information about a featured author. Interesting writing materials, such as recycled colored paper from a print shop and unusual pens and pencils, should be available. For young children, this center encourages early literacy play—an important precursor to learning to read and write (Ferguson, 1999; Isenberg, 1995; Rybczynski & Troy, 1995).

**Manipulative and Math Center.**   Manipulative materials, such as colored blocks, buttons, counting frames, and cubes, encourage children's growing mathematical understandings of number, classification, ordering, comparing, measuring, estimating, and counting. The center needs to be located near low, open shelves that contain an organized system for storing manipulatives and math games such as dominoes. Writing materials, a chalkboard, and a flannel board should also be available for children to create their own math stories and explore and practice mathematical skills and concepts. Chapter Seven contains an extensive list of appropriate manipulative materials for different ages.

**Media and Music Center.**   This center uses electronic media (e.g., computers, audio- and videotapes, records) as vehicles for play and as objects of playful expression. The media and music center needs to be located away from extreme heat, cold, and glare and near an electrical outlet. Many teachers find that laminated posters with rebus-type instructions on operating and caring for the equipment are useful. Computers should be placed on tabletops at eye level and should be arranged so that two or three children may work together at any one time (Hohman, 1985; Wright & Shade, 1994). The media center should be as open and accessible as other centers so that children can use the equipment for play and investigation. It should also contain a variety of music for children to listen to, simple musical instruments that enable children to create their own music, and experiences with music from other cultures.

**Writing Center.**   In this center, children experiment with writing and illustrating in many forms, from scribbling or drawing to composing poems and stories. Sometimes they come here from other centers to make signs or captions for their work. Good writing centers contain chalkboards, a stapler, glue, pencils, markers and crayons, and an assortment of papers in various sizes, shapes, and colors for writing and illustrating. Magazines, newspapers, old catalogues, scissors, and glue are also available for children to illustrate stories or add to their creations. Some teachers have children keep a box of children's drawings for others to use to create stories (Loughlin & Martin, 1987; Vukelich, 1991).

Centers offer children more than just good opportunities to engage in an activity; they offer children the chance to explore, investigate, and utilize their ideas in new and creative ways. It is unlikely that you will use all of these centers simultaneously. Most early childhood teachers use about six permanent centers that are aligned with their classroom, program, and school goals. Teachers periodically transform these centers to be aligned with ongoing themes and units the children are learning about. When using centers as a means of teaching and learning, particular attention needs to be paid to transitions and routines.

## Transitions and Routines

Transitions are those times during the day when children move from one activity to the next. In a classroom with centers and choices, each transition requires children to make a decision (Kohn, 1993). Routines are regular and predictable activities that form the basis of the daily schedule; they help children sense the passage of time (e.g., snack follows cleanup) and enable them to anticipate events (e.g., playing a musical selection at the end of each day).

Transitions and routines consume between 20 to 35 percent of the preschooler's day (Berk, 1976) and about 15 percent of a school-age child's day (Schickedanz, York, Stewart, & White, 1990) and are an integral part of the day for school-age children. Unless appropriately planned, they can be difficult and stressful periods for both children and teachers. Failure to plan for transition times encourages inappropriate behaviors, boredom, and increased dependence on the teacher. Planned transitions and routines that are developmentally appropriate:

1. *Facilitate children's control over the environment.* One beginning second-grade teacher was having difficulty with managing children's behavior. It seemed that each time the children moved from one activity to the next, they playfully pushed one another, tripped or knocked over materials, and constantly interrupted and asked her what to do. What was happening in her classroom? The daily schedule consisted of a series of whole-group activities requiring children to spend an inordinate amount of time waiting for a turn. Little attention was given to transitions. The teacher's mentor suggested examining the organization of the day, starting with planning for routines and transitions. The teacher replied, "It never occurred to me that I should even think about those times in the day. I just assumed children knew what was expected of them when they finished. Now I realize that I must plan for transitions just as I plan for the rest of the instructional day."

2. *Must be child-centered.* A first-grade teacher opens his morning group time with his whole class clustered around him in a large space. Following group time, the children sing a special song or chant some poetry, such as "A Wiggle in My Toe," to move from one activity to the next.

3. *Help children make connections to their ongoing, thematic activities.* During a unit on transportation, Ms. Plate sang the song "Riding in an Airplane," by Raffi, with the children. At the end of the song, she suggested that the children pretend to fly to the prepared art tables and make appropriate airplane noises along the way. This tied their study of transportation with music and art and assured a positive transition.

Planned transitions and routines that are developmentally appropriate are essential for children of all ages. They differ from other activities in purpose, length, and frequency and depend upon the age of the children and the available physical facilities. Thoughtful planning provides a structured yet flexible environment that provides predictability for children, minimizes chaos, and enables children to take charge of the day easily and comfortably (Hildebrand, 1997; Kohn, 1993). Figure 6.7 provides developmentally appropriate suggestions for managing transitions and routines for young children.

**Figure 6.7**
Ideas for Managing
Routines and
Transitions

Routines are an integral part of learning and offer both children and teacher more control over their environment.

**Arrival**

- Prepare materials and activities before children arrive.
- Be available to greet children.
- Prepare engaging and interesting activities that attract children's attention and are easy to monitor.
- In extended-day settings, be certain to communicate any unusual behaviors or concerns to staff and teachers who follow you.
- Ask parents who want to talk to stay for a moment, if feasible, or call them later to arrange a time.
- Construct an attendance chart and a center planning board so that children can sign in and choose activities as they arrive.

**Opening Group Time**

- Begin this part of the day after children have had a chance to explore the environment.
- Introduce available choices for the day and ask children to make decisions about what they will do.
- Use this time to review or create any classroom rules related to using a particular center or piece of equipment. When children help set these limits, they are more apt to internalize them.
- Demonstrate the appropriate use of new materials.

**Cleanup**

- Give notice. Children need a 10-, a 5-, and then a 1-minute warning to begin cleanup.
- Play tape-recorded music and have children listen for something special as they put away materials.
- Use a song to announce that cleanup time is approaching and sing while cleaning up.
- Organize a precleanup circle. Decide how to divide the tasks so that each child picks up a certain number of objects or a particular kind of object (e.g., everything that is smaller than a shopping bag; everything that has a metal part) or use a cleanup helpers' board.
- Model the behaviors you want to see from the children.
- Prepare an interesting activity to follow cleanup that children can anticipate with enthusiasm.
- Create rhymes to familiar tunes that refer to putting away materials or helping ("This is the way we clean up our room . . .").

*(continued)*

*Sources:* Adapted from Crosser (1992) and Hildebrand (1997).

**Figure 6.7**
*(Continued)*

| Departure |
|---|
| • Establish a departure ritual such as hearing a story or enjoying a song together. |
| • Briefly preview some of the interesting things that will take place the next day or later that week. |
| • Encourage children to bring tote or paper bags for papers, newsletters, and other forms of communication. |
| • Be available to say goodbye. |
| **Transitions from One Activity to Another** |
| • Develop a repertoire of songs and fingerplays to be used as children move from one place to another. Use a song or fingerplay (e.g., "Two little blackbirds"; ask one child to name another by color of clothing, kinds of fasteners on shoes, or name card). |
| • Have books ready for children to read while others finish their activities and get ready to join the group. |
| • Use a mystery box, puppets, a riddle ("I see something red, white, and blue with stars on it"), fingerplays, or quiet songs. |
| *For primary grade children:* |
| • Review the day and talk about tomorrow. |
| • Plan ahead on how to move from one activity to another. |
| • Have materials ready for the next activity. |

## PLANNING AND MANAGING THE OUTDOOR ENVIRONMENT

Many teachers still view the purpose of outdoor play as a release of tension and excess energy. This narrow view perpetuates the neglect of the outdoor environment as an important setting for children's creative growth and development. Outdoor environments need the same systematic attention to space, materials, and equipment as indoor environments. The best outdoor environments provide children opportunities to engage in all forms of play—exercise, dramatic and constructive play, and games with rules in an environment with natural features (Frost, 1992; Frost, Shinn, & Jacobs, 1998; Frost & Woods, 1998; Rivkin, 1995).

Think about Ms. Ogur's beliefs about her preschoolers' outdoor environment. Ms. Ogur was concerned about the quality of the play on the playground. In her school, the playground equipment included three tricycles, two balls, and a combination swing set/climbing apparatus for 15 children to share. Somehow, the children were continuously fighting over the materials. She knew that this was the year to address and solve the problem. She also knew that the children's disputes were caused, in part, by not having enough challenging materials and equipment.

After talking with other colleagues and reading professional literature on outdoor play for preschoolers, she discovered that some materials have different levels of complexity. Kritchevsky et al. (1977) classify materials as:

- **Simple units** that have a single, obvious use, with no subparts for children to manipulate or create (e.g., swings, tricycles).
- **Complex units** that have subparts of two very different kinds of materials for children to manipulate or invent (e.g., water and plastic containers, sand and digging tools). This category also includes single play materials that have many diverse possibilities (e.g., art materials such as dough and paint or a box of books).
- **Supercomplex units** that have three or more subparts that children can juxtapose (e.g., sand, digging tools, and water).

Supercomplex units hold children's attention and interest the longest because of the many opportunities children have to manipulate and juxtapose the parts and integrate them into their play themes. Simple units, on the other hand, are necessary but typically hold interest and attention only for a short period of time because they are often played with by one child in just one way, such as a Hot Wheels toy.

Ms. Ogur then decided to expand children's play by adding some complexity to the environment. She brought out a wagon, created an obstacle course from old, worn tires obtained free from the local junkyard, and made some simple traffic signs out of scrap lumber and paint. She also brought out the police officer's hat from the dramatic play center and markers and scrap paper from the literacy center. From these simple additions, the children created elaborate play themes or scenarios about accidents, traffic, parking, and speeding. Some children even created and handed out parking tickets. On other occasions, the children used the wagon as an ambulance to transport an accident victim to the hospital, where another elaborate scenario was enacted. Ms. Ogur even used the traffic signs to reinforce bicycle safety practices.

Ms. Ogur illustrates what a resourceful teacher can do to make the outdoor environment more stimulating and challenging even with limited financial resources. She also demonstrates how outdoor activities stimulate learning in all areas of development. Teachers and caregivers like Ms. Ogur, who view the outdoor environment as a support for children's development, know that activities such as balancing, crawling, and playing games contribute to children's physical development; activities that involve personal care, risk taking, and role playing contribute to children's emotional development; activities that include cooperative games, verbal dialogue, and planning promote children's social growth; while activities that include listening, experimenting, imagining, and symbolizing promote children's cognitive growth (Frost et al., 1998; Frost & Woods, 1998).

## Types of Playgrounds

Basically, there are three types of playgrounds: traditional, adventure, and creative (Frost, 1992; Rivkin, 1995). Each differs in origin, types of equipment and materials, targeted age groups, and purpose. Each also differs in promoting or constraining the amount of physical activity and social interaction of children (Barbour, 1999).

**Traditional playgrounds** originated in the early part of this century and were designed for physical exercise to emphasize gross motor play. They contain large, steel, immovable equipment (e.g., climbing bars, slides, and swings)—mostly simple units—that are designed to be used for a single purpose—exercise. The lack of variety and challenge in this type of equipment often results in boredom. Traditional playgrounds are often not well maintained or supervised, are built on dangerously hard surfaces, and are not consistent with what we know about children's learning and development, yet they are prevalent in elementary school playgrounds (Frost, 1992; Frost & Woods, 1998). Since the late 1970s, wooden superstructures with a variety of apparatuses have replaced some of this steel equipment. Traditional playgrounds favor physically able children who can take advantage of the play opportunities available. On the other hand, these playgrounds may constrain less physically able children who are reluctant to participate in these types of gross motor activities.

**Adventure or "junk" playgrounds,** originating in Denmark in the middle of the twentieth century and uniquely European, are designed to provide supervised, creative play opportunities for urban children. They contain unconnected tools and materials that enable children to build, create, and pretend with their own play structures using materials in a free and open atmosphere. Varying in size, they offer children a variety of options (e.g., building, gardening, using sand or water, cooking). Each adventure playground contains a large hut filled with a variety of typical indoor materials such as art, dramatic play materials, and music that children choose to use. Adults function as play leaders, support children's ideas, and act as facilitators. Adventure playgrounds support children's freedom to learn through discovery in an enriched environment. These types of playgrounds never were very popular in this country because of our concerns with safety and the unavailability of trained play leaders.

**Creative/contemporary playgrounds,** adapted in the twentieth century from the adventure playground concept, are a way to integrate elements of adventure playgrounds into contemporary settings. They are designed to provide children with a more stimulating environment for play than that of a traditional playground. Creative playgrounds contain a superstructure with movable parts (e.g., boards, ramps, wheels), are action-oriented, provide safe underneath surfaces, offer a variety of stimulating materials and equipment, and promote all forms of play (e.g., functional, constructive, dramatic, and games). In addition, they offer children numerous possibilities for social interaction (Barbour, 1999). Creative playgrounds are "developmentally pleasing and aesthetically rich" (Frost & Woods, 1998, p. 234).

Playgrounds that provide many play possibilities for children are important learning environments. These environments stress integrated rather than isolated equipment and extend learning from the indoor to the outdoor environment. Their design has certain features that enhance all forms of children's play.

## Developmentally Appropriate Outdoor Play Environments

Outdoor play provides many benefits for children of all ages and should be planned to be utilized year round (Frost, 1992, 2000; Frost, Shinn, & Jacobs, 1998; Rivkin, 1995). Planning a developmentally appropriate, high-quality outdoor play environment should focus on three primary characteristics: equipment and materials, safety and supervision, and storage.

### Equipment and Materials

Equipment and materials in high-quality outdoor play environments hold children's interest over time and enable them to engage in all four forms of play (Frost, 1992, 2000; National Association for the Education of Young Children [NAEYC], 1996; Wardle, 1997). Equipment should be sturdy, safe, and age-appropriate. Children who play on equipment that is not appropriate for their size, strength, and decision-making capabilities are exposed to the possibility of serious injury. High-quality equipment and materials feature loose parts; a combination of simple, complex, and supercomplex materials; a wide variety of experiences and activities; and well-defined spaces.

*Loose parts* are movable pieces that children can manipulate and use to improvise. Lightweight objects of different sizes, shapes, and textures; movable boards or ramps; and organic materials such as sand and water can be moved from place to place within the play area as children choose. They also add complexity to the environment. Moveable parts provide for flexibility, diversity, novelty, and challenge, which are all-important ingredients for creativity, socialization, and learning.

*Complexity* refers to the number of possibilities the material offers children. The more possibilities the material has, the more likely it is to hold children's interest and attention because children can do more with it (Kritchevsky et al., 1977). If too much of the play equipment is designed to be used by one child at a time or to be used in just one way, it severely limits the play area's complexity. For example, a large tire swing that can hold two or more children offers more options for play than a swing on a swing set.

*Diversity or variety* refers to the number of ways materials can be used, regardless of their complexity. It influences how children get started in their play (NAEYC, 1996). A wide slide, for example, has more possibilities than a narrow slide. A variety of materials offer children necessary choices to create their own forms of play.

*Well-defined spaces* are those in which both the amount and the arrangement of space facilitate children's play patterns. Accreditation criteria of the National Association for the Education of Young Children and the National Academy of Early Childhood Programs require a minimum of 75 square feet of play space

*The sand area should contain an assortment of digging and molding materials that invite children's experimentation and exploration.*

outdoors per child (1996). Both open and partitioned space needs to be available in the outdoor environment.

Figure 6.8 is a checklist of criteria to use in planning and managing developmentally appropriate outdoor play environments. Figure 6.9 is a list of props and "play crates" (Odoy & Foster, 1997) for the outdoor classroom. When the outdoor space is designed using these criteria, children retain ownership over their play, communicate and express thoughts and feelings, and develop feelings of satisfaction and competence. Well-planned outdoor environments meet all of their needs—physical, social, emotional, and intellectual.

Place an X under the appropriate response to see if your playground is safe for children.

**Adequate Space**            Yes   No

Does the environment

| | Yes | No |
|---|---|---|
| Stimulate all four types of play—exercise, constructive, dramatic, and games with rules—through appropriately arranged space and traffic patterns? | ☐ | ☐ |
| Provide appropriate spaces for individuals and small groups of children according to their ages, physical sizes, interests and abilities? | ☐ | ☐ |
| Develop play areas (zones), so that activities such as tricycle riding and climbing do not occur in close proximity to one another? | ☐ | ☐ |
| Ensure that movement from one zone to another will be safe and manageable? | ☐ | ☐ |
| Offer a visually pleasing area in which the natural elements and fabricated structures complement each other? | ☐ | ☐ |
| Provide overall cohesiveness rather than discrete, unconnected objects or structures? | ☐ | ☐ |
| Foster a sense of flow from one activity to another? | ☐ | ☐ |
| Provide varied ground surfaces such as hardtop for games and vehicles, grass, water, or soft mulch or sand, hilly or mounded areas, flat areas, construction areas, sunlight, and shade? | ☐ | ☐ |
| Offer easy access to coats, toilets, and drinking fountains? | ☐ | ☐ |
| Provide protected storage for equipment? | ☐ | ☐ |
| Contain space for walking, running, and skipping? | ☐ | ☐ |
| Include a shaded area with tables and benches to be used for art activities, table games, or snacks? | ☐ | ☐ |

**Materials**            Yes   No

Does the environment

| | Yes | No |
|---|---|---|
| Offer ample opportunities for a child's physical, cognitive, and social development through a dynamic, challenging, age-appropriate environment with complex materials? | ☐ | ☐ |
| Promote independent and creative uses of flexible materials such as sand, water, dramatic play, and superstructures with room for many children? | ☐ | ☐ |
| Contain equipment for active and quiet play and for solitary, parallel, and cooperative play? | ☐ | ☐ |
| Contain materials for dramatic play (e.g. car, boat, house)? | ☐ | ☐ |
| Contain materials for constructive play and experimentation (e.g., boards, ramps, tires, tools, nails?) | ☐ | ☐ |
| Provide materials for gross motor development (e.g., climbers, wide slides)? | ☐ | ☐ |
| Provide a sand area located away from people, with proper covering to protect it from inclement weather and animals? | ☐ | ☐ |
| Include a water area located near an outdoor water supply with a variety of materials for experimentation, problem solving, and exploration? | ☐ | ☐ |
| Contain a variety of balls? | ☐ | ☐ |
| Contain nonlocomotor materials for stretching, carrying, and swinging? | ☐ | ☐ |
| Contain manipulative materials for throwing, kicking and catching? | ☐ | ☐ |

*(continued)*

**Figure 6.8**   Checklist for Planning and Managing the Outdoor Environment
*Sources:* Adapted from Frost (1992), Frost, Shinn, & Jacobs (1998), NAEYC (1996), NPPS (1999).

| Activities and Experiences | Yes | No |
| --- | --- | --- |
| Does the environment | | |
| Provide for children's interactions with materials, peers, and adults through proper storage, defined spaces, and interest areas? | ☐ | ☐ |
| Offer a range of activities, experiences, and equipment with "loose parts" that children can adapt to their own play schemes? | ☐ | ☐ |
| Provide large equipment for gross motor development; loose parts and natural materials for constructive play; enclosed structures for dramatic play; linked platforms for social play; semiprivate spaces for hiding; and nature areas for gardening? | ☐ | ☐ |
| **Safety** | | |
| Are adults actively supervising the play area? | ☐ | ☐ |
| Is the equipment in good repair, in working order, and free of sharp edges? | ☐ | ☐ |
| Are there fences at least 5 feet high with lockable gates that work well? | ☐ | ☐ |
| Are there 8–10 inches of sand, mulch, or pea gravel under climbing and moving equipment? | ☐ | ☐ |
| Is there some type of edging (e.g., railroad ties) to contain the cushioning materials? | ☐ | ☐ |
| Is the area free of litter (e.g., broken glass)? | ☐ | ☐ |

**Figure 6.8**    *(Continued)*

### Safety

A safe outdoor environment is an important part of the early childhood environment. Yet national survey data reveal that today's preschool and public school playgrounds are unsafe, causing a dramatic increase in childhood playground injuries over the past two decades (Frost, & Woods, 1998; NAEYC, 1996; National Program for Playground Safety [NPPS], 1999; Rivkin, 1995; Thomason & Thrash, 1999; Thompson, Hudson, & Mack, 1998). Unsafe playgrounds:

- Are poorly designed, antiquated, and inadequately maintained.
- Lack storage facilities.
- Neglect features children prefer, such as dramatic play materials and nature areas.
- Focus entirely on motor activity.
- Are developmentally inappropriate.
- Are used without safety orientation for staff or children.

### Supervision

It has been estimated that about 40 percent of playground injuries are related to inadequate supervision. Thus, we suggest the following *guidelines for better safety and supervision* in outdoor settings:

1. Have the same ratio of adults in the outdoor environment as you do in the indoor environment. At no time should there be less than two adults

**Figure 6.9**
Props and Play
Crates for the
Outdoor
Environment

**Play crates** help you organize your materials on the playground and extend children's interests from the classroom to the outdoors. Store your materials in durable wood or plastic storage containers that are easily transportable from indoors to outdoors.

### Automobile Repair

| | | |
|---|---|---|
| Auto parts | Empty oil cans | Sparkplugs |
| Mat | Filters | Flashlight |
| Cable sets | Wiring | Gears |
| Windshield wipers | Pliers | Auto parts catalogue |
| Keys | Bicycle pump | Plastic spray bottles |
| Piece of hose | Wrench | Nuts and bolts |

### Fishing

| | | |
|---|---|---|
| Plastic boat | Stringer | Cane poles |
| Fishnet | Rod and reel | Play fish |
| Plastic worms | Rubber snakes | Spinner baits (no hooks) |
| Rubber lizards | Tackle box | Cricket box |
| Ice chest | Minnow bucket | Paddles |
| Small stool (optional) | | |

### Gardening

| | |
|---|---|
| Water cans | Seed packets |
| Small garden hoses | Gardening catalogue |
| Small rakes | Flowerpots |
| Garden tools | Labels for plantings |
| Child-sized garden gloves | Stakes |

### Beach

| | | |
|---|---|---|
| Sunglasses | Ice chest | Whistle |
| Seashells | Beach towel | Diving mask |
| Suntan lotion bottles | Snorkel | Paperback books |
| Life preserver | Air mattress | Swimming tube |
| Pail and shovel | Sun visor | |

### Camping

| | | |
|---|---|---|
| Knapsack | Sleeping bag | Canteen |
| Flashlight | Plastic dishes | Tent |
| Sticks for fire | Mosquito repellent | |

*Source:* Adapted from Odoy & Foster (1997).

*Safety is an important issue in the design and construction of outdoor playground equipment.*

supervising outdoor settings, and they should have a knowledge of injury prevention and first aid.

2. Circulate around the area rather than standing in a group and talking.
3. Set clear, reasonable limits about what children may do, such as sitting down on the slide.
4. Decide on supervision of areas in advance. Give special attention to swings or climbers where there is a lot of activity and potential for injury.
5. Place 8–10 inches of fall-absorbing material, such as pea gravel, bark mulch, or shredded tires, under and around all moving equipment (e.g., swings and rotating devices) because falls from high places are the number one cause of playground injuries to children (U.S. Consumer Product Safety Commission, 1991). Be certain to include a retaining border to hold the material and replenish it frequently.

Figure 6.10 is an acronym to help you remember the essential elements of playground safety.

### Storage

Storage facilities are essential on playgrounds for young children. They house the materials that children use to develop and extend their play. The location of the storage is critical. Storage that is accessible to the immediate play area saves time in transporting toys and encourages responsibility in children themselves. Think about storage that is:

**Figure 6.10**
SAFE Playgrounds

> **S**upervise carefully. Make sure that adults who monitor the playground have knowledge of injury prevention and first aid.
>
> **A**ge-appropriate equipment and materials. Ensure that the height, size, and complexity of the equipment is safe for the age and skill level of the children using it, such as having climbing equipment that is not taller than the children using it.
>
> **F**alls. Have landing surfaces that are resilient, such as wood chips and rubber mats, which cushion falls.
>
> **E**quipment. Periodically inspect the playground for open hooks, sharp edges, or missing parts. Also check for well-anchored equipment.

*Sources:* Adapted from NAEYC (1996) and NPPS (1999).

- Child-scaled to facilitate taking out and putting away equipment.
- Weathertight and vandalproof to protect the equipment.
- Multipurpose, contains space for teacher storage, and allows children to play on the structure.

These characteristics of high-quality outdoor environments apply to children of all ages. However, some adaptations need to be made according to children's needs, interests, and abilities.

## Outdoor Environments for Children of Different Ages and with Diverse Needs

Like indoor environments, outdoor environments must be adjusted to children's developmental levels and diverse needs and abilities. Outdoor play environments should be seen as supporting a range of learning and developmental goals, including a sense of competence and cooperation through vigorous physical activity.

### Infants and Toddlers

Playgrounds for infants and toddlers should be arranged to meet their rapidly increasing motor and social development, as well as their clear need for autonomy. While most of the safety guidelines listed in Figure 6.6 and the previous section, Safety and Supervision, are true for all children, infant and toddler playgrounds have unique safety issues (Frost, 1992; Frost & Woods, 1998). For this age group, special attention needs to be given to:

- *Ground cover* that cannot be ingested, such as pea gravel and small wood chips.
- *Hazardous material* that may have accumulated overnight, such as broken objects, sharp edges, or foreign objects. Teachers of infants and toddlers need to check the playground daily for such obstructions.
- *Swing seats* that must include strap-in seats to prevent falling and that are free from protruding elements such as bolts or acorn nuts.

- *Safety barriers* such as four-feet-high fences with self-latching gates that protect infants and toddlers from traffic, fall hazards, and pools of water.
- Providing *shade* for sun- and heat-sensitive infants.
- *Monitoring **all** water play.* Infants and toddlers can drown in even very small amounts of water (Frost, 1992).

Infants and toddlers also need opportunities for a wide range of sensory experimentation and exploration with a few simple, safe, age-appropriate choices. Adding sensory materials of different textures, such as sticks, bugs, or tree bark, on clear pathways to walk on, touch, and explore, enhances their play. They need equipment that is stimulating and close to the ground; dramatic play options; loose parts for stacking, gathering, and dumping; and natural experiences with living plants and animals (Frost, 1992; Rivkin, 1995).

Some interesting additions for toddler outdoor play include:

- Hanging large, inflatable balls or characters from a tree and having children try to "catch one" with a cardboard tube.
- Painting the pathways, equipment, or fence with small buckets of water and large brushes.
- Washing dishes and furniture with pans of warm, soapy water, sponges, and scrub brushes (Miller, 1989).

## Preschoolers and Kindergartners

Playgrounds for preschoolers and kindergartners should promote all four forms of play—functional, constructive, dramatic, and games with rules. Preschool structures must develop a wide range of skills and abilities while emphasizing dramatic play. They should contain a convenient and accessible storage facility for portable materials, a grassy area for group games, a place for privacy to accommodate children's need for solitary and parallel play, and a variety of child-sized equipment for motor development (Bredekamp & Copple, 1997; Wortham & Frost, 1990). The best outdoor environments for preschool and kindergarten children include a complex superstructure with a combination of loose parts (e.g., raw materials such as sand, water, lumber, tires, and discarded telephone cable spools).

Try some of these activities to add novelty and complexity to the outdoor environment:

- Turn wheeled vehicles into a fire engine, ambulance, or tractor by adding appropriate props nearby and stimulating dramatic play.
- Use a large, empty carton and other appropriate props to create a service station area for wheeled vehicles, a bank drive-through, or a roadside produce stand.
- Have a car wash for the wheeled vehicles. Use large buckets of warm, soapy water and add other appropriate props to stimulate imaginative play outdoors.
- Mix bubbles from 1/4 cup dishwashing detergent and 1 gallon of water. Use an assortment of recycled materials, such as berry baskets and straws, for bubble wands.

- Encourage children to paint along the fence. Clip clothespins and easel paper along the fence and use cardboard six-packs to hold paint containers in recyclable plastic containers. Leave the paintings up for an art show.
- Read *A Rose for Pinkerton* by Steven Kellogg (1981) and *Pet Show* by Ezra Jack Keats (1972) and then have a pet show with children's stuffed animals. Make judges' clipboards out of cardboard and clothespins, stands for the animals out of recycled ice-cream tubs, and prize ribbons out of used gift-wrap.
- Create nature collages. Use shoebox lids and white glue to make collages of natural materials located on or near the playground, park, or nearby woods (Miller, 1989).

### School-Age Children

Environments for school-age children should encourage natural investigation and challenge imagination. School-age children prefer structures that feature numerous physical challenges such as climbers, equipment for social development, and safe places for group games. Following are some suggestions that challenge school-age children in outdoor areas.

- Plan and conduct a scavenger hunt. Use a variety of clues that incorporate riddles, listening, or writing. Tie the scavenger hunt into the unit of study where possible.
- Provide plenty of chalk so that children can make outdoor games such as hopscotch or four square or create shadow drawings.
- Do some tie-dyeing. Tie old T-shirts with rubber bands and dip them into fabric dyes. Hang the shirts to dry along the fence. Repeat the process with another color for more complex and symmetrical designs (Miller, 1989).
- Do a shadow play in the afternoon. Invite children to enact various roles and use cardboard silhouettes for props. The audience watches the show on the ground rather than the players themselves.

The outdoor environment can be arranged to foster children's creative growth and development through a variety of planned uses of space, activities, experiences, and materials. Teachers and caregivers who believe in the power of both the indoor and outdoor environments for learning must assume roles that guide children's creative growth.

## TEACHERS' ROLES AND RESPONSIBILITIES

What we as teachers believe about creativity and play influences a vision of a creative environment. We, as teachers, would be wise to keep in mind the words of Danette Littleton (1989) as we plan, arrange, and manage creative learning environments:

> It is our own playfulness that links the child within each of us to the child we teach: the feeling child, the thinking and reasoning child, the creative child,

the compassionate child. All of these are a whole fabric woven of the unending thread of play. (p. xiii)

The following suggestions can foster a dynamic, creative learning environment. The message emanating from the environment comes from how teachers meet the challenge of creating teaching/learning places that enable children and teachers to function comfortably, productively, and effectively together by meeting their developmental needs.

1. *View yourself as a creative teacher.* Ask yourself, how creative am I? What efforts do I make to support children's creativity and build a creative learning environment? Do I have original ideas? How do I solve problems and make decisions? Do I accept children who respond in unusual ways? Could I identify the most creative children in my class? Creative teachers exhibit spontaneity, sensitivity, open-mindedness, and a high tolerance for ambiguity. They support child-initiated learning, encourage children to "live the question," reward imaginative ideas, and believe in children's self-evaluation (Edwards, 1997; Jalongo & Isenberg, 2000).

2. *Maintain an orderly environment.* An orderly environment gives children control over activity choices, helps them carry out their ideas, and builds responsibility for the care and storage of materials. Materials for children of all ages should be neatly arranged and pleasantly displayed. When children have access to materials, they also must assume responsibility for returning them to their place when finished. This means that the materials must be organized so that children understand where they belong. Most teachers separate materials by type in simple, labeled containers so that children can take responsibility for keeping materials organized.

3. *Consider the environment a powerful learning tool.* When teachers are knowledgeable about space and materials, they can often anticipate how children will use them. Predicting behavior in this way promotes children's independence, active involvement, and sustained attention (McLean, 1995).

The environment can also be used to *manage tasks.* Carefully arranged and displayed materials invite children's participation in appropriate ways with a minimum of adult intervention. One preschool teacher uses children's photographs for taking attendance and rebus recipes for preparing snacks. Such tools reduce the amount of time teachers devote to routine administrative tasks, freeing them to focus on children's creativity and learning.

4. *Plan for diversity.* Just as individuals differ in developmental level, differences in abilities or interests also influence how subject matter affects thinking. It is important to have a variety of materials and subject areas to stimulate children's imagination and diverse use of materials. Be innovative in your use of the physical environment, but keep your purpose in mind. Sometimes you might want to use an area to stimulate aesthetic appreciation; other times you might change the area to provide use of complex materials. Planning for diversity means providing a variety of center materials that respond to children's cultural backgrounds, interests, and ability levels; a balance of teacher-directed/child-initiated activities; and flexible grouping.

## ✿ PRACTICAL APPLICATIONS FOR YOUR CLASSROOM

Most early childhood classrooms have children with diverse needs, abilities, and backgrounds. Teachers' awareness of these factors is particularly important during the early years because many of children's special needs have not yet been identified. Adapting the creative environment so that all children can play means that we as classroom teachers must create appropriate surroundings that enable all children to play.

## *Experiences to Support Cultural and Ethnic Diversity*

Every early childhood setting needs to consider how the environment affects learning for students from diverse cultural backgrounds. In their book *Multicultural Literacy: Mirroring the Reality of the Classroom* (1995), Barbara Diamond and Margaret Moore describe how to design a culturally sensitive learning environment, an important way of knowing and coming to know. The following suggestions will help early childhood teachers create culturally compatible learning environments that recognize the influence of children's culture on children's learning.

**1.** *Create culturally sensitive centers that reflect learners' cultural and personal interests and experiences.* Keep in mind that the physical aspects of a culturally sensitive environment portray the visible aspects of the children's culture; the climate portrays the invisible aspects of culture (Diamond & Moore, 1995). For younger children, the media or literacy center might include recordings of favorite informational and narrative literature from different countries and cultures, such as *The Black Snowman* (Mendez, 1989), *Abuela* (Dorros, 1991), or *Chicken Sunday* (Polacco, 1990). As students read along with their recorded books and reread stories that reflect their cultural and language backgrounds, they are simultaneously gaining fluency and comprehension of text with personally meaningful material. Likewise, the writing center is a place where writing "comes alive" for children who have opportunities to express themselves with meaningful experiences. Other centers, such as the drama center, provide props such as puppets, dress-up clothing, and felt shapes that prompt children to explore language and self-expression in nonthreatening settings. (See Chapter Five for more detailed suggestions.)

A culturally sensitive environment for older children uses centers that are often more directly related to units of study. In these centers, one might find informational or biographical books, folktales, poems, or magazines to invite students to explore topics further. These centers are also good places to display cultural artifacts, games, foods, maps, books, and clothing from a specific culture. Moreover, they enable children to investigate science/math-related ideas; explore pictures, graphs, and other visual props of famous people; and become aware of the unique features of the environments of different countries such as the people, animals, weather, workers, and modes of transportation. Each of these centers containing cultural materials has the potential for becoming the basis of literacy and other powerful learning opportunities.

**2.** *Integrate play throughout the curriculum.* In play, children have the opportunity to share power with their peers and other adults, which is integral to culturally responsive teaching (Stremmel, 1997). Some teachers develop classification activities and educational games using family pictures, children's artwork, or objects from home to infuse cultural content into the curriculum through play. When children bring artifacts and toys from their home culture into their classrooms, they portray information about themselves and their culture in a meaningful way (Johnson, Christie, & Yawkey, 1999).

**3.** *Infuse children's literature and all of the creative arts to encourage an appreciation of cultural diversity.* Through books and recordings, children can experience and become enriched by a wide variety of cultures. (See Chapters Three and Five for suggested materials.)

## Experiences to Support Inclusion

A creative learning environment must address the needs of children with various disabilities. Some simple adjustments in equipment, materials, and room arrangement are necessary for children with disabilities in both the indoor and outdoor environments. The first step in adapting indoor and outdoor environments to these children's needs is to fully understand the nature and extent of each child's limitations. The next step is to adapt the environment so that each child can participate in some meaningful way—ideally, in a way that emphasizes abilities rather than disabilities.

*Children with hearing difficulties* often feel frustrated and socially isolated from other learners. As a result, they engage in less pretend play with others and are less likely to use objects symbolically (Hallahan & Kauffman, 2000; Hughes, 1999). Early childhood teachers can adapt the environment for children with hearing difficulties by:

- Seating them away from noisy backgrounds such as windows, doors, and heating and cooling systems.
- Allowing them to move freely about so that they can position themselves to hear better and see the faces of their peers.
- Reducing classroom noise with carpeting and corkboard walls.
- Minimizing classroom activities in large echoing rooms.

*Children with visual impairments* always require a physical orientation to the classroom including the location of materials, centers, and exits. Just because they are visually challenged does not necessarily mean they are unable to play. Environments for these children include:

- An orientation to the classroom from a single focal point such as their table or desk.
- An orientation to the school after they are familiar with the classroom.

- Noting which play materials, equipment, activities, and playmates are available during playtime.
- Provision of a sensory-rich play environment with a variety of sensory cues (e.g., tactile maps and tape-recorded directions could be placed in key areas of the room, which could be identified through the use of tactile material).
- Information about any changes in the physical arrangement and the use of play materials so children can become familiar with them by touch.
- A designated, sighted guide for special activities such as fire drills.
- Lighting that does not cast shadows or glare on their work and allows them to move so they can comfortably see each activity.
- Traffic patterns and pathways that are clear and free.
- Simple room arrangements.
- Encouragement of their play.

*Children with limited motor abilities* may have problems with either large or small muscles and have a slower reaction time than other children. The adaptations for them vary according to the severity and type of disability. Environments for these children should include:

- Taking apart movable playground equipment and laying it flat on the ground. Children who otherwise cannot use parts of play structures can practice walking across them when they are on the ground.
- Modifications for writing such as computers, felt-tip rather than soft lead pencils, and pads rather than sheets of paper.
- Playground designs that use smooth pathways and ramps to help them gain access to play areas.
- Wheelchair-height tables and trays so that children can use water tables and manipulatives.
- Outdoor environments that have wide gates and pathways (44 inches) and ramps to provide access to all parts of the playground for children in wheelchairs or those with impaired walking ability.

## Adaptations for Individual Learners

All children need environments that foster self-directed learning and opportunities for play in which they can plan for their own learning, identify resources and materials, and interact with one another. Following are some ways to meet the needs of individual learners.

- Prepare a *quiet space* for children who are easily distracted.
- Allow sufficient *time* for all children to plan and complete their play and creative activities.
- Plan *interest or learning centers* to promote self-directed learning and independence. These centers should provide a variety of manipulative, media, and print materials for exploration, experimentation, and long-term research (Hallahan & Kauffman, 2000). One teacher, for example, developed

an interest center about bicycling with materials for children to create bicycle paths and gain permission to build and install bicycle racks in public places.

- Use *contracts* to guide independent study and promote autonomy. Contracts allow children to make choices about what work to do, when to work, with whom to work, and where to work. After studying about the habits of different animals, some second graders contracted to extend their knowledge through art by making drawings or models of their favorite animal; others wrote original stories; still others created original play scenarios, such as "Meet My Pet Boa Constrictor." Contracts help children take responsibility for their own learning and free teachers to facilitate that learning.

Children who learn more slowly can also participate in self-directed learning activities that challenge them at their own level. Contracts help these children feel successful and offer them opportunities to choose what work to do, when to work, with whom to work, or where to work. Using this model provides more flexible grouping for all children.

## CHAPTER SUMMARY

1. Planning, arranging, and managing the creative environment is as important as planning for instruction.

2. There are three basic features of creative environments: climate, space, and time. Climate is the feeling emanating from the environment; space includes the degree to which the physical environment contributes to active, creative thinking; and time encompasses the influences of the classroom schedule on children's expression, attention span, and self-directedness.

3. Room arrangement refers to the way space is organized for children's learning and movement. When arranging the classroom environment, consider what it communicates to children; how easily the space can be supervised; how accessible the materials are; how you feel about unpredictable behaviors, and why you feel that way. Teachers also need to distinguish between the child's and adult's environment and be alert to traffic patterns.

4. There are a variety of types and uses of centers. Centers organize space and promote active learning, planning and decision making, problem solving, originality, and interaction. All early childhood classrooms should have the following centers: art, blocks, discovery/science, dramatic play, library/literacy, manipulative/math, media/music, and writing.

5. Transitions are those times during the day when children move from one activity to another. Routines are activities that occur regularly and form the basis of the daily schedule. Planned transitions and routines are essential for children of all ages to ensure predictability and a sense of security in the schedule.

6. What teachers believe about creativity and play influences how they prepare the environment as well as their vision of a creative environment. Teachers need to be creative themselves, maintain an orderly environment, use a planning or choice board, and consider the environment as the third teacher.

7. Outdoor environments need the same systematic attention to space, materials, equipment, and safety as indoor environments. They need simple, complex, and supercomplex units to hold children's interest over time and challenge their imagination.

8. There are three types of playgrounds—traditional, adventure, and creative. Action-oriented playgrounds containing a superstructure with movable apparatuses, loose parts, and safe underneath surfaces promote all four forms of play.

9. Adapting the environment for special populations of children means adjusting the basic characteristics of climate, space, and time to the particular needs of each child.

# *EXPANDING YOUR THINKING ABOUT CREATIVE LEARNING ENVIRONMENTS*

## *Discuss: Perspectives on Creative Environments*

1. Think about your most pleasurable play environment as a child. How does this relate to what you know about the importance of environments to support creative growth?

2. Visualize your ideal classroom, both indoors and outdoors. In what ways do you think your beliefs about creativity influence your mind's-eye view of the indoor and outdoor environment?

3. Refer back to the case study at the beginning of the chapter. What were Ms. Ring's reactions to the state of her classroom when she returned from leave? Were her reactions justified? On what basis? How will she go about re-creating a creative environment? If Ms. Ring's substitute asked you how she could improve her classroom, what would you suggest? Why?

4. Some teachers admit that they never think much about children's play on the playground. What do you think of this practice? Why?

5. In planning and managing your creative environment, think about how you would respond to a parent or a colleague who said, "But they are just playing! When are they going to learn something?" What would you say? Why?

## *Interview: How Teachers Plan Their Classroom Environments*

Arrange to interview a teacher of an infant/toddler, preschool/kindergarten, or primary classroom about the way he or she plans, arranges, and manages the environment. Ask the following questions and record the teacher's responses. You may wish to tape-record the responses and transcribe them immediately after the interview. Bring your responses to class to compare/contrast findings by teacher and by age group.

1.  How was the environment arranged in your setting when you first began teaching? Did you make any changes in the indoor or outdoor environment? Please describe and explain why those changes were necessary or desirable.

2.  What do you think about when you arrange the environment?

3.  Could you please share your views about centers as a part of the learning environment? How do you manage learning in a center-based environment?

4.  What features of the indoor environment are most interesting and challenging for your children? What do you suppose is the reason? Do you think room arrangement has any influence on these interests? In what ways?

5.  Could you describe how you handle transitions and routines with your class? Which is most effective for you?

## Write to Learn: Planning a New Setting

Select an age group—infants/toddlers, preschool/kindergarten, or primary. You have just been hired to teach in a brand new setting. Your principal/director has given you two weeks to purchase equipment and materials for your teaching-learning environment. Using the criteria for creative environments discussed throughout the chapter, create a working schedule and develop a floor plan for the room arrangement. Justify your selections. Present and discuss these ideas in a small group. What revisions, if any, would you make now that you have heard others' ideas?

# REFERENCES

Barbour, A. C. (1999). The impact of playground design on the play behaviors of children with differing levels of physical competence. *Early Childhood Research Quarterly, 14*(1), 75–98.

Berk, L. (1976). How well do classroom practices reflect teacher goals? *Young Children, 32,* 64–81.

Bredekamp, S., & Copple, C. (Eds.). (1997). *Developmentally appropriate practice in early childhood programs* (Rev. ed.). Washington, DC: National Association for the Education of Young Children.

Caples, S. E. (1996). Some guidelines for preschool design. *Young Children, 51*(4), 14–21.

Casey, M. B., & Lippman, M. (1991). Learning to plan through play. *Young Children, 46*(4), 52–58.

Christie, J. F., & Wardle, F. (1992). How much time is needed for play? *Young Children, 47*(3), 28–32.

Crosser, S. (1992). Managing the early childhood classroom. *Young Children, 47*(2), 23–29.

Diamond, B. J., & Moore, M. A. (1995). *Multicultural literacy: Mirroring the reality of the classroom.* White Plains, NY: Longman.

Edwards, L. C. (1997). *The creative arts: A process approach for teachers and children* (2nd ed.). Upper Saddle River, NJ: Merrill/Prentice Hall.

Edwards, C., Gandini, L., & Forman, G. (Eds.). (1993). *The hundred languages of children: The Reggio Emilia approach to early childhood education.* Norwood, NJ: Ablex.

Ferguson, C. J. (1999). Building literacy with child-constructed sociodramatic play centers. *Dimensions of Early Childhood, 27*(6), 23–29.

Frost, J. L. (1992). *Play and playscapes.* Albany, NY: Delmar.

Frost, J. L. (2000). Common issues and concerns about outdoor play environments. In M. Jalongo & J. Isenberg, *Exploring your role: A practitioner's introduction in early childhood education* (p. 177). Upper Saddle River, NJ: Merrill/Prentice Hall.

Frost, J. L., Shinn, D., & Jacobs, P. (1998). Play environments and children's play. In O. Saracho & B. Spodek (Eds.), *Multiple perspectives on play in early childhood education* (pp. 255–294). Albany, NY: State University of New York Press.

Frost, J. L., & Woods, I. C. (1998). Perspectives on play in playgrounds. In D. P. Fromberg & D. M. Bergen (Eds.), *Play from birth to twelve and beyond: Context, perspectives, and meanings* (pp. 232–240). New York: Garland.

Garreau, M., & Kennedy, C. (1991). Structure time and space to promote pursuit of learning in the primary grades. *Young Children, 64*(4), 46–51.

Gestwicki, C. (1999). *Developmentally appropriate practice: Curriculum and development in early childhood* (2nd ed.). Albany, NY: Delmar.

Hallahan, D. P., & Kauffman, J. M. (2000). *Exceptional learners: Introduction to special enducation.* (8th ed.). Needham Heights, MA: Allyn & Bacon.

Hebert, E. A. (1998, September). Design matters. *Educational Leadership,* pp. 68–69.

Hirsch, E. (1996). *The block book* (3rd ed.). Washington, DC: National Association for the Education of Young Children.

Hohman, C. (1985). Getting started with computers. *High Scope Resource, 4*(3), 11–13.

Hughes, F. P. (1999). *Children, play and development* (3rd ed.). Boston: Allyn & Bacon.

Isbell, R. (1995). *The complete learning center book.* Beltsville, MD: Gryphon House.

Isenberg, J. (1995). Whole language in play and the expressive arts. In S. C. Raines (Ed.), *Whole language across the curriculum: Grades 1, 2, 3* (pp. 114–136). New York: Teachers College Press.

Jalongo, M. R. (1992). Children's play: A resource for multicultural education. In E. B. Vold (Ed.), *Multicultural education in the early childhood classroom* (pp. 55–63). Washington, DC: National Education Association.

Jalongo, M. R., & Isenberg, J. P. (2000). *Exploring your role: A practitioner's introduction to early childhood education.* Upper Saddle River, NJ: Merrill/Prentice Hall.

Johnson, J., Christie, J., & Yawkey, T. (1999). *Play and early childhood development* (2nd ed.). New York: Longman.

Jones, E. (1977). *Dimensions of teaching-learning environments.* Pasadena, CA: Pacific Oaks.

Kinsman, C., & Berk, L. (1979). Joining the block and housekeeping areas: Changes in play and social behavior. *Young Children, 35,* 66–75.

Kohn, A. (1993). Choices for children: Why and how to let students decide. *Phi Delta Kappan, 15*(1), 8–19.

Kritchevsky, S., Prescott, E., & Walling, L. (1977). *Planning environments for young children: Physical space* (Rev. ed.). Washington, DC: National Association for the Education of Young Children.

Littleton, D. (1989). Children's play: Pathways to music learning. In B. Andress (Ed.), *Promising practices: Pre-kindergarten music education* (pp. ix– xiii). Reston, VA: Music Educator's National Conference.

Loughlin, C. E., & Martin, M. D. (1987). *Supporting literacy: Developing effective learning environments.* New York: Teachers College Press.

Loughlin, C. E., & Suina, J. (1982). *The learning environment: An instructional strategy.* New York: Teachers College Press.

McLean, S. V. (1995). Creating the learning environment: Context for living and learning. In J. Moyer (Ed.), *Selecting educational equipment and materials* (pp. 5–13). Wheaton, MD: Association for Childhood Education International.

Miller, K. (1989). *The outside play and learning book. Activities for young children.* Mt. Rainier, MD: Gryphon House.

Nash, C. (1976). *The learning environment.* Toronto: Methuen Publications.

National Association for the Education of Young Children. (1996). *Playgrounds: Keeping outdoor learning safe.* Release #5. Washington, DC: Author.

National Program for Playground Safety. (1999). *The National PTA Magazine, 25*(2), 17.

Odoy, H., & Foster, S. (1997). Creating play crates for the outdoor classroom. *Young Children, 52*(6), 12–16.

Petrakos, H., & Howe, N. (1996). The influence of the physical design of the dramatic play center on children's play. *Early Childhood Research Quarterly, 11*(1), 63–67.

Prescott, E. (1984). The physical setting in day care. In J. Greenman & R. Fuqua (Eds.), *Making day care better: Training, evaluation, and the process of change* (pp. 44–65). New York: Teachers College Press.

Readdick, C. A. (1993). Solitary pursuits: Supporting children's privacy needs in group settings. *Young Children, 33*(2), 16–23.

Rettig, M. (1998). Environmental influences on the play of young children with disabilities. *Education and Training in Mental Retardation and Developmental Disabilities, 33*(2), 189–194.

Rivkin, M. S. (1995). *The great outdoors: Restoring children's right to play outside.* Washington, DC: National Association for the Education of Young Children.

Rybczynski, M., & Troy, A. (1995, Fall). Literacy-enriched play centers: Trying them out in "the real world." *Childhood Education, 71*(4), 7–12.

Sanoff, H. (1995). *Creating environments for young children.* Mansfield, OH: BookMasters.

Schickedanz, J., York, M., Stewart, I., & White, D. (1990). *Strategies for teaching young children* (3rd ed.). Englewood Cliffs, NJ: Prentice Hall.

Sloane, M. (1998). Learning resource centers. *Childhood Education, 75*(2), 76–82.

Smith, P. K., & Connolly, K. J. (1980). *The ecology of preschool behavior.* Cambridge, England: Cambridge University Press.

Stremmel, A. (1997).Diversity and the multicultural perspective. In G. Hart, D. Burts, & R. Charlesworth (Eds.), *Integrated curriculum and developmentally appropriate practices: Birth to age eight.* Albany, NY: SUNY Press.

Tegano, D. W., Moran, J. D., III, DeLong, A. J., Brickey, J., & Ramassini, K. K. (1996). Designing classroom spaces: Making the most of time. *Early Childhood Education Journal, 30*(3), 135–141.

Thomason, C., & Thrash, D. (1999, Winter). A pre-installation checklist that could mean an injury and liability free playground. *Children and Families,* pp. 40–46.

Thompson, D., Hudson, S., & Mack, M. (1998). Child's play: Checking school playgrounds for swings, slides, and safety. *The American School Board Journal, 185*(8), 30–32.

U.S. Consumer Product Safety Commission. (1991). *A handbook for public safety.* Washington, DC: U.S. Government Printing Office.

Vukelich, C. (1991). Where's the paper? Literacy during dramatic play. *Childhood Education, 66*(4), 205–209.

Wardle, F. (1997, March/April). Playgrounds: Questions to consider when selecting materials. *Dimensions of Early Childhood,* pp. 36–42.

Wellhousen, K. (1999). Big ideas for small spaces. *Young Children, 54*(6), 58–61.

Wortham, S. C., & Frost, J. L. (1990). Introduction. In S. C. Wortham & J. L. Frost (Eds.), *Playgrounds for young children: National survey and perspectives* (pp. 1–4). Reston, VA: American Alliance for Health, Physical Education, Recreation, and Dance.

Wright, J., & Shade, D. (1994). *Young children: Active learners in the technological age.* Washington, DC: National Association for the Education of Young Children.

## *Children's Books*

Dorros, A. (1991). *Abuela.* New York: Dutton.

Keats, E. J. (1972). *Pet show.* New York: Macmillan.

Kellogg, S. (1981). *A rose for Pinkerton.* New York: Dial.

Mendez, P. (1989). *The black snowman.* New York: Scholastic.

Polacco, P. (1990). *Chicken Sunday.* New York: Simon and Schuster.

# Chapter 7

## Play Materials
## for Creative Expression and Play

*"Play materials indirectly influence development by affecting the type of play in which children engage and the content of their play. Play materials may also directly affect development by providing opportunities for learning. At the same time, children's individual characteristics, such as age, developmental level, and play styles, have an effect on how particular materials are used in play."*

James Johnson, James Christie, and Thomas Yawkey, 1999, p. 284

*"A good question to ask before investing a lot of money is, 'How many ways could the children use this?' If there are three or four rather different possibilities, it is a good indication that the children will use their imaginations to think of many more."*

Joanne Hendrick, 1996, p. 422

# TEACHERS' REFLECTIONS ON PLAY MATERIALS

### Preservice Teachers

"Before studying about play materials, I never gave much thought to it. I just assumed that providing children with store-bought toys was sufficient for their development. After observing my first graders, I am amazed at what they can do with blocks. The children used geometric shapes for food, medicine, furniture, amusement parks, and counting. This helped me see the many possibilities in just one material."

"As I was planning my student-teaching unit, I decided to add a few board games such as 'Cootie,' 'Beetle,' and 'The Very Hungry Caterpillar,' suggested in Chapter Seven, to my limited first-grade centers. I watched them practice social skills ('How many and who can play?'), problem-solve ('Since only six can play, we'll play next time'), think strategically ('I only need two more turns before . . . '), and practice school skills ('I rolled a six on the number cube . . . 1, 2, 3 . . . '). The children's responses to these games convinced me that these were appropriate materials."

"In my excitement to provide creative materials to stimulate children's art creations, I introduced a few open-ended art materials (e.g., buttons, colored yarn, paper crinkles) into the art center, but the children dumped them from their containers and played with them on the floor! How could I have expected the children to use them in art when they had no prior experience with them? That helped me understand the importance of children's exploration and investigation because eventually they used the same materials to create elaborate and complex art pieces. I continue to learn from my students."

### Inservice Teachers

"I have to admit that I was secretly delighted that few of my kindergartners were choosing to play in the block center during choice time. The center had never been one of my favorites—it is so noisy and takes forever to clean up. So, I was happy—until the night that I viewed the video in class, 'A Classroom with Blocks.' And I knew that I would never again view blocks in the same way. I realized that the number of benefits derived from block play outweighed the beauty of a 'quick cleanup' and less noise, so I redesigned my block area and my goals for children. Now I use block play for assessment as well as instruction. I will continue using these building blocks of learning!"

"Before studying about creative play materials, I thought materials for creative activities were commercial games and art materials, such as colored paper, paint, or clay. My eyes are now opened to a multitude of materials that promote convergent and divergent thinking. By using a variety of materials, I have created 'Imagination Boxes' that the children use to construct and invent objects. I now have to figure out appropriate storage for these boxes—but I know I can do that easily."

"I learned that many of the materials thought of as toys appropriate for very young children can be used to promote divergent thinking in primary age children. In my third-grade classroom, my use of Lego blocks for a community-building experience introduced me to a whole new way of thinking about creative problem solving. I used Legos as a vehicle for my students to create a three-dimensional representation of the interests of one of their friends, which meant brainstorming possible ways to do this. I think the most meaningful moments of the project were when the students were engaged in the process of figuring out how to construct something that was so abstract. In the past, I have been guilty of making all the decisions for children; with these materials and my support, children quite capably made their own decisions—decisions that satisfied their needs."

## Your Reflections

- What do you think are age-appropriate play materials, resources, and games?

- How do you think play materials nurture children's creative expression?

- How might you go about learning about the value of different types of toys and play materials?

## Case Study

### Dramatic Play in the Block and Housekeeping Areas

In the housekeeping area, three 4-year-old children are putting on dress-up clothes, while another is moving pots and pans around on the stove. They are talking about who is going to wear what. In the block area, five boys and girls are constructing a pirate ship from hollow wooden blocks. In the absence of pirate garb, the children make do with cowboy boots, vests, and construction worker hard hats. One child, sitting in front, steers the ship while the "lookout" paces about.

A child dashes from the block area to the housekeeping area, snatches the "jewelry case," then darts back to her fellow pirates.

Suddenly, the cry goes up, "Jewels! We've found the treasure! We're rich! Jewels, jewels, jewels!" With great noise and excitement, the pirates display their necklaces, bracelets, and rings. In the days that follow, the children extend this theme by adding a treasure map to assist with their forays and decorating boxes to use as treasure chests.

In these pretend play scenes, 4-year-olds used objects symbolically to initiate and carry out their pirate play theme. Their responses to materials revealed original uses of common materials (using the jewels as a treasure), role playing (acting as a lookout), and problem solving (how to create a treasure chest). As this play episode illustrates, the careful selection of materials and resources supports children's creative expression and play (Bredekamp & Copple, 1997; Hendrick, 1996; Hughes, 1999).

## THEORETICAL AND RESEARCH BASE: THE IMPORTANCE OF SELF-EXPRESSIVE PLAY MATERIALS

Play materials are as important to a child as technology and communication are to an adult. These materials are the concrete tools with which children explore, experiment, investigate, and understand their world through all forms of play. All children have the same need for play and for carefully chosen play materials to do their work well. For early childhood teachers, then, three concepts are important to understanding play materials: (1) their historical development, (2) their convergent or divergent nature, and (3) their safety.

### *History of Toys and Playthings*

Children's toys and playthings have a long history in early childhood education. In fact, the materials we provide for children reflect social, political, and cultural issues. In colonial America, for example, boys played with simulated hunting and fishing materials, while girls played with corncob dolls. Near the turn of the century, construction toys were strictly for boys; homemaker's toys were strictly for girls (Hewitt & Roomet, 1979; Mergen, 1982).

During the Industrial Revolution in the mid-1800s, toys specifically designed for children became industrialized as well. When wheeled toys, board games, dolls, and doll furniture first appeared, they were mass-produced on the assembly line. At the turn of the century, during the child-study movement, childhood was recognized as a distinct period of development and children were no longer viewed as miniature adults. As a reflection of this movement, toy manufacturers began producing educational toys. During this time, Dr. Maria Montessori also introduced an array of sensory materials for children with mental retardation. Lacing frames, knob puzzles, and graduated cylinders were just a few of Montessori's contributions to educational toys. She is also credited with originating the concept of "self-correcting" toys, toys that can be used in a particular sequence and a specified way. These materials slowly became part of some early childhood programs.

In the 1920s, toy manufacturers invited early childhood educators to help develop educational materials that would stimulate children's imagination and self-expression. Influenced by the ideas of child development specialists and educators such as John Dewey, early childhood educators provided firsthand experiences for children with concrete, self-expressive materials such as blocks, clay, paint, and wood. Additionally, they encouraged children under the age of 6 to play with language and rhythms and to invent their own games instead of playing games with rules (Monighan-Nourot, 1990).

Today, the same child may play with an heirloom set of nesting dolls from a great-grandmother's era, a Raggedy Ann doll from her grandmother's day, a Barbie doll from her mother's era, and modern-day dolls for both boys and girls.

As we approach the new millenium, the technological revolution has brought new dimensions to objects with which children can play. Children play with media-related figures that replicate what children view on television. These highly structured toys limit the imaginative possibilities of children's creative play and often increase the level of violence found in play (Levin, 1999). They also play with electronic figures that can communicate feelings and hold high appeal to young children. The advent of "digital dolls," which are similar to traditional dolls but exist only inside of a computer, and objects that children can animate once they have created them, have the potential for changing the world of play materials for young children both at home and in the classroom. While play with digital materials is quite different from the modes of play envisioned over 150 years ago by German educator Friedrich Froebel, the founder of the kindergarten movement, play with digital media and in virtual playgrounds can still have the features of make-believe and relate to children's experiences. As a stroll through a toy store or a look at an early childhood materials catalog will attest, teachers and parents need to make literally thousands of choices among materials for young children. The following sections will outline some basic considerations in selecting materials for creative expression and play.

## *Convergent and Divergent Play Materials*

The materials children use influence their growing knowledge of the physical and social world, the possibilities of their play, and the expression of ideas. Some materials lead to single or prescribed uses and encourage convergent thinking. Wind-up toys, talking dolls, and coloring books are generally considered **convergent** materials. These materials lead children to think about a single or correct way to use them. There is little opportunity to use such materials in novel ways.

Other materials lead to multiple uses and are more open-ended. Blocks, sand, and water encourage thinking about many possibilities or uses and are considered **divergent** materials (Hughes, 1999; Johnson, Christie, & Yawkey, 1999). Divergent materials invite a variety of children's responses through exploration, experimentation, and original thinking that stimulates their problem-solving ability (Yinger & Blaszka, 1995).

Think about Amy and Tony, 4-year-olds who watched with great interest as their caregiver was preparing to give away some materials. Among them was a baby carriage with wobbly wheels, prompting Amy to ask, "Could we have the wheels from the carriage to play with?" What appealed to them were the divergent properties of the wheels—the endless possibilities for expressive play. In the weeks that ensued, the wheels became a steering wheel for a camper, a home for wooden animals, and a tray for food in the children's restaurant play.

*The materials children use influence how they express their under-standings of the world.*

Divergent or open-ended materials—blocks, carpentry tools, dress-up clothes, paints and markers, modeling dough, mud, sand, and water—are usually the most valuable (Hendrick, 1996; Johnson et al., 1999). These materials:

1. *Enable children to use their imaginations in original and satisfying ways.* After 3-year-old Melissa had eye surgery, she used a spoon from the housekeeping area to operate on the eyes of a toy dog and wrapped the dog in bandages made from paper towels. She created a new use for the spoon while practicing what she knew about surgeons and having an operation.

2. *Offer children latitude for creating, manipulating, and experimenting.* When 5-year-old Jamal painted subway stops on a class mural about different types of transportation, he investigated the properties of art—color, line, form. When Jamal added a ticket booth, an engineer, and shapes for subway seats, he created what he knew about subways as a means of transportation.

3. *Encourage children to work cooperatively.* In Ms. Anderson's second-grade unit on the community, the children used blocks to build a city; sand to sculpt the terrain; paper, pencils, rulers, and protractors to make scale models of the buildings; and earth-moving toys to create roads. They learned more from

their experience than Mr. Smith's second graders, who completed dot-to-dot papers and worksheets on community helpers.

**4.** *Have no right or wrong uses, are failure-proof, and build self-esteem.* When 5-year-old Taso carefully dressed up as a cook and proudly stood before a long mirror, he exuded a sense of self-confidence and competence. The dress-up gear enabled him to view himself in a role he could not directly experience.

**5.** *Are process-oriented rather than product-oriented.* After hearing the rhyming verse of *Jamberry* (Degen, 1983), a story about a bear who rejoices in finding all kinds of berries, a group of kindergartners repeatedly chanted, "One berry, two berry, Pick me a blueberry." Their sheer delight in the rhythm and rhyme from this captivating piece of literature produced giggles and laughter as they elaborated and created other silly *Jamberry* rhymes. Here, play with language illustrates the children's interest in process over product.

## Selection and Use of Safe Play Materials

The play materials children use can either enhance or hinder children's play and creative thinking. Early childhood teachers and parents spend billions of dollars annually on play materials and equipment. Good materials for young children enable children to use their imagination and creativity in their play to understand their world. Therefore, choosing such play materials is an important task. What qualities should you look for in choosing age-appropriate materials and equipment? Are there special considerations for safety? When selecting play materials, remember it is the play itself that contributes to children's learning; the play materials can either enhance or inhibit the kind of play children do. The goal is to enhance the play, not to take control of play away from the child. Table 7.1 provides guidelines for selecting and using safe and appropriate materials that enhance creativity and imagination.

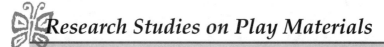

## Research Studies on Play Materials

Bagley, D., & Chaille, C. (1996). Transforming play: An analysis of first-, third-, and fifth-graders' play. *Journal of Research in Childhood Education, 10*(2), 134–142.

Ivory, J., & McCollum, J. (1999). Effects of social and isolate toys on social play in an inclusive setting. *Journal of Special Education, 32*(4), 238–246.

Malone, D. (1998). African-American and Euro-American preschoolers with intellectual disabilities: Patterns of play with toys. *Early Childhood Development, 9*(4), 393–409.

Martin, S., Brady, M., & Williams, R. (1991). Effects of toys on the social behavior of preschool children in integrated and nonintegrated groups: Investigation of setting event. *Journal of Early Intervention, 15*(2), 153–161.

**TABLE 7.1    Selecting and Using Safe and Appropriate Play Materials**

| Guideline | Example |
|---|---|
| **Choose Toys That:** | |
| • Hold children's interest and can be used in more than one way. | Construction toys that can be stacked or used to build something; modeling materials; generic toy figures |
| • Promote creativity and problem solving by enabling children to decide what to do. | Building sets that enable children to set their own tasks and solve them; board games that enable children to plan strategies; pretend materials that stimulate the imagination |
| • Can be used with other materials for changing and more complex play. | Blocks and housekeeping materials that enrich a play theme. |
| • Add new dimensions to children's play. | People and animal props; natural materials, dress-up clothes and housewares; balls; medical kits |
| • Are safe and durable. | Read labels, age and safety recommendations; check toys periodically for wear and damage; supervise for proper use of toys; store toys on shelves or safe boxes. |
| **Avoid Materials That:** | |
| • Can only be used in one way. | Programmed or mechanical toys that limit children's imaginations |
| • Promote violent and stereotypical play behaviors. | Action figures and props connected to television programs and movies |
| • Appeal to a single age or developmental stage. | Materials with very small pieces for very young children or games that require considerable academic skill; puzzles with too many pieces |
| • Are unsafe and not durable. | Outdoor toys that cannot withstand different kinds of weather; materials with toxic paint; dolls whose heads and eyes can be easily removed |

*Sources:* Adapted from Bronson (1995); Johnson, Christie, & Yawkey (1999), Levin (1999), and Moyer (1995).

Divergent play materials offer children unlimited possibilities. To capitalize on this potential, children must have opportunities to investigate and use all types of materials. The varying types of materials and their uses will be described in the next section.

 # TYPES OF MATERIALS

Two-year-old Allysun clutches a fat, red crayon and vigorously scribbles on a large piece of paper. She is absorbed with her markings and the gliding movement of the crayon across the paper's smooth surface.

Four-year-olds Lourdes and Maria, children of migrant workers in a Head Start classroom, pack, unpack, and repack boxes with dishes and food and talk about where they will next live.

Six-year-old twins, Caroline and Diana, are building tunnels and bridges with blocks as part of their unit on transportation.

Eight-year-olds Kim and Brady are engrossed in a game of checkers. They carefully contemplate their next strategic move.

Each of these children is using different types of materials in age-appropriate ways. It is important for adults to support children's growth by providing a range of materials. The following section describes different types of materials, including skill/concept, gross motor, manipulative, construction, self-expressive materials, and natural, everyday objects (Johnson, Christie, & Yawkey, 1999; Moyer, 1995; Yinger & Blaszka, 1995).

## Skill/Concept Materials

**Skill and concept materials** are prescriptive and product-oriented (Johnson et al., 1999). Children commonly practice skills such as eye-hand coordination, sorting, classifying, and counting with them. Typical materials in this category consist of board games such as Picture Lotto, simple card games such as Fish, picture books, and perception materials such as lacing beads and puzzles. These structured materials have limited possibilities for creative and divergent thinking in play.

## Gross Motor Materials

**Gross motor materials** stress large muscle activity. Children use them primarily to explore and practice motor abilities and to develop strength in large muscle coordination. Typical gross motor materials include balls, climbers, pull toys, and riding toys. As motor development increases due to activity, these materials have the potential to encourage divergent and inventive thinking when used in supportive environments.

## Manipulative Materials

**Manipulative materials** develop small muscles in children's fingers and hands, basic concepts, and eye-hand coordination. Children's use of manipulative materials provides important opportunities for early literacy and numeracy development; offers concrete experiences with basic attributes of color, size, and shape; provides opportunities for cooperative problem solving; and increases awareness of cultural diversity. Typical fine motor materials include beads, building sets, crayons, dough, geoboards, markers, jigsaw puzzles, lacing and sewing frames, pegs, pencils, pop-up boxes, and scissors.

## Construction Materials

**Construction materials** have separate pieces that can be combined in different ways. These materials include blocks (e.g., units, parquetry), building sets (e.g.,

Lincoln Logs, Tinkertoys), and woodworking materials (e.g., hammer, nails, wood scraps, white glue). Construction materials offer endless possibilities and support coordination and inventive thinking. The number of pieces influences how children choose to combine pieces and determine when their product is finished.

## Self-Expressive Materials

**Self-expressive materials** encourage children to experiment with different roles, feelings, and behaviors and express them through drama, music, and art. Materials in this category include dolls, dress-up clothes, housekeeping toys, markers, miniature life toys such as Weebles or bendable people, musical instruments, and puppets. Children determine how the materials will be used, invent personalities and roles, and respond imaginatively. As a result, self-expressive materials promote a sense of pride and accomplishment in children.

## Natural and Everyday Objects

**Everyday objects** can be natural and/or household materials that have specific, nonplay purposes (Bronson, 1995; Johnson et al., 1999; Moyer, 1995; Yinger & Blaszka, 1995). Children decide how to use them, employ imaginative and divergent thinking, and imitate and model adult roles with them. Materials in the household category might include boxes, buttons, carpentry tools, and pots and pans. Natural materials include sticks, twigs, leaves, rocks, pinecones, sand, mud, and water. Yinger and Blaszka (1995) describe a program for preschoolers in Florida that used a majority of "found" materials such as palm branches, PVC pipes, and large cardboard tubes to provide children with challenging opportunities outside as well as inside. Figure 7.1 suggests appropriate uses for recycled materials, and Table 7.2 describes the range of materials and their specific uses and lists the child's role and the potential play possibilities within each category.

   To make the most of each material, teachers need to consider other possibilities. This might involve altering the object in some way or adding materials to it. For example, think of an empty detergent bottle. A toddler might fill and empty it; a preschooler might experiment with the number and location of holes punched in it and the rate of water flowing out; a first grader might add plastic tubing and create a siphon. In this way, one recycled piece of plastic has become a challenging yet developmentally appropriate resource for each child.

## DEVELOPMENTALLY APPROPRIATE MATERIALS

**Developmentally appropriate materials** are concrete, real, and meaningful to children (Bredekamp & Copple, 1997). They are basic to the early childhood program because they support child-initiated and child-directed learning, stimulate the

| **Goals** |
| --- |
| • To help children think creatively—"Let's see what we can make!"<br>• To encourage children to work together—"Oh, no! We can't let it fall!"<br>• To get children involved in perceiving and inventing patterns—"First red, then blue, then yellow, now green again."<br>• To build children's problem-solving skills—"If I do this, I think it might . . ."<br>• To allow children to explore ideas—"I wonder what would happen if . . ."<br>• To support creating and inventing—"Teacher, look at what I made!" |
| **Sources** |
| • Ask *families* to collect decorating items (wallpaper, fabric, floor tile, paint chips, framing materials; craft and hobby items (yarn, wood scraps, lace, buttons); kitchen items (plastic containers, egg cartons, paper towel tubes, plastic milk jug caps, detergent bottles); machines and machine parts (old telephones, alarm clocks, typewriters, computer parts).<br>• Gather materials from *businesses* too:<br>   • Restaurants (bags, straws, cups, bowls, trays, spoons, corks, boxes, ice cream cartons, pizza boxes, plastic containers).<br>   • Building supply and home centers (lumber, sawdust, wood curls, nails, wire, wallpaper books, linoleum tiles, plastic pipe pieces, carpet samples, ceramic tile pieces).<br>   • Cleaners and tailors (buttons, hangers, large spools, fabric scraps).<br>   • Camera stores and frame shops (usable expired film, plastic film cylinders, matboard pieces, frame scraps).<br>   • Factories (plastic injection molders, die cutters).<br>   • Packaging companies (plastic scraps and punch-outs in a wide variety of colors and shapes, gaskets, washers, sponge-type foam, and styrofoam).<br>   • Newspaper plant or printer (card stock, newsprint, fancy papers of many types).<br>   • Grocery, drug, and department stores (boxes, divided cartons, corrugated paper, countertop displays, floor displays). |
| **Storage Suggestions** |
| 1. Create a central storage "warehouse" for materials.<br>2. Label the storage bins and involve children in sorting materials.<br>3. Provide small plastic baskets for children to transport materials from the storage area to the work area.<br>4. Develop a collection schedule so that materials arrive at predetermined times.<br>5. Make families aware of materials you need, then put labeled containers next to the door for collecting donated materials. |

**Figure 7.1**   Appropriate Uses for Recycled Materials
*Sources:* Drew (1995) and Jalongo & Stamp (1997).

TABLE 7.2 Materials for Divergent Thinking

|  | Type of Material | | | | | |
|---|---|---|---|---|---|---|
|  | Skill/Concept | Gross Motor | Manipulative | Construction | Self-Expressive | Natural and Everyday Objects |
| Illustrative Examples | Card and board games; lacing, sorting, and stacking materials. | Balls, indoor/outdoor climbers, pull and riding toys. | Puzzles, interlocking plastic and wooden sets; nuts and bolts; table blocks. | Blocks, interlocking building sets, markers, paper, scissors. | Dolls, dress-ups, housekeeping toys, markers, musical instruments, puppets. | Buttons, natural materials, pots and pans, carpentry tools. |
| Intended Use or Purpose | Teach skills and concepts. Structured and outcome-oriented. | Emphasize large muscle development. | Emphasize small muscle development and eye-hand coordination. | Contain materials with separate parts to make things. | Relate to child's role or identity and creative expression in art. | Have clear nonplay uses in the adult world. |
| Child's Role | Responds to materials with senses, both physically and intellectually. | Responds, explores, and practices gross motor skills. | Responds, explores, and practices fine motor and perception skills. | Creates with multiple pieces. Determines beginning and end of project. | Decides how to use material. Invents situations, personalities, and roles. Responds imaginatively to materials. | Determines use and incorporates into activity. |
| Potential for Divergent Thinking | Limited number of uses. Structure imposed by material. Little opportunity for creative expression. | Some opportunity for creative and imaginative input in language, depending upon the environmental conditions and the role of the teacher. | | Multiple combinations possible, depending upon number of pieces available. | Multiple possibilities to respond to, invent scenes and express language and ideas. | Self-motivating and versatile materials encourage children to imitate and model adult roles and behavior. |

imagination, facilitate recall about meaningful experiences, and aid communication. Through extensive play with real materials and interactions with others, children through the primary grades come to understand the people, events, and things in their world. Thus, all children should use materials that are commonly found in good museums and libraries. Early childhood settings should be filled with things to do, things to touch, and things to learn. These kinds of materials foster self-directed learning of which creativity is a natural by-product. In contrast, some early childhood settings are full of workbooks, worksheets, coloring books, and adult-made models of art products for children to copy that are *not* appropriate for young children. These materials do not provide children with the opportunity to pursue their interests and continue learning (Barba, 1998; Bredekamp & Copple, 1997). In the following sections, we describe developmental characteristics and age-appropriate play materials for infants/toddlers, preschoolers/kindergartners, and school-age children. We also suggest how you can use these play materials appropriately with children of different ages.

## Infants and Toddlers

Infants and toddlers learn by feedback from sensory exploration and social interaction. As infants roll, reach, grasp, and crawl they need a variety of textured objects to view and to reach. Because infants repeat interesting, pleasant experiences, they need toys and objects that make pleasant sounds (e.g., mobiles, musical toys); that are soft and squeezable (e.g., soft fabric toys with different textures, soft fabric covered balls); and that are simple and realistic (e.g., cloth picture books, bath toys) (Gestwicki, 1999).

Toddlers actively struggle with issues of independence, show great interest in children their own age, and have a high energy level. They test out materials and are fascinated by finding new and different ways to use them. Both infants and toddlers need materials for looking, feeling, listening, sucking, grasping, and moving that are carefully matched to their abilities. Toddlers also prefer:

- Action toys that *they* can make produce sounds or movements, such as musical toys.
- Toys that fit together and pull apart such as fill and dump toys and sorting boxes.
- Building toys such as blocks, reading materials, and musical toys.
- Toys that stimulate make-believe play, such as pots and pans, simple dress-ups, and empty food containers.
- Books for browsing and for reading, such as board books and photo albums.
- Gross motor toys to pull and push, such as large cartons and wagons (Gestwicki, 1999; Hughes, 1999).

Although a variety of toys is necessary, infants and toddlers need only a few at one time. Tables 7.3 and 7.4 list examples of developmentally appropriate materials for infants (birth–age 1) and toddlers (ages 1–3).

**TABLE 7.3   Developmentally Appropriate Play Materials for Infants (Birth–Age 1)**

| Type of Play Material | Appropriate Materials | Examples |
|---|---|---|
| Skill/concept | Books/records and tapes | Soft cloth and thick cardboard books; lullabies, voices of familiar caretakers |
| | Games | "Peek-a-Boo," "So Big," "Where Is the Baby?" and other socially interactive games |
| Gross motor | Active play | Push/pull toys; large balls, infant bouncers |
| Manipulative | Fine motor | Simple rattles, teethers, sturdy cloth toys, squeeze and squeak toys, colorful mobiles, activity boxes for the crib; clutch and texture balls; stacking toys; containers to fill and dump |
| Construction | Blocks | Soft rubber blocks |
| | Puzzles | Two-to-three piece puzzles of familiar objects |
| Self-expressive | Dolls and soft toys | Soft baby dolls; plush animals |
| | Puppets | Soft hand puppets |
| | Dramatic play | Large, unbreakable mirrors attached to the crib or wall |
| | Sensory | Tactile toys like soft plush animals and pillows; colorful visuals like pictures of babies; auditory toys like a music box; suitable teethers |
| Natural and everyday objects | Household | Pots and pans; plastic containers |

*Note:* For further information see Bronson (1995), Johnson et al. (1999), and Moyer (1995).

*Your Role*

The following guidelines will help you nurture infants' and toddlers' development and enhance their self-expression with materials.

**1.** *Use only toys that meet safety standards.* Avoid toys and materials that have sharp points or edges, as well as nails, wires, or pins that can be swallowed or have parts that can lodge in children's ears and throats. Be sure that toys are painted with nontoxic or lead-free paint, do not require electricity, can be easily cleaned, and cannot pinch fingers or catch hair.

**2.** *Provide a rich sensory environment.* Infants and toddlers need to experience materials with all of their senses. Teachers who create a "crawling trail" made from scraps of distinctively different textures of fabrics, such as satin, lace, corduroy, and flannel, are providing a sensory environment that intrigues and involves infants and toddlers.

**3.** *Have plenty of materials available.* Infants who use a variety of materials perform better on cognitive tasks than infants who do not use such materials

**TABLE 7.4** Developmentally Appropriate Play Materials for Toddlers (Ages 1–3)

| Type of Play Material | Appropriate Play Materials | Examples |
|---|---|---|
| Skill/concept | Books/records and tapes | Simple picture books and poems about familiar places and people; records and tapes of children's songs, folk songs, nursery rhymes, popular songs, songs from other cultures; movement and exercise music |
| | Games | Social interaction games with adults, such as "Pop Goes the Weasel," "Ring-a-Round-a-Rosy," "Round and Round the Garden" |
| Gross motor | Active play | Toys to push and pull while walking; doll carriage, wagon, toys with objects; ride-on toys allowing the child to move self along |
| | Outdoor | Low slides and climbers, tunnels of oversized cardboard boxes for crawling, variety of balls; sand and water materials |
| Manipulative | Fine motor/perception | Colored paddles, dressing dolls, activity boxes, pop-up toys operated by pushing a button, nesting and stacking toys; toys to put together and take apart; large colored beads and spools, sewing and lacing cards, large shape sorters, pegboards with a few large pegs, frames for zipping and snapping |
| | Puzzles and form boards | Simple two-to-three-piece puzzles and form boards with familiar shapes and objects; puzzles with books |
| Construction | Building sets | Small, lightweight sets of 15–25 pieces before 18 months; solid wooden unit blocks (20–40 pieces); wooden hollow blocks and accessories; interlocking building sets |
| | Carpentry | Assorted pounding toys with large wooden pegs or balls, plastic hammers, plastic pliers, thick styrofoam boards |
| Self-expressive | Dolls and soft toys | Soft-bodied or rubber dolls; simple caretaking accessories |
| | Dramatic play | Toy telephone, full-length mirror for self-awareness; miniature dishes, pots and pans; dress-up clothes; shopping cart |
| | Sensory | Soft, cuddly, easy-to-hold, safe toys; modeling dough; visual and auditory stimuli; sensory games and boxes |
| | Art/music | Rhythm instruments, bells, large crayons, markers, unlined paper |
| | Sand and water | Sponges, small shovel, pail, cups, plastic containers for dumping and filling, baster, molds |
| Natural and everyday objects | | Pots and pans, plastic containers, cooking utensils; real objects appeal to children's imagination for all categories of play and suit many types of materials |

*Note:* For further information, see Bronson (1995), Johnson et al. (1999), McKee (1986), and Moyer (1995).

(Hughes, 1999). Toddlers need plenty of materials and containers to collect, fill, dump, and stack objects. Simple, small, plastic containers of all sizes and shapes, cloth sacks, a variety of cardboard tubing, and empty wooden spools are necessary for water, sand, and manipulative play.

**4.** *Use appropriate social games.* Infants and toddlers respond positively to "Peek-a-Boo," "So Big," "Trot, Trot to Boston" and other familiar social routines. These highly repetitive games have simple rules through which infants learn the beginning of turn taking, the rhythms of conversation, and the bonds of social relationships.

**5.** *Provide attractive, everyday, safe objects.* Infants and toddlers like to use one object to represent another. Blocks, water, sand, dress-up clothes, and carefully selected, safe jewelry appeal to toddlers' imaginations.

## *Preschoolers and Kindergartners*

Preschoolers and kindergartners show an increasing social ability, a fascination with adult roles, a growing mastery over their small and large muscles, and a deep passion for make-believe play that peaks at about age 5. Their simple, unstructured play includes family roles, such as Mommy, Daddy, Grandma, and Baby, and roles

*Materials for preschoolers should support their developing social skills and increasing motor skills.*

of familiar people outside the family, such as a supermarket checker or truck driver. These children use both realistic and nonrealistic props and accessories.

Materials for preschoolers and kindergartners should support their developing social skills and interest in adult roles, growing imaginations, increasing motor skills, and rapidly expanding vocabularies (Hughes, 1999). They need:

- Dramatic play props such as discarded adult clothes, props from familiar adult roles, and literacy tools to write.
- Realistic replicas or models of useful objects such as telephones and cars.
- Construction materials, such as simple building sets, to create products.
- Sensory materials, such as sand and water, to explore.
- Manipulative materials, such as simple puzzles, to test.
- Wheeled vehicles to demonstrate gross motor skills and to facilitate social interaction.
- Picture books that capitalize on familiar themes such as transportation, families, and feelings representing people and objects from other cultures.
- Everyday objects such as boxes, cardboard tubing, and plastic bottle caps of assorted sizes, shapes, and colors.

Table 7.5 lists a variety of developmentally appropriate materials for preschool and kindergarten children.

**TABLE 7.5   Developmentally Appropriate Play Materials for Preschool and Kindergarten Children (Ages 3–5)**

| Type of Play Material | Appropriate Materials | Examples |
|---|---|---|
| Skill/concept | Books/records | Picture books, simple and repetitive stories and rhymes, animal stories, pop-up books, simple science or information books, wide variety of musical recordings |
| | Games | Socially interactive games with adults, such as "What If"; matching and lotto games based on colors and pictures, such as pictures bingo or dominoes; games of chance with a few pieces that require no reading, such as Chutes and Ladders and Go Fish; flannel board with pictures, letters, storybook characters |
| Gross motor | Active play | Push and pull toys such as wagons, wheelbarrows, doll carriages; ride-on toys such as tricycles, three-wheeled vehicles, cars, trucks; balls of all kinds; indoor slide and climber; rocking boat |
| | Outdoor | Climbers, rope ladders, balls of all sizes, old tires, sand and water materials |

*(continued)*

**TABLE 7.5** *(Continued)*

| Type of Play Material | Appropriate Materials | Examples |
|---|---|---|
| Manipulative | Fine motor | Dressing frames; toys to put together and take apart; cookie cutters, stamp and printing materials, fingerpaints, modeling dough, small objects to sort and classify; bead stringing with long, thin string; pegs and small pegs; colored cubes, table blocks, magnetic board/letters/numbers and shapes; perception boards and mosaics |
| | Puzzles and form boards | Fit-in or framed puzzles<br>For 3-year olds: from 4 or 5 to 20 pieces<br>For 4-year olds: from 15 to 30 pieces<br>For 5-year olds: from 15 to 50 pieces<br>Large, simple jigsaws; number/letter/clock puzzles |
| | Investigative | Toys, globe, flashlight, magnets, lock boxes, weather forecasting equipment, scales, balances, stethoscopes |
| Construction | Building sets | Small and large unit blocks; large hollow blocks; from age 4, interlocking plastic blocks with pieces of all sizes |
| | Carpentry | Workbench, hammer, preschool nails, saw, sandpaper, pounding benches, safety goggles |
| Self-expressive | Dolls and soft toys | Realistic dolls and accessories; play settings and play people (e.g., farm, hospital) |
| | Dramatic play | Dress-up clothes, realistic tools, toy camera, telephone, household furniture |
| | Sensory | Tactile boxes; auditory and musical materials such as smelling and sound boxes; cooking experiences |
| | Art/music | All rhythm instruments, music boxes, large crayons, paint, paste, glue, chalkboard and chalk, sewing kits, collage materials, markers, modeling dough, blunt scissors |
| | Sand and water | Sandbox tools, bubbles, water toys |
| Natural and everyday objects | | Old clocks, radios, cameras, telephones; telephone books; mirrors; doctor kits; typewriter; magazines; fabric scraps; computer; cash register and receipts; measuring cups and muffin tins |

*Note:* For further information see Bronson (1995), Johnson et al. (1999), and Moyer (1995).

*Your Role*

Teachers need to keep in mind the following guidelines when providing materials for preschoolers and kindergartners:

**1.** *Include adequate props and materials both indoors and outdoors.* Younger children and less-skilled players need more realistic props (such as miniature cars, people, or tools) to support and sustain their play. Older children and more advanced players need less-realistic materials for variety and flexibility of play themes, although they still enjoy realistic props. One preschool teacher noticed, for example, that a bridal veil, a bouquet of plastic flowers, and an old tuxedo jacket that she found at a secondhand store stimulated considerable excitement and elaborated play in the dress-up corner. Be certain to include natural and everyday objects such as puppets, hats, and boxes for children to represent their understandings. Use items that are likely to have personal significance for the child, such as a stuffed toy dog with a bowl, leash, brush, and bone.

**2.** *Model the use of open-ended materials when necessary.* As children use more highly developed make-believe skills, encourage them to use less-realistic props. Bringing a square block to the post office theme corner, one kindergarten teacher suggested: "Let's pretend this is a package that just came in the mail" or "Look what the UPS driver delivered today!" Be certain to leave the play once interactions are established.

**3.** *Develop your own imagination.* One of Mr. Phelps's kindergartners brought in a pith helmet and sombrero to add to the dress-up corner. Rather than simply leaving the gear on a hat rack, Mr. Phelps thought about the possibilities and created a game that the children loved called "Expedition." He put a piece of blue cloth on the floor and put the balance beam over it with a rubber crocodile below. He strategically positioned other animals around the room too. Soon, the children's activity took on many new dimensions—sinking in the quicksand, swinging from a pretend vine, and getting lost in the jungle. Each time Mr. Phelps introduced a new picture book, such as *Junglewalk* (Tarfuri, 1988), new themes were introduced.

**4.** *Use available resources to meet the needs of individual children.* One preschool teacher used resources as the vehicle for helping a preschool child who was

*Water play, by a 4-year-old girl.*

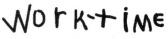

having difficulty entering group play situations learn how to join a group of play-ers. The teacher quietly suggested that the child offer a new prop for the group's play, which allowed the child successfully to become a participant. This sensitive teacher used a simple resource to support a shy child's entrance into an ongoing play episode.

## School-Age Children

School-age children are refining skills and talents that they prize, are relying more and more on support from their peer group, and are becoming more organized and logical thinkers. Each of these qualities is clearly reflected in their play. Materials for school-age children should reflect their need for realistic, rule-oriented, and peer activities. They need:

- *Organized educational or physical games with rules.* Card, board, and computer games enable them to practice school skills, strategic thinking, decision making, and problem solving. Games such as Red Rover and tag enable them to practice physical skills and teamwork.
- *Construction materials.* School-age children usually have something in mind when they begin building. They need construction and building sets as well as markers and stampers. They often create useful items such as a puppet stage and typically engage in cooperative group projects, such as building a space shuttle.
- *Props that enhance fantasy play.* School-age children's fantasy more closely resembles the reality of adults than the fantasy play of preschoolers. During the school years, children often collect their own props, create hideaways (like treehouses) and social clubs with friends, and develop secret codes.
- *Songs, chants, word games, and rituals.* Play with language and its rhythm is a hallmark of the school-age child. Games such as Scrabble, Boggle, or Word Yahtzee, as well as jokes, riddles, and tongue twisters, appeal to what Piaget called cognitive conceit, helping children to feel "in the know" and superior to those who are not so well informed. Mastery of games with rules also teaches a child how to follow instructions and preserve moral order (Hughes, 1999).
- *Puzzles.* Puzzles with 50 to 500 pieces interest school-age children. Larger puzzles make excellent long-term cooperative projects and provide opportunities for extended conversation. Table 7.6 lists a variety of developmentally appropriate materials for school-age children.

### Your Role

As elementary teachers, we must also carefully consider how to use play materials and resources to foster children's divergent thinking. Use the following guidelines to think broadly about how to use materials and resources.

**1.** *Arrange the classroom in interest centers.* As part of an integrated curriculum in one urban second-grade class, children used a sandbox as the centerpiece of the language arts center. Through their reading about knights and castles, they used the

## TABLE 7.6  Developmentally Appropriate Play Materials for School-Age Children (Ages 6–8)

| Type of Play Material | Appropriate Materials | Examples |
|---|---|---|
| Skill/concept | Books/records | Books on different cultures, recipe books, Caldecott and Newbery Award books and tapes, folktales, fables, historical fiction books in a series, biographies, jokes, riddles, tall tales; music of all types |
| | Games | Strategy and memory games such as Checkers, Tic-Tac-Toe, and Concentration; more complex board and card games for problem solving and decision making, sports games such as bocce, tetherball, soccer; word games |
| Gross motor | Active play | Organized group games such as Simon Says and Red Rover |
| | Outdoor | Jump ropes, flying disks, bicycles, rope ladders, wagons, bear bags, assorted balls, sports sets such as badminton |
| Manipulative | Fine motor | Gardening equipment, canister of buttons to sort and classify, weaving looms, sewing kits, combination locks, pick-up sticks, spirographs |
| | Puzzles | More complex puzzles with 50–100 pieces; puzzles of reproductions of paintings; form boards by famous artists |
| | Investigation | Science materials such as prisms, binoculars, microscopes; printing sets, terrariums and aquariums to create and observe, various science kits (e.g., rocks) |
| Construction | Building sets | Sets with realistic models; additional unit blocks, shapes, and accessories; props for roads and towns |
| | Carpentry | Add screwdrivers, vises, and accessories |
| Self-expressive | Dolls and soft toys | Dolls from other cultures, more detailed, smaller dolls; varied play settings (e.g., office, gas station) and action figures |
| | Dramatic play | Storybook masks and costumes, walkie-talkies |
| | Sensory | Collecting toys in sets; clay and clay tools |
| | Art/music | Small crayons, chalk, watercolors, hole punchers, staplers, all musical instruments, basket-making materials, pottery wheel, stencil and craft kits |
| | Sand and water | Add food coloring, funnels, pumps, hoses, plastic tubing, and assorted containers and utensils |
| Natural and everyday objects | | Simple cameras and film; typewriters; paper and pencils; items for "collections" such as coins, shells, rocks, cards |

*Note:* For further information see Bronson (1995), Johnson et al. (1999), and Moyer (1995).

sand table to construct their own interpretation of elaborate sand castles. They also used materials in the art center to illustrate more detailed aspects of the medieval environments they were learning about (Barbour, Drosdeck & Webster, 1987).

**2.**   *Use projects and investigative activities.* In their unit on the circus, a group of first graders worked together for several days planning and practicing circus acts and designing their outfits from available resources. Matt created a flaming hoop with a hula hoop and crepe paper streamers. Shy Sherree became a roaring lion by putting a nylon net tutu around her neck and using a knit belt as her tail. Reginald became the strong man by putting inflated balloon muscles under his T-shirt and making a barbell from a yardstick with balloons tied on each end. Later they performed circus acts for their peers.

**3.**   *Use developmentally appropriate materials.* Developmentally appropriate materials take into account children's ages, needs, interests, abilities, and cultural backgrounds. They also challenge children's creative thinking and self-expression within familiar contexts. School-age children take pride in demonstrating developing motor and intellectual skills. They are fascinated with language play, number games, riddles, and jokes. First graders are intrigued by the sound ambiguity of "knock-knock" jokes, enjoy manipulating song lyrics like Raffi's "I like to eat, eat, eat, apples and bananas; I like to oat, oat, oat oaples and banonos." Second graders also enjoy ambiguous language and such books as Fred Gwynne's *The King Who Rained* (1970), while third graders are intently interested in enacting and inventing humorous scripts (Isenberg, 1995).

## TECHNOLOGY MATERIALS AND CHILDREN'S PLAY

Many early childhood educators are uncertain about how to use technology appropriately with young children, yet it is an essential part of our daily lives. Children see computers used in the grocery store, the bank, and the service station. If we think back in time to a typical early childhood classroom about 20 years ago, few, if any, technological materials and resources were available. Consider the difference with today's ever-increasing access to such electronic materials and resources as CD-ROM encyclopedias, computers and calculators, tape recorders, and other specialized tools for solving problems and expressing ideas in early childhood settings. Technological materials are another of the many materials to be used in early childhood settings that invite new ways of playing and expressing ideas. They are tools that enable children to create and control their own playful microworlds; they invite fantasy creations by the imaginative child, and enable children to play with real-world items, such as musical instruments, dolls, and story characters (Davidson & Wright, 1994; Yelland, 1999).

Computers are only one technological tool appropriate for young children. Research (Haugland, 1999) has shown that creativity is significantly diminished in children who use drill and practice software for just 45 minutes per week. All adults who work with young children and computers, then, need to know how to choose

*Computers are a part of daily life for children and can promote playful and imaginative experiences.*

and use appropriate software that facilitates young children's self-expression as well as their own roles in facilitating children's learning with computers.

## Appropriate Software for Young Children

Certain features of software design promote children's playful and imaginative experiences. Some of these include a simple design that has many possibilities, clear instructions so that children can use the program with little adult involvement, and easy access and exit from the program (Henniger, 1999; Isenberg & Rosegrant, 1995; National Association for the Education of Young Children [NAEYC], 1996). Software that meets the needs and interests of young children and enhances children's divergent thinking and self-expression enables them to:

  **1.** *Discover, invent, and control their symbolic world.* When children play with technology, they have many opportunities to determine the outcome of their play through the use of a variety of symbols. Computer drawing programs such as *Delta Draw, Color Me, Skid Doodle,* or *Thinkin' Things Collection 2* encourage discovery as children experiment with the fill features, change colors and background, overlay colors, and invent innovative stories about their creations (Haugland & Wright, 1997). And virtual reality programs such as *I Can Be a Dinosaur Finder* in which children become paleontologists, can provide rich pretend experiences (Haugland, 1999).

**2.**   *Apply a range of skills and abilities.* Not all software programs require the same ways of thinking. Some software materials require children to use a very simple set of skills (e.g., matching and rhyming skills in *Reader Rabbit*) as opposed to the use of strategic thinking required in more open programs such as paint programs or *Kid Works2*. Programs like *Millie and Bailey Preschool* use trial and error testing to match the right shoes to different sized feet of customers. More open-ended software encourages exploration and self-directed learning that enables children to control the pace of their own learning. Software such as *Thinkin' Things Collection 2* for primary school children focuses on the development of "visual thinking." In this program, children draw a design on a two-dimensional rectangle that instantly appears in 3-D as a spinning shape. The more time children have to explore the possibilities with this program, the more intriguing the mental puzzles become to solve (Buckleitner, 1999; Isenberg & Rosegrant, 1995).

**3.**   *Enhance their social interactions.* Quality educational software is fun and easy to use, has several levels of difficulty, and encourages children to work together. In Ms. Hicks's preschool classroom, the children were fascinated by different animals, so she added the program *Fantastic Animals* to the computer center. In pairs or triads, the children playfully selected a body, head, tail, and legs to create an animal that danced across the screen. Ms. Hicks also noticed that the children were using *Delta Draw* to create their own fantastic, mixed-up animals. Some of the children even invented pretend scenarios for their animals. Other open-ended software for young children that fosters social interaction includes *Millie's Math House*, where children construct a mouse house together and take turns choosing shapes, and *Facemaker*, which enables children to create limitless kinds of faces.

**4.**   *Foster responsibility for self-directed learning.* Good software makes children want to learn. To promote self-directed learning, teachers not only must carefully select the content of the software, but also must consider children's past experiences with computers themselves. Because many programs for children have multiple parts, teachers need to introduce children to the minimal number of commands that make the program operate without frustrating or confusing the children. Initially making the program simple to use opens the door to more exploration and self-directed behavior in the children's future interactions with it. When using a drawing program such as *Color Me,* for example, a teacher may choose to introduce only the fill feature or the erase feature so that children can get started and explore new possibilities on their own, with a friend, or with another adult (Haugland & Wright, 1997).

**5.**   *Strengthen their problem-solving abilities.* Computer materials that promote problem solving provide children with possibilities for gathering information, making decisions, generating creative ideas and solutions, and testing their plans and solutions. Storyboard software, software that enables children to "build" their own stories by selecting particular backgrounds, icons, or characters, is powerful for all children because it capitalizes on children's divergent thinking and brings a story to life. With a simple click of the mouse, children can change a story's preset animals, characters, or objects to those of their own inventions. In *Wiggins in Storyland,* for example, children can explore Wiggins the bookworm's living room, play tic-tac-toe on Wiggins's windows, hear classic stories read aloud, and make a snack for Wiggins to drink. Building stories with storyboard software has limitless possibilities and fosters children's creative expression (Shade, 1995).

**6.** *Make connections to their thematic units.* During dental health week, one second-grade teacher introduced the software program *Explore-a-Story: Where Did My Toothbrush Go?* Some of the second graders created scenic backgrounds and animated characters and composed texts about toothbrushes as part of their study. They also used the program *Color Me* to create bright illustrations for their original stories about healthy teeth. Programs like *Cubby Magic: Folk Tales Around the World* use native adults to share stories, which can be read with and without Rebus pictures. Children can also make their own illustrations or use Rebus pictures to interpret multicultural ideas. The challenge for early childhood teachers is to choose software for young children that enables them to explore possibilities within a technological world (Yelland, 1999).

### Your Role
Your primary responsibility with computer materials is to ensure that technology is viewed as another powerful learning tool for all children. You can do this by providing (1) technology materials that are age-appropriate, individually appropriate, and culturally sensitive, (2) all children with equal access to computer use, and (3) software that avoids stereotypes and violence (Haugland, 1999; NAEYC, 1996). You can select software that:

**1.** *Enhances language skills,* such as *Bailey's Book House,* which enables very young children to create their own cards, *I Spy,* where children select objects to search for in a microworld, or *Storybook Weaver,* which enables older children to create their own stories with a word processor and multicultural illustrations.

**2.** *Develops and refines math, science, and logical skills,* such as *Millie's Math House,* which helps very young children learn about sizes, shapes, patterns, and seasons; *Blue's Clues 1 2 3 Time Activities,* which has children sorting food items into categories, completing patterns on colorful floats, and categorizing snacks; or *Thinkin' Things,* in which children create their own songs and games in a problem-solving environment.

**3.** *Encourages interpersonal and intrapersonal skills that enable very young children to get along with others and to better understand their own desires and feelings.* Very young children may do this with *Richard Scarry's How Things Work in Busytown* as they learn about cooperation through building roads and baking bread, while older children might respond favorably to *SimCity 2000* by designing fantasy houses of the future. Moreover, *Kid Desk! Internet Safe* now makes the Web accessible to very young children without adult assistance.

**4.** *Promotes artistic and creative expression* that develops visual-spatial perception, such as *Kid Pix2* for very young children, who create stamped designs and artwork; or *Crayola Art Studio* for older children, who use tools, stickers, and erasers to play games.

Whatever software is selected, teachers and caregivers must allow girls as well as boys, children of color, and children with disabilities equal access to this powerful technology. In the following sections, we describe other specific, divergent materials that should be available to children of all ages in every early childhood classroom regardless of resources.

## ❀ OTHER DIVERGENT PLAY MATERIALS

There are certain divergent materials that are basic for all children—blocks, modeling materials, and sand and water. These materials offer many possibilities for children to express their ideas and feelings and grow naturally with children.

## *Blocks*

In his autobiography, Frank Lloyd Wright (1932) enthusiastically recalled his kindergarten experiences with blocks: "The smooth, shapely maple blocks with which to build, the sense of which never afterward left the fingers: so form became feeling" (p. 11). With blocks, children are free to create imaginative constructions and determine what to do with them, as can be seen in a glimpse of Ms. Mitsoff's classroom. Ms. Mitsoff rearranged her entire first-grade room to double the block-building space. Throughout the year, her first graders used the blocks as the focal point for their units of study. In their unit on the farm, for example, the children conceptualized, built, and played in a farm containing stalls for cows, a henhouse, a main farmhouse, and a barn. They also assumed different farmworker roles, including those of the farmer, milker, and egg collector. Ms. Mitsoff noticed her children practicing the following concepts:

- *Science concepts* as they observed, compared, and interpreted findings on ways to collect, store, and deliver milk.
- *Math concepts* as they estimated the length of the path needed to get from the farmhouse to the henhouse.
- *Social studies concepts* as they re-created the roles of the farmworkers.
- *Literacy concepts* as they named and labeled their structures and considered books as references.
- *Art concepts* as they repeated patterns in their symmetrical buildings.

### *Types and Uses*

There are many different types of blocks—hollow blocks, unit blocks, and table blocks. **Hollow blocks** are large wooden blocks that have an opening for carrying. Children often use these blocks to build large structures. **Unit blocks** should be made from hard wood, have smooth and rounded corners and edges, and be accurate so that children can build without frustration (Hughes, 1999). To build structures, children need precisely measured unit blocks including units, double units, quadruple units, wedges, triangles, cylinders, and half-rounds. Figure 7.2 illustrates the various unit block shapes. **Table blocks** are small, colored cubed blocks that children use alone or in pairs around a table. They often include unusual shapes that invite children's inventiveness.

There are stages that children pass through in block building (Hirsch, 1996), which are summarized as follows:

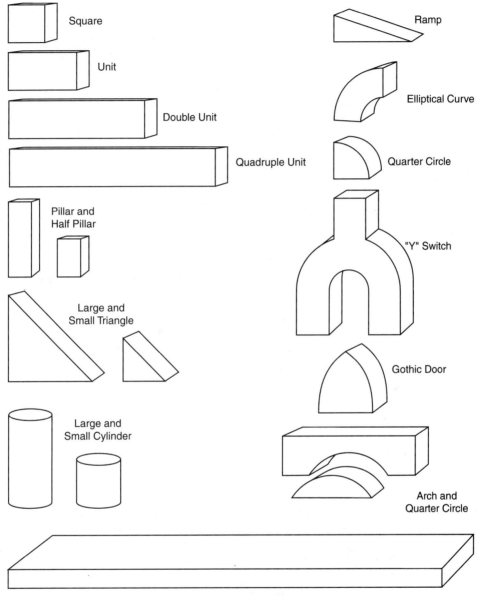

**Figure 7.2**   Illustrations of Block Shapes

- *Stage 1: Carrying*—Blocks are carried around, not used for construction. This applies to the very young.
- *Stage 2: Building begins*—Children make mostly rows, either horizontal (on the floor) or vertical (stacked). There is much repetition in this early building pattern.

- *Stage 3: Bridging*—Two blocks with a space between them, connected by a third block.
- *Stage 4: Enclosures*—Blocks placed in such a way that they enclose a space.
- *Stage 5: Decorative patterns*—When facility with blocks is acquired, much block symmetry can be observed. Buildings, generally, are not yet named.
- *Stage 6: Naming of structures for dramatic play begins*—Before reaching this stage, children may also have named their structures, but the names were not necessarily related to the function of the building.
- *Stage 7: Resembling reality*—Children's buildings often reproduce or symbolize actual structures they know, and there is a strong impulse toward dramatic play around the block structures.

*Your Role*

Block play is central to children's learning in all areas. For example, block play contributes to children's literacy development as they gain experience with symbolic representation, a basic abstract aspect of the reading and writing process; it promotes visual discrimination as children select particular blocks for their constructions; it helps children develop the fine motor strength needed for writing; and it enables children to develop their oral language skills by communicating about their plans and needs for their structures (Stroud, 1995). The following guidelines will help you maximize the potential learning in block play for children of all ages.

- Store blocks on low, open shelves for easy access.
- Provide an adequate supply of blocks—211 blocks for a group of ten 3-year-olds. A complete set of over 750 blocks is not too many for an older group of 20 children.
- Allocate enough floor space for building out of the traffic patterns, next to the housekeeping area and away from a quiet activity area.
- Provide enough time for building (45 to 60 minutes).
- Provide props and accessories such as cars and animals.
- Maintain a periodic physical presence in the area to attract children to the block center.
- Label shelves with the shape of the long side of the block in view. This helps children to locate materials quickly, to perceive the relationships of the blocks to one another, to practice classification skills, and to assist with cleanup.
- Use blocks in ways other than building, such as a matching or measuring game with blocks of a specific size.
- Develop a genuine appreciation for block playing.

# Modeling Materials

Dough and clay are three-dimensional, sensory materials that offer children possibilities for expressing thoughts and feelings. Young children enjoy pounding, squeezing, squishing, and rolling these materials. Older children do the same but also represent and/or create familiar objects or people. Where possible, let children mix the dough themselves. Figure 7.3 contains some simple recipes for modeling materials.

**Figure 7.3**
Recipes for Modeling
Materials

| Clay Substitutes | |
|---|---|
| 1 cup flour<br>1/2 cup salt<br>1/3 cup water | Mix the ingredients and knead with fingers. Add 1 teaspoon Sodium benzoate as a preservative. Refrigerate. |
| **Vegetable Dye** | |
| 1 cup flour<br>1/2 cup salt<br>1 teaspoon powdered alum<br>1/2 cup water | Mix together. Color with food coloring or vegetable dye. Keep in a covered container. |
| **Sawdust Dough** | |
| 2 cups sawdust<br>3 cups flour<br>1 cup salt<br>Water as needed | This dough dries very hard and is as breakable as other three-dimensional materials. |
| **Cornstarch Dough** | |
| 1 cup cornstarch<br>2 cups baking soda<br>1/4 cup cold water<br>food coloring | Combine cornstarch and soda. Add water and coloring. Stir until smooth. Cook to boiling point over medium heat for 1 minute. Cool and knead. Dries very hard. |
| **Play Dough** | |
| 1 cup salt<br>1/2 cup cornstarch<br>1/2 cup boiling water | Knead ingredients and place in a plastic bag for storage. |
| **Peanut Butter Dough (edible)** | |
| 1 cup honey<br>1 cup peanut butter<br>2 cups dried milk | Mix ingredients together. Form into various shapes. Add additional dried milk if too sticky. |

Modeling materials allow children to explore, manipulate, discover, create, and observe change. Children learn the attributes of modeling materials through the changes they make involving consistency (e.g., from wet to dry), color (e.g., from primary to secondary), and identity (e.g., from a ball to a snake). These first-hand experiences with transformations help children begin to make connections between actions and events, a fundamental understanding for the development of logical thinking (Goldhaber, 1992).

Children need plenty of dough for modeling to be satisfying. Be certain to focus on the process of the material and avoid pushing children to create a product.

## Sand and Water

Sand and water are readily available, inexpensive, satisfying resources that help children explore concepts and release tension. Children learn science concepts such as the effects of objects dropped on water, math concepts such as volume by guessing the number of cups of water needed to fill a larger container, and social interaction skills.

Sand and water are particularly absorbing and relaxing materials for children. Children can release tension as they pour water back and forth in containers or let sand gradually sift through their fingers. When children use sand and water, their social interactions are often quite calm and cooperative (Hendrick, 1996).

Play with sand and water should take place both indoors and outdoors. Some teachers place the sand or water in large plastic tubs or in specially prepared tables. Other teachers substitute rice, shelled corn, or birdseed for indoor sandboxes when sand is unavailable. The inside of an old truck tire laid flat makes a serviceable outdoor sandbox. Be certain to cover the sandbox when the children are not using it so that a stray animal does not foul it. Check outdoor sandboxes frequently for insect infestations too.

*Water is a particularly rewarding and relaxing material for children of all ages.*

*Your Role*

When using sand and water, consider the following:

- Use sand and water together so children can mold the mixture.
- Vary the equipment so that children are continually challenged to think of new uses. Some common materials for sand and water play include various sized molds, sponges, plastic bottles and containers of assorted sizes, flexible plastic tubing, measuring cups and spoons, and small replicas of cars, buildings, and boats. Plastic aprons are also useful.
- Ask open-ended questions such as "Why do you think the water is coming out so slowly?" or "I wonder what would happen if you added water to your sand mound?"
- Decide in advance on simple rules so that water and sand do not get tracked around the classroom. Have materials available so that children take responsibility for cleanup.

Materials of all sorts need to be matched to individual abilities. They are children's tools for understanding their world. Teachers and caregivers have a key role in ensuring a balance of appropriate materials for the release of children's creative expression. They provide a different experience from games.

## ORGANIZED GAMES

In the following scenario, think about the triplets playing games at different ages. Rosa, Dolly, and Norman are now third graders. When they were toddlers, their caregiver played social interaction games with them, such as "This Little Piggy" and "Hide the Keys." In their Head Start program, they played running and chasing games and simple spinning games of chance, such as "Hi Ho Cherry-O." In these games, rules did not matter. Now, Rosa plays soccer on the school soccer team and practices soccer skills wherever she can. Dolly, intrigued by all sorts of card and board games, actively seeks friends to play strategy games such as Rummy and Clue. And Norman thrives on memory and word games such as Twenty Questions and Scrabble.

The games Rosa, Dolly, and Norman played are typical of children during the early childhood years. Although games broaden the curriculum for children of all ages, many teachers believe games with rules foster a competitive rather than a cooperative spirit, question their value, and view them as frivolous.

## *What Is a Game?*

A **game** is a form of play in which children follow an agreed-upon set of rules, predetermine an outcome, assign players specific roles, and assign sanctions for violations (DeVries, 1998; Kamii & DeVries, 1980). Dictionary definitions usually include the elements of rules, competition, and winning.

Most children's games involve physical skill, chance, strategy, or some combination of these elements to determine the outcome. In *games of physical skill*, such as jump rope or stickball, motor skill is essential. *Games of chance*, such as the simple board game "Winnie the Pooh," rely on dice or a spin of the wheel. And *games of strategy*, such as checkers or Boggle, require decision-making skills and compel players to take turns, follow complex directions, and employ complicated strategies. Organized sports are often considered strategy games because they require a player to plan strategies and imagine oneself in the opponent's role (Hughes, 1999).

## The Value of Games

Games are one play material that contributes to children's physical, social/emotional, and intellectual development. Games themselves are motivating for many children because the desire to play comes from within. For many children, games provide a means to learn new skills and to practice known skills.

Some early childhood educators believe that organized games for young children are developmentally inappropriate, thwart creativity, and encourage competition. Others believe that they can be appropriate if teachers and caregivers positively confront the competitive element (DeVries, 1998; Hughes, 1999; Kamii & DeVries, 1980; Rivkin, 1995). When group games match children's developmental levels, children:

- *Develop cooperative behaviors and strategic thinking* by learning to understand others' thinking and relate it to their own. One second grader, for instance, talked about setting up a "double jump" in checkers, indicating her thinking in relation to her actions.
- *Practice autonomy* by choosing whether or not to play the game and to follow its rules. To illustrate, when Carmella's kindergarten friends wanted to play shadow tag, she chose another activity because she did not want to be "it."
- *Engage in problem solving* by deciding how to follow rules and play fairly. In one scenario, a group of first graders was trying to start a game of Go Fish but could not begin their play until they solved the problem of who was to go first.
- *Supervise and correct each other* by monitoring each other's actions. In a game of dominoes, it is common to hear one child tell another, "That domino doesn't have the same number of dots. You can't use that one," or to watch children's cues during "Guess Which Hand Has the Penny" (Johnson et al., 1999).

Games suitable for young children have one or two simple rules, include all children who want to participate, encourage children to figure things out for themselves, and do *not* stress being first, winning, or losing. Young children like noncompetitive guessing games such as "I'm thinking of something in the room that is . . ." simple sorting and matching games, simple board games (if they can change the rules), and basic running and chasing games.

Older children need strategy games that develop problem-solving and decision-making abilities while encouraging them to think about others' thoughts and feelings. Board games and active outdoor group games are typical of school-age children. Today, children of both sexes engage equally in these games.

When games focus on playing together rather than against one another, each player becomes important. With an emphasis on involvement, mutual enjoyment, and respect, appropriately played group games can promote basic intellectual and social skills in school-age children.

## Competition versus Cooperation

How games are presented influences their degree of competition versus cooperation. If teachers make it clear that the goal of a game is doing as well as each child can, then games can enhance cooperation. To illustrate, Ms. Ake's second graders were involved in relay races. When she reminded them that the goal of these races was to do their very best, she noticed how they urged one another on in their three-legged races as they jointly figured out ways to get quickly to the other side of the room.

Cooperation means operating together. It involves negotiating to arrive at an agreement that is acceptable to all. As a result, some disputes and conflicts are inevitable (DeVries, 1998; Kamii & DeVries, 1980). When children play games cooperatively, they construct rules for themselves as they begin to experience others' viewpoints. An emphasis on cooperative games encourages children to play together rather than against one another by focusing on group participation, sharing, giving each player an opportunity to play, and making rules that suit the players (Sobel, 1983). Cooperative games help children develop a sense of teamwork, loyalty to the group, and knowledge of how to get along with others. Because Western culture is inherently competitive, it is a challenge for teachers and caregivers to handle competition constructively in classrooms.

### Your Role

Consider this group of first graders playing Marble Run, a commercial game in which children combine small blocks with slides and intricate grooves into a course for the marble. As the first graders excitedly invented new courses, they exclaimed, "Now, let's try this" or "Look at it go!" Their teacher commented, "This is their favorite game because it has so many possibilities and combinations. When I now say, 'It's game time,' I have to be sure to say 'Only four children can use Marble Run.' It is truly the favorite game in our classroom."

The teacher's role, in this case, was that of observer and manager as she freed the children to utilize the many available combinations. There was no correct way to play the game. The children constructed the rules in ways that made sense to them (DeVries & Fernie, 1990; Kamii & DeVries, 1980).

When using games in early childhood settings, you must provide opportunities for children to modify rules and create their own games. In that way, games such as Marble Run, as they are being played, become a powerful vehicle for developing intellectual and social autonomy. You can help children modify game rules by:

**1.** *Supporting their initiatives in games.* The first graders playing Marble Run were encouraged to play the game in many different ways. Sometimes the game involved races; at other times it became a maze. Each group of players could initiate the way to play the game and then negotiate rules for it.

**2.** *Introducing noncompetitive games.* Children who compete can and do also cooperate in games as well as other activities. Appendix C describes appropriate, noncompetitive ball games, quiet games, singing games, running games, and partner games that can be introduced into the curriculum to enhance cooperation.

**3.** *Allowing them to modify rules during the game.* Even though the first graders usually started one of the Marble Run games with a race of some kind, they often decided to change it in midstream to a different game. Their teacher encouraged their ideas about all of the variations they invented.

Games are useful for active and quiet times, for transitions from one activity to another, and for fostering specific learning outcomes. Therefore, you will need to develop a repertoire of games that foster a cooperative spirit that will last children through their lives.

## CHILD-CONSTRUCTED GAMES

Child-constructed games promote children's understanding and acceptance of rules as well as their ability to cooperate and compete (Castle & Wilson, 1993). Unfortunately, children in today's world spend less time spontaneously inventing games and more time using prepared commercial games with predetermined instructions, rules, and outcomes or in organized team sports. This limits their opportunities to make, revise, and follow their own rules with their peers and to control their social interactions. In the next section, we describe the power of children's invented games on their divergent thinking, self-expression, and overall development.

### Invented Games

Inventing games makes rules meaningful and relevant for children (Castle, 1990; Castle & Wilson, 1993). Invented games help children:

1. *Become autonomous learners.* Second grader Andy made a simple baseball game from oak tag, markers, and colored dots. When other children were excited about using it and helped him to modify and perfect the game, Andy gained confidence in his ability as an independent yet collaborative learner.
2. *Practice ongoing basic skills.* Julia wanted to create her own version of hopscotch on the playground outdoors. She practiced her writing to label the asphalt with chalk and to write the game's rules; she used reading skills to read her rules to a friend; and she incorporated mathematics when figuring out the procedures and format of her hopscotch game.
3. *Develop organizational skills.* In invented games, children plan, construct, play the game with others, discover its problems, and make changes. Some of Ms. Spencer's third-grade girls invented a board game called Shopping. The object was to move along a path to purchase various department store items. While playing the game, they discovered that their rule of getting the

exact number on the dice as the number of spaces remaining on the game board left them sitting for many turns waiting to complete the game. So they agreed to change the rules.

4. *See others' ideas and points of view and develop ways to solve disagreements.* Should differences occur, children need to compromise and negotiate to reach consensus with their peers. Children need opportunities to problem-solve and negotiate without adult interference and intervention.

Invented games encourage mutual self-interest in rules and rule making and differ greatly from teacher-imposed rules. They provide an appealing and satisfying vehicle for children to apply skills, increase their understanding of rules, and improve their social interaction skills. Think about the following second graders in Mr. Green's inner-city classroom. Paolo, Kristin, and Sarah are slow readers and have some difficulty with basic arithmetic operations. For one hour every Wednesday afternoon, Mr. Green expects all of his second graders to invent their own games using assorted available materials. They choose to create a game either alone or with a partner.

Let's look at the games of Kristin, Sarah, and Paolo.

Kristin made the "Go Here and There Game" alone and then taught it to her friend. Her simple path game included starting and finishing points, some obstacles along the way, a few game cards, and an individual card for rules. During play her friend asked, "Where are the place cards?" Kristin said, "Ooops, I forgot them" and went back to make them.

Sarah's game reflects the solar system unit her class is studying. It includes all the planets, Saturn's three rings, a darkened background indicating night, and the sun and stars. She made cards for the number of spaces to move forward and back, as well as outer-space instructions like "Tack a peas [take a piece] of the moon rock and stay." She used existing dice to designate turns and dried beans for markers. Her simple rules read as follows: "RULES: Start from the moon go to the Erath and the first person to get there wens." When she tried to teach the game to a friend the next week, she quickly discovered that she had no labels on the dots telling players when to choose a card. As a result, the game could not begin. Sarah then made the necessary modifications.

Paolo's game, "Colorland," is also a simple path game containing a clear beginning and end, periodic spots to pick cards, a place labeled "card," and many cards sending players to jail or helping them escape from jail. Two of his cards read "brach owt of jail [break out of jail]" and "Go 5 steps forwerd." Paolo has played his game several times with his classmates. His final version evolved from the many questions his friends asked while playing.

Notice that in all three cases, children were refining the format or organization of their games, practicing skills in context, and collaborating with peers. Child-constructed games provide children with the opportunity to construct and use rules in relevant ways, to see others' points of view, and to figure things out autonomously or cooperatively.

*Three invented games.*

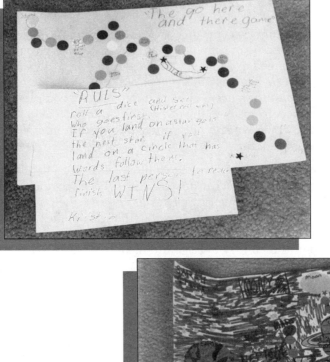

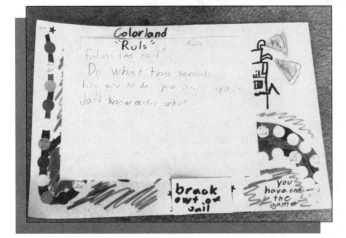

## *Making Games with Children*

The following guidelines will help you include game making your curriculum.

1.  *Find information and collect facts.* Before making a game, the children need to determine what information they need. If children are studying environmental issues, for example, this is a good time to review the content learned during the unit and clarify what they still want to know. This is also the time for children to gather books and other informational resources to verify facts.

2.  *Make a rough draft.* As in the writing process, making a rough draft of the gameboard, cards, content, and accessories frees children to plan. It provides an organizational framework for thinking and working together for a common outcome.

3.  *Make the game.* Have a variety of free and inexpensive materials available, such as file folders, poster board of all sizes and colors, beans, markers, sticky dots, labels, plastic bread ties, old magazines, calendar numbers, and assorted plastic bottle caps. Expect children to decide the type of game to make (board, card, motor) and invent it. Their games will usually look like games that are familiar to them, yet the content and the play of the game will vary.

4.  *Play the game.* Playing the games helps children notice problems and pitfalls. Children "go back to the drawing board" willingly to produce a playable game.

5.  *Revise the game to achieve more accuracy.* Revision means literally "to see again." As children revise their games, they resee and rethink them until they achieve excellence in the finished product. Because there is no correct way to make games, they provide multiple opportunities for creative expression, constructive conflict resolution, and practice in self-evaluation. By observing, recording, and comparing children's own progress with invented games throughout the year, teachers have a powerful learning, teaching, and assessment tool that appeals to children of all ages (Castle, 1990; Castle & Wilson, 1993; Surbeck & Glover, 1992).

## PRACTICAL APPLICATIONS FOR YOUR CLASSROOM

In every classroom, children from different cultures, children with special needs, and children with diverse abilities need materials that nurture their creative expression. Adapting your curriculum to meet these needs can be accomplished through simple adjustments to the materials (e.g., using large yarn balls with a child with Down syndrome who has very small hands or adding multiethnic figures or multicultural pictures of the children's families into existing interest centers).

## Experiences to Support Cultural and Ethnic Diversity

The materials that children use are powerful vehicles for multicultural education because they are visual representations of others' feelings, behaviors, artifacts, and traditions. Play materials, therefore, should reflect the individuality of children and adults in that setting (Ramsey, 1998). They contribute to children's growing awareness of cultural and ethnic diversity when teachers provide:

- *Interest centers* that reflect not only the cultural backgrounds and customs represented in the classroom but also those of other cultures, such as a celebration of the Chinese New Year, Hanukkah, or Kwanzaa. Dramatic play props, pictures, and dolls should reflect many cultures.
- *Literature* to enrich children's understanding of cultural pluralism, such as *Knots on a Counting Rope* (Martin & Archambault, 1987) or *I Hate English!* (Levine, 1990).
- *Multimedia using pictorial and visual information* to provide children with a frame of reference for learning about other cultures (Barba, 1998). After reading and talking about *Mufaro's Beautiful Daughters* (Steptoe, 1987), one teacher took her class on a trip to Zimbabwe using a self-designed "hypertext" program called "Multicultural Links" (Diamond & Moore, 1995, p. 254) as a major resource. The "journey" included clicking on maps of Africa, the continent of Africa, and the country of Zimbabwe itself. Later, the children explored topics including the country's flag, language, music, climate, and foods (Diamond & Moore, 1995).
- *Quality puzzles, books, songs, games, puppets, and dances* from other cultures or eras, such as tape recordings of music from other cultures for children to hear throughout the day, multicultural instruments such as a rainstick, an ocarina, or a guiro, and puzzles that portray animals and people from around the world.
- *Dark and light colors* for painting and bulletin boards. Refer to darker colors as positively as you refer to lighter colors. Be certain not to call brown "yucky" or "muddy" (Whaley & Swadener, 1990).
- *Art projects* including jewelry making, sand paintings, and ethnic clothing (Henniger, 1995, 1999).

To help children express themselves through materials, all teachers and caregivers need to make children from other cultures feel welcome and safe in their classrooms; cultivate their own intercultural understanding, respect, and tolerance for different social and cultural groups; help children believe in their own worth and abilities; and provide children with many opportunities to use real, concrete, and culturally relevant divergent materials in their play and in their projects.

## Experiences to Support Inclusion

Children with special needs often have a disability that affects how they approach a play situation and what kinds of play they choose. These children require materials that provide opportunities for social, physical, and cognitive interactions.

*Play materials and interest centers can contribute to children's growing awareness of cultural and ethnic diversity.*

They need a variety of materials that span various ranges of difficulty and that present individually appropriate challenges. Most materials that are appropriate for young children are also appropriate for children with disabilities, with some modifications.

*Children with sensory impairments,* for example, need tactile and auditory materials. Tactile maps for exploration, large-type print kits, and braille materials such as a braille menu for the housekeeping area might be welcome additions for these children. Ms. Risseau, a preschool special education teacher, opened a sensory table containing 15 pounds of rice. She noticed that since adding this material as a choice, the children often remained at the rice table for an entire 45-minute block of time.

*Children with communication disabilities* need opportunities to communicate about familiar people, events, and objects. Pretend play and technology offer appropriate contexts for children to communicate with their peers. Often the child who is reluctant to talk to another person directly will use the toy telephone, computer, or puppet to communicate.

Technology is often mentioned as an important resource for children and teachers in inclusive settings. For example, computers are often helpful to *children with attention deficits* by helping them concentrate on the task. Assistive devices give children access to greater social and intellectual participation in classroom experiences, enhance their interactions with peers, and facilitate the learning of particular skills and concepts. Adaptive devices such as touch-sensitive screens, condensed keyboards, or speech synthesizers promote children's abilities to express themselves to one another and to adults (Brett, 1995; Haugland & Wright, 1997).

## Adaptations for Individual Learners

In every early childhood classroom, children need a variety of materials and resources for self-expression. Providing open-ended materials that hold children's fascination, challenge their thinking, and keep them engaged supports meaningful play. Regardless of the ability or interest level of an individual child, children are, first and foremost, children. Infants and toddlers need materials that spark their emerging imaginative play. Preschool and school-age children need materials that capitalize on their unique interests and abilities and foster their sociodramatic play abilities and role-taking abilities. Because of their often exceptional verbal ability, high-achieving preschool children need to use more language play, such as riddles, jokes, and poems, and more logical, rules-oriented games.

Children who are academically talented enjoy using various forms of technology. Playing or inventing computer games that are intellectually demanding or solving advanced problems in mathematics offers children many possibilities to use their gifts. Here are some ways you can differentiate your classroom for academically talented learners. Use:

- *Problem-based learning* in which children gather resources and employ creative thinking to solve problems.
- *Higher-level thinking* during which children explore ideas, test hypotheses, and judge the quality of their solutions.
- *Self-directed learning* that enables children to develop their interest in topics through investigations, learning centers, and contracts.

See Appendix F for additional sources for free and inexpensive classroom play materials.

## CHAPTER SUMMARY

1. Throughout history, children in all cultures have played with materials. The types of play materials available are affected by economic, cultural, and political issues and strongly influence children's self-expression, inventiveness, and divergent thinking.
2. Materials that hold the most promise for creative expression and play have multiple uses, encourage inventiveness and problem solving, and are process-oriented. Playing with these materials fosters children's inventiveness.

3. Children should experience a balance of materials including skill/concept, manipulative, construction, and self-expressive materials and natural and everyday objects.

4. Developmentally appropriate materials, which are real, meaningful, and stimulating to the imagination, should be available to children of all ages. Young children need sensory materials to explore and investigate in dramatic play, art, music, construction, and manipulative play. School-age children also need realistic, rule-oriented materials.

5. Technology materials are one of many learning tools to be used in the creative classroom. They enable children to control their symbolic world, apply new and familiar skills, enhance their social interactions, foster self-directed learning, problem-solve, and connect information to what they know and are studying.

6. Organized games can be a significant aspect of the early childhood curriculum if presented and played appropriately. They can encourage autonomy, decision making, cooperation, and an understanding and use of rules.

7. Teachers should incorporate opportunities for children to invent, teach, and play their own games as part of the curriculum.

8. It is important to nurture creative expression in all children. Using a variety of open-ended materials and activities is one of the best ways for teachers to adapt the curriculum to a wide range of children's abilities, interests, and cultural backgrounds.

## *EXPANDING YOUR THINKING ABOUT PLAY MATERIALS FOR CREATIVE EXPRESSION*

### *Discuss: Perspectives on Play Materials*

1. Select, investigate, and explore a child's play material from the setting in which you are now working. Think about the possible ways children could use it. If you can, observe different children using the same material. Keep a list of your ideas and the children's uses. Compare your list with those who selected a similar material. How did infants/toddlers, preschoolers/kindergartners, and school-age children use the material?

2. Reread the quotations on page 299. How has your thinking changed since reading this chapter?

3. Incorporating invented games into the curriculum provides children many opportunities for learning. Discuss these opportunities and suggest ways to include them as part of a thematic unit.

4. Why should children use self-expressive materials? List as many types of these materials as you can think of and briefly state a rationale for including each in the curriculum.

5.  Refer to the case study at the beginning of the chapter. Why was it important for the children's teacher to provide these materials? What was her role in this play? Why do you think so?

6.  Observe a child who is introduced to a play material for the first time. Refer back to the discussion of the uses of materials in this chapter and describe his or her behaviors. How do the behaviors fit the progression?

## Interview: Play Materials: A Cross-Cultural Perspective

Throughout history, children in all cultures have played with different kinds of materials. These materials often reflect social, political, and cultural values and provide an important avenue for finding out about others' behaviors (Ramsey, 1998). Given this information, arrange to interview a person whose background is different from yours to discover the types and uses of play materials in his or her childhood years. Ask the following questions and record the responses. You may want to tape-record your interview and transcribe your responses immediately thereafter.

1.  Describe the types of play materials you used as a child. In what ways did they reflect certain values and beliefs in your culture?

2.  Did you have a favorite play material? Could you describe how you used it? Why did you find it satisfying?

3.  In your culture, did boys and girls use similar or different play materials? Could you give me some examples of what materials each preferred?

4.  What kinds of games did you play? Were they mostly indoor or outdoor games? Do you recall ever making up your own games? What were they like?

5.  Do you know what kinds of play materials children from your cultural background use today? Could you elaborate?

## Write to Learn: Responding to Parents' Concerns about Play and Creativity

You are a teacher who believes in nurturing creative expression and play in all young children. However, a group of parents has complained to your principal and to other parents that "there is too much creativity in your room." Write down your thoughts about this allegation. Explore the significance of creative expression through materials and resources, why you use divergent materials, and how they support children's learning and development. Share your writing in a small group and record the group's collective responses on a chart to report them to the whole class.

## REFERENCES

Barba, R. H. (1998). *Science in the multicultural classroom* (2nd ed.). Boston: Allyn & Bacon.

Barbour, N., Drosdeck, S., & Webster, T. (1987). Sand: A resource for the language arts. *Young Children, 42*(2), 20–25.

Bredekamp, S., & Copple, C. (Eds.). (1997). *Developmentally appropriate practice in the early childhood programs* (Rev. ed.). Washington, DC: National Association for the Education of Young Children.

Brett, A. (1995). Technology in inclusive early childhood settings. *Day Care and Early Education, 22*(3), 8–11.

Bronson, M. (1995). *The right stuff for children birth to 8: Selecting play materials to support development.* Washington, DC: National Association for the Education of Young Children.

Buckleitner, W. (1999, October/November). Making math click. *Scholastic Parent and Child,* pp. 17–18.

Castle, K. (1990). Children's invented games. *Childhood Education, 67*(2), 82–85.

Castle, K., & Wilson, E. (1993). Creativity through children's invented games. In M. Guddemi & T. Jambor (Eds.), *A right to play: Proceedings of the American Affiliate of the International Association for the Child's Right to Play* (pp. 87–90). Little Rock, AK: Southern Early Childhood Association.

Davidson, J., & Wright, J. (1994). The potential of the microcomputer in the early childhood classroom. In J. Wright & D. Shade (Eds.), *Young children: Active learners in a technological age.* (pp. 77–92). Washington, DC: National Association for the Education of Young Children.

DeVries, R. (1998). Games with rules. In D. P. Fromberg & D. M. Bergen (Eds.), *Play from birth to twelve and beyond: Contexts, perspectives, and meanings* (pp. 409–415). New York: Garland.

DeVries, R., & Fernie, D. (1990). Stages in children's play of Tic Tac Toe. *Journal of Research in Childhood Education, 4*(2), 98–111.

Diamond, B. J., & Moore, M. A. (1995*). Multicultural literacy: Mirroring the reality in the classroom.* New York: Longman.

Drew, W. F. (1995). Recycled materials: Tools for creative thinking. *Scholastic Early Childhood Today, 9*(5), 36–43.

Gestwicki, C. (1999). *Developmentally appropriate practice: Curriculum development in early childhood* (2nd ed.). Albany, NY: Delmar.

Goldhaber, J. (1992). Sticky to dry, red to purple: Exploring transformation with play dough. *Young Children, 48*(1), 26–28.

Haugland, S. (1999). The newest software that meets the developmental needs of young children. *Early Childhood Education Journal, 26*(4), 245–254.

Haugland, S., & Wright, J. (1997). *Young children and technology: A world of discovery.* Needham Heights, MA: Allyn & Bacon.

Hendrick, J. (1996). *The whole child* (6th ed.). Upper Saddle River, NJ: Merrill/Prentice Hall.

Henniger, M. (1995). Supporting multicultural awareness at learning centers. *Dimensions, 23*(4), 20–23.

Henniger, M. (1999). *Teaching young children: An introduction.* Upper Saddle River, NJ: Merrill/Prentice Hall.

Hewitt, K., & Roomet, L. (1979). *Educational toys in America: 1800 to the present.* Burlington, VT: The Robert Hall Fleming Museum/University of Vermont.

Hirsch, E. (Ed.). (1996). *The block book* (3rd ed.). Washington, DC: National Association for the Education of Young Children.

Hughes, F. P. (1999). *Children, play, and development* (3rd ed.). Boston: Allyn & Bacon.

Isenberg, J. P. (1995). Whole language in play and the expressive arts. In S. C. Raines (Ed.), *Whole language across the curriculum: Grades 1, 2, 3* (pp. 114–136). New York: Teachers College Press.

Isenberg, J. P., & Rosegrant, T. (1995). Children and technology. In J. Moyer (Ed.), *Selecting education equipment and materials for school and home* (pp. 25–29). Wheaton, MD: Association for Childhood Education International.

Jalongo, M. R., & Stamp, L. N. (1997). *The arts in children's lives: Aesthetic experiences in early childhood.* Boston: Allyn & Bacon.

Johnson, J. E., Christie, J. F., & Yawkey, T. D. (1999). *Play and early childhood development.* New York: Longman.

Kamii, C., & DeVries, R. (1980). *Group games in early education: Implications of Piaget's theory.* Washington, DC: National Association for the Education of Young Children.

Levin, D. (1999, November). Rethinking children's play: Changing times, changing needs, changing responses. *National PTA Magazine,* pp. 8–11.

McKee, J. S. (1986). Play materials and activities for children birth to ten years: People, play, props and purposeful development. In J. S. McKee (Ed.), *Play: Working partner of growth* (pp. 47–61). Wheaton, MD: Association for Childhood Education International.

Mergen, B. (1982). *Play and playthings: A reference guide.* Westport, CT: Greenwood Press.

Monighan-Nourot, P. (1990). The legacy of play in American early childhood education. In E. Klugman & S. Smilansky (Eds.), *Children's play and learning: Perspectives and policy implications* (pp. 59–85). New York: Teachers College Press.

Moyer, J. (Ed.). (1995). *Selecting educational equipment and materials for school and home.* Wheaton, MD: Association for Childhood Education International.

National Association for the Education of Young Children. (1996). Position statement: Technology and young children—ages three through eight. *Young Children, 5*(6), 11–16.

Ramsey, P. (1998). Diversity and play: Influences of race, culture, class, and gender. In D. P. Fromberg & D. M. Bergen (Eds.), *Play from birth to twelve and beyond: Contexts, perspectives, and meanings* (pp. 23–34). New York: Garland.

Rivkin, M. S. (1995). *The great outdoors: Restoring children's right to play outside.* Washington, DC: National Association for the Education of Young Children.

Shade, D. D. (1995). Storyboard software: Flannel boards in the computer age. *Day Care and Early Education, 22*(3), 45–46.

Sobel, J. (1983). *Everybody wins: Non-competitive games for young children.* New York: Walker and Company.

Stroud, J. (1995). Block play: Building a foundation for literacy. *Early Childhood Education Journal, 23*(1), 9–13.

Surbeck, E., & Glover, M. (1992). Seal revenge: Ecology games invented by children. *Childhood Education, 69*(3), 275–280.

Whaley, K., & Swadener, E. B. (1990). Multicultural education in infant and toddler settings. *Childhood Education, 66*(4), 238–240.

Wright, F. L. (1932). *An autobiography.* New York: Longman.
Yelland, N. (1999). Technology as play. *Early Childhood Education Journal, 26*(4), 217–220.
Yinger, J., & Blaszka, S. (1995). A year of journaling—A year of building with young children. *Young Children, 51*(1), 15–20.

## CHILDREN'S BOOKS CITED

Degen, B. (1983). *Jamberry.* New York: Harper & Row.
Gwynne, F. (1970). *The king who rained.* New York: Simon and Schuster.
Levine, E. (1990). *I hate English!* New York: Scholastic.
Martin, B., Jr., & Archambault, J. (1987). *Knots on a counting rope.* New York: Holt.
Steptoe, J. (1987). *Mufaro's beautiful daughters.* New York: Lothrop, Lee & Shephard.
Tarfuri, N. (1988). *Junglewalk.* New York: Greenwillow.

## CHILDREN'S SOFTWARE CITED

*Bailey's Book House.* (1993). Redmond, WA: Edmark.
*Blue's Clues 1 2 3 Time Activities.* (1999). Woodinville, WA: Humongous Entertainment.
*Color Me.* (1988). Northbrook, IL: Mindscape.
*Crayola Art Studio.* (1994). Richardson, TX: MicroGrafx.
*Delta Draw.* (1988). Cambridge, MA: Spinnaker.
*Explore-a-Story: Where Did My Toothbrush Go?* (1987). Lexington, MA: Heath.
*Facemaker.* (1986). Cambridge, MA: Spinnaker.
*Fantastic Animals: Mix-Up Puzzler.* (1990). New York: Bantam 500.
*I Can Be a Dino Finder.* (1999). Carson, CA: Educational Insights.
*I Spy.* (1997). New York: Scholastic New Media.
*Kid Desk! Internet Safe.* (1999). Redmond, WA: Edmark.
*Kid Pix2.* (1994). Novato: CA: Broderbund.
*KidWorks 2.* (1992). Torrence, CA: Davidson & Associates.
*Millie and Bailey Preschool.* (1997). Redmond, WA: Edmark.
*Millie's Math House.* (1993). Redmond, WA: Edmark.
*Reader Rabbit 1.* (1989). Fremont, CA: The Learning Company.
*Richard Scarry's How Things Work in Busytown.* (1990). Menlo Park, CA: Paramount.
*SimCity 2000.* (1994). Walnut Creek, CA: Maxis.
*Skid Doodle.* (1997). Eden Prairie, MN: KB Gear Interactive.
*Storybook Weaver.* (1992). Minneapolis, MN: MECC.
*Thinkin' Things.* (1993). Redmond, WA: Edmark.
*Thinkin' Things Collection 2.* (1994). Redmond, WA: Edmark.
*Wiggins in Storyland.* (1994). Fremont, CA: Media Vision.

## WEB SITES

*http://www.exploratorium.edu*
Hands-on exhibits devoted to inquiry-based teaching and learning.
*http://www.gateway.org*
Provides the key to one-stop, any-stop access to lesson plans, curriculum units, and other education resources.
*http://www.puzzlemaker.com*
Allows user to create puzzles and games for newsletters, flyers, handouts, or classroom assignments.

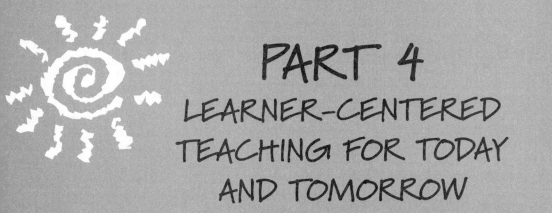

# PART 4
# LEARNER-CENTERED TEACHING FOR TODAY AND TOMORROW

# Chapter 8

## Guiding Young Children's Creative Expression and Communicating with Families

*"Quality in early childhood programs is, in large part, a function of the interactions that take place between the adults and the children in those programs. How teachers interact with children is at the very heart of early childhood."*

Susan Kontos and Amanda Wilcox-Herzog, 1997, p. 11

*"Too often, we assume that children only have the 'usual' school pressures of academic achievement, peer acceptance, and rule adherence. We assure ourselves that home is home and school is school, yet children bring home to school as easily as they tote their backpacks and lunches."*

Charlotte M. Krall and Mary Renck Jalongo, 1998/1999, p. 83

# TEACHERS' REFLECTIONS ON GUIDING CREATIVE EXPRESSION

### Preservice Teachers

"I never really thought about working together with parents as partners to co-educate children. By observing the many ways my cooperating teacher communicated with families about the way children approached their learning, I am beginning to understand their needs. I now own a poster of Albert Einstein with his quote, 'Creativity is more important than knowledge,' that I plan to hang in my own classroom as one way to send this message to families."

"I never realized there were methods for encouraging creative thinking! I saw in my student teaching classroom the effects of these strategies. In my culminating unit activity, the first graders in my classroom worked in cooperative groups to produce creative works of art, music, and drama to represent what they learned about different shelters."

"I have called parents of each of my third-grade students at least two times during my student teaching just to tell them something wonderful about their child's creative thinking. Parents seem to like this approach. Several have said that no teacher had ever called them just to say something special. One parent of a child who is challenging me has been so pleased with the conversation that she said I was doing a 'good job.'"

### Inservice Teachers

"As a Preschool Home Resource Teacher, I am now reexamining my communication with families. Sharing information about the child's creative expression has not been a common practice of mine. Now I am searching for new ways to strengthen my partnership with families by providing them with ways to become involved in their children's play and creative growth."

"This semester I have become increasingly aware of the important role of the teacher in supporting children's creative expression and how to guide parents in their understanding of play and creativity, in general. I have started to use home-school journals with my preschool parents as a place to share examples of divergent thinking, problem solving, and imagination instead of reporting on behavior and achievement. Parents are responding with such positive statements as 'I am looking at my child in a whole new way!'

"Our school just completed a museum-in-progress project, which involved the support of many parents. One teacher who was very wedded to textbooks before undertaking this project told our principal that she wasn't sure she'd ever be able to go back to 'textbook only' teaching. Her comment not only indicates that the children showed her that they really 'learn by doing research for projects' but also shows that the teacher is getting more comfortable with children learning through projects."

### Your Reflections

- What do think are some ways to support children's divergent thinking and problem-solving ability?

- How do you think a creative teacher would manage his or her early childhood setting?

- What new awareness about creative expression comes to mind for you after reading these teachers' reflections?

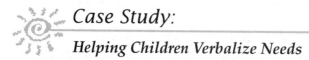

## Case Study:

### *Helping Children Verbalize Needs*

It is center time in Ms. Manning's first-grade classroom. David and Ahmad are making puppets so that they can dramatize their original stories about farm animals. When their puppets are finished, they begin tugging on each other and wrestling with their puppets. The boys become increasingly boisterous, so Ms. Manning comes over and says:

> Pardon me, David and Ahmad. Please talk with me over here. (She goes to a quiet corner, kneels down, and talks to them at their eye level.) What was in your story that made you pull on each other so roughly? (She listens intently to their responses.)
>
> **Ahmad:**   Playing pigs and robbers. The robbers were getting my pigs and we needed to catch them to get our pigs back. (David nods in agreement.)
>
> **Ms. Manning:**   David, tell me in your own words about what you were doing.
>
> **David:**   Playing pigs and robbers. But I was done with the game and didn't want to be the robber anymore, and Ahmad kept pulling on me.
>
> **Ms. Manning:**   You were done playing with your puppets for your story. Do you think when you're playing like that, when you might be wrestling or pulling, that you need to tell each other when you stop playing? (David nods.) David, did you tell Ahmad when you wanted to stop? (Shakes head no.) Look at my eyes, David. How will Ahmad know that you want to stop the game if you don't tell him? You know, next time you could say in your own words, "Ahmad, I don't want to play this game anymore." (David looks down and shakes his head.) When you leave the game, tell the person you're playing with so they know. All right? Let's go back to finishing your puppet stories about the farm animals. (All three get up and leave.)

In this scenario, Ms. Manning is guiding the behavior of two first-grade boys. She knows that David has difficulty verbalizing his needs and that conflict with peers often results. She uses this incident to talk about the need to communicate wishes ("David, did you tell Ahmad when you wanted to stop?"), model how to communicate that need ("You know, next time you could say in your own words, 'Ahmad, I don't want to play this game anymore.' "), and expresses confidence in David's ability to take charge of his own behavior (When you leave the game, tell the person you're playing with so they know. All right?"). Her appropriate guidance techniques reveal her underlying belief that children can guide their own behavior and become fully functioning individuals (Rogers, 1961).

Guiding children's creative expression can be accomplished both indirectly and directly. *Indirect guidance* on children's behavior is affected by the strategies teachers use to plan, arrange, and manage the people as well as the classroom space, materials, and schedule. These strategies were explained in detail in Chapters Six and Seven. *Direct guidance* includes the physical, verbal, and affective strategies (Gordon & Browne, 1996; Hildebrand & Hearron, 1999; Marion, 1999) teachers use to shape children's behavior and ways of thinking. This chapter explores the important role of creative growth in preparing children with real-life skills.

## THEORETICAL AND RESEARCH BASE: GUIDANCE IN EARLY CHILDHOOD SETTINGS

There are three major developmental theories that teachers use to guide children's creative expression: constructivism, humanism, and behaviorism-social learning theory. Each perspective provides a way for adults to understand how and why children think, act, and learn as they do as well as ways to respond to children's needs for appropriate guidance of their creative expression.

## *Constructivism*

Constructivists, like Piaget (1952) and Vygotsky (1976), view children as active agents in their own development. They study the mental process of creativity (that is, how children think about their world, other people, and how to behave), and are interested primarily in how children come to understand their world and solve problems they face (Papalia, Olds, & Feldman, 1999). Constructivists assume that:

- Creative growth refers to *concept building and problem solving,* which are dependent upon a child's level of cognitive development.
- Children are doers—they actively construct or build understandings of their world.
- Children think differently from adults and gradually come to understand the viewpoints of others.

For constructivists, developmentally appropriate child guidance would include the following, appropriate adult-child interactions.

- Adapting to children's different ways of working together and solving problems.
- Providing many opportunities to communicate thoughts and feelings.
- Facilitating and supporting children's investigations and experimentation with tasks and materials.
- Providing a respectful, comfortable, and accepting environment that has clear, consistent, and fair limits for all children.
- Understanding that children's emotions provide the motivation for learning.
- Facilitating the development of self-control (Bredekamp & Copple, 1997; Hyson & Christiansen, 1997).

Using constructivist theory to guide children's creative expression is most effective when the adults working with children understand their social and intellectual development, encourage children's interaction with others to increase their perspective-taking and social interaction skills, and probe children's thinking and reasoning about ideas.

## Humanism

Humanists such as Carl Rogers and Abraham Maslow believe people are capable of controlling their lives if their basic needs are met. They do this positively through choice, creativity, and self-realization (Papalia, Olds, & Feldman, 1999). Thus, how children feel about themselves strongly influences their ability to be cooperative, curious, and creative learners.

From a Rogerian perspective, human beings strive to become fully functioning individuals. Such an individual possesses four characteristics:

- Positive self-regard.
- Awareness of personal feelings and those of others.
- Acceptance of responsibility for decisions.
- Ability to solve problems (Rogers, 1961).

Children who interact with supportive, accepting adults learn to view themselves as competent and worthwhile. In contrast, children who are deprived of accepting, supportive adults do not develop such feelings and often seek approval in inappropriate ways. When teachers and caregivers draw upon Rogerian traditions, they foster children's creative growth by allowing them to think about and investigate problems, by encouraging them to express a range of feelings and emotions, and by accepting a range of solutions to problems.

Supportive, accepting, resourceful teachers facilitate children's investigative capacity. They help children talk about feelings, especially during conflicts, and guide them toward self-regulation.

## Behaviorism and Social-Learning Theory

Behaviorists view the environment as the single most important variable in shaping development. They are concerned with observable, measurable behaviors. From this perspective, children react to the forces in their environment. Consequently, behaviorist theory does not address feelings or emotional states. Behaviorists assume that:

- All behavior is learned. Learned behavior, shaped by external influences, causes development through the rewarding and recognition of observable behaviors.
- All children gradually learn how to respond to environmental influences regardless of age and developmental level.
- Adults in the environment are the major catalysts in changing or shaping children's behavior (Papalia, Olds, & Feldman, 1999).

The behavioral perspective has provided the foundation for the extensive use of behavior modification programs currently used in educational settings. The danger, of course, is that overreliance on these intrusive methods may make children more dependent upon adults to resolve problems. For example, using time-out repeatedly to allow children to regain control often does not achieve the desired behavior. Rather, children perceive it as an opportunity to gain additional attention.

Social-learning theorists view social interaction as the major influence on learning and development. Rather than relying on reinforcement to influence children's growth and behavior, social-learning theorists hold that children learn socially appropriate behavior *by observing and imitating models* in their world (Papalia, Olds, & Feldman, 1999). In this way, children are learning by example—a powerful teaching and parenting tool because children typically imitate role models in their world.

## An Eclectic Approach

Most early childhood educators rely on the assumptions and practices of several theoretical perspectives for guidance techniques, including Howard Gardner's view of multiple intelligences described in detail in Chapter One. In other words, our philosophy of child guidance tends to be eclectic. The child's characteristics, the adults' values and background, and the social context affect your decision about which strategy to use.

To understand how an eclectic philosophy operates, picture two scenarios. Mr. Keller is a substitute teacher who discovered that Lisa, a child in his class for the day, had Tourette's syndrome. Some symptoms of this poorly understood medical condition are tics, repeated tongue clicking, eye blinking, and uncontrollable verbal outbursts. Experts liken the uncontrollable nature of Tourette's syndrome to the involuntary response of sneezing; we can feel a sneeze coming on and can sometimes suppress it, but it is involuntary. Lisa suddenly shouted out in class, "Everybody, pick your nose!" Mr. Keller adopted a very humanistic and social-learning view of Lisa's behavior and did not reprimand her because he knew that this disruptive behavior was out of Lisa's control. He also adopted a constructivist stance by providing Lisa with other opportunities to express her ideas and feelings.

Ms. Olson taught a class of 4-year-olds and was challenged by Yvonne's consistently behaving aggressively when she didn't get her own way. Ms. Olson had been patiently but unsuccessfully trying to help Yvonne use words to express what she wanted. Yvonne was building a trailer in the block center and needed a large, hollow block for a door. When she grabbed one from Joseph, he took it back. She then hit Joseph with a different block, drawing blood from an area near his eye. After Ms. Olson removed Yvonne from the block area, she decided to start her on a behavior modification plan to obtain the desired behavior. She adopted a behavioral perspective to match Yvonne's needs.

Teachers often underestimate the influence of their own upbringing and value system on child guidance. Is the child who takes "silverware" from the housekeeping area to use it with the clay breaking the rules or being resourceful? To a considerable extent, our orientations derive from our experiences. We need to be aware of how the social context often determines the child guidance strategy we select.

# Research on Guiding Children's Creative Growth

Birch, S. H., & Ladd, G. W. (1998). Children's interpersonal behaviors and the teacher-child relationship. *Developmental Psychology, 34*(5), 934–946.

Broadhead, P. (1997). Promoting sociability and cooperation in nursery settings. *British Educational Research Journal, 23*(4), 513–531.

Burton, R., & Denham, S. (1998). "Are you my friend?" How two young children learned to get along with others. *Journal of Research in Childhood Education,12*(2), 210–224.

Kohn, A. (1996). *Beyond discipline: From compliance to community.* Alexandria, VA: Association for Supervision and Curriculum Development.

Porter, L. (1999) Discipline in early childhood. In L. Berk (Ed.), *Landscapes of development: An anthology of readings* (pp. 295–308). Belmont, CA: Wadsworth.

## Web Sites and Internet Addresses to Share with Families

*http://familyeducation.com*

Provides tips and resources for parenting by age level. Offers tips for special needs children.

*www.lekotek.com*

An organization for parents of children with disabilities that provides toys for children with disabilities. Lekotek has sites around the country to which parents can bring children and from which they can check out suitable toys and materials.

*www.drtoy.com*

Provides information on recommended toys and educational products and resources for children.

*www.parentcity.com*

A father-friendly Web site.

*www.families-first.org*

Provides a calendar of events and programs for parents in the Boston area.

*www.singlerose.com*

A Web site for single mothers.

*www.Ericps.ed.uiuc.edu/npin*

National Parent Information Network Web site.

*http://www.ed.gov/Family/agbts*

The U.S. Department of Education's Web site for the America Goes Back to School program. It contains tips for parents, teachers, employers, community leaders, and students about what will help children learn.

As teachers and caregivers, we must avoid dealing with all children in exactly the same way. Each child brings a rich history of experiences, cultural backgrounds, and personality traits to the classroom. Consequently, we must be as flexible as possible in guiding their creative expression.

Like an artist who selects particular paints, colors, and paper to convey an idea or image, teachers and caregivers must select the most appropriate approach and strategies to guide each child. The more educators understand the different child guidance perspectives, and their own beliefs and values about creative expression, the more able they will be to respond appropriately to children's creative ideas and behaviors. Table 8.1 presents three theoretical perspectives that affect child guidance and provides examples of each. Consider which ones reflect your current views of creative expression.

There is a growing research base that supports the importance of nurturing children's creative expression. Perhaps more than anything else, all children want to be competent learners. The research studies listed in the boxed feature will help you guide children's creative growth.

## YOUR ROLE IN GUIDING CREATIVE BEHAVIOR

Consider the different responses of these second graders to their teachers' challenge of using a blank piece of corrugated cardboard to make something. Each teacher gave the children an 8 1/2 × 11 inch piece of corrugated cardboard, asked them to think of any way to use it, design a creation, and then share how they made it. Becky quickly saw the possibility of folding the cardboard and making it into a bird feeder. She then decorated it with birds, flowers, and seeds. Sam looked longingly and sadly at the blank cardboard with tears welling up in his eyes. When his teacher asked him what the problem was, he said, "I can't do this. I don't know what you want me to make." He refused to think of any way to use the cardboard. Andrea hastily folded her piece of cardboard into a "crayon box," but after a few unsuccessful attempts to figure out how to get it to stay closed, she left the project unfinished on the table.

Clearly, children respond to creative tasks in different ways. The adult's response exerts a major influence on the way children express creative behavior. A teacher or caregiver that tells Sam "You're just not trying hard enough. Put on your thinking cap" may be providing choices and freedom, but without support. Teachers who are warm, accepting, and supportive guide children's positive creative expression. A sensitive teacher realizes that Andrea needs encouragement and recognition of her efforts to persist at a task. She might encourage Andrea with a statement such as "I like your idea of a crayon box. I wonder if this stapler would help you close those edges." On the other hand, teachers and caregivers who are not accepting or supportive make it difficult for children to develop a creative, problem-solving approach to ideas and tasks.

**TABLE 8.1  Theoretical Perspectives on Child Guidance**

| Theory | Behavioral Outcome | Teacher Role | Strategies |
|---|---|---|---|
| Behaviorism and Social Learning | Increase desired behavior. | • Direct the process. | • **Provide a cue:** Remind child before expected behavior (e.g., "Johnny, see if you can find your mailbox for your painting.")<br>• **Ignore the behavior:** Do not acknowledge minor behavioral infractions (e.g., ignore child in circle who dominates others' conversations).<br>• **Model appropriate behavior:** Demonstrate how to ask for a toy or to gain entry into an ongoing play situation. |
| Humanism | Develop a strong self-concept, which is the child's image of himself or herself. This image determines how we feel about ourselves and guides our actions. | • Guide children's ability to control and direct their own behavior. | • **Own the problem:** If the problem is an adult's, communicate that to the child with language such as, "I have a problem, and I need your help." If the problem is the child's problem, communicate that through messages such as, "It seems as though there is a problem here, do you need my help?"<br>• **Listen actively:** Listen to the message the child is conveying. Do not interrupt the child or make a judgment.<br>• **Use I-Messages:** Name the behavior causing the problem and tell the child how you feel, such as "I feel angry when I see you grab the block from Johnny." |
| Constructivism | Enable children to understand and gain control of their world through development of problem-solving abilities and conceptual understanding. | Facilitate and guide children's investigations with materials and with one another. | • **Provide opportunities to learn:** Provide infants and toddlers with many sensory opportunities and respond to their verbal and nonverbal actions. Have age-appropriate expectations.<br>• **Set clear and appropriate limits:** Focus the child's attention and give only one or two suggestions at a time. Limits should be predictable.<br>• **Redirect behavior:** Provide new options, introduce a new material or idea or limit choices, if necessary.<br>• **Take social conflicts seriously:** Be at eye level while listening to children; empathize with all children involved in the conflict.<br>• **Encourage problem-solving through dramatic play:** Use circle or meeting times for children to tell their versions of the problem to solve, talk about appropriate behaviors, and suggest alternative solutions. |

*Sources:* Adapted from Marion (1999), Papalia, Olds, & Feldman (1999), and Schreiber (1999).

## Styles of Adult-Child Interactions

There are three basic styles of adult-child interactions—autocratic, permissive, and democratic (Baumrind, 1967, 1993; Papalia, Olds, & Feldman, 1999). Each refers to how *demanding or responsive* teachers and caregivers are with children; each also cultivates typical behaviors and mind-sets to problem solving.

### Autocratic Interactions

**Autocratic** adults demand children's obedience to an inflexible set of rules and standards. The autocratic teacher:

- Maintains stern and formal interactions with students.
- Devalues adult-child verbal interactions in which there are disagreements.
- Emphasizes a "no-nonsense" classroom environment.
- Discourages individuality or autonomy in children.

When teachers are autocratic, children often become resentful and rebellious. Autocratic methods tend to develop children who have difficulty with peer relations, lack initiative, and tend to be anxious, withdrawn, and apprehensive. Because the autocratic adult is so controlling, children do not learn self-control; rather, they become dependent on the adults in their lives to control their behavior. For example, when an autocratic teacher leaves the room, children often become unruly and out of control. This behavior is children's way of expressing resentment of controlling interactions.

### Permissive Interactions

**Permissive** adults have an "anything goes" orientation. They place few demands and controls on children's decision making and problem solving in a poorly organized environment with unclear and inconsistent standards for behavior. The permissive teacher:

- Projects a laissez-faire, uninterested attitude.
- Presents an inconsistent, unpredictable environment.
- Fails to set clear, firm limits on behavior.

The methods of permissive teachers tend to create children with little self-control, self-reliance, or exploratory or investigative behavior. Because the standards for behavior are so inconsistent and the environment is so unpredictable, children cannot anticipate that their rights will be protected, or even clearly determine what their rights are.

### Democratic Interactions

**Democratic** adults believe that children need firm but reasonable limits for behavior as well as opportunities for choice, verbal negotiation, and decision making. The democratic teacher:

- Exhibits confidence in his or her ability to guide children.
- Understands child development, limits, and potentials.

- Really listens to children, and respects their ideas and opinions.
- Has high expectations for all children.
- Responds to children's initiatives and suggestions.
- Prepares the environment with choices, age-appropriate activities and materials, and plenty of time for interaction.
- Expects students to be responsible for the consequences of their decisions.

Children who live and work with democratic teachers appear to feel secure, know what is expected of them, and are self-sufficient, self-controlled, and self-assertive. They also tend to be "self-starters" who are capable of initiating and completing projects independent of adults. Democratic teachers and caregivers do more than cover material—they develop concepts and problem-solving skills in children by engaging students actively in learning and empowering students to accept responsibility for their own learning and actions. Democratic teachers embody the principles held by teachers in Reggio Emilia—that teachers facilitate children's creative interpretations of their worlds and that children are competent decision makers about what they want to learn (New, 1993).

Teachers and caregivers can look to guidelines from Reggio Emilia schools (Malaguzzi, 1993), the National Association for the Education of Young Children (Bredekamp & Copple, 1997), and the Northeast Foundation for Children (Charney, 1991) to foster children's creative expression. These guidelines provide teachers with a framework to use in encouraging children to unlock their creative potential,

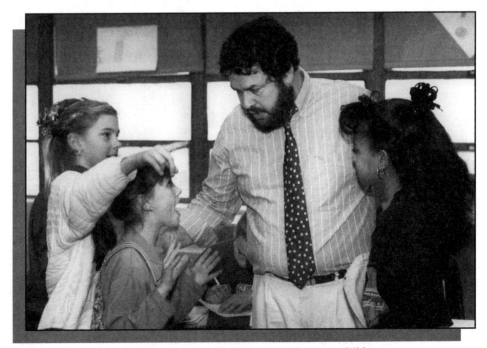

*Democratic teachers and caregivers really listen to and respect children.*

to investigate their worlds through a variety of paths, and to promote their ability to communicate in multiple forms. They also make clear that the teacher's role is one of support, acceptance, and promotion of desirable behavior through prevention, redirection, and collaboration (Bredekamp & Copple, 1997). Figure 8.1 lists several guidelines for creative expression.

Although early childhood educators have long believed in nurturing children's creative expression, many of these ideas have recently been revisited through the philosophy and values of the schools of Reggio Emilia (Edwards, Gandini, & Forman, 1993). Creative teachers guide children's expression through their active engagement in a variety of real, firsthand learning experiences, such as enactments, projects and thematic units, field trips, and community resources. They also use developmentally appropriate guidance techniques to foster children's creative expression.

## DEVELOPMENTALLY APPROPRIATE GUIDANCE

Three-year-old Hans is confined to a wheelchair, but he wants to participate in a movement activity. Justine suggests that he can be the engine when the group sings "Little Red Caboose." Five-year-old Sandy is trying to make her picture "look snowy" after the first snowfall. After listening to Sandy and realizing that it is the blanket of glistening snow that Sandy wants to re-create, Ralph remembers that they used a mixture of soap flakes, water, and silver glitter in his Sunday school class. He asks the teacher if they can try the recipe at after-school care, too. Seven-year-old Monica helps Jeffrey rig a pulley system to send messages across the room. Later, Jeffrey sends a note to Monica: It reads: "Thank you to Monica. Your friend, Jeff."

These children are all engaged in prosocial behavior—spontaneously sharing with or helping another. Prosocial behavior develops in children who live and work in supportive environments where adults model cooperative, helping behaviors. It is characteristic of children who have a high level of self-esteem, self-control, and emotional understanding. Teachers can facilitate the development of these attributes by positive guidance in the classroom community (Bredekamp & Copple, 1997; Gestwicki, 1999; Hildebrand & Hearron, 1999; Hyson & Christiansen, 1997).

## Fostering Prosocial Behavior

In creative learning environments there is mutual respect among teachers, caregivers, and children. When children see adult models of prosocial behavior, they develop cooperative, helping, and self-responsible behaviors themselves (Charney, 1991; Marion, 1999; Papalia, Olds, & Feldman, 1999).

Picture the following scenario in Ms. Payne's class of 4-year-olds. After a few days of playing in the camping center, Ms. Payne introduced the idea of fishing. She added a pup tent, a blue paper lake, and a small grill filled with crumpled

All children need adults' respect and acceptance to nurture their self-esteem. Teachers who care for them need a variety of options to meet their needs. Use these guidelines to promote children's creative growth when and where appropriate.

1. *Use positive guidance techniques,* such as setting clear limits for younger children and helping older children set their own limits, modeling appropriate behavior, and redirecting inappropriate behavior. Positive techniques enable children to imagine and *focus on what to do* rather than on what not to do and prompt children to control or regulate their behavior in age-appropriate ways.

   *Example:* Enlist children in creating and monitoring classroom rules. Introduce and model the "You can't say you can't play" rule (Paley, 1992) so that children know how to ask to join an ongoing play situation and to help children learn positive ways of communicating with one another.

2. *Prepare interesting and challenging activities that promote prosocial behavior and independent thought.* Through projects, investigative play experiences, and divergent materials, children develop positive social skills such as cooperation, negotiation, problem finding, and perseverance.

   *Example:* Children can find out information for a science project, take responsibility for care of part of the room, or choose a topic of study that helps children consciously manage their unpredictable world with new solutions and reflects the conscious beliefs of the teachers and caregivers.

3. *Model care and respect for all people in your setting.* Help children learn positive skills of sharing, cooperating, taking responsibility, showing concern, and demonstrating empathy. Care and respect for one another are created in social settings in which children talk, work, play, and solve problems together.

   *Example:* In block building, children often share ideas in deciding what structure to build and support one another in finding the appropriate places and blocks to build it.

4. *Be a creative teacher.* Creative teachers view themselves as problem solvers, risk takers, and decision makers. They expect children to share responsibility for their own learning, value their ideas, and guide children's inquiry, exploration, and experimentation with materials and ideas. In this way, they act as facilitators and are more likely to create classrooms in which creativity can thrive (Malaguzzi, 1993).

   *Example:* Before you can guide children's creative growth, you need to determine what beliefs and values you bring to your classroom. Remember: negative teachers do *not* exert a positive influence on children's creative growth. Rather, it is the positive, confident teacher who understands and accepts herself or himself who can bring out the best in children.

5. *Help children verbalize their feelings and emotions.* Children's ability to express, understand, and control their emotions and feelings takes a long time to develop. As a result, they need many opportunities to talk about and label their feelings, in order to gain control over them.

   *Example:* When a very shy child like Azra tries to enter ongoing doctor play and is "not allowed in," she sits alone in a corner looking sad and dejected. Teachers can help children like Azra by saying "I know you feel sad about not playing with the others in the housekeeping area. Let's see if they could use a pharmacist to get the sick baby's medicine."

6. *Provide children with opportunities for choices and decisions.* All children should be given some choice about when to work on a particular task, how to determine what happens in their classes, what materials to use for art projects, how to solve their own classroom problems, whether to work alone or with another child, whether to use manipulatives or play in the dramatic play area, or what message to write in a note to a sick classmate.

   *Example:* As a group, young children have less experience in making choices, so they need to begin with two or three alternatives so that they are not overwhelmed by the possibilities. The range of choices can be increased as children gain in self-confidence and experience with decision making. This gradual introduction enables students to determine which materials would work best for a particular project.

**Figure 8.1** Guidelines for Creative Growth
*Sources:* Bredekamp & Copple (1997), Hildebrand & Hearron (1999), Malaguzzi (1993), Marion (1999), and Miller (2000).

black and orange paper inside to represent a glowing charcoal fire. She developed the fishing theme by including fishing licenses, some magnetic fishing poles, a bucket, and some paper fish shapes with paper clips attached to the ends. She stimulated the children's interest in the idea by relating that she noticed people fishing nearby, so that the pond was probably well stocked with fish. In the following play text, see if you can identify examples of prosocial behavior in the 4-year-olds (e.g., cooperative, helping, sharing, supportive behaviors). What role did the teacher have in fostering such behavior? Look at the photos on the following page to better understand the children's interactions.

*Katie, Steven, Melanie, and Harold were fishing excitedly at the pond.*

**Katie:**   I need a fish. (Fishing.) Is this real water?
**Ms. Payne:**   No, it is blue paper but we are pretending it is a lake.
**Katie:**   (At the lake.) Got the fish. One, two, three . . .
**Steven:**   I need a fish. That one. (Points to the big one.) I caught a fish for myself. Look how big!
**Harold:**   Here's a fish.
**Katie:**   Pick it up. (Says to Harold) Put it over here. (Points to the bowl.) I caught that one for you.
**Steven:**   (Cutting the fish and eating.) That was good. I need more.
**Katie:**   Hey, all the fish are gone. (Everyone has caught all of the fish.)
**Steven:**   We have to put some back.
**Harold:**   We have to catch them all over again. (They put some of the fish back. Katie catches one and starts to put it back in the water.)
**Steven:**   Don't throw him back!
**Harold:**   We have to put them back after we catch them.
**Ms. Payne:**   (Passes by the camping center and adds ideas about baiting the hook to catch the fish, cleaning the fish before cooking and eating them, and throwing back those that are too small.)
**Katie:**   I am the mother and I am going to cook everything.
**Melanie:**   No, I am the mother. I want to cook.
**Katie:**   No, you can be the grandma and help me cook, but we can have only one mother.
**Melanie:**   Okay. (They both go over to the grill and start to cook fish.)
**Katie:**   Is the grill hot? Why don't we cook the fish on it?
**Melanie:**   Yes. (She puts a plastic tub on it and pretends to cook.)

***Katie:*** *If you put the plastic on there, won't it melt? The grill is real hot. Why not cook the fish right on top of the grill. Then you won't melt the plastic.*
*(Steven and Harold bring some more fish over to the grill for Katie and Melanie.)*
***Katie:*** *(To the fish) Hey, you! Don't burn! Are you done? I need a fork and a cup.*
***Melanie:*** *I'll get one. (Returns with a long stick.) We have to turn the fish with a fork. I think I burned my finger. Ouch! Ouch! (Blows on finger.)*
***Katie:*** *Come over here, Grandma. I can put a bandage on it, and it will make it feel real good. (Pretends to take out some bandages and fix the finger.)*
***Steven:*** *I want pink fish. They taste better.*
***Harold:*** *I have a pink one and I have a big fish.*
***Steven:*** *Can I have the pink one?*

*Harold:*   *I'll give you another one. You can have two and I'll have two.*

*Steven:*   *Okay. Hey, Grandma, where are the fishies? Are they done yet?*

*Melanie:*   *No, I burned them. So, now I have to clean the grill because the fish are burnt on it. (She takes the sponge and pretends to wipe it up.) All clean.*

*Katie:*   *Dinner today will be fish, macaroni, and juice.*

*Harold:*   *Mom, is it okay if we go play ball?*

*Katie:*   *Yes.*

*Harold:*   *We will probably be late for dinner.*

*Steven:*   *(Starts setting up for dinner. Then goes back to fish with Melanie. They fish and put the fish in bowls for dinner.) Mom, can I help you with dinner?*

*Katie:*   *Sure, just give everybody fish. Put two fishies on each plate.*

*Steven:*   *I passed out the fish.*

*(The children all sit down for a fish dinner).*

*Katie:*   *Wait until everyone comes. We don't want to be rude.*

*(Other children come by to join the fish dinner feast.)*

*Is everyone hungry? Boy, I sure am. Melanie, please pass the corn. (Melanie passes the corn.) Harold, do you want some?*

*Harold:*   *No, I want some fish. (Katie passes Harold some fish.)*

*Steven:*   *Pass me a napkin and cup, please. (Harold passes them to him. All the others are eating, passing different containers around, and pretending to eat and drink.)*

While this play scene may seem unimportant to the novice, it is actually rich with examples of creative and prosocial behavior. All of these children are not only drawing upon their experiences, but are also solving problems as they arise, practicing social skills, and using their fantasy and imaginations to engage in friendly interactions. From an experiential perspective, the children have shared a common episode—helping to prepare, cook, and eat food together with family and friends. They used their imaginations as they solved problems—how to cook fish on the grill and what to do when the fish were gone from the lake. They practiced social skills as they negotiated who was to play the mother when both Katie and Melanie wanted the role. And they engaged in friendly fantasy interactions as they caught fish and threw them back in the lake. In this 45-minute play episode, the children were responsible for the contents, roles, and sequence of events. After the play began, Ms. Payne intervened only once with a comment about catching, cleaning, and cooking the fish.

*We rest on mats and listen to a story during quiet time, by a 4-year-old boy.*

Using the above play text and the guidelines for creative growth in Figure 8.1, identify which episodes of the play supported children's prosocial behavior. Cite specific passages from the play text. What was the role of the teacher in this play scene?

Although it is important to recognize and respect positive behaviors in children, teachers must also prepare children to cope with conflicts that inevitably arise. How teachers interact with children in conflict situations largely determines how children will approach problem solving as adults (Beaty, 1995; Hildebrand & Hearron, 1999; Kohn, 1996).

## ❦ UNDERSTANDING CHILDREN'S CONFLICTS

In Ms. Balboa's Head Start classroom, Juanita joins Erik at the play-dough table. Within a few minutes, she rolls out a large, thick pancake shape, and the following dialogue occurs:

> *Juanita:*   *Look at my big thing! (Points to a long, snake-like shape.)*
> *Erik:*   *Oh man! That's big!*
> *Juanita:*   *I'm gonna get it even bigger. (She picks it up and shows Erik the thumbprint on the bottom.) See, on the back, Erik?*
> *Erik:*   *Whoa! (Erik leans on his rolled-out play dough, making a "tummy print." Juanita cuts biscuit shapes with a plastic cup.)*
> *Erik:*   *Hey! I need that cup!*
> *Juanita:*   *NO!*
> *Erik:*   *(In increasingly loud, angry tones) I need that cup! I need it. I need it. I'm gonna make balls and put the balls in it. So, gimme it. Gimme that. Teacher! Juanita won't let me have the cup.*

A dispute over a toy is the number one cause of conflict among preschool children. Without a doubt, conflicts hold significance for the teacher. In fact, children's inappropriate behavior is a major concern of educators, both novice and expert. But what about the children? What causes conflict? What are the consequences of various types of conflict resolution for their social and cognitive development? And what are some guidelines for conflict resolution?

## *Causes of Conflict*

Children's conflicts are a natural part of their lives. Conflict occurs when one person does something to which a second person objects. Underlying reasons for the conflict may be either intentional or unintentional. Whatever the cause, conflict is a powerful tool for creative growth because children must negotiate ideas and actions that lead to some outcome (Beaty, 1995; Kohn, 1996; Malaguzzi, 1993).

Conflicts that dominate various age groups tend to follow a developmental sequence. *Toddlers* tend to have conflicts over possessions or toys because sharing toys and materials is an essential part of group functioning in classrooms (Eisenberg-Berg, Haake, & Bartlett, 1981). *Preschool children's* conflicts continue to focus on play materials but also include struggles over playing roles; gaining access to an ongoing group, space, or number of players allowed in a space and whether the player fits the ongoing play needs by gender, size, or dress (Iseberg & Raines, 1992). For example, a preschool child expects a baby to act in certain ways. When a child does not conform to the role expectations and fails to act like a baby, peer criticism and conflict are often the result.

*Primary grade* children often disagree with their peers over rules for games, initiating interactions, and maintaining relationships (Asher & Hymel, 1981). They tend to be inflexible in thinking about rules and, as a result, often find themselves involved in disputes over them.

Most teachers are anxious to stop conflicts at all costs as soon as they arise or try to prevent them from occurring. Yet, conflict has a positive side. It is a form of interaction that offers children the opportunity to deal with their thoughts and feelings in social situations. Successful conflict resolution helps young children to develop the skills and attitudes needed for group living, to form friendships with peers, and to perceive others' behavior and ways of thinking (Bredekamp & Copple, 1997; Gestwicki, 1999; Isenberg & Raines, 1992). As teachers, we need to guide conflict to enhance children's social and intellectual development.

## Types of Conflicts in the Creative Classroom

Today, early childhood educators are spending as much time helping children learn nonviolent ways of solving problems as they spend on creating other aspects of the learning environment. Whether children are bickering over a plaything or calling one another names, conflicts are a fact of life. How teachers and caregivers face conflict affects the way they model conflict resolution for children. Your own comfort level with conflict, such as how quickly you look for solutions, how sensitive you are to hurt feelings, how much you choose to ignore a problem hoping it will go away, and how willing you are to collaborate to find mutually agreeable solutions, influences greatly how you approach conflict in the classroom (Marion, 1999; Wheeler, 2000). Table 8.2 lists some typical conflicts young children experience, describes those conflicts, and suggests strategies for prevention and intervention.

## Helping Children Resolve Conflicts

The following guidelines will help children resolve conflicts in ways that enrich their creative expression and that are developmentally appropriate. When families are invited to use these guidelines, then children receive the same messages in both home and school.

**1.** *Allow children to work through conflicts on their own, where possible, before intervening.* If teachers and caregivers are to develop children who are responsive to the needs of others, they must design environments that guide children toward caring about and helping others. You might remind older children to "look at the class suggestions about what to do when something is bothering you" or suggest to younger children that they "think about the problem and come back to it in a few minutes." Classrooms that encourage children's cooperative conflict resolution promote children's prosocial understandings (Hildebrand & Hearron, 1999; Isenberg & Raines, 1992; Wheeler, 2000).

**TABLE 8.2   Types of Children's Conflicts**

| Type | Description | Appropriate Strategies |
|---|---|---|
| Possession Disputes | Occur when children argue over ownership of a toy or material. | • Ignore the dispute, deeming it unworthy of your attention.<br>• Ask children to share the material or toy.<br>• Redirect the behavior by suggesting an alternative material or way to use that material.<br>• Discourage the practice of bringing items to school from home that children will not or should not share. |
| Power Struggle Disputes | Occur when children want to be first or force other children to play "their way." | • Suggest different ways of playing the same role or using the same materials for different purposes.<br>• Reassure children they will get a turn and be certain that they do.<br>• Keep track of turn-taking to ensure that every child really does get a turn. |
| Group-Entry Disputes | Occur when children try to join the ongoing play of another group. | • Use the "You can't say you can't play" rule to deal with problems of insiders and outsiders.<br>• Be clear that all children are expected to get along with one another.<br>• Model ways to approach an ongoing group of children already at play. |
| Aggressive Play | Occurs when violent, boisterous, play escalates in intensity and tempers flare and frustration rises. | • Set reasonable limits on play.<br>• Temporarily disband the group and redirect the children to a different activity.<br>• Establish a caring classroom where adults and children demonstrate cooperation, kindness, and respect for others.<br>• Have conversations about what kindness, cooperation, and respect mean and how they show those behaviors in the classroom. |

*Sources:* Adapted from Jalongo & Isenberg (2000), Marion (1999), and Wheeler (2000).

**2.** *Help children find solutions to problems.* Children's actions indicate their understanding of others' behavior. In conflict situations, focus on *what can be done* rather than unraveling the complex *causes* of the dispute. Ask the children questions, such as "What do you think we can do about this problem?" or "What are your ideas of how we can make this work?" Taking action will enable children to resume their activity, and this in itself is reinforcing. Eventually, children learn that making a few concessions can keep their play going instead of bringing it to an abrupt halt.

**3.** *Help children understand the consequences of their behavior* (Beaty, 1995; Dreikurs, 1969; Marion, 1999). Children need to understand the conflict from their own and another's perspective. Very young children do not understand how others feel or think. It is important, therefore, to let each child present his or her perspective on the conflict. Teachers', parents', and caregivers' comments—such as "Sarah is crying now" or "How do you think she feels after you took her doll?"—give children information about the feelings of others. Older children may also need to be reminded of others' feelings in a conflict situation.

**4.** *Encourage children to generate alternative solutions to the conflict* (Hildebrand & Hearron, 1999; Wheeler, 2000). The participants, peers, or adults in the setting may generate a variety of alternative solutions to the conflict. The adult acts as mediator, restating the suggestion for the children involved (e.g., suggesting that a child use words instead of crying when he or she needs a toy or suggesting a role for someone who has been denied access to a play situation).

**5.** *Differentiate between intentional and unintentional behavior.* Young children do not distinguish between intentional and unintentional behavior, but older children do. Teachers may help young children understand behavior by explaining unintentional behavior (e.g., "Selma did not mean to drop your cards, Harriet. It was an accident").

**6.** *Teach specific social skills to children who are aggressive, unpopular, and rejected by their peers.* Unpopular children often suffer peer rejection because they lack the skills for gaining entry into existing play groups, rely overly on adults to solve problems for them, or dominate the entire play scene. Consider, for example, a kindergarten classroom where children have been assigned to small groups to reenact "The Three Little Pigs." Dana takes *total* control. She shoves

*Teachers can help children resolve conflicts in ways that enrich their creative expression.*

the other children around and berates them if they deviate from her planned script. Just as the group is about to perform, a shy child named Rolando, who was completely excluded by Dana's stage-mother presence, says quietly to his teacher, "But *I* was supposed to be the narrator." Dana is desperately in need of guidance. She needs to see that she can experience success in the group without being overbearing. Rolando needs to have his rights protected as well. If the adults in this kindergarten classroom ignore this peer conflict, neither child's social skills will be enhanced.

   **7.** *Use group meetings to discuss how to handle conflicts.* Group meetings provide a powerful opportunity for teaching the social skills needed to manage conflicts positively, because the atmosphere is calm and children are not caught up in the immediacy of the dispute. Role playing, puppets, children's illustrations of their own conflicts, and children's literature dealing with conflict resolution provide rich opportunities for talking about conflicts and discussing ways to resolve them (Charney, 1991; Wheeler, 2000).

   Children's conflicts hold important opportunities for developing positive social interaction skills and creative growth with both peers and adults. In all early childhood settings, there are three strategies that are particularly well suited to fostering children's creative expression.

## STRATEGIES FOR GUIDING CREATIVE EXPRESSION

A major goal of the early childhood curriculum is to enable all children to become divergent thinkers. Strategies designed to meet this goal include cooperative problem-solving groups (Johnson, Johnson, & Holubek, 1990; Tegano, Sawyers, & Moran, 1989; Tudge & Caruso, 1988); investigative play (Wassermann, 1990); and project work (Katz, 1993; Katz & Chard, 1989).

### Problem-Solving Groups

Problem-solving groups involve a shared goal or interest, a difference of opinion, and an active exchange of ideas. In these groups both the child and adult work together to solve issues of concern in ways that emphasize positive interaction and individual responsibility to the group. This kind of group cooperation exposes children to different points of view, enhances their perspective-taking ability, and increases social interaction skills. Problem solving supports divergent thinking abilities, especially for minorities and women (Johnson et al., 1990; Tegano et al., 1989; Tudge & Caruso, 1988).

   All children solve problems regularly through their cooperative play as they decide how to bridge two blocks, fit two children on a swing, or paint a mural together. However, not all problems lead to cooperative problem solving, which depends upon good communication and positive relations in working through is-

**Figure 8.2**
Characteristics of
Good Problems

- Are relevant and interesting to children.
- Involve real or simulated materials and/or people.
- Require the child to modify, move, or transform the materials.
- Elicit many possible solutions.
- Can be solved by the child, yet provide interesting challenges.
- Help the child believe in his or her own problem-solving abilities.
- Encourage children to share differing points of view.
- Occur spontaneously in children's play.
- Occur in open-ended, content-specific, planned activities.

*Sources:* Atkinson and Green (1990), Bredekamp & Copple (1997), Tudge and Caruso (1988), and Wassermann (1990).

sues. Cooperative problem solving is enhanced when there are good problems to solve. Figure 8.2 describes the characteristics of good problems.

*Promoting Cooperative Problem Solving*
Use the following guidelines for problem-solving groups that contribute to children's creative growth and expression.

**1.** *Plan activities with a common goal.* Think about a group of kindergartners who were building a school bus to enact the song "The Wheels on the Bus." Before they began, their teacher encouraged them to discuss their ideas, to agree on how to build the bus, and to decide what to include on it (e.g., steering wheel, seats, horn, driver, steps, a door). Helping children work together on a common goal encourages *cooperative problem solving.*

**2.** *Encourage children's free exchange of ideas.* As part of a unit on environmental responsibility, a second-grade teacher invited children to collect clean, recyclable materials and encouraged the children to use them as they wished. Nothing much came from her suggestion. Later, she decided to try the same activity with small groups. Most children responded more favorably to this activity, because they were able to build upon one another's ideas as well as suggest their own.

**3.** *Help children agree upon common goals.* Preschool and kindergarten children are action-oriented; they do something first and then think. Two 4-year-olds at a water table illustrate this point. They were struggling to pump water from one container to another when the teacher came by and said, "I see. You're trying to get this water over there by using the tubes and funnels." After the teacher had verbalized their common goal for them, the children tested different ways to pour water from container to container using the tubes and funnels. Their play then centered on pumping water through them.

**4.** *Expect all children to participate in problem-solving groups.* Marcus is a third grader who stutters and is reluctant to share his ideas in a large group. Cooperative problem-solving groups provide a less-intimidating setting for Marcus to test his ideas.

**5.** *Provide children with specific roles and responsibilities.* To promote the necessary social, decision-making, and conflict management skills, children need to participate regularly in cooperative learning groups. By designating and rotating group members' roles as leader, recorder, questioner, or reporter, children experience different roles in a group endeavor. Participation in cooperative learning groups is particularly motivating to second-language learners by giving them more face-to-face interactions, enriching their intergroup relations and self-esteem, and improving their communication in both languages (Diamond & Moore, 1995).

All children can engage in problem-solving activities during spontaneous play, planned open-ended activities, or planned activities that are content specific, such as science investigations. Through shared exchanges of ideas, children explore new possibilities together and enhance their thinking.

## *Investigative Play*

Mr. Yoon's first graders are exploring the effect of different formulas on soap bubbles. Five groups of children are experimenting with different solutions of food colorings, liquid detergents, corn syrup, and glycerin. They are also using other materials—straws, lids, a plastic tennis racket, plastic tubing attached to a funnel, and the plastic rings from a six-pack of soda cans—to produce bubbles of various sizes. Mr. Yoon has given them an activity card with the following guidelines:

- Find out everything you can about bubbles.
- What did you observe about the different formulas? Colors?
- What solution made the biggest, strongest bubbles?
- What materials can be used to make many small bubbles? To make one huge bubble?
- Talk about what you noticed.

One group of children added glycerin to see if they could get stronger bubbles. They started with one teaspoon, and then increased to two, three, four, five, and six. Another group tried different ways of making different-sized bubbles. In both groups, there was laughter and interaction. All the children were involved in the tasks, either as investigators or as observers. Mr. Yoon functioned as a facilitator, encouraging and supporting children's investigations with such comments as "I see you are now going to try a new color of bubbles."

This activity illustrates a three-step model for organizing instruction and challenging primary grade children's divergent thinking, called **play-debrief-replay** (Wassermann, 1990). Each step is explained below.

### Play

During play, children investigate and explore materials to make predictions, observe and classify information, and make both individual and collaborative decisions. Investigative play builds children's conceptual understandings about materials and ideas and enables them to examine actively key curriculum concepts such as "Plants are living things" and "The work different people do requires special abilities and talents." In play, teachers set the stage and challenge children's learning, while children control their own learning. Wassermann reports that teachers using this model "feel exhilarated, energized and empowered" (1990, p. 28). Mr. Yoon's first graders were testing hypotheses about the "perfect" soap bubble formula. They were learning about viscosity, pressure, velocity, colors, and light—all basic concepts of physics.

### Debrief

In the second step, investigative play becomes the common base for children's reflections. In either small or large discussion groups following exploratory play, Mr. Yoon asks the children questions that encourage them to reflect upon their experiences, such as "What did you notice about the bubbles?" and "How did you figure that out?" Good questions cause children to think carefully and to add their understandings to others. In the hands of a skillful, knowledgeable teacher, debriefing-play experiences empower children as thinkers, invite new ideas, build self-esteem, and provide the foundation for future play with the new insights about the same concept (Wassermann, 1990).

### Replay

Replay occurs after debriefing. Some replay may involve the same materials; other replay may involve some new materials to move the inquiry along. A teacher might invite children to figure out the best way to transfer a bubble from one person to another without breaking it or ask children to introduce some new ways of blowing into the bubble makers. Replay provides additional practice with the concept or skill and an opportunity to replicate and verify findings. As a result, replay gradually builds children's conceptual understandings. Children's creative expression is enhanced when they can investigate objects, ideas, and events. Investigations encourage children to ask questions, explore ideas, and reflect on their thinking to make learning meaningful and powerful. They allow children to participate with their own learning styles and to begin to assess their own ways of thinking through reflection and debriefing. Play-debrief-replay is an important strategy in long-term classroom projects.

## Project Work

A third powerful strategy for strengthening creative growth is the project approach. According to Katz and Chard (1989) and Allison (2000), a **project** is a focused study of something worth learning about undertaken by one or more children for as long as they remain interested. Projects offer children opportunities to *apply* skills, *choose* what topic to study, *investigate* questions that are personally meaningful, and *revisit* theories. These four characteristics support children's creative expression.

Projects are an important teaching strategy because they foster meaningful learning, demand collaboration, require a range of skills, and can be as long or as short as children wish. In the following description of project activities related to construction, think about the possibilities for children's engagement in learning (Hartman & Eckerty, 1995).

All of the children were at the window watching. They had many questions, including "Why do they dig a hole first?" "What happens next?" and "How do they know what to do?" In response to their questions and expressed interest, Ms. Hartman developed a project on construction. Her fundamental belief that her children were capable of pursuing extended project activities and representing them in many forms led to the following scenario.

Ms. Hartman located several picture books that illustrated basic building principles, including Byron Barton's *Building a House* and Gail Gibbons's *Tool Book*. The class looked at a real blueprint, took a walking tour of the community to look for different building styles, and interviewed an architect. Ms. Hartman also brought in picture postcards of famous buildings and lavishly illustrated books from the library. It turned out that one of the teachers had built a house the previous year and had a set of photographs that documented each building stage.

In this scenario, Ms. Hartman initiated the construction project in response to children's interest and questions. She began with a class discussion about what the children already knew about construction and what they were interested in finding out. Through their investigation of books, their examination of postcards and real materials such as the blueprint, and a walking tour of the community, the children developed their own construction site to build a "class house" from blocks and boxes. Through their project and dramatic play, the children used their math and science skills (e.g., measuring space for the rooms in the house), literacy skills (e.g., making lists of materials needed to build the house), and social studies skills (e.g., exploring the interdependent roles of the architect, builder, and construction worker). They also developed clearer concepts of the complexities of building a house.

Project work can heighten creative growth by:

- Responding to children's questions.
- Fostering children's independent, creative thinking.
- Enabling children to be involved at different levels.
- Providing diverse cognitive challenges so that all children can experience success.
- Utilizing academic skills in relevant, highly motivating contexts.
- Encouraging cooperation to ensure successful completion of the project.
- Providing opportunities to increase knowledge and understandings and interpretations (Abramson, Robinson, & Ankenman, 1995; Allison, 2000; Katz, 1993; Katz & Chard, 1989).

Guidance strategies such as the project approach, investigative play, and problem-solving groups are appropriate for all children. Because they take a holistic approach to teaching and learning, these strategies make learning meaningful by relating what children are learning to what they already know. Keeping children engaged in learning makes further learning possible. In the next section, we present some ideas on communicating concepts about creative expression and play to families.

## COMMUNICATING WITH FAMILIES ABOUT CREATIVE EXPRESSION

Good communication between teachers and families makes a great difference in children's creative expression, self-esteem, aspiration levels, motivation, and view of themselves as learners both in school and out (Berger, 2000; Epstein, 1995; Greenberg, 1989). When parents understand what is going on in your classroom and what is expected of them, they will feel more comfortable with you and how you teach.

One of the challenges early childhood teachers encounter is a changing view of families. For the past two decades, an increasing amount of attention has addressed the important role parents play in their children's learning and development. To best communicate with families, teachers and caregivers must empower families in the mutual education of their children; identify the obstacles to good communication with families; and develop effective, caring strategies for enhancing communication with families.

### Empowering Families in Partnership

Involving families in children's creative growth rests on the belief that parents are the first teachers and socializers of their children. The traditional model of separating home and school in children's education does not and has not worked. As a result, educators need to learn new ways to strengthen family/school connections. This reality has led us to a partnership model in which parents are viewed as equals in children's education. A partnership model helps all children develop their creative potential and success throughout school and beyond.

Three principles should guide early childhood educators in empowering families (Berger, 2000; Epstein, 1995; Hildebrand, Phenice, Gray, & Hines, 1996; Larsen & Haupt, 1997).

**1.** *Seek out the strengths of your children's families to create a "family friendly" setting.* Using the knowledge parents have about their children and their own talents is one way to empower parents in the education of their children at school. In Reggio Emilia schools, teachers expect parents to be involved in their children's education. Teachers respect parents' knowledge about their own children and

*Families and early childhood settings together help achieve the larger goal of providing success for all children.*

continue to learn about the children by means of conferences, celebrations, photographs, and other displays. Discussions about how children represent what they know are important to both families and schools. In American schools, many teachers gain such knowledge by sending home letters inviting parents to share their expertise regarding the creation and development of a new center or project. One kindergarten teacher developed a unit on construction sites after discovering parent experts—a builder, a carpenter, and an electrician—who shared information about construction with the class. Similar expertise can be shared by cooking ethnic foods and sharing special multicultural traditions.

   **2.** *Provide comfortable ways for families to become involved in their children's play and creative expression.* One of the most important elements of supporting families relates to how teachers or caregivers understand the values, customs, and traditions typical of the cultural groups represented in their classroom settings. For example, in settings that serve Asian children, it is important for teachers to know that many Asian parents do not understand how they can become partners in their children's creative expression and play. Sending home brief but frequent notes about children's successes with art, music, or a good problem-solving idea helps parents see what children are learning. A good beginning is to show parents that help at home means encouraging, listening, and sharing children's creative and playful experiences each day. Or ask the parents themselves if you have questions, for they are the best sources of authentic information. This counters the notion that parental involvement only means help in an academic skill (Hildebrand et al., 1996; Lee, 1995).

   **3.** *Encourage a cooperative partnership.* Rather than assuming a role that implies that you know what needs to be done for a child without consulting the family, enlist the family's input in developing opportunities for the child's meaningful learning and thinking. One child-care teacher was receiving "mixed messages" from parents about learning through play. Parents would claim to agree with the school philosophy about learning through play, but would quickly add that they wished there were more academics. This thoughtful teacher decided to use a questionnaire to ask the parents to describe their views on how and what their children were learning. From the responses, she developed more specific ways of sharing with parents what their children accomplished during the day, such as saying "John used his fine motor skills today as he was lacing beads." In this way, parents had the opportunity to state what *they* needed and the teacher was able to meet those needs.

## Obstacles to Communication

Communicating with families about children's creative expression and play is important because these forms of self-expression are the vehicles for developing children's divergent, creative, and imaginative thinking. The key to communicating with families is to help them understand how creative expression and play contribute to children's physical, intellectual, social, and emotional development (Berger, 2000; Stone, 1995).

There are four obstacles that prevent teachers and caregivers from communicating effectively with parents about children's creative growth (Larsen & Haupt, 1997; U. S. Department of Education, 1994).

**1.** *Teachers and caregivers are uncertain of how to communicate with families.* Many classroom teachers and caregivers feel unprepared to respond to parents' comments that play and creative activities are frivolous. They require guidance in how to meet this challenge by demonstrating the value to parents. Many teachers and parents want to be more involved but are having difficulties arranging the time. Although it is not possible to reach all parents, all adults who interact with children must learn new ways of reaching and working with families.

**2.** *Working with families has never been a priority.* Even though school systems give lip service to working with families, they rarely provide the support teachers need to develop the skills to do so. Helping parents understand the role of play and self-expression in children's lives involves an ongoing dialogue because these experiences cannot be transported home in worksheet form. Rarely do schools reward teachers for outstanding communication with parents about creative expression and play.

**3.** *Some families do not respond to invitations to come to their child's school.* One urban teacher wondered why she should make extra effort to reach her students' families when so many of them never came to meetings or conferences. Such a negative view reveals a lack of understanding of different kinds of families. Some family members feel anxious about meeting teachers at school to discuss their children's progress. When parents have less formal education or feel less competent than teachers, they often appear passive during parent-teacher meetings or they do not bother to come at all. Language barriers also limit family-school contact. Classroom teachers must develop a new mind-set that accepts the inherent strength of families and allows parents to feel comfortable with them.

**4.** *Some parents are adversarial, uncooperative, and defensive.* Many parents view teachers as harsh judges of themselves—especially if they had a negative school experience—and as harsh critics of their children. Quite often, these parents convey negative feelings about school to their children, and children who fear failure are reluctant to try anything. As we have seen, without trial and error and without risk taking, learning and creative expression are thwarted.

When adults make a serious commitment to communicating with parents, they enhance every child's chances for success in school, meet the needs of the whole child, and share responsibility for their creative expression with their families. There are many strategies teachers can adopt to overcome the barriers to communication they face.

## *Strategies for Communicating with Families*

Communicating with families means establishing a partnership built upon mutual trust and respect. The strategies that teachers adopt to enhance communication naturally depend upon their individual beliefs and attitudes about a commitment to such communication. The following suggestions for building home–school partnerships are grouped according to three different kinds of communication. These include:

- *One-way communication*—informing parents about the school's and children's plans.
- *Two-way communication*—inviting family members to share their knowledge, interests, and concerns about their children's creative growth and the school's role in that growth.
- *Three-way communication*—collaborating among the home, school, and community to support children's creative expression.

### One-Way Communication

**One-way communication** flows from the schools to the families. Four one-way communication strategies are recommended:

   **1.** *Newsletters* communicate information about school events or projects to parents. They are well suited to conveying information. To be most useful, translate them into the family's home language. One first-grade teacher's monthly newsletter included excerpts from professional publications related to children's self-expression and play. She also included examples of particular projects children created with blocks, puppets, or music. As a result, parents came to expect information about creative arts as well as basic skills in the monthly newsletter.

   **2.** *Handbooks* provide information about school policies and procedures and available resources. A kindergarten teacher developed a special one-page insert in which she explained her emphasis on creative expression and its importance to children's overall growth and development (Berger, 2000).

   **3.** *Notes* can and should communicate news about children's positive creative growth experiences. When teachers take the time to send such notes home, it enhances communication and boosts children's self-concept. Be certain to keep paper handy to record any significant incident that illustrates creative expression, such as play with language or resolving a conflict in a constructive manner (Kuschner, 1989).

   **4.** *Photo albums or videos* documenting the processes of children's activities are especially useful to validate the importance of children's play and to give children's creative projects a sense of ownership and permanency. Ms. Alvarez photographed her preschoolers' block structures and dramatic play episodes and placed them in a class album. The children took turns taking the album home on the weekends and sharing it with their families.

### Two-Way Communication

**Two-way communication** encourages dialogue between families and schools. Five recommended two-way communication strategies follow.

   **1.** *Meetings*, such as back-to-school nights, provide an opportunity for teachers, caregivers, and parents to share general information about what and how the child is learning. They provide a good opportunity for teachers to emphasize the creative aspects of their programs and for parents to ask general questions. Ms. Daniels, a preschool director, had struggled to find a way to convince parents of the importance of play in the curriculum. She recently opened her parent meeting with the story of Richard Feynman, the physicist who won a Nobel prize. In his autobiography, *Surely You're Joking, Mr. Feynman* (1985), he tells the story of how he played with physics concepts at Cornell University. At dinner in the cafeteria, he played with dinner plates—tossing them into the air to observe their "wobble rate." In his words, "There was no importance to what I was doing, but ultimately there was. The diagrams and the whole business that I got the Nobel prize for came from that piddling around with the wobbling plate" (p. 174).

Ms. Daniels invited the parents to think about some creative problem solving they had experienced, such as reinventing a new recipe because some ingredients were missing or figuring out a temporary solution to a mechanical problem.

**2.** *Conferences* provide private opportunities for teachers, caregivers, and parents to share information and feelings about a child's progress. Many teachers include the child in the conference and invite the child's active participation. One second-grade teacher helped families to prepare for upcoming conferences and set the tone for the meeting by sending home a note. She invited the parents to share examples of their children's creative behavior in the home. Parents responded favorably to this invitation and became more focused on their children's creative behavior.

**3.** *Telephone calls and electronic mail,* like notes, provide another vehicle for sharing information briefly with parents. In the case of creative behavior, making a call or sending an e-mail to a parent to describe a child's success story sets a positive tone and keeps the lines of communication open.

**4.** *Parent visits and participation* in the classroom enable them to observe the classroom and their child. When parents do visit or volunteer to help in the classroom, invite them to participate in the children's typical activities. Select activities that require no particular preparation and contribute to the overall flow of the day (Berger, 2000).

**5.** *Home/school journals,* personal notebooks that go back and forth from home to school, enable teachers and all family members to share something positive about a child or ask a question about what is happening in a classroom and provide a quick way to communicate with families frequently (Fisher, 1998). Ms. Clare invites home/school journal use with her 4-year-old preschool class. She says, "Home/school journals are a place for families and teachers to share examples of divergent thinking, problem-solving and imagination instead of reporting on behavior and achievement." Most of the feedback from her parents is positive. One parent wrote, "I am looking at childhood, and my child, in a whole new way!"

### Three-Way and Many-Way Communication

**Three-way and many-way communication** is a team approach that includes the parents, community, and resource professionals in collaboration with one another.

These collaborations affirm the contributions that all partners bring and encourage the growth of supportive relationships (Koch & McDonough, 1999). Some of the ways you can move toward three-way communication about creative growth include the following:

- Conducting home visits that focus on play and creative expression.
- Using child-led conferences, in which a child describes a particular creative success story.
- Establishing parent-resource rooms that provide readings and photographs of children at play.
- Conveying on a regular basis "good news" to parents about a child's creative expression.
- Advocating for play in the school and community.
- Involving parents in decision making about creative activities and experiences.
- Recognizing parents and children for their creative efforts.
- Encouraging parent attendance at special events that illustrate the projects children have completed ( Jalongo & Isenberg, 2000; Larsen & Haupt, 1997).

Understanding how to communicate about creative expression and play establishes a foundation for building strong school–family connections. It is essential to addressing parents' concerns that too much play or creativity takes the place of "real learning." Parents, caregivers, and teachers have a shared responsibility in the education of their children. Every early childhood educator must develop ways to communicate this knowledge authentically to families (Brewer & Kieff, 1996/97). Appendix E contains a case study that will help you work through the dilemmas of teaching a play-based curriculum.

## PRACTICAL APPLICATIONS FOR YOUR CLASSROOM

Nurturing children's creative expression and working with families are essential aspects of the early childhood curriculum. Perhaps more than anything else, all children want to be competent learners. As early childhood educators, we must find ways to provide *all* children with opportunities for discovering unique solutions to problems, divergent thinking, investigative activities, self-control, and prosocial behavior. The following section suggests ways to guide the creative expression of all children, including those with exceptional needs (Deiner, 1993).

### *Experiences to Support Cultural and Ethnic Diversity*

All children will be better able to think divergently when learning experiences respect others. Children need many opportunities to express their cultural uniqueness, share cultural traditions, and discover their own personal identities before they can extend that learning to other cultures. The following curricular modifications strengthen self-expression in culturally sensitive ways (Miller, 2000).

**1.** *Provide opportunities for children to build new understandings about accepting others, responsibility, and their own personal identities.* Learning about families is a typical theme or unit of study in many early childhood settings. To enable children to learn more about the similarities and differences of families, one teacher read *Family Pictures,* by Carmen Garza (1990), which describes growing up in a Mexican-American community in Texas. From this story, the children explored ways the family worked together to make tamales and how the family felt about cooking together in the kitchen. The teacher reminded children that books about families often help us think about our own special memories, so she invited children to bring in personal photographs, artwork, and other important objects that they valued (Diamond & Moore, 1995).

**2.** *Role-play different problematic behaviors.* In a social studies unit on animal families, children can role-play animals' conflicts over materials and looking for food. Talk with children about similarities and differences between animal families and children's families. This is a good opportunity for children from other cultures to share a variety of family styles.

**3.** *Develop a collection of pictures depicting problem situations (e.g., two children arguing over a toy or a child locked out of the house).* Have children generate many solutions to the problems and perhaps role-play some of them. Children from other cultures can discuss why some solutions would be more appropriate in some contexts than in others.

**4.** *Adapt existing games.* Games such as lotto, bingo, and Memory can be modified using words, numbers, or significant pictures representing the cultural backgrounds of the children in your class. Invite children and their families to supply materials to adapt classroom games.

**5.** *Prepare the dramatic play area with props and clothing from different cultures represented in your room.* Try to find children's clothing, adults' clothing, jewelry, scarves, and pictures representative of these cultures. Include overnight bags for children to take pretend trips to a variety of places. Obtain travel folders and posters. Encourage children to decide how to get there, what to take, what to do there, and what language to speak. Children from other cultures will be able to share traditions and special cultural practices (Deiner, 1993).

**6.** *Use bilingual picture books to honor cultural and language differences.* Books about children with various heritages, such as the Kenyan tale *Bringing the Rain to Kapiti Plain* (Aardema, 1981), the Russian story of an Easter festival, *Rchenka's Eggs* (Polacco, 1988), or *Abuela's Weave* (Castaneda, 1996), the story of how a Guatamalan girl learns of her family traditions from her grandmother, all provide culturally sensitive experiences.

Figure 8.3 suggests additional resources for obtaining information about culturally diverse groups.

**Figure 8.3**
Additional
Teaching/Learning
Resources for
Diverse Groups

The following resources provide *free* information for classroom teachers. Be sure to mention why you need these materials and how you will use them in your early childhood setting.

African American Institute
School Services Division
833 United Nations Plaza
New York, NY 10017

Afro-American Publishing Co.
1727 S. Indiana Ave.
Chicago, IL 60616

Asian-American Studies Center
3232 Campbell Hall
University of California
Los Angeles, CA 90024

Canadian International
Development Agency (CIDA)
200 Promendade du Portage
Hull, Quebec KIA 0G4

(Provides free poster kits of children in both urban and rural settings)

Hispanic-American Institute
100 East 21st St.
Austin, TX 78705

Multiculturalism Canada
Ottawa, Ontario KIA OH5

(Provides resources for educators on multiculturalism in play)

National Information Center for Children and Youth with Disabilities (NIC-HCY)
P.O. Box 1492
Washington, DC 20013

Office of Civil Rights
U.S. Department of Education
330 C St. SW
Washington, DC 20202

(Provides free pamphlets on multiculturalism)

Single Parent Resource Center
1165 Broadway, Room 504
New York, NY 10001

The Stepfamily Association of America
602 East Joppa Rd.
Baltimore, MD 21204

*Note:* Artwork and artifacts of children, families, and colleagues provide a free and ready source of relevant resources. Moreover, many embassies and consulates provide pamphlets, maps, and posters from their countries without charge.

## Experiences to Support Inclusion

Inclusive early childhood settings benefit all children. However, children with disabilities in these settings require appropriate support to be able to participate meaningfully with their peers who do not have disabilities. The goal of curricular and environmental adaptation, discussed below, is to ensure the participation and success of children at all levels (Bredekamp & Copple, 1997; Deiner, 1993; Erwin & Schreiber, 1999).

**1.** *Provide children with opportunities for decision making on projects.* In a project on the community, for example, have children decide what kinds of buildings they wish to construct with blocks (e.g., firehouse, townhouse, prison, hospital).

Define building areas with strips of masking tape. Continue this project over the course of a few days to maximize children's sense of community. Children who have visual disabilities can feel their own work area and keep their blocks in a container to make it easier for them to build in a group. Other classmates might make braille items, such as a menu or instructions, for all to use. Children with physical disabilities can use light or small blocks to build their section of the community or build on a board at a table or wheelchair tray, then move the structure to its location on the floor.

2. *Create a classroom community that focuses on social acceptance.* A group of four teachers in a Syracuse, New York, elementary school initiated a project to support inclusion. After reading Vivian Paley's book *You Can't Say You Can't Play*, each teacher introduced the "You Can't Say You Can't Play" rule in her classroom. The kindergarten teacher modeled ways to ask to join a group and acted out ways to do so, such as tapping another on the shoulder or saying, "Excuse me, may I play?" In the first grade, which was organized in learning centers with a limited number of children assigned to each center, the teacher removed the limits because limiting the number of children who could use the center indirectly sent the message "You can't play." The teachers noticed changes in the number of children who played together, the different groups of children who now played together, and the ways that children talked to one another (Sapon-Shevin, 1998).

3. *Vary your art materials.* Try an art activity of string painting in which children dip various thicknesses of yarn into paint and make designs on paper. Children with visual disabilities can participate in the process and feel the effects when the picture is dry. Children with physical disabilities may find it easier to grip an empty spool with the yarn pulled through it rather than trying to grip the yarn itself.

4. *Provide experiences that address multiple intelligences* (Gardner, 1993). This approach to teaching enables all children opportunities to express their conceptual understandings in a variety of ways. To illustrate, you might have children close their eyes as they paint to music to support an ongoing theme (e.g., friends, circus, and music from other cultures). This activity will allow the entire class to practice interpreting auditory stimuli and will help them gain a better understanding of how children with visual impairments experience their world.

## Adaptations for Individual Learners

In an early childhood setting designed for all children to succeed, all children participate in learning experiences that address the same curricular areas but at different levels of difficulty. When children and teachers are clear about the concepts to be learned, then integrated teaching and learning with a focus on creative expression can occur for all children. Here are some examples:

1. In the same construction project on the community listed in the previous section on experiences to support inclusion, children who are high achievers can help become city planners who evaluate community needs, such as a recycling center or a traveling library, and create possible ways to meet those needs. Children

who are lower achieving might select and build the necessary buildings, make signs for the community areas, illustrate the types of buildings and equipment needed, or plan a playground.

**2.** In the unit on animal families, children who are high achieving might choose to locate more in-depth information about animals and animal behavior. They can also use imagination and fantasy to create or enact their own interpretations about particular animals. Children with language delays can participate in role enactment and produce animal sounds. And children who have difficulty with self-control can verbally discuss problems and feelings in a supportive setting.

**3.** *Select learning experiences that are designed for children at various ability levels.* Have a cooking activity and make two batches of Jell-O, using cold water in one and ice cubes in another, to figure out which jells sooner. Children at all levels can chart their predictions about the jelling process and compare their predictions to what actually happened. Have them engage in a group discussion, articulate what they observed, and give reasons why one batch jelled more quickly.

## CHAPTER SUMMARY

1. There are three fundamental theoretical perspectives that guide children's expression: constructivism, humanism, and behavioral-social learning. Constructivists view children as active agents in their own development. Humanists assume that people are capable of controlling their own lives. Behavioral-social learning theorists view individuals as products of their environment.

2. There are three basic styles of adult-child interactions—autocratic, permissive, and democratic. Each refers to how demanding or responsive teachers and caregivers are with children. Each also cultivates typical behaviors and approaches to problem solving.

3. Guiding children's creative expression includes facilitating the development of prosocial, cooperative, and helping behaviors. Democratic teachers and caregivers use positive guidance techniques that help children become more caring and self-responsible.

5. Children's conflicts are a natural part of their lives. Most conflicts among toddlers concern possessions; most preschoolers' disputes are over role playing; and many primary grade children's disagreements with peers are over rules and social interactions.

6. Helping children learn to resolve their own conflicts encourages their cognitive and social development.

7. Three culturally relevant strategies to help children become better thinkers include problem-solving groups, investigative play, and project work.

8. Communicating with families is fundamental to early childhood programs. Adults should empower families in children's creative expression as well as use a balance of communication strategies to help families understand the value of play and how children grow creatively.

# EXPANDING YOUR THINKING ABOUT GUIDING CHILDREN'S CREATIVE EXPRESSION AND COMMUNICATING WITH FAMILIES

## Discuss: Perspectives on Guiding Creative Expression

1. Refer back to the opening case study in which Ms. Manning intervenes in David and Ahmad's play. Think about the consequences of her actions. Suppose she had said, "Boys, stop that fighting right now!" What difference would that have made in their future ability to negotiate or to express feelings?

2. Imagine that you are responsible for making a presentation on parents' night that explains child guidance or the development of creativity to parents. How would you show parents what these concepts mean and enlist their active participation?

3. Brainstorm different curriculum projects that would be appropriate for collaborative problem solving. Select one project and figure out ways to identify the common goal, find the problem, test out hypotheses, and provide feedback.

4. Refer to the chapter-opening quote by Kontos and Wilcox-Herzog. After having read and discussed the material in this chapter, discuss your own views on why teacher interactions are "at the heart of early childhood." Give some examples from your own experience.

7. Using Ms. Hartman's construction project as a model, collaborate with several classmates to sketch out a two-week project for preschoolers or a three-week project for primary grade children. How would you communicate with parents about the class project? Which strategies did you select? Why?

## Interview: Concerns about Communicating with Families about Creative Expression

Early childhood educators have always considered linkages between the home and school to be important, yet many teachers and caregivers are uncomfortable about communicating with parents, particularly when it comes to creative expression and play. Interview at least two other students during class and articulate concerns about communicating with parents. Ask the following questions and record your responses to share with the group. Brainstorm ways in which you could begin to address these concerns to improve communication with families.

1. Have you had many opportunities to communicate with parents? Describe them.

2. What concerns you most about communicating with families? Why do you think this concerns you?

3. Have you ever observed (conducted) a parent-teacher conference? If so, how were children's strengths shared? How were problems or difficult areas handled?

4. How would you explain your views on creative expression and play to parents in a public meeting? How would you approach such a challenge?

5. Have you ever been concerned about including parents in your program or using them as volunteers? What concerns you?

### *Write to Learn: Characteristics of Creative Problem Solvers*

Encouraging children to figure out answers for themselves is an essential aspect of guiding creative thinking. Recall an incident that happened to you or that you observed in a setting where children were encouraged to solve a problem. Think about the following: What did the teacher or caregiver do? How did the children go about solving their problem? Write about what implications this incident has for you as a teacher. Share your writing in small groups, and compare the adult's behavior to the characteristics of a creative teacher as described in the chapter.

## REFERENCES

Abramson, S., Robinson, R., & Ankenman, K. (1995). Project work with diverse students: Adapting curriculum based on the Reggio Emilia approach. *Childhood Education, 71*(4), 197–202.

Allison, J. (2000). Ask the expert: Jeannette Allison on the project approach. In M. Jalongo & J. Isenberg, *Exploring your role: A practitioner's introduction to early childhood education.* Upper Saddle River, NJ: Merrill/Prentice Hall.

Asher, S. R., & Hymel, S. (1981). Children's social competence in peer relations: Sociometric and behavioral assessment. In J. D. Wine & M. D. Smye (Eds.), *Social competence* (pp. 125–157). New York: Guilford.

Atkinson, A. H., & Green, V. P. (1990). Cooperative learning: The teacher's role. *Childhood Education, 67*(1), 8–11.

Baumrind, D. (1967). Child care practices anteceding three patterns of preschool behavior. *Genetic Psychology Monographs, 75,* 43–88.

Baumrind, D. (1993). The average expectable environment is not good enough: A response to Scarr. *Child Development, 64*(5), 1299–1317.

Beaty, J. (1995). *Converting conflicts in preschool.* Fort Worth, TX: Harcourt Brace.

Berger, E. (2000). *Parents as partners in education: The school and home working together* (5th ed.). Upper Saddle River, NJ: Merrill/Prentice Hall.

Bredekamp, S., & Copple, C. (Eds.). (1997). *Developmentally appropriate practice in early childhood programs* (Rev. ed.). Washington, DC: National Association for the Education of Young Children.

Brewer, J., & Kieff, J. (1996/97). Fostering mutual respect for play at home and school. *Childhood Education, 73*(2), 92–95.

Charney, R. S. (1991). *Teaching children to care: Management in the responsive classroom.* Greenfield, MA: Northeast Foundation for Children.

Deiner, P. L. (1993). *Resources for teaching young children with diverse abilities* (2nd ed.). New York: Harcourt Brace Jovanovich.

Diamond, B. J., & Moore, M. A. (1995). *Multicultural literacy: Mirroring the reality of the classroom.* New York: Longman.

Dreikurs, R. (1969). *Psychology in the classroom.* New York: Harper & Row.

Edwards, C., Grandini, L., & Forman, G. (1993). *The hundred languages of children: The Reggio Emilia approach to early childhood education.* Norwood, NJ: Ablex.

Eisenberg-Berg, N., Haake, R. J., & Bartlett, K. (1981). The effects of possession and ownership on the sharing and proprietary behaviors of preschool children. *Merrill-Palmer Quarterly, 27,* 61–68.

Epstein, J. (1995). School/family/community partnerships. *Phi Delta Kappan, 76*(9), 701–712.

Erwin, E., & Schreiber, R. (1999). Creating supports for young children with disabilities in natural environments. *Early Childhood Education Journal, 26*(3), 167–171.

Feynman, R. (1985). *Surely you're joking, Mr. Feynman.* New York: W. W. Norton.

Fisher, B. (1998). *Joyful learning in kindergarten* (Rev. ed.). Portsmouth, NH: Heinemann.

Gardner, H. (1993). *Frames of mind: The theory of multiple intelligences* (2nd ed.). New York: Basic Books.

Gestwicki, C. (1999). *Developmentally appropriate practice: Curriculum development in early childhood* (2nd ed.). Albany, NY: Delmar.

Gordon, A., & Browne, K. (1996). *Guiding young children in a diverse society.* Boston: Allyn & Bacon.

Greenberg, P. (1989). Parents as partners in young children's development and education. A new American fad? Why does it matter? *Young Children, 44* (4), 61–75.

Hartman, J. A., & Eckerty, C. (1995). Projects in the early years. *Childhood Education, 71*(3), 141–148.

Hildebrand, V., & Hearron, P. (1999). *Guiding young children* (6th ed.). Upper Saddle River, NJ: Merrill/Prentice Hall.

Hildebrand, V., Phenice, L. A., Gray, M., & Hines, R. P. (1996). *Knowing and serving diverse families.* Upper Saddle River, NJ: Merrill/Prentice Hall.

Hyson, M. C., & Christiansen, S. L. (1997). Developmentally appropriate guidance and the integrated curriculum. In C. Hart, D. Burts, & R. Charlesworth (Eds.), *Integrated curriculum and developmentally appropriate practice* (pp. 257–284). Albany: State University of New York Press.

Isenberg, J. P., & Raines, S. C. (1992). Peer conflict and conflict resolution among preschool children. In J. Gittler & L. Bowen (Eds.), *Annual review of conflict knowledge and conflict resolution: Vol. 3* (pp. 21–40). New York: Garland.

Jalongo, M. R., & Isenberg, J. P. (2000). *Exploring your role: A practitioner's introduction to early childhood education.* Upper Saddle River, NJ: Merrill/Prentice Hall.

Johnson, D. W., Johnson, R. T., & Holubek, E. (1990). *Cooperation in the classroom.* Edina, MN: Interaction.

Katz, L. (1993). What can we learn from Reggio Emilia? In C. Edwards, L. Gandini, & G. Forman (Eds.). *The hundred languages of children: The Reggio Emilia approach to early childhood education.* Norwood, NJ: Ablex.

Katz, L. G., & Chard, S. C. (1989). *Engaging children's minds: The project approach.* Norwood, NJ: Ablex.

Koch, P. K., & McDonough, M. (1999). Improving parent-teacher conferences through collaborative conversations. *Young Children, 54*(2), 11–15.

Kohn, A. (1996). *Beyond discipline: From compliance to community.* Alexandria, VA: Association for Supervision and Curriculum Development.

Kontos, S., & Wilcox-Herzog, A. (1997). Influences on children's competence in early childhood classrooms. *Early Childhood Research Quarterly, 12*(3), 247–262.

Krall, C. M., & Jalongo, M. R. (1998/99). Creating a caring classroom community in classrooms. *Childhood Education, 75*(2), 83–88.

Kuschner, D. (1989). Put your name on your painting, but . . . the blocks go back on the shelves. *Young Children, 45*(1), 49–56.

Larsen, J. M., & Haupt, J. H. (1997). Integrating home and school: Building a partnership. In C. Hart, D. Burts, & R. Charlesworth (Eds.), *Integrated curriculum and developmentally appropriate practice* (pp. 389–416). Albany: State University of New York Press.

Lee, F. Y. (1995). Asian parents as partner. *Young Children, 50*(3), 4–9.

Malaguzzi, L. (1993). History, ideas, and basic philosophy. In C. Edwards, L. Gandini, & G. Forman (Eds.), *The hundred languages of children: The Reggio Emilia approach to early childhood education* (pp. 41–89). Norwood, NJ: Ablex.

Marion, M. (1999). *Guidance of young children* (5th ed.) Upper Saddle River, NJ: Merrill/Prentice Hall.

Miller, D. F. (2000). *Positive child guidance* (3rd ed.). Albany, NY: Delmar.

New, R. (1993). Cultural variations on developmentally appropriate practice: Challenges to theory and practice. In C. Edwards, L. Gandini, & G. Forman (Eds.), *The hundred languages of children: The Reggio Emilia approach to early childhood education* (pp. 215–231). Norwood, NJ: Ablex.

Paley, V. (1992). *You can't say you can't play.* Cambridge, MA: Harvard University Press.

Papalia, D. E., Olds, S. W., & Feldman, R. D. (1999). *A child's world: Infancy through adolescence* (8th ed.). New York: McGraw-Hill.

Piaget, J. (1952). *The origins of intelligence in children.* New York: International Universities Press.

Rogers, C. (1961). *On becoming a person.* Boston: Houghton-Mifflin.

Sapon-Shevin, M. (with A. Dobbelare, C. Corrigan, K. Goodman, & M. Mastin). (1998). Everyone here can play. *Educational Leadership, 56*(1) 43–45.

Schreiber, M. (1999). Timeouts for toddlers: Is our goal punishment? *Young Children, 54*(4), 22–25.

Stone, S. (1995). Wanted: Advocates for play in the primary grades. *Young Children, 50*(6), 45–65.

Tegano, D. W., Sawyers, J. K., & Moran, J. D. (1989). Problem-finding and solving in play: The teacher's role. *Childhood Education, 66*(2), 92–97.

Tudge, J., & Caruso, D. (1988). Cooperative problem-solving in the classroom: Enhancing young children's cognitive development. *Young Children, 44*(1), 46–57.

U.S. Department of Education. (1994). *Strong families, strong schools.* Washington, DC: Author.

Vygotsky, L. S. (1976). Play and its role in the mental development of the child. In J. Bruner, A. Jolly, & K. Sylva (Eds.), *Play: Its role in development and evolution.* New York: Basic Books.

Wassermann, S. (1990). *Serious players in the primary classroom.* New York: Teachers College Press.

Webster, T. (1990). Projects in curriculum: Under what conditions? *Childhood Education, 67*(1), 2–3.

Wheeler, E. (2000). Ask the expert: Edyth Wheeler on conflict resolution. In M. Jalongo & J. Isenberg, *Exploring your role: A practitioner's introduction to early childhood education* (pp. 340–342). Upper Saddle River, NJ: Merrill/Prentice Hall.

## CHILDREN'S LITERATURE CITED

Aardema, V. (1981). *Bringing the rain to Kapiti Plain.* New York: Scholastic.

Barton, B. (1981). *Building a house.* New York: Greenwillow Books.

Castaneda, O. (1996). *Abuela's weave.* New York: Lee & Low.

Garza, C. (1990). *Family pictures/Cuadros de familia.* San Francisco: Children's Book Press.

Gibbons, G. (1982). *Tool book.* New York: Holiday House.

Polacco, P. (1988). *Rchenka's eggs.* New York: Philomel.

# Chapter 9

## Assessing
## Creative Expression and Play

*"American students are the most tested and least examined students in the world. When things go badly, we just add another test—as if taking the temperature more often would heal the patient. . . . Even our best schools typically fail to yield students who understand, because we test students only on what they have been directly taught, rather than ask them to stretch their mental muscles in new and appropriate ways. "*

Howard Gardner, interviewed by David E. Fernie, 1992, pp. 226, 221

# TEACHERS' REFLECTIONS ON ASSESSMENT

### Preservice Teachers

"At the beginning of the semester, I was not aware of how important the opportunity for play and creative expression really was. When I was young, play was just 'fun time.' Now I realize the importance of play and creative expression for all areas of a child's development. Creative expression and play, as I realize now, provide a golden opportunity for informal assessment in all areas of the curriculum."

"When you start thinking about all of the things that appropriate assessment tells you as a teacher, you become convinced that it is the way to go. During my student teaching in the second grade, I did a teaching theme on celebrations. The performance assessment was for children to write and present a 60-second commercial that would include a definition of 'celebration,' common characteristics of celebrations, and one example of a celebration from that child's cultural background. I know this was a much better indicator of their understanding than a test."

### Inservice Teachers

"I have been a teacher in the public schools for four years after a year of working in child care. One of the major differences between the two jobs is the testing. I think the public schools are test-crazy! I also think that the almighty test scores are used as much to control teachers as they are to check up on students."

"I always thought that creative expression and play were learning opportunities, but I didn't ever think of all the assessment possibilities. I've always heard about enjoyment, problem-solving skills, development of language, etc., being promoted through play, but using play to assess children is one aspect I never took into account."

## Your Reflections

- How have these teachers changed the way they think about assessment?

- What relationships have they discovered between creativity, play, assessment, and curriculum?

- What issues do these early childhood teachers and caregivers raise about assessment of children's creative expression and play?

## *Case Study:*

### *Assessment Issues*

When Michael was an infant, his favorite toy was a musical mobile that played "Twinkle, Twinkle Little Star." At age 1, he began to bounce up and down and wave his arms whenever he heard his favorite television commercial jingle. During the preschool years, Michael was an enthusiastic participant in group musical activities such as fingerplays, action songs, and chants. He also sought out individual experiences with music, such as playing with musical toys or instruments, listening to recordings, improvising songs while at play, and moving spontaneously to music. Michael's favorite video was of Ella Jenkins, and he had mastered all of the lyrics and melodies for her recorded songs. When two of his teachers recited a rap version of "The Three Little Pigs," Michael remarked, "Well it's not really rap 'cause there's no dancing. There's gotta be dancing." Now that Michael is in the elementary grades, he has virtually no school experiences with dance. All of his dancing is done at home with family, friends, neighbors, and recorded music. Michael seldom has experiences with music in school either. Aside from the Christmas program performed for parents and the 30 minutes per week with the music teacher, there is no music or song. Art, another of Michael's passions, is also confined to 30 minutes per week and offers little variety. Nearly all of Michael's art experiences involve crayons, paper, and paste. Work with clay, paints, fabrics, or other materials is very rare. Throughout his school career, Michael has watched other students who are talented in reading or mathematics or sports win all of the accolades. Michael's talents remain largely undiscovered, and he will likely emerge from high school mistakenly believing that he is "not really good at anything."

All over the world, children like Michael are being deprived of opportunities to develop their abilities in the arts and to express themselves creatively. In the United States, the failure to convert talent's promise into accomplishment is exacerbated by limitations in assessment. One reason why creativity is frequently overlooked is because most people believe it is all emotion/inspiration and is therefore unmeasurable. Experts have argued that another reason why creative expression and play are undervalued is because they are seldom evaluated in some systematic way (Fowler, 1994). When educators fail to assess children's growth in play and creative expression, they virtually guarantee that these activities will be disregarded or ignored in a test-driven school system. Therefore, one way to make early childhood settings more play-based and more supportive of children's creative expression is to make it clearer how children's growth in creativity and play can be evaluated in meaningful ways.

## THEORETICAL AND RESEARCH BASE: WHAT IS PERFORMANCE ASSESSMENT?

Generally speaking, assessment is the process of discovering children's knowledge, abilities, and interests (Culbertson & Contreras, 1999). Experts have argued that our rapidly changing, high-tech, global society can no longer base education on a model of learning that "pours" knowledge into children and requires them to memorize it for tests, all the time realizing that much of it will be forgotten (Jervis & McDonald, 1996). Assessment in creative expression and play—or in any of the traditional academic subjects, for that matter—involves much more than testing. Assessment is the "continual process of observing and recording and otherwise documenting the work that children do and how they do it, as a basis for a variety of educational decisions that affect the child" (Bredekamp, 1991, p. 21). One particular type of assessment, performance assessment, "requires students to create evidence through performance that will enable assessors to make valid judgments about 'what they know and can do' in situations that matter" (Eisner, 1999, p. 659). So, instead of asking children to identify musical notes on a paper-and-pencil test, performance assessment might present children with the task of matching the pitch of a note played on the piano with their voices. In performance assessment, the proof that children have acquired an understanding or skill is assessed by competence (singing at a prescribed pitch), or knowing how to do something, rather than merely knowing about something (recognizing musical notation). Consider the many ways that a child might demonstrate understanding of musical concepts (Alper, 1999; Lewis, 1983). Young children might listen and respond by:

- Mirroring or following teachers' and peers' hand, arm, face, or torso movements which correspond to the music's tempo.
- Bouncing or rolling a large plastic ball in time to slow or moderate music.
- Writing in the air, outlining the melodic contours that they hear with their bodies or arms.

- "Freezing" when the music stops suddenly or unexpectedly.
- Using scarves to illustrate the mood, shape, or form of a piece of music.
- Playing a game called radio and showing that they understand making their singing louder or softer in response to a large cardboard dial that represents the volume control.
- Using their bodies to show that they understand different ways of responding to rhythm (e.g., cue cards that show clapping hands, snapping fingers, stomping feet).

Older children might respond by:

- Gesturing with hands to illustrate the pitch of notes (up or down on the scale).
- Playing a pattern on a melody instrument, such as a xylophone.
- Marking on the chalkboard each time they hear a pattern of musical notes.
- Representing notes on the scale as stair steps and moving up or down.

Assessing the achievement of a simple skill, such as learning to tie shoes, is relatively easy. The goal is clearly defined and so is the sequence of the steps in attaining that goal. Assessing creative expression and play, however, poses some unique challenges (Baer, 1994). Take, for example, evaluating a child's painting. First of all, the particular outcome is not predetermined. Second, there are hundreds of ways in which a quality outcome might be achieved rather than one, generally agreed-upon procedure. Thus, assessing creative expression and play poses an "ill-structured" problem (Linn, 1996) that places demands on teachers' creative resources as assessors.

In performance assessment:

- The tasks performed by children are relevant and interesting.
- Both the products and the processes used to achieve them are evaluated.
- Students develop skills in self-evaluation as they take greater responsibility for selecting their best work.
- Students' attitudes and feelings are considered as well as knowledge and skills.
- Results of the assessment are used to optimize children's learning.
- Assessment data are used to improve classroom practice and make informed instructional decisions.
- Results of the assessment produce a holistic picture of student performance.

Figure 9.1 compares/contrasts appropriate and inappropriate assessment practices.

## Purposes of Assessing Divergent Thinking

There are at least four reasons for assessing divergent thinking (Dacey, 1989; Jalongo, 1992):

**1.** *To develop deeper insight into creative growth.* One goal of assessing creative expression and play is to understand better how these abilities develop throughout life. Biographies and case studies of exceptionally creative individuals, such as

| Appropriate Assessment | Inappropriate Assessment |
|---|---|
| Recognizes the planning of instruction as main goal | Sees accountability as main goal |
| Is an ongoing process that is integrated with curriculum | Is a scheduled event that focuses on a brief episode of behavior |
| Benefits the child and expands every child's potential | Is used to justify preferential treatment for a chosen few |
| Assesses real-world abilities in naturalistic settings (i.e., writing, problem solving) | Measures isolated skills under artificial conditions |
| Respects the teacher as the assessor | Trusts only outside agencies |
| Recognizes that children need to develop at individual rates | Emphasizes normative behavior, measures skills by age and grade |
| Stresses success and understanding of errors | Stresses failures, grades, scores, and mistakes |
| Involves a concrete, hands-on approach | Is restricted to paper-and-pencil tasks |
| Focuses on the whole child | Treats the child like a disembodied intellect |
| Supports the curriculum | Drives the curriculum |
| Is process-oriented and values divergent thinking | Is product-oriented and values convergent thinking |

**Appropriate Assessment Tasks**
- Are opportunities for learning
- Enable every child to succeed at some level
- Are embedded in the curriculum
- Connect content, process, and work habits
- Acknowledge children's accomplishments
- Give children opportunities to demonstrate what they have learned
- Provide clear expectations and standards of excellence

**Appropriate Assessment Tools**
- Emphasize dialogue and self-reflection
- Are part of a comprehensive assessment plan
- Show the child's rate of progress
- Identify skills that still need to be developed
- Provide direction to teachers in planning
- Suggest ways that parents and families might support play, creative expression, and the arts at home and in the community

**Appropriate Assessment Outcomes**
- Document not only what children are learning (content, skills) but also how they are learning it (processes)
- Engage educators, other professionals, families, and communities in rich and meaningful dialogue about the value of assessment in the arts, creativity, and play
- Convince parents, families, and communities about the contributions of creative expression, play and the arts to children's lives

**Figure 9.1**  Appropriate/Inappropriate Assessment Practices

*Sources:* Adapted from Brown, N. (1995), Educators in Connecticut's Pomperaug Regional School District 15 (1996), and Isenberg & Farley (1990).

## Research on Assessment in Creative Expression and Play

Fantuzzo, J., Coolahan, K., Mendez, J., McDermott, P., & Sutton-Smith, B. (1998). Contextually-relevant validation of peer play constructs with African American Head Start children: Penn Interactive Peer Play Scale. *Early Childhood Research Quarterly, 13*(3), 411–431.

Fewell, R., & Glick, M. (1998). The role of play in assessment. In D. P. Fromberg & D. Bergen (Eds.). *Play from birth to twelve and beyond: Contexts, perspectives, and meanings* (pp. 201–210). New York: Garland.

Fishkin, A. S., & Johnson, A. S. (1998). Who is creative? Identifying children's creative abilities. *Roeper Review, 21*(1), 40–47.

Lowenthal, B. (1997). Useful early childhood assessment: Play-based, interviews, and multiple intelligences. *Early Child Development and Care, 129,* 43–49.

Plucker, J. A., & Runco, M. A. (1998). The death of creativity measurement has been greatly exaggerated: Current issues, recent advances, and future directions in creativity assessment. *Roeper Review, 21,* 36–40.

Rueda, R., & Garcia, E. (1996). Teachers' perspectives on literacy assessment and instruction with language-minority students: A comparative study. *The Elementary School Journal, 96*(3), 311–332.

Thompson, C., & Bales, S. (1991). "Michael doesn't like my dinosaurs": Conversations in a preschool classroom. *Studies in Art Education, 33*(1), 43–45.

Weinberger, L. A., & Starkey, P. (1994). Pretend play by African American children in Head Start. *Early Childhood Research Quarterly, 9,* 327–343.

Howard Gardner's (1993) investigations into different forms of human intelligence, are good examples of assessments used to gain insights about creative potential in human beings. The same principles apply to young children. When educators learn to observe the very young child carefully, their appreciation for and understanding of children's creative processes is enlarged and enlightened.

**2.** *To evaluate program effectiveness.* A second major purpose of assessment is to determine the impact of an educational program on young children's growth in creative expression and play. Take, for instance, the teacher who creates individual folders that contain representative samples of each child's drawings and writings throughout the academic year. By combining her own insights about the child's progress with the samples, this teacher is both assessing the child's divergent thinking and making judgments about the success of the program.

**3.** *To identify talents, provide enrichment, and develop potential through special programs.* Consider how an observant teacher could assess children's musical talent and potential or make inferences about a child's interest and motivation. A good teacher would notice children's responses to and interests in music, such as the child who dances spontaneously to a lively tune, invents a lullaby while rocking a baby doll, or inquires about a classical piece being played at the start of the school day. Authentic assessment always expands, rather than limits, children's options. It further develops those children who clearly have strengths in an area of the arts and provides opportunities for others to discover and explore their interests, curiosities, and motivations.

4. *To decide whether, when, or how to intervene.* Sometimes, assessments of children's play or creative expression suggest that the teacher ought to intervene. Studies of the play behaviors of children with few prior play experiences are a good example (Smilansky, 1968; Smilansky & Shefatya, 1990). These researchers found that the play of children with limited play experiences was less elaborate and social than that of their peers. Their response was to play alongside the children, thereby coaching them in more sophisticated levels of play.

By studying and assessing creative behavior, we can intervene to remediate or enrich, identify strengths, recommend new and challenging activities, and learn more about developing creative potential. "Creative processes give us valuable assessment material because they reveal not just one of two aspects of development, but rather a synthesis of many interacting factors" (Brown, 1995, p. 6).

## Difficulties with Assessment

Whenever we speak of educational assessment, there is a tendency to value "hard" data and to scorn "soft" data. But as Wassermann (1989) points out, numbers themselves do not have meaning. It takes human intelligence to make sense out of numbers. Even when we do measure and interpret a number, it can only inform us to a limited extent. We can obtain a verbal score on an achievement test, for example, but the score will not tell us if the child can create and illustrate an original story. Generally speaking, our measurement tools fall short when we try to describe complex processes. There is an old adage among psychometricians: You get what you measure. Nielsen (1990) takes the adage one step further: "Simple outcomes, simple tests, simpletons" (p. 18). This means that if educators continue to assess only low-level knowledge and skills, we run the risk of offering a program that emphasizes trivialities instead of powerful ideas.

Nevertheless, assessing play and creative expression poses some challenges for three reasons.

1. *Play and creative expression are hard to define.* Nathan is a first grader whose teacher is presenting a lesson on units of measure. She tells the children to look at several objects to be measured on a workbook page and asks, "What are some different ways that we could tell someone how long the line is without using a ruler?" Children make a variety of suggestions such as using paperclips, erasers, or fingerwidths. Then the teacher calls on Nathan, who says, "You could ask an ant to walk across the line and tell you how many steps he took." One teacher might say Nathan's response is creative; another might say it is flippant. Because imagi-

*Authentic assessment examines development in all areas: physical, so-cial, emotional, and cognitive.*

nation, creativity, fantasy, and play are difficult to define and assess, they are often misinterpreted and discouraged.

   **2.** *Play and creative expression are not adequately assessed by standardized tests.* Usually, assessment tools are product measures that focus on discrete academic skills. Even those tests that are designed to assess creativity sometimes rely rather heavily on a single creative behavior (such as artistic ability) or tend to assess prob-lem solving under very restrictive conditions. Suppose that a researcher is studying block play and provides the child with a small set of wooden blocks, then observes the child's block play during a short time period. The researcher may conclude that the child exhibits little originality. But the child may be accustomed to incorporating other miniature toys in her block play, may work exceptionally well with other children in creating large unit block structures, or may be extraordinarily imaginative with Legos at home. Because the researcher's task was so restrictive, it could not begin to tap the full range of the child's play processes. This example helps to illustrate why play and creative expression do not readily lend themselves to formal, standardized methods of assessment.

**3.** *Creative expression and play require real-life contexts to be valid.* A high score on a paper-and-pencil test of creativity does not provide an authentic, everyday indication of the child's creative expression, such as the ability to use modeling clay creatively, design an interesting collage, construct an imaginative diorama based on a favorite story, or solve a challenging mathematical problem. The ability to use creative problem solving in an actual situation is a better indicator of a person's creativity. The more removed from direct, hands-on experience that a task becomes, the less likely that it will be a good predictor of exceptional "real-world" performance. The same principles pertain to the assessment of children's creative expression and play. We need performance data collected over an extended period of time in different contexts in order for assessment to be meaningful. Figure 9. 2 provides an overview of the ways that play, the arts, and creative expression might be evaluated by three different groups: (1) the teacher, (2) the child, and (3) parents, families, and the community at large.

## CRITERIA FOR ASSESSMENT

Appraisals of children's work usually rely on one or more of six criteria (Potter, 1985). The two criteria that schools use most often are the ones that are the least applicable to creative expression and play: speed and correctness. Speed should be a criterion only when time is essential. Usually, speed is important with simple tasks and procedures, such as assembling materials and putting them away after using them. Correctness is important when there is one right answer. Suppose that a child is painting and asks for green paint, and the teacher replies, "You have red, yellow, and blue. How could you mix them to get green?" If the child says, "Mix the blue and yellow together," the response will be correct.

The four remaining criteria that are more applicable to creative expression and play are practical workability, aesthetic appeal, evidence of creativity, and attainment of standards.

* *Practical workability*—If a teacher is presenting a unit on simple machines, he or she might challenge the children to use recycled materials or construction toys to demonstrate one simple machine in action. The teacher's judgment of the children's work will be based on whether or not it works and actually demonstrates one simple machine.

---

### Prepared by the Teacher

**General Guidelines:** Observing young children's play, creative expression, and artworks is intended to provide a more holistic view of what children know and are able to do with their creative thinking processes. Teachers need to invent a system for gathering observations regularly. All observations should be dated, keyed to program goals, and filed systematically in student work portfolios to facilitate charting children's progress over time.

- **Anecdotal records** that highlight student attitudes, preferences, judgments, participation. Teacher can make notes for younger students; older students can write their own. These notes should be dated and collected over time to demonstrate patterns of growth.
- **Checklists, developmental profiles, or logs** that compare one child's progress with that of the typically developing child.
- **Conference notes** from discussions with individual children or groups of children about the content and process of their creative work that demonstrate what was accomplished during major projects.
- **Interviews** with children about their emerging understandings of creativity and the arts.
- **Documentation panels** that provide evidence of the learning that was achieved through the course of a major project. These large displays that chronicle the life cycle of a project are commercial-artist-quality documentation of children's accomplishments (Carter & Curtis, 1995; Chard, 1998; Jalongo & Stamp, 1997).

### Produced and Assessed by the Child

**General Guidelines:** In order to teach children the skills of self-evaluation, they should bear responsibility for identifying their best work and providing a rationale for its inclusion in their portfolios.

- **Self-selected work samples:** These may include one-dimensional works (e.g., paintings, drawings, writing) as well as photographs, sketches, video or audiotapes of works or displays.
- **Rating scales or checklists** that encourage children to bring their artistic decisionmaking to a conscious level as they are working on a project; to evaluate their group's performance, or to assess the overall quality of a culminating activity.
- **Child-led conferences** that enable the child to make a presentation of his or her work to parents and families.

### Assessed by the Family/Community

**General Guidelines:** Parents, families, and community members need to be involved in assessing children's growth.

- **Conferences with parents and families** that provide them with the opportunity to review the child's work over time.
- **Review of live or taped individual or group performances** that enable parents, families, and community members to see the child's/children's conceptualization, presentation, quality, personalization, and cooperation (Gardner, 1993).
- **Responses to portfolios of children's work** that give families an opportunity to provide written feedback on the child's work.

**Figure 9.2**  Overview of Assessment Methods Used by the Teacher, the Child, and Families/Communities

- *Aesthetic appeal*—As part of a unit on Mexico, some third graders are making a piñata out of papier-mâché. The quality of their piñata, to a considerable extent, will be based on its beauty, its aesthetic appeal.
- *Evidence of creativity*—In order for something to be creative, it must be both original and effective. If a teacher is observing children who are inventing a dance in response to music, each in his or her own unique way, creativity is the major criterion for assessment.
- *Attainment of standards*—Teachers and caregivers sometimes evaluate children's work in terms of how well it meets a set of criteria or standards. A good example is the peer-editing process used in writing. If the teacher sees that children are using what they have learned about editing and are providing constructive feedback to peers, then the teacher will infer that they are mastering an important aspect of the writing process.

When rendering judgments about creative problem solving, it is important to consider both the processes that children use and the products that they create. Have you ever had a mathematics teacher who would give you partial credit if you could explain the steps that you went through in attempting to solve the problem, even if the final answer was incorrect? A frequently overlooked aspect of assessment is recognizing effort, as this practice does. It is just as important to acknowledge good thinking along the way as it is to acknowledge a job that is well done.

To summarize, assessment should:

- Be accurate, appropriate, useful, and feasible.
- Improve communication between families and schools by resulting in shared understandings of the child's progress and the purposes for the program.
- Involve "real-world" tasks that have significance outside of school or testing programs.
- Give children the opportunity to self-evaluate and reflect on their progress.
- Focus not only on products but also on progress and effort.

## Assessing Creative Processes

What tasks could you imagine that would assess children's creative thinking processes? Ms. Mastalzo, a second-grade teacher, is using a treasure hunt activity (Sigel & Cocking, 1977). She begins with groups of four to six children. The first two or three children hide an object on the playground and create a "map picture," which the other group members must interpret in order to locate the treasure. The mapmakers are encouraged to take the searchers' perspective into account as they create their map. Note that both the mapmakers and the searchers are observing, gathering, and organizing data as they scrutinize the playground.

Imagine how children are using their prior knowledge to construct and read the treasure map. Perhaps they recall that "X marks the spot," that directional arrows are used, or that pictorial symbols represent landmarks. Maybe they have watched as their parents consult a map on a car trip or used an illuminated map in a shopping mall. Imagine the excitement of both groups as they recap where they are, decide what they need to do next, and discuss their assumptions and hypotheses. Finally, it is obvious that the children must create mental images; the mapmakers move from reality to symbolic representations of reality, while the searchers do just the reverse—move from symbols to reality. Children would no doubt want to have a turn at being on both the mapmaker and searcher teams, thus giving them experience in both kinds of creative thinking.

As a teacher like Ms. Mastalzo observes children during the treasure hunt activity, she can assess the creative thought process in action. Creative problem-solving tasks like the treasure hunt involve children in problem solving during which students:

- Identify the task or problem type.
- Define and clarify essential elements and terms.
- Judge and connect relevant information.
- Evaluate the adequacy of information and procedures for drawing conclusions and/or solving problems.
- Develop self-monitoring problem-solving strategies.
- Examine assumptions, reach new conclusions, and take new action (Harste, 1989).

Even though a simulation such as the treasure hunt may seem rather humble in comparison to the results of a standardized test, it actually provides more information about how children think and learn. Figure 9.3 recommends performance assessment strategies that address the eight intelligences.

**Figure 9.3**
Tools for
Performance
Assessment in the
Multiple
Intelligences

> **Verbal:** Computer printouts of children's work, audiotapes and videotapes of performances, storytelling
>
> **Visual:** Photo essays, models, maps, constructions, storyboards, posters, murals, collages, mobiles, mosaics, sketchbooks
>
> **Logical:** puzzles, mazes, sequences, patterns, analogies, time lines, computations, games
>
> **Musical:** songs, rhythms, compositions, raps, jingles, instruments, performances
>
> **Interpersonal:** group projects, observation charts, collages, murals, team tasks, group challenges, collaborative work
>
> **Intrapersonal:** journals, sketchbooks, self-assessments, reflections, interpretations, creative expression
>
> **Bodily:** body language, gestures, dramatic play, role playing, dance and movement, creative dramatics, puppetry
>
> **Naturalist:** nature walks, categorizing natural objects, conducting field studies, photographing, collecting, identifying

*Source:* Adapted from: Fogarty (1997).

## Assessing Creative Products

If we analyze high-quality, creative samples of children's work, we would notice four essential features:

1.  Children were trusted to make choices.
2.  Children's feelings were accepted.
3.  Children were challenged to grow.
4.  Children were urged to break stereotypes (Hoffman & Lamme, 1988).

It is easy to detect these differences if we look at two primary grade classrooms where children wrote friendly letters. In Room 203, every child copied a letter that the teacher printed on the chalkboard. The letters were posted on the bulletin board and never mailed. In Room 204, children used whatever writing skills they had acquired—squiggles, letterlike shapes, invented spellings, or conventional spelling—to write and illustrate real cards and letters to Julie, a classmate who had been injured in an auto accident and was now recuperating at home. Instead of becoming classroom decorations, the children's letters were actually sent to Julie, who has enjoyed the correspondence immensely and has been occupied composing answers to each one. Contrary to popular opinion, the products of imagination are not only distinctive, they are also useful. In the first classroom, they were neither; in the second classroom, they were both.

*The products of children's imagination are both distinctive and useful.*

## Assessing Multiple Intelligences

As discussed earlier in this book, Howard Gardner (1993, 1995) has proposed the theory of multiple intelligences, which includes at least eight distinctive forms of human intelligence. One major goal of Project Spectrum, which has been in operation since 1984 at Harvard and Tufts Universities, is to reform intelligence testing and promote forms of assessment that reflect the complete range of children's abilities. Rather than simply administering paper-and-pencil tests that evaluate a student's current stockpile of information in verbal and mathematical skills, assessment that respects multiple intelligences looks at three important processes that students use. These three aspects are:

- Perception—a child's unique ways of processing sensory input.
- Reflection—a child's thought processes and insights about ideas and works.
- Production—the quality of the work created by the child.

Of course, assessment of intelligence at Project Spectrum includes evaluation of children's abilities in language and numbers, but it is unique in that it also includes assessment in science, music, movement, visual arts, and social experiences. Project Spectrum aims to provide a well-rounded view of each child's assets, to investigate a means of assessment that is not culturally biased in favor of certain groups or backgrounds, and to promote a form of performance-based assessment that emphasizes problem solving, thus translating more directly to tasks that students are likely to encounter throughout their lives.

The current emphasis on the assessment of multiple intelligences, creative products, and creative processes is to discover the talents within each child and truly maximize every child's potential.

## APPROPRIATE ASSESSMENT OF YOUNG CHILDREN'S CREATIVE EXPRESSION AND PLAY

There are three basic types of assessment (Goodman, 1989) that are suited for the study of complex processes such as play and creative expression. *Observation* examines what students do as the teacher remains on the sidelines. Observation includes the informal impressions teachers and caregivers form while watching children engaged in an activity such as playing in the housekeeping area. Video or audio recordings of observations and subsequent analysis using a coding device might also be used. *Interaction* examines the ways in which a teacher responds to and communicates with students in order to determine the students' current level of performance and to pose new challenges at the right level of difficulty. Interaction includes the teacher's daily, face-to-face exchanges with students as well as more structured and planned types of interaction, such as conducting a conference or interview with a child and recording the results. *Process/product analysis* refers to gathering information and gaining insights about students from that information.

*As this child learns to read, the teacher is observing, interacting, and analyzing both the product and the process at various times.*

The teacher might collect samples of students' work at various stages, arrange them to highlight growth, and analyze them to make instructional decisions. These approaches to evaluation—observation, interaction, and analysis—may be incidental or planned, use teacher-developed materials or commercially available materials, and use different methods of recording (written, oral, or mechanically recorded).

## Observing Children's Creative Expression and Play

As Wassermann (1989) points out, "One of the most valuable yet rarely acknowledged assessment tools in educational practice is the sustained, thoughtful day-to-day observation of student behavior by a competent, professional teacher" (p. 368). Appropriate observations of young children share the following characteristics:

* Good observations use direct observational data and rely on that data for interpretations. High-inference, value-laden terminology is avoided.
* Good observations accurately record the observable behavior of the child, both verbal and nonverbal.
* Good observations describe the context in which the behavior occurred— the time, setting, circumstances, and behaviors of other children or adults related to the episode.
* Good observations are used by teachers and caregivers to plan a developmentally appropriate program.

*A 4-year-old girl's drawing of herself painting eggs.*

## *Types of Observation*

Several types of observation and examples of how teachers can use each type are described below.

### *Anecdotal Records*

Anecdotes are brief episodes of student behavior selected to highlight student growth and to provide evidence of progress toward programmatic goals. Mr. Strachota (1996) tells his second graders that he is "invisible" whenever he wears his baseball cap indoors. That way, he can concentrate on writing down what he sees for 5 to 15 minutes. Ms. Longwood, a first-grade teacher, keeps a file box of 5″ × 7″ cards on her desk. She uses this system to take brief notes on each child's progress and shares these milestones with parents during parent-teacher conferences. Mr. Jeffreys likes to use self-stick notes and a clipboard. At the end of the day, he puts the notes in each child's file. None of these teachers expects to write something about every child every day. Rather, it is sufficient to write a comment or two per child per week. Figure 9.4 is an example of anecdotal records a teacher maintained on a child in her class.

Anecdotal records can also be used to assess the value of an activity. As part of her unit on health and safety, Ms. Karyn takes her kindergarten class to visit the local hospital and creates a sociodramatic play center with a medical theme. She devotes 10 minutes each day to observing the children at play in the center, tape-records the conversations in the center, and transcribes anecdotes or pieces of dialogue that illustrate what the children are learning. She also evaluates her own ability to extend and enrich the children's play by introducing new themes, materials, and concepts. Appendix D contains some of the play texts that she collected and her interpretations of them.

Observ

Child's Name _Mo_____     Date _10/17/2000_____

Activity _Grouptime_____     Time _9 – 9:30_____

Mo and his family are recent Indochinese immigrants with limited English proficiency. After several weeks of onlooker behavior, Mo participated in circletime for the 1st time. He had mastered all of the motions and lyrics to an action song and sang out enthusiastically. Mo's peers seemed to know that this was a breakthrough for him and several made encouraging remarks ("Mo knows this one now!"; "You're a good singer."). Mo beamed with pride as I invited him to lead the group in another verse of the song.

L. M. J.

Observer

**Figure 9.4**    Example of an Anecdotal Record

### Checklists or Rating Scales

Checklists may be used to identify play skills. Teachers and caregivers may choose to study children's self-expression and levels of play, current play interests, patterns of play, levels of play, preferred materials, or interpersonal skills (e.g., entering an ongoing play episode, negotiating for materials).

Mr. Damion works in a Head Start classroom. One of his goals is to stimulate children's imagination and to document the progress that they make in imaginative play. To do this, he uses the observational scale adapted from Beaty and Garvey in Figure 9.5. There are many commercially available checklists and rating scales that teachers and caregivers can use as is or adapt to suit their needs (Seely, 1994).

**Figure 9.5**
Imaginative Play
Checklist

**Roles**
- Pretends by replaying familiar routines
- Seeks particular props to enact pretend play roles
- Assigns roles or takes assigned roles
- Takes on characteristics and actions related to role

*Explores different roles:*

_____ *Relational roles*—based on knowledge of family (e.g., parent-child)

_____ *Functional roles*—based on wider experience and defined by
        actions (e.g., "I want to be the cash register")

_____ *Character roles*—stereotypes or fictional roles based on TV and stories

_____ *Peripheral roles*—based on child's individual imagination (e.g.,
        referring to an imaginary companion)

**Themes**
- Uses language to create and sustain event-structured play themes
- Uses exciting, danger-packed themes
- Uses elaborate and creative themes, subordinates own actions to the
  goals of the group

*Fantasy themes:*

_____ Averting threat and rescuing others

_____ Communicating (telephoning, letter writing)

_____ Packing/taking a trip

_____ Shopping

_____ Cooking

_____ Dining out/entertainment

_____ Treating/healing

_____ Building/repairing

*Sources:* Adapted from Beaty (1986) and Garvey (1977).

### Interviews with Children

As part of her kindergarten writing program, Ms. Veder interviews children about their writing. When she asks Caleb the first question on the interview, "Tell me about your writing," he responds with the writing sample and explanation found in Figure 9.6. Figure 9.7 is a sample interview for the visual arts, which can be adapted for other self-expressive activities.

### Audio or Video Recordings

Mechanical means of observing become the teacher's eyes and ears while he or she continues to engage in classroom activities. Ms. Maloney, a student teacher, set up a pet store in conjunction with a unit on economics. Through the use of videotape,

**Figure 9.6**
Caleb's Writing

Caleb: This says "cat" and "dog" and that's a big "G" and one hundred and one. That's just my name and . . . yeah, my name, Caleb. And one hundred and ten and . . . uh . . . nine and six. And this is a five and a four and a fancy four and a thirteen. See? I made this pretend word and then I can find words in it. I have to underline the letters so I don't forget . . . Watch this! D-o-d—that spells dad! And m-o-m spells mom. Wait. Oh, wait. D-*a*-d spells dad! Here's a "u" and an "o." Wait, here's a fancy "u" and this is a fancy "o." Watch! This is a little "t" and this here is a littler "t" and now they're connected together!

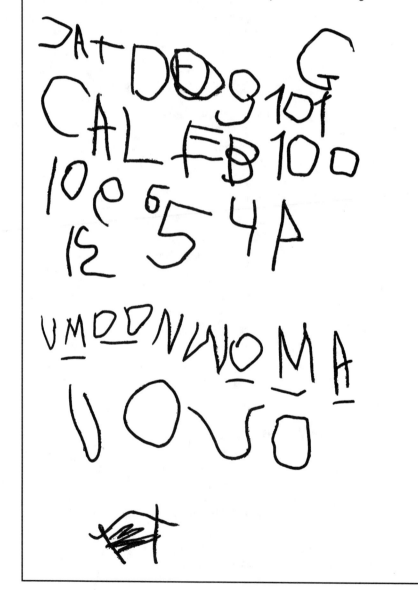

**Figure 9.7**
The Visual Arts: A
Process Interview

1. Why do people paint, draw, sculpt, weave, etc.?
2. How do you get ready to make a picture?
3. How do you decide what to make?
4. Do you ever do artwork at home? (If yes) How is art at home different from the art you do at school?
5. If you had to explain to a little child how a person makes a picture, what would you tell him or her to do?
6. Show me or tell me about your best art project. Why do you think this is your best work?

Ms. Maloney was able to analyze how divergent her questions and responses were with a second-grade girl who invited her into the play theme.

*Lori:*   This is my pet store. May I help you today, miss? Are you looking for anything in particular?
*Teacher:*   Yes, I would like to buy my nephew an unusual gift. He is going to be 10 years old on Monday.
*Lori:*   Well, isn't that just special! I hope that he is a nice boy. What kinds of animals does he like?
*Teacher:*   He likes dinosaurs and wild animals.
*Lori:*   Well, we are out of dinosaurs. I just sold the last one yesterday and I did not order any more. The animals are just too large for my store. We do have some parakeets and fish.
*Teacher:*   Do you have any parrots? They are a wild animal.
*Lori:*   Yes, I just happen to have one, beautiful colors on it.
*Teacher:*   I'll take it. He is just beautiful. Can he be taught to talk? I heard that some of them can learn to talk, is that true?
*Lori:*   First of all, before you get too confused, this is a she. This particular type of bird can be taught to talk, but it takes a lot of time.
*Teacher:*   What else do I need?
*Lori:*   You'll need a cage, food, and some items for the bird to play with.
*Teacher:*   Well, how much do I owe you for the bird, cage, food, and two toys?
*Lori:*   The total price is $125.33.
*Teacher:*   Do you take MasterCard?
*Lori:*   Yes.

By recording and watching this episode of co-playing between herself and the child, Ms. Maloney has a clearer sense of Lori's ability to take on a role, to "think

*Portfolio assessment is immediately understandable to parents, and encourages children's involvement and self-evaluation.*

on her feet," to understand basic concepts about economics as well as pet care, and to use oral communication skills. This is one reason why play-based assessment for young children is encouraged—it provides a more holistic evaluation of the children's abilities.

### Individual Case Studies

Ms. Fisher is a reading specialist whose work with Jerri, a second grader, led to a case study of an individual child. By talking with the student and her family, the teacher discovered that although Jerri's parents wanted her to learn to read, they had never read to her and there were no children's books in the home. Jerri was intellectually capable of reading, she simply saw no reason to read, other than to please adults. Instead of focusing on the skills of reading, Ms. Fisher decided that she would give Jerri a real reason to read: enjoyment. Jerri listened to and read books every day with her teacher's help, and after they discussed the book, Ms. Fisher recorded Jerri's reactions. A major breakthrough came when Ms. Fisher suggested that Jerri might like to create her own book. One of Jerri's favorites was the lift-the-flap picture book of the song *Roll Over!* by Mordecai Gerstein (1984). The edges of the pages are folded over, and by lifting them up readers can see who fell out of bed with each verse of the song. At first, Jerri used the same characters that were in the book, but as she continued to work on the project, her book became more and more original, with other animals and characters populating the pages.

After Jerri had revised her book into final form, she presented it to the class, giggling throughout at her own pleasure in the book's humor. When she was finished, the children burst into spontaneous applause and rushed up to congratulate her on her achievement.

Note how this activity meets the criteria mentioned earlier for assessing creative products. Ms. Fisher trusted Jerri to undertake a major project and accepted her work. Reading together challenged Jerri to grow; as she gained confidence in herself, she broke away from stereotypic thinking, and her work became more than just a copy.

### Published Scales

Play and creative expression can also be evaluated through more structured methods, such as published instruments. These scales provide information on children's levels of sociodramatic play (Smilansky & Shefatya, 1990), on the cognitive and social dimensions of play (Johnson, Christie, & Yawkey, 1987; Howes, 1980), on language abilities during symbolic play (Westby, 1980), or on the use of creative processes (Kulp & Tarter, 1986). Figure 9.8 lists some of the more commonly used scales and describes their purpose/focus.

## Portfolio Assessment

A technique for assembling all of the different types of observation that teachers and caregivers use is the portfolio (Graves & Sunstein, 1992). Portfolios have been used in the arts for decades. When artists apply for a job, they assemble a collection of their work to demonstrate their range and the depth of their expertise and submit the collection for review. Much the same strategy is used when compiling different types of observation of children's creative expression and play. Some common questions and answers about portfolios follow.

### Why Use Portfolios?

Portfolios reveal and document children's learning in many different modes, on real-world tasks, over a period of time. This method of assessment gives teachers and caregivers more input into assessment, is immediately understandable to parents, and encourages self-evaluation in students. The evidence collected in a portfolio also helps teachers make instructional decisions. Armstrong (1994) recommends "the 5 Cs of portfolio development" as a guide for using portfolios.

1. *Celebration.* Use portfolios to acknowledge and validate children's products and accomplishments during the year.
2. *Cognition.* Use portfolios to encourage students to reflect upon their own work.
3. *Communication.* Use portfolios to inform families, administrators, and colleagues about children's growth and progress.
4. *Cooperation.* Use portfolios as a way for groups of children collectively to produce and evaluate their own work.

---

**Creativity and Talent**

---

*Frasier Talent Assessment Profile*

Author: Mary M. Frasier                                    Publication Year: 1995

Description: A system for teachers to provide anecdotal evidence of gifted behaviors.

*Group Inventory for Finding Creative Talent* (GIFT)

Author: Sylvia Rimm                                    Publication Year: 1980

Description: A quick-scoring, individually administered, self-report questionnaire suitable for use with elementary school children.

*Student Product Assessment Form*

Authors: S. M. Reis & J. S. Renzulli                   Publication Year: 1991

Description: A set of criteria for assessing creative products.

*Torrance Tests of Creative Thinking* (TTCT)

Author: E. Paul Torrance                                Publication Year: 1990

Description: Children are provided with a simple stimulus (e.g., two parallel lines with an oval between them) and asked to make the stimulus into a picture.

*Modes of Thinking in Young Children*

Authors: M. A. Wallach and N. Kogan                    Publication Year: 1965

Description: Children are shown cards with a few lines or shapes and invited to suggest what the item might be. Points are awarded for more original, elaborate, and numerous responses.

*Screening Instrument for Identifying Artistic Talent*

Author: Merle Karnes                                   Publication Year: 1987

Description: Teachers use a simple checklist to identify giftedness in young children.

**Play Scales**

---

*Qualitative Analysis of Metaplay*

Author: Jeffrey Trawick-Smith                          Year: 1998

Description: An observational system that looks at metaplay—the process of suspending role playing to think or communicate about pretend themes from outside of the play activity. A system of 3 categories (initiations, responses, constructions) and 38 subcategories are used to observe and analyze children's play.

*Transdisciplinary Play-Based Assessment (revised)*

Authors: Toni W. Linder                                Year: 1993

Description: A play-based assessment of the cognitive, communicative, language, sensori-motor, and social-emotional areas of development for children ages 6 months to 6 years.

For more information on assessment, visit the ERIC Clearinghouse on Assessment and Evaluation at www.ericae.net

---

**Figure 9.8**   Published Play and Creativity Scales

5.  *Competency.* Use portfolios to establish a set of standards by which one child's work can be compared with other children's performance or with a benchmark established by the teacher.

### What Is Included in a Portfolio?

Children's portfolios should not be cartons filled with every imaginable item ever produced by the child during the course of the year. Rather, they should be focused and organized by learning goals. If a teacher has the language arts goal that children read and respond to a variety of picture books, for instance, the file might contain a log of the books read by the child and stories or artwork inspired by children's books. A portfolio for the visual arts focuses on content and process. It usually includes (1) sketches, studies, and preliminary works, (2) collections of images that have influenced the student artist, (3) reproductions of works by the student's favorite artists, (4) written notes and thoughts concerning the creative process (Dunn, 1995), and (5) comments about the problem solving that accompanies going from preliminary ideas to the finished product. Figure 9.9 shows a sample portfolio.

### How Should Portfolios Be Organized?

An expandable file with accordion-folded sides is a good portfolio. Individual folders that are keyed or color-coded to program goals can be placed inside the expandable file to organize the child's work. If exploring different art media is a program goal, for example, one of the folders might contain a sample of paintings, chalk drawings, batik, and a photograph of sculptures the child constructed out of clay, wood, and paper. To demonstrate the child's attainment of another art program goal, the refinement of a form, a folder might contain sketches of the work at successive stages and the finished product.

Additionally, every portfolio should include a table of contents so that teachers, administrators, parents, and children can use it. The teacher should develop the table of contents with input from the children, then give the children responsibility for maintaining their portfolios. Young children are capable of making choices about which of their works are best and which pieces belong in their portfolios. The way to build these skills in self-evaluation is to discuss children's choices with them and inquire about the reasons for their selections. By modeling how to conduct a thoughtful appraisal of one's own work, teachers are showing children how to decide which of their works is superior to others and why.

## TEACHERS' ROLES AND RESPONSIBILITIES

Perhaps the most important role of the teacher in child-centered assessment is to view children as informants about their own growth and as partners in the assessment process.

**Table of Contents**

**Goals**

*Folder 1 (blue):   Doing New Things, Using New Materials*
Shayna is a 5-year-old who is enrolled in a private school in a large suburban area. For her blue folder, she selected (1) white chalk on black paper, and (2) using markers on newsprint.

2.

1.

**Figure 9.9**   Sample Portfolios

**Figure 9.9** *(Continued)*

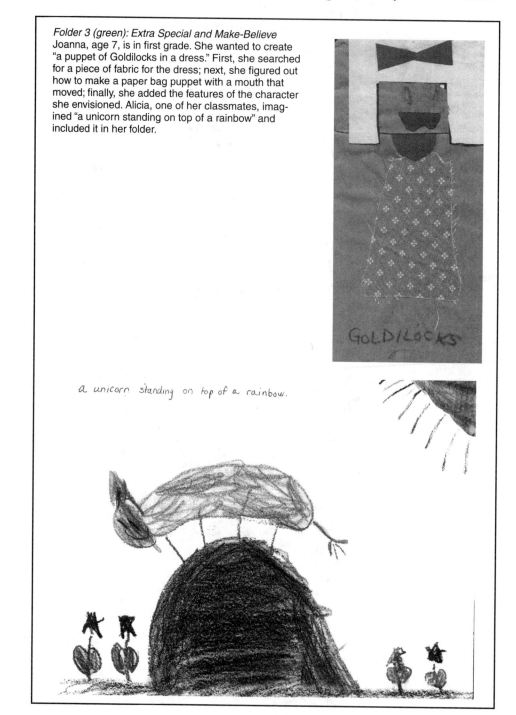

*Folder 3 (green): Extra Special and Make-Believe*
Joanna, age 7, is in first grade. She wanted to create "a puppet of Goldilocks in a dress." First, she searched for a piece of fabric for the dress; next, she figured out how to make a paper bag puppet with a mouth that moved; finally, she added the features of the character she envisioned. Alicia, one of her classmates, imagined "a unicorn standing on top of a rainbow" and included it in her folder.

**Figure 9.9**   *(Continued)*

1.

IRA Sleeps over
BEAch + Jam for Frances
Bedtime for Frances
my Goolwho Book
my First Book Peekle Juice
a may go the boats
Plai ball
The funny ride
Spot at play
The grinch who stold Christmas

Spot at play
Super fudge
Bed Time for frances
Bread and Jam for frances
Soccer
Being Selbbish
Disobaying your Paren
no girls aloud
minie + Micky

micky                    Miney

*Folder 6 (white): Books, Stories, and Letters*
Brenda (age 6) is enrolled in first grade in a parochial school. For her folder, she selected (1) an illustrated reading list, (2) a drawing inspired by *There's an Alligator Under My Bed* and (3) a letter and picture for her sister Nicole, who is away at college.

2.

There's an alligator under my Bed

3.

Brenda

adore

Me and you

Bronda

DearNichole
Imissyou
ILicyou
and Holler Das too
Iamurninghiowtooadt
Doroumiss me

Dear Nicole, I miss you. I like you and Holly does too.
I am learning how to read. Do you miss me?

**Figure 9.9**   *(Continued)*

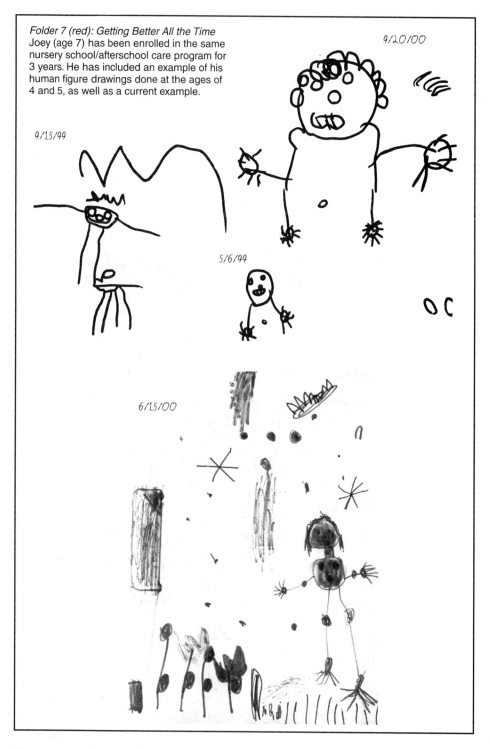

*Folder 7 (red): Getting Better All the Time*
Joey (age 7) has been enrolled in the same nursery school/afterschool care program for 3 years. He has included an example of his human figure drawings done at the ages of 4 and 5, as well as a current example.

**Figure 9.9**   *(Continued)*

## *Matching Observation Techniques to Purposes*

Teachers and caregivers can nurture play, for example, from within and without (Smilansky & Shefatya, 1990). Intervening from outside the play might include adding toy cars and people to the block area to stimulate new types of play or making comments or suggestions about a role. Intervention from inside the play means that the teacher actually gets involved in the children's play. Because entering the children's play is more intrusive, it is usually reserved for those times when children need more direct teacher intervention. Some examples of times when direct intervention is appropriate are:

- When a sociodramatic play center is first introduced.
- When the children seem to be "stalled" at a particular form of play.
- When the children have had limited experience with group play.
- When the play becomes destructive to people or property.

## *Providing Flexible Groups*

One way of balancing individual and group experiences is to provide a mixture of spontaneous group formation (such as children deciding to play with the blocks together) and teacher-designated groups (such as playing a singing game during circle time). It is also important for children to use their creative processes both individually and in groups. A child may create a painting at the easel, but she also needs experience coordinating her efforts with a small group that is creating a model of the aviary they visited, for example. A child may compose his own poem or story, but it is equally valuable for him to work with a partner or a small group to write a story or poem. A small group of primary grade children may read a story silently to themselves, but it is also appropriate for them to share that story with a child from another grade level, a parent volunteer, or a senior center volunteer. By keeping the groupings flexible, the teacher can give children experiences with a complete range of social interaction patterns as they are learning.

## *Noting Patterns*

Teachers and caregivers need to take notice of how children approach various types of play. If a child has never ventured into the block area, invite him or her in. Perhaps a child begins the day with more boisterous forms of play and may be observed listening quietly to stories and songs later in the day. Dramatic changes in a child's patterns of play may be an indication that the child is dealing with some stressful situations, such as the girl who has always insisted upon being the mother and suddenly begins to insist on playing baby's role, now that a new sibling has arrived.

Take note, also, of children's interests and role-taking preferences. Pay attention to the roles that children select for themselves. Is a particular child regularly cast in the role of victim when monsters and superheroes is the play theme? Does a child always insist upon selecting the play theme? Are sex role stereotypes present? A teacher who can readily answer these questions really knows her students.

*When materials are unfamiliar to children, teachers should intervene and demonstrate how those materials can be used.*

## Asking Good Questions

Opportunities for children to persist in exploring, discovering, and pursuing questions are essential to promote intellectual growth (Busching & Slesinger, 1995). "Questions can be stopped by answers" (VanMaanen, 1986, pp. 40–41). How can teachers and caregivers keep children's interest in the question alive? Improving the quality of learning experiences for children really demands teachers and caregivers who will allow children to take the lead; who will do less telling and more asking; who will talk less and listen more. One simple way to improve questions is to include thinking words in the questions that you ask, as illustrated in Figure 9.10.

**Figure 9.10**
Questions That
Encourage Problem
Solving

---

**For the Teacher: A Guide to Asking Better Questions**

---

Some simple changes in our ways of posing questions can encourage children to think more critically. As children hear cognitive terms in everyday use and practice the thinking skills that accompany these labels, they will begin to internalize these words and incorporate them into their own vocabularies.

Instead of saying . . .
"Let's look at these two pictures."

Say:
"Let's *compare* these two pictures."

Instead of asking . . .
"What do you think will happen when . . ."

Ask:
"What do you *predict* will happen when . . . ?"

Instead of asking . . .
"What did you think of the story?"

Ask:
"What *conclusions* can you draw about this story?"

Instead of asking . . .
"How do you know that's true?"

Ask:
"What *evidence* do you have to support . . . ?"

**A Framework for the Child's Self-Questions About Problem Solving**

---

**Circle the strategy or strategies that you used to solve the problem.**

?    I guessed.

   I looked for a pattern.

   I made a list.

   I drew a picture.

   I made a web or diagram.

   I solved a simpler problem.

   I worked backward.

   I made a table.

   I experimented with several different strategies.

   I asked somebody for clues.

   I collaborated with a group.

*Sources:* Adapted from British Ministry of Education and Costa (1993)

In a hands-on science activity on sinking and floating, Ms. Zezel used the following guidelines (Raths, Wassermann, Jonas, & Rothstein, 1986) to probe her third graders' thinking:

**1.** *Encourage children to look carefully and use what they see to support their ideas.* After equipping the children with pans of water and various objects (e.g., a cork, paper clip, pencil, coin, popsicle stick, a tennis ball, a feather, a piece of nylon net), Ms. Zezel asked: "If the goal is to find out whether objects sink or float, how will you proceed? How could we keep track of our observations?"

**2.** *Invite children to compare and classify.* After the children had completed their experiments and recorded their observations, Ms. Zezel invited them to compare and classify ("Is there anything similar about the objects that floated? the objects that sank? What differences exist between the objects that floated and sank?") and to relate new information or ideas to what they already knew ("Carl thinks that big objects sink; Kim says that light objects float. What other objects might you try to test this idea? Think about all of the things that you have seen floating in water. How would you explain the fact that they float?").

**3.** *Have children summarize and interpret.* Ms. Zezel asked the children to "recap" what they had learned so far and to explain things from their points of view ("What ideas do we now have about the properties of objects that sink? objects that float?").

**4.** *Ask children to identify assumptions and suggest hypotheses.* Ms. Zezel asked the children to articulate the assumptions they made in a low-risk environment where they felt comfortable making educated guesses ("We now have several ideas. Some people feel that floating has something to do with air inside the object. Some people have concluded that objects float or sink depending upon how heavy they are and upon the size of the body of water. We will be using the scales now to weigh each object. Refer back to your original experiment to find out if the heaviest objects always sink and the lightest objects always float.").

**5.** *Encourage children to imagine and create.* Ms. Zezel urged the children to use visualization and create mental images to help them solve the problem ("If it is true that air has something to do with floating, how does a battleship float? Imagine that your house was suddenly surrounded by deep water. What materials would you use to build something that would take you across? Why?").

## Developing New Teaching Strategies

Teachers and caregivers must constantly strive to extend their repertoire of teaching strategies. By reading professional journals and magazines and participating in other professional development activities such as workshops and conferences, teachers can remain current and get many excellent ideas. After one teacher read an article subtitled "Do You See What I Say?" (Mundell, 1987), she incorporated the following suggestions for developing children's visual images:

**1.** *Invite children to create images of concrete objects.* Talk about each child's images and compare/contrast them, emphasizing that there are no right or wrong images. For example, you might say, "Imagine the funniest hat you can think of. It should be a hat that you have never actually seen before. What is its shape and size? What does the hat look like? Who is wearing it and how does that make the hat even funnier?"

   2.   *Ask children to imagine familiar objects or scenes.* This visualization technique is a good introduction to a story. A teacher who is sharing the wordless picture book *Junglewalk* (Tafuri, 1988), for example, might discuss the first page, where the boy has just finished reading a book and is switching off the light to go to sleep: "I wonder what he was reading. Hmm. The title of his book is *Jungles of the World.* Close your eyes for a minute and imagine what sorts of things he may have seen in the book he read." In this way, the teacher assesses children's prior knowledge and improves their comprehension of a story told in pictures.

   3.   *Ask children to read or tell stories with scenes that are easy to visualize.* You might begin with familiar literary images, such as the witch's gingerbread house in "Hansel and Gretel." Following some discussion of the mental images children have created, you could move to an activity such as telling the story of Tom Thumb and then comparing the things children envisioned with the images created by artist Richard Jesse Watson (1989). Even children who are minimally proficient in English can comprehend a story that is told through vocal and facial expressions. Children who are more fluent in English can retell the story; those who are not can reenact the story in mime and words. Storytellers recognize this important advantage to listening to stories: "Somehow the very fact that they had to focus just on listening seemed to set them free" (Hinman, 1987, p. 3).

## Teacher and Learner Self-Evaluation

In order to promote more meaningful evaluation of students' work, teachers and caregivers need to engage in reflection and self-dialogue. One route to self-questioning is to consider whether your beliefs, attitudes, values, and teaching philosophy are compatible with creative teaching (see Figure 9.11).

   As we have seen, it is also necessary to build children's skills in evaluation. Just as self-discipline is the ultimate goal of discipline, self-evaluation is the ultimate goal of evaluation. In your work with young children, you will want children to grow in independence and learn how to creatively meet life's challenges. Self-evaluation is the key. Some comments and questions to help children grow in self-evaluation include:

- Tell me about how you worked in your group today.
- Describe some of the things you liked about your work.
- Which things did not work well for you?
- What are some things you could do for yourself? What did you need help with?
- What did you do to help others?
- When you had some trouble, explain how you solved the problem.
- What were some of the new ideas that you had?

**Figure 9.11**
Will You Become a
Creative Teacher? A
Self-Assessment

**Nonconformist**—Do I tend to behave, act, and think in unique ways? Am I capable of departing from routines, rules, and conventions? Am I committed to supporting children's creativity in spite of difficulties or other people's lack of support?

**Inventor**—When confronted with a daunting task, do I have the ability to generate a positive outcome through my resourcefulness and nonstereotypic thinking?

**Self-Starter**—Am I curious? Do I pursue my interests? Am I interested in knowing all that I can about something? Do I continue striving for a certain goal, not quitting until it is reached? Do I get involved in many different projects simultaneously?

**Energizer**—Am I willing to invest energy above and beyond what is required? Can I persuade others to join in?

**Player**—Do I create, understand, and take part in unexpected ideas and take pleasure in humor? Do I use humor effectively to deal with embarrassing or difficult situations?

**Observer**—Do I notice and remember details?

**Spontaneous**—Do I have the capacity to respond quickly and appropriately to unfamiliar situations?

*Sources:* Csikszentmihalyi (1996) and Dinca (1999).

- What did you do the best of all?
- Were there things that you didn't try? How did you feel about that?
- Is there a particular piece of work that you feel proud of? Tell me about it.
- Tell me what you did when . . . (adapted from Wassermann, 1990, pp. 223–224).

Communication with families, the community, and your colleagues about your approaches is a key element in teaching creatively. If you fail to help others understand why you approach teaching as you do, you are likely to be met with resistance because your ways of working with students differ from the more traditional approaches. When you begin a unit of study, be certain to let others know what you are doing, and why. Letters home are a simple, yet effective way of explaining creative approaches to teaching. Figure 9.12 is a sample letter that could be sent home to parents. Note that it has several key features. First of all, it keeps educational jargon to a minimum and is written in clear, simple language that is supported with concrete examples. Second, it explains what children are learning and how parents and families can help. Third, it has a positive tone rather than a demanding or critical tone so that families get a sense of your enthusiasm for teaching and motivating their child to learn. You may want to try writing a similar letter to accompany a thematic unit that you are planning.

**Figure 9.12**
Sample Letter to
Parents and Families

Dear Parents and Families of Kindergarteners:

Understanding patterns is an important skill for young children. Recognizing patterns is essential for learning to read and write, to create works of art, to appreciate music, to participate in dance, and to listen to stories. Next week, we will be beginning our study of patterns. Children will be learning that:

*Patterns are repetitions.* Printed fabric is a pictorial pattern, a picket fence is an architectural pattern, a jump rope rhyme is a pattern of sound, words are patterns of letters, and so forth.

*Patterns can be found everywhere.* There are social patterns, such as please and thank you; there are visual patterns, such as wallpaper; there are auditory patterns, such as clapping to the beat of music, and so forth.

*Patterns occur in nature.* The change of seasons is a pattern, a spider's web is a pattern, tracks in the snow are patterns.

*Children can make patterns.* A child can draw a border around a picture, invent motions to go with a song, or use the computer to generate patterns.

*Patterns are found in different cultures.* African Kente cloth is a pattern, Chinese characters form patterns, Navajo pottery is decorated with patterns, and company logos are patterns.

You will see your child bringing home geometric patterns that were produced on the computer, word search pages where the child highlights patterns of words, and patterns produced with a stamp pad and various stamps. Please display your child's work and invite him or her to talk with you about patterns.

Around your home and in the community, consider playing a "Pattern Hunt" game. For instance, while setting the table, you might say, "See if you can make a pattern of bowl, spoon, glass for everyone in the family." Stopped at a traffic light, you might say, "I spy a pattern—red, yellow, green. Do you see the pattern?"

Thank you for helping your child to understand patterns.

Sincerely,

## PRACTICAL APPLICATIONS FOR YOUR CLASSROOM

Assessment is being used inappropriately if the results are used to diminish children's opportunities or exclude them from special programs. In one school district with an itinerant music teacher, for example, children were routinely given a "music aptitude test" that assessed the child's potential for reading musical notation (Jalongo & Stamp, 1997). On the basis of that test score alone, large numbers of children were denied the chance to learn to play a musical instrument. Important considerations, such as the child's interest and motivation, were largely ignored. From a logical standpoint, it is questionable whether any test can accurately predict a child's musical abilities, given the wide array of musical styles and instruments that exist. Many of the rejected children accepted the school's pronouncement that they were "unmusical," and some avoided musical activities throughout their lives. Clearly, this program had a talent-scout orientation. The assumption was that music study is for a select few, rather than something to be enjoyed and experienced by all. Teachers must be convinced that all children need to have their creative processes nurtured.

## Experiences to Support Cultural and Ethnic Diversity

The story of Jane Cartagena, a 3-year-old child whose parents are migrant workers, illustrates how teachers can promote equity through the arts and authentic assessment. Jane is enrolled in a federally funded preschool program, but she has limited English proficiency and seldom interacts with the other children because they all speak English. Ms. Garner has been observing Jane each day and notes that she usually remains in the housekeeping area, performing such activities as cooking, ironing, and caring for the baby. Ms. Garner decides to try another approach. She sits outside the housekeeping corner, rings the bell on the toy telephone, and says "Hola? Hola?" Jane pauses, then picks up the telephone and begins a conversation in Spanish with her teacher. If we consider what might have happened to Jane if her teacher had no knowledge of Spanish or, worse yet, if she had labeled Jane as "nonverbal" or "uncooperative," it is easy to see how children of different cultural backgrounds can be systematically excluded from learning experiences. Good teachers figure out what their students need in order to feel accepted, to learn, and to succeed. One of the worst disservices we can do to children is to treat them as disembodied intellects evaluated purely through test performance. In order to give children a chance at success, our assessment strategies must be "based on products, progress, and effort" (Collins, 1991, p. 29).

## Experiences to Support Inclusion

Authentic assessment of children's creative work can also enable teachers to know their students better and work more successfully with them. Colin is a good example of this. He is a first grader who experienced a tragic accident last summer. His family was in an auto crash and Colin's legs and spine were so damaged that the doctors wondered if he would live, much less walk again. But even worse than his physical trauma was the emotional ordeal Colin endured. While 6-year-old Colin was in intensive care at the hospital, his mother died as a result of her injuries. When Colin began first grade in September, he didn't mention the accident. At Thanksgiving he wrote: "I am thankful that my dad and sister are still alive." Near Christmastime he wrote: "I last my mum 5 muns ago. [I lost my mom five months ago.] Please . . . that I am weak." The second sentence, he explained, "Didn't come out right . . . what I want to say is that sometimes the other kids don't understand I am weak. They say, 'Come on, can't you run any faster?' or 'You walk funny,' but I got hurt real bad and that's the best I can do. So I'm telling them, 'Please don't make fun of me.' "

Teachers and parents sometimes limit the play of a child with a physical disability such as Colin by becoming overprotective. As a result, adults frequently lower their expectations for children's play, restrict opportunities for play, and diminish the experience children have with playmates (Hughes, 1995). Sensitivity and tact are essential when breaking these barriers for children. The child who is confined to a wheelchair may find it difficult to play with unit blocks, but he or she can become the "city planner" or play with smaller blocks on a tray or at a table. A child such as Colin who has some physical limitations where speed and power are concerned can compensate for them by working to his or her strengths. The assessment of the artwork of young children with special needs, for example, requires that teachers pay attention to physical and perceptual limitations, make appropriate adaptations, and emphasize abilities rather than disabilities:

> Some children taking medication have poor eye-hand coordination, and their drawings reflect this condition. Children with neurological problems or neuro-muscular complications may not be able to hold a brush or crayon in the same way as other children. Some children with sensory processing difficulties may need carefully selected sensory input in order to focus on visual art. All efforts should be made to support the highest functioning of these children during any art activities, and especially during an assessment. (Brown, 1995, p. 6)

For guidelines on activity-based approaches to teaching and assessing young children with special needs, see resource guides such as Bricker, Pretti-Frontczak, and McComas (1999); Cavallaro and Haney (1999); and Nelson, Roberts, and Smith (1998).

## Adaptations for Individual Learners

Too often, educators have assumed that the dreary repetition of skills is appropriate for children who struggle with verbal or mathematical tasks while compelling, complex, and creative tasks are best suited for children with highly developed verbal and mathematical intelligences. But all children need authentic, engaging, legitimate, and memorable work; work that matters outside of school as well as in the classroom (Schiengold, 1991). As teachers, if we are serious in our desire to empower children, the evaluation practices we choose must provide feedback for the learners to grow on, rather than simply provide marks and grades that quantify children's performance, like eggs, into "jumbos, mediums, and cracks" (Wassermann, 1990, p. 212). A recent study of portfolio assessment of children's drawings and writings concluded that while high- and average-achieving students tended to perform equally well on standardized tests and on story-writing tasks, low-achieving children's performance on tests and on real tasks was the most disparate. As a group, the children who scored the lowest on the tests performed much better on real writing tasks than their test scores would lead one to expect (Simmons, 1991). This finding underscores the message that many of our tests, whether they are called tests of achievement, intelligence, or creativity, are actually measures of talent for paper-and-pencil types of schoolwork.

Typically, high-achieving children exhibit above-average ability, creativity, and task commitment. As a result, they need real-life experiences and activities that expose them to a wide variety of disciplines, topics, and issues; instructional methods and materials that develop both thinking and feeling processes; investigative activities and artistic productions that enable them to function as "firsthand inquirers"; and opportunities to act like practicing professionals—to become artists, scientists, writers, and so on (Hallahan & Kaufman, 1991). The teacher's role is to function as a facilitator. This involves such tasks as helping students translate a general concern into a clearly focused problem, providing children with the materials and methods necessary to resolve the problem, and assisting students in communicating their findings to authentic audiences (Hallahan & Kauffman, 1991).

Some children have less experience with more formal types of learning environments, but this does not mean that they should be "weeded out" of the educational system. Rather, the educational system must begin earlier and do a better job in preparing children for authentic learning experiences. As Hodgkinson (1991) points out, "Every dollar spent on Head Start will save taxpayers $7 in later services that the child will not need—a superb investment" (p. 15). We must make the curriculum that inaugurates the child's experience in schools a child-centered one, one that celebrates diversity and respects children. For if we stick to the "tabula rasa" mentality, low-achieving children will be blamed and will always seem deficient, and our educational system will fail them once again. Based on her interviews and surveys with elementary school children, Weinstein (1995) explains how low expectations and inappropriate assessment practices inhibit student achievement, particularly the achievement of poor and minority children:

> These students often receive barren, remedial materials, which imply the belief that they are unable to grapple with higher-order ideas. In addition, the evaluation system, which typically conveys that intelligence is stable, global, and distributed on a bell curve, implies that some are permanently less intelligent than others and that there is only one kind of intelligence. Further, educators often rely on a system of rewards and punishments to motivate poor and minority students, instead of allowing them some leeway to pursue their own interests. Similarly, these students are typically allowed little input or self-direction; they are not allowed to take responsibility for their own learning. All of these practices reflect the low expectations educators as a group hold for these students. (p. 18)

## Conclusion

Creative thinking is much more than the ability to remember bits of information. It involves using that information in an imaginative, problem-solving way. In our culture, it is common to admire the game show contestant who easily recollects fragments of knowledge or to beam with pride as a 3-year-old recites the alphabet.

But, as we have seen, such highly touted tasks do not even scratch the surface of human intellectual potential. As human beings, our strength lies in complex tasks—perceiving connections, making inferences, combining ideas, adapting materials, and so forth. Encyclopedias and computers are more efficient at storing and retrieving bits of information than are most human beings. Therefore, it makes sense to delegate more of the routine mental tasks to technology and to concentrate instead on the high-order thinking abilities that, as far as we know, only human beings can perform. By emphasizing play, creativity, and real-world performance skills in our assessments, educators are taking a major step forward in educating for the future rather than teaching for the past.

## CHAPTER SUMMARY

1.    Assessment is a highly controversial issue; many inappropriate practices are commonplace. As a result, many major professional organizations are urging teachers to use a wide range of observational methods as an alternative to the overreliance on standardized tests.

2.    Assessment is an ongoing process rather than a single paper-and-pencil test. It should include information on the child's performance of meaningful tasks over an extended period of time and should look at the learner's attitudes, processes, and effort as well as the products of learning.

3.    In general, the purposes for assessing divergent thinking are to gain insight about creativity, evaluate progress, identify talents, provide enrichment, and optimize each child's growth in creative expression and play.

4.    More child-centered alternatives to standardized tests include observations, interactions, and the analysis of products or processes. One key role for teachers is the thoughtful, day-to-day observation of children. Specific techniques include interviews, conferences, portfolios, checklists, and rating scales. The standards set forth by various organizations and published observation tools can also be used to guide assessment efforts.

## *EXPANDING YOUR THINKING ABOUT ASSESSMENT*

 *Discuss: Assessment Issues in Creative Expression and Play*

1.    An administrator decides to use a test to determine which children are "ready" for kindergarten. Many of the children who are excluded each year are those who may most need socialization experiences and an intellectually stimulating environment. What could be done to remedy this situation?

2.    Using the observations of medical play in Appendix D as evidence, build a case that children are developing physically, socially, emotionally, and intellectually through sociodramatic play.

3.   A parent who visits your classroom comments, "I expected my child to really learn something, but it looks like she's just playing. She can do that at home." How would you respond to these objections? Support your position with your readings from this textbook.

4.   Recall some occasions when you were asked to evaluate your own performance. How did that make you feel? Was your self-assessment accurate? useful? How did your self-evaluation compare with other people's assessments of your performance?

5.   Use the self-evaluation criteria in Figure 9.11 to evaluate an episode of your behavior while trying to teach a child something. Then interview the child, using the list of questions for children that appears on page 409. Did these guidelines help you to focus on teacher and learner self-assessment? Why or why not?

6.   When a large city school district announced that it would identify elementary schools for the study of music, dance, and languages, urban parents got in line the night before and literally camped out to get their children enrolled in a particular school. What does this behavior tell you about parental interest in traditionally "nonacademic" subjects? Reflect for a moment on the opening case study about Michael. What will you as an early childhood educator do to change the curriculum and assessment practices that often exclude children, particularly poor and minority children, from participating in the most inviting educational programs?

## Interview: What Thwarts and Supports Creative Expression and Play?

Begin by reading the interview questions and jotting down some of your ideas. Then work with a partner in class to conduct a peer interview. As one member of the pair answers the questions, the other should be taking notes on her or his answers. Then switch roles so that the interviewee becomes the interviewer. Be prepared to report this information when you reconvene with the total group.

1.   Reflect for a moment on all of your educational experiences over the years. Try to identify those times when you were doing something in a class that sparked your interest, something that you were enthusiastic about learning, something that "spilled over" into your life outside of school because you were completely absorbed by it. Now try to analyze the general features of those experiences. What did they have in common?

2.   Now think about the work that you have produced in various classes throughout your school career. Describe one or two examples of work you produced of which you are particularly proud. How did that work reflect your creativity? How did others respond? How did their responses affect you?

3.   Describe one of your recreational pursuits, something that you do for its own sake during leisure time. How did you learn to love this activity? Please describe the process.

4.  Think about something that you do very poorly, a subject or skill that you would prefer to avoid. How did you learn to dislike this subject or feel incompetent with this skill? What would it take for you to approach learning this subject or skill with any degree of enthusiasm and confidence? How could a good teacher be of help?

## Write to Learn: Planning and Evaluating a Child-Centered Activity

Using the description of the treasure hunt activity (pp. 400–401) as a model, design another child-centered learning activity that meets the criteria for developing higher-level thinking skills. How does your activity help children to analyze, apply, synthesize, and evaluate information? Using the questioning guidelines in Figure 9.10 as a model, make a list of open-ended questions that will encourage children to observe carefully, compare and classify, summarize and interpret, identify assumptions and suggest hypotheses, and imagine/create.

## REFERENCES

Alper, C. D. (1999). Early childhood music education. In C. Seefeldt, *The early childhood curriculum* (pp. 237–263). New York: Teachers College Press.

Armstrong, T. (1994). *Multiple intelligences in the classroom.* Alexandria, VA: Association for Supervision and Curriculum Development.

Baer, J. (1994). Why you still should not trust creativity tests. *Educational Leadership, 52*(2), 71–73.

Beaty, J. J. (1986). *Observing the development of the young child.* Upper Saddle River, NJ: Merrill/Prentice Hall.

Bredekamp, S. (Ed.). (1991). Guidelines for appropriate curriculum content and assessment in programs serving children 3 through 8. *Young Children, 46*(3), 21–38.

Bricker, D., Pretti-Frontczak, K., & McComas, N. (1999). *An activity-based approach to early intervention.* Baltimore: Paul H. Brookes.

Brown, N. (1995). Assessment through creative art activities. *National All-Day Kindergarten Network Newsletter,* pp. 6–7.

Busching, B. A., & Slesinger, B. A. (1995). Authentic questions: What do they look like? Where do they lead? *Language Arts, 72*(5), 341–351.

Carter, M., & Curtis, D. (1995). *Training teachers: A harvest of theory and practice.* St. Paul, MN: Redleaf Press.

Cavallaro, C. C., & Haney, M. (1999). *Preschool inclusion.* Baltimore: Paul H. Brookes.

Chard, S. (1998). *The project approach: Managing successful projects* [Book 2]. New York: Scholastic.

Collins, A. (1991). The role of computer technology in restructuring schools. *Phi Delta Kappan, 73*(1), 28–36.

Csikszentmihalyi, M. (1996). The creative personality. *Psychology Today, 29*(4), 36–40.

Culbertson, L., & Contreras, G. (1999). Assessment: Allowing traditional and alternative approaches to co-exist. In M. Jalongo, (Ed.), *Resisting the pendulum swing: Informed perspectives on education controversies* (pp. 49–60). Olney, MD: Association for Childhood Education International.

Dacey, J. S. (1989). *Fundamentals of creative thinking.* Lexington, MA: Heath.

Dinca, M. (1999). Creative children in Romanian society. *Childhood Education 75*(6), 355–358.

Dunn, P. (1995). *Creating curriculum in art.* Reston, VA: National Art Education Association.

Educators in Connecticut's Pomperaug Regional School District 15. (1996). *A teacher's guide to performance-based learning and assessment.* Alexandria, VA: Association for Supervision and Curriculum Development.

Eisner, E. (1999). The uses and limits of performance assessment. *Phi Delta Kappan, 80*(9), 658–660.

Fernie, D. E. (1992). Profile: Howard Gardner. *Language Arts, 69,* 220–227.

Fogerty, R. (1997). *Problem-based learning and other curriculum models for the multiple intelligences classroom.* Arlington Heights, IL: IRI/Skylight Training and Publishing.

Fowler, C. (1994, January). Quoted in J. O'Neil, Looking at the art through new eyes: Visual arts programs pushed to reach new goals, new students. *ASCD Curriculum Update,* 1–8.

Gardner, H. (1993). *Frames of mind: The theory of multiple intelligences* (10th anniversary ed.). New York: Basic Books.

Gardner, H. (1995). Reflections on multiple intelligences: Myths and messages. *Phi Delta Kappan, 77*(3), 200–203, 206–209.

Garvey, K. (1977). *Play.* London: Fontana/Open Books.

Goodman, Y. M. (1989). Evaluation of students: Evaluation of teachers. In K. S. Goodman, Y. M. Goodman, & W. J. Hood (Eds.), *The whole language evaluation book* (pp. 3–14). Portsmouth, NH: Heinemann.

Graves, D. H., & Sunstein, B. S. (Eds.). (1992). *Portfolio portraits.* Portsmouth, NH: Heinemann.

Hallahan, D. P., & Kauffman, J. M. (1991). *Exceptional children.* Englewood Cliffs, NJ: Prentice Hall.

Harste, J. (1989). Preface to M. Siegel & R. F. Carey, *Critical thinking: A semiotic perspective* (pp. vi–viii). Bloomington, IN: ERIC/Reading and Communication Skills.

Hinman, C. (1987). Quoted in B. Reed, Storytelling: What it can teach. *School Library Journal, 34*(2), 35–39.

Hodgkinson, H. (1991). Reform versus reality. *Phi Delta Kappan, 73*(1), 9–16.

Hoffman, S., & Lamme, L. L. (Eds.). (1988). *Learning from the inside out: The expressive arts.* Wheaton, MD: Association for Childhood Education International.

Howes, C. (1980). Peer play scale as an index of complexity of peer interaction. *Developmental Psychology, 16,* 371–372.

Hughes, F. P. (1999). *Children, play and development* (3rd ed.). Boston: Allyn & Bacon.

Isenberg, J., & Farley, M. (1990). *Reading assessment program review committee.* Richmond, VA: Virginia Department of Education.

Jalongo, M. R., & Stamp, L. N. (1997). *The arts in young children's lives: Aesthetic education in early childhood.* Boston: Allyn & Bacon.

Jervis, K., & McDonald, J. (1996). Standards: The philosophical monster in the classroom. *Phi Delta Kappan, 77,* 563–569.

Johnson, J. E., Christie, J. F., & Yawkey, T. D. (1987). *Play and early childhood development.* Glenview, IL: Scott Foresman.

Kulp, M., & Tarter, B. J. (1986). The creative processes rating scale. *Creative Child and Adult Quarterly, 11*(3), 166–173.

Lewis, A. G. (1983). *Listen, look, and sing* (Grades 1, 2, and 3). Morristown, NJ: Silver Burdett.

Linn, R. L. (1996). Dimensions of thinking: Implications for testing. In F. J. Beau & L. Idol (Eds.), *Dimensions of thinking and cognitive instruction* (pp. 179–208). Hillsdale, NJ: Lawrence Erlbaum Associates.

Mundell, D. (1987). *Mental imagery: Do you see what I say?* Oklahoma City, OK: Oklahoma State Department of Education.

Nelson, J. R., Roberts, M. L., & Smith, D. J. (1998). *Conducting functional behavioral assessments: A practical guide.* Longmont, CO: Sopris West.

Nielsen, R. (1990). The perils of measuring "productivity." *On Campus, 9*(7), 18.

Potter, F. (1985). "Good job!" How we evaluate children's work. *Childhood Education, 61*(3), 203–206.

Raths, L. E., Wassermann, S., Jonas, A., & Rothstein, A. (1986). *Teaching for thinking: Theory, strategies and activities for the classroom.* New York: Teachers College Press.

Scheingold, K. (1991). Restructuring for learning with technology: The potential for synergy. *Phi Delta Kappan, 73*(1), 17–27.

Seely, A. E. (1994). *Professional's guide: Portfolio assessment.* Westminster, CA: Teacher Created Materials.

Sigel, I. E., & Cocking, R. R. (1977). *Cognitive development from childhood to adolescence: A constructive perspective.* New York: Holt, Rinehart & Winston.

Simmons, J. (1991). Quoted in K. S. Jongsma, Questions and answers: Portfolio assessment. *The Reading Teacher, 1,* 264–265

Smilansky, S. (1968). *The effects of sociodramatic play on disadvantaged preschool children.* New York: Wiley.

Smilansky, S., & Shefatya, L. (1990). *Facilitating play: A medium for promoting cognitive, socio-emotional and academic development in young children.* Gaithersburg, MD: Psychosocial and Educational Publications.

Strachota, B. (1996). *On their side: Helping children take charge of their learning.* Greenfield, MA: Northeast Foundation for Children.

VanMaanen, M. (1986). *The tone of teaching.* Portsmouth, NH: Heinemann.

Wassermann, S. (1989). Reflections on measuring thinking, while listening to Mozart's *Jupiter* symphony. *Phi Delta Kappan, 70*(5), 365–370.

Wassermann, S. (1990). *Serious players in the classroom: Empowering children through active learning experiences.* New York: Teachers College Press.

Weinstein, R. (1995). In R. W. Cole (Ed.), *Educating everybody's children: Diverse teaching strategies for diverse learners* (p. 18). Alexandria, VA: Association for Supervision and Curriculum Development.

Westby, C. E. (1980). Assessment of cognitive and language abilities through play. In P. A. Broen (Ed.), *Language, speech and hearing services in schools* (pp. 154–168). Minneapolis, MN: American Language Hearing Association.

## CHILDREN'S BOOKS CITED

Gerstein, M. (1984). *Roll over!* New York: Crown.

Tafuri, N. (1988). *Junglewalk.* New York: Greenwillow.

Watson, R. J. (1989). *Tom Thumb.* San Diego, CA: Harcourt Brace Jovanovich.

# Chapter 10

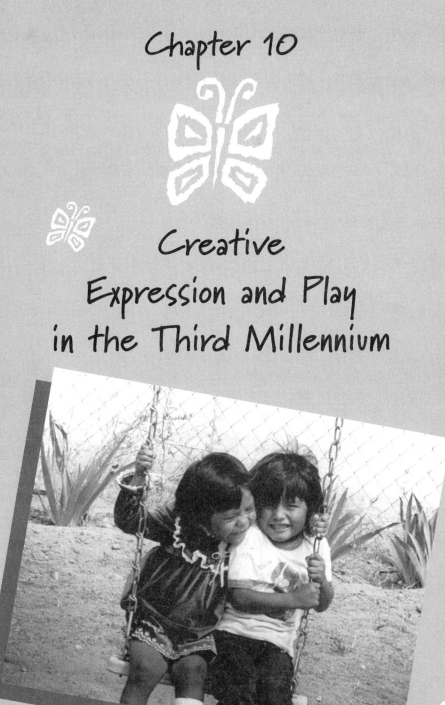

## Creative Expression and Play in the Third Millennium

*"Children are not simply 'embryonic workers.' They have value in themselves for who they are already. Children are not just 'preparatory grown-ups.' They are alive right now and must be valued, blessed, and treasured for the multitude of gifts they bring to us as a society, not for the added value they may bring to IBM. . . . Business needs team players who are not resistant or iconoclastic and do not waste precious time with metaphors or ethics. But society needs prophets, poets, troublemakers, saints and rebels, beautiful dreamers, glorious eccentrics."*

Jonathan Kozol, 1997, p. 6

# TEACHERS' REFLECTIONS ON CREATIVITY

### Preservice Teachers

"When I first scheduled this class, I thought that play was something old-fashioned, something that had been replaced by serious work. Now I realize that play is fundamental to the child's overall development. My concern after talking with some current student teachers is that not many classrooms in America support play and creative activities. Within the next few years, hopefully, teachers will see the value of offering more opportunities for creative expression and play in their classrooms."

"I attended a Saturday conference recently co-sponsored by the student chapters of the National Association for the Education of Young Children and the Association for Childhood Education International. One of the workshops that I selected was called 'Teaching to the Multiple Intelligences.' There were experienced classroom teachers in the group, but I felt like I was better informed about the topic because of the reading that I did for this class. I felt (secretly) proud that I was up-to-date and proud that the program I am in is current. That is a feeling I will work to keep throughout my professional career."

### Inservice Teachers

"I live in a small Pennsylvania coal-mining town not far from Pittsburgh. It is sad to see people who have been unemployed for months, some for years, waiting for the mines and mills to come back. When we talked in class about the type of workforce we will need in the future, I couldn't help thinking about how difficult it will be to convince those family members, neighbors, and friends that it is a new age—but I think as teachers we will have to. Otherwise, we will be getting children ready for the past and setting them up for failure."

"We had a workshop at our school about the new brain research and it really got me thinking about the importance of the early years. I mean, it's not that I had forgotten about how important early childhood is or anything, it's just that now I feel like those of us in early childhood have more scientific support for what we have been saying all along."

## Your Reflections

- As you complete this course, how have your thoughts about creative expression and play changed?

- Why is it important for early childhood educators to evaluate their personal beliefs, classroom practices, and potential biases about creative expression and play?

- How can teachers of the very young persuade others that playfulness and creativity are essential characteristics in the workforce of the future?

 *Case Study:*

### Jamal

Jamal is a second grader who has been diagnosed as having ADHD, attention deficit/hyperactivity disorder. He entered preschool as a bright, inquisitive, and animated child. In first grade, Jamal's teacher expressed concern that he "just couldn't sit still" and was disrupting the class. Now that Jamal is on medication, he is subdued and listless; in other words, he now fits the inflexible curriculum of his elementary school. Jamal's parents consented to the drug therapy for their son because they became convinced that he would fail in school without the drug. Because he is an adopted child, they worry that Jamal might have some inherited learning difficulty that can only be remedied by medication to calm him down. Yet if we really listen to Jamal, we have a different impression: "I used to think that school would be fun. Everybody kept saying, 'Oh, you're really gonna like school.' Kindergarten was fun, but it's not fun anymore. I just try real hard to be quiet, do my work, and get as many stickers as I can."

Every day, all across America, children are taking medication to make them sit still, be quiet, and listen. A few of them may truly need such treatment. But many of them are misdiagnosed or simply trapped in an unyielding, uninteresting curriculum. History is replete with examples of "problem children" who became highly creative adults—Thomas Edison, Sarah Bernhardt, Winston Churchill, Isadora Duncan, and Albert Einstein, to name a few. If those children were alive today, what would be their fate? Unless they were fortunate enough to be in classrooms with creative, caring, enlightened teachers and privileged to be the offspring of well-informed, assertive parents, they would almost certainly be on drugs designed to quell their behavior.

There are approximately 5.4 million fewer young adults and millions more senior citizens than there were ten years ago, a trend that is partly due to the postwar "baby boom" generation reaching old age and partly due to improved medical care (Haycock, 1991). This means that there are many more elderly who need support and far fewer people to support them. Clearly, every young child needs to become a highly productive member of society, yet a larger percentage than ever before—more than one-third—will be minority and poor, "the very youngsters with whom we have been least successful in assisting to master the skills they need to become productive citizens" (Haycock, 1991, p. 277).

It is a common misconception that talent is a gift—either one has it or does not. But talent is simply a *potential*. It needs the right conditions to flourish into accomplishment. A second misconception about talent is that it is always expressed as an astonishing ability in a single area. Yet, more often than not, exceptional performance is a *combination* of talents that have been used effectively. When adults look only for remarkable potential in a single area, it often leaves children with different patterns of achievement believing that they are "not good at anything." Outstanding teachers, for example, have very different profiles of talents and abilities. In the arts, it is common to refer to "mixtures and balances" that yield a satisfying outcome, and this is no less true for different patterns of strength in young children. A third misconception is that talent is more often displayed by advantaged children. Actually, talent is widely distributed among disadvantaged children. It is the absence of opportunities and resources for expressing and cultivating talents that interferes with the expression of talent. Many children and adults possess remarkable potential that remains undiscovered simply because they have not had the chance to explore and develop their talents. Finally, talent can be put to destructive, rather than positive, ends when it is suppressed. A cunning and devious criminal certainly has abilities, it is just that these abilities were channeled into socially inappropriate outlets. The one thing that can avert the subversion or loss of talent is for us to become talented teachers ourselves and work to develop the creative potential in every child. The final chapter of this book is about becoming teachers who foster the abilities that children will need in order to thrive in a rapidly changing society that is approaching the third millennium. We cannot afford to be shortsighted, to consider only the task of preparing youngsters for the next grade level. Rather, we need to prepare children to function as adults in later life. Although it is difficult to make any definite predictions about what the future will be like, there is one thing we can be sure of: there will be a demand for sensitive, creative, flexible problem solvers.

The way that you envision the future of the children in society influences the curriculum that you design and the quality of life within your classroom or center. In the past, society's goal was to produce consensus and conformity. A large number of simple tasks needed to be performed in precise ways by reliable, attentive workers in factories, mills, and mines. Conversely, the technological era is far more complex. It is a society encompassing an overwhelming array of choices in food, clothing, media, work, and leisure. Under these conditions, it is less important for children to be unquestioningly obedient and more important for them to learn to function autonomously as decision makers (Csikszentmihalyi, 1993; Toffler, 1970, 1980). Moreover, to excel in tomorrow's international workplace, we need a different type of citizen, one who is capable of generating new ideas.

As an early childhood educator, you prepare children for their uncertain futures by emphasizing divergent thinking skills that ask students to come up with different, rather than similar, solutions and break through the true-false, name-this, memorize-that confines of public education. For every problem there may be many correct answers. This kind of reasoning is far more often the case in the real world, where there are often many ways to do any one thing well. An effective work force needs both kinds of reasoning, not just the standardized answer.

> When we involve students in creative problem solving, we invite their participation as partners in the learning process. . . . Such figuring-out requires critical thinking, analysis, and judgment. . . . Being able to think independently is the basis of creativity. (Fowler, 1994, p. 6)

Children today experience a world quite different from the one their parents grew up in—global awareness, technological advances, and different family structures are just a few of the most obvious differences (Howe, 1993; Papert, 1993). A first grader can get on the World Wide Web and communicate with another first grader two continents away. The personal computers that were a marvel a few years ago are now as commonplace to contemporary children as pencils were to their parents. The family structures that children's elders thought of as troubled are now the norm. Additionally, today's children form a stronger peer culture because they find it increasingly difficult to relate to the experiences of their parents or other adults.

In consideration of all these factors, it is helpful to reflect upon one fundamental question as you think about the role of creative expression and play in children's futures: What kind of human beings do we hope that children will become? Figure 10.1 presents a list of human characteristics that adults might consider to be important for children to develop. Look through the list and reflect upon the top five traits that you hope to nurture in your students. How does your list of five compare with the lists that other students produce? We have used this exercise from Elizabeth Jones (1986) many times with groups of preservice and inservice teachers around the globe and, generally speaking, there is considerable agreement among early childhood educators about what is really

What kind of adult do you hope children will become? Read through the list and put a star next to those characteristics that ought to be encouraged. Then select the five most important traits, those to be encouraged above all others.

| | |
|---|---|
| _____ Adventurous | _____ Negativistic |
| _____ Affectionate | _____ Never bored |
| _____ A good guesser | _____ Obedient |
| _____ Altruistic | _____ Persistent |
| _____ Always asking questions | _____ Physically attractive |
| _____ A self-starter | _____ Physically strong |
| _____ Athletic | _____ Proud |
| _____ Attempts difficult jobs | _____ Quiet |
| _____ Becomes preoccupied with tasks | _____ Rebellious |
| _____ Careful | _____ Receptive to ideas of others |
| _____ Cautious | _____ Refined |
| _____ Competitive | _____ Regresses occasionally (playful, childish) |
| _____ Completes work on time | _____ Remembers well |
| _____ Conforming | _____ Self-assertive |
| _____ Considerate of others | _____ Self-confident |
| _____ Cooperative | _____ Self-satisfied |
| _____ Courageous | _____ Self-sufficient |
| _____ Creative | _____ Sense of beauty |
| _____ Critical of others | _____ Sense of humor |
| _____ Curious | _____ Sensitive |
| _____ Desires to excel | _____ Sincere |
| _____ Determined | _____ Socially well adjusted |
| _____ Domineering | _____ Spirited in disagreement |
| _____ Emotional | _____ Strives for distant goals |
| _____ Energetic | _____ Stubborn |
| _____ Fault finding | _____ Talkative |
| _____ Fearful | _____ Thorough |
| _____ Gets good grades | _____ Timid |
| _____ Healthy | _____ Unwilling to accept things on others' say-so |
| _____ Independent in judgment | _____ Versatile |
| _____ Industrious | _____ Visionary |
| _____ Intelligent | _____ Willing to accept judgments of authorities |
| _____ Intuitive | _____ Willing to take risks |
| _____ Likes school | |
| _____ Likes to work alone | |

**Figure 10.1** What Traits Do You Hope to Foster in Young Children?

*Source:* Adapted from Jones (1986).

important. After you have compiled the most frequently chosen five traits for the entire class, think about this question: Which of these traits, based on what you have read in this book, would be supported by creative expression and play? Usually, the answer is "All of them."

According to many experts and leaders in the field, the twenty-first century will demand:

1.  Students who possess "resilience and flexibility, a creative and integrative way of thinking, and a certain psychological sturdiness in the way they face new circumstances in the company of other people" (Minuchin, 1987, p. 254).

2.  A school curriculum that encourages "experimentation, risk-taking, flexibility, autonomy" and children who have acquired "a mode of learning that places responsibility on them and that allows them the freedom to try, to test, to innovate, and to be creative" (Tetenbaum & Mulkeen, 1986, p. 99).

3.  A workforce that is responsible and self-disciplined, can move from one challenge to another, adapt quickly to change, produce innovative solutions to problems, and acquire expertise in more than one area (Research and Policy Committee, 1985; Tetenbaum & Mulkeen, 1986). Tomorrow's workers must be able to "figure out what they need to know, where to get it, and how to make meaning of it" (Task Force on Teaching as a Profession, 1986, p. 20).

4.  A "knowledge society" (Drucker, 1994) in which our most important product is knowledge produced by workers who can read, write, and compute at high levels; analyze and interpret data, draw conclusions, and make decisions; and function as part of a community (Boyer, 1995; Etzioni, 1993). To illustrate how much more advanced the skills of future workers must become, William Daggett (1994) points out that in 1950, 60 percent of available jobs in America were unskilled; in 1994, that percentage fell to 35 percent. Currently, only 15 percent of jobs in the United States are unskilled. More than ever before, our democratic ideal of education for all must become a reality so that "no child is left behind." Despite all of these societal demands, developmental studies suggest that human creativity is eroded, rather than strengthened, as children mature and gain additional experience in schools (Runco & Pritzker, 1999).

One important influence on all of these ideas is a revolution in understandings about the human brain and how it operates. Figure 10.2 will familiarize you with highlights of the research on the human brain and its implications for early childhood educators.

## THEORETICAL AND RESEARCH BASE: THE HUMAN BRAIN

Historically speaking, many deeply rooted dichotomies have dominated Western philosophy. Most people still believe, for example, that the following pairs of words are opposites: reason/imagination, science/art, cognition/emotion,

- There are more than 15 million American children under the age of 4 (Kantrowitz, 1997).

- Researchers report that approximately one-half of the child's critical brain development occurs before kindergarten (Simmons & Sheehan, 1997).

- According to a study conducted by the National Goals Panel, the major risk factors for children under the age of three are inadequate prenatal care, isolated parents, substandard child care, poverty, and insufficient attention (Carnegie Corporation, 1994).

- A child is born with 100 billion neurons, which make over 50 trillion connections, called synapses. During the first three years of life, many more neural connections are made, literally trillions more than the brain can possibly use. Over time, those that are rarely or never used are eliminated, a process called "pruning." (Begley, 1997; Nash, 1997).

- The way in which the child is raised affects how the child's brain is wired; in other words, the early years are "when we create the promise of a child's future" (Simmons & Sheehan, 1997).

- A young child's brain development suffers if the child is not permitted to live in a healthy, safe, and stimulating environment. Researchers at Baylor College of Medicine found that children who don't play much or who are rarely touched develop brains 20 to 30 percent smaller than normal for their age (Nash, 1997).

- Research on the human brain suggests that three things contribute significantly to a child's well-being: (1) good prenatal care, (2) warm and loving attachments between young children and adults, and (3) positive, age-appropriate stimulation from the time of birth (Newberger, 1997).

- The connection between early experience and later experience is so strong that it led researchers to conclude that "early social and emotional experiences are the seeds of human intelligence" (Hancock & Wingert, 1997, p. 36).

- Neuroscientists have identified "windows of opportunity," particular time periods when the brain's circuitry matures. "We now know that different regions of the brain are actively developing and maturing according to certain timetables, and that during these periods, there is heightened sensitivity to environmental influences (Puckett, Marshall, & Davis, 1999).

**References**

Begley, S. (1997, Spring-Summer). How to build a baby's brain. [Special Issue]. *Newsweek, 129,* 28–32.

Carnegie Corporation. (1994). *Starting points: Meeting the needs of our youngest children.* [On-line]. Available: *http://www.carnegie.org/starting_points/startpt1.html*

Hancock, L., & Wingert, P. (1997, Spring-Summer). The new preschool. [Special Issue]. *Newsweek, 129,* 36–37.

Kantrowitz, B. (1997, Spring-Summer). Off to a good start. [Special Issue]. *Newsweek, 129,* 6–9.

Nash, J. M. (1997, February 3). Fertile minds. *Time, 149*(5), 48–56.

Newberger, J. J. (1997). New brain development research—A wonderful window of opportunity to build public support for early childhood education! *Young Children, 52*(4), 4–9.

Puckett, M., Marshall, C. S., & Davis, R. (1999). Examining the emergence of brain development research: The promises and the perils. *Childhood Education, 76*(1), 8–12.

Simmons, T., & Sheehan, R. (1997, February 16). *Brain research manifests importance of first years. The News & Observer* [on-line]. Available: *http://www.nando.net/nao/2little2late/stories/day1-main.html*

**Figure 10.2**   Facts and Figures about Brain Research

and facts/values. Even contemporary thinking contributes its own potential set of dichotomies by oversimplifying the results of brain research. According to this research, the left side of the brain is analytical and practical, while the right side is intuitive and holistic. The erroneous conclusion that the left side of the brain is scientific while the right side is creative perpetuates the sort of either/or thinking that has adverse consequences for creativity and innovation (Bruer, 1997; Lindsey, 1998, 1999; Shore, 1997). As a society, we need to put these fragments back together again and recognize that the same brain that thinks also feels, that the same brain that stores factual information also imagines what is not yet possible.

Complete this sentence: "The brain is like _____." If you are like most of your contemporaries, you said "a computer." If the same sentence-completion task had been posed in the 1950s, most people would have said "a machine." Examining the symbols or metaphors that we use to describe the human brain provides a glimpse into society's depth of understanding about the brain and its functioning. Now that we have increasingly sophisticated research about the brain, neither of these comparisons is adequate. A machine is too simple, and a computer too linear. Now the human mind is conceived as an incredibly powerful parallel processor, always doing many things at once (Caine & Caine, 1991, 1997). Consider an ordinary task such as signing your name. Exactly what did you do when producing your signature? Analyze every detail of what is involved—the knowledge and skills that you needed, the experiences you had previously, every step involved in the task. If you brainstorm a list of everything involved, such as holding the pen, positioning the paper, forming each letter of the alphabet, making your signature distinctive, and knowing where to sign, you could probably come up with dozens of facts, subskills, actions, beliefs, values, and attitudes. Yet you probably did not think about any of those abilities in isolation or consciously analyze what you were doing (Neve, Hart, & Thomas, 1986). Your brain handled all of the necessary steps for you (Kline, 1995). While you were signing, your brain was helping you think about other things as well, such as the fact that you need to do some laundry, that it's raining outside, and that your chair is uncomfortable—in other words, your brain is processing many other "programs" or chains of thought simultaneously (Neve, Hart, & Thomas, 1986). In fact, your brain could assemble a new pattern instantly if you were called upon to sign 30 cover letters for job applications versus signing a thank you note to a friend, versus signing your name on a marriage license. From this point of view, (1) the brain's primary drive is to relate things to the real world, (2) the human brain is exceptionally effective at perceiving and processing patterns, and (3) learning is actually the acquisition of useful programs or chains of thought (Carnine, 1990; Kline, 1995).

Therefore, teaching in a way that is consistent with how the human brain works is compatible with everything that you have learned from this book thus far about creative expression and play. It also supports developmentally appropriate practice because, as Boyer (1995) points out, "Young children don't think about categories of knowledge. They follow their curiosity wherever it leads. They are,

*Teaching in a way that is consistent with the way the brain works supports developmentally appropriate practice.*

above all, natural, integrative learners" (p. xvii). "Brain-compatible" teaching would be:

- *Low-risk*—a nonthreatening climate where children have psychological freedom (internal) and psychological safety (external).
- *Hands-on*—encouraging exploration and manipulation of a vast array of materials from which students can extract patterns.
- *Interactive*—emphasizing genuine communication in the language arts as a way of interacting with other people.
- *Real-world*—emphasizing problems, examples, and contacts that are real and can be put to actual, productive uses.
- *Respectful of natural thinking*—counteracting the traditional school overreliance on linear thinking, academic subjects, and verbal/ mathematical skills by emphasizing intuitive thinking, a grasp of useful patterns, aesthetic activities, and nonverbal interests (adapted from Kline, 1995, p. 40).

Figure 10.3 is an overview of the environmental, mental, emotional, and developmental conditions that foster creativity and respect the brain's natural way of functioning.

**Figure 10.3**
Conditions That
Support Creativity

| Environmental | Room arrangement that facilitates hands-on learning |
| | Independent access to materials |
| | Variety of media and resource materials |
| Mental | Flexible and stimulating environment |
| | Challenging (but not overwhelming) tasks |
| | Activities adapted to children's special needs |
| Emotional | Respect for children's contributions |
| | Support to take risks with new ideas and activities |
| | Honest, individualized praise |
| Developmental | Children's rates and styles of growth expected to vary |
| | Individual differences prized; cultural differences celebrated |

*Source:* Adapted from Shallcross (1981).

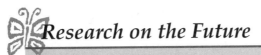 *Research on the Future*

Dyson, A. H. (1998). Folk processes and media creatures: Reflections on popular culture for literacy educators. *The Reading Teacher, 51*(5), 392–402.

Kagan, J. (1999). *Three seductive ideas.* Boston: Harvard University Press.

Lindsey, G. (1998/99). Brain research and implications for early childhood education. *Childhood Education, 75*(2), 97–100.

Morgan, A. D., & Mantranga, M. (1998). What issues will confront public education in the years 2000 and 2020? Predictions of chief state school officers. *Clearing House, 71*(6), 339–342.

Yelland, N. (1999). Technology as play. *Early Childhood Education Journal, 26*(4), 217–220.

### Web Sites

ArtsEd Net

*http://www.artsednet.getty.edu*

What's New at Project Zero?

*http://pzweb.harvardedu/HPZpages/Whatsnew.html*

Federal Interagency Forum on Child and Family Statistics (1999). *America's children: Key national indicators of well-being.*

*www.childstats.gov*

## How Basic Is Creative Thinking?

Think about the kindergarten child whose teacher held up a piece of purple construction paper and said, "What color is this?" Cris thought for a moment, then answered, "graple." The teacher who is thinking literally and convergently moves on, saying, "Can somebody help Cris?" But the teacher who really listens and respects children thinks about Cris's answer. It makes perfect sense. Cris has noticed—perhaps through direct experiences with popsicles or lollipops or beverages—that grape is the flavor associated with the color purple and has invented a word to make sense out of this observation. A good teacher might marvel out loud, saying with a tone of pleasure and surprise in her voice, "Grape-flavored things are usually purple, aren't they?" Cris's response falls somewhere between the historical dichotomies: between reason and feeling, between logic and imagination, between "left brain" and "right brain." That largely uncharted territory between what are incorrectly regarded as bipolar opposites is where genius lies. Every child—not just the compliant, the economically advantaged, or the gifted and talented—has creative potential just waiting to be set free by a great teacher.

As an early childhood educator, you will systematically overlook the genius of childhood if you allow your penchant for rationality and logic to overshadow the child's natural affinity for nonliteral thinking (Egan, 1988). Rollo May (1975) poses a question that every educator should take to heart: "In our day of dedication to facts and hardheaded objectivity, we have disparaged imagination. . . . What if imagination and art are not frosting at all, but the fountainhead of human experience?" (pp. 149–150). Perhaps we have had it backwards. Skills mastery is not the price of admission to creativity. Rather, it is the opportunity for joyful creative expression that inspires us to refine our skill.

Consider, for example, two children from different families who are learning to play the piano. Zhu is an 8-year-old who has been taking lessons since she was 5, and she says in complete candor to a visitor: "Please, just don't ask me to play the piano. I hate it." Justin, the second child, first became interested in the piano as a toddler because he liked to sit on his grandfather's lap and experiment with the sounds made by the different keys. Sometimes they would sing songs together. Because there was a talented piano player in Zhu's ancestry, her parents believe that early, intensive drill on the technical skills will enable Zhu to surpass even her illustrious ancestor's achievements. But which child is more likely to use music to enrich life? And who is more likely to develop the individual, interpretive style that is the hallmark of a great pianist? Teachers and parents must remember that although mastery of techniques is important, it should not be developed at the expense of creativity (Hope, 1990).

This describes the human resources we need in the future, but what can teachers expect from their teaching careers in the future? The next section describes some of the most recent speculations about the characteristics of tomorrow's children and classrooms.

## *Educational Reform*

Throughout the nineties, there have been repeated calls for educational reform. Elliot Eisner (1992) has summarized the five dimensions of reform, which we apply here to the field of early childhood education.

1. *The intentional.* The serious, studied examination of what really matters in young children's learning and what we are doing to make certain that our programs reflect these priorities.

2. *The structural.* Rethinking the diverse settings in which we work and the quality of the work life of early childhood educators. Examining closely the characteristics of the workplace, how programs are structured, how roles are defined, and how time is allocated—all in ways that influence the scope of possibilities for what can be done to nurture the very young.

3. *The curricular.* Focusing attention on ideas that matter, skills that count, and the means through which children will engage ideas and skills. Emphasizing not simply what children will learn, but how and why they learn it.

4. *The pedagogical.* Emphasizing the quality of teaching and reconceptualizing work with young children as an art. Providing professional development opportunities for early childhood educators so that they can better serve young children.

5. *The evaluative.* Recognizing that assessment practices are a major mechanism for school improvement. "If our evaluation practices do not reflect our cherished values, they will undermine the values we cherish" (Eisner, 1992, p. 5).

Of course, in order for these dimensions to exert an influence on schools, they will need to be translated into practices. Marie Carbo (1995) summarizes five sweeping changes that are implicit in the reform movement. As you read about these five fundamental changes, think about how an emphasis on creative expression and play supports each transition.

Contemporary schools need to:

- Emphasize concept development, depth of learning, and interpretation of meaning rather than the learning of isolated facts.
- Increase opportunities for social interaction, collaborative problem solving, and group process skills.
- Include and value the contributions of many ethnic groups.
- Offer an interdisciplinary curriculum in which skills such as reading, writing, mathematics, and oral communication are used as tools for understanding history, the humanities, and science.
- Support diversified teaching and learning strategies that reflect students' interests, backgrounds, and learning styles.

## TEACHERS' ROLES AND RESPONSIBILITIES

Imagine for a moment what teaching young children will be like as you complete your degree program. Do you predict that there will be an increase or a decline in enrollment? What do you think your first year's class or a group of students you have not yet met will look like? Describe them as a census taker would in terms of race, ethnic background, socioeconomic status, family structure, and home environment. Now compare your responses with the following statistics (Federal Interagency Forum on Child and Family Statistics, 1999; Hodgkinson, 1991):

- In 1998, there were 69.9 million children in the United States, 0.3 million more than in 1997. Children now make up 26 percent of the population. The child population is expected to increase to 77.6 million by 2020.
- The racial distribution of children is changing dramatically. Currently, more than one-third of the students in America will be African-American, Asian, or Hispanic. In many schools across America, students from these backgrounds are already the majority (Boyer, 1995). In 1998, Hispanic children outnumbered black, non-Hispanic children for the first time. The number of Hispanic children grew from just 9 percent of the population in 1980 to 15 percent in 1998. It is estimated that by 2020, more than one in five children will be Hispanic.
- About 19 percent of American children live in extreme poverty, defined as an annual income of $8,200 or less for a family of four. Children living in extreme poverty were much more likely to experience hunger and poor nutrition, less likely to be considered in very good or excellent health, and more likely to have difficulty performing everyday activities.
- In 1998, 68 percent of children lived with two parents, almost 25 percent lived with only their mothers, 4 percent only with their fathers, and 4 percent with neither parent. Thirty-two percent of all births were to unmarried women in 1997.

This changing composition of students will influence how teachers teach in the future.

## The Realities of Teaching

In 1970, Charles Silberman noted that it is impossible to spend any prolonged period visiting public school classrooms without being appalled by the destruction of spontaneity, the joy of learning, the pleasure of creating, and self-esteem. What has been done to change this situation during the last three decades? Some would argue that very little progress has been made, pointing to trends in education such as the "back to basics" backlash or minimum competency testing as evidence of our schools' fixation on low-level skills (Sarason, 1995). What can be done to improve teaching, foster children's creativity, and prepare for the changes ahead? As an initial step, you must prepare yourself for the realities of teaching.

In comparison with other professional groups, teachers tend to be altruistic, committed to serving others. At a time when 75.6 percent of incoming college freshmen identify "being well off financially" as a major life goal (Higher Education Research Institute, 1991), those who enter the teaching profession know full well that the education field does not offer the promise of wealth. In spite of their altruism and idealism, however, many preservice and new teachers are shocked by several things. Typically, beginning teachers' culture shock is a response to such factors as the stamina required of the job, the amount of paperwork, the range and

*The changing composition of students will influence how teachers teach in the future.*

intensity of students' needs, parents who lack confidence in their children, and the lack of support for their efforts within the school and district (Ryan, 1986). If the demographic trends are any indication, the pressures on today's teachers are likely to intensify rather than abate. Student teachers can often be heard to say, "Nobody told me how hard this would be." As authors, we want to go on record as having explained some of the challenges that you will face as a professional dedicated to nurturing the very young. Some aspects of teaching that every early childhood educator must consider as she or he prepares for teaching in the twenty-first century include the following (MacDonald, 1991):

1. Recognize that you will be in a confined setting surrounded by a culturally diverse and demanding group of young children. Much of your work will be done in relative isolation from other adults.
2. Realize that managing the classroom will require the ability to concentrate on several events simultaneously, to make thousands of "instant decisions" each day, and to adapt quickly and flexibly to change.
3. Understand that you will have to take abstract, nonsituational knowledge and make it meaningful for young learners, many of whom have few prior academic experiences and some of whom will arrive at the early childhood setting with not even their most basic needs met.
4. Know that you are entering a "helping profession," an occupation that draws upon and sometimes drains emotional and interpersonal resources. You will be as tired from a day of teaching as you have ever been in your life—not so much physically tired as exhausted from the relentless bids for your attention and the fact that your brain is on full-time circuitry overload as it runs hundreds of "programs" simultaneously.
5. Accept the fact that your success is determined by your influence on the attitudes and behaviors of other people—children, of course, but also families, colleagues, and the community at large.
6. Be aware that the best teachers are the most avid learners. Unless you become a lifelong learner, take charge of your own professional development, and become a "model learner" whom young children want to emulate, your effectiveness will surely be diminished (Jalongo, 1991).

## Redefining the Teacher's Role

Most of the characteristics that will enable you to become an outstanding teacher depend upon your creative thinking processes. Teachers for the future will need:

- A repertoire of alternative teaching strategies that encourage student self-expression and intrinsic motivation.
- Well-developed powers of communication.
- A dynamic conception of human learning that uses personalized, learner-centered techniques.
- The adaptability to facilitate learning in a highly diverse mix of students.

- The personal stamina and resourcefulness to face challenging teaching responsibilities.
- Patterns of professional involvement that make the best use of creative energies (MacDonald, 1991, p. 25).

Two critical resources for dealing with all of these issues are (1) to understand your role as a mediator of children's learning and (2) to develop your own creativity so that you can facilitate the creativity of children.

## Teachers as Mediators of Learning

When someone says the word *teacher*, what image does your mind produce? Is it a stereotype—a conservative, middle-class, white woman? Is it another stereotype—an adult standing in front of rows of desks, putting children through their paces? These inaccurate, outmoded images of teachers must be left behind if we are to move forward:

> Today, we are asking teachers to stop teaching students isolated facts, to stop emphasizing rote learning, and to stop just covering material and preparing for multiple-choice tests. Instead, we are asking them to start teaching students how to apply skills, how to understand concepts and solve problems, how to work collaboratively and how to take responsibility for learning. In other words, we want teachers to give students the skills they will need to function in the workforce and society (David, 1991, p. 39).

One useful way of reconceptualizing the teacher's role is to think of it as a mediator. A mediator of children's learning would use the following strategies:

1. Mediators *share their intentions and goals* with children.
2. Mediators *emphasize connections,* connections between the immediate situation and other situations remote in time or space.
3. Mediators *model the search for meaning*—in all its forms—affective, motivational, and value-oriented.
4. Mediators *build children's sense of competence and control* by helping every child to experience success and guiding the child in regulating his or her behavior (Feuerstein & Hoffman, 1982).

In order to appreciate the difference between a mediator of learning and a teacher, consider a very common lesson, teaching the difference between fantasy and reality. Ms. Clark prepares several short statements such as "a flying dog" and "a barking dog." She tells the children to listen carefully and decide whether or not what she says could really happen, then polls the group. But if Ms. Clark were truly working to young children's strengths, she would have used a very different approach, one that capitalizes on the children's imaginations and casts her in the role of mediator.

A better and more challenging way of understanding the difference between fantasy and reality focuses on the transformative aspect of children's play. Matthews (1977) found that children's transformations fell into several categories and that the fantasy/reality distinction could be highlighted through skillful questions.

*These boys practiced cooperative, creative, and flexible problem-solving skills by building this block structure.*

- *Substituting a real object for an imaginary one.* A child might use a cylindrical block for a "telescope" when her teacher says, "What can you see with your telescope? It's fun to pretend."
- *Attributing a pretend function to a real object.* If a child puts on a hat and announces, "This is a magical hat," the teacher might ask, "What can you do with its magic?"
- *Ascribing animate characteristics to an object.* If a child is walking around and talking out loud to a toy, the teacher might pause, introduce herself to the toy and address it directly, then wait to see how the child responds. The child might begin talking in a funny voice as if the toy were speaking, the child might answer for the toy like a doting parent, or the child might remain silent, imagining what the toy would say.
- *Referring to nonexistent objects.* If a child moves around the room making engine sounds and pretending to drive a car and his friend says, "Okay, buddy, pull your car into my garage and I'll see if I can fix it," the teacher might ask, "What do you think is wrong with it?" or suggest some additional props to create a car garage center.
- *Referring to nonexistent situations.* If children say, "We're going to a fancy restaurant," the teacher might ask, "What food do they serve there?" or "How can we make this look like a restaurant? What will you need?"

*Holding hands with my teacher, by a 4-year-old boy.*

- *Directly adopting or assigning a role.* If children are playing and choosing roles (e.g., "You be the queen now and I'll be the princess"), a teacher might remark, "What are some things that make a person look like a queen or princess?" and plan to share some children's books that depict royalty.

Notice how this play-based way of developing the distinction between fantasy and reality allows children to retain ownership of the learning process. Ownership, as defined in problem solving, involves three things: (1) *influence,* the opportunity for the child to take action and test hypotheses; (2) *interest,* the personal investment in and concern about the task; and (3) *imagination,* the drive for innovation and the development of new ideas and constructive actions (Isaksen & Treffinger, 1985).

## Teachers' Own Creativity and Teacher Empowerment

What makes one teacher more effective than another? Why does the performance of some teachers grow with experience while the performance of others declines over the years? Figure 10.4 highlights the major influences on teachers' creativity.

→ **Education**

Teachers without specific training in creativity are not well equipped to serve as models of creativity for their students.

Conversely, teachers who are well informed about creative thinking processes can exert a powerful influence on their students' work.

→ **Expectations**

When teachers feel pressured to teach only the material that is tested, used to rank schools, or used to decide who is a "good" teacher, this inhibits their willingness to try new things.

Conversely, when teachers work in settings that expect and support new and interesting things from them, they are more likely to attempt new things and approach challenges positively.

→ **Resources**

When materials are in very scarce supply, it can interfere with planning for instruction and providing opportunities to be creative.

Conversely, when inviting materials are readily available, teachers are more likely to put them to use in their classrooms.

→ **Recognition**

When teachers' efforts to do more than follow the book and cover the material are disregarded, they sometimes give up and fall into the well-traveled ruts of marginal or "burned-out" teachers.

Conversely, when teachers gain the respect of their peers and leaders for daring to be different, they are more likely to continue to grow and develop as creative practitioners.

→ **Hope**

When teachers feel oppressed by the lack of freedom, they feel disrespected and become apathetic and disaffected.

Conversely, when teachers are given choices, challenges, and support, they are more likely to rise to the occasion.

→ **Opportunities**

When teachers are deprived of opportunities for professional development in the area of creativity, they tend to teach the same things in the same ways, year after year.

Conversely, when teachers have opportunities to learn about and try out creative teaching strategies, they are more likely to expand their teaching repertoires beyond the ordinary.

→ **Rewards**

When teachers struggle to do more than what is minimally required and do not receive intrinsic or extrinsic rewards, their motivation to teach creatively is diminished.

When teachers enjoy the satisfaction of a job well done and the admiration of others, they feel validated, encouraged, and energized to continue teaching creatively.

**Figure 10.4**   Influences on Teachers' Creativity
*Sources:* Csikszentmihalyi (1996), Piirto (1992), and Rodd (1999).

Contemporary researchers contend that experts from all walks of life have acquired highly specialized knowledge and skill, which they organize into episodes, events, or cases (Carter & Doyle, 1989). Researchers further contend that it is the number, richness, and flexibility of the "scripts" teachers bring to the classroom setting that will ultimately determine their effectiveness. In other words, we use story structures to capture the essence of what we have come to know through experience (Jalongo & Isenberg, 1995). What appears to be most essential about using these cases or scripts as tools for learning, however, are the teachers' reflections upon their experiences. It is easy to see how a teacher's own creativity would affect the ability to learn from experience. A teacher who is overly literal in her or his thinking would lack the imagination to reflect upon experience in ways that enrich professional growth. Thus, creative thinking for teachers is more than dreaming up interesting lesson plans. It is a tool for professional development and an antidote to apathy. If teachers' creativity is so essential, why doesn't it flourish?

Imagine that you are assigned to write a lesson plan and urged to "be creative." Think about all of the influences that might inhibit rather than facilitate your own creativity. Usually, our insecurities about thinking more creatively fall into three categories (Adams, 1986):

1. *Fear of taking a risk.* Often, college students do not feel sufficiently safe and secure to "break out" and take the risks associated with being different. External pressures such as grades, peer ridicule, or the censure of the instructor might make us overly fearful of making a mistake. Internal feelings, such as not wanting to appear foolish or not wanting to be noticed, also inhibit creativity.
2. *Premature criticism.* Preservice and inservice teachers sometimes become prematurely critical of their efforts and judge ideas before they are even considered. Students who are writing a lesson plan might begin over and over again, trying to make the plan perfect from the very start rather than playing with ideas, allowing themselves to generate many ideas at first before selecting the best ones later. It is only after many possibilities are generated that teachers should begin to exercise their more judgmental side.
3. *Need for control.* If educators follow the safe, predictable path, they feel more in control of the situation. Writing a plan that is dry and ordinary, yet meets the minimal requirements, is a way of exercising control over uncertainty. Another possible reason for teachers' confusion about producing a "creative lesson plan" has to do with conflicting ideas about what constitutes creative teaching.

One way of understanding teachers' creativity is to ask them to characterize their teaching through a metaphor. If you interview several veteran teachers and ask them what interferes with teaching more creatively, some may use the metaphor of being "beaten down by the system." Others might tell you that they just "go along with the program" to "avoid rocking the boat." Still others will use agricultural metaphors and say that they have to wait for children to "grow" or "bloom." All of these expressions are very revealing. They suggest not simply what a teacher knows, but also the beliefs and values that undergird that educator's practices and points of view. Each of these perspectives is affected by the teachers' sense of power to exert a positive influence on students, the school, and the social system. There is little question that teachers confront a variety of challenges as they work with increasingly needy groups of children, limited resources, parents who do not understand their efforts, administrators who do not understand developmentally appropriate practices, politicians who make education a whipping boy, and a popular press that makes sweeping, unsubstantiated pronouncements about schools. Despite all of these forces that erode teachers' power, however, teachers have tremendous power within the confines of their classrooms and the children they teach.

As Raywid (1995) points out, teachers are powerful in their abilities to:

- Establish and control the social dynamics of the classroom.
- Exert an emotional influence over children's self-appraisals.
- Exercise power over the content of a child's mind.
- Arbitrate the meaning of dialogue in the early childhood settings.
- Function as a role model of habits of mind and work.

With this power comes enormous moral responsibility for the lives of young children. Raywid (1995) explains five specific moral obligations that accompany your profound responsibility as an early childhood educator:

> First, a teacher's obligations extend to all the youngsters in the classroom— not just to the eager and attractive and cooperative ones, but equally to those who appear least responsive and appealing. Indeed, because the least successful and least "worthy" student may be the neediest—and the one whom the teacher has the greatest capacity to help—such children may be precisely our most compelling moral obligation.
>
> Second, since we know that children and adolescents—and perhaps even adults—need teachers to care about them, it appears that teachers have an obligation to at least try to establish personal relationships with their students. . . . Third, perhaps teachers have an obligation to share their power. Given what we know about the role of power in eliciting the interest and engagement essential to learning, this may be necessary to teacher effectiveness and student accomplishment. . . .
>
> Fourth, beyond the objective of enhancing teaching and learning, there is another reason that the teacher ought to deliberately devolve some of his or her power to students. Doing so is a prime way of helping them to learn major lessons and acquire vital truths about the conduct of human affairs. . . .
>
> Finally, and perhaps most fundamentally, the teacher's possession and constant exercise of such awesome power impose an obligation of continuing consciousness of it. . . . They can never allow themselves the luxury of what has been called "compassion fatigue." (pp. 83–85)

What is this "compassion fatigue?" Put simply, it means that everyone who goes into teaching starts out intending to exert a positive influence on children's lives. Yet some teachers drift away from their original intentions and sink into indifference. One of the best antidotes to stale or destructive teaching is to give yourself many opportunities to grow and learn and become a more creative human being. Cohen and Gainer (1995) put it this way: "Creativity is one of the most precious qualities human beings possess, and so is intelligence. These two qualities are needed by society to help us deal with the enormously complicated problems we constantly face" (p. 195).

## Creative Teaching in the Future

Ask a group of teachers what it means to teach creatively, and many of them will describe clever activities or visual aids that are used in the classroom. But teaching creatively is actually very different than this. It is the process of facilitating children's creative expression rather than something a teacher makes or does. In other words, fostering creativity is an inside-out operation.

The hallmark of the creative teacher is the high-quality work that her or his students produce. What makes one product more creative than another? Creative products are:

- *Novel,* meaning that they are unusual and original.
- *Appropriate,* meaning that they are consistent with the goals of the person who created them.
- *Meaningful,* meaning that they are significant rather than trivial.
- *Satisfying,* meaning that the person who created them takes pleasure from having done so.
- *Parsimonious,* meaning that they are elegant in their simplicity (Amabile, 1989).

When teachers slavishly follow a prepackaged curriculum, they cannot nurture children's creativity and spontaneity. When children must rigidly follow someone else's plan, creative teaching cannot occur.

David (1991) describes teaching creatively in the twenty-first century this way:

> Curriculum and instruction must change from an emphasis on isolated facts, skills, and coverage to a focus on integrated content, on the application of skills, and on the development of conceptual understanding. Teaching must change from dispensing information and rewarding right answers to creating activities that engage students' minds and present complex problems with multiple solutions. (p. 39)

In order to teach creatively, teachers must be resourceful. A teacher in a parent cooperative nursery school who wished for a program rich in opportunities for creative expression through the visual arts decided that she would work on her dream rather than complain that the school could not supply all of the materials she needed. She created tabletop easels by using three sides of a cardboard box and taping them into a freestanding triangular shape. Then she put binder clips at the top of the easel to hold the children's work. Additionally, she sent home letters to parents asking for all sorts of "beautiful junk" to be used in collage and construction. She cut out paint smocks from heavy gauge plastic trash bags. Instead of sending in sugary treats on their child's birthday, she asked parents to donate art materials. Notice how this teacher changed negative messages into positive ones, turned dreams into action plans, and sought gradual improvement rather than instant, dramatic change (Kriegel & Patler, 1991). One of the best ways to teach children to be creative problem solvers is to model those behaviors ourselves as teachers.

Teachers of young children also bear responsibility for functioning as advocates, and Figure 10.5 provides guidelines for demonstrating your leadership in supporting creativity and the arts.

**Leadership through Advocacy**
- Learn to articulate your beliefs about the value of creative expression and play, even to those who are skeptical or nonsupportive.
- Take action to defend children's right to safe and healthy opportunities for play by engaging in activities such as cleaning up and painting an urban playground.
- Band together with respected colleagues to propose programs and policies that support children's creativity and play.

**Administrative Leadership**
- Join a task force, committee, or service organization that focuses on children's creative expression and play.
- Revamp the curriculum to infuse more opportunities for children to express themselves creatively and have time to play.
- Lead a group of colleagues in taking action to make your center or school an environment more conducive to children's and teachers' creativity.

**Community Leadership**
- Work with the community to develop an attractive display of children's work at the mall, in the local bank, at a festival or fair.
- Join a discussion group on the Internet and share what you have learned about children's creative expression and play with parents and families.
- Seek sources of funding support for arts projects, including business sponsorship, grants, and other means of financial backing for the arts.

**Conceptual Leadership**
- Write a position paper on some area of children's creative expression, have it reviewed carefully by experts, then post it on the Web.
- Develop an informative bulletin board, newsletter, flyer, or other means of communication that can be shared with the general public.
- Join a group of classmates and a faculty member in making a professional conference presentation on children's creative expression and play.

**Leadership through Career Development**
- Join a professional organization that supports children's creative expression and play, such as the National Association for the Education of Young Children, the Association for Childhood Education International, or the Reggio Emilia network.
- Scan the professional journals, such as *Early Childhood Education Journal, Childhood Education,* and *Young Children,* and surf the Net regularly for new information from organizations such as the Council for Exceptional Children, Americans for the Arts, and Music Educators National Conference.
- Further your education by volunteering to offer arts experiences for children, participating in conference sessions on creativity and play, and pursuing an advanced degree.

**Figure 10.5**   Leadership Activities to Support Children's Creativity and the Arts
*Source:* Kagan & Bowman (1997).

## AN AGENDA FOR THE FUTURE OF CREATIVE EXPRESSION AND PLAY

The Association for Childhood Education International (ACEI) has issued position papers on the child's right to creative expression and play (Isenberg & Quisenberry, 1988; Jalongo, 1990). The key recommendations of those policy papers were:

**1.** *Every child has a right to opportunities for imaginative expression.* Imaginative expression is not the exclusive province of special programs for the gifted and talented. It is not a curricular "frill" to be deleted when time is limited. Nor is imagination synonymous with enrichment, something reserved for those children who have already completed their "work." Rather, imagination is a capacity in every child that merits deliberate and careful nurturing by adults.

**2.** *Educating the child's imagination is a societal contribution of the first order.* One thing we can be certain about in our culture is change. The "personal inclinations required by the arts" are well suited to the demands of a rapidly changing society. These include play with images, ideas, and feelings; recognizing and constructing the multiple meanings of events; looking at things from different perspectives; and functioning as risk takers (Eisner, 1976). Educating a child's imagination is therefore an important way to prepare children for the future.

**3.** *The educated imagination is the key to equity and intercultural understanding.* Creative productivity can be social rather than isolationist, and its outcomes need not be money-saving, labor-saving, or even artistic. Imagination dramatizes the inner workings of our minds by giving our ideas form and making our thoughts visible to others (Rosen, 1980). What is less well understood is how the imagination serves as the foundation for and undercurrent of human interaction (Rosen, 1980). For after we gain insight into ourselves, we can use imaginative powers to identify with others, first to empathize and then to enact creative solutions to social problems (Hanson, 1986). Imagination, then, is the foundation for intercultural understanding and multicultural education.

**4.** *Children's creative productivity is qualitatively different from adults'.* We must resist "childism," the tendency for adults to look condescendingly upon children's ideas and feelings, to regard them as less real or important than their own (Lightfoot, 1978). Children's creativity is different from adults', not inferior to adults'.

**5.** *Creative expression should permeate the entire curriculum.* When we speak of basics in education, people immediately think of reading, writing, and arithmetic. But is that what is basic? If *basic* means something that is fundamental to the experience of all children, then other things would surely be basic. Play would certainly be basic (Moyer, Egerston, & Isenberg, 1987). Telling and enacting stories would be basic (Nelms, 1988). Drawing, painting, and sculpting would surely be basic, because even before children can read, write, or calculate, they use these ways of communicating their ideas, emotions, and individuality. Music and dance are basic, because even before a child can speak, he or she can listen and move to music. Thus, in the sense of being fundamental, the arts are every bit as basic as the three Rs.

*Imagination is the key to artistry in teaching and excellence in our schools.*

**6.** *Imagination is the key to artistry in teaching and excellence in our schools.* American educators continue to search for the panaceas in education. Teachers are jaded by these bandwagons, tired of legislative mandates, weary of standardized tests that dictate the curriculum. What is worse, our schools have been sapped of their ability to surprise, so much so that the overwhelming impression after thousands of hours of observation in classrooms is that they are routinized, predictable, and "emotionally flat" (Goodlad, 1984).

Where does the solution lie? Many prominent educators state that our schools need artistry, creativity, intuition, insight, inspiration, and reflection (Rubin, 1985; Schon, 1983; Sizer, 1984)—all qualities that are intimately connected with imagination.

**7.** *We must refashion our schools for the twenty-first century.* School reform must, in the view of the National Educational Association, recognize that the industrial model is obsolescent in our information age. We need to shut off the rapid assembly line of textbooks, tests, schedules, and paperwork in favor of cooperative learning and interesting projects. Schools need to go beyond tolerating imagination and begin to value and nurture it. Schools in the twenty-first century should encourage children to select relevant topics, to reflect imaginatively, and to learn about their own creative processes as well as those of others.

**8.** *Children's play is the foundation for a high-quality early childhood curriculum.* In an ACEI policy paper on children's play, it was recommended that every program provide:

- Appropriate play activities and equipment
- Safe and inviting environments
- Appropriate, planned outdoor play environments
- Carefully planned curricula that capitalize on children's natural playfulness
- Responsible teacher/parent roles in supporting children's play

In 1970, Toffler wrote that we would live in a world of overchoice. Unless we prepare children to cope with these choices by teaching them to make decisions, they will find the number of options to be overwhelming.

## PRACTICAL APPLICATIONS FOR YOUR CLASSROOM

In a school committed to creative expression and play, children are active participants. They learn how to bring order out of chaos, to use their multiple intelligences, to interpret symbols, to be open to feelings, to develop a tolerance for ambiguity, and to seek problems as well as solutions. If a school nurtures children's imagination and creativity, it means that children function more autonomously as they meet challenges in a supportive environment (Kamii, 1988). It means that teachers function as enablers who share their power, inviting children to manage their own learning processes and giving them time to revise their tentative notions about the world (Isaksen & Treffinger, 1985), deferring judgment until children are satisfied with their work (Klein, 1984). Education for the third millennium begins with the engagement of the child as a learner rather than the delivery of a curriculum. As Charles Silberman (1970) argued 30 years ago, "Education should prepare people not just to earn a living but to live a life—a creative, humane, and sensitive life. This means that the schools must provide a liberal, humanizing education" (p. 114). Teachers who can make a contribution to that sort of education and life value creative expression and play. Figure 10.6 illustrates the humanizing influence of creative expression and aesthetic experiences for young children.

Take, for example, our current concerns with violence in schools and society. How might opportunities for creative expression and play support prevention efforts? The word *violence* originates in a word meaning life force; it has the same root word as *vital*. Originally, the word *violence* did not have the host of negative meanings that we attribute to it today. If we begin to think about violence as an outburst of life, we begin to see connections between creativity, or the life force put to good use, and the contemporary understanding of *violence*, or the life force put to destructive purposes. The goal of education never should be to cause children to become emotionally "flat." Rather, it should channel their interests, passions, and curiosities into socially acceptable and productive outlets. The child who is angry can express that anger by pounding clay into a shape rather than behaving aggressively toward a peer. The child who is frustrated by learning to read can regain patience and focus by building something at the woodworking center. The child who feels frightened can "play out" those fears via sociodramatic play. In every case,

| FROM | TO |
|---|---|

**Fear and Chaos**     ➜     **Joy and Control**
*Example:* A child may resist using fingerpaints because they are "messy" and they have been told to stay neat, yet with protective clothing, encouragement, and experimentation, that same child can relish the opportunity to make a fingerpainting.

**Boredom and Routine**     ➜     **Engagement and Surprise**
*Example:* Young children are immersed in cartoon-style art at discount stores, as holiday decorations, at fast-food restaurants, and in the media, yet when they are given real works of art to examine closely and discuss, they break away from the ordinary and develop an aesthetic response to what is extraordinary and highly valued in society.

**Frustration and Low Self-Esteem**     ➜     **Mastery and Pride in Attainment**
*Example:* When first learning a simple folk dance, the child may find it confusing or awkward, yet when they have supportive guidance and opportunities to practice, they experience the joy of mastering the dance and performing it gracefully.

**Other Directedness and External Evaluation**     ➜     **Self-Directedness and Self-Evaluation**
*Example:* Many of the questions and tasks that young children encounter in school have one correct answer. Opportunities for creative expression give children greater responsibility for selecting tasks, pursuing them at their own pace, and evaluating both processes and products in terms of their personal satisfaction and sense of completeness.

**Isolation and Exclusion**     ➜     **Belonging and Community**
*Example:* Many creative children are cast in the role of outsiders in a society that values conformity and compliance, yet with opportunities to creatively address problems, to pursue a passion in the arts, or to participate in dramatic play, the strengths and talents of students who do not fit someone else's mold can be revealed and appreciated.

**Figure 10.6**   The Humanizing Influence of Opportunities for Creative Expression

play, creative problem solving, and the arts supply appealing alternatives to anti-social behavior.

## Experiences to Support Cultural and Ethnic Diversity

Ms. Ochoa teaches kindergarten in an economically depressed area where many of the children live in trailer courts. She overhears two children who are building a house with blocks as they discuss their concept of a habitat:

> **Bradley:**   *No, you can't live in a trailer, you've got to live in a house.*
> **Carol Ann:**   *But I do live in a trailer.*
> **Bradley:**   *A trailer is for camping. You've gotta live in a house, or maybe an apartment.*

*Encouraging students to share their cultural backgrounds and beliefs helps promote understanding of diversity in the classroom.*

Ms. Ochoa could ignore the children's dilemma, leaving Carol Ann with the feeling that her home was inferior and a source of shame. Instead, Ms. Ochoa initiates a "Where do they live?" bulletin board/collage. Her sources for pictures come from real estate advertising booklets and magazines such as *National Geographic, Life,* and *Old House Journal.* She also finds that UNICEF has a set of notecards called "International Neighbors" and calendars that contain both photographs and children's drawings of homes from around the world. The children use these materials as resources to create their own impressive display of different habitats for human beings. To extend the project even further, Ms. Ochoa invites a Habitat for Humanity volunteer to speak with the children about her work and to share photos of the homes that she has helped to refurbish through the program, including the volunteer's own home. As a result of Ms. Ochoa's efforts, every child's concept of what a home can be or look like is extended. Additional guidelines for building intercultural awareness, understanding, and acceptance are highlighted in Figure 10.7.

President Franklin Delano Roosevelt once said, "Inequality may linger in the world of material things, but great music, great literature, great art, and the wonders of science are, and should be, open to all." These words should guide you as you work with diverse groups of young children in various settings. In order to function in a culturally pluralistic society, you will need to have a commitment to all of the cultural groups in which you participate, function in more than one culture simultaneously, and be able to examine your own culture from an outsider's perspective

1. *Be aware that multiculturalism starts with you.* Your attitudes and values will be communicated to students, and you will teach more by your example than by what you say. Give children a role model to emulate rather than empty words. Be aware also that multicultural understandings are pertinent in every classroom, not just in schools where many distinct cultural groups are represented. If the children in your class happen to be rather similar in background, they may need multicultural education most of all to function in the larger society.

2. *Know your students and their cultural backgrounds.* Too often, teachers refer to distinct groups as if they were one group, for instance, referring to Japanese, Chinese, and Vietnamese as "oriental." Each of these groups has its own identity.

3. *Expect conflict and model conflict resolution.* There will be inevitable clashes between children with different life experiences—the boy who thinks "girls can't be doctors" or the girl who thinks "only mommies can take care of babies." Understand that children base these assumptions on what is admittedly limited personal experience. The way to resolve such conflicts is to create what Piaget called "disequilibrium" by offering compelling evidence of examples that are contrary to the child's concept.

4. *Bring the outside world into the classroom and help parents to see the value of play firsthand.* It is important to put parents back in touch with how *they* learned as children. Parents will be more accepting of your curriculum if you show rather than tell them how the things that their children are doing are challenging and relevant. A parent may initially think that the sociodramatic play themes of camping and doctor in Chapters 8 and 9 are a waste of time. But if you share the rich dialogues and problem-solving behaviors that these play themes elicit, parents are more likely to recognize that authentic learning is taking place.

5. *Present modern concepts of families and occupations.* The American family has changed dramatically since the '50s. The family structure of a father who works and a mother with two or three children who devotes full time to child care and homemaking is found in less than 10 percent of contemporary families. Avoid holding up one type of family structure as the "standard" by which others are judged. Be careful about the terminology you use to describe families too. Do not refer to children's homes as "broken" or to their remarried parents as "stepparents." These terms are emotionally loaded and leave the impression that the family is defective or the parents are less caring than "real" parents. Use more positive terminology such as "single parent family" or "blended family."

6. *Use children's literature to enrich children's play and understandings about cultural pluralism.* There are many excellent picture books that help children to sense both the rich cultural diversity and the universality of human experience. Use these books to make every child feel like a valued member of your classroom community.

**Figure 10.7**   Embracing Cultural Diversity: Guidelines for Teaching
*Source:* Jalongo (1991).

(Ramirez, 1983). Contrary to popular opinion, understanding cultural diversity is not simply "knowing about" other cultures, and certainly not about merely tolerating them. Education that promotes intercultural understanding and global awareness would lead to a celebration of diversity in which the contributions of various cultures are regarded as assets that are just as valuable as those of the dominant culture. By modeling these attitudes, we build children's self-esteem, give children a sense of their heritage, and promote intercultural understanding (Jalongo, 1991).

## Experiences to Support Inclusion

Adapting the curriculum to address the needs of all children is essential. "If we deny children's needs, we deny our humanity. The greatest need today is to reestablish respect for human worth. A widespread decline in the reverence for human life and loss of respect for the dignity of the individual has led to an independence toward the welfare of children. . . . In dedicating ourselves to children, perhaps we can start a general renaissance of the human spirit" (Pifer, 1982, p. 1).

In the past, there has been an emphasis on life skills for children with handicapping conditions. In the future, it will become clear that our definition of life skills has been far too narrow. Although it is undeniably important for a child who cannot speak to learn to communicate, it is equally, if not more, important for that child to use those communication skills to create. Likewise, although it is important for children to master self-help skills such as feeding or dressing or washing themselves, it is equally important for those children to apply and practice these motor skills in play situations with peers. The media routinely report about children who far exceeded routine expectations—children who compensated for their intellectual or physical handicaps. We have just begun to get a glimpse of what a child with Down syndrome is capable of achieving. That knowledge has developed because somebody somewhere cared enough. These adults cared so much about the child with Down syndrome that they refused to be limited by what the child was supposedly capable of doing. The future will teach us even more about human potential and ways of enhancing that potential in children with handicapping conditions.

## Adaptations for Individual Learners

One of the worst assumptions a teacher can make is that creativity is a form of snobbery and elitism, a way of making a few select individuals more refined, cultured, or better than the rest. Rather, we should "do what can be done to crack the old forbidding codes, to break through these artificial barriers that have so long served to exclude" (Greene, 1988, p. 53). These issues pertain to giftedness as well.

Giftedness is usually defined as an interaction among three clusters of traits: above-average general abilities, high levels of task commitment, and high levels of creativity (Renzulli, Reis, & Smith, 1981). But as the demographics in this chapter suggest, many of the children in our classes will be in poverty or arrive at school with few prior experiences that have stimulated them intellectually. Therefore, it is doubly important that we as teachers use that definition of giftedness not as a label, but as a goal. The goal is for every child, regardless of his or her achievement record, to acquire new abilities, to learn to work diligently in completing a task, and to learn how to use creative processes. As Vivian Paley (1990) points out, "Those of us who presume to teach must not imagine that we know how each student begins to learn" (p. 78). For even though we know pedagogy and child development, each child is an individual. Good teachers watch, listen, and learn from their students; they trust children and work to the strengths of every child. We do children a terrible disservice when we characterize some as creative and others as not creative. In the model schools of Reggio Emilia, teachers describe their philosophy this way:

> What we like to do is to accompany a child as far as possible into the realm of the creative spirit. . . . At the end of the path is creativity. We don't know if the children will want to follow the path all the way to the end, but it is important that we have shown them not only the road, but also that we have offered them the instruments—the thoughts, the words, the rapport, the solidarity, the love— that sustain the hope of arriving at a moment of joy. (Gallamine, Kaufman, & Ray, 1992, p. 83)

Perhaps the greatest contribution of creativity to human life is that it enables us to recognize the potential for genius in one another. As Armstrong (1998) explains, "Every student is a genius. I do not mean this in the psychometric sense of the word, in which an individual must score above the 99th percentile on a standardized measure of intelligence to qualify. . . . nor do I mean it in the sense of every student as a grandmaster chess champion, a virtuoso on the violin, or a world-class artist" (p. 1). There is a type of genius that every human being can possess, and cultivating it should be a major mission of education (Sternberg & Lubart, 1996). Figure 10.8 highlights the 12 qualities of genius that all of us can achieve. People rarely learn to recognize genius in themselves and others unless their own fledgling creative processes were nurtured early on; therefore, honoring creativity is a special responsibility of adults who care about children. Early childhood educators must be fully prepared to articulate their philosophy and to defend the child's right to creative expression.

During the last decade, behaviorism has dominated educators' thinking. But research has shown that the indiscriminate use of extrinsic rewards—such as teacher praise—or tangible reinforcers—such as stickers or stars—tends to diminish children's interest in a subject over time. Instead of enjoying a book for its own sake, they have their eyes on the prize: the hamburger or pizza. Rose (1989) contends that we have created an educational system that encourages high-achieving students to become cynical grade collectors and alienates most low-achieving children. Teachers for the twenty-first century must embrace a different philosophy. Our job is not to rank-order children's intellects and judge them like cattle in a 4-H competition. Our job is to convince children that they are capable of doing high-quality work and to give them a sense of their own power as learners. Teaching is not simply conveying information. If it were, a television course could take the place of today's teachers. The real talent in teaching is bringing out the best in every child, in showing—by our own example—that being a learner is a joy in itself and offers enduring intrinsic rewards. In all of your teaching, keep in mind that:

> We are creatures of feeling as well as thought, and schools that recognize that basic fact and address it are better schools. . . . Our spirit needs as much nurturing as any other part of our mind. Schools that ignore it are cold and desolate places. Remember: If we fail to touch the humanity of students, we have not really touched them at all. (Fowler, 1994, p. 4)

In the first chapter of this book, we talked about children's natural curiosity, their vivid imaginations, and the relative ease with which they move from fantasy

1. **Curiosity:** A full-scale, active exploration of the world and ideas driven by the urge to make meaning and gain understanding.

*We speak of young children's active imaginations, their natural curiosity.*

2. **Playfulness:** Experimenting with things and ideas in a spontaneous, intrinsically motivated way that is not bound by others' rules.

*Young children, even in the desperate circumstances of a war-torn country or natural disaster, manage to make playthings from the rubble.*

3. **Creativity:** The ability to look at things differently, make surprising connections, and generate useful products.

*Young children are particularly adept at connecting the seemingly unconnected and creating interesting juxtapositions.*

4. **Wonder:** Being awestruck by the world and astonished by what others might take for granted.

*Young children experience the world afresh and are amazed by what they encounter even when it seems commonplace to adults.*

5. **Imagination:** Producing rich and varied images, even of things that do not exist.

*Young children's eidetic imagery—the richness of their mental images—is so strong that a frightening picture comes alive and nightmares seem real.*

6. **Wisdom:** Delving beneath the surface to get to the heart of the matter.

*Young children have a fresh way of looking at things that often escapes their elders, who rely on years of experience.*

7. **Inventiveness:** Producing surprising results from "hands-on" creativity.

*Young children are discoverers. They put the simplest materials to funny and sometimes bizarre uses. They play with the wrappings while the expensive gift sits idly by.*

8. **Vitality:** Being awake to sensory input, responding to it fully, and actively engaged in experiences.

*Young children are noted for their energy levels and the passion with which they pursue their interests.*

9. **Sensitivity:** Responding vividly to stimuli, thereby enriching what is experienced.

*Young children have a deep, yet naive response to music, literature, and art.*

10. **Flexibility:** Capitalizing on the plasticity of the mind.

*For the young child, the lines of demarcation produced by adults' literal thinking are dotted. Children move easily between fantasy and reality, between the inner world and outer world.*

11. **Humor:** Breaking out of routine and leaving behind seriousness.

*The young child's sense of humor is at first slapstick, then incongruity, then word play.*

12. **Joy:** Something that emanates from within when new connections, insights, feats, or skills are made.

*The young child finds delight in simple accomplishments.*

**Figure 10.8**   12 Qualities of Genius in Every Child: Implications for Early Education
*Source:* Based on Armstrong (1998).

to reality and back again. Instead of wringing these traits out of them in the quest for evidence of logical thinking, teachers of young children must cherish and cultivate these talents. As contemporary society begins the third millennium of human history, creative expression and playfulness are surely attributes that will be prized in the future.

## CHAPTER SUMMARY

1.  Every child has talent. Such talent will be of great importance in the next millennium, which will be characterized by diversity and complex challenges.
2.  The technological era requires individuals who can think critically and independently. Education should foster the development of these traits in order for children to participate fully in tomorrow's society.
3.  There is a need to teach children in ways consistent with brain research. We know that young children learn in a natural and integrative manner. Play, social interaction, and psychological safety and freedom all contribute to children's learning and creative expression.
4.  Fostering creativity in children and in ourselves as teachers is crucial as we confront the rapid-paced and challenging times ahead. Teaching is a moral craft because a teacher's power over children's lives in classrooms makes educators ethically and morally responsible for them.
5.  Teachers must function as mediators and design a curriculum that works to the child's strengths. A curriculum that respects children's active imaginations and capitalizes on their natural playfulness is developmentally appropriate.
6.  Every early childhood practitioner bears responsibility for developing the creative genius in every child and unlocking each child's talents.

## *EXPANDING YOUR THINKING ABOUT THE FUTURE OF CREATIVE EXPRESSION AND PLAY*

 *Discuss: Creative Expression and Play in the Future*

1.  Compare/contrast the "traditional" teacher's role with the role of a teacher in the twenty-first century. What specific strategies will you use to become more future-oriented as an educator?
2.  Howard Gardner says that in the future, schools and teachers will become almost like "brokers" who put families and children in contact with the necessary social services, organizations, and programs. Describe some practical ways that you could function as a "broker" who would alert families to resources and opportunities within the community that would promote children's play, creativity, and experiences in the arts.
3.  In reconceptualizing early childhood education for the future, how would you nourish a different view of learning and develop confident children who

become lifelong learners? How would your instructional strategies and child guidance techniques help children to function more autonomously?

4.   What have you done as an educator that gave you a sense of efficacy—a belief in your own power to affect children's lives for the better? Be prepared to discuss this with a small group in class.

## Interview: The Ideal Educator

In Louis Rubin's (1985) research with administrators, he identified several teacher characteristics that were highly valued. While there was general agreement that knowledge, skills, and overall competence were basic requirements, administrators identified four teacher attributes that differentiated superlative teachers from "ordinary" classroom teachers: spontaneity, perceptivity, originality, and insight. Interestingly, these four attributes all have a clear connection to creative expression and playfulness. Conduct your own interview with a teacher or administrator by asking her or him to reflect on two things: the "basic" requirements for becoming a good teacher and the abilities or traits necessary to become a superlative teacher. Then give the interviewee a copy of the information in the box below.

---

**Teacher Characteristics**

Consider two categories of teachers, those who are marginally competent and those who are outstanding. Rate the following attributes in terms of their importance for teachers on a scale of 1 to 10, where 10 is of the utmost importance and 1 is of the least importance.

| | Importance for average teacher (1–10) | Importance for outstanding teacher (1–10) |
|---|---|---|
| Dependability/reliability | | |
| Knowledge of subject-specific content | | |
| Understanding of children's growth and development | | |
| Interpersonal effectiveness | | |
| Organizational abilities | | |
| Ability to plan for effective instruction | | |
| Spontaneity | | |
| Flexibility/adaptability | | |
| Perceptivity and insight | | |
| Creativity and originality | | |
| Dependability/reliability | | |
| Understanding of educational settings (educational philosophy, organizational mission, institutional policies) | | |

Now compile the results of the entire class. How did your findings compare with those obtained by Rubin?

## Write to Learn: Confronting Bias and Stereotypes

Use the self-evaluation that follows to evaluate your beliefs, values, and attitudes concerning children's creative expression and play. Based on the results of your self-evaluation, write a brief narrative statement about your strengths and weaknesses as a child-centered teacher. What biases do you have? How can you go about reducing your personal prejudices concerning children's creative expression and play?

---

**Self-Assessment**
**Beliefs and Practices about Creative Expression and Play**

Instructions: Rate each item on a scale from Strongly Agree to Strongly Disagree.

**Beliefs about Creativity and Play**
*Creative expression and play provide opportunities for:*

| | | | | | |
|---|---|---|---|---|---|
| Emotional release | SA | A | U | D | SD |
| Enjoyment | SA | A | U | D | SD |
| Physical development | SA | A | U | D | SD |
| Intellectual development | SA | A | U | D | SD |
| Social development | SA | A | U | D | SD |
| Problem solving | SA | A | U | D | SD |
| Gender/sex role development | SA | A | U | D | SD |
| Communicative abilities | SA | A | U | D | SD |
| Decision-making skills | SA | A | U | D | SD |
| Literacy development | SA | A | U | D | SD |
| Investigation | SA | A | U | D | SD |
| Other | SA | A | U | D | SD |

**Curricular Issues**
*Creative expression and play:*

| | | | | | |
|---|---|---|---|---|---|
| Provide choices | SA | A | U | D | SD |
| Foster feelings of competence | SA | A | U | D | SD |
| Expand learning goals | SA | A | U | D | SD |
| Integrate subject areas | SA | A | U | D | SD |
| Foster language growth | SA | A | U | D | SD |
| Other | | | | | |

*(continued)*

---

---

**Self-Assessment**
**Beliefs and Practices about Creative Expression and Play,** *continued*

---

**Assessment Issues**
*Creative expression and play can be used to:*

| | | | | | |
|---|---|---|---|---|---|
| Encourage divergent thinking | SA | A | U | D | SD |
| Document children's work | SA | A | U | D | SD |
| Gain insight about creative processes | SA | A | U | D | SD |
| Evaluate the program | SA | A | U | D | SD |
| Identify talents | SA | A | U | D | SD |
| Guide social development | SA | A | U | D | SD |
| Guide intellectual development | SA | A | U | D | SD |
| Other | | | | | |

**Problems with Creative Expression and Play**
*The things that are most troublesome about creative expression and play are:*

| | | | | | |
|---|---|---|---|---|---|
| Conflict between children over play (toys, roles, use of space) | SA | A | U | D | SD |
| Potential for chaos | SA | A | U | D | SD |
| Lack of materials | SA | A | U | D | SD |
| My difficulty in generating new ideas for play themes | SA | A | U | D | SD |
| The influence of television | SA | A | U | D | SD |
| Transitions in and out of play | SA | A | U | D | SD |
| Other | | | | | |

**Barriers to Creative Expression and Play**
*Major impediments to more child-centered teaching are:*

| | | | | | |
|---|---|---|---|---|---|
| Lack of administrative support | SA | A | U | D | SD |
| Physical environment | SA | A | U | D | SD |
| Scheduling constraints | SA | A | U | D | SD |
| State regulations and policies | SA | A | U | D | SD |
| Limited budget | SA | A | U | D | SD |
| Standardized tests | SA | A | U | D | SD |
| Lack of parental support | SA | A | U | D | SD |
| Other | | | | | |

*(continued)*

**Self-Assessment**
**Beliefs and Practices about Creative Expression and Play,** *continued*

**Evidence of Creative Expression and Play**
*In my classroom, I encourage:*

| | | | | | |
|---|---|---|---|---|---|
| Freedom to create | SA | A | U | D | SD |
| Child-initiated activities | SA | A | U | D | SD |
| Large blocks of time | SA | A | U | D | SD |
| A wide array of materials | SA | A | U | D | SD |
| A low-risk, nurturing environment | SA | A | U | D | SD |
| Opportunities for make-believe | SA | A | U | D | SD |
| A challenging outdoor environment | SA | A | U | D | SD |
| Mutual respect between and among teachers and children | SA | A | U | D | SD |
| Less teacher talk and more child talk | SA | A | U | D | SD |
| Other | | | | | |

**Evidence of Appropriate Assessment**
*In my classroom, I:*

| | | | | | |
|---|---|---|---|---|---|
| Focus on the whole child | SA | A | U | D | SD |
| Strive to communicate effectively with parents | SA | A | U | D | SD |
| Value divergent/lateral thinking | SA | A | U | D | SD |
| Use developmentally appropriate practices | SA | A | U | D | SD |
| Use observational skills | SA | A | U | D | SD |
| Compile children's work into portfolios | SA | A | U | D | SD |
| Guide children in self-evaluation | SA | A | U | D | SD |
| Other | | | | | |

**Roles and Responsibilities**
*I see my most important roles in children's creative expression and play as:*

| | | | | | |
|---|---|---|---|---|---|
| Facilitating children's growth | SA | A | U | D | SD |
| Observing children's processes | SA | A | U | D | SD |
| Preparing the physical environment | SA | A | U | D | SD |
| Providing appropriate materials | SA | A | U | D | SD |
| Educating parents about creative expression and play | SA | A | U | D | SD |
| Defending the value of play to others in the field of education | SA | A | U | D | SD |
| Evaluating the outcomes of children's creative expression and play | SA | A | U | D | SD |
| Other | | | | | |

## REFERENCES

Adams, J. (1986). *Conceptual blockbusting* (3rd ed.). Reading, MA: Addison-Wesley.

Amabile, T. M. (1989). *Growing up creative.* New York: Crown.

Armstrong, T. (1998). *Awakening genius in the classroom.* Alexandria, VA: Association for Supervision and Curriculum Development.

Boyer, E. L. (1995). *The basic school: A community for learning.* Princeton, NJ: Carnegie Foundation for the Advancement of Teaching.

Bruer, J. (1997). Education and the brain: A bridge too far. *Educational Researcher, 26*(8), 4–16.

Caine, R. N., & Caine, G. (1991). *Teaching and the human brain.* Alexandria, VA: Association for Supervision and Curriculum Development.

Caine, R. N., & Caine, G. (1997). *Education at the edge of possibility.* Alexandria, VA: Association for Supervision and Curriculum Development.

Carbo, M. (1995). Educating everybody's children. In R. W. Cole (Ed.), *Educating everybody's children: Diverse teaching strategies for diverse learners.* Alexandria, VA: Association for Supervision and Curriculum Development.

Carnine, D. (1990). New research on the brain: Implications for instruction. *Phi Delta Kappan, 71*(5), 372–377.

Carter, K., & Doyle, W. (1989). Classroom research as a resource for the graduate preparation of teachers. In A. E. Woolfolk (Ed.), *Research perspectives on the graduate preparation of teachers* (pp. 51–68). Englewood Cliffs, NJ: Prentice Hall.

Cohen, E. P., & Gainer, R. S. (1995). *Art: Another language for learning* (3rd ed.). Portsmouth, NH: Heinemann.

Csikszentmihalyi, M. (1993). *The evolving self: A psychology for the third millennium.* New York: HarperPerennial.

Daggett, W. (1994). Make the curriculum fit the future. *Education Digest, 60*(4), 8–11.

David, J. L. (1991). Restructuring and technology: Partners in change. *Phi Delta Kappan, 73*(1), 37–40, 78.

Drucker, P. F. (1994, November). The age of social transformation. *The Atlantic Monthly,* p. 64.

Egan, K. (1988). The origins of imagination. In K. Egan and D. Nadaner (Eds.), *Imagination and education* (pp. 91–127). New York: Teachers College Press.

Eisner, E. (1976). *The arts, human development and education.* Berkeley, CA: McCuthen.

Eisner, E. W. (1992). The reality of reform. *English Leadership Quarterly, 14*(3), 2–5.

Etzioni, A. (1993). *The spirit of community: Rights, responsibilities, and the communitarian agenda.* New York: Crown.

Federal Interagency Forum on Child and Family Statistics. (1999). *America's children: Key national indicators of child well-being.* Washington, DC: U.S. Government Printing Office.

Feuerstein, R., & Hoffman, B. (1982). Intergenerational conflict of rights: Cultural imposition and self-realization. *Journal of the School of Education, Indiana University 58,* 44–63.

Fowler, C. (1994). Strong arts, strong schools. *Educational Leadership, 52*(3), 4–9.

Gallamine, D., Kaufman, P., & Ray, M. (1992). *The creative spirit*. New York: Dation.

Gardner, H. (1983). *Frames of mind: The theory of multiple intelligences*. New York: Basic Books.

Goodlad, J. (1984). *A place called school: Prospects for the future*. New York: McGraw-Hill.

Greene, M. (1988). What happened to imagination? In K. Egan & D. Nadaner (Eds.), *Imagination and education* (pp. 45–56). New York: Teachers College Press.

Hanson, K. (1986). *The self imagined*. London: Routledge & Kegan Paul.

Haycock, K. (1991). Reaching for the year 2000. *Childhood Education, 67*(5), 276–279.

Hodgkinson, H. (1991). Reform versus reality. *Phi Delta Kappan, 73*(1), 9–16.

Hope, S. (1990). Technique and arts education. *Design for Arts in Education, 91*(6), 2–14.

Howe, H. (1993). *Thinking about our kids: An agenda for American action*. New York: The Free Press.

Isaksen, S. G., & Treffinger, D. J. (1985). *Creative problem solving: The basic course*. Buffalo, NY: Bearly Ltd.

Isenberg, J. P., & Quisenberry, N. L. (1988). Play: A necessity for all children. *Childhood Education, 64*(3), 138–145.

Jalongo, M. R. (1990). The child's right to the expressive arts: Educating the imagination as well as the intellect. *Childhood Education 66*(4), 195–201.

Jalongo, M. R. (1991). Children's play: A resource for multicultural education. In E. B. Vold (Ed.), *Multicultural education in the early childhood classroom* (pp. 52–56). Washington, DC: National Education Association.

Jalongo, M. R., & Isenberg, J. P. (1995). *Teacher's stories: From personal narrative to professional insight*. San Francisco: Jossey-Bass.

Jones, E. (1986). *Teaching adults*. Washington, DC: National Association for the Education of Young Children.

Kagan, S. L., & Bowman, B. T. (Eds.). (1997). *Leadership in early care and education*. Washington, DC: National Association for the Education of Young Children.

Kamii, C. (1988). Autonomy or heteronomy: Our choices of goals. In G. F. Roberson & M. A. Johnson (Eds.), *Leaders in education: Their views on controversial issues* (pp. 97–108). Lanham, MD: University Press of America.

Klein, B. (1984). Power and control, praise and deferred judgment. *Journal of Creative Behavior, 17*, 9–17.

Kline, L. W. (1995). A baker's dozen: Effective instructional strategies. In R. W. Cole (Ed.), *Educating everybody's children: Diverse teaching strategies for diverse learners* (pp. 21–41). Alexandria, VA: Association for Supervision and Curriculum Development.

Kozol, J. (1997). Students' needs or corporate greed? *Education Digest, 63*(1), 3–6.

Kriegel, R. J., & Patler, L. (1991). *If it ain't broke . . . break it!* New York: Warner.

Lightfoot, S. L. (1978). *Worlds apart: Relationships between families and schools*. New York: Basic Books.

Lindsey, G. (1998/99). Brain research and implications for early childhood education. *Childhood Education, 75*(2), 97–100.

MacDonald, R. E. (1991). *A handbook of basic skills and strategies for beginning teachers: Facing the challenge of teaching in today's schools*. New York: Longman.

Matthews, W. S. (1977). Modes of transformation in the initiation of fantasy play. *Developmental Psychology, 13,* 212–216.

May, R. (1975). *The courage to create.* New York: Norton.

Minuchin, P. (1987). Schools, families and the development of young children. *Early Childhood Research Quarterly, 2,* 245–254.

Moyer, J., Egerston, H., & Isenberg, J. (1987). The child-centered kindergarten. *Childhood Education, 63*(3), 235–242.

Nelms, B. (1988). *Literature in the classroom: Readers, texts and contexts.* Urbana, IL: National Council of Teachers of English.

Neve, C. D., Hart, L. A., & Thomas, E. C. (1986). Huge learning jumps show potency of brain-based instruction. *Phi Delta Kappan, 68*(2), 143–148.

Paley, V. G. (1990). *The boy who would be a helicopter: The uses of storytelling in the classroom.* Cambridge, MA: Harvard University Press.

Papert, S. (1993). *The children's machine: Rethinking school in the age of the computer.* New York: Basic Books.

Pifer, A. (1982, October). Children—A national resource. *High/Scope Research, 2*(2), 1.

Ramirez, M. (1983). *Psychology of the Americas: Mestizo perspectives on personality and mental health.* New York: Academic.

Raywid, M. A. (1995). A teacher's awesome power. In W. Ayers (Ed.), *To become a teacher: Making a difference in children's lives* (pp. 78–85). New York: Teachers College Press.

Renzulli, J. S., Reis, S. M., & Smith, L. H. (1981). The revolving door model: A new way of identifying the gifted. *Phi Delta Kappan, 62*(9), 648–649.

Research and Policy Committee. (1985). *Investing in children.* Washington, DC: Committee for Economic Development.

Rodd, J. (1999). Encouraging young children's critical and creative thinking skills: An approach in one English elementary school. *Childhood Education, 75*(6), 350–354.

Rose, M. (1989). *Lives on the boundary: A moving account of the struggles and achievements of America's educational underclass.* New York: Penguin.

Rosen, H. (1980). The dramatic mode. In P. Salmon (Ed.), *Coming to know.* London: Routledge & Kegan Paul.

Rubin, L. (1985). *Artistry in teaching.* New York: Random House.

Runco, M. A., & Pritzker, S. (1999). *Encyclopedia of creativity.* San Francisco: Academic Press.

Ryan, K. (1986). *The induction of new teachers.* Bloomington, IN: Phi Delta Kappa (Fastback #237).

Sarason, S. B. (1995). *Parental involvement and the political principle: Why the existing governance structure of schools should be abolished.* San Francisco: Jossey-Bass.

Schon, D. A. (1983). *The reflective practitioner.* New York: Basic.

Shallcross, D. (1981). *Teaching creative behavior.* Upper Saddle River, NJ: Prentice Hall.

Shore, R. (1997). *Rethinking the brain: New insights into early development.* New York: Families and Work Institute.

Silberman, C. E. (1970). *Crisis in the classroom: The remaking of American education.* New York: Random House.

Sizer, T. (1984). *Horace's compromise.* Boston: Houghton Mifflin.

Sternberg, R. J., & Lubart, T. (1996). Investing in creativity. *American Psychologist, 51*(7), 677–686.

Task Force on Teaching as a Profession. (1986). *A nation prepared: Teachers for the 21st century.* Washington, DC: Carnegie Forum on Education and the Economy.

Tetenbaum, T. J., & Mulkeen, T. A. (1986). Computers as an agent for educational change. *Computers in the Schools, 2*(4), 91–103.

Toffler, A. (1970). *Future shock.* New York: Random House.

Toffler, A. (1980). *The third wave.* New York: Morrow.

# Appendix A

# Dance Prop Box

## THEME: DANCE/MOVEMENT

### GOALS FOR CENTER

- To provide opportunities to move from thinking and feeling to the physical expression of thought and emotion.
- To provide opportunities for role-playing experiences such as aerobics instructor, ballet dancer, or square dancer.
- To encourage oral language expression in describing different kinds of dances and feelings about dancing.
- To provide opportunities for talking about health, fitness, and relaxation.

### MATERIALS IN PROP BOX

| | | |
|---|---|---|
| Mats | Hats | Mats |
| Feathers | Headdress | Assorted dance shoes |
| Tiaras | Gloves | Leotards |
| Boas | Balloons | Tights |
| Bandannas | Tutus | Dance recital costumes |
| Ribbons | Pompoms | Tambourines |
| Long skirts | Baton | Masks |
| Balls | Vests | |

## SUGGESTED SUPPLEMENTS AND MATERIALS

| | | |
|---|---|---|
| Book or story about dance | Hand mirror | Record player |
| Records or tapes for dance | Full-length mirror | Cubes |
| Posters of dancers | Tape player | Ballet bar |

## VOCABULARY

| | | |
|---|---|---|
| Aerobics | Circle right | Modern dance |
| Arabesque | Folk dancing | Plié |
| Ballerina | Jazz | Positions of the feet |
| Ballet | Jumping jacks | Recital |
| Choreographer | March | Rhythm |
| Circle left | Mask | Square dance |

## CHILD-MADE MATERIALS

Tambourines

Signs about the dance

Masks or headdresses

## RESOURCE PEOPLE AND FIELD TRIPS

Fathers, mothers, and friends of students who are dancers could come to class and tell what they do during a day of work. The class could visit a local dance studio or children's dance theater, watch a video, or attend a film or a ballet.

## INTRODUCTION OF CENTER

"Welcome to the Dance Center"

Discuss what the children know about dance and about why people dance.

Explain different types of dance (e.g., ballet, folk, modern, jazz, and square dancing).

Ask the students how many have seen or participated in a dance.

Discuss the different roles they can play at the dance center: ballerina, modern dancer, tap dancer, ballroom dancer, aerobics teacher, or choreographer.

Set a limit of four children in the center. As space becomes available, children may choose to join the dancers.

Model different dance forms to introduce some of the vocabulary, if appropriate.

## ACTIVITIES

Inform the families of the new center and invite them to share dance experiences with their children.

Encourage children to try out all roles in the dance center.

Use photographs of children dancing to add to the dance book.

## EXTENSION

Visit an aerobics studio or watch a videotape of dance performances. Encourage children to imagine themselves as dancers, draw pictures, or write a story about themselves as dancers.

Ask children to choreograph their own dance. Read "I Like Me!" "I Dance in My Red Pajamas," and "The Camel Dances" from Arnold Lobel's *Fables*.

## ADDITIONAL IDEAS FOR PROP BOXES

### Doctor's Office
Telephone, appointment book, tongue depressors, prescription pads and empty bottles, cotton balls, stethoscope, pencils, examination mat, dolls, doll bed, bandages

### Space
Sleeping bag, Ziploc bags for food, telescope, steering wheel, control panel, space suit, helmet

### Birthday Party
Candles, streamers, markers, paper, cake pans, wrapping paper, boxes, invitations

### Library
Children's books with pockets made from cut envelopes, videotapes, library cards, pencils, signs for story hours, cards for book pockets, date stamp and ink pad, cash register, money, book-return box

### Restaurant
Aprons, chef's hat, menus, tray, pitcher, silverware, dishes, stove top (bottom of box), play money, cash register, pencils and order pads

### Gas Station
Spray bottles and paper towels, used and cleaned motor parts, hammer, oil funnel, flashlight, old rags, keys, automobile supply catalogues, hoses

## PROP BOXES FOR FAIRY TALES

*Little Red Riding Hood*
Tape recording and book of the story, red sweater or cape, basket for red apron, bow, spoon for mother, ball cap with ears for wolf, axe and hat for woodcutter, bonnet for grandmother

*The Three Bears*
Tape recording and book of the story, three different-sized bowls, spoons, blankets, three different hats for bears, hat or collar for Goldilocks, three stuffed bears

*The Elves and the Shoemaker*
Tape recording and book of the story, a few pairs of old shoes, shawl for old woman, apron for old man, doll clothes for elves, piece of brown or black felt representing leather

*Cinderella*
Tape recording and book of the story, apron for Cinderella, high-heeled shoe for slipper, hats for stepaunts, crown for prince

*Hansel and Gretel*
Tape recording and book of the story, hat and axe for father, scarf for stepmother, bonnet for Gretel, hat for Hansel, witch hat for the witch, dog bone (block)

*Snow White and Rose Red*
Tape recording and book of the story, apron for mother, white and red plastic flowers, scissors from classroom, bags or boxes of beads for jewels, pixie hat for gnome, brown garbage bag for bear, crown for prince, red and white collars

*Source:* Courtesy of Dorothy Nadeau.

# Appendix B

# Published Rating Scales to Evaluate Preschool Settings

Frost, J. L. (1986). Playground rating system: Ages 3–8. In J. S. McKee (Ed.), *Play: Working partner of growth* (pp. 66–67). Wheaton, MD: Association for Childhood Education International.

*The rating system contains 39 items to evaluate three different areas of playground quality. It evaluates what the playground should contain, the condition and safety of the equipment, and the degree and quality of challenge and learning opportunities for children. Each item is rated on a scale from 0 ("Does Not Exist") to 5 ("Excellent; All Elements"). A score may be obtained for each individual area, as well as a total playground rating score.*

Harms, T., & Clifford, R. M. (1989). *Family day care rating scale.* New York: Teachers College Press. 39 pages.

*This scale defines family day care comprehensively and can be used for evaluating family day care settings. It provides ratings for space, materials, and learning activities among the six categories addressed to ensure that the environment is developmentally appropriate for young children. Each item is described in four levels of quality ranging from "Inadequate" (does not meet custodial needs) to "Excellent" (high-quality care).*

Harms, T., & Clifford, R. M. (1995). *School-age care environment rating scale.* New York: Teachers College Press.

*The SACERS provides a resource for identifying high-quality environments offered by schools and other organizations. The scale contains 49 items; organized within seven categories that include Space and Furnishings, Health and Safety, Activities, Interactions, Program Structure, and Staff Development.*

Harms, T., Clifford, R. M., & Cryer, D. (1998). *Early childhood environment rating scale* (Rev. ed.). New York: Teachers College Press. 44 pages.
*This rating scale provides guidelines for assessing the quality of the physical and social environments for young children in seven areas. Detailed guidelines are provided for room arrangement, furnishings, and displays, as well as for creative activities.*

Harms, T., Cryer, D., & Clifford, R. M. (1990). *Infant/toddler environment rating scale.* New York: Teachers College Press. 48 pages.
*This rating scale contains assessment criteria for children in group care up to 30 months of age. Criteria for furnishings and displays for children, space, learning activities, and program structure are among the seven categories rated from "Inadequate" (not meeting custodial care needs) to "Excellent" (describing high-quality care).*

Jones, E. (1977). *Dimensions of teaching-learning environments.* Pasadena, CA: Pacific Oaks.
*This rating scale describes the physical setting and the teacher's behavior along four dimensions: soft/hard, simple/complex, intrusion/seclusion, and high mobility/low mobility. It views these dimensions along a continuum and explores the possibilities of arranging environments within them.*

National Association for the Education of Young Children. (1998). *Accreditation criteria and procedures of the National Association for the Education of Young Children.* Washington, DC: Author.
*Contains standards for early childhood programs set by the profession. A portion of these standards describes nine aspects of the physical environment. The scale focuses on the arrangement of the environment, selection of materials, and interactions between adults and children.*

# Appendix C

# Noncompetitive Games for Children

## BALL GAMES

### Preschoolers/Kindergartners

#### Call Ball
Form a circle with one child in the center who tosses the ball while calling another child's name. This child tries to catch the ball after the first bounce. The child continues with other children.

#### Basket Ball
Children stand before a plastic basket and toss the ball into the basket. The game may be played individually, in pairs, or in groups. Emphasis is on trying to hit the mark rather than keeping score, so move the basket closer or farther away to adjust the challenge level.

### School-Age Children

#### Letter or Number Ball
As players pass a small ball around a circle, have them say a letter or a number. Players may count or say the alphabet in unison if they go in order.

#### Tennis
Make "rackets" out of a nylon stocking stretched over a coat hanger. Children can bat a ping-pong ball back and forth using the racket.

#### Lap Ball
Players form a circle and sit close to one another, with shoulders touching. They try to pass a ball around the circle from lap to lap without using their hands.

# QUIET GAMES

## *Preschoolers/Kindergartners*

### *Nursery Rhymes*
Say the rhyme and follow up with action. For example: "Jack and Jill went up (children reach up high) the hill. Jack falls down (children touch the ground)." Other favorite nursery rhymes include "Humpty Dumpty," "Mary Had a Little Lamb," and "Baa Baa Black Sheep."

### *Toyshop*
Have children pretend they are toys. When called on, each child imitates the sound and action of the toy and continues until someone guesses the name of the toy.

### *Clap and Tap Names*
In this game, say a child's name and have the group repeat it several times, establishing a rhythm for the name. Then have the children clap the rhythm of the name while they say it. Ask them to use their feet while saying the name and, last, to move forward on that rhythm.

## *School-Age Children*

### *On My Way to School . . .*
Form a circle with one child in the center who says, "On my way to school this morning, I saw . . . " and then imitates what he or she saw. Others guess the imitation. The one guessing correctly goes into the center, and the game begins again.

### *Buzz*
Players take turns counting one number at a time. Whenever they have to say a number with seven in it, they say buzz instead. If a player accidentally says *seven* (or *seventeen*, or *twenty-seven*), then the game begins again at number one.

# SINGING GAMES

## *Preschoolers/Kindergartners*

### *Charlie over the Water*
Players join hands in a circle. One player, Charlie, is in the center. The circle moves to the left while chanting:

> *Charlie over the water,*
> *Charlie over the sea,*
> *Charlie caught a blackbird*
> *But he can't catch me.*

On the word *me* the players quickly squat. Charlie tries to tag a player before he or she gets into the squat position. The tagged child then becomes "Charlie."

### Round and Round Went the Gallant Ship

In this game, children dance around in a circle with clasped hands, reciting the following verse and "bobbing" down quickly as the ship goes to the bottom of the sea:

> *Three times round went our gallant ship,*
> *And three times round went she;*
> *Three times round went our gallant ship,*
> *Then she sank to the bottom of the sea.*

A tumble as the ship goes down adds much to the spirit of the play.

### Did You Ever See a Lassie?

One child is in the middle of a circle. Other children grasp hands and circle around the child in the center while singing the first two lines. During lines three and four, the children drop hands and imitate the child in the middle, who thinks up some special way to hop.

> *Did you ever see a lassie (laddie), a lassie, a lassie,*
> *Did you ever see a lassie, do this way and that?*
> *Do this way and that way, and this way and that way,*
> *Did you ever see a lassie do this way and that?*

## School-Age Children

### Riggety Jig

The children form a standing circle. One child begins to skip inside the circle to the following tune:

> *As I was going down the street*
> *Down the street, down the street*
> *As I was going down the street*
> *Hi Ho, Hi Ho, Hi Ho.*
> *A handsome fellow (pretty girl) I chanced to meet*
> *Chanced to meet, chanced to meet*
> *A handsome fellow (pretty girl) I chanced to meet*
> *Hi Ho, Hi Ho, Hi Ho.*

With the chosen partner, both children skip around the circle to the following tune:

> *Riggety jig, jig, and away we go*
> *Away we go, away we go*
> *Riggety jig, jig, and away we go*
> *Hi Ho, Hi Ho, Hi Ho.*

Others clap the tune.

*Singing Syllables*

After one player leaves the room, the rest of the group decides on a word to sing. If the word is *November,* for example, some players will sing "No No No," some will sing "vem vem vem," and the rest will sing "ber ber ber," all at the same time.

Now the player who left the room returns and tries to figure out what the word is. Everyone gets a turn to be the guesser, with, of course, a new word sung each time.

# RUNNING GAMES

## *Preschoolers/Kindergartners*

### *Squirrel and Nut*

The children sit in a circle with heads down and hands open. One child, the squirrel, drops the "nut" (a piece of chalk or crayon) into the hands of any other child. That child immediately gets up and tries to catch the squirrel, who is safe by reaching the place of the second child. If not caught, the other child becomes the squirrel.

### *Cat and Mice*

The cat hides behind something. Four or five "mice" creep up to the cat's hiding place and start scratching on the floor. Their scratching is the signal for the cat to start chasing them, and they are safe only on reaching their holes (places). Any mouse who is tapped becomes the cat. Other mice are then chosen, and the game begins again.

### *Drop the Handkerchief*

One child runs around the circle and drops a handkerchief behind another player. That player picks up the handkerchief and runs around the circle in the direction opposite to that of the first player. The one who reaches the vacant place left in the circle becomes "it." Then the game is repeated.

### *Musical Chairs*

One version of musical chairs is to play music and have children find a chair *or* a lap when the music stops. A chair is removed each time, but everyone finds a seat (by sitting on a lap).

## *School-Age Children*

### *Numbers Change*

Players stand in a large circle and are numbered consecutively. One player, in the center, calls two numbers (not his or her own). The center player tries to secure one of their places. The one who is left without a place now becomes the center player.

In the classroom, the number caller (who also has a number) stands in front of the room and calls two numbers. While players change places, the caller tries to take a seat vacated by one of the runners whose number was called.

### Kitty in the Corner

The children form a circle on the floor. Four chairs are placed in four corners of a square. A fifth child is in the middle. When the teacher calls "Kitty in the corner," the children in the chairs change places while the child in the center seeks to get into one of the chairs. The displaced child then chooses someone to take his or her place until all have had a turn.

### Squirrels in Trees

The group is divided and numbered in threes. Numbers 1 and 2 join hands to represent the tree. Number 3 is the squirrel and stands in the circle formed by the other two. There should be one or more odd squirrels without trees. The groups of threes are scattered over the play space. At a signal from a leader or the teacher, the squirrels attempt to get into trees. Only one squirrel is allowed in one tree at the same time. Someone is always left without a tree. As soon as all trees are full, the game is repeated.

## PARTNER GAMES

## *Preschoolers/Kindergartners*

### Repeat

One player says a word that the other player repeats. Continue repeating the same word until one player wants to stop, which is the tricky part.

### Finish My Action

One player begins an imaginary action, such as brushing teeth or raking leaves. When that player stops, the partner finishes the action. Then the partners switch roles.

## *School-Age Children*

### Copycat

With a partner, decide who will be the mirror and who will be the copycat. Players must face each other as they stay together mirroring actions.

### Puppeteers

One player is the puppet on the ground, unable to move. Along comes the puppeteer, who brings the puppet to life with pretend strings. The puppeteer pulls the strings, and the puppet responds to every tug. Allow everyone a chance to be the puppeteer as well as to be the puppet.

### Ali Baba and the Forty Thieves

Two players stand facing each other a few feet apart. One of the players sings the words "Ali Baba and the forty thieves" to any made-up tune, at the same time doing a hand movement, such as clapping. When the singer is finished, the second player repeats the song and the motions exactly; at the same time, the first player sings the phrase again and does something different with his or her hands—hitting one arm with the opposite hand, for example.

For the next round, the second player must copy this second set of movements, along with continuing to sing, and so on, with both players singing "Ali Baba and the forty thieves" over and over, each doing a different hand movement. The activity continues until one of the players forgets the line.

# REFERENCES

Gregson, B. (1984). *The outrageous outdoor games book.* Carthage, IL: Fearon.

Kamii, C., & DeVries, R. (1980). *Group games in early education: Implications for Piaget's theory.* Washington, DC: National Association for the Education of Young Children.

Orlick, T. (1978, 1982). *The cooperative sports and games book* and *The second cooperative sports and games book.* New York: Pantheon.

Rowe, S., & Humphries, S. (1994). *Playing around: Activities and excursions for social and cooperative learning.* London: Forbes.

Sobel, J. (1983). *Everybody wins: Non-competitive games for young children.* New York: Walker.

# Appendix D

# Observations of Medical Play

### April 8: Getting started

**Nick (doctor):**  Come in, come in! (Puts stethoscope around neck.) Where's your heart?
**Allen:**  Right here.
**Nick:**  Nurse, get me the blood pressure kit.
**Amanda:**  Where's my hat? A nurse can wear a hat, but I don't have one. Well, I'll put this nice new pretend hat on. There! How do I look?
**Teacher:**  Amanda, you look just like the nurse at my doctor's office.

### April 15: Drawing on prior experience

**Teacher (mother):**  It won't hurt my baby? Are you sure?
**Markus (doctor):**  Hold on to him, Mommy. Where do you think he should get his shot at?
**Teacher:**  How about his arm?
**Markus:**  How about his foot? I got a shot in my foot one time for stepping on a nail. A tennis shot.
**Teacher:**  Do you mean a tetanus shot?
**Markus:**  Yeah, that's it.

### April 22: Building vocabulary

**Mallory:**  What's that? I can't remember, and I need to use it.
**Teacher:**  That's a thermometer. It tells you the temperature of your body.
**Mallory:**  Oh, yeah, I remember.
**Jeremy:**  Where's the heart thing? I want to listen to someone's heart.
**Teacher:**  Here's the stethoscope.

*April 27: Reality testing*

**Allen:**   My leg hurts, Doc.
**Nick:**   I'll put this on. (Puts an Ace bandage on for a few seconds.) Now it's time to take it off and see if your leg is better. (Allen begins removing the bandage.)
**Teacher:**   Allen, would the patient take off his own bandage?
**Allen:**   Whoops. Hey, Doc, take off my bandage!
**Nick:**   Your leg's all better, but I have to give you a shot. Now lay down. Now I'm gonna give you a shot, but I'm gonna put these cotton balls in your mouth first. (Giggles and starts to move toward Allen's mouth.)
**Teacher:**   Nick, when you go to the doctor, how does he really use the cotton ball?
**Nick:**   (Begins to rub Allen's arm with the cotton ball.)

*April 29: Introducing new materials and concepts*

**Teacher:**   I am a blood pressure kit salesperson. I would like to demonstrate how to use our new and improved blood pressure kit. First, you have the patient hold out her arm. Then you carefully put the arm cuff on like this. Next, you put the end of the stethoscope right under the cuff and hold it. Then you pump it up only three times and watch the needle. That's how you use this new kit. If you have any questions, just call me.

*May 4: The high price of medical care*

Today the theme of medical costs was introduced by Markus, who was playing the doctor and charged exorbitant rates. When the patient paid him, he said, "I'm rich! I'm rich!"

**Teacher:**   How much do I owe for today's visit?
**Kara:**   You owe me $235. Pay me now. (Holds out hand.)
**Teacher:**   Here you go.

*May 6: Negotiation*

Kara and Michelle started to argue about who will play the doctor and who will be the nurse.

**Michelle:**   Okay, you can look at his throat and ears, and I'll do the eye chart and see how tall he is.
**Kara:**   And you can do the blood pressure, and I'll give him a shot and listen to his body.
**Michelle:**   Allen, stand against the wall here. (She puts her hand just above his head and looks at the chart.) Allen, move away. You are four feet one inch.

Later, Kara was the patient.

**Allen:**   Okay, Kara, cover your eye and say those letters.
**Kara:**   Those are small letters. Ready? (Reads all the letters.) There, I did it! (Big smile.) And I didn't even miss one. (Checks the chart with both eyes uncovered.)

## May 9: Incorporating new vocabulary

Greg was the nurse. He said that he had a telephone call and needed to go to the scene of an accident. I asked him if nurses usually did that. He wasn't sure. I explained that the people who go to accidents in an ambulance are called *paramedics*. Later, Greg got another accident call and said, "I'm sorry, I can't come. You need the paramedics. I'll call 911 and get a ambulance with paramedics on it. They'll save 'em."

(Notepads, an appointment book, and a ballpoint pen were added to the center.) Michelle is playing the role of doctor and asks, "Why do I have paper?"

The teacher answered: "Did you ever see doctors write a prescription? The doctor writes down what kind of medicine you should take."

**(Later) Michelle:**   I got my paper to write stuff out. Who needs a prescription? Who needs a bill?

**Melanie:**   What do you do with a prescription?

**Michelle:**   You take it to a drugstore and they give you the medicine you need from what's written on the paper.

## May 13: Connecting with life

Letha has been in and out of the hospital because she was diagnosed as having cancer (now in remission). When she returned to school, I changed the center to a veterinarian's office during our pets theme. Throughout the children's play, I heard her refer to her hospital experiences. Some examples of statements she made were "Is this like a people hospital? I was in a people hospital a long time."

When Brandon tried to give her a shot, she said, "Not me! I had enough shots already in the hospital. I got blood taken lots of times. The thing they used looked just like this, except longer." Their conversation continued:

**Brandon:**   I never had that done. I'll take some blood from the dog to examine.

**Letha:**   I'll show you how, okay? You need to put on your mask like real doctors do.

**Brandon:**   What is the mask for?

**Kurt:**   My bear broke his head. He was standing on his chair and fell off.

**Brandon:**   I'll x-ray his head. But I gotta put my mask on first.

**Kurt:**   Why?

**Brandon:**   So I don't spit my gum on him. No. To keep out the germs.

**Maryjane:**   Germs? Did I hear someone say germs? This is a hospital. There should not be germs. Get out, get out.

**Markus:**   Guys, I got a . . . I got a . . . I need something. I got a sick fox here.

**Brandon:**   Wait, I'm taking care of this one.

**Amanda:**   I had a pet rabbit one time, I mean, a long time ago at home. His name was Henny. He was really sick, and he died a long time ago. My mom thought he would die, and he did.

**Melanie:**   I had a gerbil, and my mom thought he was gonna die because we forgot to feed him.

*May 16: Symbolic play*

**Shawn:**   I'm the doctor today.
**Scott:**   No, I am.
**Shawn:**   We both are. It's a big petpital.
**Scott:**   What's a petpital?
**Shawn:**   It's a hospital for pets.
**Allen:**   When my brother went to the doctor's, they found out how much he weighed and how tall he got.
**Teacher:**   Maybe we could do that for one of our animals.
**Jeremy:**   Yeah. Let's see. I'll use this block for the uh, what's that thing called?
**Letha:**   A scale.
**Jeremy:**   (Brings over a toy duck.) We need to weight him.
**Shayna:**   I'm the nurse. Put your duck on the scale, and I'll measure him.
**Letha:**   My duck is a girl.
**Shayna:**   Sorry. She weights, uumm . . .
**Jeremy:**   Twenty-five million pounds!
**Letha:**   She does not. Your scale must be broke.
**Jeremy:**   Okay, 13 pounds.
**Shayna:**   She's 1 foot tall, too.

*May 18: Sex role stereotypes*

**Dee:**   Can I play?
**Scott:**   No, we have two doctors and nurses. That's enough.
**Teacher:**   I think we can find something for Dee to do.
**Dee:**   I could be the ambulance driver.
**Scott:**   No, you cannot.
**Dee:**   Why?
**Scott:**   Because! You're a girl, and girls can't be ambulance drivers.
**Amanda:**   They can too!
**Shawn:**   Can not.
**Teacher:**   Scott and Shawn, why do you think that girls can't be ambulance drivers?
**Scott:**   Because men drive better.
**Shawn:**   Yeah.
**Amanda:**   No, they do not.
**Maryjane:**   Men drive lousy.
**Teacher:**   Girls can be ambulance drivers just like boys. Girls can be doctors and boys can be nurses. My doctor is a woman.
**Dee:**   I'm gonna find something to use for my—*my* ambulance. Whoo, whoo, ambulance comin' through. Hey, there's a sick fox over here. What kind of hospital is this anyway? I said I got a sick fox over here!
**Maryjane:**   Oh! Hey, we need a doctor over here. We have a patient.
**Shawn:**   I'm coming. Hold your pants on. (Children from the camping play center come over.) I wish these guys would stop coming and bugging me and my patient. This is a hospital, not a picnic. Geez.

# Appendix E

## Case Study: Dittos and Elegant Costumes

Case methodology is a form of problem-based instruction for adults. Cases help learners experience situations that they are *likely to experience* in their professional settings. Use this case to help you analyze problems of communicating about play to parents and colleagues, to set goals about play for your own professional setting, and to share your ideas about appropriate ways to respond to parental concerns about too much play in the classroom.

## DITTOS AND ELEGANT COSTUMES

"What do you think of this, Clara?" asked her principal, setting a three-page single-spaced letter from a parent in front of Clara just a few minutes before school began one morning. Clara, her assistant, and her student teacher were busy preparing the room for the students' arrival, and the contents of the letter came as a complete surprise to her. As she read she felt her anger rise and a flush move from her neck up to her cheek then to her forehead as she tried to hold on to some sense of composure.

"We want Lauren moved from Miss Sparks' kindergarten class immediately," the letter began. "There is no comparison between the two classes. All Lauren does is play, play, play. She is not learning a thing. The class never does anything. The children in Mrs. Wolfe's class put on a play just last week with elegant costumes. Each child had memorized long parts and lots of songs. Our neighbor's child is in Mrs. Wolfe's class, and his pictures come home looking like they are supposed to. And the ditto sheets that they do are really helping him learn."

There was more, but Clara looked up at the principal with hurt in her eyes. "Lauren's parents just don't understand. They don't want to understand that there are other ways of teaching young children besides elaborate productions and ditto sheets—perhaps even better ways. What shall we do?"

"I don't know, Clara. I need to think about it for awhile. But I know that I will need to talk with Lauren's parents soon."

"I have talked with them so many times myself," said Clara, "but somehow it just doesn't do any good. I hate it, being put on the defensive this way."

The principal left, leaving Clara to try to salvage what remained of her morning. Soon the children arrived, and she became swept up in the momentum of the day's activities. She had no time to reflect on her own teaching philosophy and style until much later, during free choice activity time. She looked out over her class busily engaged in learning activities of their own choosing: on the floor, at tables, standing up, sitting down, moving around, quiet and chatty.

Her eyes caught Jenny. Jenny was up to her elbows in soapsuds, her face intent, her eyes sparkling. There was a daub of white at the end of her nose. "A, B, C, D, E," Jenny sang to herself as she wrote letters in the soap on the table's surface.

Clara walked over to Tommy. His eyebrows were puckered, and his whole countenance concentrated on his task. Tommy was hammering a nail at the woodworking table.

"Look, Miss Sparks! With one nail, the pieces wiggle. Two nails hold it steady," he exclaimed.

Sally and Louise then approached Clara, their heads covered with scarves, each carrying a basket.

"We're on our way to Grandma's house, Miss Sparks," said Louise. "Would you like a cookie?"

"Only if you'll be careful never to talk with strangers," replied Clara.

"Oh, we won't. We never do," the girls answered, moving on again around the room, the path invisible to all but their own eyes.

Clara continued to watch the children, jotting down a note here and there for her anecdotal records, involving herself where necessary to keep the flow of learning strong and creative. As she worked, she felt her confidence return, and at the end of the free choice time she continued her day with renewed vigor. She liked what she was doing. She was convinced that her child-centered approach to teaching was right for children.

On the way home that afternoon Clara gathered her anecdotal records about Lauren. She needed to touch base with the principal before leaving the building to clarify her own role in the matter and to find out what the principal planned to do next.

She walked out past the other kindergarten room with its displays of children's work on the walls, each one a carbon copy of the next.

"Good night," Clara called to her colleague, Mrs. Wolfe, still in her classroom.

"Oh, Clara, could we talk a minute?" Mrs. Wolfe answered. Clara stopped and went in.

"I don't know how to say this, Clara, so I'll just say it," Mrs. Wolfe began. "Lauren's mother stopped in to see me today and told me that she asked to have Lauren moved to my room. She said that many of her neighbors feel the same way about you, and that the discussions about kindergarten in the neighborhood are angry ones. They're out to get you, Clara, and I thought you'd want to know."

Clara looked at her colleague, stunned. . . .

## Study Questions

Think about the above case and write down your thoughts about these questions. Be prepared to use your responses to share with your group at another class meeting.

1. What is the problem here? Why? Explain what you mean.
2. What are the issues in this case? Explain. Give an example from the case to illustrate each one.
3. How powerful is the neighborhood gossip mill? What are some appropriate ways to deal with it?
4. To what and to whom is Clara responsible? Explain.
5. What is the role of the principal? Why?
6. If you were Clara, what would you do and why?

*Source:* Courtesy of George Mason University Case Writing Team.

# Appendix F

# Resources for Play Materials

## SELECTING AND USING SAFE PLAY MATERIALS

Bronson, M. (1995). *The right stuff for children birth to age 8.* Washington, DC: National Association for the Education of Young Children.
*Provides a detailed list of age appropriate materials that are organized by different types of play.*

Moyer, J. (Ed.). (1995). *Selecting educational equipment and materials for school and home.* Wheaton, MD: Association for Childhood Education International.
*Contains lists of materials and equipment for classrooms for children ages birth through age 10 as well as a listing of developmentally appropriate materials that promote each type of play.*

U.S. Consumer Product Safety Commission (1993, 1994). *Which toy for which child? A consumer's guide for selecting suitable toys: Ages birth through five* and *Which toy for which child? A consumer's guide for selecting suitable toys: Ages six through twelve.*
*List basic safety guidelines and age-appropriate toys and materials. For additional information, write to: U.S. Consumer Product Safety Commission, Washington, DC 20207.*

## FREE CLASSROOM PLAY MATERIALS

For 120 decks of cards and 100 sets of dice to use as number cards for math and that are free of charge, write a letter stating you are a teacher and would like to have the cards and dice for use in your classroom. Include your name and address and send to:
Sands Hotel-Casino
136 S. Kentucky Ave.
Atlantic City, NJ 08401 (Allow 4 months for processing your request.)

# FOLKLIFE AND CULTURAL ARTIFACTS

For advisory information on folklife resources and cultural artifacts, contact the following national, regional, or local agencies.

## *National Agencies*

American Folklife Center
Library of Congress
101 Independence Ave. S.E.
Washington, DC 20540-4610
(202) 707-5510

New York Center for Urban Folk Culture
72 E. 1st St.
New York, NY 10003
(212) 529-1955

## *Regional Agencies*

Southern Arts Federation
1401 Peachtree St. N.E., Suite 460
Atlanta, GA 30309
(404) 874-7244

Western Folklife Center
P.O. Box 1570
Elko, NV 89803
(775) 738-7508

## *State and Community-Based Agencies*

Most states and local communities support a Council on the Arts that should be able to assist you with materials and other useful resources for classroom applications. Be sure you tell the contact person you are an early childhood educator.

## *Company That Produces Multicultural Materials*

Mastercommunications/Asia for Kids, (800) 765-5885

# Glossary

Note to the student: A glossary should be used to help you remember terms with which you are familiar. For a deeper understanding of any of these terms, we encourage you to reread the chapter sections in which those terms appear. The chapter reference is in parentheses.

**active learning** Concrete experiences that are "hands-on," challenging, and relevant to the learner. (Chapter 2)

**adventure or "junk" playgrounds** Collections of tools and materials which allow children to build, create, and pretend using these items outdoors. (Chapter 6)

**aesthetic** Having to do with feelings, ideas, and perceptions about beauty. (Chapter 4)

**affective** Feelings or emotional responses. (Chapter 4)

**autocratic** Demanding obedience, following specific rules, and imposing inflexible standards on behavior. (Chapter 8)

**behaviorism** The view that a person's environment is the most important variable in shaping his or her development. (Chapter 8)

**brainstorm** Generating as many ideas as possible without evaluating them in order to enhance creativity. (Chapter 5)

**center-based classroom** Rooms arranged into various areas each containing interesting and accessible materials that offer children choices and support their independence. (Chapter 6)

**child-centered** Activities and programs that base decisions and policies on the needs of the children and place concerns about the learners first. (Chapter 6)

**classical theories** Theories about play that sought to explain the causes and purposes of play from the nineteenth century through World War I. (Chapter 2)

**climate** The feeling tone created by a learning environment. (Chapter 6)

**cognitive** Having to do with knowledge, understanding, and intellectual growth. (Chapter 4)

**cognitive-development theory** Jean Piaget's view of how children's intellectual abilities develop and progress through a series of stages. (Chapter 2)

**complex units** Units with subparts made of two totally different elements for children to manipulate or invent. (Chapter 6)

**conflict resolution** A problem-solving process enabling children to understand and resolve their disputes or disagreements peacefully. (Chapter 8)

**construction materials** Varied materials that children can combine and recombine to build something. (Chapter 7)

**constructive play** Creating or engaging in problem-solving behavior according to a preconceived plan. (Chapter 2)

**constructivism** The belief that children are more than passive recipients of information and actively build their own understandings. Based on Piaget's cognitive-developmental theory. (Chapter 8)

**controlled scribbles** Scribbles with a definite shape that are produced when the child has better control over the writing implement. (Chapter 3)

**convergent or closed** Materials or experiences that lead children to think about a single answer or one right way of arriving at a solution. (Chapter 7)

**cooperative learning** A group of persons who work collaboratively to achieve a common goal. (Chapter 8)

**creative playgrounds** Superstructures with moveable parts that are action-oriented, provide safe underneath surfaces, and promote all forms of play. (Chapter 6)

**creative teachers** Educators who are committed to supporting children's play and facilitating children's creative expression. (Chapter 8)

**creativity** A thinking and responding process that involves connecting with our previous experience, responding to stimuli, and generating at least one unique combination. (Chapter 1)

**democratic** Having high expectations, understanding child development, showing and expecting respect, allowing decision making, and setting reasonable limits for behavior and practices. (Chapter 8)

**developmentally appropriate materials** Materials, experiences, and activities that are carefully matched to the children's developmental levels. (Chapter 7)

**divergent or open-ended** Materials and experiences designed to elicit many different student responses that promote exploration, experimentation, and problem-solving. (Chapter 7)

**dramatic play** The child's use of props, plot, and roles to symbolize real or imaginary experiences. Also referred to as pretend, fantasy, make-believe, or symbolic play. Dramatic play is typical of 2- to 7-year olds. (Chapter 2)

**enactive stage** The developmental stage during which physical activity and music are intertwined. (Chapter 4)

**enactment** Adopting actions, feelings, thoughts, and behaviors of people in particular situations. This ability typically begins at age 3. (Chapter 5)

**formal or scripted drama** The most structured dramatic form, which includes a prepared script used in a practiced production and is viewed by an audience. (Chapter 5)

**functional play** Simple, pleasurable, repeated movements with objects, people, and language to learn new skills or to gain mastery of a physical or mental skill. It is also referred to

as sensorimotor, practice, or exercise play and is typical of infants and toddlers. (Chapter 2)

**game** A form of play in which children follow a set of predetermined rules and procedures and assign players specific roles. (Chapter 7)

**gross motor** Refers to large muscle activity/ coordination and activities designed to foster these skills. (Chapter 7)

**hands-on materials** Manipulatives that children can use to enhance their understanding and learning; learning by doing. (Chapter 5)

**hollow blocks** Large wooden blocks with an opening for carrying. (Chapter 7)

**humanism** The belief that people are capable of controlling their lives through choice, creativity, and self-realization (Chapter 8)

**iconic stage** The developmental stage during which children use pictures and real objects to represent ideas and experiences. (Chapter 4)

**imagination** The ability to form rich and varied mental images or concepts of people, places, things, and situations that are not present. (Chapter 1)

**indirect guidance** Child-centered strategies teachers use to plan, arrange, and manage people and classroom space, materials, and schedules. (Chapter 8)

**informal drama** Spontaneous enactments that include dramatic and sociodramatic play, pantomime, and movement activities. (Chapter 5)

**investigative play** Actively exploring and experimenting during play. (Chapter 8)

**learner-centered art** Allowing children to direct their own work, valuing the process as much as the product, and fostering originality rather than conformity. (Chapter 3)

**manipulative materials** Concrete materials that aid small muscle activity in the fingers and hands, basic concepts, and eye-hand coordination (Chapter 7)

**medium** The means or channel through which the artist conveys a message. (Chapter 3)

**modern theories** Theories of play, prominent after World War I, that emphasize the consequences of play for children. (Chapter 2)

**multicultural education** Learning that respects and celebrates children's diversity (e.g., ethnic, racial, religious). (Chapter 5)

**naming of scribbling** Children's verbal labeling of a scribble they have produced. (Chapter 3)

**nonrepresentational drawing** A stage in children's drawing where the drawings do not resemble the items being represented. (Chapter 3)

**one-way communication** A focus on messages from the school to the family. (Chapter 8)

**permissive** Having a disinterested attitude that results in an inconsistent environment and fails to promote children's self-control. (Chapter 8)

**play-debrief-replay** Wassermann's three-step model for organizing instruction and challenging primary grade children's divergent thinking. (Chapter 8)

**practice theory** A theory that proposes that play prepares children for the future roles and responsibilities needed to survive in their culture. (Chapter 2)

**preschematic** Children's drawings that are just beginning to represent the object being depicted yet are difficult for adults to interpret without the child's explanation. (Chapter 3)

**process** An emphasis on the way something (e.g., a piece of artwork) is produced, including the problem-solving strategies used and the originality or inventiveness exhibited. (Chapter 3)

**project** An in-depth study that is usually initiated, planned, and evaluated by the children. (Chapter 8)

**prop boxes or dramatic play kits** Collections of real items or props that have a relation to one another. For example, a chef's hat, apron, cookware, and plastic food could be in a prop box for a restaurant center. (Chapter 5)

**psychoanalytic theory** A theory that perceives play as an important outlet for emotional release and for developing self-esteem as children learn to control their thoughts, bodies, objects, and social behaviors. (Chapter 2)

**random scribbling** Random marks that are produced by toddlers when the writing implement happens to make contact with the writing surface. (Chapter 3)

**readers theater** A form of interpretive drama during which a group of readers assumes a role, read, and orally interpret the parts of the story that relate to their role. (Chapter 5)

**recapitulation theory** A theory that proposes that play enables children to revisit activities of their ancestors and shed any negative behaviors in order to prepare them for living in today's world. (Chapter 2)

**recreation/relaxation theory** A theory that suggests that play replenishes or "re-creates" energy used in work. (Chapter 2)

**referent** An object or symbol that stands for something else. (Chapter 3)

**repeated shapes** A stage in children's drawing where scribbling is well controlled and small geometric shapes are repeated, almost like designs. (Chapter 3)

**representational drawing** A stage in children's drawing where the drawings begin to resemble the items being depicted. (Chapter 3)

**representational use** Children's intentionally planning and acting upon ideas and ways familiar to their world. (Chapter 7)

**room arrangement** The way space is organized for children's learning and movement. (Chapter 6)

**schematic** A category of children's drawings in which the child's work clearly resembles the object(s) drawn. (Chapter 3)

**self-expressive materials** Resources that encourage children to experiment with various roles, feelings, and behaviors and express them through drama, music, and art. (Chapter 7)

**simple units** Play materials that have no apparent use with no subparts for children to manipulate or create. (Chapter 6)

**skill and concept materials** Materials that are prescriptive and product-oriented. (Chapter 7)

**sociocultural theory** A view that learning occurs in a social context and is fundamentally social in nature. The major vehicle for learning is interaction with an emulation of role models. (Chapter 2)

**sociodramatic play**  Symbolic play that involves two or more children who communicate verbally about the play episode and enact social roles. (Chapter 2)

**space**  The degree to which the physical environment is arranged to develop active, creative thinkers. (Chapter 6)

**story drama or story retelling**  Interpretive drama creating a rendition or reenactment of someone else's ideas and words, often based on children's literature. (Chapter 5)

**story play or story dictation**  Guided drama using children's original stories as the content for enactment. (Chapter 5)

**supercomplex units**  Play materials having three or more subparts that children can juxtapose. (Chapter 6)

**surplus energy theory**  A view that human beings have certain amounts of energy to be used for survival and the excess energy not spent forms a surplus that is expended through play. (Chapter 2)

**symbolic play**  The child's use of props, plot, and roles to symbolize real or imaginary experiences. Also referred to as pretend, dramatic or sociodramatic, fantasy, or make-believe play. Symbolic play is typical of 2- to 7-year-olds. (Chapter 2)

**symbolic stage**  The developmental stage during which a child uses abstract symbols, es-

pecially language, to represent ideas and experiences. (Chapter 4)

**table blocks**  A variety of small, colored cubed blocks used alone or in pairs on a table or hard surface. (Chapter 7)

**three-way communication**  Collaborating among the home, school, and community to support children's creative expression. (Chapter 8)

**time**  A feature of creative environments that conveys a clear message about the importance of an activity or experience. (Chapter 6)

**toys**  Materials specifically designed for children's play and learning. Toys and playthings reflect their society, politics, and cultural issues. (Chapter 7)

**traditional playgrounds**  Playgrounds containing large, steel, immovable equipment designed for physical exercise outdoors. (Chapter 6)

**two-way communication**  A dialogue between schools and families that encourages and respects families' contributions to the interaction. (Chapter 8)

**unit blocks**  A set of large, smooth hardwood blocks in a wide array of shapes used for constructive play and large building projects on the floor. (Chapter 7)

**water table**  A raised frame that holds a large container of water so that several children can stand next to it and engage in water play with toys, various types of plastic containers, or tubing. (Chapter 7)

# Index

*Note:* Page numbers followed by letters *f* and *t* indicate figures and tables, respectively.